FOURTH EDITION

PERSONAL FINANCE

An Integrated Planning Approach

Bernard J. Winger
Ralph R. Frasca
University of Dayton

Prentice Hall, Upper Saddle River, New Jersey 07458

To those we love:
Sue, Mike, and Bob
Crystal, Matthew, Anthony, Michael, and Christina

Acquisitions Editor: Paul Donnelly
Editorial Assistant: MaryBeth Sanok
Editor-in-Chief: James Boyd
Assistant Editor: Gladys Soto
Marketing Manager: Sandra Steiner
Production Editor: Judith Leale
Production Coordinator: Renee Pelletier
Managing Editor: Carol Burgett
Manufacturing Supervisor: Arnold Vila
Manufacturing Manager: Vincent Scelta
Senior Designer: Ann France
Design Director: Patricia Wosczyk
Interior Design: Levavi & Levavi, Inc.
Cover Design: Lorraine Castellano
Illustrator (Interior): Hadel Studio
Composition: Pine Tree Composition, Inc.
Cover Photo: David Roche, Nawrocki Stock Photo, Inc.

Library of Congress Cataloging-in-Publication Data
Winger, Bernard J.
Personal finance: an integrated planning approach/Bernard J. Winger, Ralph R. Frasca.—4th ed.
p. cm.
Includes bibliographical references and index.
ISBN 0-13-269630-4
1. Finance, Personal. I. Frasca, Ralph R. II. Title.
HG179.W545 1997
332.024—dc20 96-23941
CIP

Prentice-Hall International (UK) Limited, *London*
Prentice-Hall of Australia Pty. Limited, *Sydney*
Prentice-Hall Canada, Inc., *Toronto*
Prentice-Hall Hispanoamericana, S.A., *Mexico*
Prentice-Hall of India Private Limited, *New Delhi*
Prentice-Hall of Japan, Inc., *Tokyo*
Simon & Schuster Asia Pte. Ltd., *Singapore*
Editora Prentice-Hall do Brasil, Ltda., *Rio de Janeiro*

Printed in the United States of America

10 9 8 7 6 5 4 3 2 1

Brief Contents

Contents

Preface

Our primary aim in writing this text is to help the reader plan for a successful financial future. Planning has never been easy, and in recent years it has grown increasingly difficult. Slow rates of economic growth, corporate restructures and downsizing, and an ever-changing tax law are among the many factors influencing today's personal financial plans. Moreover, a new attitude seems to be taking hold—we cannot rely upon our government or employers for financial security; instead, we must rely upon ourselves.

As with previous editions, we attempt to reflect changes in the financial environment throughout the text. Many changes have been made to reflect the new mood of self-reliance, update the material, clarify explanations, and sharpen the decision-making focus. Moreover, the text's outline and topic development have been thoroughly revised to reflect important changes.

Part 1 presents a basic framework to help individuals plan their financial futures by focusing on *organizing* and *managing* personal financial resources. Part 2 covers insurance planning and stresses the importance of *protecting* financial resources. Part 3 explains the importance of effective investing to *grow* financial resources over time. And Part 4 covers the basic reason why financial planning is important—to *enjoy* our financial resources, both currently and in the future.

We believe the text's current organization works best in most classroom situations; however, the major parts can certainly be rearranged to accommodate other teaching plans. Moreover, most chapters are self-contained and can be easily omitted. The text is very flexible, and instructors will have no difficulty in selecting material for their specific course developments.

Although coverage is flexible, we have continued the text's tradition of providing thorough topical discussions and analyses. It is our belief that a text in any discipline owes its adopters this type of coverage, allowing them the option to cover a topic in less depth if they so choose. Personal financial planning is not easy, and we do our students a disservice if we present it as such.

DISTINGUISHING FEATURES

DECISION-MAKING APPROACH We continue using a four-part approach to decision making that involves setting goals, listing alternatives, measuring performance, and evaluating achievement. Important in this process are the concepts of opportunity costs and marginal analysis. These topics are introduced and explained in Chapter 1 and are used extensively throughout the text.

AN EMPHASIS ON RISK AND RETURN At the core of financial decision making is the balancing of risk and return. This concept applies in particular to investments, but it is also useful in other decisions that involve uncertainty; thus, there is an expanded discussion of risk management in the insurance section. In the investment section, we treat risk in such a way that students can use the concept when making investment decisions. Readers thus gain a practical tool as well as an understanding of the basic principles.

INTEGRATION WITH THE INTERNET The enormous growth in popularity of the Internet has changed considerably the way many people now derive and use personal financial information. Recognizing the importance of the Internet, we have integrated it within this edition of the text. Internet addresses (web sites) are listed at the end of each chapter, along with the *Supplementary Internet Exercises* that accompany the text. This helps students connect the addresses to the topical coverage within the chapter. We feel strongly that the Internet can be a valuable tool in enhancing student interest in personal finance, and we want to help with the instructor's task of making this tool available for students.

A FOCUS ON THE TIME VALUE OF MONEY The growing importance of achieving long-term goals through investing has increased the need for students to grasp the time value of money. *New to this edition:* An expanded coverage of the topic begins in Chapter 1 and appears in all later chapters where time-value-of-money techniques are needed in making important decisions. Our explanation and use of these techniques are simple and well within the grasp of most students.

THE USE OF ACTION PLANS An action plan is a written, step-by-step approach to solving a financial problem. The use of action plans encourages students to think analytically about problems, rather than memorizing answers. *New to this edition:* All action plans developed in previous editions have been revised and updated to reflect changes in the financial environment.

AN ILLUSTRATIVE FAMILY As part of the decision-making approach, we continue to highlight a typical American family, the Steeles. Their financial situation is far from perfect, and, like most of us, they make mistakes. *New to this edition:* The Steeles' financial situation has been updated and revised. They still manage to live a reasonably comfortable and financially secure life, but they are encountering growing financial pressures as they consider their future needs to educate their children and to provide an income for themselves in retirement. The Steele family appears in nearly every chapter, where they encounter problems common to most families. As they deal with them and make decisions, so does the reader. In many cases, an action plan details a concrete approach to the problem, allowing the student to participate in solving it.

BOXED FEATURES Each chapter contains featured items that have been selected specifically for this edition to add interest and to provide background. All boxes have been selected to fit into three themes: Saving Money, Simplifying Financial Planning, and Personal Finance News. These themes focus student attention and often include practical and useful information.

MARGINAL NOTES The text is enhanced by marginal notes. All marginal notes provide key term definitions, which would benefit students in understanding concepts and preparing for exams.

THE USE OF COLOR, GRAPHICS, AND OTHER VISUAL AIDS The sophisticated graphic treatment in this text is meant to heighten interest in the topic at hand and to illustrate the concept in a concrete and effective way. The illustrations are both analytical and inviting.

AN INFORMAL WRITING STYLE To help the reader comprehend the many complex aspects of personal finance, we employ an informal writing style that brings the student into the discussion without simplifying the concepts involved. We have been careful to explain new or unfamiliar terms, to use examples where appropriate. and to speak engagingly to the student.

A COMPLETE COMPLEMENT OF END-OF-CHAPTER LEARNING AIDS Each Chapter concludes with the following study aids:

- *Summary.* A brief review of the major topics discussed.
- *Key Terms.* A list of important concepts in each chapter, accompanied by the page number where each key term is introduced and defined. To help the reader locate them, the key terms appear in boldface type within the chapter.
- *Problems and Review Questions.* A list of questions meant to provide the basis for a review of textual material and to stimulate thought and discussion on the chapter's content. *New to this edition:* The list of questions and problems has been expanded. Also, all items have been updated to reflect changes in the financial environment.
- *Cases in Personal Finance.* Two cases that, when completed, provide additional insight into the topics covered. These study aids are more challenging than the problems and re-

view questions, requiring a firm grasp of the fundamentals and more computation. *New to this edition:* All cases have also been revised to reflect changes in the financial environment.

- *Helpful Contacts.* A list of addresses and phone numbers of institutions providing help in financial planning. *New to this edition:* A list of Internet addresses.

SUPPLEMENTARY MATERIALS This text is accompanied by a complete list of supplementary teaching aids for both the instructor and the student.

- *Student Study Guide.* Paul Allen of Sam Houston State University has prepared the Study Guide to assist students in completing this course. For each chapter of the text, the guide contains highlights, a review of key terms, and test questions. The self-test items consist of matching concepts, sentence completions, true-false statements, multiple-choice questions, and learning exercises.
- *Instructor's Manual.* The Instructor's Manual, also by Paul Allen, includes extensive summaries that highlight essential points in each chapter. Also included are answers to the end-of-chapter questions and sample solutions for the cases.
- *Test Bank.* The test bank includes over 1,400 questions (all written by the authors). The questions vary in rigor and type, from term identification to problem solving, and they should provide adopters a wide array of choices in preparing tests. For those adopting this text, the test bank is also available on a computer disk, along with complementary software for generating examinations keyed to chapters in the text.

We usually learn by doing, and this text gives students plenty of opportunities to both do and learn. The decision-making approach enlivens the classroom, simplifies the teaching process, and encourages independent analysis on the part of the student. *Personal Finance: An Integrated Planning Approach* presents personal finance in a way that is easy to understand, easy to teach, and interesting to learn. We hope that you enjoy this text.

ACKNOWLEDGMENTS

This edition is a collaborative effort of many people—teachers, students, and financial planners—who have contributed numerous suggestions, criticisms, and helpful insights. To begin with, we are grateful to Rick Deus (Sacramento City College), David D. O'Dell (McPherson College), Steven E. Huntley (Florida Community College), Daniel T. Winkler (University of North Carolina–Greensboro), Clarence C. Rose (Radford University), Cliff Olson (Southern College), Robert C. Waldron (Southern Illinois University–Carbondale), William S. Tozer (Washington State University), and Richard Trieff (Des Moines Area Community College) for reviewing this edition. We acknowledge again the many reviewers for the first, second and third editions. This text is unquestionably strengthened by their contributions, and we welcome this opportunity to publicly thank them and acknowledge their efforts: Paul Allen (Sam Houston State University), Anne Bailey (Miami University), Emerson R. Bailey III (Casper College), James W. Baird (Community College of the Finger Lakes), A. Frederic Banda (The University of Akron), Robert J. Bond (Los Angeles Valley College), Benny D. Bowers (University of North Carolina at Charlotte), Patrick J. Cusatis (Pennsylvania State University), Mary Ellen Edmondson (University of Kentucky), Loren Geistfeld (Ohio State University), George L. Granger (East Tennessee State University), Vickie L. Hampton (University of Texas at Austin), Donald Johnson (College for Financial Planning), Walter H. Johnson (Cuyahoga Community College), Jerry L. Jorgensen (University of Utah), Robert F. Kegel, Jr. (Cypress College), Robert W. Kilpatrick (University of Connecticut), Anthony J. Lerro (Winthrop College), Joseph T. Marchese (Monroe Community College) William C. Marrs (Morton College), Jerry Mason (Texas Tech University), Randolph J. Mullis (University of Wisconsin), Emily Norman (Delta State University), Dennis D. Pappas (Columbus State Community College), Myron S. Pharo (Penn State University), J. Franklin Potts (Baylor University), Jean R. Robinson (Cornell University), Joe Samprone (Purdue University), Michael Solt (University of Santa Clara), Mary J. Stephenson (University of Maryland), Skip Swerdlow (University of Nevada–Las Vegas), and Rosemary Walker (Michigan State University).

We also thank George Euskirchen and Thomas E. Davidson for their contributions and Laura Abrams for her assistance.

Finally, the members of Prentice Hall's staff should be recognized for their work and, more important, for their enthusiasm for the project. Special thanks are due MaryBeth Sanok, Teresa A. Cohan, Judith Leale, and Margo Quinto. Their commitment to successful completion went beyond what an author usually expects from a publisher.

Bernard J. Winger
Ralph R. Frasca

Personal Finance

Part 1

THE BASIC FRAMEWORK: Organizing and Managing Your Financial Resources

We usually think of financial success as making the most of what we have. We can achieve it through planning: setting goals, establishing priorities, and making effective decisions. Our goals are likely to be both financial and nonfinancial. Indeed, nonfinancial goals, those pertaining to love, family, and religion, are probably more important. But our success in achieving financial goals often enables us to enrich the nonfinancial aspects of our lives.

Part 1 deals with effective planning techniques, the key to financial success. We begin, in Chapter 1, by outlining the planning process and presenting several basic concepts that can help you effectively evaluate financial choices. Among other issues, we consider the uneven match between income and needs during the life cycle, which requires us to respond by shifting resources through time to accommodate present and future needs.

Long-run financial success is usually accomplished by achieving short-run goals. Budgets and financial statements, the subjects of Chapter 2, help you do just that. Financial statements show you where you are now so that you can plan effectively for the future; they help determine your existing worth and show how you managed your income in the past. Budgeting, on the other hand, helps you manage your future income, thereby increasing your net worth.

Chapters 3 and 4 cover your most pervasive financial activities—maintaining adequate liquidity and using short-term credit. Our emphasis is upon performing these activities in the most cost-effective manner.

Part 1 concludes with a discussion of taxes, emphasizing the federal personal income tax. Chapter 5 familiarizes you with tax law, as well as tax-minimizing strategies.

Chapter 1

Financial Planning: Why It's Important to You

Objectives

1. To understand why setting goals is an important first step in financial planning
2. To appreciate that trends in the financial environment—inflation, taxes, and economic cycles—affect financial success and enhance the need for planning
3. To see why life-cycle financial planning is important and to understand the nature of a planning approach
4. To understand what is meant by marginal analysis and opportunity costs and to know how these concepts are used in financial decision making
5. To understand the time value of money and the techniques of compounding and discounting
6. To meet the Steele family, a family we will follow through the text

Many of us would prefer avoiding financial problems or turning them over to someone else. Managing financial resources is time consuming, usually difficult, and sometimes not successful. We have often asked the federal, state, and local governments for help; Social Security retirement and federally funded health care are examples. But there is growing evidence that governments are no better—and perhaps are worse—at solving these problems than we are. If you are a young adult ready to start pursuing the American Dream, you will face some challenges far more formidable than those that faced your parents. The Dream is becoming ever more elusive.

Many people of your parents' generation never worried much about health care and retirement. If they had a job, their employers provided health insurance; and Social Security will be waiting for them at retirement. Many of you are unlikely to have these assurances. If there is one dominant social theme in recent years it is *self-reliance*. Self-reliance, though, is not a trait inherited at birth; rather, it is an acquired skill. Which leads us to personal finance. Becoming self-reliant financially begins with knowledge, and your decision to take a personal finance course was a wise one; it may be one of the most important decisions in your life.

WHY STUDY PERSONAL FINANCE

You probably decided to take a personal finance course because financial success is important to you and you realize that in most cases it doesn't come easily. But what is financial success, and how is it measured? To some, it means making a lot of money—the sooner, the better. If that is your goal, then we are afraid this text won't help you very much; nor, we might add, will any other. You might as well save your time and go to Las Vegas or Atlantic City and hope for the best. **Financial success,** often elusive to define, is usually thought of as *obtaining the maximum benefits from limited financial resources*. This means you can be a financial success (or failure) regardless of your income level. A widow with many children and an income below the poverty line may be quite successful in allocating her very limited resources to achieve the goals her family feels are important, whereas a millionaire might misallocate most of his resources and achieve nothing.

Financial success: Obtaining maximum benefits from limited financial resources.

Your Goals in Life

If personal finance deals with achievement of goals, then you might ask: What goals does it try to achieve? Does it suggest, for example, that we all should save as much as we can? Do we measure success in terms of our weekly contributions to the bank account? Not necessarily. Obviously, what we plan to do during our lifetimes differs considerably. You may want to have a big family and enjoy entertainment activities with the kids while they are young and growing; you might also want to provide for their education. We, on the other hand, might be skinflints who love money for money's sake and have virtually no other interests in life. (We're really not.) As Figure 1.1 indicates, we can categorize goals as either nonfinancial or financial.

NONFINANCIAL GOALS We should realize that many of our aspirations in life are nonfinancial. We hold moral, family, social, religious, or political ideals that have little or no connection to finance. You can't put a price tag on these goals, and you

Nonfinancial	Financial
• Moral	• Current consumption
• Family	• Future consumption
• Social	• Savings
• Religious	
• Political	

Figure 1.1
Life's goals.

don't try. In fact, an attempt to buy a vote or a preferred position in the hereafter is considered illegal or sacrilegious. Oscar Wilde once defined a cynic as someone who knows the price of everything and the value of nothing. As students of personal finance, let us not become cynics. On the other hand, the extent to which we succeed in achieving our financial goals might determine how much time and energy are available to pursue the nonfinancial. Sociologists tell us, for example, that one of the primary reasons for divorce is financial stress in the family. Achieving financial goals doesn't assure a happy life, but the evidence suggests that it helps far more than it hinders.

FINANCIAL GOALS Financial goals form the basis for financial planning. Indeed, without financial goals, planning is impossible. Setting goals and incorporating them in annual budgeting are important topics discussed in depth in Chapter 2. However, it is useful to introduce the topics here.

Financial independence: Having sufficient income or resources to be self-reliant.

Very broadly, one might list the most important financial goal as **financial independence;** that is, to have enough income or resources to be self-reliant. However, a goal defined this broadly really doesn't help us plan for the future. What does self-reliant mean? You might understand it as having a job with little threat of a layoff, while someone else sees it as never going into debt. Actually, there are two more-concrete goals to shape financial plans: a consumption goal—current and future—and a savings goal.

Current consumption: Goods and services used in a current time period.

Current consumption. **Current consumption** refers to goods and services that we use in a current period of time, such as this year. These goods and services measure our scale of living. A low consumption budget means we use fewer of them and (probably) have a lower level of satisfaction than someone with a high consumption budget. If Mary's consumption budget is twice that of John's, chances are very good she has more consumption satisfaction than he. But she might not have twice as much. Economists often point out the **principle of diminishing marginal satisfaction,** which means that current consumption satisfaction increases as current income increases but usually at a decreasing rate. This principle explains why we begin to look more favorably at future consumption after we have achieved reasonable levels of current consumption.

Principle of diminishing marginal satisfaction: A decreasing *rate* of satisfaction in relation to increasing income.

Future consumption: Goods and services to be used in future periods.

Future consumption. **Future consumption** refers to goods and services to be used in future periods. By itself, future consumption is less desirable than current consumption. Would you rather enjoy a good meal today or 20 years from today? In fact, if your annual income were to remain constant throughout your life, you might very well choose to spend a higher proportion on consumption while you are young, rather than waiting until you are old. But our incomes are seldom the same from year to year. Usually, they are quite low when we start our careers, increase substantially as we move into our most productive years, and then decline as we enter retirement. If we were forced to consume all our income each year, a very uneven consumption pattern would result. Fortunately, there is no such requirement. We try to smooth current consumption over time in order to get the highest overall consumption satisfaction throughout our lifetimes. This means we borrow heavily when we are young and repay our debts in later years.

Savings: The portion of current income *not* consumed.

Savings. **Savings** is simply the portion of our income *not* spent on current consumption. We have just mentioned one important reason for saving—to enjoy future consumption, perhaps in retirement—but there are others. One of the more important of these is to leave an estate to our heirs. Another might be to increase our investment assets, thereby gaining greater financial independence.

Important Economic Trends

Achieving financial goals would be much simpler if we lived in a predictable economic environment. But, we don't. There are, however, certain trends that are likely to continue in the future. Let's see what they are.

CONTINUING INFLATION Inflation is a perennial problem. We are not likely to repeat in the near future the double-digit inflation numbers of the 1970s and early 1980s, but more-modest amounts are very possible. Recent annual rates have been between 2 and 4 percent (see Figure 1.2), a range that is likely to continue. Although these numbers suggest a tame inflationary environment, over long periods of time they can seriously erode the value of your savings. Your investments must earn more than the inflation rate if you hope to grow your wealth in real terms. Unfortunately, many people have been content to leave too much of their money in low-yielding savings accounts that often only match, or fall short of, inflation rates. We hope you won't make that mistake.

Figure 1.2
Annual inflation rates.
SOURCE: Federal Reserve Bank of St. Louis, *National Economic Trends,* August 1995, p. 7.

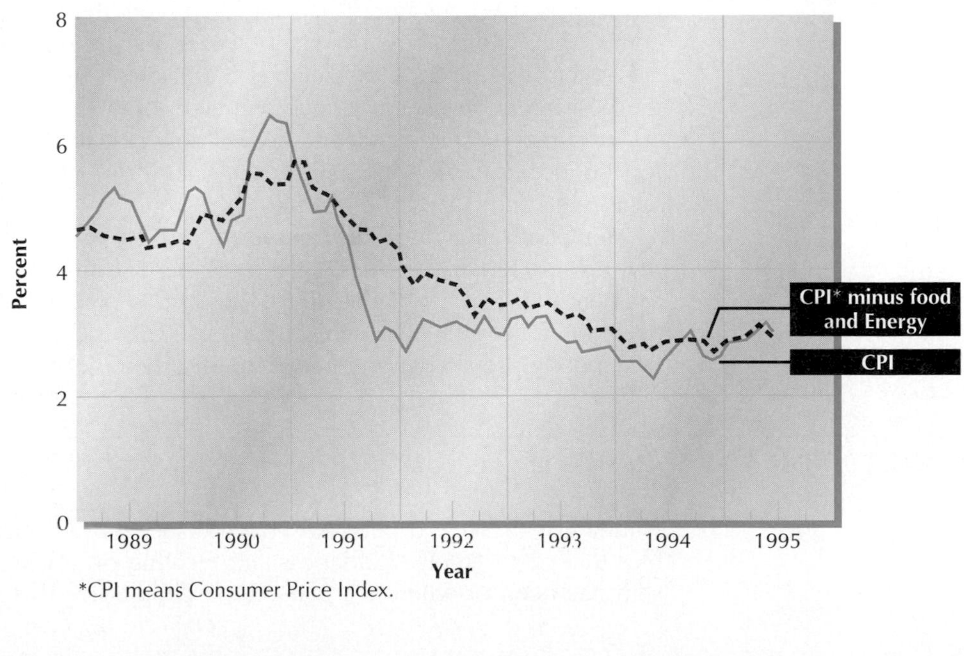

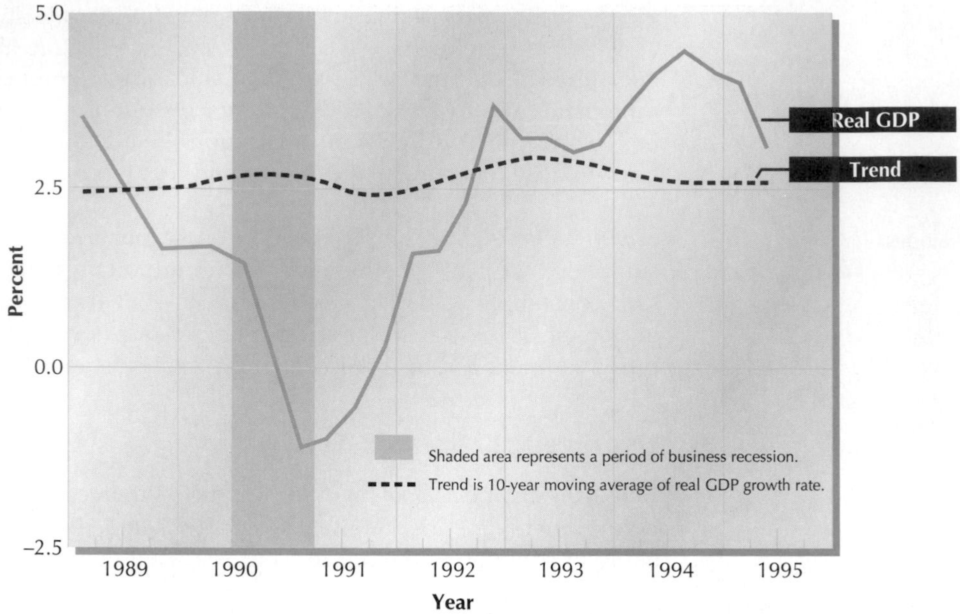

Figure 1.3
Changes in real gross domestic product (GDP).

SOURCE: Federal Reserve Bank of St. Louis, *National Economic Trends,* August, 1995, p. 3.

PERSISTENT BUSINESS CYCLES Figure 1.3 provides a measurement of our economy's performance in recent years. We selected it to show the 1990–1991 recession, which had a serious impact on many American families, in terms of layoffs, reduced incomes, and spending cutbacks. About every four years or so (the cycle has been longer lately), we get a recession, and there is no reason to suspect the pattern will stop. So you should develop financial plans that allow for economic instability. Build enough wealth to survive a financial shock and hold it in investments that aren't devastated in value by the cycle.

A HIGH AND SELECTIVELY REWARDING TAX SYSTEM The Republican congressional victories in 1994 suggested to some observers that sizable tax cuts were soon to come. They hadn't come by mid-1996, and maybe they never will. Our sociopolitical system still places considerable emphasis on government spending, and even the best intentions to scale back will take years to achieve significant results. The tax laws may change—indeed, there is now talk of substituting a consumption tax for the income tax—but whatever the final forms of taxation, they are likely to be very high.

Along with high rates, the tax system is likely to continue to incorporate features that reward certain activities, such as saving and investing for retirement. The government will play a smaller direct role in this process, offering instead the incentives for us to plan our own retirements. This is a scary proposition, considering how poorly prepared many people are for the tasks ahead.

ACHIEVING FINANCIAL GOALS THROUGH PLANNING

Planning is the key to personal financial success. Without it, your situation resembles that of an empty, rudderless ship floating on a lake. You can't tell where the ship has been or where it's going. Few people live this aimlessly, but many have

Box 1.1

PERSONAL FINANCE NEWS

Late Edition

For Whom Do the Bells Toll? For the Baby-Boomer Generation!

Some 80 million Americans, those born between 1946 and 1962, are in deep trouble. A generation not accustomed to the word *no* where spending is concerned are getting ever closer to retirement with very little in savings. And, it's starting to dawn on them that $1,500 a month from Social Security is petty cash to a family used to spending $4,000 a month to keep happy.

A recent study by the brokerage firm Merrill Lynch shows that the average amount of financial assets (savings accounts, bonds, mutual funds, stocks, and others) held by the average baby-boomer family is $2,600. Even though this amount excludes employer pension funds, it is still amazingly low. So how will the baby boomers make it?

Unfortunately, many families pursue retirement planning as though they live in Oz. Some plan to *never* retire; now, that's a realistic approach, particularly if you have a job that is physically or emotionally demanding and not much fun. Others are counting on Mom and Dad to leave them a bundle. True, there are trillions of dollars of savings held by the over-55 generation; but most of that belongs to a handful of very wealthy families. The average baby-boomer family will probably get around $25,000—just enough to buy a new car. And, no kidding, some families actually believe that a winning ticket in the state lottery will bail them out in the end.

If you are a member of a younger generation, observe today's situation and take note. You or one of your friends may have a parent who was forced into early retirement through corporate restructuring or "rightsizing." Surely, the news stories in the media have given plenty of examples. It's not a pretty sight to see a family devastated by a job loss, with $2,600 in the bank and little in retirement accounts.

Avoiding such a situation requires a thoughtful savings-investment plan. As the table below shows, the sooner you start, the easier the task. A $250,000 nest egg is not an excessive amount for two spouses who are likely to live 15 to 20 years beyond age 65. The 4 percent column is the most realistic when inflation is taken into consideration, but no tax-savings retirement plans (such as IRAs or 401(k)s) are used; if such plans are available, you could achieve the 6 or 8 percent columns. You would have to be very lucky to earn an inflation-adjusted 10 percent rate of return.

REQUIRED MONTHLY SAVINGS TO ACCUMULATE $250,000 BY AGE 65

	Interest Rate Earned on Investments			
Age You Begin to Invest	4%	6%	8%	10%
25	$ 211	$ 125	$ 71	$ 39
35	359	248	167	110
45	680	539	422	327
55	1,692	1,518	1,358	1,210

only very hazy and poorly defined ideas about what they hope to accomplish financially. Waking up one morning in your mid-forties and realizing you'd better do something about retirement is a poor approach. You may not have enough time to accumulate an adequate retirement nest egg, and you also lose all the income tax advantages that were available during the lost years, plus the earnings that earlier investments could have provided. A dollar saved and properly invested in your twenties could easily be the equivalent of $10 saved and invested during your forties. This view of planning as a lifelong process is called **life-cycle planning.**

Life-cycle planning: A view of financial planning as a lifelong process.

Life-Cycle Planning

People go through different phases during their lives, as Figure 1.4 shows. Goals change in importance as we enter different phases, but the key to life-cycle planning is that *all* our lifelong goals are recognized and attended to at *each* phase in the cycle. The sooner a goal is stated and solidified, the better. Retirement (as in

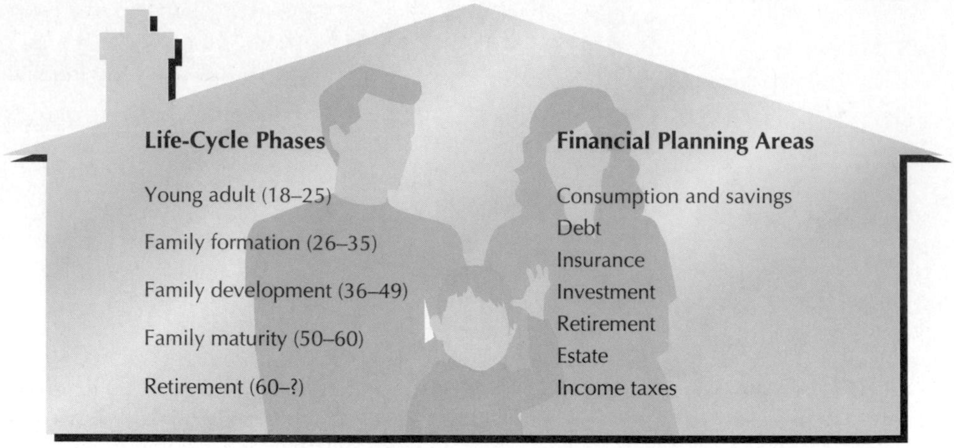

Figure 1.4
Life-cycle financial planning.

the preceding example) or the children's educations, or a trip to Tahiti, are more easily and effectively accomplished when lead times are longer.

Major Financial Planning Areas

Certain areas require constant attention in all life-cycle phases. These areas are: consumption and savings planning, debt planning, insurance planning, investment planning, retirement planning, and estate planning. Threaded throughout all of these areas is income tax planning. The government's share of your success is a fact of life that is probably already familiar to you. It certainly will become more familiar as this course progresses. The sections that follow discuss each type of planning.

CONSUMPTION AND SAVINGS PLANNING Consumption and savings planning is an integral part of your strategy to achieve lifelong goals. As mentioned previously, you must decide each year how much of your income to allocate to current consumption and how much to save for the future. Two important activities related to consumption and savings planning are preparing periodic personal financial statements—an income statement and a balance sheet—and an annual budget. The latter is the instrument you use most often to make sure you are moving toward your goals. Financial statements and budgeting are covered in Chapter 2. Also, the most important consumption expenditures, those for consumer durables and housing, are discussed in Chapters 15 and 16.

DEBT PLANNING Very few people avoid debt throughout their lives—nor should they. Debt is the vehicle that allows us to even our lifelong consumption. In addition, it is a shopping convenience, and it can help us hedge against inflation by permitting us to buy assets that match or beat the inflation rate. But debt must be managed carefully. We must avoid excessive debt and make sure we tap the lowest-cost sources of credit. Why borrow at 18 percent if you have access to funds costing 8 percent or less? Unfortunately, many Americans do. Debt management is discussed in Chapter 4.

INSURANCE PLANNING Life's uncertainties create continuous insurance needs. As a young adult with few obligations and no dependents, your primary asset is your ability to work and earn income. Therefore, you must protect yourself against the loss of that ability; that is, you need disability insurance. As you go through later phases of the life cycle, other insurance needs increase in importance. The needs of your dependents in the event of your death create a demand for life insurance, and as you accumulate assets—a house, automobiles, household furnishings, and others—you need more property and personal liability insurance. And, most important, you need medical insurance to protect against health or accident problems. The "average" illness can lead to hospital and doctor bills large enough to wipe out your entire savings, and then some. Insurance planning is explained in Chapters 6, 7, and 8.

INVESTMENT PLANNING While saving part of our income each year, we must decide how to invest it. Choices here seem almost limitless, ranging from simply letting our bank account grow to speculating in raw land or commodity futures contracts. Successful investment often spells the difference between achieving our lifelong goals (and maybe even exceeding them) and failing to do so. An important first investment goal is to provide sufficient liquidity; this topic is discussed in Chapter 3. You can then turn your attention to riskier investments that offer potentially higher returns, discussed in Chapters 9, 10, 11, 12, 13, and 14.

RETIREMENT PLANNING Retirement planning consists primarily of estimating future consumption and other needs and then determining how you will meet those needs when you are no longer working. Most of us rely on Social Security and employer-sponsored retirement plans for retirement income, but we also realize that supplemental sources may be necessary to maintain a suitable lifestyle in retirement. We must invest during our working years to accumulate a retirement nest egg. The federal government has recognized these supplemental retirement efforts and has enacted favorable tax legislation to help achieve them. Retirement planning is the subject of Chapter 17.

ESTATE PLANNING If you live forever, you can avoid the problem of estate planning: how to minimize taxes while giving away your wealth. Since the odds in favor of earthly immortality are not encouraging, your next best strategy is to make sure you have your financial house in order when you make the grand exit. Essential to this plan are a proper will and a sound tax strategy, which might mean distributing part of your wealth in the form of gifts while you are still alive. Estate planning is, appropriately enough, our final subject, and it appears in Chapter 18.

INCOME TAX PLANNING Almost no aspect of our financial lives is untouched by federal income taxes. The federal government will become a partner in all the income you earn. There are ways to minimize the tax bite, but it is up to you to find out what they are and how and when to use them. Two people with identical incomes and family situations could wind up with $100,000 difference in their assets after 30 years or so because of effective versus ineffective tax planning. With this much at stake, it's worth your effort to become familiar with the income tax law, and Chapter 5 will give you a good start.

A Planning Approach

As shown in Figure 1.5, planning involves four steps. First, you must state your broad goals in specific and concrete terms. For example, if buying a home is an

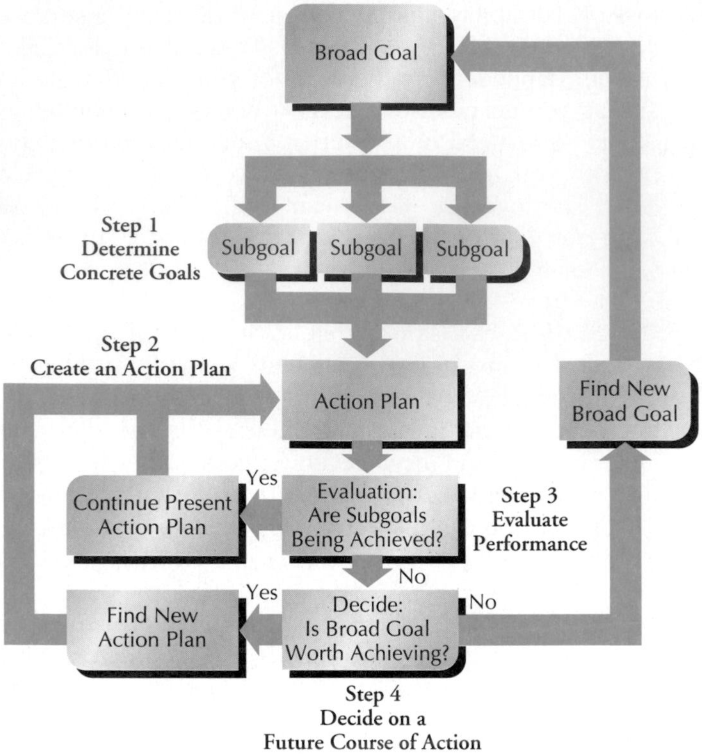

Figure 1.5
Steps in the planning approach.

important goal, you must decide eventually when you will buy it, how much to pay for it, the size of your down payment, and how to finance it. The second step is to create an action plan, which sets out in detail how you will achieve your goal. To achieve the goal of buying a home, you must save a portion of your income each year and invest the funds temporarily. After you have set a specific date to buy a home, you can decide which temporary investments are best suited to help achieve the goal. If the purchase date is relatively far in the future (say, five years or longer), you might choose investments that are somewhat riskier (with potentially higher yields) than you would choose if you intended to buy next year. The third step in the planning process involves evaluating your performance toward the goal. This step would be unnecessary if we lived in an unchanging world—but we do not. The type of home you want might increase in price, or financing costs might go up, or other changes could frustrate your effort to buy the home. The fourth and final planning stage forces us to decide if the goal is still worth achieving or if we should abandon it and search for another broad goal. If you decide the home is still worth the effort, for example, you must then revise your action plan, by increasing the annual savings or perhaps by choosing other temporary investments offering higher returns. (The latter approach could be very risky, though.)

Using the above four steps does not guarantee success, but you will certainly achieve goals far more easily if you use this method rather than a haphazard approach. Effective planning puts you at the rudder of the ship on the lake, and it gives you the navigational aids you need to bring the ship to its destination.

Box 1.2 SIMPLIFYING FINANCIAL PLANNING
Five Simple Steps to Start Your Financial Life

Financial planning is not easy, particularly when it must be tailored to a specific family. But its complexities should not deter you from taking important steps as your financial life begins in earnest after graduation. The following five steps are generalizations that may need to be changed as your situation evolves. But they should get you off on the right foot.

1. *Save 10 percent of your pretax income.* Try to have the amounts deducted automatically from your paycheck and invested directly so that you aren't tempted to slacken for a tempting expenditure.

2. *Use tax-deferred investment plans.* After you save 10 percent, try to invest as much as possible in tax-deferred plans, such as IRAs or 401(k)s. If your employer matches (fully or partially) your contributions to a 401(k), invest as much as you can even if the amount exceeds 10 percent; if you can't afford it, consider borrowing from your parents or another low-cost source. When an employer matches your contribution, you double your rate of return immediately—and that's hard to pass up.

3. *Take manageable risks with your investments.* Don't be afraid to invest in common stocks through a good mutual fund. To keep things simple until you can evaluate mutual funds, use index funds such as those offered by the Vanguard Group of Valley Forge, Pennsylvania. The percentage to invest in stocks is 100 minus your age; if you are 24, put 76 percent in stocks and 24 percent in high-quality corporate bonds (again, using mutual funds).

4. *Don't borrow on your credit cards.* You are likely to pay between 10 and 21 percent borrowing on credit cards in today's market, and these rates are simply too high, given current inflation and interest rates in general. You can't afford an item if you must borrow to buy—it's that simple.

5. *Buy term life insurance.* Don't buy *any* life insurance if you have no dependents who might be impoverished by your untimely death. But if you have dependents, you need life insurance—and probably far more than you think ($500,000 is not too much). Term insurance is far cheaper than cash value insurance, and with it you can probably afford $500,000 protection. That much cash value insurance is far too expensive for beginners. After you learn more about life insurance, you may want to switch.

The Building Blocks of Success

An important part of financial planning is setting priorities. All through life you will encounter both opportunities and risks, and you need to put them in perspective. Suppose you are a young person with family obligations and very little savings. A friend who has recently become a securities salesperson calls and tells you how you can double your money in a speculative investment. There is a strong temptation to take the offer, even though you know if it fails you will have to give up or delay other important goals. But if it succeeds, you can do so much more! Most financial advisers will tell you to forget risky propositions such as this until you have satisfied those goals you have already decided are the most important.

"Building-block" approach to personal finance: Sequential investing, starting with a low-risk foundation and then moving to riskier investments.

Setting priorities and sticking to the long-run plan suggests a **"building-block" approach to personal finance,** as illustrated in Figure 1.6. You begin with the lowest blocks, which means you first build a strong foundation of support. You proceed to the first investment level *after* the lowest blocks are secure. Likewise, go to riskier investments only after you have a suitable level of safe ones, deferring the very riskiest until last. Remember that if you fail at a higher level, the goals supported by success at the lower levels will not be achieved. You might have decided, for example, to invest in government bonds that will guarantee enough future return to put your kids through the state university. If you abandon this plan and put the money instead into speculative growth stocks, you might eventually have enough to put them through Harvard—or you might have to tell them there is very little available to support their educations anywhere. You must make the choice, but at least understand the risks involved and the potential consequences of your choice.

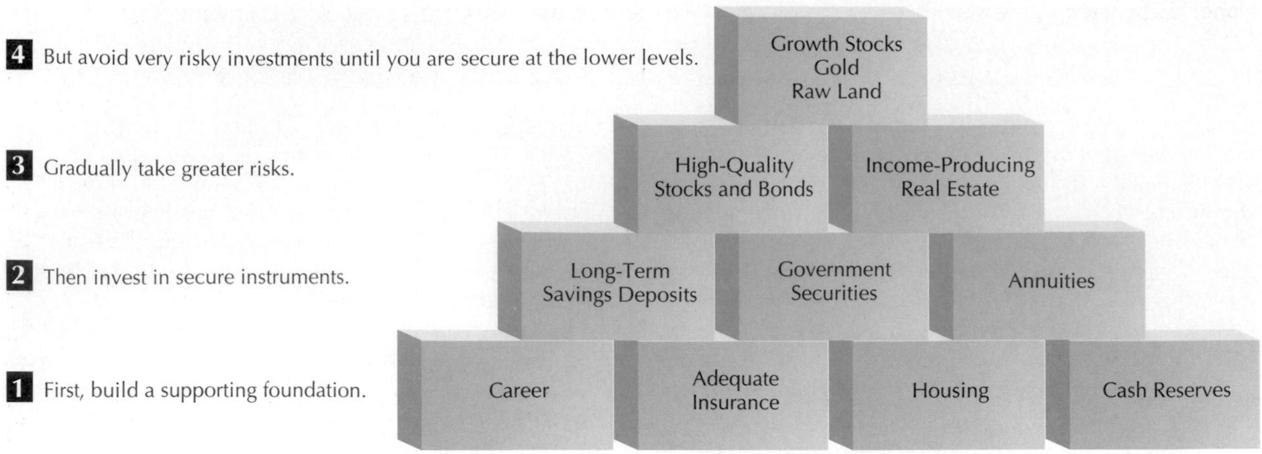

Figure 1.6 The building blocks of success.

Making Financial Decisions

Making a decision is a complex process. To decide is to choose among alternatives. You probably have encountered many situations in which making a choice was difficult; indeed, your biggest problem may have been simply identifying what choices were available. Then you had to find some basis for evaluating the expected outcomes of each alternative. With all that done, you must pick one alternative as the best. Consider how difficult choosing a major in college can be; unfortunately, we face equally difficult financial decisions most of our lives. Although each decision is made in its own set of circumstances, all decisions involve techniques that can help you. Each technique—using marginal analysis, determining opportunity costs, and considering the time value of money—is explained below.

Marginal analysis: Evaluating *changes* in important variables in relation to controllable decision inputs.

MARGINAL ANALYSIS **Marginal analysis** means looking at *changes* in important variables that are related to changes in decision inputs you can control. For example, suppose you are ready to graduate and you are investing in a wardrobe you will need for your first job. You know that two good business suits are a must but a third might be a luxury. To decide whether to buy the third suit requires that you compare the benefits it provides against its cost. If you think the added benefits are worth it, buy the third suit; if not, then don't buy it. But definitely do not consider benefits that the first and second suits provide, because they are totally irrelevant to the decision.

Marginal analysis should always be employed whenever a decision involves comparing different approaches to a problem. For example, suppose you are considering buying two different automobile insurance policies that differ with respect to coverage and cost. The two plans have the same basic coverage, but one includes protection against certain perils whereas the other does not. The former also has a higher yearly premium. In deciding between the two, you don't have to look at the total coverages and total premiums of each; all you have to do is to compare the extra (marginal) coverage with the extra (marginal) premium. Then decide if the more-comprehensive policy is worth the extra cost.

Opportunity costs: Benefits given up when one alternative is chosen over another.

OPPORTUNITY COSTS **Opportunity costs** are benefits that you give up when you choose one alternative over another. If you decide to work during the Christmas holidays, you might give up a skiing trip to Colorado. The opportunity cost of the job is the fun you lose by not choosing the skiing trip, and the opportunity cost of the skiing trip is the income you won't earn by turning down the job. Sometimes opportunity costs are obvious; at other times they are identified only by thoughtful consideration. For example, what is your opportunity cost of taking a course in personal finance, assuming you need the hours for graduation? It is not the tuition cost of the course; rather, it is the information and learning offered by another course that you can't take because you are taking this one.

These examples might seem trivial, but opportunity costs arise in big decisions as well as small. Examples: What are the opportunity costs of choosing one career over another? What are the opportunity costs of your undergraduate education? What are the opportunity costs of renting versus buying a home? Consider carefully your responses to these questions. Some of the costs are clearly economic and probably easy to measure; others involve personal preferences and can be measured only by expressing personal value judgments. To get on the right track when using this technique, ask the following question: What do I give up if I choose one alternative over another? The answer will give you the opportunity cost for the alternative under consideration.

THE TIME VALUE OF MONEY

Many of our important financial decisions involve long periods of time. Consider this example: You make retirement investments in your early twenties that you will not touch for 30 or even 40 years. But there are so many investments available today offering different rates of return and different levels of risk, how do you evaluate alternatives unless you have a clear understanding of how an investment's return influences its growth in value over time? Consider a second example: You are thinking of buying a life insurance policy that will offer a cash value 10 years from its purchase. You must decide whether the annual premiums you pay to buy the policy are reasonable amounts, given the policy's insurance protection benefits and its future cash value.

Each of the above examples requires some knowledge of time-value-of-money techniques to make an intelligent decision. Indeed, so many financial decisions involve both time and money that we must acquire the basic time-value-of-money skills, which are called compounding and discounting. Each is discussed in the following sections.

Compounding (Finding Future Values)

Compounding: The process of accumulating value over time from a single payment.
Annuity: A series of equal payments.
Future value: A sum of money received or paid in the future.

Compounding refers to the process of accumulating value over time. Two cases are considered: first, the accumulation of value from a single payment (*payment* is a more general term than *investment*); second, the accumulation of value from a series of equal payments, called an **annuity.**

FUTURE VALUE OF A SINGLE PAYMENT A sum of money received or paid in the future is called a **future value.** For example, you might be considering an investment that costs $1,000 today and returns the same amount to you at the end of three years. Is it a good investment? Of course not! Why be content just to get your money back when other investments pay interest? If someone wishes to use our money, we insist on a return—one at least as good as those available on equal-risk, alternative investments. Suppose the borrower offered to give your $1,000 back at the end of three years along with $200 in interest. Is that acceptable, if you think you could earn 10 percent annual interest somewhere else? To answer the question we must calculate the future value (FV) of $1,000 invested elsewhere. This calculation is shown below.

$$FV \text{ at end of year } 1 = \$1{,}000 + 0.10(\$1{,}000) = \$1{,}100$$
$$FV \text{ at end of year } 2 = \$1{,}100 + 0.10(\$1{,}100) = \$1{,}210$$
$$FV \text{ at end of year } 3 = \$1{,}210 + 0.10(\$1{,}210) = \$1{,}331$$

An alternative quick calculation is:

$$FV = (\$1{,}000)(1.0 + i)(1.0 + i)(1.0 + i)$$

where i = your required investment rate each period. Then

$$FV = (\$1{,}000)(1.1)(1.1)(1.1) = (\$1{,}000)(1.331) = \$1{,}331$$

An even quicker calculation (assuming you use a calculator) is:

$$FV = (\$1{,}000)(1.0 + i)^n$$

where n = the number of periods you earn the rate i. Then,

$$FV = (\$1{,}000)(1.1)^3 = (\$1{,}000)(1.331) = \$1{,}331$$

In the above example, your $1,000 grows to $1,331 if you can invest it (and all the subsequent interest earned) at 10 percent. Comparing $1,331 with the $1,200 offered by the other investment tells us the other investment should be rejected.

Compound interest: A future value that includes interest on interest.

Simple interest: An assumption that interest earned in a period is withdrawn in that period.

The $331 of interest calculated above is called **compound interest.** It includes "interest on interest," which means that interest earned in earlier periods is assumed to be reinvested to earn interest in future periods. **Simple interest** assumes that interest earned in each period is withdrawn and not reinvested. The formula below is used to calculate simple interest:

$$\text{Simple interest} = (\text{principal}) \times (\text{rate}) \times (\text{time})$$

Using the above data, simple interest would be $300 as calculated below:

$$\$300 = (\$1{,}000) \times (0.10) \times (3)$$

You can use either method to calculate interest, depending on which one is more appropriate to what you actually will do with earned interest. However, in most financial planning illustrations the compound method is used.

The importance of additional yield. The future values of different investments are crucial to many financial decisions. For example, suppose you are considering investments A and B. A offers an 8 percent yield and has virtually no risk on either a short- or long-term basis. *B* offers a 10 percent yield and is about as risky as *A* on a long-term basis, but somewhat riskier short-term. (You might pay a penalty for early withdrawal, for example.) Since you plan to hold each investment for a long period of time, *B*'s added risk is not of major concern to you. On the other hand, you aren't sure that a mere two percentage points is enough marginal yield to pick *B* over *A*. By looking only at the difference of two percentage points, you may fail to see the substantial difference in future values between the two. Figure 1.7 shows this difference in dramatic detail. (The amounts were calculated using the compound interest techniques explained above.) At the end of three years, you will have only $71 ($1,331 minus $1,260) more with investment *B*, but at the end of 40 years you will have an extra $23,535—more than twice as much!

The importance of additional time. Figure 1.7 also dramatizes the importance of investing early to achieve certain goals, such as retirement. Suppose you are 25 and plan to retire at age 65. You are considering investing now for retirement but wonder how much difference it would make if you waited 10 years to start. Assuming the 10 percent investment rate, the answer is $27,810 ($45,259 minus $17,449). You accumulate considerably more in the last 10 years than you do in the first 30!

Time-value-of-money tables. Future value calculations are easy to make with a hand calculator, following the procedures just explained. As an alternative, many people use a *future-value-of-$1 table*. A portion of such a table is shown as Table 1.1. (More-detailed tables appear in Appendix A.) A future-value table shows the future value of $1 invested for a specified number of periods and at a specified investment rate each period. To use the table, simply multiply the future value of $1 by the number of dollars you invest. If you invest $100, multiply $100 times 1.3310; if $200, multiply $200 times 1.3310, and so forth. You can see from Table 1.1 how the values in Figure 1.7 were determined.

Figure 1.7
Future value of $1,000 invested at 8 and at 10 percent.

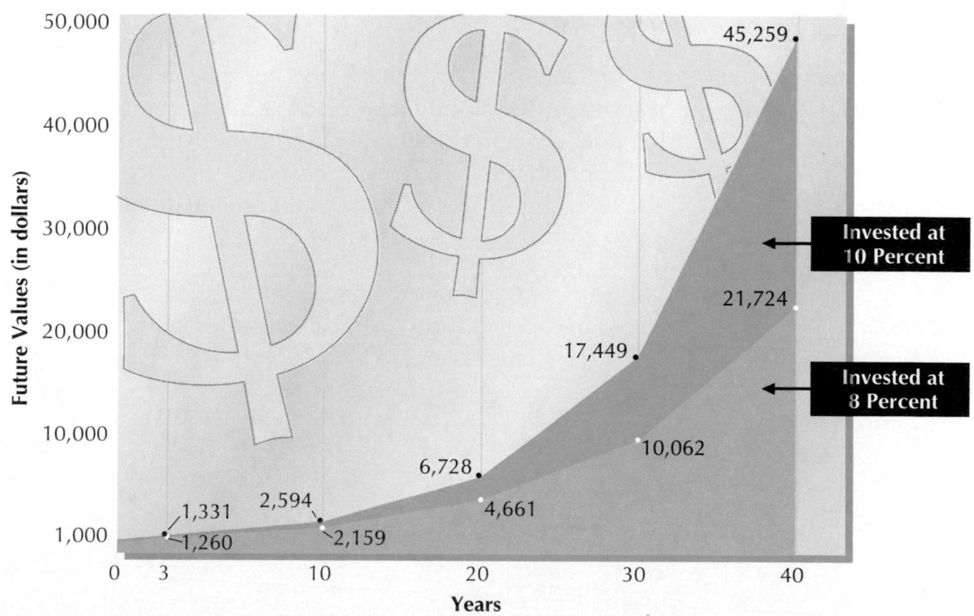

TABLE 1.1 • PORTION OF A FUTURE-VALUE-OF-$1 TABLE (See Appendix A, Table A.1 for an expanded table.)

Number of Periods (*n*)	Interest Rate		
	6%	8%	10%
1	1.0600	1.0800	1.1000
3	1.1910	1.2597	1.3310
10	1.7908	2.1589	2.5937
20	3.2071	4.6610	6.7275
30	5.7435	10.0620	17.4490
40	10.2850	21.7240	45.2590

FUTURE VALUE OF AN ANNUITY Recall that an annuity is a series of equal payments. Many financial products, such as investments and insurance policies, involve making annual payments. So, suppose an investment requires a payment of $1,000 a year for the next three years, with payments made at the *end* of each year. How much will this investment accumulate at the end of the three years, assuming an annual investment rate of 10 percent?

Let's break the investment down to three separate single payments—one occurring a year from now (with two years to accumulate), one occurring two years from now (one accumulation year), and one occurring three years from now (no accumulation time). The accumulations are as follows:

First payment: $1,000 × 1.1 × 1.1 =	$1,210
Second payment: $1,000 × 1.1 =	1,100
Third payment: $1,000 × 1.0 =	1,000
Total	$3,310

The answer is $3,310. It could have been found much more quickly by referring to a future-value-of-$1-annuity table, an example of which appears in Table 1.2. As you see, the future value of a $1 annuity invested at 10 percent for three years is 3.310. Multiply this figure by the annuity amount—$1,000—and you have your answer. You have found the future value of an ordinary annuity (FVOA).

Ordinary annuity: An annuity with end-of-period payments.

Annuity due: An annuity with beginning-of-period payments.

If payments take place at the end of the period, the annuity is called an **ordinary annuity;** if they take place at the beginning of a period, it is called an **annuity due.** An annuity due simply involves one more compounding period than an ordinary annuity, thereby increasing the total accumulation. Let's return to the above example and calculate the accumulation.

TABLE 1.2 • PORTION OF A FUTURE-VALUE-OF-$1-ANNUITY TABLE (See Appendix A, Table A.2 for an expanded table.)

Number of Periods (*n*)	Interest Rate		
	6%	8%	10%
1	1.0000	1.0000	1.0000
3	3.1836	3.2464	3.3100
10	13.1800	14.4860	15.9370
20	36.7850	45.7620	57.2750
30	79.0580	113.2800	164.4900
40	154.7600	259.0500	442.5900

First payment: $1,000 × 1.1 × 1.1 × 1.1 = $1,331
Second payment: $1,000 × 1.1 × 1.1 = 1,210
Third payment: $1,000 × 1.1 = 1,000
Total $3,641

The sum—$3,641—is called the future value of an annuity due (FVAD). Of course, there is a much easier way to find this value. Simply find the accumulation with an ordinary annuity and multiply it by 1.0 plus the interest rate (*i,* expressed as a decimal); that is,

$$FVAD = (1.0 + i) \times FVOA = (1.0 + 0.10) \times FVOA$$
$$FVAD = (1.10) \times \$3{,}310 = \$3{,}641$$

Since converting a FVOA to a FVAD is so easy, we present only an FVOA table in Appendix A.

Discounting (Finding Present Values)

Discounting: The process of reducing future values to present values.

In compounding we are finding future values, given present values; in contrast, **discounting** is the process of reducing future values to present values. Again, two cases are considered: first, finding the present value of a single sum that will be received or paid in the future; and second, finding the present value of an annuity to be received or paid in the future.

PRESENT VALUE OF A SINGLE PAYMENT Discounting is simply the reverse process of compounding. So, revising the above example, suppose an investment that requires an immediate $1,000 payment will pay us $1,331 three years from now. Is it a good investment? The answer depends on the interest rate (now called a discount rate) we think should apply to the investment. Let's find the present value (*PV*) of the $1,331 future value (*FV*), discounting at 10 percent (*i*). The easiest approach is to use a present-value-of-$1 table, an example of which appears in Table 1.3. As you see, the present value of $1 received three years in the future and discounted at 10 percent is $0.7513 (about 75 cents). Multiplying 0.7513 times the future value of $1,331 gives us the present value of the investment—$1,000.

The answer should reinforce the statement above that discounting is simply the reverse process of compounding. We showed earlier that $1,000 *compounds* to $1,331 when invested at a 10 percent annual rate for three years. Clearly, then,

TABLE 1.3 • PORTION OF A PRESENT-VALUE-OF-$1 TABLE
(See Appendix A, Table A.3 for an expanded table.)

Number of Periods (*n*)	Interest Rate		
	6%	8%	10%
1	0.9434	0.9259	0.9091
3	0.8396	0.7938	0.7513
10	0.5584	0.4632	0.3855
20	0.3118	0.2145	0.1486
30	0.1741	0.0994	0.0573
40	0.0972	0.0460	0.0221

$1,331 *discounts* to $1,000 when it is received three years from now and 10 percent is the annual discount rate.

Is the investment a good one, then? Actually, it's right at the margin between good and bad—a situation we often describe as a "fairly priced" asset. For example, if you use an 8 percent discount rate, you get a present value of $1,056.55 (0.7938 × $1,331). Now, we could say the investment is a good one because the present value exceeds the $1,000 required to buy it. In contrast, if you discount at 12 percent, the investment turns bad because the present value is now only $947.41 (0.7118 × $1,331).

PRESENT VALUE OF AN ANNUITY Finally, we can find the present values of ordinary annuities and annuities due. Again, the easiest method is to use the present-value-of-$1 annuity table (see Table 1.4). As an example, suppose you are evaluating an investment that pays you $5,000 a year (end of year) for the next three years. What is the present value of the investment (ordinary annuity), assuming an annual discount rate of 6 percent? From Table 1.4, we find the discount factor for three years and 6 percent; it is 2.6730. So, the present value of an ordinary annuity (*PVOA*) = 2.6730 × $5,000 = $13,365.

Table 1.4 shows discount factors for ordinary annuities. If the investment required beginning-of-year payments, its present value (*PVAD*) would be $14,166.90. As before:

$$PVAD = (1.0 + i) \times PVOA = (1.0 + 0.06) \times PVOA$$
$$PVAD = (1.06) \times \$13{,}365 = \$14{,}166.90$$

Is this a good investment? The answer depends on its cost. Suppose the cost is $13,700 and payments are received at the end of years. Then it is a bad investment because the present value of what you receive is only $13,365; in effect, you lose $335 ($13,365 − $13,700) if you buy it. But if payments begin immediately (annuity due), it's a good investment and you make $466.90 ($14,166.90 − $13,700.00). Receiving the payments one year earlier makes the difference.

Time-Value-of-Money Applications in the Text

We could provide many more applications of time-value-of-money techniques at this point in our discussion. However, they would be redundant because we will use the techniques in future chapters when they are needed to evaluate specific financial products or strategies. At those points, we will explain solutions using the

TABLE 1.4 • PORTION OF A PRESENT-VALUE-OF-$1 ANNUITY TABLE
(See Appendix A, Table A.4 for an expanded table.)

Number of Periods (*n*)	Interest Rate		
	6%	8%	10%
1	0.9434	0.9259	0.9091
3	2.6730	2.5571	2.4869
10	7.3601	6.7101	6.1446
20	11.4699	9.8181	8.5136
30	13.7648	11.2578	9.4268
40	15.0463	11.9246	9.7791

simplest and most direct approaches. For now, learn the basics and become familiar with the four tables.

THE STEELE FAMILY

As we start our journey into personal financial planning, we would like to introduce you to the Steele family. You will meet them from time to time in the succeeding chapters as they help us illustrate the application of financial planning techniques. The Steeles represent a composite of the characteristics of a typical American middle-class family. Sharon and Arnold are both professionals in their mid-thirties with two children, two cars, and a dog.

By most measures, the Steeles have achieved a certain level of success. Arnold, 37, is a chemist with a major paint manufacturer and is currently next in line for vice president of plant operations. Sharon, 35, is a CPA and works part time at a local accounting firm. As the time demanded by the two children, Nancy, 9, and John, 7, has declined, her part-time work has steadily expanded. In a few years she hopes to return to full-time employment.

Box 1.3 SAVING MONEY
What's a Professional Financial Planner—And Do You Need One?

The growing complexities of financial planning over the past 20 years have created a demand for a new professional—the **financial planner.** This person has a broad understanding of tax laws, insurance, investments, and finance in general. He or she is not necessarily an expert in any one area but is sufficiently knowledgeable in all to recognize problems and to suggest specialized professional help, if it is needed. The planner's main function is to create a financial plan to help clients achieve their goals. This profession is not yet as organized and regulated as other professions, such as medicine, law, or accounting, and anyone can adopt the title of professional planner. But there is a growing trend toward regulation and, as the table below shows, there are a number of self-regulatory organizations that are active in establishing standards and a professional code of ethics.

Do you need a professional planner? Of course, the answer to that question depends on the complexity of your financial situation and how much of your own time you are willing to devote to the job. Assuming you have an average financial situation and you carefully complete this text (and the course, if you are using the text as part of a course), you should be able to develop your own financial plans. However, the professional planner may be able to add insights to a problem or use a computer to develop and evaluate your financial plans. These services could be worth their costs, which usually start at about $300 for a simple evaluation and could go to several thousand dollars for someone with complex financial problems.

Some companies provide financial planning services to their employees as a fringe benefit. If you use this service, make sure the contact person is truly a financial planner and not a commissioned salesperson who may promote his or her products, whether they are appropriate for you or not.

Organization	Certification/Membership
International Board of Standards and Practices	Certified Financial Planner (CFP)
American College	Chartered Financial Consultant (ChFC)
International Association of Financial Planning	Member of the Registry
International Association of Registered Planners	Registered Financial Planner (RFP)
National Association of Personal Financial Advisors	Association of Fee-Only Planners
American Institute of Certified Public Accountants—Personal Financial Planning Division	Certified Public Accountant—Accredited Personal Financial Planning Specialist (CPA–APFS)

Like many people, the Steeles are not experiencing any unusual financial stress. They live a comfortable life in their own home near a relatively large Midwestern city. Also, like most of us, they have achieved all this without much in the way of serious financial planning. Of course, they have some general idea of what their monthly inflows and outflows are, but they never really sat down as a family to specify their financial goals and come up with an orderly plan for achieving them.

Lately, they have come to the conclusion that a casual review of their expenditures and income might not adequately prepare them for future and long-term needs. As of now, they have not yet fully considered how they will provide for the children's college educations or for their own support in retirement. These and other related questions are too important for the casual planning they have done so far. The tools developed in this text will help them plan for whatever may be on their financial horizon.

SUMMARY

Planning for personal finance needs is necessary for all of us. In this chapter we have introduced you to the planning process, a process that involves setting concrete goals, devising action plans to achieve goals, evaluating performance, and deciding which goals are worth continuing to pursue. We have also explored several basic techniques and concepts that form the framework for making financial decisions—marginal analysis, opportunity cost, and the time value of money. Finally, we have considered the nature of the financial environment, identifying broad trends that are likely to continue in the future.

KEY TERMS

annuity (p. 13)
annuity due (p. 16)
"building-block" approach to personal finance (p. 11)
compound interest (p. 14)
compounding (p. 13)
current consumption (p. 4)
discounting (p. 17)
financial independence (p. 4)
financial planner (p. 19)
financial success (p. 3)
future consumption (p. 4)
future value (p. 13)
life-cycle planning (p. 7)
marginal analysis (p. 12)
opportunity costs (p. 13)
ordinary annuity (p. 16)
principle of diminishing marginal satisfaction (p. 4)
savings (p. 5)
simple interest (p. 14)

PROBLEMS AND REVIEW QUESTIONS

1. Give a definition of financial success, and discuss how it may be measured.
2. Discuss the choice of financial and nonfinancial goals and the part each may play in personal financial planning.
3. Identify important economic trends that are likely to continue in the future.
4. What are the phases of the life cycle, and how are they related to financial planning?
5. Explain the steps involved in financial planning, and list the eight major planning areas.
6. What does a building-block approach to success entail, and how does it reduce the risk of failure?
7. Explain marginal analysis and opportunity cost, and then indicate why they are important concepts in financial decision making.
8. How would you measure the cost of spending a night at home watching television?
9. How does simple interest differ from compound interest?
10. You deposit $100 in a bank account earning 8 percent a year compounded once *annually*. Assuming you have not withdrawn anything, how much do you have in the ac-

count after two years? How much would you have if you withdrew each year's interest? Calculate your interest earned in each case.

11. Explain the difference between compounding and discounting.
12. What is an annuity? Distinguish between an ordinary annuity and an annuity due.
13. Find the following future values, using Table 1.1 or 1.2:
    (*a*) $500 invested today at a 6 percent rate and held for 20 years,
    (*b*) $800 invested at the end of each of the next 10 years to earn 10 percent,
    (*c*) $300 invested at the beginning of each of the next 40 years to earn 8 percent.
14. Find the following present values, using Table 1.3 or 1.4:
    (*a*) $6,000 received 30 years from now, discounted at 10 percent,
    (*b*) $4,000 to be received at the end of each of the next 10 years, discounted at 6 percent,
    (*c*) $2,000 to be received at the end of each of the next three years, discounted at 8 percent.
15. Suppose an investment has been offered to you that requires an initial outlay of $10,000. Ten years from now the investment will pay you $20,000. If you think an investment of this type should offer a return of 8 percent, should you make the investment? Explain, showing your analysis.
16. You can buy an annuity contract that will pay you $1,000 a year (end of year) for the next 10 years. The contract costs $6,000 today. If you think you should earn 6 percent on such investments, should you buy the contract? Explain, showing your analysis.

Case 1.1 The Haggertys' Financial Planning

Jan and Mickey Haggerty graduated from college several years ago. Each majored in biology, and they were fortunate to receive good job offers at graduation; their combined income last year was over $50,000. The Haggertys enjoy a high level of current consumption, but they also have saved about $6,000, which is invested in a bank savings account. They would like to buy a house eventually, but they are not certain when. Jan thinks they should have a definite plan for buying the house. This plan would indicate the date of purchase, the down payment, the expected purchase price, and other important details. Jan is so enthusiastic over the purchase that she thinks they should take their money out of savings and invest in growth stocks. She has heard that you ought to get 20 percent on these stocks, which certainly beats the 6 percent they are getting at the bank.

Mickey thinks Jan worries too much about buying a house. He questions the necessity of a financial plan, believing instead that they should just continue saving in the future as they have in the past. Besides, he heard at work that a recession could be coming, and, if it does, he thinks it might be a good idea to delay buying stocks until their prices come way down. He heard you make money in the stock market by buying low and selling high. Jan would like to buy the house within five years; Mickey thinks setting a date is not wise. If the stocks work out well, they get it sooner; if not, they have to wait. Besides, a friend of Mickey's told him he should worry more about all the income taxes he and Jan are paying, since they already are in a 28 percent tax bracket.

QUESTIONS

1. Without knowing more about the Haggertys, would you say they might benefit from financial planning? Cite specific examples.
2. What do you think of Jan's idea of investing in growth stocks? What additional information about the Haggertys would you like to have before you give a final answer to this question?
3. What is your opinion of Mickey's idea to delay buying common stocks until their prices fall? Do you think his source of information at work is a reliable forecaster? And do you think it's a good idea in general to base the success of your financial plans on accurately forecasting future economic events? Explain.

Case 1.2 Lou Pirella and Vicki Wright: Two College Students

Lou Pirella and Vicki Wright are taking a course in computer science together. They have been good friends for some time, and each will graduate at the end of the current term. Lou is going directly into the work force, and Vicki plans to earn an MBA degree at a university near her hometown. She is trying to convince Lou to join her, but he feels four years of college is enough—at least for a while.

Lou and Vicki have been talking quite a bit about their plans after graduation. Vicki is relying on her MBA to earn a good income in the future, although she also plans to invest, but only in very secure investments. Lou will take a more aggressive approach to investing, and he told Vicki he will probably earn two percentage points more than she each year. Vicki hardly thinks that's worth the effort; after all; 2 percent on a thousand dollars is only $20. Big deal. Both agree, though, they will take care of their insurance, housing, and liquidity needs before they start investing.

QUESTIONS

1. How should Vicki look at the opportunity costs of her MBA degree? Explain.
2. Do you agree that an extra 2 percent return is trivial and hardly worth taking any additional risk for? Illustrate your answer with a good example.
3. Suppose that when Vicki registers at the university, she learns that she can pay a flat tuition of $3,000 a semester and take up to 15 credit hours (but no more). Or she can elect simply to pay $250 per credit hour and take as many hours as she wants each semester. Assuming it takes 60 hours to graduate and also assuming she could handle 20 hours a semester without threatening her grades, what is the marginal cost of the second option—that is, paying $250 per credit hour? What might be the opportunity costs of the first option? Explain.

HELPFUL CONTACTS

American College
270 Bryn Mawr Avenue, Bryn Mawr, PA 19010

American Institute of Certified Public Accountants
1211 Avenue of the Americas, New York, NY 10036 (telephone 800–969–7371)

The International Board of Certified Financial Planners
5445 DTC Parkway, Englewood, CO 80111 (telephone 303–850–0333)
If you are interested in a career in financial planning, ask for their publication "Financial Planning as a Career." If you are thinking of using a financial planner, ask for their publication "How to Select a Financial Planner."

INTERNET ADDRESSES

Consumer Information Center of the U.S. General Services Administration (publishers of the Consumer Information Catalog, which provides information on a wide range of consumer activities, from buying a car to repaying student loans)
http://www.pueblo.gsa.gov/

Consumer Law Page (brochures and resources on legal issues affecting consumers)
http://www.seamless.com/talf/txt/intro.html

Consumer Line (Federal Trade Commission publications concerning consumer fraud)
http://www.ftc.gov/bcp/conline/conline.htm

Consumer World (over 900 of the most useful consumer resources on the Internet)
http://www.consumerworld.org/

Federal Reserve Bank of St. Louis (good source of economic data)
http://www.stls:frb.org./fred/

Gabelli Funds, Inc. (financial calculator for periodic investments)
http://www.gabelli.com/Gab_phtml/mfund/saving1.html perinv

GNN: Global Network Navigator (excellent site that provides links to financial newspaper and magazine web sites)
http://gnn.com//gnn/wic/wics/persfin.nmn.html

LifeNet (sources for insurance and financial services)
http://www.lifenet.com/

The Money Advisor (provides a variety of both general and task-specific financial calculators: consumer loans, savings, mortgages, and many others)
http://www.moneyadvisor.com/calc/

USA Today Personal Wealth Section (provides a variety of financial news stories and investment strategies)
http://web.usatoday.com/money/wealth/mw001.htm

Wall Street Journal (inspect the Personal Finance Library by signing up for the Money and Investing Update)
http://www.wsj.com/

Yahoo (Yahoo is the best known compiler of web sites. It lists sites covering topics from the Arts to Society and Culture. If you are just beginning to "cruise the net," you should start here.)
http://www.yahoo.com/

Chapter 2

Financial Statements and Budgets: Where Are You Now and Where Are You Going?

Objectives

1. To understand the importance of the balance sheet as a tool for measuring personal wealth
2. To prepare a balance sheet by identifying and valuing assets and liabilities
3. To prepare an income statement and to recognize its role in measuring financial performance
4. To evaluate financial performance by using appropriate financial ratios
5. To prepare an annual budget by constructing a master budget worksheet and a monthly income and expense plan
6. To monitor monthly activities by creating a system for recording actual income and expenses and then comparing them with budgeted amounts
7. To evaluate and control expenses during the year through a monthly review process

You learned in Chapter 1 that financial planning is a four-stage process: First, financial goals are set; second, action plans are devised for achieving those goals; third, a system is developed to measure the degree to which success is achieved; and fourth, on the basis of an evaluation of achievement, goals and action plans are reexamined to determine whether they should be dropped, modified, or left unchanged. In this chapter, our attention is directed toward the third task—measuring achievement. We are helped in this effort by accountants, who have devised three particularly useful statements that measure success. These are the balance sheet, the income statement, and the cash budget. Each is structured to answer a specific question about financial performance. The balance sheet determines your financial position *at a particular point in time,* usually at the end of the year. The income statement shows your income, expenses, and contribution to savings *over a past period of time,* usually the preceding year. The cash budget details estimates of your income, expenses, and contribution to savings *in the upcoming period,* usually the next year. Each of the three statements plays an important role in helping us achieve our financial goals.

THE BALANCE SHEET

Personal balance sheet: A statement designed to measure someone's wealth.
Assets: Items of value owned by the balance sheet preparer.
Liabilities: Bills and other obligations of the balance sheet preparer.
Net worth: Wealth of the balance sheet preparer (assets minus liabilities).

What are you worth? It's a good practice to ask yourself this question periodically. A loan officer at a bank most certainly will ask it if you apply for a loan. She will also ask you to prepare a **personal balance sheet** to aid her in determining whether you should get the loan. The balance sheet is designed to determine someone's wealth. It has three components: **assets,** items that are owned and are measured by their fair market values; **liabilities,** bills and other obligations owed creditors that must be paid in the future; and **net worth,** the difference between assets and liabilities. (Net worth is actually the accounting term for wealth.) A simple balance sheet for Mike Mason, a second-year college student, appears in Figure 2.1. Mike has only a few assets, the most important being his stereo unit and tape and record albums, and he has only two liabilities—$20 he owes Ed Bates and the balance due on his Visa card. Since the total value of Mike's assets is $1,311, and his liabilities are only $96, he has a net worth of $1,215 ($1,311 – $96) on December 31, 1996.

The word *balance* in balance sheet suggests a particular relationship among its three components. As Figure 2.1 shows, the balance is between assets on the one

Figure 2.1
A balance sheet for Mike Mason prepared as of December 31, 1996.

Assets		Liabilities and Net Worth	
Cash on hand	$ 18.00	Loan from Ed Bates	$ 20.00
Balance in the checking account	75.00	End-of-month balance on Visa card	76.00
Clothing inventory	237.00		
Textbooks, school supplies, and similar items	81.00	Total liabilities	$ 96.00
Stereo unit and tape and record albums	900.00	Net worth	$1,215.00
Total assets	$1,311.00	Total liabilities and net worth	$1,311.00

hand and the sum of liabilities and net worth on the other. Arithmetically, it is shown by the equation

$$\text{Assets} = \text{liabilities} + \text{net worth}$$

The equality always holds, because net worth can be either positive or negative. It is positive when the market values of assets are greater than the total value of all liabilities; its is negative when the reverse is true.

Listing liabilities ahead of net worth on the right-hand side of the balance sheet is done for a purpose, too: It reflects the legal claims creditors have in assets. Specifically, it means that in most cases (except bankruptcy), their claims to your assets rank before your own claims. This relationship can be seen with an example. Suppose you purchase a new car for $10,000, putting down $2,000 and financing $8,000 with a local bank. If we ignored all other balance sheet items, immediately after the purchase your balance sheet would appear as below:

$$\$10{,}000(\text{assets}) = \$8{,}000(\text{liabilities}) + \$2{,}000(\text{net worth})$$

After the first year of ownership, you may have paid off $2,000 of the loan, but if the car depreciated by $3,000, the new balance sheet would be:

$$\$7{,}000(\text{assets}) = \$6{,}000(\text{liabilities}) + \$1{,}000(\text{net worth})$$

If the car had to be sold at this point to raise cash, the bank's $6,000 loan balance would be satisfied first. After that is taken care of, then you can take what is left—in the above example, $1,000. You should also be able to see how negative net worth arises. If the car depreciated by $5,000 in the first year while the loan payoff remained at $2,000, net worth would now be a negative $1,000. Before we look more closely at assets, liabilities, and net worth, it should be remembered that financial planning aims to maximize net worth; it does not attempt to maximize assets. As you can see, regardless of how much your assets are worth, if your liabilities are greater, you have negative net worth. Technically and legally, you're insolvent.

Assets

Assets are things you own that have market value. They might have physical substance, such as jewelry or a house; or they may be pieces of paper, such as stocks and bonds, that give you rights to receive income or other benefits. Determining the total value of your assets takes two steps. First, you must identify and count all the items you own, and second, you need to determine each item's market value. This second step is often harder, even though some assets' values are easily determined: For example, a quick glance at the morning newspaper will tell you what a share of IBM stock is worth. But other assets, such as a diamond engagement ring purchased many years ago, have market values that can be only roughly approximated unless an expert is consulted.

Assets and liabilities are often grouped on the balance sheet to make evaluation easier. A balance sheet for a business firm, for example, normally lists assets according to their liquidity, beginning with the most liquid assets and progressing toward the least liquid. This approach is appropriate for a personal balance sheet as well, but it is also helpful to group assets according to their use. In this respect, there are three main categories: assets to satisfy liquidity needs, assets that are a part of our lifestyles, and investment assets that can increase net worth or provide income for current use or for retirement. We now take a closer look at these three categories.

Liquid asset: Cash or any other asset easily convertible to cash with no loss in market value.

LIQUID ASSETS A **liquid asset** is cash or any other asset that can be converted to cash with a minimum amount of inconvenience and with no loss in market value. Currency and coins, of course, are the most liquid of all assets, and most people carry them to meet daily expenses, such as lunch, the dry cleaning bill, and many others. Since currency and coins provide no return and are easily lost or stolen, we usually try to minimize the amount held. To pay *larger* bills, and possibly to earn interest on daily balances, we use checking accounts; and finally, after we determine our minimum requirement here, we then can place our funds into many other kinds of liquid deposits that offer potentially higher returns. Examples of these are deposits offered by banks and other financial institutions, such as savings accounts, money market deposits, and certificates of deposit. Managing liquid assets is a very important part of personal financial management, and the topic is discussed thoroughly in the next chapter.

Figure 2.2 shows a comprehensive balance sheet for the Arnold and Sharon Steele family, whom you met in Chapter 1. You will become better acquainted with them in this chapter as we use their financial situation in 1996 to explain the balance sheet, income statement, and budget. Arnold and Sharon have $16,240 in liquid assets, with most of it being held in their passbook savings account and certificates of deposit.

Lifestyle assets: Things that help us achieve our desired quality of life.

LIFESTYLE (USE) ASSETS Things that help us achieve the quality of life we want are our **lifestyle assets** (also called use assets). Most families hold the greatest percentage of their total assets in them. This is particularly true if a house is purchased, since it is such a large investment. But many other similar assets are also "big ticket" items, such as household furniture and furnishings, appliances, automobiles, and possibly hobbies like coin and stamp collections. Naturally, ownership of these assets varies considerably from one family to another, depending upon family members' interests and activities.

Referring to Figure 2.2, you can see that of the Steeles' total lifestyle assets of $261,500, $205,000 is in their home. They determined this value by observing the selling prices of homes similar to theirs and then deducting 7 percent to allow for a realtor's commission.

Investment assets: Assets that provide income or increase our net worth.

INVESTMENT ASSETS **Investment assets** are purchased for the purpose of providing additional income or increasing your net worth over time. Your ultimate goal might be to provide adequate funds for retirement, or it may be to accumulate an estate to pass on to your heirs. You may also be investing for shorter-range purposes, such as providing for your children's college education. Whatever the reason, you need to invest your funds in assets that will provide a return that is at least equal to the inflation rate. Naturally, you would like to do even better than that, if you can.

The Steeles have accumulated a reasonable amount of investment assets. They own 400 shares of a mutual fund and have invested in other common stocks, including those of the company Arnold is with, InChemCo. The stocks are quoted on the financial pages of their local newspaper, so finding their values at December 31, 1996, was quite simple. It was also easy to determine the cash surrender value of Arnold's life insurance policy, because that value is printed in the policy. To find

BALANCE SHEET at *December 21, 1996*	
For *Arnold & Sharon Steele*	
ASSETS	
Liquid Assets:	
Coins and currency on hand	$ 240
Checking account balances	2,400
Other deposits at financial institutions:	
Savings account	5,600
42-month certificate of deposit	5,000
	—
Money market mutual funds	—
U.S. Series EE or HH bonds	3,000
Other liquid assets:	
none	—
none	—
Total liquid assets	$ 16,240
Lifestyle Assets:	
Residence	205,000
Vacation home	—
Furniture, household furnishings, and appliances	20,000
Automobiles and recreational vehicles:	
1995 Voyager van	16,000
1993 Honda sedan	11,000
1991 Coleman camper	2,100
Jewelry	4,000
Clothing	1,400
Sporting equipment	600
Hobbies and collections *(stamp collection)*	400
Other lifestyle assets:	
1994 Toro riding mower	1,000
Total lifestyle assets	$ 261,500
Investment Assets	
Preferred stocks	$ —
Common stocks	16,000
Corporate bonds	—
Government bonds	—
Mutual funds *400 shares of Fidelity Fund*	6,800

Figure 2.2
Balance sheet for the Steele family.

the cash value of Arnold's retirement fund at InChemCo, however, he had to call the company's personnel office. The Steeles realize that they must increase their investment assets if they are to achieve their retirement goal and the goals they have for educating John and Nancy.

Adding the total of investment assets to the total of lifestyle assets and liquid assets determines total assets. As you can see in Figure 2.2, for the Steeles this was $325,540.

Business interests		—
Cash value of life insurance		4,000
Cash value of annuities		—
Cash value of retirement fund		21,000
Individual retirement accounts (IRAs):		
Arnold – none		—
Sharon – none		—
Total investments assets	(c)	47,800
TOTAL ASSETS = (a) + (b) + (c) =	(d)	325,540
LIABILITIES		
Current Liabilities:		
Unpaid bills Gas and Electric, Telephone		460
Credit card balances due		1,720
Estimated taxes due		1,750
Installment loan balances due in one year:		
Autos		4,424
Others:		
none		—
Other current liabilities:		
none		—
Total current liabilities	(e)	8,354
Noncurrent liabilities:		
Installment loan balances due after one year:		
Autos		4,966
Others:		
none		—
Mortgage loans		152,829
Loans on life insurance policies		2,000
Debit balances on margin accounts with stockbrokers		—
Other noncurrent liabilities:		
none		—
Total noncurrent liabilities	(f)	159,795
TOTAL LIABILITIES = (e) + (f) =	(g)	168,149
NET WORTH = (d) – (g) =	(h)	157,391
TOTAL LIABILITIES AND NET WORTH = (g) + (h) =	(i)	325,540

Figure 2.2 Continued.

Liabilities

At any point in time, most people have debt obligations. These obligations arise for a variety of reasons. You might use a bank credit card because of its convenience. If you don't want to use all your liquid assets to pay for one item, you might arrange an installment loan. Because you simply don't have enough resources, you obtain a mortgage loan to buy a house. Liabilities such as these are usually arranged on the balance sheet as current or noncurrent.

Current liability: A debt that must be paid within one year.

CURRENT LIABILITIES A **current liability** is any debt that must be paid within one year. There are two sources of current liabilities. First are unpaid bills. These come from your use of credit cards, or from direct purchases, as in the case of gas, electric, and telephone bills. The Steeles had $2,180 ($460 + $1,720) of these items. The second source consists of portions of installment loans that are due within one year. The Steeles are paying off two car loans over four years. The current liability portion is $4,424. We distinguish between current and noncurrent liabilities in order to better evaluate the Steeles' liquidity position, a topic we'll explain in more detail later in this chapter.

Noncurrent liabilities: Debt obligations beyond one year.

NONCURRENT LIABILITIES **Noncurrent liabilities** are all debt obligations beyond one year, and they are also of two types. The first type represents the noncurrent portion of loans with specific repayment schedules. Examples are installment loans on automobiles, furniture, and major appliances, or credit card balances being paid off on an installment basis. To illustrate, one of the Steeles' car loans extends into 1999 with portions payable in 1998 and 1999, which explains their $4,966 noncurrent liability. Another important example is a mortgage loan on a house or other property. The second kind of noncurrent liability consists of loans that do not have repayment schedules. A loan on your life insurance policy, such as the $2,000 loan the Steeles have an Arnold's policy, is an example. While these loans do not require repayment, you do pay interest on them periodically. Adding noncurrent and current liabilities gives total liabilities; for the Steeles, this figure is $168,149 ($8,354 + $159,795).

Net Worth

As indicated previously, net worth is the difference between total assets and total liabilities. Even though this form of measurement has its problems, it is still the single best estimate of one's wealth. The Steeles' net worth at December 31, 1996, was $157,391. This figure was calculated in Figure 2.2 by subtracting total liabilities (item *g*) from total assets (item *d*). Net worth plays a crucial role in estimating financial strength, so we need to understand how it can change from one period to the next. Net worth can be changed in two ways:

Positive contribution to savings: Increase in net worth.
Dissavings: Reduction in net worth.

First, net worth increases whenever cash income exceeds cash expenses during a period. This situation is called a **positive contribution to savings;** conversely, if expenses exceed income, a negative contribution—call it **dissavings**—occurs, and it reduces net worth. Second, changes in net worth also occur when the market values of assets you own at the beginning of a period increase or decrease during the period. For example, if you own a home that increases in value, your net worth increases by an equal amount. (This assumes, of course, that you do not increase your mortgage or other loans.)

THE INCOME STATEMENT

Income statement: Detailed breakdown of cash income and expenses over a past period.

The **income statement** (sometimes called the statement of cash flows) presents a detailed breakdown of cash income and expenses over a past period. In doing this, it also provides a figure for the period's contribution to savings, and thus it becomes an important companion statement to the balance sheet. The income statement provides the opportunity to review how well you have done financially in the past period and to help you budget your income and expense items for the upcoming period. The Steeles' income statement for 1996 is shown in Figure 2.3 and discussed in the sections below.

Income

Income: Cash inflows, consisting primarily of salaries and wages.

Income usually consists of cash inflows. As Figure 2.3 shows, there are many potential sources of income. For many people, Arnold and Sharon included, by far the largest percentage of their total income consists of wages and salaries. Arnie has a full-time position with InChemCo, but Sharon works only during the tax season—roughly January through April—with a CPA firm. The data arrangement in Figure 2.3 shows gross wages rather than after-tax, or take-home, wages. You probably will do your financial planning with the take-home figure, but it is also instructive to detail the actual amount of taxes you pay. This puts the total expense in perspective and underscores the need for effective tax planning. It is surprising how few people actually know how much in total taxes they pay—much less their effective tax rates—because they focus exclusively on take-home pay. You should look carefully at both.

The Steeles' total wages in 1996 were $75,600. Deducting from this the total payroll taxes of $14,570 leaves their combined take-home salary of $61,030. Arnold's and Sharon's salaries have increased rather nicely in the last several years, making it easier for them to achieve their financial goals.

The Steeles' $937 of interest income came from their passbook savings account, certificates of deposit, and U.S. Series EE bonds. They did not actually withdraw the interest earned on any of these deposits (you have limited access to the latter two), but instead allowed it to accumulate. The $1,090 of dividend income was earned on their common stocks and Fidelity Fund shares, and they did receive those dividends in cash. Adding the interest and dividends to their wages and salaries gives their total income of $77,627.

Expenses

Expenses: Cash outflows that sustain our scale of living.

Expenses are cash outflows that sustain our scale of living. They do not include all cash outlays, however. You would not, for example, consider the purchase of investment assets as expenses. Payments made on installment and mortgage loans are viewed as expenses even though formal accounting rules would probably require us to distinguish between payments of interest and payments of principal in measuring income. (We are required to do this for tax purposes, because interest is an itemized deductible expense whereas principal payments are not. But our focus here is not on taxes.)

The breakdown of expenses in Figure 2.3 is typical of most income statements you are likely to encounter in loan applications and elsewhere. The list of expenses is fairly comprehensive, although you might prefer to arrange them differently. We'll distinguish between inflexible and flexible expenses when budgeting is discussed later, but it is useful to introduce and explain these terms here.

Inflexible expenses: Expenses that are hard to control in the short run.

INFLEXIBLE EXPENSES **Inflexible expenses** (also called fixed expenses) are often defined as those over which you have very little control in the short run. Some expenses are perfectly inflexible, meaning they never change in amount. Such expenses arise typically from contractual arrangements requiring payments of so

INCOME STATEMENT for the Period *Year Ended 12/31/96*
For *the Arnold and Sharon Steele Family*

			Percent
INCOME			
Wages and Salaries:			
Arnold – InChem Co		$ 60,200	
Sharon – Todd and Talbot CPAs		15,400	
Total wages and salaries	(*a*)	75,600	97.4%
Other Income:			
Interest		$ 937	
Dividends		1,090	
Capital gains or (losses)		none	
Others		none	
Total other income	(*b*)	$ 2,027	2.6%
TOTAL INCOME = (*a*) + (*b*) =	(*c*)	$ 77,627	100.0%
EXPENSES			
Housing:			
Rent		$ none	
Mortgage payments		18,285	
Maintenance fees on condo or cooperative		none	
Maintenance and home furnishings		3,500	
Total housing expenses	(*d*)	$ 21,785	28.0%
Transportation:			
Automobile loan payments		$ 5,688	
Gas, oil, other maintenance and repairs		2,100	
License, parking, and other auto		210	
Other transportation		none	
Total transportation expenses	(*e*)	$ 7,998	10.3%
Food and Other Consumption Items:			
Food and household supplies		$ 6,300	
Meals eaten out		1,210	
Personal care—barbers and beauticians		720	
Others		none	
Total food and other consumption items	(*f*)	$ 8,230	10.6%
Utilities:			
Telephone		$ 540	
Gas and electric		$ 2,280	
Water and sanitation		510	
Garbage pickup		none	
Cable TV		420	
Others		none	
Total utilities	(*g*)	$ 3,750	4.8%

Figure 2.3 Income statement for the Steele family.

			Percent
Taxes:			
Payroll		$ 14,570	
Real estate and personal property		3,500	
Others		none	
Total taxes	(*h*)	$ 18,070	23.3%
Insurance:			
Health and medical withheld from wages		$ none	
Life		480	
Property and liability		$ 570	
Automobile		1,470	
Disability		none	
Others		none	
Total insurance	(*i*)	$ 2,520	3.3%
Leisure and Entertainment:			
Theater and sporting events		$ 870	
Health club memberships		none	
Newspapers, magazines, etc.		430	
Vacations		2,380	
Hobbies		280	
Sporting equipment		160	
Others *Family Christmas gifts*		890	
Total leisure and entertainment	(*j*)	$ 5,010	6.5%
Clothing:			
New clothing		1,830	
Laundry and dry cleaning		290	
Others		none	
Total clothing	(*k*)	$ 2,120	2.7%
Others:			
Gifts and charitable contributions		$ 2,080	
Dues and subscriptions		200	
Tuition, books, other education expenses		390	
Babysitters		540	
Family members' personal allowances		1,300	
Unreimbursed medical–dental		1,040	
		—	
		—	
		—	
Total others	(*l*)	$ 5,550	7.2%
TOTAL EXPENSES = (*d*) + (*e*) + (*f*) + (*g*) + (*h*) + (*i*) + (*j*) + (*k*) + (*l*) =	(*m*)	75,033	96.7%
CONTRIBUTION TO SAVINGS = (*c*) – (*m*) =	(*n*)	$ 2,594	3.3%

Figure 2.3 Continued.

much per period. As you review the expense categories in Figure 2.3, you most likely will pinpoint the following as examples: the mortgage payments of $18,285, the automobile loan payments of $5,688, and maybe the life insurance premiums of $480. These expenses are often called **sunk costs** because the fixed amount must be paid regardless of what happens in the future; the only way out of them is to drop, pay off, or renegotiate the underlying contracts. Other inflexible expenses are not fixed in amount from period to period, but they are nevertheless difficult to control. The Steeles' taxes of $18,070 are a good example of this type; we know they must be paid each year, but the actual amounts might differ each year, or even in each month of the year.

Sunk costs: Costs that cannot be avoided regardless of what happens in the future.

FLEXIBLE EXPENSES **Flexible expenses** (also called variable expenses) are those over which you have some control, at least in the short run. A good example is home maintenance. Of course, some of these expenses are more flexible than others. Home maintenance expenses, along with doctors' and dentists' bills, are very irregular and are the most troublesome to deal with in budgeting. Others, however, are far more predictable, such as purchases of food and household supplies. Some flexible expenses might be paid in such a way that they become inflexible expenses. For example, gas and electric usage can be billed in equal monthly payments regardless of seasonal variations. Also, some flexible expenses go up or down along with your income. For example, if you use your car on the job, and you work more hours during a period, your car expenses will increase as your income rises.

Flexible expenses: Expenses that are generally controllable in the short run.

Figure 2.4 shows a breakdown of the Steeles' $75,033 of total expenses in 1996. As you can see, the larger percentage is in the inflexible category, indicating that quite a bit of their expenses were set and predictable during the year.

Contribution to Savings

As explained earlier in this chapter, the excess of income over expenses is a positive contribution to savings (or savings, for short). It increases net worth and is a

Figure 2.4 A breakdown of the Steeles' 1996 expenses.

Inflexible Expenses		Flexible Expenses	
Mortgage payments	$18,285	Family members' allowances	$ 1,300
Automobile loan payments	5,668	Leisure and entertainment	5,010
Car licenses	210	Home maintenance and furnishings	3,500
All utilities	3,750	Gas, oil, and car repairs	2,100
All taxes	18,070	All food and other consumption items	8,230
All insurance	2,520	Clothing, laundry, and dry cleaning	2,120
Dues to professional societies	200	Gifts and charitable contributions	2,080
Tuition and books	390	Babysitters	540
		Medical-dental expenses	1,040
Totals	$49,113		$25,920
Total Expenses		$75,033	

Percentages
Inflexible = $49,113/$75,033 = 0.66, or 66%
Flexible = $25,920/$75,033 = 0.34, or 34%

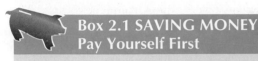

Box 2.1 SAVING MONEY
Pay Yourself First

Most financial planners agree that if saving money is truly important to you, then put savings in a proper focus—first, and not last—in the budget. In short, pay yourself first out of each paycheck. Seriously, when you get paid, take whatever percentage amount you have targeted and put it in a savings vehicle; then, spend the rest.

This strategy works even better if you never get your hands on the money. So consider using a "forced savings" approach. For example, many employers let you channel funds into U.S. savings bonds, mutual funds, or optional retirement plans. Or your bank may have automatic transfer plans that reposition cash from your checking account to a savings account. If you own mutual fund shares, choose the option to reinvest all dividends and capital gain distributions. Also, some companies have dividend-reinvestment plans; if you own shares in them, take the option. If you are very poor at voluntary savings, consider buying whole life, rather than term, insurance. This type of policy has a built-in savings feature.

Millions of Americans willingly choose to have more taxes withheld from their paychecks than the IRS requires and then count on the tax refund for extra spending or saving funds. Of course, this is the least effective way to do it, since you give up interest on money that could go into interest-earning assets. If you are currently allowing overwithholding, check with your employer to see if an alternative savings arrangement is available.

Finally, some people argue that buying a home is the ultimate forced savings, since living in rented housing produces nothing more than canceled checks. Frankly, this argument stretches the point a bit. Buying versus renting is a complex problem, where the forced-savings feature might be considered, but should not dominate, in making a decision.

source of increases in assets or reductions in liabilities. In 1996, the Steeles made a positive contribution to savings of $2,594. Placing the contribution to savings figure last in the income statement seems to foster the notion that savings are something left over after everything else has been bought. Actually, this is a poor view toward savings that frequently leads to no savings at all, since there is usually some expenditure offering a quicker and more immediately satisfying return than savings. Placing savings last is meant to highlight its importance not to diminish it. Like all other expense items, savings should be planned. It also helps to determine just how much you should save in relation to your income.

PLANNED SAVINGS Many people view savings as a fixed expense; that is, each period they make sure the amount they wish to save is placed into an investment vehicle. A helpful technique is to establish specific savings goals and to open an investment account for each goal. Although it is relatively inconvenient, this approach does have merit in that it allows for goals that are expected to be achieved at different dates in the future. A deposit appropriate for a goal you hope to achieve next year may not be appropriate for a goal targeted for 10 years in the future. You may want to put your money in a very safe place for next year's goal, whereas the goal 10 years away might call for a riskier and potentially more profitable investment. The key piece of advice is: Set specific goals and use specific savings instruments to achieve them.

HOW MUCH SHOULD YOU SAVE? The amount you save depends on two factors: the importance of savings in your overall financial plan and your level of income. This text's approach to the first factor does not promote savings over all other activities in life. Your long-run health may depend as much on an enjoyable vacation in the mountains as it does on a "mountain" of savings. Each should be evaluated by you and your family members as to its relative importance.

The average savings rate for all U.S. families has changed from time to time, but in recent years it has been around 4 percent of disposable (after-tax) income. Thus, if the average family income in 1996 is $40,000, the annual contribution to savings for the average family should be $1,600. In 1996, the Steeles saved 3.3 percent of their $77,627 gross income and 4.1 percent of their after-tax income. The Steeles are quite unhappy with their savings performance in recent years, and they realize that attaining education and retirement goals may be impossible unless they save more. Accordingly, they plan to increase savings substantially in 1997, as we shall soon learn.

EVALUATING PAST FINANCIAL PERFORMANCE

Financial ratios: Yardsticks to measure financial strength and progress.

Ultimately, your financial performance can be judged successful or unsuccessful only within the framework of your personal goals. If your plans call for buying a house or a new car, or saving $5,000, then you are successful if you achieve those goals. Apart from this personal evaluation, however, there also are objective yardsticks, called **financial ratios,** to measure present financial strength and its growth over time. Actually, to an outsider, such as a bank from which you are seeking a loan, your personal goals are not important. The bank must evaluate your request with an impersonal, objective attitude, asking whether you are a good credit risk. In attempting to answer this question, the bank relies on, among other things, certain ratios that can be calculated from the balance sheet and income statement. Even if your financial picture is not being evaluated by outsiders, it is worthwhile for you to use similar objective criteria to assess your situation. Three areas that are particularly important to evaluate are your financial performance as compared with the annual inflation rate, the liquidity of your assets, and your level of debt.

Matching or Beating the Inflation Rate

It is always sound financial management to compare the annual inflation rate with annual changes in both your income and net worth. In periods of high inflation, such as the early 1980s, it is doubly important, because failure to match inflation will lead to an eroding scale of living and a diminished real net worth.

Nominal income: Actual income received.

Real income: Nominal income adjusted for inflation.

Sticker shock: Consumers' surprise at the amount of price inflation when a durable item, such as a car, is replaced.

INCOME AND THE INFLATION RATE Let us suppose that your **nominal income** (the amount you actually receive) increases by 5 percent during a year when prices in general are increasing by 10 percent. In real terms—that is, in terms of what your nominal income buys—your **real income** (the amount your nominal income is worth) has declined by 5 percent. You are worse off this year because you have not kept up with the inflation rate. You may not feel much worse off, at least not immediately, because some items in your budget are fixed, as we explained earlier. So, you will continue to make the same payments on your auto or furniture loans, or on your home loan, as you did in the past, and you may continue to meet your savings goals. But eventually many of the items being financed will need to be replaced, and we then confront the reality of a deteriorated financial condition. This happened with such regularity in the late 1970s and early 1980s that a phrase was coined to describe it: **sticker shock.** It referred to the surprise of consumers who hadn't looked at a price sticker on a new automobile for five or six years.

An important first test, then, is to compare your increase in nominal income with the inflation rate for the year. The simplest approach is first to calculate a percentage change in nominal income, as shown below:

$$\% \text{ change in nominal income} = \left(\frac{\text{this year's nominal income}}{\text{last year's nominal income}}\right) - 1.0$$

After you have this figure, compare it with the inflation rate (which is frequently reported in the newspaper and on television) to judge your relative performance. Using the Steeles as an example, and assuming that the 1996 inflation rate was 4.0 percent, we have

$$\begin{matrix}\% \text{ change in} \\ \text{nominal income}\end{matrix} = \frac{\$77,627}{\$71,788} - 1.0 = 1.0813 - 1.0 = 0.0813, \text{or } 8.13\%$$

Thus, we know that the 8.13 percent increase in the Steeles' nominal income was about twice the inflation rate.

NET WORTH AND THE INFLATION RATE Inflation's impact is not limited to your income. If the market values of your assets do not increase at inflation's rate, your real net worth will decline. The same arithmetic procedures shown above can be used to calculate the change in real—as opposed to nominal—net worth. To prevent a decline in net worth, you must own assets that appreciate in value equal to the inflation rate. In the past, personal residences and common stocks have performed well in this respect.

Maintaining Adequate Liquidity

Adequate liquidity means having sufficient liquid assets to pay your bills on time. You may have a very high net worth, but if most of it is represented by assets with poor liquidity, such as your house, you still could be illiquid. To avoid becoming illiquid we often hold a portion or our total assets in cash or other liquid assets, such as savings accounts. Two ratios are frequently used to measure liquidity: the ratio of liquid assets to take-home pay and the ratio of liquid assets to current liabilities.

LIQUID ASSETS TO TAKE-HOME PAY Financial advisers often use the rule of thumb that you should hold liquid assets equal to three to six months of take-home pay to serve as such a buffer. If you have good loss-of-income protection through your employer or union, then the low figure might be adequate. If protection is poor, you should strive for the higher amount.

Liquid assets to take-home pay ratio: A liquidity measurement.

Using data for the Steeles, we can calculate their **liquid assets to take-home pay ratio.** Recalling (from page 31) that their 1996 take-home pay was $61,030 and their liquid assets at December 31, 1996, were $16,240 (see Figure 2.2), we have:

$$\begin{matrix}\text{Liquid assets to} \\ \text{take-home pay ratio}\end{matrix} = \frac{\text{liquid assets}}{\text{take-home pay}} = \frac{\$16,240}{\$61,030} = 0.266$$

The number can then be expressed as months of the year; for example, 0.266 means about 27 percent of 12 months, or about 3.2 months. (Notice that an answer of 0.5 indicates half the year, or six months.) Thus, the Steeles fall at the lower rule-of-thumb figure of three months, suggesting they should build their liquid reserves. Since Arnold does have rather good loss-of-income protection at InChemCo., the lower figure is the more appropriate one for them to use. (We should note that take-home pay is an appropriate value to use if there are no other major sources of income, as in the Steeles' case. If there are other major sources, they should be included in the denominator, after allowing for related income taxes.)

Liquidity ratio: Liquid assets divided by current liabilities.

LIQUID ASSETS TO CURRENT LIABILITIES The ratio of liquid assets to take-home pay does not consider the level of existing liabilities. Another family may show an identical ratio to the Steeles' but be in far worse shape because their existing current liabilities are much greater. To augment the first ratio, then, it is helpful to calculate another ratio, called the **liquidity ratio,** which measures liquid assets against current liabilities. For the Steeles, it is:

$$\text{Liquidity ratio} = \frac{\text{liquid assets}}{\text{current liabilities}} = \frac{\$16,240}{\$8,354} = 1.94$$

This number tells us the Steeles have $1.94 of liquid assets for every $1.00 of existing current liabilities. There is no hard-and-fast rule indicating what this ratio should be, but any number greater than 1.0 shows fairly good strength, assuming

Box 2.2

PERSONAL FINANCE NEWS

Late Edition

Our National Savings Rate—Our National Disaster

Many families in America are headed for financial disaster; ironically, many know it but seem powerless to stop the march. The root problem: We spend too much and save too little. Our national saving rate—personal savings as a percent of disposable personal income—has waffled between 3 and 6 percent since 1980. This is not only the lowest by a long shot among all industrialized countries of the world (the Japanese save about 20 percent), it is also only half of our own savings rate during the highly inflationary decade of the 1970s. Why are we such big spenders?

Part of the answer rests in the fact that our population is now dominated by baby boomers—people born between 1946 and 1962. Having matured during times of plenty, boomers are accustomed to consuming—not to saving. Unfortunately, their habit is learned quickly by their children. Mom and Dad want Porsches and Saabs and the kids want $150-a-pair Nikes.

Many families earn the incomes to afford such luxuries, *if* they don't have to worry about retirement. But, of course, that's when the fiddler gets paid. No matter how much we make during our working years, saving 3 percent of our income will leave a huge shortfall at retirement, if we plan to have a lifestyle then that's even remotely close to what we enjoy now.

The above warning is not newly made, and it has not fallen on deaf ears. People realize the problem, and conversations at expensive cocktail parties or cruises often turn to the topic of saving more; somehow, the connection isn't made that a prerequisite is spending less. Some boomers are hoping that their parents will bail them out (What are *they* supposed to live on in retirement?); others are counting on larger Social Security payments (dream on!); and a growing number have simply given up the notion of ever retiring and plan to work until they drop. Solutions like these suggest that a reality check is seriously needed.

the ratio of liquid assets to take-home pay is also adequate. Of course, the larger the number, the better the liquidity. With a ratio of 1.94, the Steeles are in reasonably good shape.

Avoiding Excessive Amounts of Debt

Adequate liquidity protects you from temporary cash emergencies, and liquidity ratios are designed to warn you of liquidity problems. However, they do not tell us whether total debt is being used properly or is excessive. *Excessive* doesn't mean too much debt in absolute dollars, but rather, in relation to your underlying assets and income that support the debt. Two important ratios are often used to evaluate total debt: the ratio of total liabilities to total assets and the ratio of take-home pay to debt repayment obligations.

TOTAL LIABILITIES TO TOTAL ASSETS Technically, you are judged insolvent when your total liabilities exceed your total assets. Being insolvent doesn't automatically mean you are illiquid; you might still have sufficient cash to pay your bills for a while. What it does mean is that, unless the situation changes, you will ultimately not have enough assets to pay all your bills. Many people in this position eventually file bankruptcy as a means of settling with creditors or establishing an orderly plan for paying their bills over an extended period of time.

Debt ratio: Total liabilities divided by total assets.

Bankruptcy (discussed more fully in Chapter 4) is not to be taken lightly or viewed as a convenience to avoid paying obligations. You should look for early signals of impending troubles. The **debt ratio,** which measures total liabilities against total assets, is one such signal. Using the Steeles' data from Figure 2.2 as an example, it is calculated below:

$$\text{Debt ratio} = \frac{\text{total liabilities}}{\text{total assets}} = \frac{\$168{,}149}{\$325{,}540} = 0.517$$

This number tells us that the Steeles have about $0.52 in total debts for each $1.00 of total assets. Looking at it in another way, the value of their assets could shrink up to 48 percent (1.00 – 0.52) before the Steeles would encounter insolvency problems. The smaller the ratio, the better from a safety point of view, but again, there is no iron-clad rule telling us what the ratio should be in every instance. The less volatile the market prices of your assets, the higher the ratio could be, all other things considered. In general, we like to see ratios below 0.5, to be on the relatively safe side. The Steeles are right at the margin.

DEBT SERVICE COVERAGE Your capacity to carry debt is reflected not only in the market value of assets you own but also by the relationship of your take-home pay to your total debt-servicing charges. By debt service, we mean monthly (or yearly) payments of both principal and interest on those loans requiring periodic repayment. The debt service coverage ratio measures take-home pay against total debt service charges. The Steeles have two auto loans and their home mortgage. In addition, they borrowed $2,000 on Arnold's life insurance policy. Although this loan does not require periodic repayments, they pay interest of $160 each year. The total annual payments are $24,133 ($18,285 + $5,688 + $160), and the following **debt service coverage ratio** can be calculated:

Debt service coverage ratio: Take-home pay divided by debt service charges.

$$\text{Debt service coverage ratio} = \frac{\text{take-home pay}}{\text{debt service charges}} = \frac{\$61,030}{\$24,133} = 2.53$$

This number indicates that the Steeles earned $2.53 in take-home pay for each $1.00 of required debt repayment and interest. Higher ratios, of course, indicate greater debt-carrying capacity than low ones. A ratio of 1.0 means that all of your after-tax income is needed to repay existing debts, and a ratio less than 1.0 indicates that your income will not even cover your existing repayments. (Again, if other major sources of income exist, they should be included, on an after-tax basis, in the numerator.)

A single number is never enough to distinguish strength from weakness, but it is usually felt that a ratio of 3.0 or better signals adequate strength and reasonable flexibility in future budgeting. In such a situation, a large portion of your income will not be committed to repaying existing debt. The Steeles' ratio of 2.53 indicates some weakness in this area.

Review of the Steeles' Financial Situation

Now that you have learned about financial statements and have seen them applied to the Steeles' financial situation for 1996, what impression do you have? Are they a wealthy family? Are they "sailing right along" with few financial concerns? Actually, their situation is not quite so successful as it might first appear.

True, they have a net worth of over $157,000. But there are a number of areas of concern. First, their residence of $205,000 is almost two-thirds of their total assets. Housing prices do often increase over time at the inflation rate or greater, but real estate markets can become very soft in the short run. A decline of 10 or 20 percent over several years, while not likely, would decrease their net worth substantially.

Second, Arnie and Sharon have $27,000 invested in late-model automobiles, which depreciate in value rather rapidly. If they continue to turn over their cars after three or four years, they will perpetually carry a rather high amount of expensive installment debt. As our ratio analysis revealed, they are probably already at their debt limit, and it would be helpful to reduce debt somewhat.

Third, and most important, the Steeles are enjoying a high-consumption budget that produces very little savings in relation to their income. At their current pace, they will not accumulate sufficient funds to educate Nancy and John or to achieve other important future goals. Put simply, the Steeles must rethink their priorities, or become smarter consumer-investors, or do both. We will follow them in this process as the remaining chapters unfold. But their most pressing immediate need is to learn the budgeting process.

ACHIEVING GOALS THROUGH BUDGETING

Budget: A plan indicating financial goals and how resources will be allocated to achieve them.

What is a **budget?** Put very simply, a budget is any plan—simple or complex—that expresses your financial goals and how you will allocate your limited resources to achieve them. A budget can be so simple that you keep it on the back of an envelope to monitor your monthly progress with checkmarks. Or it can be as complex as the one the federal government prepares each year, detailing how almost $2 trillion will be spent. But size is no guarantee of success. Your envelope approach might work, and there are many critics who feel the federal budget never has. We'll discuss principles of effective budgeting in this chapter, but before doing so, we will set forth some simple rules for budgeting success. Our discussion will revolve around these rules:

- *Set realistic budget goals.* The plural is important here. The budget is a device for achieving all your important goals; it is not a straitjacket to produce only savings.
- *Stick to simple procedures.* A $25 journal or an expensive computer is nice if you use it properly, but a waste of money if you don't. Trying to categorize every conceivable expense misses the whole point of budgeting and creates an unnecessary work burden that makes budgeting unpleasant.
- *Use the budget to control and direct expenses.* The main strength of a budget does not lie with its record-keeping function, although that is a necessary part. A budget allocation, say, for dining out, is a commitment you and your family make to an underlying activity. If you exceed the budget amount, ask yourself why. If the answer is because you want to, then you need to reexamine your goals to see if more funds should be allocated to this activity and less to others. If the answer reflects a temporary "overindulgence," then cut back next month to bring the activity back within budget. The simple acts of knowing you have exceeded budget and then deciding what to do about it are the essence of successful budgeting.

Goal Setting

Goal setting: A complex process that involves a hierarchy of wants—abstract at the top and tangible at the bottom.

When you set goals, you are effectively managing your finances rather than merely letting them take place as you go about your routine activities. Actually, **goal setting** is a rather complex process, and it has been studied by professionals from many disciplines, including social psychology, economics, and behavioral management. Goals can be viewed in a type of hierarchy, with very general and abstract goals at the top and more-specific and tangible ones at the bottom. Figure 2.5 illustrates such a hierarchy of financial goals. At the top is the general goal of attaining financial independence for each member of the family. But what does this mean?

Figure 2.5 A hierarchy of personal financial goals.

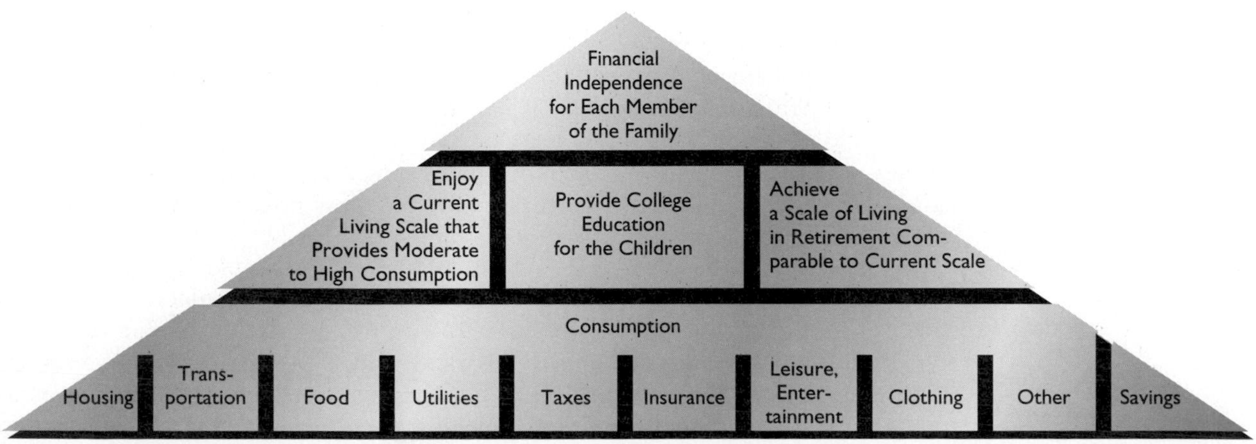

You might understand it to mean sufficient wealth to be self-reliant; another person might understand it as having a job free of possible firing or other layoffs. To be meaningful, the general goals must be expressed in specific terms. For example, in Figure 2.5 financial independence is structured into three distinct goals: to enjoy a current living scale that reflects a moderate to high level of consumption, to provide a college education for the children, and to achieve a scale of living in retirement that is on a par with the current living scale. As we move to the lowest level on the triangle, goals become even more specific and can be broken down to yearly savings and current consumption targets. Things to be acquired in the future—the children's education and retirement funds—must be saved for out of current income. Savings must be budgeted if these goals are to be achieved.

LONG- AND SHORT-RUN GOALS Since all our goals are not achieved in the current year, you could also classify goals in terms of when they are expected to be achieved. Thus, we have short-range goals that might span, say, the next five years; intermediate-range goals that arrive in 5 to 15 years; and long-range goals that mature beyond 15 years. Referencing goals to the year when we hope to accomplish them allows us to plan for the use of funds we must accumulate during the waiting period. Table 2.1 shows important goals of the Arnold and Sharon Steele family and when they expect those goals to be accomplished. They prepared this list at the end of 1996 in connection with their planning for 1997 and beyond. Keep in mind that these are their major goals that will require savings to be achieved, and they do not include those goals that are a part of their annual consumption expenditures. For example, their cars must be replaced periodically, but this will be a part of their annual expenditure budget.

DETERMINING THE REQUIRED ANNUAL SAVINGS As you can see in Table 2.1, Arnold and Sharon must save an average of $9,500 a year to accomplish all their major goals. However, they expect their savings to be somewhat below this average in the earlier years and above it later on. For simplicity they are assuming that savings will start at $8,000 and increase by $500 over each four-year period. Also for simplicity, they are not including their current investment assets (the common stocks and mutual fund shares). If they considered them, the total required savings would be approximately $23,000 less, or $243,000.

Along with the amount that must be saved each year, the balance in savings and investments assets should also be estimated. If this balance ever turns negative, the Steeles will have to borrow to achieve their goals. Table 2.2 shows estimates for the Steeles and indicates that their balance grows steadily to $55,000 in the year 2005 (the year before Nancy starts college) but falls to $14,500 in the year 2011 (John's last year in college); it then builds to the required $100,000 in the year 2024, when Arnold plans to retire.

It should be pointed out that the above figures are not adjusted for inflation, but on the other hand, they do not include any earnings on the investment assets. Obviously, for greater accuracy, the Steeles should review both of those factors each year and make appropriate adjustments.

Preparing the Annual Budget

Armed with a clear understanding of the importance of expressing goals, you are in position to prepare the annual budget. It is this budget and your willingness to stick with it that will determine your success in goal achievement. There are two

TABLE 2.1 • THE STEELES' MAJOR GOALS

Goal	Approximate Amount Required	Year Goal Will Be Accomplished	Age at That Time: Arnold's	Age at That Time: Sharon's
1. Down payment on a vacation condo in the Smoky Mountain area	$ 15,000	1999	40	38
2. Family vacation in Hawaii	5,000	2001	42	40
3. College expenses for Nancy and John	96,000	2006–2011	47–53	45–51
4. Add patio and greenhouse to home; also do major landscaping	40,000	2016	57	55
5. European vacation for Arnold and Sharon	10,000	2019	60	58
6. Accumulate additional investment assets to supplement retirement income	100,000	2024	65	63

Total required savings	$266,000
Remaining years	28
Average savings per year	$ 9,500

Estimated savings by four-year periods:

1997–2000	$ 8,000
2001–2004	8,500
2005–2008	9,000
2009–2012	9,500
2013–2016	10,000
2017–2020	10,500
2021–2024	11,000

Master budget worksheet: Budget allocations detailing planned income, expenses, and contribution to savings.

Monthly income and expense plan: A monthly breakdown of amounts listed on the master budget worksheet.

parts to budget preparation: the **master budget worksheet,** which details planned income, expenses, and contribution to savings in total for the budget year; and the **monthly income and expense plan,** which shows how each month's income, expenses, and contribution to savings will take place.

THE MASTER BUDGET WORKSHEET Budgeting begins each year by trying to forecast what your total income and expenses will be in the budget year. Some income and expense items are easy to forecast because they are known in advance (recall our previous discussion of fixed expenses): your mortgage payments on the house, for example. Others can vary widely and will be much more difficult to estimate: Dentist or doctor bills are good examples here, as is home maintenance. Despite the difficulties, estimates must be made and the budget finished.

Figure 2.6 illustrates a master budget worksheet the Steele family prepared for 1997. You probably recognize immediately that the budget has the same format as the income statement shown in Figure 2.3. The budget for a year should lead directly to the same kind of actual income and expense items after the year is over. In fact, budgeted and actual figures should be compared very closely at the end of

TABLE 2.2 • HOW THE STEELES PLAN TO ACHIEVE THEIR MAJOR GOALS

Year	Annual Contribution to Savings	Outflow	Balance in Savings and Investment Assets
1997	$ 8,000	—	$ 8,000
1998	8,000	—	16,000
1999	8,000	$15,000	9,000
2000	8,000	—	17,000
2001	8,500	5,000	20,500
2002	8,500	—	29,000
2003	8,500	—	37,500
2004	8,500	—	46,000
2005	9,000	—	55,000
2006	9,000	12,000	52,000
2007	9,000	12,000	49,000
2008	9,000	24,000	34,000
2009	9,500	24,000	19,500
2010	9,500	12,000	17,000
2011	9,500	12,000	14,500
2012	9,500	—	24,000
2013	10,000	—	34,000
2014	10,000	—	44,000
2015	10,000	—	54,000
2016	10,000	40,000	24,000
2017	10,500	—	34,500
2018	10,500	—	45,000
2019	10,500	10,000	45,500
2020	10,500	—	56,000
2021	11,000	—	67,000
2022	11,000	—	78,000
2023	11,000	—	89,000
2024	11,000	—	100,000

a budget year, both for evaluating results for the year just ended and for preparing a budget for the upcoming year.

It goes almost without saying that budget figures should be determined as realistically as possible. Each line item should be reviewed and some reason found for making the estimate; that is, your figure should be defensible. A common mistake is to set a consumption item unrealistically low. If you think there is a good chance you will spend $40 a week on dining out, and if that is what you want to do, then don't budget this activity at $20 a week. Doing so will only lead to frustration and eventual discarding of the budget.

THE MONTHLY INCOME AND EXPENSE PLAN After the master budget worksheet has been prepared, the next budgeting step is to determine how income and expense items will occur during the year. Usually, this is done on a monthly basis. Some expenses occur sporadically and in rather large amounts. It is important to plan for these expenses so that sufficient funds are available when these expenses must be paid. The monthly income and expense plan details income, expenses, and contributions to savings on a month-to-month basis. Arnold and Sharon Steele

MASTER BUDGET WORKSHEET for the period *Upcoming Year 1997*
For *the Arnold and Sharon Steele Family*

INCOME			
Wages and Salaries:			
Arnold—expect 5% raise this year			$ 63,216
Sharon—expect 10% raise and more hours			18,000
Total wages and salaries		(a)	81,216
Other Income:			
Interest	*should be about 7% on average balance*		$ 984
Dividends	*expect 10% increase*		1,200
Capital gains or (losses)			*none*
Others			*none*
Total other income		(b)	$ 2,184
TOTAL INCOME = (a) + (b) =		(c)	$ 83,400
EXPENSES			
Housing:			
Rent			$ *none*
Mortgage payments	*fixed*		18,285
Maintenance fees on condo or cooperative			*none*
Maintenance and home furnishings	*cut back a bit*		2,400
Total housing expenses		(d)	$ 20,685
Transportation:			
Automobile loan payments	*fixed*		$ 5,688
Gas, oil, and other maintenance and repairs	*say $200 a month*		2,400
Licenses, parking, and other auto	*should be about $20 a month*		240
Other transportation			*none*
Total transportation expenses		(e)	$ 8,328
Food and Other Consumption Items:			
Food and household supplies	*about $550 a month*		$ 6,600
Meals eaten out	*lets budget $80 a month*		960
Personal care—barbers and beauticians	*about $60 a month*		720
Others			*none*
Total food and other consumption items		(f)	$ 8,280
Utilities:			
Telephone	*this should be $45 a month*		$ 540
Gas and electric	*last year was $190 a month; go higher*		2,400
Water and sanitation	*last year was $128 a quarter; go higher*		720
Garbage pickup			*none*
Cable TV	*$35 a month last yaer; will go higher*		480
Others			*none*
Total utilities		(g)	$ 4,140

Figure 2.6
Master budget worksheet for the Steeles.

programmed their personal computer to show their monthly income and expense plan; it is shown in Figure 2.7.

Estimating the monthly activity. Some of the expense items were estimated in total by determining a budget monthly figure and then multiplying by 12. The monthly allocation, then, is this same monthly figure. For example, the Steeles' telephone

Taxes:			
Payroll	*estimates based on 1996 estimated income*		$ 15,600
Real estate and personal property	*last year's; didn't go up*		3,500
Others			*none*
Total taxes		(*h*)	$ 19,100
Insurance:			
Health and medical withheld from wages	*InChem Co pays*		$ *none*
Life	*fixed; don't anticipate more insurance*		480
Property and liability	*budget 5% over last year*		600
Automobile	*budget 5% over last year*		1,560
Disability	*InChem Co pays*		*none*
Others			*none*
Total insurance		(*i*)	$ 2,640
Leisure and Entertainment:			
Theater and sporting events	*budget $70 a month*		$ 840
Health club memberships	*not interested*		*none*
Newspapers, magazines, etc	*budget $40 a month*		480
Vacations	*count on four weeks camping*		1,800
Hobbies	*buy one small antique*		240
Sporting equipment	*soccer shoes, tennis equipment*		240
Others	*Christmas gifts*		$ 800
Total leisure and entertainment		(*j*)	$ 4,400
Clothing:			
New clothing	*let's budget $150 a month*		1,800
Laundry and dry cleaning	*estimate $20 a month*		240
Others			*none*
Total clothing		(*k*)	$ 2,040
Others:			
Gifts and charitable contributions	*budget $180 a month*		$ 2,160
Dues and subscriptions	*last year's amount*		200
Tuition, books, other education expenses	*expect big increase*		480
Babysitters	*estimate at $50 a month*		600
Family members' personal allowances	*we agree on this*		1,200
Unreimbursed medical–dental			—
	InChem Co pays all		—
	figure the worst on braces		1,200
			—
Total others		(*l*)	$ 5,840
TOTAL EXPENSES = (*d*) + (*e*) + (*f*) + (*g*) + (*h*) + (*i*) + (*f*) + (*k*) + (*l*) =		(*m*)	$ 75,453
CONTRIBUTION TO SAVING = (*c*) – (*m*) =		(*n*)	$ 7,947

Figure 2.6 Continued.

bill was budgeted at $45 a month, so that figure is entered for each month. Notice in Figure 2.7 those expenses that do not occur uniformly. For example, all the insurance bills come in January and February; real estate taxes are paid in February and August, and dental-medical bills are expected in February and September. Notice further that Sharon's salary comes only in January through June and again in December and that dividends are received quarterly. In planning the monthly activ-

Figure 2.7 Monthly income and expense plan for the Steele family for 1997.

Income	Jan	Feb	Mar	Apr	May	June	July	Aug	Sept	Oct	Nov	Dec	Total
Arnold's salary	5,268	5,268	5,268	5,268	5,268	5,268	5,268	5,268	5,268	5,268	5,268	5,268	63,216
Sharon's salary	2,000	3,000	4,000	4,000	2,000	1,000	—	—	—	—	—	2,000	18,000
Interest	82	82	82	82	82	82	82	82	82	82	82	82	984
Dividends	—	—	300	—	—	300	—	—	300	—	—	300	1,200
Total income	7,350	8,350	9,650	9,350	7,350	6,650	5,350	5,350	5,650	5,350	5,350	7,650	83,400
Expenses													
House mortgage	1,524	1,524	1,524	1,524	1,524	1,524	1,524	1,524	1,524	1,524	1,524	1,524	18,285
Maintenance and furnishings	200	200	200	200	200	200	200	200	200	200	200	200	2,400
Auto loan	474	474	474	474	474	474	474	474	474	474	474	474	5,688
Gas, oil, maintenance	200	200	200	200	200	200	200	200	200	200	200	200	2,400
Licenses, parking	20	20	20	20	20	20	20	20	20	20	20	20	240
Food, household items	550	550	550	550	550	550	550	550	550	550	550	550	6,600
Meals eaten out	80	80	80	80	80	80	80	80	80	80	80	80	960
Personal care	60	60	60	60	60	60	60	60	60	60	60	60	720
Telephone	45	45	45	45	45	45	45	45	45	45	45	45	540
Gas and electric	200	200	200	200	200	200	200	200	200	200	200	200	2,400
Water, garbage	180	—	—	180	—	—	180	—	—	180	—	—	720
Cable TV	120	—	—	120	—	—	120	—	—	120	—	—	480
All payroll taxes	1,400	1,500	1,700	1,600	1,400	1,200	1,100	1,100	1,100	1,100	1,100	1,300	15,600
Real estate taxes	—	1,800	—	—	—	—	—	1,700	—	—	—	—	3,500
Life insurance	480	—	—	—	—	—	—	—	—	—	—	—	480
Property insurance	—	600	—	—	—	—	—	—	—	—	—	—	600
Auto insurance	—	1,560	—	—	—	—	—	—	—	—	—	—	1,560
Theater, sports	70	70	70	70	70	70	70	70	70	70	70	70	840
Newspapers, magazines	40	40	40	40	40	40	40	40	40	40	40	40	480
Vacations	—	—	—	300	—	400	600	—	—	—	—	500	1,800
Hobbies, Christmas gifts	—	—	—	120	—	—	—	120	—	—	—	800	1,040
Sporting equipment	—	—	—	120	—	—	—	120	—	—	—	—	240
New clothing	150	150	150	150	150	150	150	150	150	150	150	150	1,800
Laundry, dry cleaning	20	20	20	20	20	20	20	20	20	20	20	20	240
Gifts, contributions	180	180	180	180	180	180	180	180	180	180	180	180	2,160
Dues and subscriptions	50	—	—	—	50	—	25	25	25	25	—	—	200
Tuition, books, etc.	—	—	—	—	—	—	—	480	—	—	—	—	480
Babysitters	50	50	50	50	50	50	50	50	50	50	50	50	600
Personal allowances	100	100	100	100	100	100	100	100	100	100	100	100	1,200
Dental-medical	—	600	—	—	—	—	—	—	600	—	—	—	1,200
Total Expenses	6,193	10,023	5,663	6,403	5,413	5,563	5,988	7,508	5,688	5,388	5,063	6,563	75,453
Contribution to Savings	1,157	−1,673	3,987	2,947	1,937	1,087	−638	−2,158	−38	−38	287	1,087	7,947

ity, you should try to determine as well as you can when the expected income or expense will occur.

Getting through the lean months. Because of the irregularity of some income and expense items, it is possible that your expenses will exceed your income in a given month. Of course, you must have the funds available to meet the deficit, and you may have to borrow to do so. In looking at Figure 2.7 you see that the Steeles will have five deficit months. The other seven months show positive contributions to savings. By knowing they are likely to need extra funds in these five months, the Steeles can be alert to the need for effective cash management. For example, if we assume that their checking account balance is at a bare minimum as they begin 1997, then they should be careful how they deposit the expected surplus of $1,157 in January. It would not be wise to put all of it into some type of account—say, a certificate of deposit—that is not readily available for withdrawals, because they will need $1,673 in the next month. Unquestionably, the year's activity will not unfold exactly as the Steeles see it in Figure 2.7; there are sure to be some surprises

Box 2.3 SIMPLIFYING FINANCIAL PLANNING
Budgeting with Envelopes and Play Money

At first glance, the bulletin board in Mark and Carla Spielman's kitchen looks pretty much like anyone else's—but there's a difference. Along with the reminders, recipes, and other assorted notes usually adorning bulletin boards, theirs has nine letter-size envelopes, one for each of the most important ways the Spielmans spend money; there's also a red envelope for savings, red meaning: "Stop before entering." In each of the 10 envelopes Mark and Carla put a predetermined amount of play money at the beginning of each month, which represents their monthly allotment for the activity marked on the envelope; for example, the Entertainment envelope starts each month with $100 in it.

These envelopes are the Spielmans' complete budgeting system. Every evening they go together to the bulletin board and withdraw money from the appropriate envelopes to represent the money they spent that day, whether by check or cash. At the end of the month all the envelopes should be empty, except those that include things such as vacations, where funds are being temporarily saved for later use. If all goes exactly to plan, every envelope should be empty, except savings, on December 31. But what happens if the money runs out before a month is over? Unless they come up with a good reason for transferring from one envelope to another (but never from the red one unless it's an absolute emergency), that activity is shot for the month. So if $100 is taken out of the Entertainment envelope by midmonth, the Spielmans watch a lot of television or find other things to do for the rest of the month.

The envelope system of budgeting probably dates back to the time envelopes were invented. Of course, the system itself doesn't guarantee success, but supposedly the discipline you gain by touching and feeling the money as you slip it out of the envelope makes you more budget-conscious than do other approaches, such as writing things down on a budget worksheet, or, in today's environment, punching data into your home computer. But what about play money? Will you have the same emotional reservations about spending it as you have about spending real money? Some financial planners think so, and if you haven't done well at budgeting in the past, it's worth a try. It has several big advantages over the real thing: It's not that important if you lose some, and hardly anyone wants to steal it. And, just as important, you can leave your actual cash in the bank to earn interest. Don't take this last advantage lightly. If you have an expense budget of $3,000 a month and pay expenses uniformly over a month, your average balance for the month—and for the year as a whole—is $1,500. If you had a NOW account earning 4 percent, you would give up $60 a year by stuffing cash in those envelopes. So, use play money and sleep at night—and have a good night on the town with the interest you earn.

along the way to change things, but the Steeles are now in a far better position to cope with these changes than they would be without their monthly income and expense plan.

Monitoring and Controlling Activities

With the master budget worksheet and the monthly income and expense plan finished, the first phase of budgeting is completed. You now have a road map to guide your financial activities through the year. The second phase of budgeting begins as the year unfolds and events take place. This phase involves three separate tasks: First, you need a system to record your actual income and expenses. Second, you must periodically update your income and expense accounts to see if actual amounts received and spent are in line with amounts planned. (This is usually done on a monthly basis.) Third, you need to evaluate and control activities as the year progresses.

RECORDING INCOME AND EXPENSES Record keeping is perhaps the most unpleasant aspect of budgeting, but it is necessary. Our concern should be primarily with how to do it most efficiently, since most people resent doing extensive bookkeeping each evening or weekend. The following list of suggestions might help you simplify the work.

Don't use cash. Pay as many bills as you can with checks or by charges to your credit cards (assuming neither method induces you to spend more). These will give you a written record of expenses that can be recorded at the end of the month. Paying bills with cash means, in effect, that you must create your own record, either by saving invoices or by writing things on odd pieces of paper. Both of these activities are time consuming, and the records are easily lost. Whenever you do pay with cash, standardize the recording by creating your own little "voucher," which can be a small piece of paper like the one shown in Figure 2.8. You can make many of these if you have access to a copying machine. Stick a few in your pocket each day and get in the habit of using them.

Code income and expense accounts. Assign an account number to each line item (particularly those used frequently), and, as you pay a bill, code the check stub with the appropriate number. This practice will facilitate summing expenses by category each month. Also, code your income items as you make bank deposits in order to identify the income source. If you receive a check from someone and cash

Figure 2.8
A simple voucher to record cash expenses.

it instead of depositing it, you also will have to record the amount received and identify the source. It is almost always better to deposit all checks and cash to your checking (or other) account so that they can be identified; if you need cash, write a check to get it.

See if your bank can help. Ask if your bank provides computerized services in summarizing your checks and deposit slips. Some banks do (and the trend is grow-

Figure 2.9 Monthly budget update for the Steeles for the first quarter, 1997.

	January			
Income	**Budgeted**	**Actual**	**Variance**	**Cumulative Variance**
Arnold's salary	$5,268	$5,268	$ 0	$ 0
Sharon's salary	2,000	2,375	375	375
Interest	82	84	2	2
Dividends	0	0	0	0
Total Income	$7,350	$7,727	$ 377	$ 377
Expenses				
House mortgage	$1,524	$1,524	$ 0	$ 0
Maintenance and furnishings	200	188	12	12
Auto loan	474	474	0	0
Gas, oil, maintenance	200	210	−10	−10
Licenses, parking	20	23	−3	−3
Food, household items	550	548	2	2
Meals eaten out	80	88	−8	−8
Personal care	60	73	−13	−13
Telephone	45	41	4	4
Gas and electric	200	195	5	5
Water, garbage	180	188	−8	−8
Cable TV	120	120	0	0
All payroll taxes	1,400	1,531	−131	−131
Real estate taxes	0	0	0	0
Life insurance	480	480	0	0
Property insurance	0	0	0	0
Auto insurance	0	0	0	0
Theater, sports	70	62	8	8
Newspapers, magazines	40	37	3	3
Vacations	0	0	0	0
Hobbies, Christmas gifts	0	0	0	0
Sporting equipment	0	40	−40	−40
New clothing	150	161	−11	−11
Laundry, dry cleaning	20	27	−7	−7
Gifts, contributions	180	180	0	0
Dues and subscriptions	50	50	0	0
Tuition, books, etc.	0	0	0	0
Babysitters	50	67	−17	−17
Personal allowances	100	100	0	0
Dental-medical	0	0	0	0
Total Expenses	$6,193	$6,407	$−214	$−214
Contribution to Savings	$1,157	$1,320	$ 163	$ 163

ing), and if you simply number-code your checks and deposits for each income and expense classification, the bank's monthly statement can provide you with the following information: (*a*) income and expense by each code number, (*b*) number of entries in each code number, (*c*) a percentage breakdown of income and expenses by code number for the month, and (*d*) an update of income and expense items by code number for the year. There probably will be a modest charge (say, $6 to $12 a month) for this service.

February				March			
Budgeted	Actual	Variance	Cumulative Variance	Budgeted	Actual	Variance	Cumulative Variance
$ 5,268	$ 5,268	$ 0	$ 0	$5,268	$ 5,268	$ 0	$ 0
3,000	3,475	475	850	4,000	4,425	425	1,275
82	80	−2	0	82	77	−5	−5
0	0	0	0	300	300	0	0
$ 8,350	$ 8,823	$ 473	$ 850	$9,650	$10,070	$ 420	$1,270
$ 1,524	$ 1,524	$ 0	$ 0	$1,524	$ 1,524	$ 0	$ 0
200	160	40	52	200	230	−30	22
474	474	0	0	474	474	0	0
200	225	−25	−35	200	232	−32	−67
20	27	−7	−10	20	24	−4	−14
550	596	−46	−44	550	593	−43	−87
80	102	−22	−30	80	91	−11	−41
60	66	−6	−19	60	63	−3	−22
45	43	2	6	45	43	2	8
200	208	−8	−3	200	176	24	21
0	0	0	−8	0	0	0	−8
0	0	0	0	0	0	0	0
1,500	1,647	−147	−278	1,700	1,910	−210	−488
1,800	1,800	0	0	0	0	0	0
0	0	0	0	0	0	0	0
600	620	−20	−20	0	0	0	−20
1,560	1,630	−70	−70	0	0	0	−70
70	80	−10	−2	−70	−76	−6	−8
40	37	3	6	40	56	−16	−10
0	0	0	0	0	0	0	0
0	0	0	0	0	0	0	0
0	0	0	−40	0	0	0	−40
150	133	17	6	150	174	−24	−18
20	28	−8	−15	20	26	−6	−21
180	178	2	2	180	173	7	9
0	0	0	0	0	0	0	0
0	0	0	0	0	0	0	0
50	64	−14	−31	50	79	−29	−60
100	100	0	0	100	100	0	0
600	470	130	130	0	0	0	130
$10,023	$10,212	$−189	$−403	$5,663	$ 6,044	$−381	$ −784
$−1,673	$−1,389	$ 284	$ 447	$3,987	$ 4,026	$ 39	$ 486

Use a personal computer. If, like the Steeles, you have a personal computer, determine if a home budgeting software package will be helpful. These vary in capability, but all provide data manipulation similar to the bank's service mentioned above. In addition, your personal computer has capabilities to store all the data and make them readily available for other purposes, such as comparing one month's expenses in a given category with similar monthly expenses of the previous year. And much more can be done; for example, the budget can be connected directly to your year-end balance sheet and income statement, so that making entries on the computer keyboard is virtually all you ever have to do for the entire financial recording process. All data manipulation and storage—and even printed copies—are provided automatically by the computer.

Variance: Actual income or expense item differs from the budgeted amount.
Income variance: Income item variance—favorable when actual exceeds budgeted; unfavorable in the reverse situation.
Expense variance: Expense item variance—favorable when actual is less than budgeted; unfavorable in the reverse situation.
Cumulative variance: Monthly accumulation of variances.

UPDATING INCOME AND EXPENSE ACCOUNTS After all income and expense items have been accounted for, the next step is to update your monthly income and expense plan by recording actual amounts and then comparing them with the budget. This is usually done monthly, and it is done best with an income and expense plan update, such as the one shown in Figure 2.9 (pages 50–51). If the actual amount for a line item differs from the budgeted figure, it is called a **variance.** Variances can then be either favorable—meaning they assisted in the saving effort—or unfavorable—meaning they detracted from it. An **income variance** is favorable whenever actual exceeds budgeted; it is unfavorable when the reverse is true. An **expense variance** is favorable whenever actual is less than budgeted, and it is unfavorable in the reverse case. Unfavorable variances are indicated in Figure 2.9 by a minus sign in front of the amount. The **cumulative variance** figure results from adding the current month's variance to variances of previous months; thus, the cumulative variance for maintenance—the second expense item—in February is a favorable $52, which is the sum of the favorable $40 variance in February and the favorable variance of $12 in January. In March, maintenance showed an unfavorable variance of $30, and subtracting this from February's cumulative variance gives a new cumulative variance of $22 at the end of March.

Figure 2.9 shows the Steeles' activity for the first three months of 1997. Although you see all three months at once, you should assume that each month's activities were recorded separately. The flow of data gives you a fairly good picture of how the Steeles' financial events took place during the quarter. Sharon began working more hours than she anticipated, which led to most of the favorable income variance in January, and this continued in February and March. By the end of the quarter, Sharon had earned $1,275 more than budgeted. The estimates for Arnold's salary and dividends were accurate, and the interest variance is trivial.

EVALUATING AND CONTROLLING ACTIVITIES Being able to stay within budget means you are continuously adjusting your expenses during the year. Evaluating and controlling activities really make the budget work; an elaborate recording system does little good if we choose to ignore the information it provides. For example, the Steeles went $11 over their budget for new clothing in January. This tells them they have only $139 ($150 − $11) to spend in February. You must subtract the cumulative variance (add, if it's favorable) from the current monthly budget figure to determine how much of current funds is available for a given line item. In February, the Steeles went $17 under budget for new clothing, which offset the unfavorable $11 variance, leaving a $6 favorable variance for March. However, March's figure was $24 over budget, meaning the Steeles ended the first quarter with a cumulative unfavorable variance of $18 in this account. Unless their goal is changed here, they should try to reduce this variance to zero by the end of June.

Even though you are monitoring activities and calculating cumulative variances at the end of each month, a year-end review can be helpful. It serves mainly to assist in making budget estimates for the next year. It also provides an opportunity to prepare the current year's income statement, because the figure for each line item on this statement is simply the budget amount for the year plus its cumulative variance at December 31.

SUMMARY

Financial Statements are prepared to measure financial performance and to assist in future planning. There are three major financial statements: the balance sheet, the income statement, and the cash budget. A balance sheet measures your net worth, which is the difference between the market values of all the assets you own and your liabilities. Net worth is the best measurement of your wealth, even though it is difficult to place market values on some assets. It is important to understand not only the level of net worth, but also how net worth changes over time. These changes can come about if your income exceeds your expenses or if the market values of assets held at the beginning of a period increase during the period.

An income statement shows income, expenses, and contribution to savings over a period of time. Income is cash inflow from wages or salaries, interest, dividends, gains or losses on sale of securities, business or partnership profits, and other sources; expenses are cash outflows that sustain a living scale. Financial performance is evaluated periodically to objectively assess one's financial strength. A first test is a comparison of percentage changes in income and net worth with changes in inflation. A second test measures one's liquidity, and a third evaluates a person's total debt to see if it is being used excessively.

A budget is a plan expressing goals and allocations of limited resources to achieve them. Whether simple or complex, budgeting is likely to be successful if it (*a*) sets realistic goals, (*b*) sticks to simple procedures, and (*c*) serves to control and direct expenses. In order to be useful for budgeting, goals must be set in specific terms. It is important to have a schedule of major future goals showing when the goal will be accomplished and the amount of annual savings required for accomplishment. An annual budget is usually prepared with the aid of two schedules: the master budget worksheet and the monthly income and expense plan. The master budget worksheet lists all expected income and expenses for the upcoming year. The monthly income and expense plan takes the total income or expense for the year and shows the individual amounts received or spent in each month. These monthly amounts are useful because they pinpoint how funds will be used each month, thereby helping to control future activities. Monitoring and controlling activities make up an important phase of budgeting, which begins by recording monthly income and expenses. The year-end review completes budgeting activities for the year.

KEY TERMS

assets (p. 25)
budget (p. 40)
cumulative variance (p. 52)
current liability (p. 30)
debt ratio (p. 39)
debt service coverage ratio (p. 39)
dissavings (p. 30)
expenses (p. 31)
expense variance (p. 52)
financial ratios (p. 36)
flexible expenses (p. 34)
goal setting (p. 41)
income (p. 31)
income statement (p. 30)
income variance (p. 52)
inflexible expenses (p. 31)
investment assets (p. 27)
liabilities (p. 25)
lifestyle assets (p. 27)
liquid asset (p. 27)
liquid assets to take-home pay ratio (p. 37)
liquidity ratio (p. 38)

master budget worksheet (p. 43)

monthly income and expense plan (p. 43)

net worth (p. 25)

nominal income (p. 36)

noncurrent liabilities (p. 30)

personal balance sheet (p. 25)

positive contribution to savings (p. 30)

real income (p. 36)

sticker shock (p. 36)

sunk costs (p. 34)

variance (p. 52)

PROBLEMS AND REVIEW QUESTIONS

1. Explain the following elements of a balance sheet and give an example of each.
   (*a*) liquid assets,
   (*b*) investment assets,
   (*c*) lifestyle assets,
   (*d*) current liabilities,
   (*e*) noncurrent liabilities.
2. Explain how asset values are determined on the balance sheet and whether these valuations are made easily.
3. What is net worth? Does it have anything to do with wealth? Explain two factors that can change net worth from one period to the next.
4. Explain the difference between a current and a noncurrent liability. Give an example of each. Explain whether liability amounts are difficult or easy to determine.
5. Lisa Rich spent every cent she had and then borrowed $1,000 to purchase an elaborate wardrobe worth $2,000. Ignoring all of Lisa's other assets and liabilities, construct her balance sheet after the purchase. Suppose that, a year later, Lisa's wardrobe—now completely out of style—is worth only $100. If Lisa has paid off $500 of her loan, what does her balance sheet look like now? Comment on her present financial position.
6. What is an income statement, and what are its component parts? In your answer, distinguish between flexible and inflexible expenses.
7. Would you classify the following expense items as flexible or inflexible? Which one(s) would you consider "sunk costs"?
   (*a*) property taxes,
   (*b*) house mortgage payments,
   (*c*) clothing,
   (*d*) car licenses,
   (*e*) insurance,
   (*f*) family members' personal allowances.
8. Explain how planned savings differs from savings as something "left over"?
9. The following items, arranged alphabetically, belong to either the income statement or the balance sheet. Put them in their correct place and then construct each statement. (You must also calculate net worth and contribution to savings.)

Automobile (1994 Ford)	$6,000
Automobile loan payments	1,200
Cash value of life insurance	2,000
Coins and currency	300
Credit card balances due	500
Federal income taxes withheld from wages	4,000
Food and household supplies	6,000
Gas and electric expenses	2,200
Gifts	400
Hobbies and collections	650
Installment loan balances due in one year	1,200
Interest	700

Jewelry	[illegible]
Mortgage loan on residence	60,000
Mortgage payments	6,200
Property and liability insurance	300
Real estate taxes	1,200
Residence	80,000
Telephone	240
Theater and sporting events	700
Tuition	1,100
U.S. Series EE bonds	1,600
Unpaid bills	700
Wages and salaries	26,000

10. You are given the following data for Kim Zerussen:

	1995	1996
Income during the year	$30,000	$32,000
End of year: Assets	50,000	60,000
Liabilities	40,000	49,000

Assuming that inflation was 10 percent during 1996, evaluate Kim's financial performance for that year.

11. Explain a financial ratio and then identify the ratios below, indicating what they are supposed to test. How would you evaluate each, given its specific numbers? After you complete that assignment, discuss whether you think the person to whom these ratios apply is a good credit risk.
    (*a*) liquid assets to take-home pay = 0.08
    (*b*) liquidity ratio = 0.75
    (*c*) debt ratio = 1.20
    (*d*) debt service coverage ratio = 1.10
12. Explain three simple rules that often lead to success in budgeting. Do you agree that the more complex a budget is, the more successful it will be? Explain.
13. Discuss the process of setting goals. List several general goals that you think will be important to you after graduation and then indicate which specific goals you will use in your annual budgets.
14. Describe the master budget worksheet, indicating some expenses you believe might be easy to forecast and some that are more difficult.
15. Explain how you would forecast the following expense items for an upcoming budget year:
    (*a*) mortgage payments,
    (*b*) food and household items,
    (*c*) income and other payroll taxes,
    (*d*) family members' personal allowances.
16. How does a monthly income and expense plan help in managing your cash and checking account?
17. Explain how a budget helps us achieve effective cash management.
18. Briefly describe four procedures that might simplify bookkeeping activities connected with recording monthly income and expense amounts.
19. Explain the relationship among the budget, the income statement, and cumulative variances. Also, discuss possible situations that might warrant making changes in your budget during the year.
20. Below are budget and actual figures for selected income and expense accounts for the month of June and cumulative variances for each account through May. (Parentheses indicate an unfavorable variance.)

	Cumulative Variance through May	June Budgeted	June Actual
Salaries	$(1,600)	$3,000	$3,400
Expenses:			
Rent	(100)	300	320
Transportation	85	200	215
Food	125	550	575
All others	(160)	850	780
Payroll taxes	400	900	1,000

Assuming that the accounts listed above are all that need to be considered, answer the following questions.

(*a*) Calculate June's variances and the cumulative variances through June.

(*b*) If the budgeter planned at the beginning of the year to save an equal amount each month and has not revised that plan, how much has he or she actually saved through June? (Show your work.)

Case 2.1 Can Arnold and Sharon Afford a Vacation Condominium?

At the end of 1995, Arnold and Sharon Steele were considering buying a condominium in Gatlinburg, Tennessee. Gatlinburg is a resort town next to the Great Smoky Mountain National Park area, where the Steeles have often camped. The condo they particularly liked was priced at $67,000, and the seller offered to finance 90 percent of the purchase price with a first mortgage loan requiring monthly payments of $597 during the first year. To make the $6,700 down payment, and $2,200 of closing costs the Steeles planned to sell both their Coleman camper (which would have been worth $2,500 at that time) and their U.S. Series EE bonds (then worth $2,800). The balance of $3,600 would be borrowed from Sharon's parents, who would not expect regular repayments of the loan but would charge interest of $288 each year. Arnold and Sharon decided against the purchase for a number of reasons, one of which involved finances. They felt that the condo would have placed an excessive strain on their budget, given their alternative goal of adding to their investments and liquid assets.

QUESTIONS

1. Using the data given above and elsewhere in this chapter, calculate what the Steeles' contribution to savings would have been in 1996, if they bought the condo on January 1, 1996. (Assume that expenses, including income taxes, not related to the purchase remain the same.)
2. Prepare a new balance sheet at December 31, 1996, for the Steeles, again assuming that they made the purchase on January 1, 1996, and that total interest payments on the mortgage loan were $6,935 and payments of principal were $229 for the year.
3. Using the four ratios given in this chapter to evaluate liquidity and total debt, make new calculations for the Steeles, assuming the condo purchase, and compare them with those calculated in the chapter. Discuss the comparisons.
4. Do you agree with the Steeles that the purchase would have been a financial strain for them? Explain your answer.

Case 2.2 The Terrels' Budget for 1997

Donna and Sherman Terrel are preparing a budget for 1997. Donna is a systems analyst with an airplane manufacturer, and Sherman is working on a master's degree in educational psychology. The Terrels do not have any children or other dependents. Donna estimates her salary will be about $36,000 in 1997; Sherman expects to work only during the summer months, doing painting and remodeling work for a building contractor. He anticipates an income from those activities of $2,400 a month in June, July, and August. Sherman does have a scholarship that pays his tuition and also provides $2,400 a year, payable in equal amounts in October and February. The Terrels don't expect to have any other income in 1997.

Donna and Sherman have listed their expected total expenses in 1997 below:

Housing (rent)	$ 5,760
Transportation	4,800
Food (includes dining out)	7,920
Utilities	2,880
Payroll taxes:	
Donna	10,800
Sherman	1,200
Insurance:	
Life—payable in May	600
Auto—payable in January	1,320
Leisure and entertainment:	
Vacation in May	1,152
All others	1,728
Clothing	1,296
Others	3,840
Total Expenses	$43,296

The Terrels will begin 1997 with about $1,200 in liquid assets, and they prefer not to draw this balance below $600 at any time during the year.

QUESTIONS

1. Prepare a monthly income and expense plan for the Terrels in 1997.
2. On the basis of the plan you have just prepared, discuss the Terrels' expected financial situation in 1997. Explain if you foresee any difficulties.
3. During the quarter break in April, Sherman's employer landed a major remodeling project and asked for Sherman's help. Sherm agreed, and he expects to earn $1,800 from the job before taxes, but probably won't receive a check until early June. Discuss how this unexpected event might affect the Terrels' activities and their budget for the balance of 1997. It is not necessary to prepare a revised monthly income and expense plan, but do refer to specific accounts and amounts (make appropriate assumptions) in your discussion.

HELPFUL CONTACTS

The National Foundation of Consumer Credit helps people who have credit problems to prepare budgets. Call 800–338–2227 for a member consumer credit counseling office near you.

INTERNET ADDRESSES

Bureau of Labor Statistics (good source of information on the CPI, including monthly updates)
gopher://una.hh.lib.umich.edu/ll/ebb/price

Gabelli Funds, Inc. (financial calculator for determining needed investment amounts to provide for college)
http://www.gabelli.com/Gab_phtml/mfund/saving2.html

Internet Vals (deals with consumer attitudes, values, and lifestyles)
http://future.sri.com/

Oakland University's Software Repository (download budgeting software from SimTel, the Coast to Coast Software Repository®)
http://mars.acs.oakland.edu/oak/

Chapter 3

Cash Management: Funds for Immediate Needs

Objectives

1. To identify the important deposits for holding cash balances and the advantages and disadvantages of each
2. To determine how much liquidity is usually necessary, given your income and preferences for safety
3. To decide on the appropriate type of checking account and to learn how to make transactions with your account and reconcile it each month
4. To understand how compounding makes your deposits grow over time and why deposits with long maturities are riskier than those with short maturities
5. To devise a strategy for managing your total liquid asset portfolio

Cash management strategy: A plan determining how much cash to hold, in what form, and in which financial institutions.

Many of us began our financial lives by opening a savings or checking account with a local bank. The need to have cash readily available to pay bills or make investments continues from then on for the rest of our lives. Cash is the most liquid asset we hold. Because it is so liquid, it often offers either no return or one below what might be available on other investments, such as stocks and bonds. This difference in return is the price (opportunity cost) we pay to be liquid, and it makes sense to keep this price as low as possible. Achieving this goal requires a **cash management strategy,** which is a plan determining how much cash to hold, in what form, and in which financial institutions. This chapter discusses the important aspects of cash management.

MEETING CASH NEEDS

Few of us hold the same amount of cash. Your income might be far greater than mine, or you might be more conservative in your financial outlook. Despite such differences, people share some common characteristics that determine their cash needs. And to satisfy them, most of us keep some pocket money and hold the rest of our cash in either checking or savings accounts.

Why Hold Cash?

In a barter system, cash would be unnecessary, but life would be much more difficult. If you had fish and wanted corn, you would have to find someone who had corn and wanted fish. And if you didn't consume or trade all your fish, you would find it difficult to hold—or save—the excess supply. All developed countries eventually evolve complex monetary systems in order to facilitate trade and commerce. After a while, these systems appear so complicated that people without training in finance usually give up trying to understand them. These people usually deposit their cash on the basis of the advice of a friend or relative. Before looking at the kinds of deposits available, though, it is helpful to understand the primary reasons why cash must be held in the first place. These reasons are threefold: to undertake transactions, to have a cash reserve in case of an emergency, and to have a temporary store of value. Each of these will now be examined.

Pocket money: Coins and currency a person holds.

UNDERTAKE TRANSACTIONS Each day you make small transactions. You may have bought lunch at the cafeteria; perhaps you stopped at a vending machine to buy a candy bar or some other item. It took cash—specifically, **pocket money** (coins and currency)—to do these things. How much pocket money do most people have on hand? Normally, they keep enough to get through a week or two; so, if you spend an average of $10 a day, you might cash a check each week for $70. Or if you have access to an automated teller machine (an ATM), you can use your bank card to make withdrawals, and this method is usually more convenient than cashing a check. Actually, it is convenience, along with safety, that dictates how much pocket money to have on hand: The more convenient it is to get it, the less you need to hold. Since pocket money is easily lost or stolen, it is usually worthwhile to put up with some inconvenience to keep your balance low.

Checking account: Funds held with a financial institution and available upon demand.

These inconveniences lead most people to open a **checking account** to pay larger monthly bills, such as the rent or utilities. You wouldn't want the risk of losing currency in the mail or the inconvenience of visiting the creditor just to pay the bill in cash. Moreover, a canceled check serves as evidence of having paid the bill. The advantages of checking accounts so heavily outweigh any of their disadvantages that a much larger portion of our total liquid assets are held in them than in coins and currency.

EMERGENCY RESERVES In addition to needing cash for everyday transactions, most people want to hold a portion of their assets in liquid form in case of emergencies. An illness, the loss of a job, or any other unfortunate event can severely strain a family's budget, and without some liquid assets, the family could be forced to sell other assets, such as the house or automobile, to meet daily living expenses. While most people agree that some cash should be held for **emergency reserves,** *how much* should be held isn't clear. Individual circumstances must dictate the amount. If you have disability income insurance or other protection that would maintain your income at close to its previous level while you are unemployed, you need a smaller emergency reserve than does someone whose income stops altogether. Important, too, is the amount of medical insurance carried: The more you have, the less cash you need. Many financial planners recommend a reserve equivalent to three to six months' after-tax income; so if you take home $2,000 a month, a reserve of $6,000 to $12,000 is suggested. Remember, though, this is only a rule of thumb.

Emergency reserves: Liquid deposits held to meet unexpected cash needs.

Since emergency reserves are not intended to be used for making transactions, they should be held in deposits that offer the highest potential return consistent with reasonable liquidity. Holding them in a checking account that pays no interest, for example, would be a mistake.

STORE OF VALUE You may be saving to make a major purchase in the future: a house, a new automobile, a personal computer, or a vacation. Until you have enough money, you need to save each pay period and then hold your savings in a form that will earn a return. You should be aware, though, that if you are holding funds for a fairly long period of time, the return on your deposits may not match the inflation rate on the item you are saving to buy. In this case, the deposit has not served well as a store of value. It is important to balance earnings against liquidity in the savings effort; in order to achieve your target, you may have to give up some liquidity to capture a higher return.

In addition to saving for a major purchase, some people hold cash balances as temporary "parking places" for their money. They really plan to reinvest their funds in less liquid investments in the future but are waiting for the investment environment to improve. Whatever the motive for holding cash, it must be held in specific kinds of deposits, to which we now turn our attention.

Fundamental Deposits

Many people meet their cash needs by holding deposits in checking and NOW accounts and passbook savings accounts. These are the basic deposits, but other types are often used as well. Table 3.1 shows frequently used deposits and grades them in terms of availability, safety, liquidity, and yield. In this section and the next we will explain these deposits, but first, remember that what makes a deposit liquid is your ability to withdraw it easily, with no delays or other complications, and your ability to withdraw it with *no loss in principal.* This last feature rules out many kinds of investments for serving liquidity needs. Common stocks, for example, can be sold quickly and relatively inexpensively—but there is never a guarantee they

TABLE 3.1 • A SCORECARD FOR LIQUID DEPOSITS AND ACCOUNTS

Deposit	Availability	Safety	Liquidity	Yield (Average Rate)[a]
Regular checking account	A+ (no minimum)	A+	A+	F (-0-)
Savings account	A+ (no minimum)	A+	B+	D (2.0%)
NOW account	A (small minimum)	A+	A+	D (1.5%)
Super NOW account	C (fairly large minimum)	A+	A+	C (2.0%)
Money market deposit account	C (fairly large minimum)	A+	B+	B– (2.8%)
Money market mutual fund	B+ (minimum varies)	A to C (depending on securities held)	A+ to B (depending on checkwriting privileges)	B– (5.5%)
Certificates of deposit (CDs)	A (minimum varies)	A+	C (early withdrawal penalties)	A (5.5%)[b]
Series EE bonds	A (small minimum)	A+	B	B+ (5.3%)

[a]Approximate amounts at mid-July, 1995.
[b]On 60-month CDs; longer maturities offered higher rates, shorter maturities less.

can be sold without loss, so they fail the liquidity test. Some of the deposits examined below are much more liquid than others. Certificates of deposit are the least liquid because of their interest penalties for early withdrawal.

Closely related to the issue of losing principal is the question of safety. Many depositors view safety as their most crucial concern because a large portion of their total investments may be in liquid accounts. Certainly a major advantage of holding deposits in most banks, savings and loans, and credit unions is the availability of federal insurance.

Indeed, the failure of some financial institutions during the 1980s clearly indicates that you could make a tragic mistake by using a nonfederally insured institution. Be sure, then, to look for the abbreviations below when opening an account.

- *FDIC* (Federal Deposit Insurance Corporation)—insures commercial banks
- *SAIF* (Savings Association Insurance Fund)—insures savings and loans and mutual savings banks
- *NCUA* (National Credit Union Administration)—insures credit unions

It is important to know also that insurance is provided up to $100,000 for the *depositor* not for the deposit. So, if you are fortunate enough to have more than $ $100,000, you should open a second account with a different institution, or you could make additional deposits with the same institution in another person's name.

NOW (negotiated order of withdrawal) account: Interest-earning checking account, usually with a minimum balance requirement.

Super NOW account: NOW account paying high interest but with a large minimum balance requirement.

CHECKING AND NOW ACCOUNTS Checking and NOW accounts are used primarily to satisfy transaction needs. While there is a slight technical difference between a regular checking and a **NOW (negotiated order of withdrawal) account,** for all practical purposes they are identical. Their major difference to you is that a NOW account pays interest on balances in the account, whereas a regular checking account does not. Most banks advertise their NOW accounts and **super NOW ac-**

counts (these pay higher interest) with names such as *Checking Plus* or *Checking Plus More,* to indicate that interest is earned on the account. The interest may be paid in several ways. Amounts below a minimum (usually between $500 and $5,000) earn interest at a relatively low rate, and amounts above the limit earn higher rates. The higher rates are usually pegged to current money market rates, which means the interest you receive depends on the level of interest rates in general; as these go up, so does the amount earned. Of course, the reverse is also true.

If you can meet the minimum balance requirement of a NOW account it is usually the best choice. However, get complete information on all accounts the bank offers before making a choice. Then compare their benefits and costs.

Savings account: Account with virtually no restrictions but with no checkwriting privileges.

Passbook rate: Interest rate on a savings account; usually the lowest savings rate offered by a financial institution.

SAVINGS ACCOUNTS Many Americans have had a **savings account** at one time or another. They were often called passbook accounts because a record of your activity in the account was recorded in a passbook. These books are now mostly replaced by the type of statements used for checking accounts. However, the rate of interest earned on passbook accounts is still called the **passbook rate.** Because these accounts require no minimum balances, they are used frequently when only small deposits can be made. The passbook rate is generally the lowest rate of interest available, and it may be to your advantage to invest funds in alternative liquid accounts if you have enough cash to qualify for one of them. But shopping around may be to your advantage, even with savings accounts. For example, your credit union might offer a higher rate than your bank or savings and loan.

Other Deposits

In addition to checking and savings accounts, investors have access to a variety of other deposits. These are explained briefly in the following sections.

Money market deposit account (MMDA): Savings account whose interest rate is tied to money market rates of interest.

MONEY MARKET DEPOSIT ACCOUNTS **Money market deposit accounts (MMDAs)** offer current money market rates and easy access through checkwriting privileges, usually limited to three checks (or six transfers in total) a month. Federal depository insurance also enhances their appeal, as does access through automated teller machines. Unfortunately for small depositors, they have minimum deposit balances. Also, in very recent years, banks have lowered the rates on MMDAs substantially below market rates. Notice the relatively low yield of 2.8 percent in Table 3.1, compared with 5.5 percent for money market mutual funds.

Money market mutual fund: Pooling arrangement that invests in money market securities having very large denominations.

MONEY MARKET MUTUAL FUNDS **Money market mutual funds** pool the resources of many investors to purchase short-term securities issued by the U.S. Treasury, large commercial banks, and financially strong corporations (more information about mutual funds is provided in Chapter 13). Most people cannot afford to purchase such securities directly because they are sold only in very large denominations, such as $10,000 for a U.S. Treasury Bill and $100,000 for a commercial bank certificate of deposit. Since most of these investments are very safe, so too are the money market mutual funds that invest in them. Nevertheless, your deposit is not insured as it is in a money market account or other federally insured deposit. A unique money market fund is one that invests in municipal bonds with very short maturities. Such funds appeal to depositors in high tax brackets, because the earnings are exempt from federal income tax. All money market mutual funds have a minimum balance requirement, which is usually $1,000, although some are as low as $500.

Certificate of deposit (CD): Savings account with a set maturity and restricted access to funds until maturity.

CERTIFICATES OF DEPOSIT **Certificates of deposit (CDs)** are somewhat different from money market deposit accounts or money market mutual funds. When you buy CDs, you are in effect freezing your money for the maturity of the deposit, which can vary from seven days to eight years, or even longer. For instance a 60-month deposit of $1,000 might be purchased to yield 8 percent. At the end of 60 months you will get $1,469.33, which is the principal plus interest (assuming annual compounding). But suppose you need the money before the 60 months end. You will then pay an interest penalty, the amount depending upon when withdrawal takes place. A very early withdrawal can mean you get less back than your initial deposit. Naturally, this penalty discourages investors from using these deposits indiscriminately to obtain higher rates. The interest rate at the time of purchase is locked in for the entire term of the deposit. If interest rates fall during that period, you benefit by having your money invested at the higher rate. But if interest rates rise, the certificates will have been a poor choice.

U.S. Series EE bonds: Treasury-issued bonds with indexed interest rates, low denominations, and other attractive features.

U.S. SERIES EE BONDS **U.S. Series EE bonds** are very attractive short-term investments, particularly for small investors. They now offer returns pegged to interest paid on U.S. Treasury securities. If you hold the bonds less than five years, their yield is set at 85 percent of the yields earned on *6-month* Treasury securities; if you hold them for five years or longer, their yield is set at 85 percent of *5-year* Treasury securities. Yields are determined twice a year, at May 1 and November 1. Series EE bonds formerly had a minimum return of 4 percent, but that feature was eliminated effective May 1, 1995.

The interest you earn on Series EE bonds is free of state and local income taxes and can be deferred for federal income tax purposes until you redeem the bonds. Moreover, federal income taxes may be avoided altogether if interest on the bond is used to pay for a child's college or vocational education. Currently, single individuals earning $40,000 or less and married couples jointly earning $60,000 or less earn

Box 3.1 **PERSONAL FINANCE NEWS** *Late Edition*

Banking by Computer: Has Electronic Banking Finally Arrived?

About a dozen years ago, we heard that banking by phone was the wave of the future. It never happened. Now we hear that in the near future most U.S. families will bank by computer, and there is growing evidence that indeed they will. The pieces are all coming together: First, by the year 2000, half of all U.S. homes are likely to own personal computers; second, the number of homes hooking up to on-line data services such as Prodigy or the Internet is growing exponentially; and, third, easy-to-use software such as Intuit's Quicken is being integrated into on-line banking services.

The big advantage of computerized banking is the ease of paying bills. With a PC, you pay bills by writing checks on the screen and clicking a payment box. Data for payees that you pay frequently, such as the telephone company, are held in memory, which means you don't even have to write the on-screen check—just click another box. Your electronic check can be sent in one of two ways. You may have a service that actually writes a check and mails it to the payee. Or the payee may have an electronic hookup to your bank, in which case the funds are simply transferred from your account to the payee's.

Naturally, PC banking involves charges. In some cases you pay a fee to the on-line provider in addition to its regular monthly fee. Also, there is usually a per-check charge for all checks above a minimum number. A ballpark estimate of cost is $9 to $15 a month for 30 checks. This method offers scant dollar savings over the old way, but it should save your time. Moreover, you may have instant access to your account to determine its balance, outstanding checks, or other information. Last, but not least, you avoid licking those gruesome postage stamps.

PURCHASE PRICE	• $25 to $5,000; maximum investment is $30,000 per individual
YOUR RETURN	• Indexed to 6-month U.S. Treasury securities, if held less than 5 years • Indexed to 5-year U.S. Treasury securities, if held 5 years or longer
WHERE TO BUY	• Through payroll deduction plans • At most banks and other financial institutions • Through the mail from Bureau of Public Debt, Washington, DC 20226
REDEMPTION	• Redeem at any bank
OTHER ADVANTAGES	• No buying or selling charges, fees, or commissions • Income taxes can be deferred until redemption, or possibly avoided altogether if bond interest is used for a child's education • No state or local income taxes

Figure 3.1 Important facts about U.S. Series EE savings bonds.

a full exclusion of all Series EE bond interest. For incomes from $40,000 to $50,000 (single return) and $60,000 to $90,000 (joint return), partial exclusion is available; and for incomes over $50,000 and $90,000, no exclusion is allowed. Clearly, this possible avoidance of taxes on Series EE bonds makes them very attractive.

Interest is earned on the Series EE bond by redeeming it for an amount greater than what was paid to purchase it. Another important consideration in purchasing Series EE bonds is their widespread availability. They can be bought or redeemed at most federally insured commercial or mutual savings banks or savings and loans. Some basic information about U.S. Series EE bonds is shown in Figure 3.1.

U.S. Series HH bonds: Treasury-issued bonds that pay a fixed semiannual interest; available only through exchange of U.S. Series EE bonds.

U.S. SERIES HH BONDS **U.S. Series HH bonds** are also issued by the Treasury. You cannot buy them, however; you can acquire them only by exchanging Series EE bonds (or series E bonds, an older version of Series EE). This exchange is referred to as a Series EE rollover. The HH series differs from the EE series in that interest is paid semiannually and is determined at the time of the exchange; the bonds mature in 10 years (but can be extended to 30 years). An appealing feature of HH bonds is that deferred interest on EE bonds can be continued by the exchange. However, semiannual interest is taxable.

USING YOUR CHECKING ACCOUNT

The convenience of paying bills by checks, rather than with cash, was noted earlier in this chapter. Maintaining a checking account properly, however, involves some work. Care must be taken in making deposits and writing checks, and it is important to keep an adequate balance in the account, both to avoid overdrafts and to stay above any minimum that applies to the account. In addition, each month the bank will provide a statement of activity in the account, which you should reconcile with your activity records to ensure that neither you nor the bank has made a mistake. The first order of business, though, is to select a bank. We use the term **bank** to refer to any financial institution that offers checking account services. These could be commercial banks, savings and loans, mutual savings banks, or credit unions.

Bank: Any financial institution offering checking account services.

Selecting a Bank

Your choice of bank is usually determined by a variety of factors. Perhaps the most important of these is convenience, but very often the range of services provided by the bank is also considered. Finally, what the bank charges to service the account and what it offers in interest on average balances must be evaluated. Shop around to find a checking account that fills your needs best.

GEOGRAPHIC CONVENIENCE Depositors often cite geographic convenience as the single most important factor in choosing one bank over another. Although many transactions can be made indirectly through such means as preauthorized savings or bill payments, people nevertheless still conduct most of their banking business by direct contact with the bank. They visit it frequently to cash checks, make deposits, pay off loans, and so forth. It's not surprising, then, that geographic convenience still matters the most. But closely related to the geographic convenience of the main office and branches is the existence of automated teller machines at convenient locations. Many people now rely upon them as a source of cash and as a means of making other transactions. Finally, convenience and courtesy at the bank will probably influence your choice to open or keep an account there. Drive-in window facilities are obviously important to many of us, judging by the long lines of automobiles we often see at banks.

BANK SERVICES Full-service banks and many other institutions now offer a wide array of services to their depositors, as Figure 3.2 shows. You might notice the items of convenience, such as the arrangements available for paying bills and transferring funds. A particularly intriguing service is the "Answer Bank," which provides useful information about many personal financial questions.

SERVICE CHARGES AND EARNED INTEREST Competition among banks has led to significant differences in service fees and interest paid on deposits. So comparative shopping is essential. There is little reason to pay any fee, no matter how small, for a service, when you can get the same service free elsewhere. However, if a bank's charges are low for some services, they might be high for others. Decide which services are important and then do your shopping.

Checking Account Procedures

Using a checking account is a relatively simple process if you are careful. Once an account is opened, you will make periodic deposits to increase your balance, and you will draw it down by writing checks. A record of these transactions is kept in a check register, which may be a journal but is more often simply stubs to the checks written. Regardless of what forms are used to keep records, it is a good idea to take a little extra time to record all pertinent data. Very often a check is written in haste at a crowded checkout line, for example, and the stub is left for our memory to fill in later. Unfortunately, memories fade with time, particularly with respect to the exact amount of the check, and after several such instances, we have no idea how much is in the account. Along with filling out the stub completely as the check is written, it is also a good idea to earmark certain expenditures if they have particular importance. For example, many people use a checkmark or other symbol to identify tax-deductible expenses. This identification helps when next year's tax return needs to be filed.

Bank

Savings

- Passbook accounts
- Money market deposit accounts
- Certificates of deposit—maturities of one week to ten years
- Savings reserve, to protect against accidental overdrafts
- IRAs

Loans

- Personal loans—autos, trucks, recreational vehicles, home improvements
- Business loans—lines of credit, term loans
- Mortgage loans—business and residential (conventional, FHA, VA)

Major Credit Cards

- American Express Gold Card/Executive Credit
- Mastercard/Visa

Other Services

- Automated teller machines
- Safe deposit boxes
- Trust services
- Business services—payroll, accounting, leasing, direct deposit
- "Answer Bank"—free personal financial advice to 50 commonly asked questions
- Preauthorized savings—automatic transfers from checking to savings
- Direct deposit of retirement checks (Social Security, Civil Service, or Railroad Retirement)
- Direct deposit of payroll checks
- Wire transfers
- Bank by mail
- Money orders, cashier's checks, traveler's checks
- Utility payments
- Home banking by home computer

Figure 3.2
A partial list of services offered by a large Midwestern bank.

Right of survivorship: An owner of an account has access to all funds upon the death of a co-owner.

Tenants in common: An owner of an account has a legal claim only to his or her share of an account upon the death of a co-owner.

OPENING THE ACCOUNT Opening a checking or savings account requires nothing more than filling out a simple signature card. If a joint account is opened, both (or all) signatures are required. It is important to use your legal name on any account. A married couple should consider a joint account rather than separate accounts for several reasons. First, the monthly service charges on two accounts are generally higher than for only one account. Second, and more important, if one of the spouses were to die, the funds in a joint account would pass immediately to the remaining spouse. This **right of survivorship** is associated with most bank accounts. However, in some states a joint account that does not specifically state right of survivorship will presume that **tenants in common** applies, in which case the survivor receives only his or her share of the account. Be sure to inquire about right of survivorship when you open an account.

MAKING ADDITIONAL DEPOSITS AND ENDORSING CHECKS Making deposits to a checking account is a regular activity. These deposits consist of currency, coins, and checks written to you. Deposits are made with a deposit slip, such as the one illustrated in Figure 3.3. Notice that the deposit is for $600, consisting of $100 in currency and a check for $500. The arrangement of numbers 01–4/435 is the bank transit number on the check deposited. This number is of no particular importance to you, but it is used in the Federal Reserve's check-clearing process, and it should

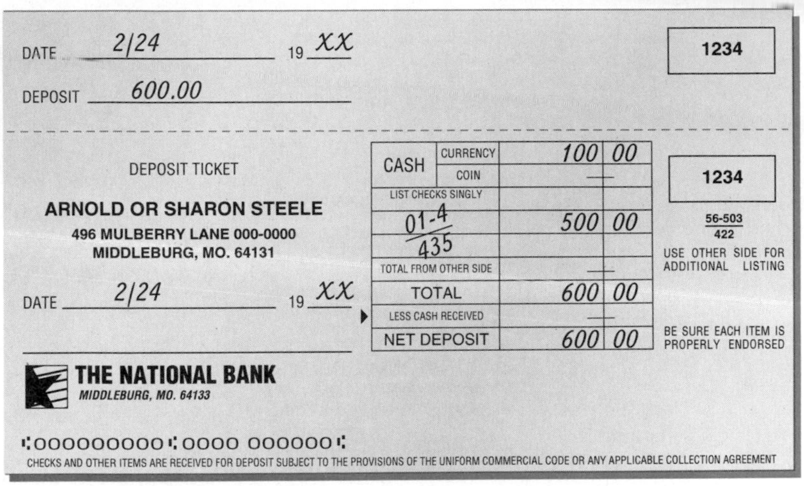

Figure 3.3
A deposit slip.

be listed carefully to help this process. Also, use a separate line for each check deposited even if all the checks are from the same bank.

Blank endorsement: Unrestricted endorsement of a check; anyone possessing the check can cash it.

Restrictive endorsement: Limits the use of a check to a single purpose, usually to make a deposit.

Special endorsement: Using a check to pay a third party.

Checks can be endorsed (signed on the back) in three different ways, as shown in Figure 3.4. You use a **blank endorsement** when withdrawing cash from the account, but remember that once you sign a check it becomes a negotiable instrument and can be used as such by anyone. If you happen to lose the check, all the finder needs to do is sign it under your signature and cash it. As a safeguard, don't sign the check until you are at the bank and ready to make the withdrawal. A **restrictive endorsement** limits the use of the check to a single purpose. "For deposit only" is written on a check when it is deposited by mail. If the check is lost in the mail and subsequently found, it cannot be cashed. A **special endorsement** is used when you use the check to pay someone else. All that you need do is indicate the payee and sign, as shown in Figure 3.4. It is usually not a good idea to pay bills in this manner, however, since you will not have a record of the payment unless you take the time to make one. Remember, the check will be returned to the person who issued it, not to you.

WRITING CHECKS Writing a check is a simple procedure illustrated in Figure 3.5. As mentioned above, the stub should be filled in at the same time the check is written, and, naturally, they should be in agreement. Your account number is printed on the bottom of the check, as well as on the deposit slip. This number identifies the account and is needed whenever inquiries about the account are

Figure 3.4
Ways to endorse a check.

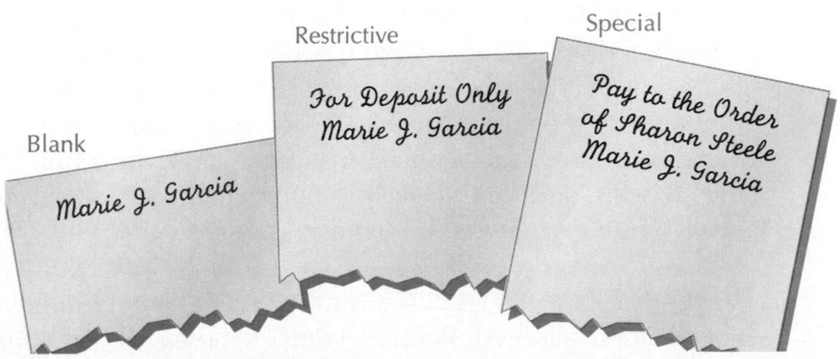

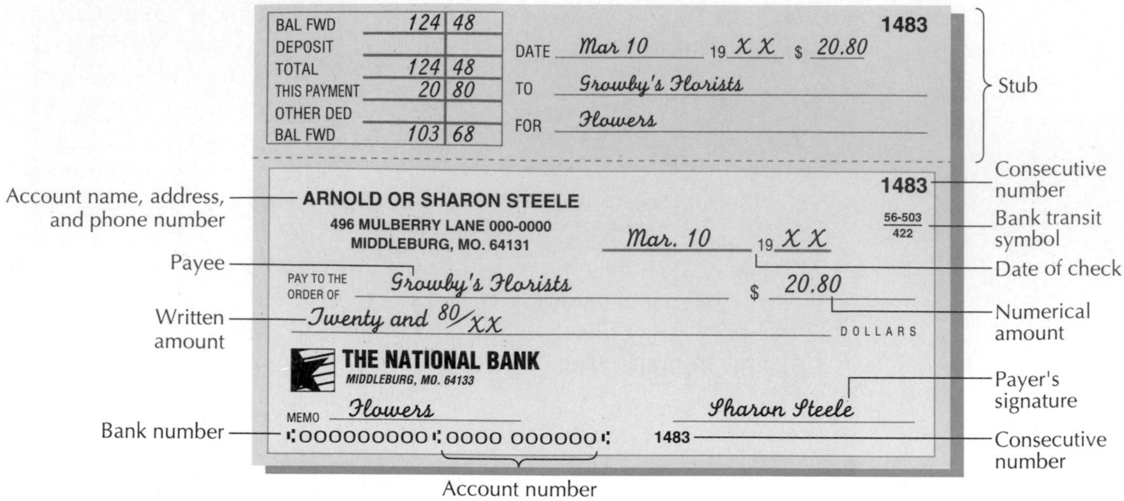

Figure 3.5 A sample check.

made. As a safeguard, the amount of the check is indicated both numerically and in written form. Be particularly careful about the written amount, because it is the legally binding figure. Also, your signature should appear exactly as you signed the signature card to open the account.

Overdraft (bounced check): A check lacking sufficient funds to cover it.

"BOUNCING A CHECK" If you happen to write a check without sufficient funds to cover it, you will have an **overdraft,** commonly referred to as a **bounced check.** It's an expensive oversight, since most banks charge about $20.00 for each such check. Moreover, it can lead to a poor credit rating. Either of these factors should motivate you to balance your account accurately on a timely basis. After writing one or two overdrafts, some people go to the opposite extreme and keep an excessive balance to avoid the problem in the future. But this practice is costly if the account does not pay interest. Another precautionary step is to arrange a savings reserve that ties the checking account to a savings account and automatically transfers funds from the latter to the former whenever an overdraft takes place. Although this arrangement is better than "overloading" the checking account, it too has a drawback if interest earned on the savings account is only at the passbook rate. You might get a better rate than this in another account. A third alternative is to arrange for a loan that will cover the overdraft. This is the worst alternative, since interest is typically charged at your credit card rate, which is usually 18 percent or more.

AVAILABILITY OF FUNDS Current federal law requires all banks to comply with the following standards in making funds available after deposits have been made to the account: Cash, wire transfers, government checks, cashier's checks, and certified checks must be available on the next business day. Checks written on a local bank or other local financial institution must be available two business days after the deposit day, and checks written on a nonlocal financial institution must be available five business days after the deposit day.

STOPPING PAYMENT ON A CHECK Sometimes it is necessary to stop payment on a check already issued. Perhaps you paid someone for merchandise and after inspec-

Stop-payment order: Directive to a bank not to pay a check.

tion found it defective or incomplete. You simply go to the bank and fill out a form, called a **stop-payment order,** directing the bank not to pay the check. You are charged for this service, so it shouldn't be used casually. It's a better idea not to issue a check until you are satisfied with the service or merchandise in question.

You should not issue a stop-payment order for a lost or stolen check. Contrary to what you may have heard, such checks are the bank's responsibility and not yours; that is, the bank is supposed to verify your signature before honoring a check. So there is no reason for you to incur a charge to benefit the bank. Naturally, you should inform the bank—both as a courtesy and to close the old account while opening a new one (which may involve a charge). The same advice applies to a check you forgot to sign. Let it process, and the bank may honor the check anyway. If it doesn't, write another check to the payee.

End-of-Month Activities

At the end of each month, the bank will send you a monthly statement showing all transactions the bank has recorded in your account. It is important to reconcile this statement each month, both to update and audit your records for accuracy and to make sure the bank hasn't made a mistake.

Bank reconciliation: End-of-month analysis comparing the cash balance per bank statement with the cash balance per checkbook.

BANK RECONCILIATION A **bank reconciliation** means that the end-of-month balance as shown on the bank statement is the same as the end-of-month balance shown in the check record. Figures 3.6, 3.7, and 3.8 illustrate the steps in the reconciliation process. Figure 3.6 shows the stubs from a series of checks, numbers 1483 through 1488, written from the account. Notice that the running balance is maintained and that the end-of-month balance is $134.48. Figure 3.7 shows the bank statement sent to the depositor at the end of the month. A glance at it reveals several bits of information. First, the bank has deducted a service charge of $2.00, which wasn't known and therefore was not recorded up to now. So the first task is to reduce the book balance from $134.48 to $132.48. Second, you can see that of the six checks written during the month, only four have cleared; checks 1486 and 1488 are still outstanding. That is why the bank's balance is so much greater than the book balance. Figure 3.8 is a reconciliation form that appears on the back of this particular bank statement. By following steps 1 through 4, you should be able to reconcile the statement. Notice that after the outstanding checks are deducted from the bank's balance, the book balance (after the service charge has been deducted) of $132.48 is confirmed. This reconciliation is a fairly simple one, since there are only six checks to review, no deposits in transit, and no other activity to make things more difficult. However, before you start a reconciliation, it is a good idea to compare each cleared check with the data recorded on the stub, because errors seem to occur no matter how carefully we try to keep our books. Cross-checking before you start to reconcile can prevent a headache later on if the two balances fail to agree after a first reconciliation attempt.

Truncation: The bank retains a payer's checks.

FILING AND STORAGE After reconciliation, the bank statement can be filed for later reference. Most banks will return the canceled checks along with your statement, although the trend today is toward **truncation,** which simply means that the payer's bank retains the checks and forwards only a bank statement. This statement, however, does indicate the name of the payee on each check, along with the check number and dollar amount. Many depositors prefer truncation because it reduces the bulky records they must keep. Be careful to save whatever documents

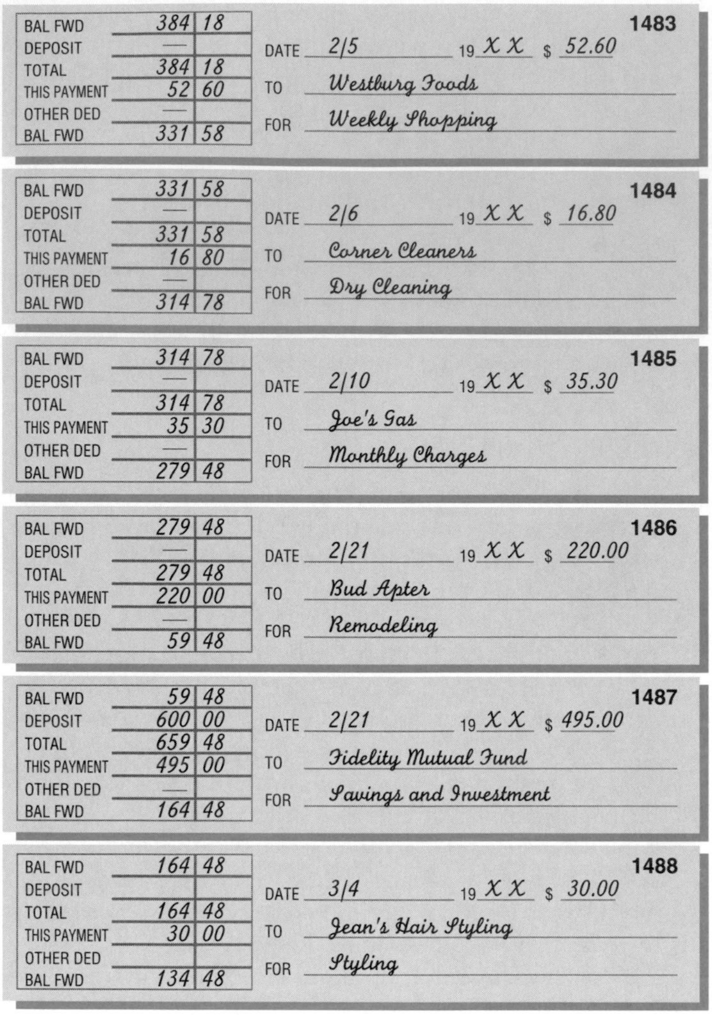

BAL FWD 384 18
DEPOSIT —
TOTAL 384 18
THIS PAYMENT 52 60
OTHER DED —
BAL FWD 331 58
1483
DATE 2/5 19 X X $ 52.60
TO Westburg Foods
FOR Weekly Shopping
BAL FWD 331 58
DEPOSIT —
TOTAL 331 58
THIS PAYMENT 16 80
OTHER DED —
BAL FWD 314 78
1484
DATE 2/6 19 X X $ 16.80
TO Corner Cleaners
FOR Dry Cleaning
BAL FWD 314 78
DEPOSIT —
TOTAL 314 78
THIS PAYMENT 35 30
OTHER DED —
BAL FWD 279 48
1485
DATE 2/10 19 X X $ 35.30
TO Joe's Gas
FOR Monthly Charges
BAL FWD 279 48
DEPOSIT —
TOTAL 279 48
THIS PAYMENT 220 00
OTHER DED —
BAL FWD 59 48
1486
DATE 2/21 19 X X $ 220.00
TO Bud Apter
FOR Remodeling
BAL FWD 59 48
DEPOSIT 600 00
TOTAL 659 48
THIS PAYMENT 495 00
OTHER DED —
BAL FWD 164 48
1487
DATE 2/21 19 X X $ 495.00
TO Fidelity Mutual Fund
FOR Savings and Investment
BAL FWD 164 48
DEPOSIT
TOTAL 164 48
THIS PAYMENT 30 00
OTHER DED
BAL FWD 134 48
1488
DATE 3/4 19 X X $ 30.00
TO Jean's Hair Styling
FOR Styling

Figure 3.6
Sample check stubs.

the bank returns to you. These items—not your check stubs or other documents that you generate—are necessary to support a claim that payment has been made. For example, the Internal Revenue Service requires these source documents to support your personal income tax deductions.

Checks That Guarantee Payment

On occasion you may need a check that guarantees payment. Maybe you are buying something from a person who doesn't know you and is also not familiar with your bank. Conversely, there are instances when you want to be sure a check you are receiving will not bounce. There are three popular approaches to guaranteeing a check: have a personal check certified, buy a cashier's check, and buy traveler's checks.

Certified check: Bank verification that a payer has sufficient funds to cover a specific check.

CERTIFIED CHECK A person can take a personal check to his or her bank and ask to have it certified, making it a **certified check.** This means that the bank will verify that sufficient funds are in the account to cover the check. After this verification,

THE NATIONAL BANK

YOUR BANKING NO. 211 4003

ARNOLD OR SHARON STEELE
496 MULBERRY LANE
MIDDLEBURG, MO 64131

STATEMENT PERIOD	PAGE
FROM 2/04/XX TO 3/07/XX	1

CHECKING

TYPE	PREVIOUS BALANCE	DEPOSITS & CREDITS NUMBER	DEPOSITS & CREDITS AMOUNT	CHECKS & DEBITS NUMBER	CHECKS & DEBITS AMOUNT	NOW INTEREST	SERVICE CHARGE	CURRENT BALANCE
FREE&EASY 02	384.18		600.08	1	601.70		2.00	382.48

DAY	AMOUNT	CHECK NO. OR DESCRIPTION	DAY	AMOUNT	CHECK NO. OR DESCRIPTION	DAY	AMOUNT	CHECK NO. OR DESCRIPTION
07	2 00	SERVICE CHARGE						
05	52 60	1483						
08	16 80	1484						
18	35 30	1485						
24	600 00	DEPOSIT						
25	495 00	1487						

Figure 3.7 Sample bank statement.

the bank deducts the amount of the check from the account, making the funds immediately available to the payee. A certification is then stamped on the check.

Cashier's check: A check issued by a bank against itself.

CASHIER'S CHECK People without checking accounts often use a **cashier's check** to pay bills. Such a check is also used when the amount involved is very large. It is written by a bank against itself and is accordingly much more acceptable than a personal check. There is a small service charge for a cashier's check unless you are a special customer to the bank, in which case the charge might be waived.

Traveler's check: Check purchased from a bank, usually when a payer is traveling away from home.

TRAVELER'S CHECKS A **traveler's check** is generally used when you are traveling away from home. These checks can be purchased at any bank or other financial institution in denominations that usually range from $10 to $100. At the time you buy these checks, you sign each one in the presence of a bank officer; later, when you cash one of them, you sign again in the presence of the person cashing it. The payees can thus compare signatures to guard against forgery. You also get a small journal to record the check serial numbers and other pertinent information. It's a good idea to keep this journal somewhere other than where you keep the checks, since theft or loss of the checks must be reported to the bank to stop payment. If the journal and checks are lost or stolen together, you may not know what specific checks are actually missing. Traveler's checks are accepted practically everywhere throughout the world. They are a wise purchase (some banks will provide them free) whenever you travel.

To balance your checking account:

Step 1 Subtract from your checkbook balance all charges or other transfers that are shown in the checking section on the front of the statement such as, Service Charges, Automatic Transfers, Reorder of Checks or Others. Your Checking Plus Loan Payment is shown in the bottom right section on the front of your banking statement. Subtract only the payment amount from your checkbook balance. Add your NOW Account interest to your checkbook balance.

Step 2 Compare checks shown on this statement to your checkbook records and list checks outstanding by dollar amount.

Step 3 Enter Current Balance shown on this statement $ 382.48

Add Deposits made after Statement Period $ —

Total $ 382.48

Subtract total of checks outstanding $ 250.00

Step 4 This Balance should agree with your checkbook $ 132.48

Checks Outstanding	
Date or No. 1486	$ 220.00
1488	30.00
Total	$ 250.00

Figure 3.8 A bank reconciliation.

Electronic Banking

Growing computer and electronics technologies have created important changes in the way banking transactions can be made. As mentioned before, it is now possible to do much of your banking business with your telephone hooked up to your personal computer. Most of us are already familiar with **automated teller machines (ATMs).** With these, you use a plastic ID card and a personal access code to conduct a number of bank activities such as withdrawing cash (in limited amounts only), transferring funds from one account to another, or paying routine monthly bills. You should exercise care in using an ATM, because it is a fertile area for consumer fraud and theft. For example, don't leave your access card in the machine or in other unprotected places, and don't use obvious code numbers such as your street address or phone number.

Automated teller machines (ATMs): Machines that perform certain banking functions.

Electronic funds transfer systems (EFTS) extend beyond ATM services. The same access card can also be used to pay bills at stores that have point-of-sale terminals. In this way, funds are transferred automatically from your account to the vendor's. There are still other forms of electronic transfers: You may have an arrangement whereby your payroll check is wired directly to your bank; or, if you are a retiree, you may receive your Social Security check through an electronic transfer. Although electronic banking lacks a personal touch, it does add convenience.

Electronic funds transfer systems (EFTS): Electronic payment of bills and other transfers of cash.

Box 3.2 SAVING MONEY
Understanding the Blizzard of New Service Charges

Before opening a checking or savings account, make sure you understand how the account works with respect to service charges. You might be surprised to learn that such charges often apply to services that once were provided free or at low cost. Some potential trouble spots are indicated below. Consider them and how you intend to use your account. If it seems likely that you will run up a sizable monthly total, you should consider a simpler account, even though it may offer fewer services.

ATM Users

If you use an ATM, you are likely to be charged if you use a "foreign" machine (one that's not part of the bank's system). These charges can be as high as $2 a transaction. Even if you use an in-system machine, expect to pay charges for many regularly made transactions such as cash advances. While many banks levy a 2 percent charge, most cap the charge at $10 or $20; however, some do not, and this means an exorbitant fee for a cash advance. Also, if you open an ATM-only account, expect to pay a stiff fee if you make a teller-assisted transaction.

Dealing with a "Live" Teller

Amazing as it seems, some banks are now charging for the luxury of dealing with a person rather than an ATM. First National Bank of Chicago initiated a $3 fee per transaction and Key Bank in Colorado charges $25 an hour if you need help with your account. Although such fees are not widespread at the moment, you should ask if the bank has such charges before opening an account.

Credit Cards

Most banks charge an annual fee of $20 or so for a credit card. In addition, you may face a similar charge if you exceed your credit limit or if your monthly payment is late. Of course, the big cost is the high rate of interest charged on most cards—from 18 to 21 percent. The persistence of these high rates is remarkable considering that interest rates in general have declined substantially in recent years and are now considered low.

Handling Mistakes

Transactions involving the bank often lead to mistakes that can be costly. If you overdraw your account, expect a charge of $10 to $20. Issuing a stop-payment order on a check is likely to incur a similar fee. Finally, you might be charged $5 (or more) if you are unsure of the current account balance and ask the bank for such information.

UNDERSTANDING HOW YOUR ACCOUNT EARNS INTEREST

What does a financial institution mean when it offers to pay you, say, 12 percent interest on your account? On the surface, this looks like a simple enough calculation: If you put $1,000 in the account, you get back $1,120 a year later, which is the initial $1,000 plus $120 (0.12 × $1,000) of earned interest. Simple as it seems, complications can arise if your account is structured differently from the one above, and many are.

One source of confusion in the simple interest calculation is that it assumes that interest is paid only once—at the very end of the year. But you probably have seen accounts that advertise interest paid weekly, daily, or even continuously. Do you earn more with these accounts? If so, how much more? To answer these questions we need an understanding of basic interest calculations. Finally, suppose you make periodic deposits and withdrawals to and from an account. Will interest be earned on the deposit balance at the beginning of the month, at the end of the month, on the average for the month, or just what? Clearly, these questions, too, must be asked before you open an account.

How Interest Is Calculated

The actual interest dollars ($\$I$) earned on a deposit depend on three factors: the amount you invest ($\$P$); a stated interest rate (i), expressed in decimal form; and the length of time (t) the deposit is held, expressed as a fraction or multiple of a year. This relationship is shown below:

$$\$I = (\$P)\,(i)\,(t)$$

Thus, in the earlier example we have

$$\$120 = (\$1{,}000)\,(0.12)\,(1)$$

If the deposit were held for only six months, then the interest earned would be

$$\$60 = (\$1{,}000)\,(0.12)\left(\frac{6}{12}\right)$$

The future value ($\$FV$) of any deposit is simply the sum of principal invested and interest earned; that is,

$$\$FV = \$P + \$I$$

The *$FV* for the deposit held 12 months is $1,120 ($1,000 + $120), and it is $1,060 ($1,000 + $60) for the six-month deposit. Which of these two deposits would you rather have? If you thought that at the end of six months you could take the $1,060 and reinvest it at a 12 percent annual rate for another six months, you would clearly prefer the two six-month deposits to the one 12-month. Why? To find out, calculate the *$FV* of the six-month deposit at the end of the second six months. You must first calculate *$I,* which is

$$\$63.60 = (\$1{,}060)\,(0.12)\left(\frac{6}{12}\right)$$

Then, *$FV* is $1,123.60 ($1,060 + $63.60). What you have determined is the future value of a deposit with a 12 percent stated interest rate (also called the *nominal rate*) *compounded semiannually.* In comparison with the annual compounding, it provided $3.60 more over the one-year holding period. From this illustration, you probably also recognize that the more often compounding takes place, the greater is the future value of any given deposit for any given stated interest rate. Table 3.2 shows future values for a $1,000 deposit and an 8 percent stated rate for various compounding periods, assuming the deposit is held for 1, 2, 4, 8, or 16 years. As you see, more frequent compounding leads to greater future values. The table also shows a fairly common phenomenon in compounding. Small differences compounded over a long period of time eventually become a big difference. For example, daily compounding added only $3.28 more than annual compounding for one year, but over 16 years the difference grows to $170.19 ($3,596.13 – $3,425.94). *Continuous compounding* may not be familiar to you. It assumes that interest is calculated even more frequently than every second of every day. It sounds impressive but, as Table 3.2 shows, it adds little above daily or weekly compounding.

TABLE 3.2 • FUTURE VALUES OF $1,000 INVESTED AT 8 PERCENT STATED RATE WITH INTEREST CALCULATED UNDER VARIOUS COMPOUNDING PERIODS

Frequency of Compounding	Number of Years Deposit Is Held				
	1	2	4	8	16
Annually	$1,080.00	$1,166.40	$1,360.49	$1,850.93	$3,425.94
Semiannually	1,081.60	1,169.86	1,368.57	1,872.98	3,508.06
Quarterly	1,082.43	1,171.66	1,372.79	1,884.54	3,551.49
Weekly	1,083.22	1,173.37	1,376.79	1,895.55	3,593.11
Daily	1,083.28	1,173.49	1,377.08	1,896.35	3,596.13
Continuously	1,083.30	1,173.51	1,377.13	1,896.48	3,596.62

Determining Interest on Your Account

All savings accounts are not alike in the way interest is determined on them. Differences arise with respect to the length of time balances in the account are judged to qualify for earning interest. In some cases, if a deposit is not held for an entire quarter, it earns no interest at all, even if it was withdrawn on the very last day of the quarter. Four different methods are in general use: (*a*) day of deposit to day of withdrawal (or daily interest), (*b*) minimum balance, (*c*) FIFO, and (*d*) LIFO. Table 3.3 illustrates those four methods. It is assumed that a deposit of $1,000 is made on the first day of the quarter; another $1,000 is made on the 30th day; and a $900 withdrawal takes place on the 60th day. The account has a stated interest rate of 6 percent.

TABLE 3.3 • QUARTERLY INTEREST EARNED UNDER FOUR DETERMINATION METHODS WITH A 6 PERCENT STATED INTEREST RATE

Activity in the Account

Day	Deposit (Withdrawal)	Balance
1	$1,000	$1,000
30	1,000	2,000
60	(900)	1,100
90	Closing	1,100

Interest Calculations

1. Day of deposit to day of withdrawal:
   a. $1,000 × 30/360 × 0.06 = $ 5.00
   b. $2,000 × 30/360 × 0.06 = $10.00
   c. $1,100 × 30/360 × 0.06 = $ 5.50
   Total $20.50
2. Minimum balance:
   $1,000 × 90/360 × 0.06 = $15.00
3. FIFO:
   a. $ 100 × 90/360 × 0.06 = $ 1.50
   b. $1,000 × 60/360 × 0.06 = $10.00
   Total $11.50
4. LIFO:
   a. $1,000 × 90/360 × 0.06 = $15.00
   b. $ 100 × 60/360 × 0.06 = $ 1.00
   Total $16.00

Day-of-deposit to day-of-withdrawal method: Pays interest on the average daily balance in an account.

DAY-OF-DEPOSIT TO DAY-OF-WITHDRAWAL METHOD The **day-of-deposit to day-of-withdrawal method** is the fairest method to a depositor, and, fortunately, competition is forcing most institutions to offer it. In effect, interest is computed on the account each day; but notice, this method is not the same as daily compounding. As we saw above, daily compounding would mean each day's interest is reinvested at the stated rate. The calculations in Table 3.3 do not assume daily compounding. The $20.50 of total interest results from having $1,000 invested for 30 days; then, after the second deposit is made, $2,000 is invested for another 30 days; and after $900 is withdrawn, $1,100 is invested for the final 30 days. With this method, you earn the actual stated rate of interest on the account. With the other methods, you might earn something less, but never more, than the stated rate.

Action Plan for the Steeles: Cash Management

Background In late December 1996, the Steeles had about $16,000 in liquid deposits, which equaled roughly three months of their combined take-home pay. This seemed a reasonable amount, given their medical insurance coverage and loss-of-income protection at Arnie's job. They always kept a rather sizable balance in their checking account because they are antique buffs and never know when they might come upon an attractive purchase and need the funds to buy it. They used a regular checking account with a $300 minimum balance requirement but no service charges. Their actual balance in the account, however, was never below $1,000 and averaged about $2,000 a month. They also had $5,600 in a savings account they opened when they married and added to over the years. Arnie also purchased U.S. Series EE bonds through payroll withholding and had approximately $3,000 in these, measured at current market value. The balance of their liquid deposits was in 42-month certificates of deposit that were about to mature.

The Problem The Steeles wanted to arrange their deposits to get a maximum yield consistent with reasonable safety and liquidity. They were hesitant to forecast future interest rates but felt the chances were high that rates would increase over the planning period. They realized this was only a guess, but it was the best they could do. They were willing to take some risks to capture a higher return.

The Plan The first step was to gather information on what deposits were available and their current rates. These are shown in the schedule of deposits, which also indicates the suggested arrangement of new deposits. As you see, the financial planner recommended the following changes: (*a*) eliminate the savings account and transfer these funds to a newly opened money market account; (*b*) reduce the balance in regular checking by about $600 and transfer these funds also to the new money market account; (*c*) as the CDs mature, use the funds to acquire additional U.S. Series EE savings bonds.

Schedule of Deposits

	Rates (%) Assumed to Exist at December 31, 1996	Current Balances	Suggested Balances
1 Regular checking	-0-	$ 2,400	$ 500
2 Savings account	2.5	5,600	-0-
3 42-Month CDs	6.0	5,000	-0-
4 U.S. Series EE bonds	5.5	3,000	8,000
5 Money market account	5.7	-0-	7,500
Total		$16,000	$16,000

Rationale for the Plan The Steeles have sufficient resources to avoid the low-yielding savings account, and replacing it was to be their first priority. The money market account gave them a far better yield and, in fact, easier access to their funds than did the savings account. It also provided sufficient cash reserves (for the occasional antique uncovered at a garage sale), thereby allowing them to reduce their checking account balance to a more sensible level.

The CDs would be a bad choice if interest rates were expected to increase. The savings bonds are a better choice because their rates are indexed to market rates on other Treasury securities. Moreover, the bonds offer far better liquidity, since there are no early withdrawal penalties. Overall, the plan involved very little liquidity risk. This is desirable if interest rates are expected to rise. By maintaining liquidity, the Steeles will be in a position to invest in the future at the expected higher rates. And if rates do not rise, they still will earn reasonable returns on the money market account and savings bonds.

Minimum-balance method: Pays interest only on the minimum (lowest) balance in an account.

MINIMUM-BALANCE METHOD The **minimum-balance method** pays interest for the entire quarter—but only on the minimum balance in the account during the quarter. The minimum balance in our example is the beginning deposit of $1,000; thus, all deposits made after that, in effect, earn nothing. Similarly, withdrawals that do not reduce the minimum balance do not enter into the interest determination. In the example, then, interest earned is simply 6 percent of the opening balance for 90 days, or $15.00. With an account such as this, it would make no sense whatsoever to add deposits *except* right before the beginning of a quarter.

FIFO method: Withdrawals from an account reduce the earliest account balance.

FIFO METHOD FIFO stands for *first in, first out*. It is an assumption as to how withdrawals are deducted against account balances. Specifically, the **FIFO method** assumes that any withdrawal reduces your earliest balance first and then works toward the more recent balances. This assumption works to your disadvantage, as Table 3.3 illustrates. Here, the $900 withdrawal made on the 60th day goes back and reduces the opening $1,000 deposit. As a result, you have only $100 invested for the full 90 days. The $1,000 deposit on the 30th day, however, is undisturbed and continues to earn interest for the full 60 days it is on deposit. Only $11.50 was earned with the FIFO method in this example, and it is usually the most undesirable method. It should be avoided if you expect to make withdrawals from your account.

LIFO method: Withdrawals from an account reduce the most recent balance.

LIFO METHOD In contrast to FIFO, LIFO means *last in, first out*. The **LIFO method** presumes that any withdrawal reduces the most recent deposit first and then works backward until the entire balance is exhausted. It is an improvement over FIFO, but is still not a fair representation of actual funds on deposit during the period. In the example, the $900 withdrawal reduced the last $1,000 deposit to $100, which then earned interest for 60 days. The first $1,000 deposit was undisturbed and continued to earn interest for the full 90 days. The total interest earned is $16.00, which comes closest to the true interest of $20.50 but is still quite short of it.

CASH MANAGEMENT STRATEGY

At the beginning of this chapter we said that the object of cash management is to minimize cash balances while maintaining an adequate level of liquidity. By now you can see that the problem is made more complex by the many forms of liquid deposits. No one would argue against keeping currency and coin holdings to a minimum, but differences of opinion arise over how other cash should be held. If you want to manage your cash actively, rather than putting it all into one account, then you should follow these steps:

1. Resolve to your own satisfaction which direction you think interest rates will move in the planning period.
2. Obtain current information about various deposit accounts, particularly current interest rates and possible account restrictions.
3. Allocate your liquid funds among the accounts to satisfy your preferences for yield, safety, and liquidity.

Keep in mind: The more yield you want, the less safety and liquidity you must take. These three aspects are brought together in the action plan for the Steele family, but we should emphasize the instability of interest rates.

Interest Rate Volatility

The advent of money market funds introduced many of us to the volatile behavior of interest rates. Up to that time, most saving deposits were in passbook accounts with their virtually constant rates. However, when yields on money market funds rose into the double-digit range in 1979 and then almost to 18 percent by mid-1981, deposits by the billions flowed out of passbook accounts and into the funds. But these exceptionally high rates didn't last; by the end of 1982 they were down to around 8 percent, and by the end of 1993 they were down to about 3 percent. While the trend in interest rates since 1981 has been downward, there have been periods of sharp increases. For example, rates skyrocketed during 1994, and many funds were offering close to 6 percent by year end—almost twice their yields of a year earlier.

Such volatility in rates makes cash management very difficult. For example, when rates are low, there is a temptation to shift your money into higher-yielding accounts, such as two-year certificates of deposit, to "pick up" the higher yield. But doing that could be a mistake if rates then increase. For example, in early 1994 investors could have earned about 4 percent on two-year CDs, a pickup of 1 percentage point over money market funds—not a trivial increase in interest earned. But it would have been a bad choice since the average yield on the funds over the two-year period was close to 5.2 percent. By selecting the money market fund with its variable rate, you earned 1.2 percentage points over the CD's fixed rate.

An Action Plan for the Steele Family

We introduced the concept of an action plan in Chapter 1. An action plan is simply a device for achieving a specific financial goal. It defines the problem, lists alternative ways to solve the problem, then selects a particular strategy to be implemented. An action plan goes beyond the mere thinking about a problem; indeed, to be effective, the plan should be made concrete by being expressed in written form. If a goal is important to you, it deserves more than casual conversation. Moreover, creating a written action plan allows you to monitor activity to determine if the plan is working.

Sharon and Arnie Steele are like many Americans who were caught in the volatility of inflation and interest rates. Not paying attention to the new types of deposits, they held relatively large balances in their traditional passbook and checking accounts. The action plan on pages 76–77 describes their situation and the changes suggested by one financial planner. Improving the yield on $16,000 of liquid assets is very important to the Steeles. They discussed making changes for too long; now, it's time for action!

SUMMARY

People hold cash to meet three liquidity needs: to undertake transactions, to have emergency reserves, and to have a store of value. Fundamental deposits for meeting these needs are checking, NOW, and savings accounts. Other major deposits are money market deposit accounts, money market mutual funds, certificates of deposit, and U.S. Series EE savings bonds. An important consideration to depositors is the availability of federal insurance on deposits up to $100,000 at federally insured commercial banks, mutual savings banks, savings and loan associations, and credit unions.

A checking account is used primarily to pay bills. Geographic convenience and the package of services offered are usually important criteria to depositors in selecting a bank. Interest earned on a checking or savings account depends on two key factors: first, the frequency of compounding; and second, the method the financial institution uses to determine which balances qualify for interest.

A cash management strategy considers how much total cash should be held and in what forms. The expected rates of interest over the holding period determines whether deposits should be held in accounts with floating interest rates, or whether they should be held in CDs with fixed rates. The volatility of interest rates makes this decision a difficult one.

KEY TERMS

automated teller machines (ATMs) (p. 72)
bank (p. 64)
bank reconciliation (p. 69)
blank endorsement (p. 67)
cashier's check (p. 71)
cash management strategy (p. 59)
certificate of deposit (CD) (p. 63)
certified check (p. 70)
checking account (p. 59)
day-of-deposit to day-of-withdrawal method (p. 76)
electronic funds transfer systems (EFTS) (p. 72)
emergency reserves (p. 60)
FIFO method (p. 77)
LIFO method (p. 77)
minimum-balance method (p. 77)
money market deposit account (MMDA) (p. 62)
money market mutual fund (p. 62)
NOW (negotiated order of withdrawal) account (p. 61)
overdraft (bounced check) (p. 68)
passbook rate (p. 62)
pocket money (p. 59)
restrictive endorsement (p. 67)
right of survivorship (p. 66)
savings account (p. 62)
special endorsement (p. 67)
stop-payment order (p. 69)
super NOW account (p. 61)
tenants in common (p. 66)
traveler's check (p. 71)
truncation (p. 69)
U.S. Series EE bonds (p. 63)
U.S. Series HH bonds (p. 64)

PROBLEMS AND REVIEW QUESTIONS

1. Explain the reasons for holding cash. How much pocket money (coins and currency) do most people hold? What advantages does a checking account have over pocket money?
2. List and briefly explain three fundamental deposits and five other popular types of deposits, ranking them according to availability, safety, and liquidity.
3. What is a *federally insured* deposit? Is deposit insurance important to you? Explain.
4. Explain all the advantages of U.S. Series EE bonds. Identify several advantages that are most important to you.
5. A local bank offers a "free" checking account if you maintain a minimum balance of $1,000. Is the account really free? Explain.
6. What institutions are "banks"? What makes an institution a bank, according to the text?
7. Discuss factors that should be considered in choosing a bank.
8. Identify or explain the following items:
   (*a*) Series EE rollover,
   (*b*) bank,
   (*c*) right of survivorship,
   (*d*) bounced check,
   (*e*) stop-payment order,
   (*f*) truncation,
   (*g*) certified check, cashier's check, traveler's check,
   (*h*) ATM,
   (*i*) EFTS.
9. Explain three ways to endorse a check; explain which is the riskiest and why.
10. Explain what is meant by interest rate volatility and then discuss the risk of investing in CDs in periods of interest rate volatility.
11. Juan Mendez has just opened a savings account that pays interest at a 4 percent annual stated rate, compounded semiannually. If he puts $1,000 in the account, how much will he get back a year later? After he opened the account, Juan learned that another account was also available that quoted a rate of 4.25 percent, compounded annually; now he isn't sure whether he got the best deal. Did he?
12. Lori Shaw opened a savings account at her credit union that paid interest at 4 percent a year, compounded annually; it used the minimum balance method for computing interest. Activity in her account for the quarter was as follows:

Opening balance at day 1	$1,000
Deposit, 60 days after day 1	500
Withdrawal, 75 days after day 1	600
Balance at end of the quarter	900

Calculate Lori's interest earned. Also, calculate the interest she would have earned under the other methods of determining interest: (*a*) day of deposit to day of withdrawal; (*b*) FIFO; (*c*) LIFO.

Case 3.1 Mark's First Checking Account

During his junior year in college, Mark Sutherland opened a checking account at the First National Bank of Westerly, Nebraska. His account does not have a minimum balance requirement, but he does pay a monthly service charge of $3.00. Mark has just received his first monthly bank statement and notices that the end-of-month balance on the statement is quite different from the end-of-month balance he shows in his check record. He has asked your help in explaining this difference and has provided you with the bank statement and his check record shown below.

ACCOUNT:	Mark J. Sutherland	PERIOD:	January 3, 1996 through January 31, 1996
ACCOUNT #:	43967		

Bank Statement of Activity This Month

Beginning Balance	Deposits and Other Credits to Your Account	Checks and Other Charges to Your Account	Ending Balance
00.00	300.00	163.80	136.20
03 Deposit	300.00		
05 100	16.50		
07 101	20.00		
12 103	42.96		
14 104	16.87		
17 105	5.00		
17 106	11.43		
19 107	25.00		
24 108	14.04		
28 109	9.00		
31 Service Charge	3.00		

Mark's Check Record

Date	No.	Payee	For	Amount	Balance
1/3		Deposit		300.00	300.00
1/3	100	Harmon Foods	food	16.50	283.50
1/4	101	Cash		20.00	263.50
1/5	102	VOID			
1/7	103	Mel's Sporting Goods	gym shoes	42.96	220.54
1/10	104	Valley Cleaners	dry cleaning	18.67	201.87
1/13	105	Sharon Mackey	birthday present	5.00	196.87
1/14	106	University Bookstore	supplies	11.43	190.44
1/14	107	Cash		25.00	175.44
1/19	108	Harmon Foods	food	14.04	161.40
1/24	109	Mom	repay loan	9.00	152.40
1/25	110	Poindexter's Cafe	Sharon's birthday party	20.00	132.40
1/26		Deposit		50.00	182.40
1/28	111	Exxon	monthly statement	12.96	169.44

QUESTIONS

1. Reconcile Mark's account for him, and explain the difference between his balance of $169.44 and the bank's of $136.20.
2. How careful was Mark in keeping a record of his checking activities? Discuss.

Case 3.2 Choosing Liquid Accounts for Marcia and Philip Helm

Marcia and Phil Helm have been married for several years. They have no children, and each has a professional career. Marcia is a trainee for a management position at a large department store, and Phil is an engineer at an electronics firm. Their careers have promising futures, but neither has exceptionally good income protection in the event of a layoff. The Helms have saved around $8,000, and $7,400 of it is in a 3.5 percent savings account at the credit union where Phil works. They have about $600 in a regular checking account (with Mid-City Bank) that doesn't have a service charge or monthly minimum requirement, but also doesn't pay any interest. The Helms' combined take-home pay is about $2,500 a month, and Phil thinks they should take the $7,400 out of their savings and invest in the stock market to earn a better return. He points out that, excluding their life insurance policies, they have no other investments. Marcia thinks this plan might be too risky, but she does agree that the 3.5 percent yield is not very good. Recently, at a party, a friend suggested they take out certificates of deposit (CDs) with long maturities, since they were paying around 6 percent. The Helms liked her advice and stopped at Phil's credit union to get more information on the CDs. After talking with the office manager for a while, though, they became even more confused. He didn't favor CDs, although the union had them available. He pointed out that interest rates on the new money market accounts were around 4 percent and didn't require "freezing" your money for a year or more. He also indicated that the union could offer a super NOW account that would allow the Helms to close their current unproductive checking account with Mid-City. This account would give them unlimited checkwriting privileges with no service charges and would pay 3 percent interest; however, it would require a minimum balance of $2,500. If their balance went below the minimum in a month, interest would be only 2 percent.

The Helms left the credit union without taking any action. They have asked you for advice on managing their liquid deposits.

QUESTIONS

1. Explain the relative risks and potential advantages of CDs. Explain under what condition(s) you would recommend them for the Helms.
2. Do you agree with Phil that some of their funds should be invested in the stock market? Explain.
3. Prepare and defend a cash management plan that you think is most appropriate for the Helms.

HELPFUL CONTACTS

1. Disputes or other issues involving commercial banks, federally chartered savings and loans, and federally chartered credit unions:
   a. Comptroller of the Currency, Consumer Affairs Division, Washington, DC 20219 (if the bank is nationally chartered)
   b. Board of Governors of the Federal Reserve System, Division of Consumer Affairs, Washington, DC 20551 (if the bank is state chartered but a member of the Federal Reserve System)
   c. Federal Deposit Insurance Corporation, Office of Bank Consumer Affairs, Washington, DC 20429 (if the bank is state chartered but not a member of the Federal Reserve System and offers Federal Deposit Insurance)
   d. Federal Home Loan Bank Board, Washington, DC 20552 (federally insured savings and loan)
   e. National Credit Union Administration, Division of Consumer Affairs, Washington, DC 20456 (federally chartered credit unions)
2. U.S. Savings Bonds:
   a. Legal or technical questions: Bond Consultant Branch, Bureau of the Public Debt, Parkersburg, WV 26106 (telephone 304–420–6102)
   b. Current rate information: 800–US–Bonds
   c. Commercial banks provide information; a particularly helpful publication is *The Savings Bonds Question and Answer Book.*

INTERNET ADDRESSES

Browser called Wimsey (provides data on competitive CD rates offered by various banks throughout the U.S.)
http://vanbc./wimsey.com/~emandel/BankCD.html

Credit Union National Association (information on credit unions)
http://www.cuna.org/

CUNA (National trade organization for credit unions)
http://www.cuna.org:80/

Department of the Treasury, Bureau of Public Debt (provides a full explanation of series EE bonds)
gopher://gopher.gsa.gov:70/00/cic/money/invstinf

Exec–PC and MMR software (savings bond calculator that calculates the values of series EE bonds)
http://www.execpc./com/~mmrsoft/

FamilyPC (reviews of personal finance software)
http://www.zdnet.com/~familypc/print/9507/familyt/ftsoft/finance.html

FDIC (information about FDIC-insured banks in each state and details about deposit insurance, specifically distinguishing insured bank deposits from uninsured bank deposits)
http://www.fdic.gov/

FDIC (consumer information on federally insured bank deposits)
http://www.fdic.gov/

Federal Reserve System (the central bank for the U.S. government)
http://www.stls.frb.org/fedsystm.html

Network Payment Mechanisms and Digitial Cash (references payment systems involving the Internet)
http://garges.cs.tcd.ie/mepeirce/project/html

USA Today Saver's Scoreboard (shows the highest yielding bank and many fund deposits)
http://web.usatoday.com/money/savebox.htm

WIC Select:Personal Finance:Banking and Credit Cards (lists sites offering a variety of bank services and products)
http://gnn.com/wic/wics/persfin.bank.html

Chapter 4

Consumer Credit: Buying Now and Paying Later

Objectives

1. To evaluate reasons for and against using credit and decide whether or not credit is appropriate for you
2. To be able to take the necessary steps to establish credit and develop a credit history
3. To identify what is meant by sales credit and how it is used
4. To understand how to use credit cards properly and to know your legal rights as a borrower against credit mistakes
5. To identify what is meant by cash credit and how it is used and to learn the important characteristics of installment loans
6. To compare the various sources of credit and to learn what to do if you experience credit problems

Opening a checking and a savings account is the first step in establishing your credit worthiness. Credit can be a useful tool for managing your expenses and your household budget. There are, however, unfortunate examples of those who have let credit work against them, rather than for them. With some care, credit can become a useful instrument in financial planning. Borrowing to purchase assets, such as a home, which are likely to increase in value, can be a wise investment strategy. On the other hand, borrowing to increase present consumption, or to purchase assets that will decrease in value, places a burden on our future ability to consume. Too much, and it can result in a vicious cycle, with an ever-increasing burden of obligations as we attempt to repay old debts with new loans.

All of us use credit in one form or another. When the paper boy or girl delivers your newspaper each day and stops by only at the end of the month to collect, he or she extends credit to you for the month's bill. The same is true for the local gas and electric company or any other business that does not demand immediate payment for its product or service. Much of this credit—called **service credit**—we take for granted, probably because it is readily available and usually provided without cost. The forms of credit we are more aware of—sales credit and cash credit—are more difficult to obtain and often carry interest and other expenses; these forms of credit are the topics of this chapter.

Service credit: Credit extended by the merchant from whom you have purchased the good or service.

We live in an era of what appears to be abundant credit: about $8,000 for each household in the United States, not including home mortgages. It is hard to imagine that not too many years ago you probably would have been advised to avoid all forms of credit, with the possible exception of a mortgage loan to buy a home. Borrowing was a sign of financial weakness: If you had cash to buy something, you shouldn't have to borrow; and if you didn't have the cash, then you couldn't afford the item and you shouldn't buy it. This thinking led to the popular observation that only those who don't need credit can get it. We still experience a similar type of contradiction. If you fail to qualify for credit, you will feel it is in short supply; but once you qualify, you will be swamped by lending institutions willing to loan you funds almost at the drop of a hat. So there always seems to be either too much or too little of it. But in either case, credit must be planned and managed effectively.

ARRANGING AND USING CREDIT

Before applying for credit, you should consider carefully why you want it in the first place and what possible disadvantages are connected with its use. It is important to avoid too much debt, as this often leads to serious financial problems, including the possibility of bankruptcy.

Reasons for Using Credit

People sometimes think that the only reason for using credit is a lack of sufficient cash to pay for a purchase. Although this factor can be important, it may not be the only one. Furthermore, your lack of sufficient cash does not necessarily mean that the item's cost exceeds all the cash you have. You may have more than enough to pay for it, but in so doing you would reduce your cash reserves below what you consider a safe level. Furthermore, you would give up the potential earnings on those reserves. So you may choose not to use cash in order to maintain adequate liquidity and earnings. You might choose credit over cash for other reasons, too, and these are discussed below.

AS A SHOPPING CONVENIENCE Using credit instead of cash can make shopping much more convenient. You avoid the risks of loss or theft associated with carrying cash, and your end-of-month statement provides a clear and complete record of expenses to help with budgeting and income tax preparation. Moreover, if you are one of a store's credit customers, you will receive information about its future sales or other promotional events. A credit card also simplifies shopping by phone or returning merchandise. A national credit card, such as Visa or MasterCard, allows you to enjoy many of these advantages throughout the entire United States, even throughout the world.

TO INCREASE TOTAL CONSUMPTION BENEFITS Borrowing allows people to consume in a given year at a level greater than their incomes would otherwise permit. This consumption in turn can lead to a higher scale of living and greater satisfaction from total consumption over time. This point is illustrated in Figure 4.1, in which we show a four-year period to keep things simple. Assume that you would like to have an even amount of consumption over the four years, as indicated by the line *AB,* and also assume your total consumption for the four years equals your total income; that is, assume zero savings over the four years. If your income is low at the beginning and then rises, as shown by the line *CD,* and if your consumption is tied to your income, it would also be low at the start and higher at the end. However, borrowing allows you to even out consumption and achieve your goal. You borrow in years 1 and 2 and repay the loans in years 3 and 4. The illustration does not consider interest, which would reduce total consumption, since part of your income would be needed to pay it, but the added satisfaction you gain from an even level of consumption might far outweigh the satisfaction you lose by paying interest.

Figure 4.1 Consumption and credit over time.

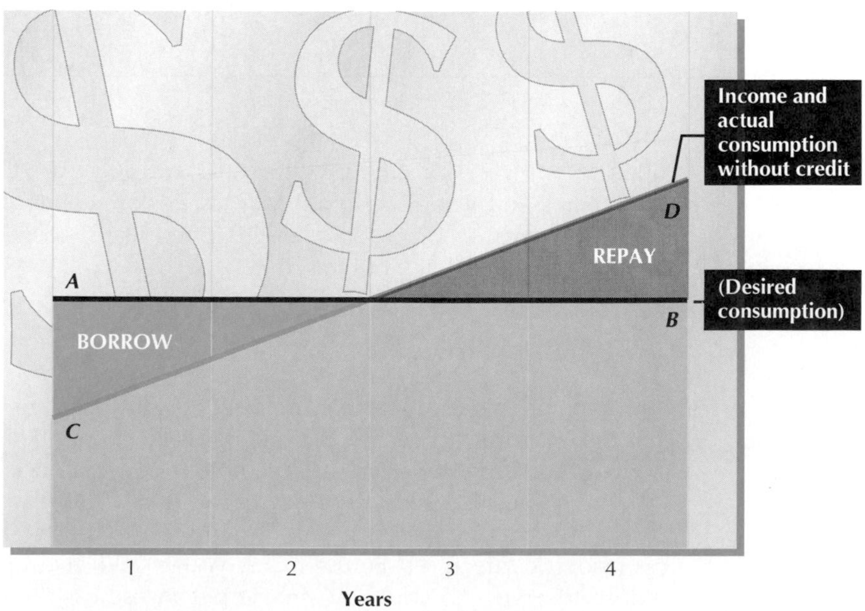

AS AN INFLATION HEDGE When the rate of inflation increases, many people tend to use credit in an effort to soften its impact. We hear such expressions as "paying back your debt with cheap dollars," and "buy now and avoid higher future prices." All too often, these words have been true and symbolic of a high-consumption approach toward life. Credit makes this approach possible. Buying now to avoid higher future prices, however, is often not as simple as it appears, since a high inflation rate is almost always accompanied by a high rate of interest on money borrowed.

Table 4.1 illustrates the "buy now or buy later" purchase decision. In columns 1 and 2 we are assuming that a shopper is trying to decide whether to use consumer credit to buy an item now or wait one year until she has sufficient cash to buy it without borrowing. Because she does not yet have enough cash, using credit is the only way she can buy it now. As you can see in column 2, the item is expected to increase 10 percent in price over the year, so waiting will add another $10 to the cost of the item. In this case, the inflation rate must be weighed against the cost of borrowing, the interest expense of $18 in column 1. In effect, the net real marginal cost of borrowing is $8 ($18 – $10); therefore, the shopper must decide if the $8 saving is worth not having the use of the item for one year.

In columns 3 and 4 we are assuming that the shopper has sufficient cash to buy the item now. However, to do so she would have to give up the opportunity of placing those funds in an investment, assumed to be earning a taxable return of 9 percent. The shopper now has three options; she can either buy now and pay cash, buy now and finance the purchase, or delay the purchase for one year. If the shopper wants to purchase the item now, her next decision is whether to pay cash or finance it. If she looks only at the $100 explicit cash cost in column 3, she might conclude that she saves $18, the total interest expense in column 1, by paying cash now rather that borrowing to finance the purchase. This does not take into account, however, the entire opportunity cost of paying cash. The opportunity cost listed in column 4 incorporates the cost of all lost opportunities. This includes not only the explicit cash expense of $100, but also the implicit after-tax income she could have earned had she not used these funds.

Her marginal tax rate is the tax rate on an additional dollar of earnings. If she could have earned $9 on a $100 investment and her marginal tax rate is 28 percent, then the after-tax income she could have earned would equal $6.48 ($9.00 –

TABLE 4.1 • DECIDING WHETHER TO BUY NOW OR BUY LATER

	Cash Is Not Available Now		Cash Is Available Now	
	Buy Now (1)	Buy Later (2)	Explicit Cost (3)	Opportunity Cost (4)
Cost of item to be purchased	$100.00	$110.00	$100.00	$100.00
Interest expense at 18%	18.00			
Interest earned on investment fund at 9%				9.00
Less income tax on interest earned (marginal tax rate = 28%)				(2.52)
Net cost	$118.00	$110.00	$100.00	$106.48

$2.52). Thus, the opportunity cost of presently using cash to make the purchase would equal $106.48 ($100 + $6.48). If we compare the net opportunity cost of using cash ($106.48) with the net cost of financing the purchase ($118.00), we can see that even after taking into consideration the implicit cost of lost investment income, it is still cheaper for her to pay cash.

Assuming that she intends to make the purchase eventually, we can also observe that it is probably not worthwhile for her to delay the purchase. Given that the cost of the item will rise by $10 over the next year, and that her after-tax return on the invested cash is only $6.48, she can save $3.52 ($10.00 – $6.48) by purchasing with cash today.

AS A SOURCE OF EMERGENCY FUNDS Having easy and quick access to credit gives you funds that could be used in case of emergency if your available liquid assets were not adequate. Some people regard this feature as the single most important advantage of credit, since it allows them to hold a larger portion of their total investments in nonliquid assets, where yields have historically been higher. It would be a mistake, though, to rely upon credit too much or for too long a period of time. Borrowed funds must be repaid, meaning that eventually you must sell nonliquid assets and suffer potential losses if their prices are low when you sell them.

Disadvantages of Using Credit

After considering the reasons for using credit, you should also become aware of some of its disadvantages. The final decision to use credit—and how much to use—rests on a comparison of its advantages and disadvantages. The most important disadvantages are discussed in this section.

A TEMPTATION TO OVERSPEND As mentioned before, after you qualify for credit, you will probably be surprised at how willing lenders are to extend credit. Given these temptations, and without proper credit planning, you are in real danger of allowing the consumption component of your budget to get far out of hand. The only solution to this problem is to develop the discipline to stay within a planned budget, as we discussed in Chapter 2. Also, some people become so accustomed to using credit cards that they often forget purchases they made during a month. Consumption quite naturally becomes excessive, and the rude awakening arrives with the monthly statement. To guard against this form of overspending, some financial planners urge you to maintain a credit card expense journal, which is similar to the check stubs in a checking account. After each credit purchase, write down all pertinent information—payee, date, amount, reason for purchase, etc.—as you would on a check stub. Keep a weekly running total of credit card expenses and parenthetically deduct the end-of-week total from your checking account balance. You can then approximate what your cash balance will be after paying your monthly statement.

CREDIT COSTS The biggest cost associated with credit is the interest you pay, if your loan carries interest. At a minimum, you should know what the annual percentage rate (APR) is on the loan, how interest will be calculated, and what will be the total interest paid over the life of the loan. We'll cover those topics in detail later in this chapter. Occasionally there may be expenses directly connected with credit, such as an annual maintenance fee on your account. Indirect costs can be

Truth in Lending Act (TILA): Sets rules regulating credit market. It also sets limits on your credit-related financial responsibilities.

important, too. If your loan involves a credit card, you must be concerned about its safety: If it is lost or stolen, it can be used by someone else, with you paying the bill. The **Truth in Lending Act (TILA)** limits your loss to $50 per account, but this amount could be substantial if you lost five or six cards. You will also have the aggravation of notifying creditors and taking other steps to be protected under the law. Another indirect cost is the time it takes to review creditors' monthly statements for accuracy and then to write and mail your checks. Many people are not concerned with these indirect costs, but they may be important to you.

LESS FLEXIBILITY WITH FUTURE BUDGETS The more we spend in one period, deferring payment until a later one, the less flexible is our future budget. In effect, we increase the fixed-expense component of the future budget. By itself, this practice isn't necessarily bad; but it sometimes happens that items purchased with credit fail to satisfy us as we thought they might at the time we purchased them. Holiday gifts

Box 4.1 SIMPLIFYING FINANCIAL PLANNING
A Credit Card Register

If you update the register each time you write a check, your check register should indicate just how much you have in your checking account. Unless you or the bank make a mistake, you are not likely to be surprised by your monthly checking account statement. The same people, however, who keep excellent check registers are often surprised by the outstanding balance on their charge account, because they fail to keep similar information on their credit card use.

The first sign of credit card misuse is an unexpectedly large credit card balance. If you use "plastic money" often, you are likely to forget just how much you have charged. You might keep the receipts in your wallet with the good intention of periodically totaling your charges, but somehow that gets put off until the credit card statement arrives. By then it is too late: You have already overspent your budget.

You may have heard of food diets in which you are required to keep a running list of everything you eat. If each little snack is added to the list, you may eventually come to the realization that all those little snacks add up to one big eating spree. The same should hold true for a credit diet. If you maintain a running tally of your credit charges, you must inevitably confront your own excesses and reduce your overspending. You can do this by creating a credit card register that you update just as you would a check register.

Credit card companies, which have an interest in seeing you run up your outstanding balance, do not supply a credit card register. However, you can create your own out of an unused check register by using the accompanying illustration as a guide. Each time you charge a purchase, receive a credit for returned merchandise, or make a monthly payment, enter the transaction in the register and update the outstanding balance. If you get in the habit of making entries with each use of the account, you will eliminate the unexpected by knowing just how much you owe at any time.

Date	Description	Credit for Returns and Payments	Amount of Charge	Balance
				$ 74.20
1/2/96	Marshalls—sweater		$56.19	130.29
1/6/96	Sunoco—gas and milk		18.75	149.14
1/8/96	Kmart—return of defective garden hose	$11.08		138.06
1/9/96	Lotus Blossom—dinner with the Williams		48.96	187.02

usually come to mind as examples here. In these cases, we are left with the bills to pay, along with the temptation to buy new items to satisfy current consumption demands. An overreliance on credit can strain your future budget.

How to Get Credit

Having decided you want credit, the next step is to apply for it. You can apply in person or by mail, but in either case, you probably will be asked to complete an application form that asks for personal and financial information. It is important to know what a lender looks for in a credit applicant and what steps you can take to begin a credit record. If you are a woman, you may face special problems in this effort.

WHAT THE LENDER LOOKS FOR Put simply, the only concern of the lender is your ability to repay the loan along with any related expenses. To assess this ability, lenders often look at the three Cs of credit—your *character, capital,* and *capacity*. Character has to do with how you have handled yourself in previous financial dealings. Do you have checking and savings accounts and use them regularly? Do you use them properly, or are there frequent overdrafts? Have you used credit properly before by repaying your debts on a timely basis? These are some of the questions lenders frequently ask to judge creditworthiness. Capital refers to your financial strength, usually measured by net worth, a topic discussed in Chapter 2. Capacity means your ability to repay debt out of your future income. Here the lender looks not only at the amount of such income but also at future commitments that might restrict it.

Lenders may apply rules of thumb before granting a loan. For example, only consumers with monthly mortgage loan payments less than 25 percent of income and total loan payments less than 30 percent of income may be deemed creditworthy. Others may use a more specific evaluation technique to weigh important factors in the credit-granting decision and arrive at a numeric guide as to whether credit should be made available to you. The scoring system will be based on the lender's bad-loan experience. Factors that are likely to weigh in your favor include home ownership, residential and job stability, education, and income. The use of other factors such as age, gender, and marital status has been abolished by antidiscrimination laws.

Equal Credit Opportunity Act (ECOA): Ensures that you cannot be denied credit because of your race, color, age, sex, or marital status.

Regardless of the system lenders use to evaluate your credit application, the **Equal Credit Opportunity Act (ECOA)** insists that fairness be applied. You cannot be discriminated against because of race, color, age, sex, marital status, or related other factors. This does not mean that someone is automatically given a loan because of one or several of these characteristics; what it does mean is that lenders may not *deny* him or her a loan because of any one of them. ECOA also ensures that lenders do not use such factors in credit-scoring formulas. Age may matter, but if you are 62 or older, you must be given at least as many points as someone under 62. Finally, you are entitled by ECOA to receive a response from a creditor within 30 days after your application indicating whether your request has been approved or denied. If it was denied, the response must be in writing, and it must either explain the reasons for the denial or indicate your right to an explanation. If you have had a loan request denied, by all means determine why. Knowing the reason will help you remedy a situation that might prevent your access to credit in the future. If the lender's reasons do not seem justified and you feel you have been discriminated against, cite the law to the lender. If the loan is still denied, you should contact a federal enforcement agency for assistance or consider legal action against the lender.

BEGINNING A CREDIT RECORD Being aware of the factors lenders look at to assess your creditworthiness helps you improve your score and your chances of receiving credit. There are some practical things you can do.

- Open both checking and savings accounts (if you don't already have them) and, of course, use them properly. This means no "bounced checks" and a history of regular deposits to the savings account.
- Open a retail charge account with a local store or major oil company. These accounts are often easier to obtain than other loans. Then use the card and make sure you are prompt in remitting the monthly balance due. Not all creditors report to credit bureaus. Make sure that yours do. In this way you will begin to build a credit history.
- If you qualify for a small installment loan, take it even if the funds are not needed immediately. Repaying such a loan promptly each month helps establish a good credit record. If you don't need the funds, invest them in a short-term account and use the interest earned to offset interest on the loan.
- If you have recently moved, write for a summary of any credit record kept by a credit bureau in your former town. It will be helpful in establishing credit in your new town.
- Have a telephone installed; this item often appears as a factor in credit-rating formulas.

You may face special problems in getting credit if you are a woman, so you should take additional steps:

- Always use your own name when applying for credit. If you are Nancy Brown, who marries Edward Hall, you should use *Nancy Hall* or *Nancy Brown Hall* as your legal name, if you choose to use your husband's last name. You are not required to do so, however, and you can continue to use your maiden name. But definitely do not use a social title such as *Mrs. Edward Hall*. Not only could other women have this name, but also any credit information under it goes to your husband's credit file and does not benefit you individually.
- Make sure all credit information is reported under your name as well as your husband's. The ECOA guarantees this for all joint accounts opened after June 1, 1977. With a **joint credit account** both spouses are responsible for the debt. Obviously, if you are separated or divorced, you should immediately cancel all joint accounts. On an **individual credit account** only you are responsible for the debt, and the account will appear only on your credit report.
- If you are recently married, you should inform creditors accordingly and indicate that you wish to maintain your own credit record. For individuals who live in a community-property state, a creditor may consider your spouse's credit history. Nevertheless, you should make certain that the local bureau has a separate file in your name.

Joint credit account: Both spouses are responsible for the debt.

Individual credit account: Only you are responsible for the debt.

Once you begin using credit, you will establish a **credit history.** Many lenders do not maintain their own credit-investigating facilities, but instead use such services provided by major credit bureaus. In all likelihood, one or more of these bureaus will keep your credit history.

Credit history: A record of credit previously granted you. It should also indicate how responsible you were in handling that credit.

THE ROLE OF THE CREDIT BUREAU The United States has approximately 2,000 credit bureaus that function as clearinghouses for information about borrowers' credit histories. These bureaus are connected to five major firms by way of a computer hookup, so if you wish to make a credit card purchase in California, the seller can check your credit history even if you have never used your card outside of New York. The largest of these firms, TRW Credit Data, maintains over 90 million credit files. It is sometimes believed that the credit bureau decides whether you receive credit, but this is not true. A credit bureau only stores information about how you have handled credit in the past and about any legal actions against you that might impair your financial strength in the future. As part of their review of your credit application, lenders may buy from the credit bureau a **credit report** about you. They use this report in their decision to extend you credit, although it is not the only factor they consider, and a good credit record doesn't automatically guarantee that credit will be given.

Credit report: A credit history record provided by a credit bureau to a prospective lender.

The credit report includes the credit accounts that you have with banks, retailers, credit card issuers, and other lenders. Information on each account states your credit limit, the loan amount, and the account balance. Public record information such as bankruptcies, tax liens, and monetary judgments are also included. Bankruptcy information may remain on your credit report for up to 10 years, and other negative information may remain up to seven years. The report also indicates if anyone besides you is responsible for paying the account. Finally, it lists everyone who obtained a copy of the report for the last two years.

Fair Credit Reporting Act of 1971: Sets down your rights to a fair and accurate credit report and establishes procedures for correcting an inaccurate report.

IF YOU ARE DENIED CREDIT The **Fair Credit Reporting Act of 1971** entitles you to a fair and accurate credit report. If you have been denied credit, insurance, or employment because of your credit report, you have the right to obtain a free copy of your report within 30 days of denial. If the facts are correct but you feel they do not present your side of the story fairly, you may submit your own statement to be included in your file. You have a right to have information on a bankruptcy that is more than 10 years old and other adverse information that is more than seven years old removed from your report. You can insist that all those who have requested a credit report within the past six months be notified of any unsubstantiated or incorrect entry.

A credit report can determine whether you get that next job or next promotion. Since 1988 most businesses have been prohibited from using lie-detector tests to screen applicants. Their response to this prohibition has been to rely more heavily on credit checks. Companies are required to notify you if you were rejected because of a poor credit rating. Some companies, however, have failed to follow this rule, so it is a good idea to check your credit report before you begin a job search.

You can review your credit report, even if you are just curious about it. The credit reporting company will provide you with a copy of your report for free, or at most a minimal fee. The bureaus in your area can be found in the Yellow Pages under such headings as "Credit" or "Credit Reporting Agencies."

If you have trouble handling credit, you may consider credit counseling, discussed later in this chapter. However, be wary of credit repair clinics that claim they can reestablish your good credit for an exorbitant fee. They can accomplish no more than you can by contacting the credit bureau directly. Professional help for repaying your creditors and managing your debt can be obtained from the Na-

Box 4.2

PERSONAL FINANCE NEWS

Late Edition

Credit Card Risk–Based Repricing

Pay your credit card a little late or exceed your credit limit and you might expect to be charged a penalty fee. Now banks are going one step further and charging a penalty rate on credit card balances. They call it "risk-based repricing."

American Express introduced risk-based pricing for the Optima card in 1992, lowering rates for their most favored cardholders. Now other card issuers have taken up the idea. But instead of lowering rates for preferred customers, they seem to be more concerned with raising rates on those who can least afford it.

Cardholders who are singled out for such punishment can end up with an annual percentage rate that is twice as high as the one they signed up for. But cardholders who clean up their act might see their rates lowered after about a year.

In some cases, you don't even have to do anything wrong to get charged a higher rate. The card issuer may examine your credit record to see how creditworthy you are. If you carry a lot of debt or if you have had trouble repaying other cards or loans, they might decide you belong in the high-risk category and raise the interest rate on your card.

Some banks run credit histories through a computer scoring program. Cardholders who raise a red flag by exceeding limits on risk factors have their card rates readjusted.

The card issuer's right to charge you a higher rate is explained in the cardholder agreement you receive when you sign up for a card or renew your old card. Typically, notice of a rate change is sent out 35 to 40 days before a new rate becomes effective.

If you are charged a punitive rate, you have a right to a free copy of your credit report and the reason for the rate change. In 17 states you can avoid paying the higher rate by simply canceling the card. The laws in those states prohibit the lender from applying the higher rate to your previous balance if the card is no longer in use.

Customers who feel they have been unfairly assigned higher rates should seek out other credit cards. With low promotional rates on many cards, and a competitive market bidding for your business, there is no reason to pay a punitive rate unless your credit is really poor.

The banks claim risk-based pricing helps offset the cost of servicing tardy repayments and bad loans. The way the card issuers see it, they intend to make those customers bear their fair share of the increased costs. If they are right, it should lower the cost to the rest of us who pay on time and are not overburdened with debt.

Secured credit card: A credit card secured by funds held at the bank issuing the card. Useful for those who are establishing credit or who are trying to overcome a poor credit history.

tional Foundation of Consumer Credit listed under Helpful Contacts at the end of this chapter.

A **secured credit card** can be helpful if you are trying to reestablish a good credit record. The card is secured by funds that you have on deposit at the bank, assuring the bank repayment for your purchases. Consequently, banks that might not consider issuing you a typical credit card will have no problem granting you a secured credit card. For a small fee, a list of secured card issuers can be obtained from Bankcard Holders of America, listed under Helpful Contacts.

SALES CREDIT

Sales credit: Any credit arising from the sale of merchandise or services.

Sales credit arises from the sale of merchandise or services. Traditionally, most of this credit was offered by merchants, such as department stores, major oil companies, automobile dealerships, and furniture and appliance dealers, in an effort to expand their sales. While they are still important in supplying such credit, the major bank credit cards—Visa and MasterCard—have also become important sources. Sales credit is often symbolized by a credit card that is used to make service or merchandise transactions, although many of these cards can now be used for financial transactions as well, such as making a cash loan.

Kinds of Accounts

Open-end account: A credit agreement that establishes an ongoing line of credit covering future purchases. One agreement may cover a multitude of purchases.

Closed-end account: A credit agreement covering a single purchase with a set repayment schedule.

Regular charge account: A credit account with a merchant in which complete payment at the end of the billing cycle usually avoids all interest charges.

Revolving credit account: An open-end account with an established line of credit and rules for minimum monthly payments and interest charges on the unpaid balance.

You can obtain sales credit in three different forms; first, as a regular (or 30-day) account; second, as a revolving account; and third, as a retail installment account. The first two are called open-end credit accounts; they are discussed below. The third is referred to as a closed-end account, and it is discussed in a later section. When you establish an **open-end account,** you will sign an agreement that covers all credit purchases and cash advances made in the account. This one agreement is binding as long as the account is open. In contrast, a **closed-end account** requires a separate retail installment contract for each purchase, but these are usually for large amounts and longer periods of time.

REGULAR CHARGE ACCOUNT People who use a **regular charge account** are typically those who view credit as a shopping convenience. Your purchase transactions for a month are accumulated and sent to you at the end of the month. You agree with the terms of this account by paying the total amount billed within 10 to 30 days after the billing date, and you avoid interest by so doing. Interest can be charged for late payment, however.

REVOLVING ACCOUNT A **revolving credit account** allows you to make purchases up to a credit limit that is usually determined by your credit record and net worth. If you then pay the full amount due at the end of the month, you are using the account as a regular account. Often, though, you will make a partial payment, the amount of which depends upon how much credit you have used and the interest charged on the account. As the balance is reduced by payments, you may again make purchases up to the limit, so the account may never actually be paid off. Interest is charged each month on the unpaid balance. Your monthly payments are presumed to cover interest first and cover principal only if the payment exceeds the interest. The Truth in Lending Act requires the creditor to inform you each month as to the interest rate applicable that month, the applicable rate expressed as an annual percentage rate (APR), and the method used to determine the balance upon which the monthly rate is applied. Along with telling you how monthly interest will be charged, a revolving credit agreement will also include information about:

- the time available to pay your balance due without being charged interest;
- the minimum amount you must pay each month, and what happens if you don't pay it; and
- permission you give the creditor to investigate your credit history.

You will receive a monthly statement for each credit account you have. An example of such a statement is shown in Figure 4.2, where the period covered is the month of July 1996. This statement is patterned after one used by a major bank card, but it is typical of most monthly statements. Notice that the borrower made three purchases during the month and one payment; there were no credits for returned merchandise. The lender charged interest of $4.32 for the month, based on the monthly rate of 1.65 percent (which is an annual percentage rate of 19.80 per-

Reference Number	Date	Description of Transaction		Amounts (Credits indicated by –)
89453987	7/05	K Mart 7549	Centerville, OH	$ 38.15
42874908	7/10	Payment		20.00–
69426933	7/12	Days Inns 033M	McDonough, GA	32.50
75538521	7/20	Mendelsons Retail	Dayton, OH	17.64

FINANCE CHARGE	Computed on an Average Daily Balance of	MONTHLY PERIODIC RATE	ANNUAL PERCENTAGE RATE	Payment Due Date	Statement Closing Date
$ 4.32	$ 261.83	1.65%	19.80%	8/15/96	7/31/96

Previous Balance	Payments	Credit Transactions	Debit Transactions	FINANCE CHARGE	New Balance
$ 215.00	$ 20.00	$ -0-	$ 88.29	$ 4.32	$ 287.61

Credit Limit: $1,000
Available Credit: $712.39
Minimum Monthly Payment: $20.00

Figure 4.2 A monthly statement for a revolving credit account.

cent). The sum of this interest and purchases was $92.61 ($4.32 + $88.29). Subtracting the $20.00 payment made during the month gives the net change during the month of $72.61; this amount is then added to the $215.00 beginning-of-the-month balance to arrive at the end-of-the-month balance of $287.61. This amount or the minimum monthly payment of $20.00 must be paid by August 15, 1996. Also, notice that the borrower has a **credit limit** (the most that can be borrowed) of $1,000, and there is $712.39 ($1,000 – $287.61) of credit available at the beginning of August.

Credit limit: You may have outstanding charges up to this amount. Charges in excess of the credit limit may result in a penalty.

We mentioned above that it might be the borrower's intent to use a revolving account as a somewhat permanent form of credit. Before doing that, a person should consider other sources of credit that might be less expensive. In the preceding example, the APR was a rather high 19.80 percent. In July 1996, many consumer installment loans were being made at somewhat lower rates than this, and other loans, such as margin account loans or second mortgage loans, were substantially lower. Generally, revolving credit is expensive credit if it is used on a permanent basis, although there may be exceptions during periods when interest rates are rising rapidly and lenders are not adjusting their rates to match. That situation occurred during the late 1970s, but is unlikely to happen again because lenders have far greater flexibility in adjusting rates. Moreover, most lenders now use an average daily balance method for determining interest. This method takes each day's activities into account, which—as we'll see in the next section—eliminates any advantage in the time lag between your purchase and when interest is charged.

DETERMINING INTEREST ON A REVOLVING ACCOUNT Interest on a revolving charge account is determined by applying the monthly rate to the balance in the account. It seems simple enough, except that there are various ways of determining what this balance is. The three most commonly used methods are the previous balance

Previous balance method: The interest rate is applied to the outstanding balance at the end of the previous billing period.

Adjusted balance method: The interest rate is applied to the previous balance less any payments or returns made during the current billing cycle.

Average daily balance method: The interest rate is applied to the average outstanding balance over the billing cycle.

method, the adjusted balance method, and the average daily balance method. Using data from Figure 4.2, each of these methods is illustrated in Table 4.2.

The **previous balance method** is the simplest of the three. The rate is applied to the balance at the end of the previous month. As you see in Table 4.2, this means you multiply the rate, 1.65 percent, by the previous balance, $215.00, to arrive at the month's interest of $3.55. This method works to your advantage if you have considerable charges in the current month.

The **adjusted balance method** is more favorable than the previous balance method. The adjusted balance is equal to the previous balance less any payments or returns you made during the current billing cycle. Thus, in Table 4.2, the adjusted balance is simply $215 less the credit payment of $20. Applying 1.65 percent to $195 determines a finance charge of $3.22. This is the most advantageous method for cardholders.

There are two variations to the **average daily balance method;** one includes purchases for the current billing cycle, the other does not. The *average daily balance method including current purchases* gives the most correct balance for applying interest. In this procedure, you weight a balance for the number of days it is

TABLE 4.2 • THREE METHODS FOR COMPUTING INTEREST ON A REVOLVING CREDIT ACCOUNT (BASED ON DATA FROM FIGURE 4.2)

I. Previous Balance Method

Interest is charged on the previous balance

1.65% × $215.00 = **$3.55**

II. Adjusted Balance Method

Interest is charged on the previous balance less any current credits

1.65% × ($215.00 – $20.00) = **$3.22**

III(a). Average Daily Balance Method (including current purchases)

Interest is charged on the updated balance considering the day a charge or credit takes place

Period	(a) No. of Days	(b) Balance	(c) (a) × (b)
7/1–7/4	4	$215.00 + $ -0- = 215.00	$ 860.00
7/5–7/9	5	215.00 + 38.15 = 253.15	1,265.75
7/10–7/11	2	253.15 – 20.00 = 233.15	466.30
7/12–7/19	8	233.15 + 32.50 = 265.65	2,125.20
7/20–7/31	12	265.65 + 17.64 = 283.29	3,399.48
	31		$8,116.73

$$\text{Average daily balance} = \frac{\$8{,}116.73}{31} = \$261.83$$

1.65% × $261.83 = **$4.32**

III(b). Average Daily Balance Method (excluding current purchases)

Interest is charged on the updated balance considering the day a current payment is made but ignoring current purchases or returns

Period	(a) No. of Days	(b) Balance	(c) (a) × (b)
7/1–7/9	10	$215	$2,150.00
7/10–7/31	21	$215.00 – $20.00 = 195	4,095.00
			$6,245.00

Average daily balance = $6,245.00/31 = $201.45

1.65% × $201.45 = **$3.32**

outstanding. In the example, the beginning balance of $215.00 was applicable only for the four days, 7/1 through 7/4. Thereafter, other balances were appropriate for varying numbers of days. By weighting each balance for the number of outstanding days, you arrive at the total weighted balance of $8,116.73, which is then divided by 31 to arrive at the $261.83 average daily balance. This figure multiplied by 1.65 percent gives the interest amount of $4.32.

The other variation is the *average daily balance method excluding current purchases*. Again an average daily balance is computed. However, in this variation of the average daily balance method the finance charge is less because new purchases are not included in the daily balance. As indicated in Table 4.2, the finance charge is only $3.32 when new purchases are excluded.

Grace period: Period in which interest charges are forgiven on the condition that the outstanding balance is fully repaid.

Lenders traditionally provide a **grace period** of 25 days during which interest on the loan balance is forgiven. This usually applies only when you have fully paid off the previous month's balance. The grace period normally lasts between the statement closing date and the payment due date. Recently, some lenders have eliminated the grace period; others have offered their customers a choice between credit accounts with or without a grace period. Finance charges on the account with the grace period are based on a higher annual percentage rate, making it less desirable for someone who does not regularly pay off the entire amount due.

Two-cycle average daily balance method: Collects interest over two billing periods when an unpaid balance is begun.

Some major card issuers are now applying a **two-cycle average daily balance method.** This eliminates any grace period applied in a previous month when you fail to completely pay off the balance in the present month. Thus, the creditor can in effect go back two months to collect interest on unpaid balances. If you pay your balance in full each month or you carry a balance from month to month, your interest payments are the same as under the one-cycle average balance method. Those hit the hardest with increased interest charges are consumers who pay off their balances in alternating months. For example, suppose a consumer with no balance in the first month charges $1,000 and then makes a 2.7 percent minimum payment. In the next month, the cardholder charges another $1,000 but pays off the entire balance. If this is repeated three more times during the year, a study by Bankcard Holders of America indicates that at a 19.8 percent interest rate, the cardholder would pay $196.20 in finance charges with the two-cycle method and $132 under the one-cycle method. That is almost a 50 percent increase in finance charges.

For each revolving account you have, you should determine how the monthly balance is calculated and verify the monthly statement to make sure it is correct. Of course, you aren't likely to go through all the calculations for the average daily balance method, and it may not be necessary that you do. A quick glance between this month and last month should indicate if the number is approximately correct. A last piece of fairly obvious advice is to use those accounts that determine the monthly balance to your best advantage.

Major Issuers of Credit Cards

"Plastic money" is indeed an appropriate name for what we use to purchase many goods and services. Over 100 million Americans use credit cards regularly, and each user has about 5.2 cards. Of the number of cards issued, retail store cards are in first place. Over one-half of all families hold at least one retail store card. Most retail store cards are charge cards issued in conjunction with a regular charge account. Next in number of cardholders are bank credit cards. Over one-half of all households have at least one bank credit card. The major names of issuers include Visa, MasterCard, and Discover.

Bank credit cards: Credit cards, such as MasterCard and Visa, that are issued by banks.

BANK CREDIT CARDS The **bank credit cards**—MasterCard and Visa—are by far the largest suppliers of consumer installment credit. When you use one of these cards, you are actually borrowing from a bank, perhaps a local one, or you may have a card issued by one of the major banks, such as Chase Manhattan. We illustrated and discussed a typical credit card account earlier, which showed how the card is used to make purchases. But bank cards can also be used to make financial transactions. For example, you may be able to get cash advances from money machines with your card, and in some places you can use it to buy securities, such as stocks or bonds. A worksheet, like that in Figure 4.3, can be used to compare the costs and benefits of various cards.

Affinity card: Returns a small percentage of sales to the sponsoring organization.

A bank card that carries the name of a sponsoring organization is known in the industry as an **affinity card.** The card's sponsor receives a small percentage of card sales. Part of this may be returned to cardholders in the form of frequent flyer miles, discounts on purchases, or a cash rebate. Some sponsors, such as environmental groups and alumni organizations, utilize the revenues from affinity cards to support socially desirable causes. Visa estimates that 22 percent of their cardholders have these cards.

Travel and entertainment (T&E) cards: Credit cards issued by finance companies catering to businesspeople and travelers.

TRAVEL AND ENTERTAINMENT CARDS Traditionally, **travel and entertainment (T&E) cards,** such as American Express, have catered to travelers—usually businesspeople—who frequently buy goods and services away from their hometowns. The cards are used to pay for hotel and motel accommodations, to buy airline tickets, and to pay restaurant bills. However, the T&E cards are expanding their services. The usual annual fee of $50 or more for a T&E card is much higher than that of a bank credit card, and it is questionable whether it is worth it, since bank credit cards are so universally acceptable.

OTHER CARDS We mentioned above that many retail establishments issue their own credit cards. These stores generally prefer that you use their card rather than a bank card (many will not accept bank cards), since consumer credit is often a profitable part of their business.

For some people, the card used most frequently is their oil company card. While these are usually used on a 30-day basis with no interest charge, they can also be used on a revolving basis for major purchases of tires, batteries, or service work. At some stations, credit card users pay a higher price for gas than cash customers. Is it worth it? At a four-cent differential and an average price of $1.00 a gallon, and assuming you can defer payment for 30 days, the implicit interest rate is 4 percent per month and about 48 percent a year ($4 \times 12 = 48$)—a very expensive form of credit. You would be better off getting a cash advance on your bank credit card and buying your gas with cash.

Debit card: Unlike a credit card, the price of a purchase is deducted immediately from your bank deposit.

CREDIT CARDS CONTRASTED WITH DEBIT CARDS A credit card should not be confused with a debit card even though they may look identical. For example, the MasterCard II—a **debit card**—is a perfect clone of the MasterCard credit card. It is unfortunate that they look alike, because they are quite different in terms of their impact on your cash flow and on the protection you have under federal law. You can use a debit card at an automated teller machine or point-of-sale terminal. (Such terminals are located at numerous retail outlets and allow you to make transactions such as paying the retailer or obtaining cash.) Whenever you use the card, your bank deposit is reduced immediately. By contrast, a credit card transaction puts you in debt to the bank; you reduce the debt later by paying your monthly state-

CARD ISSUER:		
	Cost Comparison	
Charge	**Description**	**Cost**
Annual membership fee[a]	Typically about $25 for bank credit cards, and higher for travel and entertainment cards.	
Annual percentage rate[a]	One-twelfth of the annual rate is applied to the outstanding balance to determine the monthly finance charge. If an introductory rate is offered, the regular rate should also be disclosed. The APR on cash advances is likely to be higher than the APR on credit purchases. Some issuers also practice *tier pricing,* whereby the APR is higher on balances above a certain amount.	
Variable rate information[a]	If the interest rate is variable, the disclosure will indicate the index or formula and the spread or margin that determine the APR. If there is a cap or a floor on the APR, this should also be indicated.	
Grace period[a]	The free period within which the credit extended must be repaid in order to avoid finance charges will be indicated. If the card issuer does not provide a grace period, that fact must be disclosed.	
Balance computation method[a]	Method used to compute the balance upon which finance charges will be based.	
Minimum finance fee[a]	Minimum fee applied whenever there is a finance charge.	
Transaction fee[a]	Fee applied to each purchase.	
Cash advance fee[b]	Fee imposed for an extension of credit in the form of cash.	
Late payment fee[b]	Fee imposed for late payment of minimum monthly payment.	
Over-the-limit	Fee imposed for exceeding the credit limit.	
Replacement fee[c]	Fee for replacing a lost credit card.	
Return check charge	Fee for a check returned because of insufficient funds.	
Copy charge[c]	Fee for receiving a photostatic copy of receipt on sales or cash advance.	
Fees for optional services[c]	May include such things as credit life insurance, disability insurance, unemployment insurance, and credit card registration. See the benefits section below for a description of some of these benefits.	

Figure 4.3 Worksheet for credit card comparison.

ment. A debit card is actually a form of checking account, which is how you should view it when considering its use. Make sure you know whether you're using a credit card or a debit card. The difference is important, because whenever you use a debit card, your bank balance is immediately reduced.

Over the last decade, as illustrated in Figure 4.4, there has been tremendous growth in debit card transactions. They are convenient for the consumer because using them reduces trips to the bank or money machine and time at the checkout

Benefit Comparison		
Benefit	**Description**	**Value**
Credit Limit	If your credit balance exceeds this amount, you will be charged an over-the-line fee.	
Credit life insurance	Pays off the outstanding balance up to some set limit at the time of death.	
Total disability insurance	May pay off your account balance or make minimum monthly payments if you become totally disabled.	
Unemployment insurance	If you are involuntarily terminated from your employment, this may cover your minimum monthly payment during the period of unemployment.	
Rebates and discounts	Some cards offer a small percentage rebate on all credit purchases. Others offer discounts on special purchases such as airline tickets.	
Purchase price protection	If you charge something and then see the same product advertised elsewhere at a lower price within a specified time period, your account will be credited with the difference. This may be difficult to document and inconvenient to collect. In addition, there may be a limit on refunds.	
Accident insurance	Small amounts of coverage for accidental injuries.	
Rental car collision insurance	This may already be provided under your personal auto insurance.	
Merchandise warranty protection	The period of warranty may be extended by the card issuer.	
Credit card registry	Service that arranges for cancellation and replacement of credit cards in the event of loss.	
Merchandise loss protection	Replaces the cost of lost or stolen items that were charged up to a specified limit. Insurance lasts for only a specified period after purchase and may be secondary to protection under other insurance policies.	

[a]Information must be disclosed in a prominent table.
[b]Information must be disclosed somewhere on the application form.
[c]Information need be provided only upon request.

Figure 4.3 Continued.

counter. Consequently, debit card transactions are the most numerous for small-ticket items at grocery stores and gas stations, where customers are in a hurry. The convenience, however, comes at the cost of giving up some of the benefits related to credit card use. Most credit cards have a grace period over which no interest is charged. Depending on when the purchase is made and when the bill comes due, this grace period can provide the consumer with up to a month's free credit. Electronic transfers, which clear over a much shorter period, leave little or no room between expenses and revenues. On the other hand, for consumers who have had trouble controlling their expenditures, replacing a credit card with a debit card can be a plus. Available funds must exist before the purchase is made.

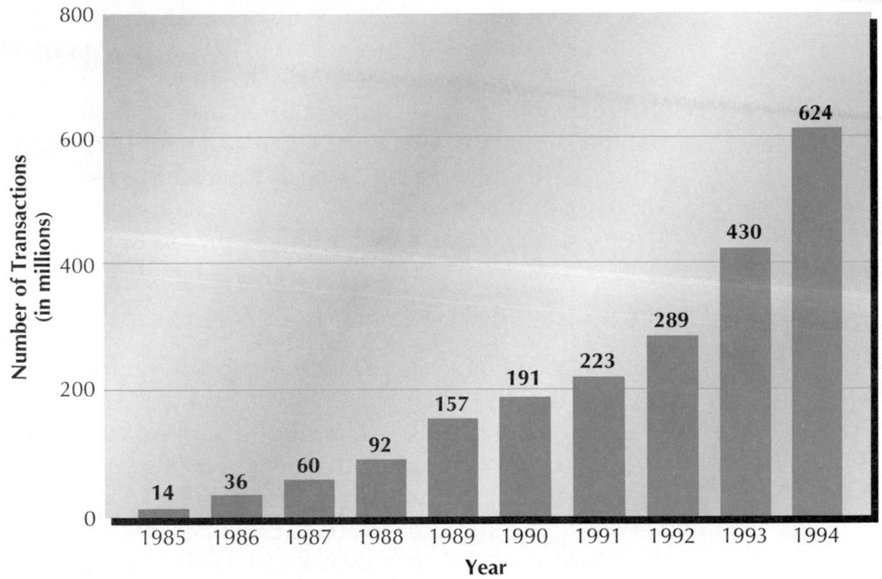

Figure 4.4
Debit card transactions

SOURCE: U. S. Bureau of the Census, *Statistical Abstract of the United States, 1994 and 1995,* Table 801and Table 814.

Losses due to a lost or stolen credit card are limited to $50 under the Truth in Lending Act. With a debit card, you can lose up to $500 if you fail to notify the debit card issuer within two business days after learning of the theft. Moreover, if you wait until 60 days or more after a bank statement has been mailed, your losses may be unlimited. Given a choice between using a debit or credit card, it is hard to see why you shouldn't always choose the credit card.

SELECTING A CREDIT CARD Many people who are good credit risks find their mailboxes overflowing with solicitations from credit card companies. Their major problem is not in getting credit but rather in selecting the best credit from among the numerous offers. In order to make comparison shopping easier, and also to eliminate potentially misleading sales practices, Congress passed the Fair Credit and Charge Card Disclosure Act in 1988. The act empowered the Federal Reserve Board to set down rules governing the information that credit card companies must furnish potential consumers. The rules enacted under this law have provided for detailed and uniform disclosure of rates and other cost information in applications and solicitations to open credit and charge card accounts.

Unfortunately, disclosure rules have not standardized charges. The cost of credit can vary significantly among issuers and over time in response to changing conditions in credit markets. In addition to interest charges, the cost of using a credit card will include maintenance fees and other specialized charges. Many of these costs are described in the credit card comparison worksheet in Figure 4.3. Information on most of the items listed is typically disclosed prominently on the application form.

The benefit section of the worksheet in Figure 4.3 indicates the many types of services that card issuers have provided in an effort to attract customers. The value of many of these items is rather small. You would be wise to select from among offers of credit cards on the basis of an assessment of the relative costs itemized in the cost section of the worksheet.

The best credit card for you will depend on your credit practices. If you intend to pay off the entire balance each month, a card with a grace period and a low annual membership fee would be favored. Given the high cost of finance charges on credit cards and the relatively lower cost of credit from other sources, this is probably the best strategy for most people. However, if you do intend to incur finance charges on your credit card, then you may be better off by paying a higher annual membership fee in exchange for a lower APR. For example, if your average outstanding balance is $1,000, then a 1 percent reduction in the APR would save you $10 a year. Therefore, if the annual membership fee on this card is no more than $10 above the fee on a card with a higher APR, it could be your best choice.

Protection against Credit Card Fraud

We mentioned previously that the Truth in Lending Act limits your losses from unauthorized uses of your credit cards to $50 per card; but, if your purse or wallet is stolen and if it contains several cards, your loss can be more than trivial. So it pays to be careful with them, and the following are suggestions that can help in this effort.

- Record card numbers, their expiration dates, and the phone number and address for each card company in a safe place.
- Destroy old bills, receipts, and carbons, because these have your credit card number imprinted on them. Also destroy all credit cards you do not use, and sign each new card as soon as it arrives.
- Watch clerks carefully while they are using your card to make sure they do not run impressions on other sales checks. Of course, ask the clerk to return your card immediately after it has been used.
- Make sure the sales check you sign is completed correctly, including the addition of separate line items; then, save your receipts, compare them with your monthly bill, and report any discrepancy immediately.
- Be extra careful in giving your number over the phone unless you initiate the phone call and want to charge the purchase. Any calls purporting to be "conducting a credit card survey" should be completely avoided. If a caller claims to be with the credit card company and is attempting to correct an error with another account that is somehow related to yours (you both have the same names, for example), ask for his or her name and number and offer to call back after you confirm the authenticity of the inquiry. It's a good bet the caller is a fraud.

If your cards are stolen or lost, contact each issuer immediately. This means keeping a list of addresses and phone numbers in a convenient and safe place; but remember, accidents such as these often happen on vacation, and your list will not do much good if it is at home. Getting ready for a vacation is hectic enough, but try to remember the list and don't store it in your wallet or purse, because that is what is usually lost or stolen.

Correcting Credit Mistakes

Despite the care taken by you or the credit issuer, mistakes do occur. It is important for your sake that they are corrected immediately, not only to save money if it's an overcharge but to protect your good credit rating. Both the Truth in Lending Act and the Fair Credit Billing Act give you considerable legal protection against credit mistakes. Since it is very important that you understand what your protections are, some of them—billing errors, defective goods, prompt payment, and credit blocking—are discussed below. This material is adapted from the *Consumer Handbook to Credit Protection Laws,* published by the Board of Directors of the Federal Reserve System.

BILLING ERRORS The law defines a billing error as any charge:

- For something you didn't buy or for a purchase made by someone not authorized to use your account
- That is not properly identified on your bill or is for an amount different from the actual purchase price or was entered on a date different from the purchase date
- For something that you did not accept on delivery or that was not delivered according to agreement

Billing errors also include:

- Errors in arithmetic
- Failure to reflect a payment or other credit to your account
- Failure to mail the statement to your current address, provided you notified the creditor of an address change at least 20 days before the end of the billing period
- A questionable item, or an item for which you need additional information

If you think your bill is wrong, or you want more information about it, follow these steps:

1. You may want to call the card company to correct the problem, but phoning is not sufficient because it does not trigger your legal safeguards. Notify the creditor *in writing* within 60 days after the bill was mailed. Be sure to write to the address the creditor lists for billing inquiries, and tell the creditor: your name and account number; that you believe the bill contains an error and *why* you believe it is wrong; and the suspected amount of the error or the item you want explained. Finally, send the letter by certified mail with a return receipt requested.
2. Pay all parts of the bill that are not in dispute. But, while waiting for an answer, you do not have to pay the amount in question (the "disputed amount") or any minimum payments or finance charges that apply to it.

   The creditor must acknowledge your letter within 30 days, unless your bill can be corrected sooner. Within two billing periods—but in no case longer than 90 days—either your account must be corrected or you must be told why the creditor believes the bill is correct.

   If the creditor made a mistake, you do not pay any finance charges on the disputed amount. Your account must be corrected, and you must be sent an explanation of any amount you still owe.

   If no error is found, the creditor must promptly send you an explanation of the reasons for that determination and a statement of what you owe, which may include any finance charges that have accumulated and any minimum payments you missed while you were questioning the bill. You then have the time usually given on your type of account to pay any balance.
3. If you still are not satisfied, you should notify the creditor within the time allowed to pay your bill.

A creditor may not threaten your credit rating while you're resolving a billing dispute. Once you have written about a possible error, a creditor is prohibited from giving out information to other creditors or credit bureaus that would damage your credit reputation. And, until your complaint is answered, the creditor also may not take any action to collect the disputed amount.

After the creditor has explained the bill, you may be reported as delinquent on the amount in dispute, and the creditor may take action to collect if you do not pay in the time allowed. Even so, you can still disagree in writing. Then the creditor must report that you have challenged your bill and give you the name and address of each person who has received information about your account. When the matter is settled, the creditor must report the outcome to each person who has received information. Remember that you may also place your own side of the story in your credit record.

DEFECTIVE GOODS OR SERVICES You may withhold the remaining payment on any damaged or shoddy goods or poor-quality services purchased with a credit card, as long as you have made a real attempt to solve the problem with the merchant. Your withholding of payments results in what is called a **chargeback,** whereby the card issuer charges the disputed amount back to the merchant. At this point the merchant can dispute the chargeback. The card issuer must then decide whether to reissue the bill to you or to proceed against the merchant for repayment.

Chargeback: A disputed amount charged back to the merchant by the credit card company.

This right to withhold payment may be limited if the card was a bank or a travel and entertainment card or any card *not* issued by the store where you made your purchase. In such cases, the sale must have totaled more than $50 and must have taken place in your home state or within 100 miles of your home address.

PROMPT CREDIT PAYMENTS AND REFUNDS FOR CREDIT BALANCES If you can avoid finance charges on your account within a certain period of time, it is obviously important that you get your bills, and get credit for paying them, promptly. Check your statements to make sure your creditor follows these rules:

Prompt billing. Look at the date on the postmark. If your account is one on which no finance charge is added before a certain due date, then creditors must mail their statements at least 14 days before payment is due.

Prompt crediting. Look at the payment date entered on the statement. Creditors must credit payments on the day they arrive, as long as you pay according to payment instructions.

Stores often give you a credit on your bill instead of cash when you return a purchase. If this results in a credit balance on your account, a store must make a refund in cash if you request it.

CREDIT BLOCKING If you were ever in the embarrassing position of having a purchase denied because you had exceeded your credit limit, you may have been a victim of **credit blocking.** This is a perfectly legal practice. It can happen when you use your credit card to check into a hotel or to rent a car. The clerk will contact the card issuer with the estimated cost. Your line of credit is then reduced by this amount with what is termed a "block" or "authorization." When you pay your bill with the same credit card, the block is typically removed in a few days. However, using a card different from the one you used to initiate the transaction could

Credit blocking: Credit limit is reduced by the amount of the expected purchase.

create a credit problem. The credit limit on the first card might remain blocked for as long as 15 additional days. Consequently, if you use a different card to pay the bill, be sure to tell the clerk to unblock the first card.

CASH CREDIT

Cash credit: Credit extended in the form of cash.

Cash credit simply means borrowing money; as we have seen, sales credit involves borrowing in connection with buying something. The distinction is a tenuous one since, in most cases, cash borrowed is also used to make purchases. The major distinction between sales and cash credit is the way you repay the debt. Cash credit is repaid either with a single payment at the end of a period of time or by a series of uniform payments called installments. You might remember that earlier we said a form of sales credit is the retail installment account. This account is virtually identical to an installment cash loan, which is why it is explained now rather than before.

The Contract

Retail installment contract: A contract between a borrower and a lender establishing periodic repayment of the amount borrowed.

Promissory note: A contract binding a borrower to future repayment of the amount borrowed.

Security agreement: Establishes the creditor's security interest in the good for which the credit was extended.

The agreement between you and a person selling an item is call a **retail installment contract.** If you purchase the item by obtaining a cash loan from a bank, savings and loan, consumer finance company, or credit union, the agreement is called a **promissory note.** Although promissory notes can be unsecured—and in fact, many are—their use in consumer credit is almost always on a secured basis, with the purchased item serving as collateral. The retail installment contract is always on a secured basis. The creditor obtains a security interest in the property with the **security agreement,** which is a separate instrument.

INFORMATION THAT MUST BE PROVIDED The Truth in Lending Act requires that each credit contract gives you the following information:

1. The amount financed
2. The total number of payments, the amount of each payment, and due dates
3. Finance charges expressed both as a dollar amount and as an annual percentage rate
4. The date when finance charges begin, if that date is different from the transaction date
5. An itemized list of all charges not included as part of the finance charge
6. The charges for late payments or default
7. A description of security held by the creditor
8. How finance charge refunds are determined in the case of prepayments
9. A description of prepayment penalties, if any

Creditors are also required to supply the following additional information when merchandise is purchased on time:

1. A description of the merchandise
2. The cash price
3. The deferred payment price
4. The down payment, including any trade-in

How Interest Charges Are Determined

Although the Truth in Lending Act requires lenders to state in writing the interest you must pay on a loan—both in dollars and as an annual percentage rate (APR)—it is still important that you know how these calculations are made. Three approaches are in general use: the simple interest method, the discount method, and the add-on method. These are explained below, along with several techniques you can use to approximate the true APR on a loan.

Simple interest method: The interest payment is computed by applying the annual percentage rate to the outstanding loan balance.

SIMPLE INTEREST METHOD Under the **simple interest method,** the interest payment is computed by applying a percentage rate to the outstanding loan balance during each payment period. This is the usual method for calculating a finance charge on a revolving credit account like that discussed earlier. It is also used by many banks and credit unions for computing the interest due on automobile installment loans and home mortgages.

A loan of $1,000 to be paid off in 12 equal monthly installments of $88.85 is illustrated in Figure 4.5. Using the simple interest method, the monthly finance charge in column 3 is equal to the outstanding balance in column 1 times the monthly interest charge of 1 percent. The excess of the monthly payment in column 2 over the finance charge in column 3 serves to reduce the outstanding balance. You should notice that as the loan is repaid, the finance charge in column 3 declines. You should also notice that, given the equal monthly installments and the declining monthly finance charge, a larger portion of each subsequent monthly installment is devoted to loan repayment. Thus, the loan is paid off more rapidly toward the end of the monthly payments.

Discount method: The interest payment is deducted from the credit extended at the beginning of the loan.

DISCOUNT METHOD Under the **discount method,** the lender deducts the interest to be paid on the loan from the credit extended to you at the beginning of the loan. Therefore, the face amount of the loan will exceed the amount you want to finance. To finance a purchase of $1,000, you have to borrow more than $1,000. On a one-year loan, your total payments are determined by the following formula:

Figure 4.5
A 12-month installment loan with annual simple interest of 12 percent, or 1 percent monthly.

Month	Outstanding Balance (1)	Monthly Payment (2)	Monthly Finance Charge (3)	Monthly Loan Repayment (4)
1	$1,000.00	$ 88.85	$10.00	$ 78.85
2	921.15	88.85	9.21	79.85
3	841.51	88.85	8.42	80.43
4	761.08	88.85	7.61	81.24
5	679.84	88.85	6.80	82.05
6	597.79	88.85	5.98	82.87
7	514.92	88.85	5.15	83.70
8	431.22	88.85	4.31	84.54
9	346.68	88.85	3.47	85.38
10	261.30	88.85	2.61	86.24
11	175.07	88.85	1.75	87.10
12	87.97	88.85	0.88	87.97
Total		$1,066.19	$66.19	$1,000.00

$$\frac{\text{Total payments}}{\text{on discount loan}} = \frac{\text{amount financed}}{1-(\text{discount rate} \times t)}$$

$$\$1,136.36 = \frac{\$1,000}{1-(0.12 \times 1)}$$

where t is the term of the loan in years. Thus, to finance a $1,000 purchase for one year, at a discount rate of 12 percent you must repay $1,136.36. If this were a 12-month installment loan, you would owe $94.70 ($1,136.36/12) per month. The true interest rate on this discount installment loan would be much higher than 12 percent, because you would not have the full use of $1,000 during the entire year. As indicated in the cost comparison in Figure 4.6, the annual percentage rate on this loan is 24.28 percent, about twice the discount rate.

Add-on method: Interest is added to the amount financed in order to determine total payments.

ADD-ON METHOD The add-on method is by far the most widely used method for determining finance charges on consumer loans. Under the **add-on method,** the lender adds the interest to the value of the purchase you are financing to determine your total payments using the following formula:

$$\text{Total payments on add-on loan} = \text{amount financed} \times [1 + (\text{add-on rate} \times t)]$$

$$\$1,120 = \$1,000 \times [1 + (0.12 \times 1)]$$

If the add-on rate is 12 percent per year and you intend to borrow $1,000 for one year, the interest charge of $120($1,000 × 0.12 × t), where t is the term of the loan in years, is added to the original principal of $1,000 to determine total repayments of $1,120 ($1,000 + $120). The monthly payments would equal $93.33 ($1,120/12). You should notice that an add-on rate of 12 percent is more costly than a similar loan with a simple interest rate of 12 percent. The monthly payments of $88.85 on the simple interest loan are $4.48 less per month than the $93.33 monthly payment for a comparable add-on loan.

As with the discount loan, the true interest rate on an add-on loan is far greater than the add-on rate of 12 percent. Again, you are being charged as if you had the full use of $1,000 for the entire year. However, you have the use of a full $1,000 only for the first month. Since you repay principal with each payment, the total amount borrowed declines with each payment. In the current example, an add-on rate of 12 percent would entail the same monthly payments as a simple interest rate of 21.46 percent.

ANNUAL PERCENTAGE RATE Regardless of how the lender determines the interest charge, the government requires that the lender provide the borrower with the in-

Figure 4.6 Comparative interest on credit of $1,000 to be repaid in 12 equal monthly installments.

Method	Contract Rate	APR	Monthly Payment	Total Interest Paid
Simple interest	12%	12.00%	$88.85	$ 66.19
Discount interest	12%	24.28%	94.72	136.36
Add-on interest	12%	21.46%	93.33	120.00

Annual percentage rate (APR): The rate charged on the outstanding balance; the ratio of the finance charge to the average amount of credit extended over the life of the loan expressed as a rate.

formation on the true interest rate, or what is officially termed the annual percentage rate. The **annual percentage rate (APR)** is the ratio of the finance charge to the average amount of credit extended to you over the life of the contract, expressed as a percentage rate per year. Since the simple interest charge is also based upon the amount of credit extended in each period, the annual simple interest rate and the APR are the same.

Unfortunately, there is nothing simple about calculating the APR on installment loans. The actuarial method is the most accurate method for calculating the APR. It entails the use of either complicated formulas, annuity tables, or a financial calculator. Two simpler but less accurate approaches to calculating the APR are illustrated in Table 4.3 for the add-on example discussed previously. As you can see, the constant-ratio method is less complicated, but always overstates the true rate. The *N*-ratio method results in a rate very close to the true APR of 21.46 percent.

The APR is the rate you should use to judge the relative cost of credit. As indicated in Figure 4.6, identical contract rates can result in widely different interest payments and annual percentage rates. If you are comparing loans for identical amounts of credit and identical maturities, the loan with the lower APR will also have the lower finance charge.

AREAS OF SPECIAL CONCERN In addition to recognizing how the finance charges are computed, it is important that you read the entire credit agreement carefully and understand each of the several clauses that may be included in the contract. The areas discussed in the following paragraphs should receive special consideration.

Rule of 78: A method for computing the interest refunded upon early repayment. This method is highly favorable to lenders.

Prepayment and the rule of 78. Credit agreements will include a statement indicating how interest is to be calculated if you decide to repay the loan at any earlier date than scheduled. Agreements that utilize the add-on method for computing installment payments usually determine your interest refund by the so-called **rule of 78.** An example will show how this rule works to the lender's advantage. Suppose, as before, you have a $1,000 add-on loan for one year that carries total interest of $120. If you repaid the loan as scheduled you would make 12 monthly payments of $93.33 for total payments of $1,120.

TABLE 4.3 • TWO METHODS FOR ESTIMATING APR

APR = annual percentage rate
M = number of payment periods in one year
N = number of scheduled payments
C = dollar cost of credit
P = value of purchase financed

Example: A $1,000 loan with add-on finance charges of $120 to be repaid in 12 monthly payments of $93.33.

Constant-Ratio Method	*N*-Ratio Method
$APR = \frac{2MC}{P(N+1)}$	$APR = \frac{M(95N+9)C}{12N(N+1)(4P+C)}$
$= \frac{2 \times 12 \times 120}{1,000(12+1)}$	$= \frac{12 \times [(95 \times 12)+9] \times 120}{12 \times 12 \times 13 \times (4,000+120)}$
$= \frac{2,880}{13,000}$	$= \frac{1,654,560}{7,712,640}$
$= 22.15\%$	$= 21.45\%$

Suppose that after making three payments you receive an unexpected amount of cash and you are considering using that cash to pay off your loan. How much interest will you save? You might guess $90, reasoning that interest is charged uniformly each month, in which case you would save 9/12 of the total (9/12 of $120 = $90). Good guess, but wrong. The rule of 78 allows lenders to earn interest at the quicker pace indicated by column 6 in Figure 4.7.

Under the rule of 78, the monthly interest earned by the lender is determined by the monthly interest factor in column 4. If we multiply the monthly interest factor by the total interest due on the scheduled loan, we can calculate the interest earned in each month in column 5. In Figure 4.7 the monthly interest factor for the third month is 10/78. Therefore, the interest earned by the lender in the third month is $15.38 ([10/78] × $120).

To determine the monthly interest factor we first add up the digits for the total number of payments on the loan. This is equal to the sum of the payment numbers in column 1 of Figure 4.7 (1 + 2 + . . . + 12 = 78). For a one-year loan with monthly payments, the digits sum to 78. The sum of the digits (*SD*) for a loan of any number of years can be determined with the following formula:

$$SD = N\left(\frac{N+1}{2}\right)$$

where *N* is equal to the number of months. For example, the sum of digits for a four-year loan is 1,176 (48 × [49/2] = 48 × 24.5 = 1,176).

The sum of the digits is the value in the denominator of the fraction in column 4 of Figure 4.7. To obtain the value in the numerator of the monthly interest factor we list the digits for the payments in reverse descending order. In reverse descending order the digits for the first payment would be 12, the second 11, and so on. Consequently, the interest earned by the lender in the first month equals 12/78 of $120 ($18.46), and the interest earned in the second month equals 11/78 of $120

Figure 4.7
A 12-month installment loan with an annual add-on interest rate of 12 percent. Initial amount refinanced = $1,000.

(1) Monthly Payment Number	(2) Monthly Payment	(3) Total Payments	(4) Monthly Interest Factor	(5) Monthly Interest Earned ($120 × Col. 4)	(6) Total Interest Earned	(7) Interest Refund ($120 – Col. 6)
1	$ 93.33	$ 93.33	12/78	$ 18.46	$ 18.46	$101.54
2	93.33	186.67	11/78	16.92	35.38	84.62
3	93.33	280.00	10/78	15.38	50.77	69.23
4	93.33	373.33	9/78	13.85	64.62	55.38
5	93.33	466.67	8/78	12.31	76.92	43.08
6	93.33	560.00	7/78	10.77	87.69	32.31
7	93.33	653.33	6/78	9.23	96.92	23.08
8	93.33	746.67	5/78	7.69	104.62	15.38
9	93.33	840.00	4/78	6.15	110.77	9.23
10	93.33	933.33	3/78	4.62	115.38	4.62
11	93.33	1,026.67	2/78	3.08	118.46	1.54
12	93.33	1,120.00	1/78	1.54	120.00	0.00
Total 78	$1,120.00		1	$120.00		

Loan payoff: The amount needed to eliminate your loan indebtedness during the term of the loan.

($16.92). To find the total interest earned by the lender through any payment month, as illustrated in column 6, we add up the monthly interest earned by the lender through the time of the loan payoff. For example, the total interest earned through month 3 is $50.77 ($18.46 + 16.92 + 15.38).

To calculate the **loan payoff** (the amount needed to eliminate the loan) at any point in time, you start with the original amount of the loan, excluding the add-on charge. To this amount you then add the interest the lender is entitled to receive and subtract all payments you have made. In the current example, the loan payoff immediately following the third payment of $770.77 can be calculated as follows:

Original loan principal, excluding add-on interest	$1,000.00
Interest owed lender: (total interest factor × add-on interest = 33/78 × $120)	+50.77
	$1,050.77
Less payments made to date (3 × $99.33)	−280.00
Loan payoff	$ 770.77

You should always know your interest savings before deciding to prepay. If you do not prepay the loan, you have the opportunity of investing these funds elsewhere. It is optimal to prepay the loan only if the interest savings on the loan exceed the value of your lost opportunities. The interest you would save by early repayment of the loan is listed in column 7 of Figure 4.7. It is equal to the add-on interest charge less the interest earned by the lender through the given point in time. In the current example, with repayment at the end of month 3, the interest saved is $69.23 ($120 – $50.77).

Of course, if you choose to pay off the loan, you will be giving up the opportunity of using these funds elsewhere. When the after-tax earnings on the alternative use of these funds exceeds the $69.23 in interest savings, you are better off not prepaying the loan. For example, suppose you could invest these funds at an annual after-tax rate of 8 percent, or 0.67 percent per month. We can estimate the return from the alternative use of these funds by first adding the cost of a monthly payment to the amount of the loan payoff and dividing the sum by 2. This approximates the average amount you would have in the investment account over the remaining term of the loan (nine months), assuming you placed the required payoff amount of $770.78 in the fund and withdrew from it to make each monthly payment. This average balance is then multiplied by the rate of return earned over the investment period. In the current example the calculations are as follows:

$$\frac{\text{Loan payoff} + \text{monthly payment}}{2} = \text{average balance}$$

$$\frac{\$770.78 + 93.33}{2} = \$432.06$$

$$\text{Average balance} \times \frac{\text{after-tax}}{\text{monthly rate}} \times \text{months} = \text{return on investment}$$

$$\$432.06 \times 0.67\% \times 9 = \$26.05$$

Therefore, if we chose not to pay off the loan, we could earn $26.05 in additional investment income. However, this is less than the $69.23 we could save in interest charges. In this example, the best choice is early loan repayment.

Acceleration clause: A late payment entitles the lender to demand that the entire unpaid balance be paid immediately.

The acceleration clause. If you miss just one payment on a loan, the **acceleration clause** makes the entire unpaid balance due immediately. If you can't pay this entire amount, you stand a chance of having the loan collateral repossessed. Repossession is guided by state law, but it usually means the lender is free to sell the item for its best market price. From this amount are deducted any expenses connected with the sale, and the difference is applied to the credit balance. If it is greater, the lender remits the difference to the borrower; if it is less, the borrower is still required to pay the difference. Your main concern here is the price the lender receives in selling the repossessed item. Under forced sale conditions, it could be very low, and you would bear the loss. Lenders do not usually apply the acceleration clause immediately, preferring instead to rely upon penalties for late payments, but it is not a factor to take casually.

Add-on clause: Allows the lender to repossess all goods financed under the agreement in the event of a missed payment.

The add-on clause. Suppose you purchase some kitchen appliances from an appliance dealer and finance the deal with an installment loan for one year. Six months later you return to the same dealer and purchase a television set and tape recorder as part of an add-on to your earlier agreement. Eight months after that purchase, financial problems set in and you stop making payments on the loan. With an **add-on clause,** the dealer can repossess all the appliances he or she sold you, even though your total payments may have been more than enough to have paid for the earlier purchase. Fortunately, courts seldom enforce this clause.

Balloon payment: An amount larger than other periodic payments that is due as the last installment payment.

The balloon payment. The **balloon payment** is usually the last installment payment, and it is for an amount much greater than the other monthly payments. The problem with the balloon is that borrowers may not prepare sufficiently to make the payment and so may require new financing when it is due or may have the item repossessed. Balloon clauses sometimes were used in the past as a means of defrauding borrowers, and this abuse led some states to make them illegal.

OBTAINING CREDIT AND RESOLVING CREDIT PROBLEMS

Once you understand how credit works, the next step is to find a lender. After you are successful in arranging credit, the final step is to use it properly to avoid credit problems. Unfortunately, even the most financially prudent people can face these problems, and you should know how to deal with them.

Sources of Credit

There are many suppliers of credit, ranging from commercial banks at the top of a list to friends and relatives at the bottom. The discussion that follows will not attempt to explain detailed features of each but will focus instead on their most important characteristics. Comparative shopping is important in the credit market. We are in an era of volatile interest rates, and, although it is true that similar lenders tend to charge about the same rates for similar loans, differences can exist. And don't underestimate the importance of saving 1 or 2 percent on the loan. For example, a 48-month installment loan for $5,000 will cost about $250 more at 16 percent than at 14 percent.

Interest rates charged on consumer loans from 1984 to 1993 are illustrated in Figure 4.8. Over this period there was a general downward trend in loan rates,

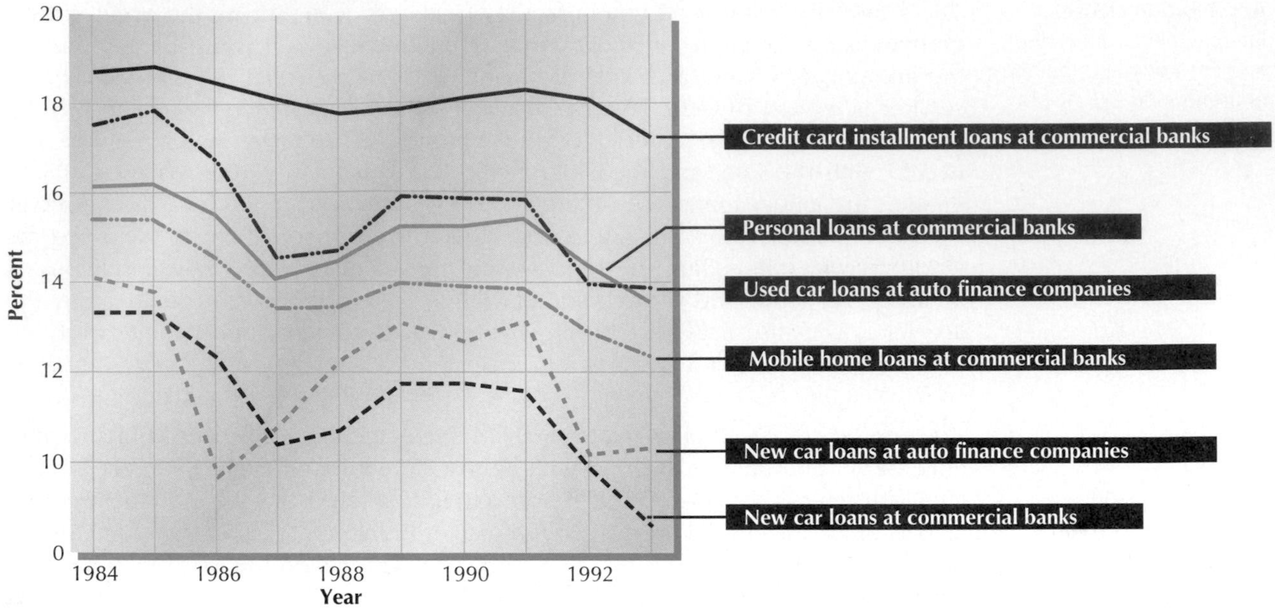

Figure 4.8 Interest rates on consumer loans.
SOURCE: Federal Reserve Board Online Data, 1996.

with an increase in the spread between the highest and the lowest. Credit card rates came down only slightly, making them much less attractive than other sources of funding. Before you run up the balance on your charge card, it would be wise to check out other less-expensive sources of credit.

BANKING INSTITUTIONS Commercial banks, savings and loan associations, and credit unions all compete for your consumer credit dollar with similar offers. In addition to credit cards, these institutions generally provide revolving credit at lower interest rates in the form of overdraft protection credit lines, unsecured personal credit lines, and home equity credit lines.

Overdraft protection credit line: Credit is automatically extended to cover excess withdrawals from a checking account.

Unsecured personal credit line: An unsecured credit line upon which you can withdraw cash.

Home equity loan: A loan secured by the ownership in your home in the form of a second mortgage.

The financial institution where you have a checking account may offer you an **overdraft protection credit line.** If you write a check for an amount that exceeds the funds available, the bank automatically extends you a loan to cover the excess amount up to some predetermined credit limit. In addition to providing you with a convenient source of credit, the overdraft protection credit line has the advantage of saving you the embarrassment and cost of a bounced check.

An **unsecured personal credit line** is separate from your checking account. You must apply for it by submitting a loan application. After you are approved for an unsecured personal credit line, you access the credit line by writing specially issued checks or utilizing a special credit card. Each month you receive a statement indicating the amount you owe, the amount of credit still available, your finance charges, and your minimum monthly payment.

With a **home equity loan,** your credit is secured by your ownership in your home. Banks typically let you borrow up to 75 to 80 percent of the equity in your home. Home equity loans come in two forms, closed-end credit and open-end credit. With an *open-end home equity line of credit,* you can borrow up to a predetermined credit limit on a revolving charge account. A *closed-end home equity loan* is the same as a second mortgage on your home. You borrow a fixed amount for a set period of time.

Home equity loans have become extremely popular because interest charges on home equity loans up to $100,000 may be taken as an itemized deduction on federal income tax returns. Interest payments on all other consumer loans are presently nondeductible. Moreover, home equity loans are typically available at much lower interest rates than other consumer loans. In addition, loan repayment may be stretched out over many years, producing small monthly payments. On the negative side, home equity loans may entice some consumers into making long-term payments on purchases that provide short-lived satisfaction.

CONSUMER FINANCE COMPANIES There are two types of consumer finance companies: those that offer specialized loans, such as GMAC on General Motors automobiles, and those that offer general-purpose loans, both secured and unsecured. The specialized lenders are dominant forces within their particular areas, and they usually offer interest rates at or below bank rates. Sometimes they are substantially below bank rates when they are part of auto dealers' sales promotion programs. Of course, the question then is whether you are getting the best price on the item purchased. Try to bring financing into the discussion as a separate topic after the price has been agreed upon. The objective is to get the best price *and* the best financing.

The general-purpose consumer finance companies are more willing to loan to first-time borrowers and to make loans on unsecured terms. Their administrative costs tend to be higher because they make many small loans, and their delinquency costs are also higher because of the poorer quality of the loans they make. As a result of these factors, you can expect their interest rates to be higher on these kinds of loans, but they may be competitive with higher-quality loans.

OTHER SOURCES Some sources are not typical lenders to consumers but are nevertheless important. You can borrow on your ordinary life insurance policy up to its loan value, usually at a rate that could be far lower than any other available rate if

Box 4.3 SAVING MONEY
Early Redemption of a Certificate of Deposit: An Alternative Source of Funds

Certificates of deposit at banking institutions often represent an attractive short-term investment; they are essentially riskless when federally insured, and they often pay rates of return exceeding those on savings and money market accounts. The downside, of course, is that in a credit crunch you may find that you need to redeem a certificate of deposit before it has matured. When this occurs, most banks will levy a six-month interest penalty upon early withdrawal. This can amount to a significant dollar loss. For example, on a $10,000 CD at an APR of 8 percent, the interest penalty would equal $400.

The same bank that issued the CD may offer you a better alternative. Many banks will provide you with a personal loan secured by the CD. The APR on the CD-secured personal loan is often dependent on the rate you are earning on the CD. Some banks extend such secured loans at an interest rate 2 percentage points above the rate on the CD. If the rate you are earning on the certificate of deposit is 8 percent, then the rate on the personal loan will be 10 percent. The net interest rate on the loan principal after deducting interest income on the CD will equal only 2 percent.

In the present example, the interest penalty for early redemption on a $10,000 certificate is $400. The annual net interest charge on a $10,000 loan secured by the CD is equal to $200 per year ($1,000 in interest paid minus $800 in interest earned). If the CD matures in the next two years, or if other funding becomes available within that time frame, then net interest charges on a loan will be less than the interest penalty on early redemption, making the loan the better alternative. The consideration of taxes can slightly complicate this analysis. Interest earned is taxable, and interest penalties are tax deductible.

the policy is older than, say, 10 years. These loans are exceptionally easy to make, requiring you to do nothing more than write a letter. And you never have to repay them, but, of course, if you die your beneficiaries will receive only the face value of the policy less the amount of the loan outstanding. Insurance companies very often emphasize this fact to persuade you not to borrow in the first place or to repay any outstanding loans. Actually, a loan on your life insurance policy offers no greater hardship to your heirs than any other loan outstanding at your death. They all must be repaid, and it makes no sense to single one out and argue that it should be repaid before the others. You must be watchful, however, that the loan plus unpaid interest does not exceed the cash value on the policy. If it does, the policy will be canceled.

If you own stocks or bonds, you should consider using them as collateral for a loan. A bank will accept securities as collateral, or you can open a margin account with a stockbrokerage firm. In either case, you can usually borrow up to 50 percent of the market value of the securities pledged. The interest rate on such a loan will probably be one to two points above the prime rate (the rate a bank charges its most creditworthy customer). This arrangement can be risky in a volatile market. Should the market price of the stocks fall, you may get a call for additional collateral. If you fail to provide the requested funds, the broker may force the sale of your stocks at a market low.

If you are really desperate and have something of value, consider a pawnshop. Pawnbrokers are willing to make loans on practically any item they feel can be resold if you fail to reclaim it after a specified period of time, usually 60 to 90 days. You will be able to borrow only a fraction of the item's market value and can expect to pay the very highest interest rates allowed. They are bad places to borrow, but pawnshops can be good places to buy if you are willing to take some risks on product quality and service.

As a last (or maybe first) resort, friends and relatives might extend credit to you. Before taking this alternative, bear in mind that credit misunderstandings have ended many friendships. The best advice if you do borrow (or lend) is to put the arrangement in writing, complete with all pertinent details that are found on other credit contracts. A "pay-me-back-when-you-can" loan is bad for both the borrower and the lender, because neither then knows how to budget for the loan. Also, remember that if either borrower or lender dies, heirs will be left to resolve the loan. Although the two parties involved may know and trust each other, their heirs may not.

A Credit Management Strategy

If your financial life is just beginning, you may be satisfied to simply get credit wherever you can. That situation doesn't last long, however, and as your assets and income grow, so does your access to credit. Now your problem is to use credit discriminatingly, and you will be better able to do so if you have an overall approach—that is, a strategy—for managing credit. Credit management is similar in many respects to cash management, discussed in the previous chapter. There, the objective was to maximize the return on short-term investments while achieving a reasonable degree of liquidity. Here, the objective is to minimize the cost of credit while simultaneously achieving both the target amount needed and a reasonable level of shopping convenience. Since we differ in how much credit we want and in our attitude toward convenience, our strategies for managing credit will also differ. But the following guidelines apply in most cases.

1. Use as much of the grace period as you can, but be sure to avoid late payment penalties. You can thus keep your money in an interest-earning account longer than if you pay bills with cash.
2. Do not have revolving charge accounts, or if you have one, use it as a 30-day account. We mentioned previously that most often this is expensive credit, and it should be used only if other credit is unavailable.
3. Take a broad view toward credit; that is, do not think in terms of borrowing here to buy this or borrowing there to buy that, but think instead of a total borrowing requirement. Then, search for the cheapest sources of credit to meet this requirement. For example, you might take a home equity mortgage and with it buy a car, send your kid to summer camp, and enjoy a vacation. The interest on this loan could be far less than an installment loan on the car and personal loans for the other two activities—and no riskier.
4. Be careful of variable-rate loans if you think that interest rates may rise. The initial interest rate on a variable-rate loan is lower than on a fixed-rate loan. The variable rate, however, is indexed to other market rates of interest and automatically rises as they do. Without a cap on how high the rate may rise, you may wind up making much higher monthly payments that you expected. Under all circumstances you should try to avoid getting into a vicious credit cycle. This occurs when the interest payments on the debt become a burden, forcing you to search for other sources of credit just to repay the previous debt. Keeping track of your personal debt ratios can help you avoid this trap.

Resolving Credit Problems

The easiest way to resolve a credit problem is not to let it begin in the first place. This means limiting your credit to an amount your income can support. Credit counselors often feel this limit is about 20 percent of your take-home pay for consumer credit, not including your home mortgage. The 20 percent is applied in two ways: First, your monthly credit payments should not exceed 20 percent of your monthly take-home pay; and second, your total consumer credit should not exceed 20 percent of your total take-home pay for the year. If you exceed either one of these limits, you are courting financial danger. You can keep credit within the 20 percent limit by always figuring the impact of any new credit arrangement on your budget *before* you make a loan. If it does not fit in the budget then, it won't fit later, either.

Despite all precautions, you may still run into credit problems. If you do, the first step is to seek outside help. If that fails, you may have to consider bankruptcy. Also, the law entitles you to protection from lender harassment while you are having credit difficulties, or at any time, for that matter.

CREDIT COUNSELING You cannot resolve a credit problem by avoiding lenders. As a first step you should explain the nature of your problem to them and try to get their cooperation while you attempt to remedy the situation. Most lenders prefer being repaid in full, even if extra time is needed, rather than forcing you into bankruptcy, where they may collect only a fraction of their loans. Recognizing their common interest in helping troubled borrowers, many lenders support the activities of **credit counseling** services, over 200 of which are sponsored by the National Foundation of Consumer Credit. These counseling centers provide two levels of service. First, they work with the borrower to help him or her develop a reasonable plan for repaying debts. This plan often includes a budget. Second, if this

Credit counseling: Helps consumers with credit problems by rescheduling loans and eliminating negative behaviors.

budget indicates that income will not be sufficient to meet both living expenses and the existing debt repayment load, the counselor will work out a new plan between the borrower and lenders, with a new repayment schedule. The borrower then gives the counselor a certain percentage of each week's income, and this in turn is given to the lenders. This service is essentially free to borrowers, regardless of their income, as are other counseling services. If you have a credit problem, contact the Better Business Bureau or the Chamber of Commerce in your town and inquire about credit counseling assistance. By all means, though, avoid any private credit counselor who supposedly specializes in working out your credit problems. The fee for this service can be as high as 35 percent of your total debt.

Action Plan for the Steeles: Credit Card Balances

Background The Steeles had every intention of paying their credit card balance each month. However, given unexpected medical and auto bills, their monthly income in some months has fallen behind their monthly cash outflow. They dealt with these intermittent cash crunches by making the minimum payment on their credit card and letting the outstanding balance grow.

The Problem The Steeles currently have an outstanding credit card balance of $1,720. With a 19 percent APR, their monthly finance charge is now up to $27.23. Moreover, future purchases may push them over the credit card limit of $3,000, in which case they would have to pay an overlimit fee of $10. They would like to reduce their credit card balances but are not sure how best to go about it.

The Plan The Steeles should immediately pay off the outstanding balance on the credit card. The monthly finance fee of $27.23 may not sound like a lot of money, but it adds up to $326.76 a year. Credit cards typically represent high-cost credit. The Steeles can eliminate their credit card debt either by substituting lower-cost credit or by utilizing some of their liquid assets. They are likely to save money either way. The worst strategy is to do nothing and simply make the minimum payment on the outstanding debt.

In the future, the Steeles should try to improve their budgeting by estimating medical and auto expenses more generously. Unfortunately, there will always be some unexpected expenses. The family's liquid assets held as an emergency fund can be used to cover such unanticipated and unusual needs. By avoiding expensive debt that drains future income and managing the cost of debt more effectively, the Steeles will avoid a major financial planning pitfall.

The Rationale If the Steeles decide to substitute lower-cost debt, there are numerous choices open to them. Obvious sources for families like the Steeles include home equity loans, insurance loans, loans on retirement accounts, margin loans on stocks, and checking account overdrafts.

They could even consider utilizing the 42-month CD that is about to mature. If they turn in the CD before maturity, their bank will levy a six-month interest penalty. However, they can avoid this penalty by using the CD as collateral for a personal loan. The bank that issued the CD will offer them such a loan at two points above the rate paid on the CD. On an 8 percent CD the bank will charge a 10 percent APR, a rate significantly below that charged on the credit card.

Using liquid assets to pay off the credit card debt is also a wise choice when the interest you save is more than the interest you lose on your depleted assets. When undertaking this analysis, you must remember that interest charges on consumer debt are paid out of after-tax dollars, whereas investments generate dollars on which taxes are due. Therefore, the best use of your funds will depend on a comparison of the after-tax interest rate on your debt and the before-tax interest rate on your investments. Given the interest rate on consumer debt, the following formula can be used to find the equivalent before-tax rate:

$$\text{Equivalent before tax interest rate} = \frac{\text{interest rate on consumer debt}}{1 - \text{marginal tax rate}}$$

$$26.39\% = \frac{19\%}{1 - 0.28}$$

The marginal tax rate is the fractional amount of any additional dollar of income that must be paid in taxes. In the Steeles' 28 percent marginal tax bracket, they would have to achieve a before-tax return of 26.39 percent in order to earn an after-tax return of 19 percent. If you also take the potential overlimit charge into account, the necessary before-tax rate would be even greater. Since they are not earning this high a return on any of their investments, using savings to reduce their credit card debt is a cost-saving choice.

BANKRUPTCY Over 800,000 Americans file bankruptcy each year. Many people continue to regard bankruptcy as a calamity to be avoided at any cost. Others view it as an easy way to avoid all the bills that result from an enjoyable buying binge. Regardless of your viewpoint, bankruptcy is a serious step, and you should seek credit counseling before taking it. We cannot cover the whole scope of the bankruptcy act in this introductory text, but you should know certain general facts.

You can file for bankruptcy under either Chapter 7 of the bankruptcy code, called a straight bankruptcy, or under Chapter 13 of the bankruptcy code, called a wage earner plan. In most instances, neither can be used to avoid payments for alimony, child support, taxes, or recent student loans.

Straight bankruptcy: A Chapter 7 bankruptcy in which most assets are sold off, most debts are discharged, and a fresh start is provided.

Over 70 percent of personal bankruptcies are filed under Chapter 7 as **straight bankruptcies.** This discharges all of your debts and thus provides you a fresh start. A straight bankruptcy may require you to sell off most of your assets. However, you are not left a complete pauper, and in most cases few assets are actually sold. Under federal exemptions, which may be more or less generous than state laws permit, you may keep from creditors up to $15,000 of homeowners equity or personal property and additional amounts of specific assets. These exemptions are for each individual, and therefore double for a married couple.

If you have been through a straight bankruptcy, you cannot file again for another six years, and the record of the bankruptcy remains on your credit report for 10 years. During this period it may be difficult for you to get credit or enter into normal everyday contracts such as rental agreements or purchase contracts. It may even hurt your employment prospects if potential employers access your credit records.

Wage earner plan: A repayment schedule established under Chapter 13 bankruptcy that allows debtors to retain their property while repaying all or part of their obligations.

Under a Chapter 13 filing, the court creates a **wage earner plan.** This is a court approved and administered repayment schedule for employed persons with regular income. This allows debtors to retain their property and to repay all or part of their obligations over a three- to five-year period with protection from creditors. It will remain on your credit report for seven years. On the plus side, it indicates that by filing under Chapter 13 rather than Chapter 7, you made a sincere attempt to repay your debts.

The Banking Reform Act of 1994 encourages individuals to file a Chapter 13 wage earner plan rather than a Chapter 7 straight bankruptcy by raising the credit debt limits on persons who are eligible to $250,000 of unsecured debt and $750,000 of secured debt. In addition, the dollar limits on property exempt from creditors is now indexed to consumer prices. This means that every three years, the limits should automatically increase as the cost of living rises.

To stem the rising tide of bankruptcies, legislators made significant changes in the bankruptcy laws in 1984. First, petitioners must now list their current income and expenses, and judges can dismiss petitions that, in their view, represent "substantial abuses" of the system. However, since the law does not spell out what abuses are, this option has not been vigorously applied. Second, not all debts may be discharged in a Chapter 7 filing. Income taxes, child support payments, alimony, debts incurred in anticipation of bankruptcy, and damage awards to accident victims may all survive bankruptcy proceedings.

Fair Debt Collection Practices Act: Limits the tactics that creditors may employ in attempting to collect overdue loans.

PROTECTION FROM LENDER HARASSMENT The **Fair Debt Collection Practices Act,** passed on March 20, 1978, entitles borrowers to be treated fairly by debt collectors. You are entitled to a written notice from the debt collector describing your debt in detail and what to do if you feel you do not owe the debt. You then have 30 days to send a letter to the debt collector denying the debt. The debt collector cannot continue collection efforts until you receive a written verification of the debt. Among other things, the debt collector cannot use abusive language, threaten you, harass you at work, or attempt to collect the bill through trickery. Finally, you can keep a debt collector from communicating with you by providing written notification that all contacts must cease.

A Summary of Federal Credit Legislation

We have alluded to most of the federal legislation in consumer credit as we discussed the various topics in this chapter. However, it is helpful at the end to have a summary of this legislation and, more important, to show the governing agencies that can assist you with a credit problem. Table 4.4 presents this summary. In addition, the Board of Governors Publications Services provides helpful pamphlets on consumer credit (see Helpful Contacts).

SUMMARY

Most people use credit every day, but effective use requires both planning and management. You must balance credit's advantages and disadvantages in deciding whether to use it, and you may have to take special steps to begin a credit record. Once you begin using credit, a credit bureau will maintain your credit history and will send credit reports to all lenders to whom you apply for credit. You have the right to review your credit history and should do so periodically to ensure its accuracy.

Sales credit is supplied by merchants, banks, and other institutions in the form of charge accounts and installment contracts; cash credit refers to money borrowed rather than borrowing as a result of a purchase. Major sources of credit in the United States are banking institutions, consumer finance companies, and credit unions. Other sources are ordinary life insurance policies, margin accounts with stockbrokerage firms, pawnshops, and friends and relatives. In using all these sources, it is wise to have a credit management strategy. Despite prudence and caution, credit problems can still arise. If they do, a first step is to seek the assistance of a credit counselor; a final step is filing bankruptcy. You are given certain legal protections against lender harassment during periods when repaying debts is difficult.

TABLE 4.4 • U.S. CREDIT LEGISLATION		
Act (Date Effective)	Major Provisions	Governing Agencies
Truth in Lending (July 1, 1969)	• Provides specific cost disclosure requirements for the annual percentage rate and the finance charge as a dollar amount • Requires disclosure of other loan terms and conditions • Regulates the advertising of credit terms • Provides the right to cancel a contract when certain real estate is used as security	The following federal agencies are responsible for enforcing all of these acts. The agency to contact for information or in case of a complaint depends on the particular creditor involved. Store or business: • If a retail store, department store, consumer finance company, gasoline credit card, travel and entertainment card, or a state-chartered credit union is involved, contact one of the FTC regional offices, or Federal Trade Commission, (name of the act), Washington, DC 20580. If a bank is involved, contact one of the following: • If it is a nationally chartered bank, contact: Comptroller of the Currency, Consumer Affairs Division, Washington, DC 20219. • If it is a state-chartered bank and a member of the Federal Reserve System, contact: Board of Governors of the Federal Reserve System, Division of Consumer Affairs, Washington, DC 20551. • If it is a state-chartered bank and is insured by the Federal Deposit Insurance Corporation, but is *not* a member of the Federal Reserve System, contact: Federal Deposit Insurance Corporation, Office of Bank Consumer Affairs, Washington, DC 20429. • If a federally chartered or federally insured (FSLIC) savings and loan association is involved, contact: Federal Home Loan Bank Board, Washington, DC 20552. • If a federally chartered credit union is involved, contact: National Credit Union Administration, Division of Consumer Affairs, Washington, DC 20456. On a state level, contact: • The Attorney General's office • State banking department
(January 25, 1971)	• Prohibits credit card issuers from sending unrequested cards • Limits a cardholder's liability for unauthorized use of a card to $50	
(October 1, 1982)	• Requires disclosures for closed-end credit (installment credit) be written in plain English and appear apart from all other information • Allows credit customer to request an itemization of the amount financed, if the creditor does not automatically provide it	
Fair Credit Reporting Act (April 24, 1971)	• Requires disclosure to consumers of the name and address of any consumer reporting agency that supplied reports used to deny credit, insurance, or employment • Gives a consumer the right to know what is in his file, have incorrect information reinvestigated and removed, and include his version of a disputed item in the file • Requires credit reporting agencies to send the consumer's version of a disputed item to certain businesses or creditors • Sets forth identification requirements for consumers wishing to inspect their files • Requires that consumers be notified when an investigative report is being made • Limits the length of time certain information can be kept in a credit file	
Fair Credit Billing Act (October 28, 1975)	• Establishes procedures for consumers and creditors to follow when billing errors occur on periodic statements for revolving credit accounts • Requires creditors to send a statement setting forth these procedures to consumers periodically • Allows consumers to withhold payment for faulty or defective goods or services (within certain limitations) when purchased with a credit card • Requires creditor to promptly credit customers' accounts and to return overpayments if requested	
Equal Credit Opportunity Act (October 28, 1975)	• Prohibits credit discrimination based on sex and marital status • Prohibits creditors from requiring women to reapply for credit upon a change in marital status	*(continued)*

TABLE 4.4 • U.S. CREDIT LEGISLATION, Continued

Act (Date Effective)	Major Provisions	Governing Agencies
	• Requires creditors to inform applicants of acceptance or rejection of their credit application within 30 days of receiving a completed application • Requires creditors to provide a written statement of the reasons for adverse action	
(March 23, 1977)	• Prohibits credit discrimination based on race, national origin, religion, age, or the receipt of public assistance	
(June 1, 1977)	• Requires creditors to report information on an account to credit bureaus in the names of both husband and wife if both use the account and both are liable for it	
Fair Debt Collection Practices Act (March 20, 1978)	• Prohibits abusive, deceptive, and unfair practices by debt collectors • Establishes procedures for debt collectors contacting a credit user • Restricts debt collector contacts with a third party • Specifies that payment for several debts be applied as the consumer wishes and that no monies be applied to a debt in dispute	
Home Equity Loan Consumer Protection Act (June 7, 1989)	• Requires creditors to provide consumers with extensive information on open-end credit plans secured by the consumer's dwelling and imposes substantive limitations on these plans • Information must be provided at time of application on payment terms, fees imposed under the plan, and, for variable-rate loans, information about the index and a 15-year history of the changes in the index • Limits the type of index that can be used for variable-rate plans • Limits the creditor's rights to terminate a plan and accelerate repayment of any outstanding balance	
Fair Credit and Charge Card Disclosure Act (April 3, 1989)	• Requires credit and charge card issuers to provide disclosures to consumers in solicitations and applications • Renewal notices including credit disclosures must be provided before fees are imposed to renew credit and charge card accounts	

KEY TERMS

acceleration clause (p. 111)
add-on clause (p. 111)
add-on method (p. 107)
adjusted balance method (p. 96)
affinity card (p. 98)
annual percentage rate (APR) (p. 108)
average daily balance method (p. 96)
balloon payment (p. 111)
bank credit cards (p. 98)
cash credit (p. 105)
chargeback (p. 104)
closed-end account (p. 94)
credit blocking (p. 104)
credit counseling (p. 115)
credit history (p. 91)
credit limit (p. 95)
credit report (p. 92)
debit card (p. 98)
discount method (p. 106)
Equal Credit Opportunity Act (ECOA) (p. 90)
Fair Credit Reporting Act of 1971 (p. 92)
Fair Debt Collection Practices Act (p. 118)
grace period (p. 97)
home equity loan (p. 112)
individual credit account (p. 91)
joint credit account (p. 91)
loan payoff (p. 110)
open-end account (p. 94)
overdraft protection credit line (p. 112)
previous balance method (p. 96)
promissory note (p. 105)
regular charge account (p. 94)
retail installment contract (p. 105)
revolving credit account (p. 94)
rule of 78 (p. 108)
sales credit (p. 93)
secured credit card (p. 93)
security agreement (p. 105)
service credit (p. 85)
simple interest method (p. 106)
straight bankruptcy (p. 117)
travel and entertainment (T&E) cards (p. 98)
Truth in Lending Act (TILA) (p. 89)
two-cycle average daily balance method (p. 97)
unsecured personal credit line (p. 112)
wage earner plan (p. 117)

PROBLEMS AND REVIEW QUESTIONS

1. Explain how credit serves as:
   (*a*) a shopping convenience,
   (*b*) a means to increase total consumption benefits,
   (*c*) a hedge against inflation,
   (*d*) a source of emergency funds.
   What are several disadvantages of credit?
2. Describe the three Cs of credit and why lenders feel they are important in evaluating a loan request. Then list five steps you can take to begin a credit record; list three extra steps that might be necessary if you are a woman.
3. What function does the credit bureau perform in the lender's evaluation of your credit application?
4. Shirley Szczesniak uses her credit card to purchase gasoline each month. She drives her car a lot and buys about 100 gallons a month. She has been paying about $1.20 a gallon lately but notices that if she paid with cash, she could save three cents a gallon. Would you advise Shirley to use cash or continue using her card? Explain.
5. Is a credit card about the same thing as a debit card? Explain.
6. List steps you can take to protect yourself against credit card fraud.
7. Suppose you review your monthly statement of credit card activities and discover that you have been charged for an item you didn't buy. Explain in detail what you should do.
8. Describe the information a lender must provide you on a credit contract. Why should you be particularly concerned about the following items:
   (*a*) the rule of 78,
   (*b*) the acceleration clause,

(c) the add-on clause,
(d) a balloon payment?

9. Explain several steps you can take to avoid credit problems.
10. If a good friend of yours has had serious financial misfortunes lately and is unable to meet her debt payments, what advice can you give? Be sure to include the topic of bankruptcy, since she has heard that it eliminates all your credit problems. In your discussion, distinguish between straight bankruptcy and a wage earner plan.
11. Indicate the actions you should take if you are denied credit or employment because of an unfavorable credit report.
12. Which method for determining the outstanding balance on a revolving credit account is likely to determine the lowest outstanding balance? Which method is likely to determine the highest outstanding balance?
13. Under what circumstances would you decide to obtain a credit card with a lower APR but a higher annual maintenance fee?
14. Suppose you were deciding whether to prepay a loan. Discuss the important facts that must be taken into consideration in order to make the least-cost decision.
15. Explain why home equity loans have become an important source of consumer credit.

Case 4.1 Should the Caseys Use Credit?

Mike and Helen Casey are a young couple, married about four years. They have no debts other than the usual monthly bills such as gas and electricity, the telephone, and newspapers. Both Mike and Helen work, and their incomes are quite good. Their approach to personal financial management has been to avoid all consumer credit, which they felt was the safest way to stay within their budget. However, they are beginning to wonder if this is really the correct approach. For one thing, all their friends have several credit cards that they use frequently, and they also appear to make most of their major purchases with installment credit. For another, using cash all the time is often inconvenient, particularly when they are away from home and merchants are reluctant to accept their personal checks.

The Caseys are considering using credit extensively. To start, they think they might open regular charge accounts with local stores where they shop regularly. By doing so, they probably could put about $300 a month on this credit and be able to defer payment for an average of 30 days. Second, in the upcoming year they would like to buy some furniture and major appliances that will cost $4,000. They had initially vetoed this idea, preferring to wait until the following year, when Helen expects to receive a distribution from her deceased grandmother's estate. Now they are not so sure this is a good idea, because they believe that by waiting one year, they may have to pay 8 percent more for the same items. If they wish to buy now, they can obtain a personal cash loan for one year at 15 percent simple interest.

QUESTIONS

1. Would you advise the Caseys to open the regular accounts where they intend to spend $300 a month? Explain if they will save (or earn) any money by doing so.
2. If the Caseys are in a 28 percent tax bracket, do you think they should buy now, using the personal cash loan, or should they wait one year?
3. Assume that the Caseys have $4,000 in an investment fund (earning 9 percent interest), which they could use without impairing their liquidity position. Explain whether you think they should buy now instead of waiting; and if they buy now, should they use the cash loan or withdraw the funds from their savings account?

Case 4.2 Evaluating Nancy Tai's Revolving Account

Nancy Tai has recently opened a revolving charge account with MasterCard. Her credit limit is $1,000, but she has not charged that much since opening the account. Nancy hasn't had the time to review her monthly statements promptly as she should, but over the upcoming weekend she plans to catch up on her work.

In reviewing October's statement she notices that her beginning balance was $600 and that she made a $200 payment on November 10. She also charged purchases of $80 on November 5, $100 on November 15, and $50 on November 30. She can't tell how much interest she paid in November because she spilled watercolor paint on that portion of the statement. She does remember, though, seeing the letters APR and the number 16 percent. Also, the back of her statement indicates that interest was charged using the average daily balance method, including current purchases, which considers the day of a charge or credit.

QUESTIONS

1. Assuming a 30-day period in November, calculate November's interest. Also, calculate the interest Nancy would have paid with: (*a*) the previous balance method, (*b*) the adjusted balance method.
2. Going back in time to when Nancy was just about to open her account, and assuming she could choose among credit sources that offered the different monthly balance determinations, and assuming further that Nancy would increase her outstanding balance over time, which credit source would you recommend? Explain.
3. In talking with Nancy, you have learned that she can also get credit through her credit union. An advertisement from the union shows that Nancy could take a personal cash loan at 14 percent on a discount basis or an installment loan at 12 percent add-on. Each is a one-year loan. Would you advise Nancy to use one of these to pay off her November balance with MasterCard? (Assume the 14 and 12 percents are not APRs.) Nancy doesn't believe she will have enough funds to reduce the November balance until the end of next October.

HELPFUL CONTACTS

Bankcard Holders of America, 460 Spring Park Place, Suite 1000, Herndon, VA 22070
Information on secured credit cards for a small fee. Mediates disputes between members and creditors.

Board of Governors, Publications Services, Division of Support Services, Washington, DC 20551
Copies of pamphlets on consumer credit are available on request.

National Foundation of Consumer Credit. Call 800–338–2227 for a member consumer credit counseling office near you.

INTERNET ADDRESSES

American Express, Inc. (credit card company)
http://www.americanexpress.com/

Bankruptcy Reform Act of 1994 (prepared by the law firm of Hale and Dorr)
http://www.haledorr.com/newsletters.html

Consumer Credit Counseling Service, Inc. (member of the National Foundation of Consumer Credit)
http://www.pe.net/~cccs/

Debt Counselors of America (Sm) (nonprofit organization assisting families with credit problems)
http://dca.org/

Electronic Credit Repair Kit (Shareware guide to credit repair information)
http://www.primenet.com:80/~kielsky/credit.htm

Equifax, Inc. (credit reporting agency)
http://www.equifax.com/

Federal Trade Commission (articles on consumer credit)
gopher://gopher.ftc.gov:70/11/ConsumerLine/publications/credit

MasterCard International, Inc. (credit card company)
http://www.mastercard.com/

National Institute for Consumer Education (clearinghouse for consumer information at Eastern Michigan University)
http://www.emich.edu/public/coe/nice/mission.html

TRW, Inc. (credit reporting agency)
http://www.trw.com/iss/is/isdiv.html

Visa, Inc. (credit card company)
http://www.visa.com/

Chapter 5

Taxes: The Government's Share of Your Rewards

Objectives

1. To understand the basic approach used by the Internal Revenue Service to determine your yearly federal income tax liability
2. To be able to calculate your yearly federal income tax liability following directions and guidelines provided by the Internal Revenue Service
3. To recognize the role the Internal Revenue Service plays in enforcing the income tax law and to know when to seek professional help in income tax matters
4. To understand and use important strategies that help you save federal income taxes or defer them to later years
5. To identify other important taxes that you currently pay or will pay in future years

Taxes are an important part of our everyday lives. We pay sales and excise taxes on many items that we purchase to consume. Our houses, automobiles, and other assets—tangible and intangible—are subject to property taxes. The income we earn is taxed, and when we die, our estates are taxed. Figure 5.1 indicates the size of the "tax bite" in relation to income; it should be noted that the table considers only so-called direct taxes levied on households. When all taxes are considered, the percentages are considerably higher. Indeed, the average family must work about five months each year to support government services. The largest single tax is the federal income tax, and Figure 5.1 gives a clear indication of the federal government's role in American society. Not only does its size make it important, but it is structured in such a fashion that most people can reduce their tax liability through effective tax planning. But planning is difficult. Despite the good intentions of many past presidents and Congresses, the tax law grows increasingly complex, as evidenced by the comprehensive 1986 Tax Reform Act and the more recent Revenue Reconciliation Act of 1990. Some call these tax laws the "full employment acts for accountants," a description they probably deserve. Despite their complexities, you can become aware of simple strategies to reduce your tax liability. With effort, you too can find "tax scholarships" or other tax-minimizing devices. This chapter will help you.

DETERMINING YOUR FEDERAL INCOME TAX

The federal income tax follows the approach—or formula—illustrated in Figure 5.2. To begin with, many items that you might look upon as income are not considered taxable income by the Internal Revenue Service (the IRS). From the total of the included gross income items, you then are allowed certain deductions to arrive at adjusted gross income. From this total, two other deductions are allowed: personal

Figure 5.1 Federal income taxes as a percentage of adjusted gross income.
SOURCE: Individual Income Tax Returns, 1993 (Washington, DC: U.S. Dept. of the Treasury, Internal Revenue Service).

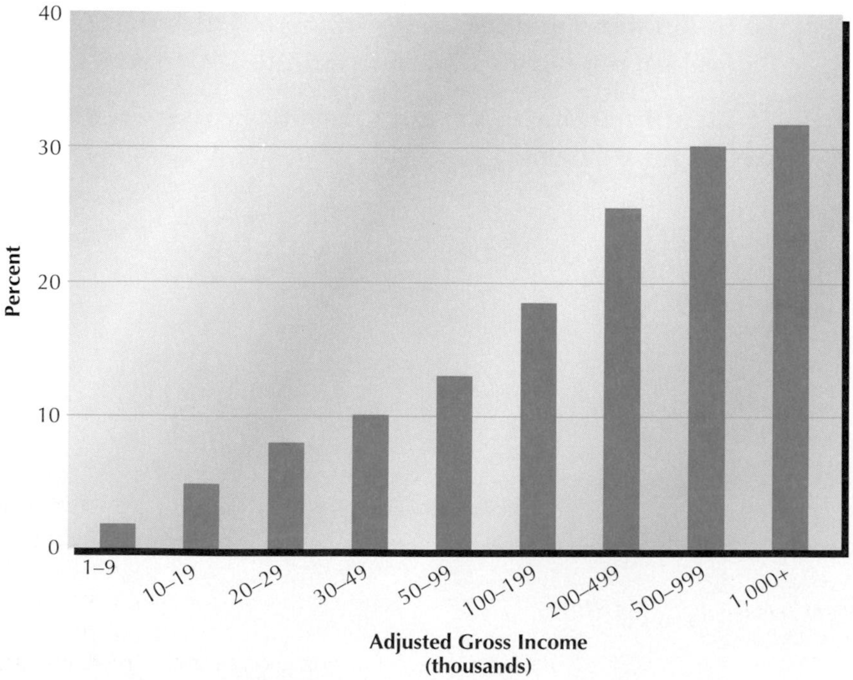

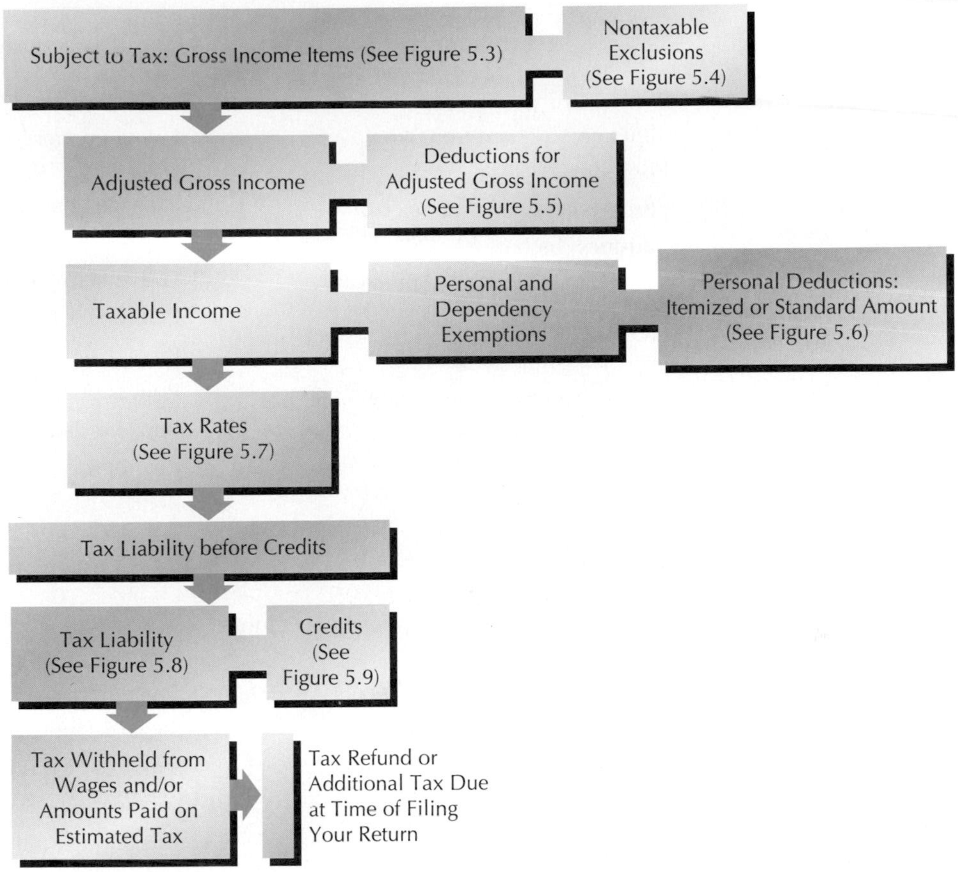

Figure 5.2
The federal income tax formula.

and dependency exemptions and personal deductions, either itemized or taken as a standardized amount. You now have taxable income, which is then subjected to specific tax rates to arrive at your tax liability before tax credits for the year. From this amount, tax credits are deducted to arrive at your tax liability. Since most of us have income taxes withheld (or paid in advance, using estimates), this liability may have been paid before filing time. If it has, a refund is claimed when the return is filed. If withholding falls short of the liability, as shown in Figure 5.2, we must pay the balance due along with the return. The entire process is explained in greater detail in the following sections, and later we'll illustrate the topic by showing Arnold and Sharon Steele's income tax return.

Gross Income Items

Gross income items: Sources of income that are subject to the federal income tax.

Nontaxable exclusions: Items that are *not* includable as gross income.

Basically, any compensation you receive for the use of your labor or capital is a taxable income item. If you take the time to enter a contest and are fortunate enough to win, the prize is income and not a gift, which you would prefer because gifts are not taxable. A partial list of **gross income items** is shown in Figure 5.3, and a partial list of **nontaxable exclusions** is shown in Figure 5.4.

Some of the excluded items are important in tax strategy and should be identified and explained here. Notice that municipal bond interest is an excluded item. All other factors the same, it is to your advantage to own municipal bonds as opposed to those whose interest payments are fully taxable. Also, such items as

Alimony	Hobby income
Awards	Interest
Back pay	Jury duty fees
Bargain purchase from employer	Living quarters, meals (unless furnished for employer's convenience)
Bonuses	Mileage allowance
Breach of contract damages	Military pay (unless combat pay)
Business income	Partnership income
Clergy fees and contributions	Pensions
Commissions	Prizes
Compensation for services	Professional fees
Death benefits in excess of $5,000	Punitive damages
Debts forgiven	Reimbursement for moving expenses
Director's fees	Rent
Dividends	Retirement pay
Embezzled funds	Rewards
Employee awards	Royalties
Employee benefits (excepting certain fringe benefits)	Salaries
Employer-paid disability benefits	Severence pay
Estate and trust income	Social Security benefits (partial inclusion)
Farm income	Strike and lockout benefits
Fees	Supplemental unemployment benefits
Free tour	Tips and gratuities
Gains from illegal activities	Travel allowance
Gains from sale of property	Unemployment compensation
Gambling winnings	Wages
Group term life insurance, premium paid by employer (coverage over $50,000)	

Figure 5.3
A partial list of gross income items.

group term life insurance and health insurance are often offered as fringe benefits by employers (or as part of a salary-reduction plan). You should see that if you must provide these benefits yourself, it will take more of your income than if you receive them as fringes. Why? Because you cannot deduct such payments in calculating your tax liability and, therefore, they are bought with after-tax dollars. For example, if you are in a 28 percent tax bracket and purchase $1,000 of such insurance, you must earn $1,389 to net the $1,000. (You get this figure by dividing the $1,000 by 1.00 minus the tax bracket; that is, 1,389 = 1,000/[1.00 − 0.28].) Clearly, if your employer gives you a choice between the $1,000 or the insurance, choose the latter if you intend to buy the insurance anyway.

Adjustments to Income

Adjusted gross income: Gross income plus or minus certain adjustments.

The tax law requires certain adjustments to arrive at **adjusted gross income.** Most of these adjustments are expenses related to earning income, but some simply reflect the intent of Congress to provide equity or incentives in the tax law. A

Accident insurance proceeds	Life insurance paid on death
Annuities (to a limited extent)	Long-term capital gain on personal residence—$125,000 one-time exclusion
Casualty insurance proceeds	Meals and lodging (furnished for employer's convenience)
Child support payments	Military allowances
Compensatory damages	Moving and storage expenses paid by employer
Cost-of-living allowance (for military)	Municipal bond interest
Damage for personal injury or sickness	Qualified employer-provided educational assistance
Death benefits (up to $5,000)	Relocation payments
Disability benefits	Scholarship grants (to a limited extent)
Disability pensions (to a limited extent)	Veterans' benefits
Fellowship grants (to a limited extent)	Welfare payments
Gifts	Workers' compensation
Group term life insurance, premium paid by employer (coverage not over $50,000)	
Health insurance proceeds not deducted as a medical expense	
Inheritances	

Figure 5.4
A partial list of exclusions from gross income.

list of the adjustments is shown in Figure 5.5, and a discussion of the more important ones follows.

MOVING EXPENSES You can deduct certain moving expenses if your new job is at least 50 miles from your previous home and these expenses are incurred within one year of the date on which you began your new job. These deductions are available to both individuals changing jobs and those entering the job market for the first time. Generally, you can deduct the cost of traveling to your new home and the cost of moving your furnishings.

IRAs and Keogh plans: Retirement plans that reduce gross income.

IRAs AND KEOGH PLANS **IRAs** and **Keogh plans** will be explained in greater detail in Chapter 17, but a few words about each are appropriate here. A Keogh plan can be established by anyone with self-employed income; that is, income from a business. Such plans are used by many small business operators and professionals, such as artists and writers. Allowable contributions to a Keogh are considerably greater than IRA contributions, so if you earn self-employed income, you should become familiar with the Keogh provisions.

The IRA (Individual Retirement Account) can be used by anyone (employed or self-employed) whose income does not exceed certain limitations. IRAs became

Figure 5.5
Adjustments to income.

- Alimony paid
- IRA deduction
- Keogh and SEP (Simplified Employee Pension) plan contributions
- Moving expenses
- Penalty for early withdrawal of savings
- Self-employed health insurance deduction
- Self-employment tax (half)

extremely popular in 1982, after Congress liberalized its provisions in the 1981 Tax Act. Its intent is to encourage individual retirement planning, and it accomplishes this aim by allowing deductions to qualified IRA investments. Most investments people make—such as deposits in banks and savings and loans, common and preferred stocks, bonds, certain partnership interests, and more—are qualified investments. A single taxpayer (or each spouse) can deduct up to $2,000 invested in these each year if he or she (or each) has that much in wages, alimony, or other earned income, which does not include interest, dividends, or other items (all these are defined as unearned income). A married couple in which one spouse has all the earned income can deduct up to $2,250. It goes almost without saying that the IRA is one of the easiest and most generous tax concessions provided by Congress. Many tax advisers call it the best tax shelter for the middle-income family.

Not only is the IRA a generous deduction, it's virtually the only one you can take even after the tax year is over, since you have until April 15 of the following year to make your investment. Unfortunately, if your income exceeds certain limits, the deductibility of an IRA is gradually eliminated. Specifically, the income limits are $40,000 for a married couple filing a joint return and $25,000 for a single filer (see Chapter 17 for more details).

Alimony payments: Added to gross income to the receiver, but a reduction of the payer's gross income.

ALIMONY PAID In general, **alimony payments** must be included as income by the person receiving them and are deductible by the ex-spouse making them. Such payments must be the result of a court decree of divorce or separation and also must satisfy all of the following requirements. They must be based on your marital status or family relationship, paid after the decree, and paid periodically instead of in a lump sum. Divorce or separation often involves deep emotional feelings, and the last thing on the spouses' minds is how to structure the divorce to minimize future tax liabilities. This is unfortunate, because a cooperative approach can benefit each partner. You need good tax advice in this area, and it's usually worth retaining an attorney or CPA to help with the settlement.

Adjusted Gross Income

Making all the adjustments to income from the total gross income items leaves adjusted gross income. It is an important figure because some itemized deductions have maximum limits based upon it.

Taxable Income

Taxable income: Adjusted gross income less personal and dependency exemptions and allowable personal expense deductions.

Personal and dependency exemptions: Deductions from adjusted gross income based on the number of people in a household, their ages, and eyesight quality.

Taxable income consists of adjusted gross income less **personal and dependency exemptions** and deductions for personal expenses. This latter item consists of either taking a standardized amount or itemizing allowable deductions.

PERSONAL AND DEPENDENCY EXEMPTIONS The law allows most taxpayers a personal exemption. The amount was $2,500 in 1995. It is *indexed* to the price level; therefore, the exemption is adjusted upward each year to reflect the current rate of inflation. For example, if the rate of inflation were 3 percent, the new amount would be $2,575 ($2,500 × 1.03).

Each spouse on a joint return is entitled to the exemption, and it also applies to any of the taxpayer's dependents. Therefore, a married couple with four dependents could claim $15,000 in exemptions for tax year 1995. It is important to note that someone claimed as a dependent on another's return, such as parents claiming a dependent child, cannot also take the personal exemption. A working college student, for example, might provide most of his or her own support, thereby earning the exemption amount but preventing the parents from taking it. If the parents are in a high tax bracket, this is poor tax strategy.

We should note that personal and dependency exemption deductions are gradually eliminated when taxable income exceeds certain limits. For a married couple filing a joint return the threshold income was $172,050 for 1995 returns; and, at an income level of $297,500 all exemption deductions were eliminated. Comparable figures for a single filer were $114,700 and $239,700.

Standard deduction: Deduction from adjusted gross income based on the taxpayer's filing status.

THE STANDARD DEDUCTION In addition to personal and dependency exemptions, the law also allows a **standard deduction** for personal expenses. The deductible amount depends upon taxpayer filing status as indicated below. Standard deduction amounts also are inflation indexed.

If you are:	Standard Deduction Amount 1995
1 Married filing jointly, or a qualifying widow or widower	$6,550
2 Head of a household	5,750
3 Single	3,900
4 Married filing separately	3,275

Age and impaired sight allow taxpayers *additional* standard deduction amounts beyond those just described. For the 1995 tax year, an unmarried taxpayer 65 or older was allowed an additional $950; if he or she was also blind, the amount was increased another $950. For a married couple, the deduction was $750 for each spouse 65 or older or blind. For example, for a married couple with both spouses over 65 and one blind, the additional amount was $2,250 and the total 1995 standard deduction was $8,800 ($6,550 + 2,250).

Box 5.1 SIMPLIFYING FINANCIAL PLANNING
How Do Your Deductions Compare?

At right are average amounts written off by taxpayers who claimed these deductions on 1993 returns filed in 1994. Note: This does not mean that taxpayers with $40,000 to $49,999 in income averaged $4,547 in medical deductions. Most such persons did not qualify for medical write-offs. The figure instead is the average deduction among those who *could* deduct medical expenses.

Adjusted Gross Income (thousands)	Medical-Dental	State and Local Taxes	Interest Deducted	Contributions
$ 20–24	$ 3,614	$ 2,128	$ 5,040	$ 1,347
25–29	3,751	2,360	5,059	1,349
30–39	3,632	2,772	5,503	1,384
40–49	4,547	3,322	5,738	1,541
50–74	4,632	4,442	6,618	1,739
75–99	5,986	6,220	8,282	2,319
100–199	10,842	10,035	11,389	3,427
200–499	28,991	22,655	17,772	8,207
500–999	62,266	52,462	27,605	20,635
1,000+	98,265	173,490	60,427	108,883

SOURCE: *Statistics of Income Bulletin, A Quarterly Statistics of Income Report, Spring 1995* (Washington, DC: U.S. G.P.O., 1995) pp. 25–27.

Itemized deductions: Deductions from adjusted gross income based on actual amounts spent by a taxpayer.

ITEMIZED DEDUCTIONS In general, the IRS does not allow personal expenses as deductions except in those cases where the tax law clearly indicates to the contrary. Most allowable personal deductions reflect activities regarded as socially desirable (giving to charity, for example) or alleviating undue financial hardship (medical expenses). Some are allowed probably because strong vested interests were influential in having them included in the tax law. Figure 5.6 indicates the more common deductions. The total of **itemized deductions** is taken as an offset to adjusted gross income. While it is important to keep good records to support all items on your tax return, it is particularly so in the case of itemized deductions. A lack of supporting evidence—canceled checks, invoices, or carefully written logs—will often lead to a disallowance of the claimed deduction.

There are limits on the amounts you can deduct for medical expenses, charitable contributions, casualty losses, and miscellaneous expenses. You can take only amounts greater than 7.5 percent of your adjusted gross income for medical expenses, which include hospital and doctor bills, payments to health insurance plans, and drugs and medicines. Special rules apply if charitable contributions exceed 20 percent of adjusted gross income. Also, for a charitable contribution to qualify, it must be made to an IRS-recognized charity; gifts made to individuals do not count as deductions. You may claim a deduction for a contribution of $250 or more only if you have a receipt from a qualified charitable organization.

As is the case with personal and dependency exemptions, taxpayers lose a portion of itemized deductions when their incomes exceed certain limits. The law becomes somewhat involved here, and if you are fortunate to have a taxable income in excess of $114,700 you should refer to an appropriate tax publication or consult with a tax professional.

Determining Your Tax Liability before Tax Credits

After taxable income has been calculated, you are ready to determine your tax liability before tax credits. To do this you will use either the tax table or Tax Rate Schedules X, Y, or Z. You must use the tax table—a portion of which is shown in Figure 5.7—if your taxable income is less than $100,000. To find the tax, simply

Figure 5.6 Frequently claimed itemized deductions.

- Medical expenses (including payments to medical insurance) in excess of 7.5% of adjusted gross income
- State and local income taxes
- Property taxes
- Personal property taxes
- Interest on home mortgage (possible limitations)
- Charitable contributions (subject to limitations)
- Casualty and theft losses (subject to limitations)
- Miscellaneous expenses in excess of 2% of adjusted gross income:
  - Union dues
  - Professional dues and subscriptions
  - Certain educational expenses
  - Tax return preparation fee
  - Investment counsel fees
  - Unreimbursed business expenses

If line 37 (taxable income) is—		And you are—			
At least	But less than	Single	Married filing jointly *	Married filing separately	Head of a household
		Your tax is—			
36,000					
36,000	**36,050**	7,052	5,404	7,552	6,025
36,050	**36,100**	7,066	5,411	7,566	6,039
36,100	**36,150**	7,080	5,419	7,580	6,053
36,150	**36,200**	7,094	5,426	7,594	6,067
36,200	**36,250**	7,108	5,434	7,608	6,081
36,250	**36,300**	7,122	5,441	7,622	6,095
36,300	**36,350**	7,136	5,449	7,636	6,109
36,350	**36,400**	7,150	5,456	7,650	6,123
36,400	**36,450**	7,164	5,464	7,664	6,137
36,450	**36,500**	7,178	5,471	7,678	6,151
36,500	**36,550**	7,192	5,479	7,692	6,165
36,550	**36,600**	7,206	5,486	7,706	6,179
36,600	**36,650**	7,220	5,494	7,720	6,193
36,650	**36,700**	7,234	5,501	7,734	6,207
36,700	**36,750**	7,248	5,509	7,748	6,221
36,750	**36,800**	7,262	5,516	7,762	6,235
36,800	**36,850**	7,276	5,524	7,776	6,249
36,850	**36,900**	7,290	5,531	7,790	6,263
36,900	**36,950**	7,304	5,539	7,804	6,277
36,950	**37,000**	7,318	5,546	7,818	6,291

Steeles' taxable income → (36,300–36,350)

Example → (36,650–36,700)

Figure 5.7
A portion of the 1995 tax table.

find the appropriate income bracket and move over to the column corresponding to your filing status. For example, if your taxable income is \$36,311 and you are married filing a joint return, the tax is \$5,449.

If your taxable income is greater than \$100,000, you must use one of the tax rate schedules shown in Figure 5.8. You will calculate your tax by following directions in the schedule. For example, suppose you are a single taxpayer with a taxable income of \$120,000. Your tax would be calculated from Schedule X as follows:

$$\begin{aligned}\text{Tax} &= \$31{,}832.50 + [0.36(\$120{,}000 - \$117{,}950)] \\ &= \$31{,}832.50 + \$738 \\ &= \$32{,}570.50\end{aligned}$$

Tax Credits

Tax credit: A dollar-for-dollar offset against the tax liability.

A **tax credit** is a direct deduction against your tax liability. There are a number of such credits, which are shown in Figure 5.9. Most tax credit calculations follow specific formulas established in the tax law. It is necessary to follow these formulas to determine both whether you qualify for a credit and how much you can claim.

Your tax liability for the year is determined by subtracting the total of your credits from the taxes you calculated using the tax table or one of the schedules. This tax liability is an important figure—one you should be very much aware of as you make financial decisions. An even more important figure to know is your marginal tax rate, which we'll explain shortly. The withholding system, although convenient, very often does not show in bold terms either what our actual liability is or at what rates our incomes are being taxed.

1995 Tax Rate Schedules

Caution: *Use **only** if your taxable income (Form 1040, line 37) is $100,000 or more. If less, use the **Tax Table**. Even though you cannot use the tax rate schedules below if your taxable income is less than $100,000, all levels of taxable income are shown so taxpayers can see the tax rate that applies to each level.*

Schedule X—Use if your filing status is **Single**

If the amount on Form 1040, line 37, is: *Over—*	*But not over—*	Enter on Form 1040, line 38	*of the amount over—*
$0	$23,350	.... 15%	**$0**
23,350	56,550	**$3,502.50 + 28%**	**23,350**
56,550	117,950	**12,798.50 + 31%**	**56,550**
117,950	256,500	**31,832.50 + 36%**	**117,950**
256,500	....	**81,710.50 + 39.6%**	**256,500**

Text example

Schedule Y-1—Use if your filing status is **Married filing jointly** or **Qualifying widow(er)**

If the amount on Form 1040, line 37, is: *Over—*	*But not over—*	Enter on Form 1040, line 38	*of the amount over—*
$0	$39,000	.... 15%	**$0**
39,000	94,250	**$5,850.00 + 28%**	**39,000**
94,250	143,600	**21,320.00 + 31%**	**94,250**
143,600	256,500	**36,618.50 + 36%**	**143,600**
256,500	....	**77,262.50 + 39.6%**	**256,500**

Steeles' bracket

Schedule Y-2—Use if your filing status is **Married filing separately**

If the amount on Form 1040, line 37, is: *Over—*	*But not over—*	Enter on Form 1040, line 38	*of the amount over—*
$0	$19,500	.... 15%	**$0**
19,500	47,125	**$2,925.00 + 28%**	**19,500**
47,125	71,800	**10,660.00 + 31%**	**47,125**
71,800	128,250	**18,309.25 + 36%**	**71,800**
128,250	....	**38,631.25 + 39.6%**	**128,250**

Schedule Z—Use if your filing status is **Head of household**

If the amount on Form 1040, line 37, is: *Over—*	*But not over—*	Enter on Form 1040, line 38	*of the amount over—*
$0	$31,250	.... 15%	**$0**
31,250	80,750	**$4,687.50 + 28%**	**31,250**
80,750	130,800	**18,547.50 + 31%**	**80,750**
130,800	256,500	**34,063.00 + 36%**	**130,800**
256,500	....	**79,315.00 + 39.6%**	**256,500**

Figure 5.8 Partial tax schedules for 1995.

Do You Get a Refund or Owe More Taxes?

The amount you receive or pay depends upon how much tax has been withheld from your wages. (Or, if you earned income not subject to withholding, how much you have paid in estimated taxes. By the way, if you expect to earn such income you are required to file an estimated tax. Failure to do so can lead to both penalties and interest.) If withholding was greater than your tax liability, you are entitled to a refund; if the reverse is true, you must pay additional tax. Every employer is required to provide employees an annual report of their wages and all the taxes (and

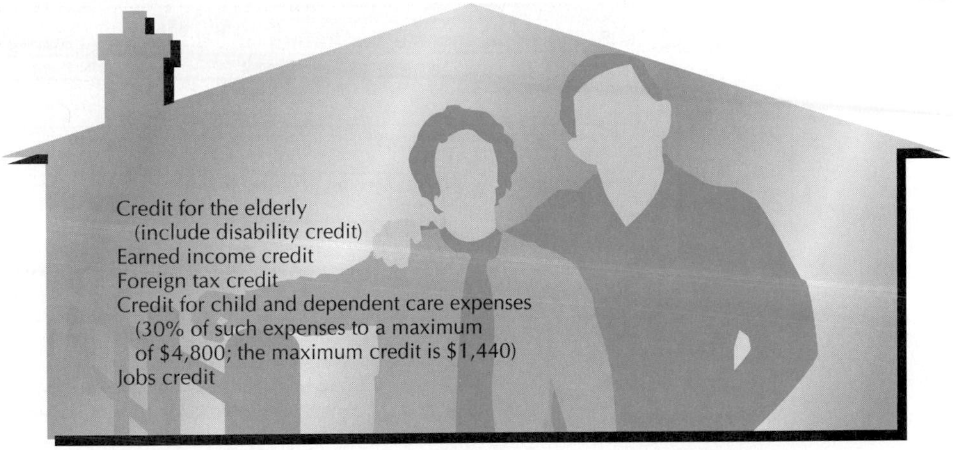

Credit for the elderly
(include disability credit)
Earned income credit
Foreign tax credit
Credit for child and dependent care expenses
(30% of such expenses to a maximum
of $4,800; the maximum credit is $1,440)
Jobs credit

Figure 5.9
Tax credits.

W-2 form: A form prepared by an employer showing an employee's earnings and withholdings.

W-4 form: A form signed by an employee to claim exemption allowances for payroll withholding purposes.

possibly other items) withheld from their wages. This report is called a **W-2 form,** and you should review yours each year to make sure it is correct. Also, you need the carbon copies to attach to your federal and state income tax returns.

Keep in mind that the IRS does not pay interest on excess withholding. Despite this fact, many taxpayers claim fewer exemptions than they need to on withholding forms filed with their employers (called a **W-4 form**). They do this because it is a form of forced savings or because they enjoy getting a big refund. Actually, this is very poor financial management. In many cases, it is just as easy to have your employer withhold from your salary each week and invest the money in a way that offers you a return. Savings plans with Series EE bonds, for example, are very popular; there are many others. Before you allow excess withholding, see if any plans are available and select one that fits your investment objectives.

Determining the Steeles' 1995 Income Tax

In 1996, Arnold and Sharon Steele had the following items to consider in preparing their 1995 income tax return. Arnold earned $55,380 at InChemCo and had $5,048 of federal income tax withheld from his salary. Sharon earned $13,800 at Todd and Talbot and had $654 of such taxes withheld. They received $861 in interest on savings accounts and $812 in dividends on stocks they owned. During the year they sold some stocks Sharon received from her parents as a gift. There was a $935 gain on the sale. The Steeles itemized their deductions and arrived at an allowable total of $25,476.55. They also paid $600 in child-care expenses. With the above information, the Steeles are ready to prepare their return. They used Form 1040 (the so-called long form), which is shown in Figure 5.10.

FILING STATUS AND EXEMPTIONS The Steeles are filing a joint return, and they are claiming four exemptions. They could have filed under option 3—married filing separate returns—but they found their tax liability would have been greater. This isn't always the case, so you should check your liability each way to determine the appropriate option.

TOTAL INCOME The Steeles' total income was $71,788.

ADJUSTMENTS TO INCOME None.

Form **1040** Department of the Treasury—Internal Revenue Service
U.S. Individual Income Tax Return (L) **1995** IRS Use Only—Do not write or staple in this space.

For the year Jan. 1–Dec. 31, 1995, or other tax year beginning , 1995, ending , 19 | OMB No. 1545-0074

Label (See instructions on page 11.) **Use the IRS label.** Otherwise, please print or type.

LABEL HERE

Your first name and initial: *Arnold S.*	Last name: *Steele*	**Your social security number** *000 : 00 : 0000*
If a joint return, spouse's first name and initial: *Sharon R.*	Last name: *Steele*	**Spouse's social security number** *000 : 00 : 0000*
Home address (number and street). If you have a P.O. box, see page 11.: *496 Mulberry Lane*	Apt. no.	**For Privacy Act and Paperwork Reduction Act Notice, see page 7.**
City, town or post office, state, and ZIP code. If you have a foreign address, see page 11.: *Middlebury, Missouri 64131*		

Presidential Election Campaign (See page 11.)

	Yes	No	
Do you want $3 to go to this fund?	✓		**Note:** *Checking "Yes" will not change your tax or reduce your refund.*
If a joint return, does your spouse want $3 to go to this fund?		✓	

Filing Status (See page 11.) Check only one box.

1 ☐ Single
2 ☑ Married filing joint return (even if only one had income)
3 ☐ Married filing separate return. Enter spouse's social security no. above and full name here. ▶
4 ☐ Head of household (with qualifying person). (See page 12.) If the qualifying person is a child but not your dependent, enter this child's name here. ▶
5 ☐ Qualifying widow(er) with dependent child (year spouse died ▶ 19). (See page 12.)

Exemptions (See page 12.)

6a ☑ **Yourself.** If your parent (or someone else) can claim you as a dependent on his or her tax return, **do not** check box 6a. But be sure to check the box on line 33b on page 2

b ☑ **Spouse**

No. of boxes checked on 6a and 6b *2*

c **Dependents:**

If more than six dependents, see page 13.

(1) First name Last name	(2) Dependent's social security number. If born in 1995, see page 13.	(3) Dependent's relationship to you	(4) No. of months lived in your home in 1995
Nancy J. Steele	*000 : 00 : 0000*	*D*	*12*
John L. Steele	*000 : 00 : 0000*	*S*	*12*

No. of your children on 6c who:
- **lived with you** *2*
- **didn't live with you due to divorce or separation (see page 14)**

Dependents on 6c not entered above

d If your child didn't live with you but is claimed as your dependent under a pre-1985 agreement, check here ▶ ☐

e Total number of exemptions claimed

Add numbers entered on lines above ▶ *4*

Income

Attach Copy B of your Forms W-2, W-2G, and 1099-R here.

If you did not get a W-2, see page 14.

Enclose, but do not attach, your payment and payment voucher. See page 33.

Line	Description	Line	Amount
7	Wages, salaries, tips, etc. Attach Form(s) W-2	7	*69,180 00*
8a	**Taxable** interest income (see page 15). Attach Schedule B if over $400	8a	*861 00*
b	**Tax-exempt** interest (see page 15). DON'T include on line 8a 8b		
9	Dividend income. Attach Schedule B if over $400	9	*812 00*
10	Taxable refunds, credits, or offsets of state and local income taxes (see page 15)	10	
11	Alimony received	11	
12	Business income or (loss). Attach Schedule C or C-EZ	12	
13	Capital gain or (loss). If required, attach Schedule D (see page 16)	13	*935 00*
14	Other gains or (losses). Attach Form 4797	14	
15a	Total IRA distributions 15a — b Taxable amount (see page 16)	15b	
16a	Total pensions and annuities 16a — b Taxable amount (see page 16)	16b	
17	Rental real estate, royalties, partnerships, S corporations, trusts, etc. Attach Schedule E	17	
18	Farm income or (loss). Attach Schedule F	18	
19	Unemployment compensation (see page 17)	19	
20a	Social security benefits 20a — b Taxable amount (see page 18)	20b	
21	Other income. List type and amount—see page 18	21	
22	Add the amounts in the far right column for lines 7 through 21. This is your **total income** ▶	22	*71,788 00*

Adjustments to Income

Line	Description	Line	Amount
23a	Your IRA deduction (see page 19)	23a	
b	Spouse's IRA deduction (see page 19)	23b	
24	Moving expenses. Attach Form 3903 or 3903-F	24	
25	One-half of self-employment tax	25	
26	Self-employed health insurance deduction (see page 21)	26	
27	Keogh & self-employed SEP plans. If SEP, check ▶ ☐	27	
28	Penalty on early withdrawal of savings	28	
29	Alimony paid. Recipient's SSN ▶	29	
30	Add lines 23a through 29. These are your **total adjustments** ▶	30	

Adjusted Gross Income

Line	Description	Line	Amount
31	Subtract line 30 from line 22. This is your **adjusted gross income**. If less than $26,673 and a child lived with you (less than $9,230 if a child didn't live with you), see "Earned Income Credit" on page 27 ▶	31	*71,788 00*

Cat. No. 12600W Form **1040** (1995)

Figure 5.10 The Steeles' federal income tax Form 1040.

Form 1040 (1995) Page **2**

Section	Line	Description	Amount
Tax Computation (See page 23.)	32	Amount from line 31 (adjusted gross income)	32: 71,788 00
	33a	Check if: ☐ **You** were 65 or older, ☐ Blind; ☐ **Spouse** was 65 or older, ☐ Blind. Add the number of boxes checked above and enter the total here ▶ 33a	
	b	If your parent (or someone else) can claim you as a dependent, check here ▶ 33b ☐	
	c	If you are married filing separately and your spouse itemizes deductions or you are a dual-status alien, see page 23 and check here ▶ 33c ☐	
	34	Enter the **larger** of your: **Itemized deductions** from Schedule A, line 28, **OR** **Standard deduction** shown below for your filing status. **But if you checked any box on line 33a or b,** go to page 23 to find your standard deduction. If you checked **box 33c,** your standard deduction is zero. • Single—$3,900 • Married filing jointly or Qualifying widow(er)—$6,550 • Head of household—$5,750 • Married filing separately—$3,275	34: 25,476 55
	35	Subtract line 34 from line 32	35: 46,311 45
	36	If line 32 is $86,025 or less, multiply $2,500 by the total number of exemptions claimed on line 6e. If line 32 is over $86,025, see the worksheet on page 23 for the amount to enter	36: 10,000 00
If you want the IRS to figure your tax, see page 35.	37	**Taxable income.** Subtract line 36 from line 35. If line 36 is more than line 35, enter -0-	37: 36,311 45
	38	Tax. Check if from a ☑ Tax Table, b ☐ Tax Rate Schedules, c ☐ Capital Gain Tax Worksheet, or d ☐ Form 8615 (see page 24). Amount from Form(s) 8814 ▶ e	38: 5,449 00
	39	Additional taxes. Check if from a ☐ Form 4970 b ☐ Form 4972	39
	40	Add lines 38 and 39 ▶	40: 5,449 00
Credits (See page 24.)	41	Credit for child and dependent care expenses. Attach Form 2441 — 41: 120	
	42	Credit for the elderly or the disabled. Attach Schedule R — 42	
	43	Foreign tax credit. Attach Form 1116 — 43	
	44	Other credits (see page 25). Check if from a ☐ Form 3800 b ☐ Form 8396 c ☐ Form 8801 d ☐ Form (specify) ____ — 44	
	45	Add lines 41 through 44	45: 120 00
	46	Subtract line 45 from line 40. If line 45 is more than line 40, enter -0- ▶	46: 5,329 00
Other Taxes (See page 25.)	47	Self-employment tax. Attach Schedule SE	47: —
	48	Alternative minimum tax. Attach Form 6251	48: —
	49	Recapture taxes. Check if from a ☐ Form 4255 b ☐ Form 8611 c ☐ Form 8828	49: —
	50	Social security and Medicare tax on tip income not reported to employer. Attach Form 4137	50: —
	51	Tax on qualified retirement plans, including IRAs. If required, attach Form 5329	51: —
	52	Advance earned income credit payments from Form W-2	52: —
	53	Household employment taxes. Attach Schedule H	53
	54	Add lines 46 through 53. This is your **total tax** ▶	54: 5,329 00
Payments Attach Forms W-2, W-2G, and 1099-R on the front.	55	Federal income tax withheld. If any is from Form(s) 1099, check ▶ ☐ — 55: 5,702 00	
	56	1995 estimated tax payments and amount applied from 1994 return — 56	
	57	**Earned income credit.** Attach Schedule EIC if you have a qualifying child. Nontaxable earned income: amount ▶ ____ and type ▶ ____ — 57	
	58	Amount paid with Form 4868 (extension request) — 58	
	59	Excess social security and RRTA tax withheld (see page 32) — 59	
	60	Other payments. Check if from a ☐ Form 2439 b ☐ Form 4136 — 60	
	61	Add lines 55 through 60. These are your **total payments** ▶	61: 5,702 00
Refund or Amount You Owe	62	If line 61 is more than line 54, subtract line 54 from line 61. This is the amount you **OVERPAID**	62: 373 00
	63	Amount of line 62 you want **REFUNDED TO YOU** ▶	63: 373 00
	64	Amount of line 62 you want **APPLIED TO YOUR 1996 ESTIMATED TAX** ▶ 64	
	65	If line 54 is more than line 61, subtract line 61 from line 54. This is the **AMOUNT YOU OWE.** For details on how to pay and use **Form 1040-V,** Payment Voucher, see page 33 ▶	65: —
	66	Estimated tax penalty (see page 33). Also include on line 65 — 66	

Sign Here — Keep a copy of this return for your records.

Under penalties of perjury, I declare that I have examined this return and accompanying schedules and statements, and to the best of my knowledge and belief, they are true, correct, and complete. Declaration of preparer (other than taxpayer) is based on all information of which preparer has any knowledge.

Your signature	Date	Your occupation
Arnold Steele	4/2/96	Chemical Engineer
Spouse's signature. If a joint return, BOTH must sign.	**Date**	**Spouse's occupation**
Sharon Steele	4/2/96	Accountant

Paid Preparer's Use Only

Preparer's signature	Date	Check if self-employed ☐	Preparer's social security no.
Firm's name (or yours if self-employed) and address		EIN	
		ZIP code	

Printed on recycled paper *U.S.GPO:1995-389-060

Figure 5.10 Continued.

TAX COMPUTATION The Steeles' adjusted gross income is reduced first by their net itemized deductions of $25,476.55. Then this subtotal of $46,311.45 is further reduced by the $10,000 of exemptions (four exemptions claimed times $2,500 per exemption) to arrive at their taxable income of $36,311.45. Their tax liability before tax credits is $5,449, which is found in the tax table.

CREDITS AND REFUND The Steeles had one credit in 1995. It is the credit for child and dependent care expenses. The amount of this credit is related to your total qualifying expenses and level of adjusted gross income. The maximum is $2,400 if you have one qualifying dependent, and $4,800 if you have two or more. The Steeles' credit in 1995 was 20 percent of the $600 of qualifying expenses, or $120.

Average tax rate: Total tax liability divided by total income.

Marginal tax rate: Additional tax liability divided by additional income.

At this point, Arnold and Sharon reflect upon their tax situation. Their tax liability is $5,329 out of their pretax total income of $71,788. Therefore, they paid 7.42 percent ($5,329.00/$71,788.00) of their income in 1995 in federal income taxes. This is their **average tax rate,** but a far more useful figure is their **marginal tax rate.** This rate is more or less buried in the tax table, so Arnold and Sharon found it by using Schedule Y to calculate their tax (see Figure 5.8). This schedule clearly highlights their marginal rate, which is 15 percent. The marginal rate, as you should see, is the rate being applied to the bracket in which taxable income falls. If the Steeles' taxable income rose enough to put them into the next higher bracket, their marginal rate would jump to 28 percent. The marginal rates are the ones to consider in making financial decisions concerning future sources of income or deductions, because additional income will be taxed, or additional deductions will save taxes, at the marginal rate. For example, suppose Sharon has considered working additional hours at

Box 5.2 SAVING MONEY
Do Your Own Tax Return

Why do so many Americans not prepare their own tax returns? Completing the 1040EZ usually takes no more time and is no more challenging than completing a credit application. The 1040A is only a bit more involved, and even the so-called long form—the 1040—should be relatively simple for most taxpayers, considering that 60 percent of 1040 users do not itemize deductions. Is it fear of the IRS, unwillingness to undertake an unpleasant task, or simple year-to-year inertia? Some people feel that the signature of a professional preparer on the return lessens their chance of being audited, although there is no evidence to support this belief. Why you use an outsider is unimportant; what matters is that you will pay anywhere from $25 to $2,000 when you go for outside help.

If you have used outsiders in the past, the trick is to break the cycle by deciding to go it alone this year. It is extremely helpful to have a copy of your previous year's return when you begin. In most cases, doing this year's return is no more involved than following last year's return but using this year's numbers. (If your preparer did not give you a copy of last year's return, call and ask for one.) Along with "plugging in" the new numbers, you should read the information booklet mailed to you along with your return. This will alert you to any current-year changes.

Actually, the IRS booklets are easy to read and reasonably clear in indicating the steps to take in preparing a return. They are keyed to the line items on the returns, which makes it easy to start at the beginning and work toward the end. If you have a question and cannot find a suitable answer in the booklet, you can call the IRS assistance line (800–829–1040). *Money* magazine annually tests the correctness of IRS responses and finds the service has improved substantially.

Whether you go it alone or use an outsider, it is important to keep good records along with the documents provided by your employer or financial institutions. These latter items indicate your wages and interest or dividends earned during the year. They also will show any mortgage interest that can be deducted. It's a good idea to put the documents in a large envelope or box as soon as you receive them; also, put your tax returns there when they arrive.

Finally, file your return early. You should have all your needed documents by January 31, so set mid-February as your target. Waiting until April accomplishes nothing and may create a feeling of desperation that you won't be able to finish the return on time by yourself.

Todd and Talbot, and she could earn $1,000 more by doing so. Should she work the additional hours? If she does, the Steeles' taxable income will increase by $1,000. Assuming that everything else remains the same, they will pay $150 more in taxes, and their after-tax income will increase by only $850. Of course, they must decide if the additional $850 is worth the extra time and effort on Sharon's part.

Finally, since the Steeles had $5,702 of taxes withheld from their wages, they overpaid their 1995 tax liability by $373. They could have applied this overpayment to a 1996 estimated tax, but chose a refund instead.

OTHER ASPECTS OF THE FEDERAL INCOME TAX

In addition to understanding how the federal income tax formula is used to determine your tax liability, it is important to be familiar with other aspects of the tax. In the sections below, we will explain capital gains and losses, loss limitation rules, and the role of the Internal Revenue Service (the IRS). Finally, we discuss the issue of seeking outside help in preparing your return.

Capital Gains and Losses

As your income and wealth increase, you can expect to have a growing number of transactions involving the sale or exchange of capital assets. Almost always, an exchange results in either a gain or a loss that may have to be reported in filing your annual return.

Capital gain or loss: Gain or loss resulting from the sale of a capital asset.
Capital assets: Assets held for personal pleasure or investment.

WHAT IS A CAPITAL GAIN OR LOSS? A **capital gain or loss** results whenever you sell a capital asset for more or less than what you paid for it (or your "basis" in the asset if you received it as a gift). The next logical question is: What are **capital assets?** For the most part, everything you own and use for personal purposes, pleasure, or investment is a capital asset. Examples are stocks, bonds, and other securities; your house, car, and household goods; or your hobbies, such as stamp and coin collections, and fishing gear.

TAX TREATMENT OF CAPITAL GAINS AND LOSSES Important provisions apply to the tax treatment of capital gains and losses. The maximum tax rate on capital gains is 28 percent, as opposed to 39.6 percent on ordinary income. Any gain on the sale of property held for personal use—your car, for example—must be reported and is taxed in full. Any losses on the sale of such assets, however, cannot be deducted against other income. Of course, you seldom sell personal property at a gain, but it is possible.

Investment assets are treated similarly to personal-use assets, but with one distinction: You can deduct up to $3,000 of any losses (all gains are reported in full). Moreover, if losses in a year exceed $3,000, the unused portion can be carried forward to future years and taken as deductions. However, the maximum allowable deduction in any year is $3,000. This includes carry-forward amounts and current-year losses.

SELLING YOUR HOME Your home is a personal property, so it is also subject to capital gain taxation. However, special provisions have been written into the law to soften the tax's impact. To begin with, you can defer any gain from selling your existing home by buying (or having built) another one within 24 months from the time you sold the first one. Second, you are allowed a one-time exclusion of \$125,000 (\$62,500 if you are married and filing an individual return) if you are 55 or older at the time of sale (and if you meet other tests). For example, suppose Alice Dean buys a home in 1966 for \$20,000; she then sells it in 1986 for \$90,000 and buys another three months later for \$95,000. In 1995, when she is 60 years old, she sells this home for \$155,000 and retires to Florida. Alice has a \$70,000 gain in 1986, but she doesn't pay tax on this gain in 1986 because she purchased another home at a higher price within 24 months. In 1995 she realizes a \$60,000 gain on the sale of the second home, which, combined with the deferred gain of \$70,000, gives her a \$130,000 total gain. Her one-time exclusion of \$125,000 reduces the taxable gain to \$5,000.

It is obvious that a home is a tax-advantaged investment. This feature, coupled with the fact that home prices have increased considerably over the years, has made home ownership a very attractive investment. This aspect is explained more fully in Chapter 15.

Loss Limitation Rules

Many investment and business activities produce income or losses other than capital gains and losses. The tax law also has special provisions dealing with their treatment for tax purposes.

Earned income: Employment income or income earned in the direct operation of a business.
Portfolio income: Income earned on intangible investments (stocks, bonds, savings accounts).
Passive income: Income from a business in which the taxpayer does not materially participate.

EARNED, PORTFOLIO, AND PASSIVE INCOME First, there are important distinctions depending on the source of your income. **Earned income** refers to income received through employment or in the direct operation of a business. Common forms of this income are wages, salaries, bonuses, commissions, and business profits. **Portfolio income** describes income earned on investment assets such as stocks, bonds, and deposits at financial institutions. Dividends and interest are common forms of this income. **Passive income** (or loss) is any income that results from passive activities. These activities include the conduct of any trade or business in which the taxpayer does not materially participate, including the rental of tangible property (such as real estate). It is your responsibility to provide evidence of active participation; without such proof, the IRS will assume you are inactive.

The distinctions are critical because you cannot use any passive losses to offset earned or portfolio income. This was a common practice before the 1986 Tax Reform Act. Investors with high tax rates often invested in so-called tax shelters to earn substantial losses that were used to offset other income. Although such shelters are still available under limited conditions in the oil and gas industry, they have been eliminated everywhere else.

MAXIMUM ALLOWABLE LOSS Even if you are active in managing your business, you cannot offset more than \$25,000 of losses against earned or portfolio income. Moreover, the maximum deduction is gradually eliminated—\$0.50 for each \$1.00—as income exceeds \$100,000, being fully exhausted at \$150,000. To illustrate: Suppose you earn \$120,000 in wages and interest. You also run a business that shows a \$40,000 loss. Your loss offset is \$15,000, determined as follows: \$25,000 (maximum) less 0.5 × \$20,000 (amount over \$100,000) = \$25,000 less \$10,000 = \$15,000. Taxable income is then \$105,000 (\$120,000 less \$15,000). Again, keep in mind that if you were an inactive owner, there would be no loss offset.

The Role of the Internal Revenue Service

Internal Revenue Service (IRS): Federal agency assigned the task of administering the federal income tax.

The **Internal Revenue Service (IRS)** a division of the Treasury Department, is the federal agency assigned the task of administering the federal income tax. Two of its most important functions are providing taxpayer assistance and auditing tax returns. In addition to understanding these functions, you should be aware of the filing deadline and extensions, and the statute of limitations as it applies to the federal income tax.

TAXPAYER ASSISTANCE The IRS attempts to make filing your return as easy as possible. (Don't blame the IRS if the return itself is difficult to complete; blame Congress, because the tax law is its responsibility.) If you have filed a return in the past, you are automatically sent a tax form for the current year. If you have never filed a return, or if you need to file one different from the previous year, you can find forms at practically every public library and many banks or savings and loans. Forms and instructions are also available from the IRS home page on the Internet and on several electronic information servers (see Helpful Contacts and Internet Addresses). The IRS may have an office in your town, which you can call or visit for forms or taxpayer assistance. If an office is not convenient, you can call 1–800–829–1040 for assistance. In addition to Form 1040 (illustrated with the Steeles' example), there are two simpler forms—1040A and 1040EZ—that many taxpayers can use.

It is often helpful to read IRS publications to handle a tax item properly. The instruction booklet that accompanies your tax return contains a list of IRS publications and forms and shows where to write in your state to get them. We strongly recommend Publication 17, *Your Federal Income Tax,* as a handy and reliable general reference on many tax matters. All IRS publications are free, so don't hesitate to ask for any that you might need. They can be ordered at no charge by calling the IRS toll-free at 1–800–829–3676. A descriptive list of publications can be found in the IRS's *Guide to Free Tax Services*. The IRS also operates Tele Tax, an automated service providing recorded tax information on 140 topics. Through this system you can also access the current status of an expected refund.

If you file Form 1040EZ or Form 1040A, the IRS will figure the tax for you, if you wish. You must provide all the relevant information, however. The IRS will also figure your tax on Form 1040 if you meet certain tests. These are too involved to discuss here, but if you file a 1040 you can read the instructions guide that comes with it to see if you meet these tests. Actually, once you have gathered all the necessary information, filing the return involves very little extra work. As a tip, we suggest you do it in pencil (assuming you'll make a mistake or two) and then make photocopies to send the IRS.

IRS AUDITS The strength of our tax system rests upon the integrity of millions of taxpayers to file an honest and reasonably correct return. An important function—the IRS audit—is to ensure that such filing takes place. Actually, the IRS has three basic audit approaches: the field audit—where an IRS agent visits your premises to examine your return; the office audit—where you visit an IRS center; and the self-audit—where the IRS essentially questions some aspect of your return and asks you to examine the item again to determine its appropriateness.

An audit may involve questioning just one item on your return, or the whole return might be audited, which means you must have documentary support for each line item. Returns selected for audit are determined by a formula (known only to the IRS) and random procedures. But, as Figure 5.11 shows, your odds of being audited increase substantially with your income and if you are self-employed.

It is illegal to file a fraudulent return, or not to file a return at all, and stiff penalties can be assessed in each case. A mistake or an alternative interpretation of the law may not lead to a penalty, but you will pay interest on any deficiency. The interest rate changes periodically, depending on market rates of interest. For assessments of additional taxes, the interest period begins on the due date of the return—not from the time the deficiency is found.

Automatic extension: An extension of time for filing an income tax return, given automatically by the IRS.

FILING DEADLINE AND EXTENSIONS Your tax return must be filed before April 16. If you can't meet that deadline, you can get an **automatic extension** for four months. However, before April 15 you must file Form 4868 asking for the extension. Remember, though, an automatic filing extension does not extend the time you have to pay your tax. You must estimate your tax for the year and pay any tax due along with Form 4868. There is a penalty for late payment unless you have reasonable cause for not paying your tax when due. You can request extensions beyond the automatic four-month extension, but you must meet certain tests before the IRS will grant them.

ELECTRONIC FILING As an alternative to mailing in your tax return, you can have it electronically filed. If you would otherwise file Form 1040EZ, you can do this yourself by using a touch tone telephone and the IRS's Telefile system. The IRS plans to mail informational packages to those who may be eligible. To use the system, you dial an IRS toll-free number and punch in responses to a computer automated series of questions. The program immediately tells you if you owe taxes, how much you owe, or how much you overpaid. The personal ID contained in the informational package serves as your signature.

If you file anything more complicated than a 1040EZ, you will have to use an electronic filing service. Fees can range from $5 to $50. To do this, take your return and W-2 forms to a qualified tax preparer and sign Form 8453, which authorizes

Figure 5.11
Chances of an audit.

SOURCE: IRS data for 1992 examinations, U.S. Bureau of the Census, *Statistical Abstract of the United States, 1995,* Table 531.

	Percent of Returns Examined by			
Adjusted Gross Income	Revenue Agents (field audit)	Service Centers (office audit)	Tax Auditors (self-audit)	Total %
1040A income under $25,000	0.03	0.31	0.36	0.69
Non-1040A, income under $25,000	0.09	0.11	0.45	0.64
$25,000–$49,999	0.09	0.11	0.39	0.59
$50,000–$99,999	0.20	0.21	0.59	1.01
$100,000 and over	1.48	1.99	1.44	4.92
Self-employed income: gross receipts				
Under $25,000	0.45	0.07	0.97	1.49
$25,000–$99,999	0.87	0.18	0.94	1.99
$100,000 and over	2.64	0.59	0.73	3.95
All returns	0.18	0.26	0.47	0.91

transmission of the tax data. You may also use one of the commercial on-line services, such as CompuServe or America Online. These may be set up to accept data directly from a tax preparation software package on your home computer.

You are not required to use the filing service's tax preparer's assistance in preparing your return; you can complete the return yourself. By electronically filing, you typically receive your return within two to three weeks, instead of the usual five to six weeks. If you can't wait that long, a number of preparers will make you a **refund anticipation loan** of $300 to $3,000. In this case, you receive a direct deposit following the acknowledgment by the IRS that you have filed a valid return. Naturally, you should determine if the fees associated with electronic filing and a refund anticipation loan are worth the benefit. Unless you need the refund desperately, determine the equivalent annual interest on the latter item. For most individuals, this will be an unreasonably high rate. Consequently, it has not proven popular among middle- and upper-income tax filers.

Refund anticipation loan: A loan provided by a tax preparation service based on a taxpayer's refund.

Not exactly electronic filing, but close to it, is printing out a 1040PC on your computer. It is a printed form provided by most tax software preparation packages. The printout is more compact than Form 1040 and can be electronically scanned by the IRS computers. It still must be mailed in like the traditional 1040; however, the computer printout saves you the time and trouble of transferring data to paper by hand.

Statute of limitations: A period of three years given the IRS to impose additional taxes on a filed return.

THE STATUTE OF LIMITATIONS The **statute of limitations,** as it generally applies to the federal income tax law, gives the IRS three years from the time a return is filed to impose additional tax liabilities. This fact suggests that tax records should be kept at least this long. But a special six-year limitation applies if you omit a gross income item that is greater than 25 percent of reported total gross income. Moreover, the statute of limitations does not apply if a return is never filed or if a fraudulent return is filed.

Also, be forewarned that if you overpaid taxes in a given year, you must file a claim for a refund within three years from the date the return was filed or two years from the date the tax was paid, whichever is later. Failure to file within these periods usually leads to loss of the refund.

Getting Outside Help

Preparing returns has become a very big business, and you are probably familiar with H & R Block, the largest tax preparation service in the United States. Should you use an outside firm? The answer to that question depends upon several factors. If you have a rather complex tax question that cannot be answered by referring to Publication 17 or a tax reference manual at the public library, and if the item is large enough to matter, then an expert's opinion is needed. Second, you may not care to spend the time doing your return. There are two broad types of preparers: the tax service companies such as H & R Block and professionals such as CPAs and attorneys.

TAX SERVICE COMPANIES Many tax service companies open their offices in January and close them in May. Others remain open all year in some of their locations. Fees for their services vary, but a Form 1040 with several supporting schedules will usually cost between $50 and $100. The short forms cost less, but there are additional charges for state and local income tax returns. While most of these companies do a good job in filing your return, you should know that most of their work consists of simply entering the data you give them in appropriate places on the return. While they claim their staff is instructed to ask the right questions to save you taxes, you shouldn't count on it.

After you finish this chapter, if you get Publication 17 and also keep reasonably alert to newspaper and magazine articles on how to reduce your taxes, you will have a good chance of doing a better job on your return than many of these preparers will. Actually, you're more likely to save taxes by planning throughout the year rather than finding clever loopholes at year's end. You're not likely to get effective tax planning from these companies for the modest fees involved. And if you want such planning, you must either inform yourself or turn to the experts.

CPAs AND ATTORNEYS CPAs and attorneys with specialized training in federal income taxation are the tax experts. If you are fortunate to have a high income, or if you are involved in activities with many income tax implications (running a business, for example), you probably need a professional. As just mentioned, you may want his or her services to guide you throughout the year. You most likely want assistance not only in preparing the return but also in setting up trusts or gifts, or advising you about the income tax implications of various investments, including self-employed retirement plans (if they are applicable). Fees for these services are very high: Count on \$75 to \$150 an hour, or an annual retainer of \$500 as a minimum.

FINANCIAL PLANNERS Many financial planners do not specialize in income tax advice, although they may have contact with people who do. Also, a number of business firms are now engaging financial planners to advise their employees on financial planning. Their services are offered as a fringe benefit to employees. You might ask if this service is available at your company and, of course, take advantage of it if it is. The financial planner may not do tax returns, but he or she should be able to help with tax planning.

TAX PUBLICATIONS AND SOFTWARE If you decide to prepare your own tax return, consider buying books that offer tax advice. The oldest, and still one of the best, is J. K. Lasser's *Your Income Tax* (around \$15; published annually by Macmillan Publishing Co.). However, there are several other excellent guides at modest prices.

Using computer software to prepare your return can save you considerable time. A good program will lead you through the return by providing information on likely deductions and signaling probable omissions. Most of the major programs sell for less than \$50, a modest cost for the added convenience. When selecting software, be sure to check out the following features:

- The ability to report and print a Form 1040PC that can be mailed to the IRS.
- The ability to complete both federal and state tax returns. (Most software packages charge an extra price for a state module.)
- The capability of importing data from your existing word-processing or spreadsheet programs into the tax software. Some tax packages accept data directly from the popular budget management programs.
- Telephone support providing information on both software and tax questions.
- The cost of an annual upgrade.

Special Considerations for Students

The IRS publishes several specialized information bulletins for students. These include: *Student's Guide to Federal Income Tax,* Pub. 4; *Scholarships and Fellowships,* Pub. 520; and *Educational Expenses,* Pub. 508.

If you are under 24 and a full-time student, you may be claimed as a dependent on your parents' return. This is typically advantageous, because they are likely to be in a higher marginal tax bracket. Being listed as a dependent on your parents' tax form does not necessarily relieve you of the responsibility of also filing a return. In general, you must file a federal income tax return if you had earned income of more than $3,800 (in 1994) or if you had combined interest income and earned income that totaled more than $600.

Scholarships and fellowships may or may not be included in taxable income. If you are in a degree program and those awards cover purely educational expenses such as tuition, fees, books, supplies, and equipment then they are most likely tax exempt. However, if part of these payments are meant to cover your noneducational living expenses such as room and board then that part is taxable. One exception is an ROTC subsistence allowance paid to students participating in advanced training.

A *qualified tuition reduction* is tax free. This is a reduction in tuition provided an employee, or the wife and child of an employee, by the educational institution. This exemption also applies to graduate students who perform research or teaching activities. This service must, however, be for education furnished by that institution and does not represent payment for services.

If you are working your way through school, *qualifying educational expenses* that meet certain restrictive requirements are deductible. The education must be required by your employer or serve to maintain or improve your skills in your present work. Moreover, it must be related to your present work. It doesn't qualify if it is needed to meet minimum education requirements for your present job or its purpose is to prepare you for a new trade or business. The deduction reduces your taxable income only if you itemize and your total job-related deductions exceed 2 percent of your adjusted gross income.

Some employers pay for part-time schooling under a *qualified educational assistance plan*. Either a portion or all of these payments may be tax exempt. Your employer can tell you if the plan is qualified. If you do receive tax-exempt payments, then you must reduce your *qualifying educational expenses* by this amount. You cannot receive both a reimbursement and a tax deduction for the identical expense.

PLANNING TO REDUCE YOUR INCOME TAXES

Effective tax planning is an ongoing process. Among other things, it requires selecting investments carefully, holding them for a sufficient length of time, and then selling them at the most opportune time for tax purposes. It also means that you must use provisions of the income tax law that are specifically designed to lower your tax liability. Tax planning attempts to either avoid taxes altogether or defer them to a later time. It works within the tax law, not outside of it as is the case with tax evasion. Following are some of the more common and useful tax-planning techniques.

Invest Where You Receive Tax-Advantaged Income

The tax law favors some forms of income over others. You can reduce your taxes by investing first in those favored investments, which are discussed below.

Municipal bonds: Bonds paying interest that are exempt from federal income tax.

BUY MUNICIPAL BONDS All interest on **municipal bonds** is tax exempt. These bonds are explained in more detail in Chapter 12, but you should see at this point that the after-tax yield on a municipal bond is the same as its pretax yield.

BUY A HOME We have already explained the income tax treatment of your personal residence. In effect, you can enjoy a $125,000 tax-free, long-term capital gain. It's hard to beat that anywhere. Also, most mortgage interest is deductible as an itemized expense. The investment quality of a personal residence is explained in depth in Chapter 15.

BE AN ACTIVE INVESTOR IN REAL ESTATE Despite the disadvantage of limited deductibility of business losses, actively managing your own business, such as real estate, offers certain tax advantages to taxpayers with incomes under $150,000. As discussed, you can deduct up to $25,000 if your income is under $100,000. The appeal of real estate rests in the fact that a large portion of many losses is represented by a noncash charge called depreciation. This means that even though the property shows a loss for tax purposes, you might still have a decent cash return. The Steeles were considering a real estate investment, and their experiences are described in Chapter 13. If you have further interest in the topic, you should review the details in that chapter.

Take Capital Losses Quickly

If you have a capital loss, it is usually to your advantage to take it before a tax year ends. Even if you believe the security's price might rebound and eliminate the loss, you should consider selling the security you own and replacing it with a similar security. For example, suppose you buy Exxon common stock, and after your purchase its price falls to half of what it was. You believe the international oil companies will do well in the future, but the year is about to end. Consider selling Exxon and buying Mobil, another international oil. You will then be able to deduct all the loss in Exxon (up to $3,000), and the tax savings will enable you to buy that many additional shares of Mobil. Why not just sell Exxon and buy it right back? You can't; that's called a *wash sale.* You must wait at least 30 days, which also may not be a bad idea if you think Exxon is a far better stock than Mobil over the long run. This strategy works well for stocks, but it works even better with bonds since their characteristics are more similar from one bond to another.

Split Your Income

Dividing income among family members so that it is taxed at a collectively lower marginal rate is a favorite tax-avoidance technique. If you are in a 28 percent tax bracket and your child is in a 15 percent tax bracket, then the family will save 13 cents on each dollar of income earned by the child rather than the parent. This approach is used often when people wish to establish educational funds for their children. It can also be used to create retirement income for aging parents, who may also have high medical expenses. The two most frequently used techniques are making outright gifts and setting up trusts.

GIFTS A husband and wife can give someone as much as $20,000 a year without incurring any gift tax; and since it is a gift, it is not income to the recipient. Regardless of the amount given, any future earnings on the invested funds become income of the recipient. Suppose you are interested in providing funds for your child's education. It's a simple matter to set up a **custodial account** (at a bank or other financial institution) and make a gift each year, the amount depending on how much you wish to accumulate.

Custodial account: An account set up by parents in their children's names.

For minors under 14 years of age, the first $500 of income from gifted assets (or any assets) is tax free by virtue of a modified standard deduction. The next $600 of income is taxed at the minor's rate, which is usually 15 percent; then, all amounts over $1,200 are taxed at the parents' rate. Even though only $1,200 of income receives favorable tax treatment, shifting income still can result in substantial tax savings. Savings are greatest if a gifting arrangement is started early—ideally, when a child is born. Also, for minors 14 years of age or older, all income is taxed at their

Box 5.3

PERSONAL FINANCE NEWS

Late Edition

Get Ready for the Self-Audit

The letter from the IRS is reasonably friendly: Some aspect of your return doesn't seem quite right and you now have the chance to audit the return, assessing yourself for any unpaid taxes, penalties, and interest. Does the IRS really expect you to respond something like this: "You were right. I caught myself for overstating travel and entertainment expenses. I reported a $2,000 deduction but half of that actually was for entertaining my family—not business clients." Yes, in a way that is exactly what the IRS expects. Or at least it hopes that its friendly letter will scare you enough to come clean.

The self-audit is an attempt by the IRS to use its resources more efficiently since Congress has limited its budget allocations. The program is currently being evaluated for effectiveness, and if it passes muster it will likely be continued. At best, the IRS now can audit only around 1 percent of all returns; but the self-audit could be administered to a far greater number.

What characteristics of your return might invite the self-audit? While the IRS does not disclose its formula for spotting potential underreporters, the following are generally recognized as "red flags":

- Itemized deductions in excess of average amounts deducted
- Operation of a business that typically has cash transactions—a restaurant, for example
- Operation of a business that continuously shows losses or very meager profits in relation to sales
- Claiming a business loss on an activity that appears more like a hobby. Even a hobby with profit might be a flag, since it can be used to write off expenses that have nothing to do with the hobby. For example, you restore old cars and sell them, so you write off a family vacation to Disney World because you "consult" with an expert in Orlando on how to repair a 1965 Mustang
- Claiming a dependent who does not live with you or a dependent who is not your child
- Showing less dividend or interest earned on your return than the amount shown on 1099 returns provided by financial institutions (this is almost sure to be questioned)
- Failing to report an IRA distribution (another sure questioning)
- Reporting a large amount of travel and entertainment expenses

If your return features one or more of the above items, you have nothing to fear if you reported correctly on the return and if you have good documentation supporting the item. If you don't, and if your self-audit seems uninspiring to the IRS, they may send an agent to show you how an audit should be conducted—on your return.

rates, and not the parents'; thus, it makes sense to increase gift amounts for these individuals.

Be careful when you set up a custodial account to name as legal custodian someone who will not make contributions to the account: a friend or relative, for example. Also, keep in mind that once you make gifts to your children, they become the children's property. In effect, you lose control of the money and cannot legally get it back. Finally, anyone who sells securities that have appreciated in value to finance their children's college costs is simply throwing money down the drain. At the very least, they should give the securities to the children, who can then sell them.

TRUSTS A trust is a legal arrangement that allows assets to be managed by a trustee for the benefit of individuals called beneficiaries. Trusts are more expensive to establish than a gifting program, but they can be structured in many ways, making it wise to seek legal advice in establishing one. Trusts are often used to provide income for someone who is aged or infirm and in need of medical or other care. Funds provided the beneficiary are derived from income earned on trust assets, which is taxed at a lower rate than the one applying to the trust creator. For example, if your marginal rate is 28 percent and the beneficiary's rate is 15 percent, 13 percent savings can be realized on income earned.

Stagger Income and Expenses

If you can control the timing of expenses and income, you may be able to reduce taxes. For example, you may have a very large doctor or hospital bill that can be paid in either 1995 or 1996. But you might find that even by paying the bill in 1995, you don't have enough other itemized expenses to exceed the standard deduction. If you pay the bill in 1995 anyway, you may lose benefit of the deduction in 1996. By delaying payment, you hold the expense until 1996, when you may be able to itemize.

Even if you itemize in both years, it could be advantageous to stagger as many itemized expenses as you can into one of the two years. Again, this difference results from the income tax's progressive rate structure: A large total in one year could put you in a lower tax bracket that year, whereas taking an approximately even amount each year might leave you in the same bracket each year. As the months of November and December get closer, you should review your tax situation and see if expenses can be staggered profitably. Of course, staggering income—if that's possible—should also be considered.

Defer Income to Later Years

Deferring income to be taxed in later years is different from avoiding taxes altogether. However, deferring can be as attractive as avoidance, for several reasons. First, deferred income is free to accumulate, and it will grow to a substantially larger sum than income that is taxed each year. Second, your marginal tax rate when you recognize the income (usually during retirement) might be lower than your current marginal rate. Some commonly used income-deferring investments are IRAs and Keogh and 401(k) plans; tax-deferred annuities; and U.S. Treasury Series EE bonds. In addition to these formal plans, any investment that defers your return to the future offers tax advantages. For example, a growth stock typically pays little or no current dividends that would be taxable. Rather, you can enjoy your total return as a capital gain when you sell the stock in the future. True, you might pay the same amount of tax as you would with, say, a savings account; but with the growth stock, taxes are deferred until the stock is sold. The "saved" taxes can be invested and earn a return during the entire investment period.

IRAs, KEOGHS, AND 401(K) PLANS We explained IRAs and Keoghs earlier in this chapter. A 401(k) is an option retirement plan many employers make available to their employees. It also may be better than an IRA, depending upon the options offered. We will discuss each of these in far greater depth in Chapter 17. Certainly one of the major advantages of these plans is the deduction against current income of amounts invested.

With IRAs, you should be aware you can always take your money out of an IRA before retirement. If you do, though, you must pay a 10 percent penalty on amounts withdrawn, and you also must include the withdrawals in determining taxable income in the withdrawal year. (Remember: You excluded the IRA investment in the year you made it.) Even with the penalty, though, it may be to your advantage to use the IRA if your funds can remain invested for a sufficient period of time. But what period of time is sufficient? This is a rather difficult question to answer, so we'll defer the response to Chapter 17.

Tax-deferred annuity: An investment, usually sold by insurance companies, that allows tax deferral on current interest earned.

TAX-DEFERRED ANNUITIES A **tax-deferred annuity** is an investment that is usually written by an insurance company. It also defers income to later years, but in contrast to IRAs, Keoghs, and 401(k)s, you cannot take a deduction on your current return for amounts invested, which makes them less attractive. Moreover, the financial collapse of Baldwin United—one of the leaders in writing tax-deferred annuities—in 1983 created doubts in the minds of many investors about their safety. However, the 1986 Tax Reform Act rekindled interest in annuities because so many other tax shelters were eliminated.

U.S. TREASURY SERIES EE BONDS Series EE bonds give you the option of either reporting income as it accrues on the bond each year or reporting it when you cash the bond. The main advantage of this bond is its flexibility. You choose when to cash it and pay the tax, and choosing a year when your marginal tax rate is low can save taxes. These bonds are explained further in Chapter 12.

Income Tax Planning for the Steeles

Arnold and Sharon Steele have done virtually no income tax planning. They hope to help John and Nancy with college costs, and they should already be considering making gifts or using trusts for that purpose, even though funds won't be needed for about eight more years. The Steeles are interested in purchasing a vacation condominium, which they hope to rent for most of the year, and they are considering buying a rental property. Each of these investments has certain tax-sheltering aspects that must be reviewed in depth; we'll look at them in Chapter 13, giving detailed attention to the rental property.

The Steeles also intend to accumulate about $100,000 for a retirement nest egg. This means they should begin taking advantage of tax deferrals as soon as possible. While most of their savings through 2006 will be earmarked for the vacation condo and the children's education, they will still have some savings that can be invested for retirement. To date, the Steeles have invested in a mutual fund, Fidelity, and have bought $16,000 of InChemCo common stock through the company's share-purchase plan. They might consider selling the Fidelity shares and some of the InChemCo shares and reinvest the funds in tax-deferred annuities, although advantages from this switch seem minimal. The Steeles have not clearly identified the purposes for buying the InChemCo and Fidelity shares—something they really should do—but if retirement is one of those purposes, they need to examine the expected future accumulations with the shares versus accumulations with tax-deferred annuities.

OTHER IMPORTANT TAXES

Although the federal income tax is the most important tax to most of us, others should also be understood. For example, people in low- or middle-income brackets might pay more in Social Security taxes than in personal income taxes; if you are very wealthy, you will pay substantial estate and inheritance taxes when you die or gift taxes if you try to give the estate away before you die. The growing fiscal needs of state and local governments have brought forth an array of income, sales, and property taxes at these levels.

Social Security Taxes

Most of us are familiar with the Social Security system. We are counting on it as an important part of our retirement income or for survivor benefits to our families if something happens to us. But, as you probably also know, it has come under financial stress because benefits seem to be outpacing revenues. As a result, Social Security taxes have escalated rapidly and will continue to do so in the future.

FICA taxes: Taxes collected for Social Security purposes.

The taxes withheld from your wages for Social Security are called **FICA taxes;** FICA means Federal Insurance Contributions Act. FICA taxes consist of two components, one for old age (OASI) and disability insurance (DI) and the other for health insurance (HI). There is an adjustable annual limit on the taxable base for each of these components. In 1995 wages up to $61,200 were taxed at 6.2 percent to pay for OASI and DI, and wages up to $135,000 were taxed at 1.45 percent to pay for HI.

Your FICA taxes depend on the tax rate and the base amount of your wages subject to the tax. Each of these has changed over time. It is important to realize that you might overpay FICA taxes. This could happen if you change employers during the year or if you work for two or more employers. You can claim excess payments as a credit against your federal income tax liability at the time you prepare your return. By all means, check the W-2 forms your employer gives you in January to make sure you have not overpaid. However, both spouses must pay the full amount of the tax, so you cannot have an overpayment simply because the sum of the two exceeds the maximum.

Also, you should be aware that your employer must pay FICA tax equal to the amount withheld from your wage. This is an expensive payroll cost for employers. Self-employed individuals must also pay FICA tax, and their rates have been extremely high in recent years: 15.3 percent in 1995.

Estate and Gift Taxes

Federal estate tax: A tax levied on a decedent's estate.

The **federal estate tax** is levied on the value of a decedent's estate at the time of death. The tax follows a fairly complicated formula that is explained in greater detail in Chapter 18. Provisions of the federal estate tax have been liberalized in recent years, and in 1996 your estate must have exceeded $600,000 before any tax would have been levied.

Inheritance taxes: State taxes levied on the heirs to an estate.

Federal gift tax: Excise tax levied on the transfer of property; supplements the federal estate tax.

In addition to the federal estate tax, each state has its own inheritance and estate tax. **Inheritance taxes** are levied somewhat differently than estate taxes in that heirs are classified according to their relationship to the decedent. The tax depends on this classification, with more distant relationships leading to greater taxes.

The **federal gift tax** is an excise tax charged on the transfer of property. A gift tax is necessary to supplement an estate tax, otherwise you would be able to transfer wealth during your lifetime and so avoid the estate tax. Like the federal estate tax, the federal gift tax follows a specific formula, but it does permit a "modest" gift each year of $10,000 per donee ($20,000 for husband and wife donors). For most families the "modest" gift provision allows a substantial transfer of their wealth each year.

State and Local Taxes

The maze of state and local taxes in most states not only takes a fairly large amount from your bank account but also creates considerable confusion as to what is being taxed and for how much. Very few people thoroughly understand all these taxes; in fact, some of the taxes are buried in the prices of items that we buy. There is little that can be done about the situation except to make the best of it. Table 5.1 gives an indication of how tax burdens vary among different cities. Of course, governments that collect high taxes may also provide high levels of services. In this sense, then, high taxes aren't necessarily bad.

INCOME TAXES All the states except Florida, Alaska, Nevada, South Dakota, Texas, Washington, and Wyoming levy income taxes. These are usually withheld from your wages, but you must file an annual return, similar to the federal return, to calculate your tax liability and to determine any over- or underpayment. The tax bases and rates vary among the states, and they can be quite high. A New York

TABLE 5.1 • ESTIMATED STATE AND LOCAL TAXES PAID BY A FAMILY OF FOUR IN SELECTED CITIES: 1992

	Total Taxes Paid by Gross Family Income Level			
City	$25,000	$50,000	$75,000	$100,000
Atlanta	2,838	5,593	9,107	12,019
Baltimore	4,068	8,246	12,791	16,659
Chicago	2,954	5,938	9,326	12,084
Detroit	4,723	9,680	14,773	19,290
Milwaukee	3,274	7,288	11,425	15,071
New York	2,603	6,579	11,199	15,247
Philadelphia	3,956	7,610	11,361	14,755
Portland	2,428	5,369	8,623	11,542
Salt Lake City	2,038	4,682	7,564	10,020
Washington, DC	2,278	5,041	8,416	11,556
Median	1,970	4,306	7,253	9,921

SOURCE: U.S. Bureau of the Census, *Statistical Abstract of the United States, 1994,* Table 480.

City resident whose income is in the highest bracket will pay over 20 percent in combined state and city income tax.

Many local governments—mostly cities and villages—impose income taxes. While these are often called payroll taxes, they are imposed on all forms of income. These also require filing an annual return if you have taxable income not subject to withholding. It is not uncommon for someone in Ohio or Pennsylvania (such as a sales representative) to file more than a dozen returns if he or she earned income in 12 different communities. To make matters more confusing, there is always the question of whether you pay tax to the city where the income was earned or the city in which you live, assuming they are different. In general, the tax follows the place of employment unless the city of residence imposes a higher tax rate; then you usually pay the difference between the two rates to the city of residence. Of course, you must file a tax return with that city.

PROPERTY TAXES Property taxes are still the mainstay of local governments, particularly school districts. All states have taxes on real property (houses and buildings), and most also tax personal property (equipment, furniture, fixtures, and the like) of businesses; some also tax household personal property. Many impose taxes on intangible property, such as stocks and bonds. The property tax rate that you pay depends very much upon the community where the property is located. Rates can vary widely even within a county or other geographic area. One city's rate might be $60 per $1,000 valuation, while a neighboring city might charge only $30 per $1,000. And comparisons between states show even more dramatic differences: You'll pay about $50 per $1,000 in Boston and $8.00 per $1,000 in Phoenix.

SALES TAXES Forty-five states and the District of Columbia have sales taxes. Some tax all consumption items—services as well as commodities—and others omit services. Some tax necessities, such as food; others do not. The sales tax rates vary among states, and even within states when local governments enact their own taxes to "piggyback" the state tax.

SUMMARY

The federal income tax is the largest source of revenue for the federal government. As applied to individuals, it follows a specific formula that beings with gross income items and ends with additional taxes due the IRS or with a refund for overpayments. A gross income item is any compensation you receive for the use of your labor or capital. From the total of gross income items, you may make certain adjustments; the balance is called adjusted gross income. Taxable income is calculated by subtracting personal deductions—by either itemizing or using the standard amounts—and exemption allowances from adjusted gross income. Your tax liability is then determined by finding the tax associated with your taxable income and subtracting from it any allowable tax credits. Your tax liability is then compared with the amount of taxes withheld from your wages and estimated taxes paid during the year to determine if you overpaid or underpaid during the year.

Other aspects of the federal income tax should also be understood. Only $3,000 of capital losses can be deducted each year. Also, other loss limitation rules apply to investments and business interests. The Internal Revenue Service (the IRS) is the federal agency responsible for administering the income tax. In so doing, it provides taxpayer assistance and periodic audits of returns. You can get outside help in preparing your return from either the tax service companies, such as H & R Block, or CPAs and attorneys, and effective planning can reduce your income taxes.

The federal income tax is not the only important tax you must pay. Social Security (FICA) taxes are growing rapidly, and many people pay more in these taxes than they do in federal income taxes. Estate and gift taxes are levied by both the federal and state governments. State and local governments also have many other taxes, such as income taxes, property taxes, and sales taxes. The amounts collected by states and local areas vary considerably throughout the United States.

KEY TERMS

adjusted gross income (p. 128)

alimony payments (p. 130)

automatic extension (p. 142)

average tax rate (p. 138)

capital assets (p. 139)

capital gain or loss (p. 139)

custodial account (p. 147)

earned income (p. 140)

federal estate tax (p. 150)

federal gift tax (p. 151)

FICA taxes (p. 150)

gross income items (p. 127)

inheritance taxes (p. 151)

Internal Revenue Service (IRS) (p. 141)

IRAs and Keogh plans (p. 129)

itemized deductions (p. 132)

marginal tax rate (p. 138)

municipal bonds (p. 146)

nontaxable exclusions (p. 127)

passive income (p. 140)

personal and dependency exemptions (p. 130)

portfolio income (p. 140)

refund anticipation loan (p. 143)

standard deduction (p. 131)

statute of limitations (p. 143)

taxable income (p. 130)

tax credit (p. 133)

tax-deferred annuity (p. 149)

W-2 form (p. 135)

W-4 form (p. 135)

PROBLEMS AND REVIEW QUESTIONS

1. Arrange the following items in their appropriate sequence according to the federal income tax formula:
   (*a*) adjusted gross income,
   (*b*) adjustments to income,
   (*c*) itemized deductions,
   (*d*) tax credits,
   (*e*) gross income items,
   (*f*) nontaxable exclusions,
   (*g*) federal income taxes withheld,
   (*h*) exemptions.
2. What is the amount allowed for each exemption? Is the exemption amount indexed? Explain what this means.
3. Suppose you and your spouse work and have wages of $16,000 and $5,000, respectively. Calculate the maximum deduction for IRAs. Calculate it if your income was $21,000 and your spouse's was zero.
4. Chrissy, Jack, and Janet share an apartment. Jack and Janet have grown fond of each other and are thinking of marrying. Chrissy has told them, however, that if they do, their income taxes will increase. Jack and Janet don't see how that's possible. Assume each made $37,000 and took the standard deduction in 1995. Using the tax schedules given in this chapter, determine whether Chrissy is right.
5. John is 66 years old and blind. He lives with his wife Clara, who is also 66 but has good vision. John had $8,000 of income in 1995. Will he and Clara pay any tax? If so, how much?
6. Steve has a 28 percent marginal tax rate. What is it worth to him to have:
   (*a*) an additional itemized deduction of $100,
   (*b*) an additional $100 invested in an IRA,
   (*c*) an additional tax credit of $100?

7. Explain how capital losses are treated. Also, explain the loss limitation rules as they apply to actively—and inactively—managed investments.
8. Miguel purchased a home in 1979 for $30,000. He sold it in 1984 for $70,000 and immediately purchased another one for $80,000, which he sold in 1995 for $135,000. How much taxable capital gain, if any, does Miguel have?
9. Identify, explain, or elaborate upon the following items:
   (*a*) functions of the IRS,
   (*b*) automatic extension of time for filing,
   (*c*) statutes of limitations,
   (*d*) assistance in tax-return preparation,
   (*e*) income splitting,
   (*f*) staggering expenses,
   (*g*) avoiding taxes,
   (*h*) deferring taxes.
10. How are FICA taxes calculated? Is it possible to overpay them? If your answer is yes, what should you do?
11. What are estate, gift, and inheritance taxes?
12. Identify frequently levied state and local taxes.

Case 5.1 Preparing Becky Sell's First Tax Return

Becky Sell graduated from a Midwestern college in 1995 and immediately began work as a marketing manager trainee for a large consumer products company. Becky had never prepared her own tax return before, but she was determined to do it for the first time. Becky got all pertinent information together in February 1996, and it appears below.

1. Data on two W-2 forms (Becky worked part-time prior to graduation) showed wages of $24,000 and federal income tax withheld of $1,600. In addition, they showed she paid $600 in state and city income taxes and $1,836 in FICA taxes.
2. Becky paid most of her bills with checks and kept all canceled receipts for purchases. Examination of these and her check stubs shows the following major classifications of expenses: rent = $5,000, charitable contributions = $500; interest on installment loans = $1,900; food and clothing = $8,000; dues to professional marketing society = $200; hospital and doctor's bills = $1,000; state sales tax = $600; contributions to a political candidate in her hometown = $110; contributions to a panhandler she often sees outside the office of the political candidate = $50.
3. Becky received $12,000 in gifts at graduation, and with it she purchased shares of GM stock in April. Three months later she sold these shares for $8,500.

Becky wants to file a return that will minimize her 1995 tax liability. She has cash from the GM stock sale that could be used for an IRA investment, but she isn't sure of the maximum allowed.

QUESTIONS

1. If Becky itemized personal expenses, how much can she deduct? How much is her standard deduction?
2. Using the tax form and tax schedules presented in this chapter, and taking the standard deduction, determine Becky's 1995 tax liability. (Assume she will make a maximum IRA investment.) How much will Becky owe or have refunded?
3. Determine Becky's marginal tax rate and explain to her what this rate means.
4. Becky worked for two employers; did she overpay her FICA taxes? Explain.

Case 5.2 The Brittens' Investment Alternatives

Bernie and Pam Britten are a young married couple beginning careers and establishing a household. They will each make about $30,000 next year and will have about $40,000 to invest. They now rent an apartment but are considering purchasing a condominium for $60,000. If they do, a down payment of $10,000 will be required.

They have discussed their situation with Lew McCarthy, an investment adviser and personal friend, and he has recommended the investments detailed below:

1. The condominium—expected annual increase in market value = 10 percent.
2. Municipal bonds—expected annual yield = 8 percent.
3. High-yield corporate stocks—expected dividend yield = 12 percent.
4. Savings account in a commercial bank—expected annual yield = 5 percent.
5. High-growth common stocks—expected annual increase in market value = 12 percent; expected dividend yield = 0.

QUESTIONS

1. Calculate the after-tax yields on the above investments, assuming the Brittens have a 28 percent marginal tax rate.
2. How would you recommend the Brittens invest their $40,000? Explain your answer.

HELPFUL CONTACTS

Internal Revenue Service (the following 800 numbers are available in most locations):
General information and assistance: 800-829-1040
Publications: 800-829-3676
Tele Tax: 800-829-4477

INTERNET ADDRESSES

Income tax information on the Internet (an extensive list of tax-related resources on both federal and state taxes)
http://www2.best.com/~ftmexpat/html/taxsites.html

IRS, The Digital Daily (download tax returns and tax information)
http://www.irs.ustreas.gov/prod/cover.html

J. K. Lasser's *Your Income Tax Online* (useful tax information, but a subscription is needed for full access)
http://www.mcp.com/bookstore/jklasser/

Taxing Times (electronic compendium of information related to tax preparation)
http://www.scubed.com/tax/tax.html

U.S. Tax Code On-Line (the complete document in hypertext format)
http://www.tns.lcs.mit.edu/uscode/

Part 2

INSURANCE PLANNING: Protecting Your Financial Resources

Before you go forth to make your millions, you should ensure that nothing can deprive you or your family of the basic necessities of shelter and support. In the first chapter of this text, we discussed a building-block approach to success, in which you first create a solid foundation upon which you can build subsequent successes. One of the stones in that foundation is adequate insurance protection. Without it, later financial successes may unexpectedly crumble, leaving you or your family with nothing but debt. In Part 2 you will learn how insurance can protect you against many of life's common financial disasters.

Insurance is one area in which a wrong purchase is very easy to make. The objectives are complicated, the terminology is confusing, and the sales agent may not be working in your best interest. Moreover, if you buy without adequate forethought, your mistake will become apparent only after it is too late. What good does it do to realize you purchased the wrong kind or amount of insurance *after* the auto accident, *after* the home fire, or *after* the disabling illness?

Insurance is purchased for many reasons. However, the basic and most important purpose of insurance is to protect you against financial catastrophe. No matter what kind of insurance you're examining—be it life, health, or property—you should keep this primary objective in mind. With this, and a good understanding of the chapters that follow, you should be able to select the amount and type of insurance protection you and your family really need.

Chapter

6

Life Insurance: Protecting Your Dependents

Objectives

1. To know how to estimate the maintenance requirement for dependent survivors
2. To calculate your life insurance protection needs
3. To understand the important provisions in a life insurance policy
4. To describe the major kinds of life insurance
5. To judge the relative merits of different insurance plans
6. To learn how to make cost comparisons on life insurance plans
7. To be able to choose the type and amount of protection that is best for you

Life insurance is a topic that most people would rather not discuss. Anything that questions our own mortality is almost always distasteful. In addition, we confront a special language we don't understand and costs that are difficult to compare. Moreover, we are sometimes subjected to high-pressure sales tactics from aggressive life insurance agents. It would be very nice if the whole problem of life insurance would just go away. Unfortunately, avoidance is often not the best policy.

The life insurance decision requires a considerable amount of effort. You must first examine the reasons why you might need life insurance. If you feel you do need insurance, you must then decide upon the appropriate kind and amount of insurance protection. This means gathering information on the life insurance market. Life insurance policies differ widely in both cost and coverage, and you can easily misunderstand what is being offered to you. Finally, you must be able to conduct a cost comparison so as to satisfy your insurance needs at the lowest possible cost. Most people do not devote this much effort to the life insurance decision. This is the reason for the industry adage, Life insurance is sold, not bought.

This is unfortunate, because a more positive attitude can produce substantial rewards. Life insurance is an integral part of a well-thought-out financial plan. It can provide your dependents with security against possible financial hardship resulting from your premature death. Without life insurance these contingencies must be covered by your present savings. If you first had to accumulate substantial savings before providing this security, you might be overly cautious in your career decisions and your financial investments.

Effort taken in the life insurance decision can give you substantial cost savings, in addition to peace of mind. The Federal Trade Commission has estimated that billions of dollars have been lost by holding life insurance policies that paid below-market rates of return and by prematurely terminating policies with high surrender charges. With a little knowledge, you can avoid these pitfalls.

FUNDAMENTAL INSURANCE CONCEPTS

Life insurance is only part of a bag of tools you can use to manage financial risk. To understand how this tool and others, such as health, disability, and property insurance, can best be applied, you should first review a few basic concepts in insurance and risk management. Given this foundation in the principles of insurance, the information provided in this and the next two chapters should help you avoid many of the major financial catastrophes that can occur.

Risk

It is impossible, and probably not even desirable, to eliminate all risk from your life. Every day brings you unexpected pleasures and unforeseen disappointments. Without them, life would be bland and unexciting. That new job can be rewarding or frustrating. The new car can provide hours of enjoyment or hours in the shop. Everything you do involves some risk.

Speculative risk: Exists when there is the opportunity for both gain and loss.

You willingly undertake certain risks because they provide the possibility of financial gain. In the stock and bond markets you accept **speculative risks** in the hope that you will receive a compensating return on your investments. Speculative risk exists when both gain and loss are possible.

There are some risks, however, that you certainly could do without. These risks provide only the opportunity for loss, with no possibility of gain. Examples include the risk that your home might burn to the ground or that your car might go off the road. Each represents a potential financial drain on your resources and is said to contain pure risk. **Pure risk** exists when only loss is possible and the loss is the result of accidental circumstances. You may undertake certain precautions to reduce these risks, such as keeping a fire extinguisher in your home and driving only in good weather. However, individual action may not be enough to significantly reduce pure risk. In some circumstances, group action in the marketplace may be necessary. It is pure risk we seek to protect against when we purchase insurance.

Pure risk: Exists when only loss is possible and the loss is the result of accidental circumstances.

POOLING OF RISK All market insurance involves a pooling of risk. For each of us individually, the future is highly uncertain. However, when we combine many individuals, functioning under similar circumstances, future events affecting the group as a whole become highly predictable. It is difficult to forecast with any certainty whether you will have an auto accident on a given weekend. However, it is not too difficult to predict how many accidents will take place nationally on that weekend. This ability to forecast with great certainty the likelihood of events for large numbers of individuals allows us to join together and pool our risks.

If we can estimate total losses suffered by a given group of individuals, then we know the necessary amount of financial reserves that will reimburse these same individuals for their expected losses. When group members share the cost of this reserve, by each member's paying what is termed a *premium,* they share the group's losses. Each member is committed to paying a certain premium but is also freed from the possibility of a larger financial loss. The premium represents the cost of the risk transfer.

The premium should be based upon the average loss experience for the group as a whole. When using past loss experience to project future losses, insurance companies must be wary of adverse selection. **Adverse selection** is the tendency for those with higher than average risk to desire insurance coverage. If, over time, those at high risk either purchase insurance or continue coverage to a greater extent than those at low risk, then average losses must rise. The insurance company will then find that the premiums it has collected do not adequately cover the losses it had insured. If the insurance company is unable to meet its obligations, it is insolvent. This may result in widespread financial loss and great hardship for many policy holders who had paid premiums for nonexisting protection. It is hard to think of a greater tragedy than to have suffered a loss, only find that the insurance protection you were depending on is not there.

Adverse selection: The tendency for those with higher than average risk to seek or continue insurance coverage.

Underwriting is the process of selecting and classifying risk exposure. The person who does this is called an *underwriter*. It is the underwriter's responsibility to guard against adverse selection by denying coverage to those who are at greater risk than that of the insured group. This can lead to negative publicity for the insurers, who are often accused of being heartless because they deny coverage to those who most need it. In doing this, however, the underwriter is protecting not only the interest of the insurance company. The underwriter is also guaranteeing the continued protection of the many policy holders who are relying on this company to be there in time of need.

Underwriting: The process of selecting and classifying risk exposure so that an insurance company may decide which applications for insurance it will accept.

Obviously, if everyone in the group suffered a loss at the same time, the reserves could not cover all the losses. Consequently, we cannot successfully insure ourselves against risks that affect the group as a whole; we can only insure against risks that are personal in nature. For this reason, private market insurance does not cover losses resulting from wars, nuclear accidents, or floods. Where such insurance does exist, it is viable only when backed by a government with the power to levy taxes and print money.

In the marketplace, the insurance company manages the reserve pool of funds. In doing so, it incurs some transaction costs and some financial risks. The company must receive adequate compensation for processing and policing the many claims and for assuming the risk that the pooled reserves may not be adequate to meet all of the claims. Consequently, insurance companies will receive more in premiums than they pay out in claims. This doesn't mean that insurance is a bad deal. It does mean there is an expected cost attached to using the marketplace. Therefore, you should decide whether the transfer of risk is worth the additional cost before purchasing insurance.

Insurable interest: An interest in which you may experience financial loss and an interest for which you can purchase insurance protection.
Gambling: Wagering on a risky event in which you have no insurable interest.

INSURABLE INTEREST In order to have an **insurable interest,** you must be related to the insured event in such a way that if the event occurs, you will incur a financial loss. Without this requirement, you would be **gambling,** not purchasing insurance. For example, I cannot purchase insurance against loss of the space shuttle. I have no financial interest in the enterprise. If it were lost, I would not suffer any financial harm. An agreement whereby I would receive payment if the shuttle were unsuccessful would be a gamble rather than an insurance contract. However, companies having payloads aboard the shuttle can and do enter into insurance contracts dependent on the shuttle's success. The financial loss these companies would suffer if the shuttle mission were unsuccessful represents an insurable interest.

Indemnification: The restoration of the financial state that existed before you incurred a loss.

INDEMNIFICATION Another way in which insurance differs from gambling is that payment under an insurance contract should not exceed the value of the loss. At most, insurance is meant to provide **indemnification;** that is, a return to your financial status before the loss. You should not receive a net financial gain when an insurance policy pays off. For this reason, you should not insure an article for more than it is worth. Overinsurance is a waste of money, because an insurance company will not pay out more than the market worth of the loss.

Of course, no fair market value can be placed on a human life. Consequently, the amount of life insurance we can take out on ourselves and our relatives is practically unlimited. The concept of indemnification, however, is important when we take out life insurance on our business associates. In business relationships, the amount of life insurance must be limited by the amount of financial harm.

Risk Management

Risk management: The process of identifying, evaluating, and deciding how to deal with risk.

Risk management consists of identifying, evaluating, and determining how to handle your risks. Your health, property, and ability to generate income are constantly at risk from numerous sources. You need to enumerate these risks and then determine how threatening each is to you and to your family's financial survival. You must then choose the best method or combination of methods for dealing with each of your risk exposures. There are four basic techniques for managing risk: risk reduction, risk avoidance, risk transfer, and risk retention.

Risk reduction: Reducing the probability of loss through preventive action.

RISK REDUCTION You engage in **risk reduction** when you lower the probability of a loss by taking preventive action. Examples of personal risk reduction include the use of car bumpers, football helmets, seat belts, and smoke and burglar alarms. Each reduces the probability of major property damage, the probability of loss of life, or both.

Risk avoidance: Reducing or eliminating risk through behavior modification.

RISK AVOIDANCE **Risk avoidance** involves reducing or eliminating the probability of a loss by avoiding the cause of the loss. If you avoid smoking and the heavy use of alcohol, you avoid severe risks to your health.

Risk avoidance is termed a conservative strategy because it calls for a change in our behavior. Sometimes, the cost of changing our behavior is just too high for us to accept. You could avoid the risk of flying by not flying, but this would limit both your business career and your vacation alternatives. Furthermore, you must be careful that the avoidance of one risk does not increase another. By not flying, you may be accepting greater risks by driving.

Risk retention: Accepting risk as the least costly, best course of action.

RISK RETENTION When the cost of eliminating the risk far exceeds the benefits of eliminating the risk, your best decision may be **risk retention.** This can be true for both major losses and minor losses. For example, it would be prohibitively expensive—if not impossible—to insure your property against loss to war or insurrection. Consequently, you must assume the risk.

You can insure against the cost of appliance repairs with a service contract. The expected cost of repairs, however, is typically much less than the cost of the service contract. In addition, when the appliance does need repairs, it is usually a minor inconvenience rather than a major financial catastrophe. Your optimal strategy is to retain small risks but transfer the large ones.

Risk transfer: Eliminating the possibility of probabilistic loss through the purchase of insurance.

RISK TRANSFER By purchasing an insurance contract, you engage in **risk transfer.** With life, health, auto, and homeowners' insurance the associated risks of major financial loss are transferred from you and your family to the insurer. Transferring risk is an important tool for eliminating major risks that cannot be feasibly disposed of through risk reduction or avoidance. No matter how moderate and healthful your lifestyle may be, there is still the possibility of a disabling sickness or premature death. The resulting expense and loss of income could lead to drastic changes for both you and your family. For protection against risks such as this, transferring risk through market purchase insurance is the best risk management strategy.

ESTIMATING YOUR LIFE INSURANCE NEEDS

The two most important reasons for buying life insurance are that it can serve as a convenient means of saving and it can provide financial security for dependents. You must judge its performance as a form of savings against all alternative methods. However, there is no substitute for the death protection it provides. You may *want* to use life insurance as a savings vehicle, but you *need* it for the insurance protection. Therefore, we will first examine ways in which you may estimate your own need for life insurance protection.

The American Council on Life Insurance estimates that the average household has a little more than $100,000 in life insurance protection. This may sound like a significant amount of death protection. However, it is only about twice the average disposable income per household. For families with dependent children or dependent spouses, this is probably not enough to provide for the interim care of those dependent family members.

Young adults are often sold life insurance when they graduate from college. Many times, these policies are purchased from other recently hired and inexperienced alumni. The insured later tend not to review the adequacy of their coverage. The paradoxical result is that those who don't need protection have too much, and those who really need the protection have too little. To avoid this situation, you should probably sit down and calculate your life insurance needs at least once every three years. You should also recalculate whenever the family undergoes a significant change, such as the birth of a child or the purchase of a home.

The needs of the survivors may be many and varied. Funds will be necessary for death-related expenses. In addition, the survivors may require continuing financial support and funds for specialized needs such as educational expenses. The dollars to cover all of these expenses must come either from the liquidation of your family's present net assets or from your life insurance proceeds. After you decide what assets might be used to support your survivors, any needs in excess of this amount must either remain unsatisfied or be covered by life insurance. The accompanying worksheets and text will help you judge your life insurance protection needs and the adequacy of your present coverage.

The Clean-Up Fund

Clean-up fund: Funding for expenses that will be incurred at the time of death.

Expenses that are related directly to the death and that must be paid for at the time of death may be budgeted for in the **clean-up fund.** This fund should also include any liabilities that would be convenient or preferable to liquidate at this time. The typical items included in a clean-up fund are listed on the sample worksheet in Figure 6.1.

FUNERAL AND BURIAL COSTS The price of a funeral and burial can vary widely, depending on your style of departure. A standard funeral and burial cost between $3,000 and $5,000. However, you can hold this expense down to about $1,000, if you decide on an inexpensive cremation.

ESTATE TAXES Both the state and the federal government may collect taxes on the death estate. These are discussed in Chapter 18 on estate planning.

Under federal estate tax laws, an unlimited amount may be transferred to your spouse tax free. If you have a substantial estate—over $600,000—and a nonspousal estate transfer, you will have to estimate your tax liability at this point. This is particularly important if you own a business. Covering the tax liabilities will allow your beneficiaries to avoid a forced sale in a possibly depressed market.

PROBATE COSTS The lawyer who wrote your will can probably estimate the probate costs associated with the validation of your will and the distribution of your estate. As a second-best estimate, you may calculate probate costs at 4 percent of

Figure 6.1
Clean-up fund worksheet.

	Sample Entries	Your Entries
1. Funeral and burial costs	$3,500	_____
2. Estate taxes	-0-	_____
3. Probate costs	3,200	_____
4. Uninsured medical costs	1,300	_____
5. Outstanding loans due	6,000	_____
Total clean-up fund	14,000	_____

the value of the assets distributed through the probate process. For example, you would incur about $3,200 on an estate with $80,000 in assets. These assets should not include life insurance proceeds, since life insurance payouts to beneficiaries other than the estate avoid probate.

UNINSURED MEDICAL COSTS Your estimate of uninsured medical costs will depend upon the quality of your health insurance coverage (see Chapter 7). You can generally count on the cost of your medical care at death exceeding deductibles on your medical insurance policy. Therefore, you should enter any deductibles as an uninsured medical cost. In addition, you might enter another $500 to $1,000 for expenses that are medically related but not covered by medical insurance. Consequently, if you had a $300 deductible on your medical insurance, you might conservatively enter $1,300 for uninsured medical costs.

OUTSTANDING LOANS DUE The amount you enter under *outstanding loans due* will be equal to the value of the loans you would like to see paid off at the time of your death. Generally, it is a good idea to include any consumer-type loans you may have. These are probably at high rates of interest and will represent an unnecessary burden on your dependents. If you had $1,000 payable on your charge cards and a $5,000 auto loan, you might enter $6,000 for outstanding loans due.

The outstanding balance on a home mortgage may or may not be included in the clean-up fund. The payments on any loan that is not included in the clean-up fund must be covered under the family maintenance fund.

The Family Maintenance Fund

Family maintenance fund: Funding for the ongoing support of dependent family members.

The most important of your insurance protection needs is the **family maintenance fund.** It will insure the viability of the dependent family unit. The size of the fund will reflect the level of living you would like to see maintained. You want to budget an amount at least large enough to eliminate the need for major financial adjustments. On the other hand, you don't want to budget an amount that makes you worth more to your family dead than alive.

THE MULTIPLE-OF-SALARY APPROACH Because your family's living needs will depend upon future prices, estimation can be extremely difficult. In an effort to simplify the process, life insurance planners have devised tables indicating your income maintenance needs as a multiple of your gross earnings. This information has been published by major banks and life insurance companies. The calculations in these tables are usually based upon the following assumptions:

1. The family requires 75 percent of its previous after-tax income to maintain its standard of living.
2. There is a surviving spouse with two children.
3. The support will continue until the insured reaches age 65.
4. The dependents are eligible for Social Security benefits.

Table 6.1 contains examples of salary multiples based on these assumptions. According to these estimates, a worker at age 35 with gross annual income of $40,000 would need 11 times the gross income of $40,000, or $440,000, in the family maintenance fund. This multiple is found by locating the row with the closest gross income and the column with the closest age to that of the insured.

TABLE 6.1 • INSURANCE REQUIREMENTS TO REPLACE 75% OF EARNINGS AFTER TAXES TO INSURED'S AGE 65 (as a multiple of gross annual pay)*

Gross Annual Pay	Age of Insured						
	25	30	35	40	45	50	55
$ 20,000	14	13	12	10	9	7	6
30,000	14	13	12	10	9	7	5
40,000	13	12	11	10	9	7	5
60,000	12	12	11	9	8	6	5
80,000	12	11	10	9	8	6	4
100,000	11	10	9	8	7	5	4
150,000	10	10	9	8	7	5	4
200,000	9	9	8	7	6	5	5

*After-tax income varies among individuals. Factors such as investment rate of return, inflation rate, and individual debt, needs, goals, and retirement benefits should be determined on a personal basis.

THE NEEDS APPROACH If you desire a more exact method of determining your maintenance fund, you can try the needs approach. In over half the families in the United States, both the husband and the wife work outside the home. In these families the surviving spouse may or may not be able to provide partial income maintenance at the death of the insured. Under such circumstances, the 75 percent income replacement typically assumed in a multiple-of-salary chart may tend to under- or overestimate the required amount of insurance protection. If, for this or any other reason, the assumptions employed in a multiple-of-salary chart do not fit your own situation, you may have to employ a more complicated needs approach in calculating your family maintenance requirements. The following steps and the worksheet in Figure 6.2 will lead you through the computations.

Step 1: Calculate the monthly expenses for the dependent family unit. If you keep a family budget, you can estimate the monthly living expenses for the surviving family members on the basis of these data. Be sure to include all items that are jointly consumed and exclude only those items that are independently consumed by the insured. For example, the home must still be heated and maintained, but the family may no longer need that second car.

Figure 6.2
Family maintenance fund: needs approach.

		Sample Entries		Your Entries	
Step 1.	Monthly survivors' expenses		$ 4,000		
Step 2.	Monthly survivors' take-home pay	$ 670			
Step 3.	Monthly survivors' benefits	1,980			
	Total contribution by survivors		– 2,650		
Step 4.	Monthly maintenance requirement		$ 1,350		
Step 5.	Calculate size of maintenance fund		× 12		× 12
	(a) Annual requirement		$ 16,200		
	(b) Multiply by number of years until the youngest child is independent		× 10		
	Family maintenance fund		$162,000		

If you have not kept track of your monthly expenses, or you find it difficult to identify marginal expenses for the insured, you might rely on data based upon average family budgets. Various studies tend to support the percentage of income consumed by the head of household presented in Figure 6.3. To estimate the amount spent for the exclusive support of the insured, multiply total family take-home pay by the appropriate percentage. If you subtract the resulting amount from the family's take-home pay, you are left with the approximate expenditures necessary to provide for the continued support of the surviving members in a typical household.

The entries in Figure 6.2 assume combined take-home pay of $5,000 per month and a family with three dependent children. Consumption by one of the adult family members in a three-child family would be equal to 0.20 × $5,000, or $1,000 per month. Therefore, the dependent family would require $4,000 per month in maintenance expenditure.

After you have arrived at monthly living expenses based upon current expenditures, you may want to add in any additional expenditures the family might incur with the death of the insured. This may include additional homemaking expenses and lost fringe benefits. For example, many workers receive family medical insurance as a fringe benefit, but this coverage may lapse at their death. In this situation, the monthly cost of medical insurance should be added to living expenses in order to assure the family's continued protection.

Step 2: Calculate total monthly survivors' take-home pay. You will have to estimate the amount the surviving family members can contribute to their own support. After the death of the insured, survivors may find new sources of income. On the other hand, the additional homemaking responsibilities placed on the surviving spouse may reduce that person's ability to participate in the labor market. The example in Figure 6.2 assumes that the surviving spouse will bring home part-time earnings of $670 per month.

Step 3: Calculate total monthly survivors' benefits. If you have worked, paid Social Security taxes, and earned enough "credits" (see Appendix B), certain members of your family may be eligible for monthly survivors' benefits. These may be paid to a(n):

Figure 6.3
Family head's consumption expenditure as percentage of family income.

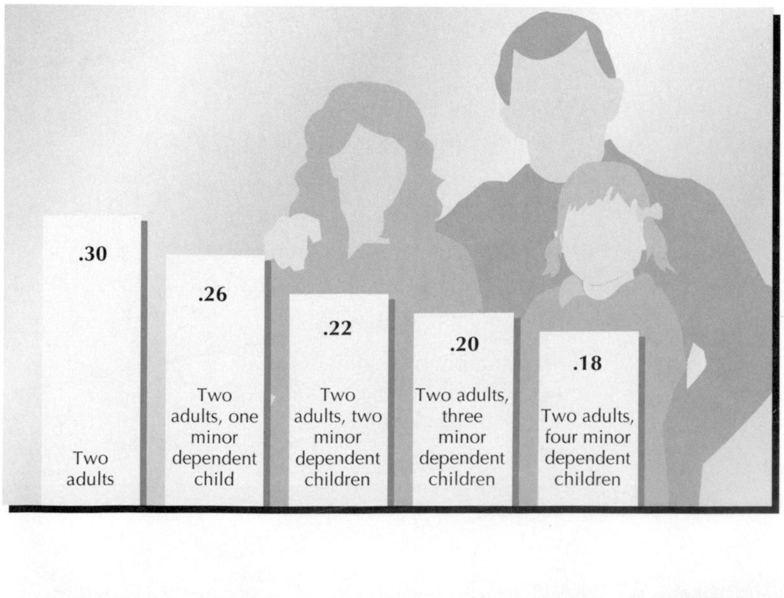

- Widow, widower, or divorced spouse at age 65 or reduced benefits as early as 60. A disabled widow, widower, or divorced spouse can get benefits at 50–60.
- Widow, widower, or divorced spouse at any age if she or he takes care of your child who is under 16 or disabled.
- Unmarried child under 18 (or up to age 19 if he or she is attending elementary or secondary school full time). Your child can get benefits at any age if he or she was disabled before 22 and remains disabled. Under certain circumstances, benefits can also be paid to your stepchildren or grandchildren.
- Dependent parent age 62 or older.

You should recognize that a surviving parent will receive benefits until the children finish high school. He or she then enters a blackout period during which benefits are discontinued. Later, when he or she reaches age 60, benefits may again be paid under a widow(er)'s pension.

The local Social Security office will prepare a "Personal Earnings and Benefit Estimate Statement" for you. This will include an estimate of your survivors' benefits as well as estimates of retirement and disability benefits. As a temporary alternative if you have not yet received your statement, you may use the following ballpark estimates for your life insurance calculations.

ESTIMATES OF MONTHLY SOCIAL SECURITY BENEFITS FOR DEPENDENT SURVIVORS

	Average Annual Social Security Covered Earnings				
	Less than $10,000	$10,000–$20,000	$20,000–$30,000	$30,000–$50,000	$50,000 and over
One surviving child	450	600	730	940	1,150
Parent and one child	900	1,190	1,450	1,880	2,300
Maximum family benefit	900	1,420	1,770	2,190	2,680

Include benefits for each of the surviving children in your calculation as long as the total is less than the maximum amount the family is permitted to receive. Do not include Social Security benefits for the surviving spouse if he or she plans to earn more than about $8,200 per year. At earnings above this, spousal benefits are sharply reduced.

If you have a private insurance plan that provides monthly survivors' benefits, you will want to add this to any Social Security benefits to arrive at total survivors' benefits. For example, if Social Security provides $1,880 per month and a private pension plan provides $100 per month, then total monthly benefits will be $1,980.

Employer-sponsored retirement plans will often provide some type of benefit for the surviving spouse. In fact, when retirement annuities are offered employees, both preretirement and postretirement spousal survivorship benefits are in most instances required under the Retirement Equity Act of 1984. These benefits are mandatory and can be withdrawn only with the consent of the nonemployee spouse. For those who die after retirement, the surviving spouse must receive a monthly benefit equal to at least one-half the amount they had received jointly. If the employee dies before retirement, but after rights to a retirement annuity have been earned, the surviving spouse must receive a reduced annuity from either the date of the employee's death or the date of the earliest possible retirement, whichever is later.

Step 4: Calculate the monthly maintenance requirement. The monthly maintenance requirement is equal to the difference between the expenditure needs of the dependent family unit and the support provided by potential income and benefits. To calculate this amount, add survivors' take-home pay in step 2 and survivors' total benefits in step 3, and subtract the sum from total monthly expenses in step 1. For the sample data, the monthly maintenance requirement is $1,350.

The requirement may change over time. However, some of the changes may offset each other; for example, Social Security benefits are reduced as children become self-supporting. Thus, your estimate of a monthly maintenance requirement for the present age structure of your family may hold up reasonably well until the youngest child reaches age 16. If the surviving spouse does not expect to become self-supporting after the youngest child reaches age 16, you may want to calculate a separate monthly maintenance requirement for the surviving spouse over the years that Social Security benefits are blacked out.

Step 5: Calculate the size of the maintenance fund. The monthly maintenance requirements must be paid out of the maintenance fund. In estimating the appropriate size of the maintenance fund, you should consider two important facts: one, with inflation, monthly expenses will rise over time; and two, the maintenance fund will be invested and will earn an interest return. If you sum up the maintenance requirements over the years of dependency, you will have arrived at the necessary size of the maintenance fund under a very special assumption; the after-tax interest return on the maintenance fund is just equal to the rate of inflation. This is termed the **offset method.**

Offset method: Present value of future dollars based on the assumption that the after-tax return on investments equals the rate of inflation.

If you want to assume that your dependents can beat the rate of inflation on their investments, then more complicated financial techniques (see Appendix A) can be used to estimate a reduced size for the maintenance fund and the specialized funds that follow. The purpose here, however, is to apply a method that is both simple and conservative. Try not to be too optimistic when assuming an after-tax return on your death estate. Although you may be an experienced investor, it is your survivors who will be making the investment decisions. Furthermore, you should not employ an interest assumption that requires speculative investments. Your life insurance objective is to reduce risk not to increase it.

Specialized Funds

You might consider setting up various specialized funds to meet temporary needs that are not covered by the maintenance fund. Special funds for emergencies, education, and retirement are definitely worth thinking about and are listed on the specialized fund worksheet in Figure 6.4.

AN EMERGENCY FUND You may want to be fairly generous in estimating the size of your emergency fund, since emergencies might be more difficult to handle in a single-parent household. A good rule of thumb is three to six months of the survivors' expenses included in Figure 6.4. If most of these expenses are guaranteed by survivors' benefits, a multiple of 3 should be sufficient.

AN EDUCATIONAL FUND College students over 18 years of age are no longer entitled to survivors' benefits under Social Security. Therefore, if you plan to provide a college education for your children, you should consider the need for an educational fund. Tuition and fees, room and board, books and supplies, transportation,

Figure 6.4
Specialized fund worksheet.

		Sample Entries		Your Entries
Emergency fund		$ 12,000		______
Educational fund				
Cost per child	$36,000		______	
Number of children	×3		×	
		$108,000		______
Retirement fund				
Annual requirement	$ 3,000		______	
Multiply by 20 years	× 20		× 20	
		$ 60,000		______
Other funds		-0-		______
Total specialized fund		$180,000		______

and personal expenses for a resident student are now about $9,000 per year at public institutions. Thus, a four-year college education can cost about $36,000.

A RETIREMENT FUND If you think that pension benefits from private plans and Social Security might not provide enough support for the surviving spouse, you might want to set an additional amount aside in a retirement fund to eliminate this deficiency. If you multiply the annual deficiency in support times 20 years, you will have a decent estimate of the amount needed in the retirement fund, assuming retirement at age 65. More accurate techniques for estimating a retirement fund are contained in Chapter 17 on retirement and pension planning.

The Insurance Protection Gap

Once you have estimated the total needs of the dependent family—consisting of the clean-up fund, the maintenance fund, and specialized funds—the next task is to determine how these needs will be met. Figure 6.5 contains a worksheet for calculating the insurance protection gap.

Figure 6.5
Worksheet: the life insurance gap.

	Sample Entries		Your Entries	
Funding Needs				
1. Clean-up fund	$ 14,000		______	
2. Family maintenance fund	$162,000		______	
3. Specialized fund	$180,000		______	
Total funding needs		$356,000		______
Less Funding Sources				
1. Financial investments	$ 56,000		______	
2. Tangible goods	10,000		______	
3. Life insurance				
(a) Group insurance	$ 50,000		______	
(b) Individual insurance	-0-		______	
(c) Social Security	250		$ 250	
Total sources		($116,250)		(______)
Unfunded Needs		$239,750		
Unfunded Estate Liquidity		-0-		______
Life Insurance Protection Gap		$239,750		______

1. *Financial investments.* These should be counted at present market value after taxes. You should include your personal portfolio, plus any lump-sum distributions from retirement plans that pay out upon death.
2. *Tangible goods.* You may have some items the family will no longer require. These should be valued at their market price after taxes and selling costs.
3. *Life insurance.* The face amount of your present policies, minus outstanding loans on those policies, is available for future support. You should also include any group coverage you have at work, plus the $250 death benefit under Social Security.

Funding needs less funding sources represents your survivors' unfunded needs. You obviously will have to provide sufficient insurance protection for your survivors' unfunded needs. However, covering only their unfunded needs may not protect your survivors adequately from immediate financial hardship. Your survivors may be hard-pressed to convert the funding sources into cash in order to meet immediate death-related expenses such as estate taxes. For this reason, you should check your funding needs and sources in Figure 6.5 to ensure that your liquid resources—those readily convertible into cash—are sufficient to cover the clean-up fund, which should include all immediate death-related expenses. The deficiency in liquid resources must be entered under unfunded estate liquidity.

Life insurance protection gap: Unfunded needs plus unfunded estate liquidity.

Your survivors' unfunded needs plus their unfunded estate liquidity equals your **life insurance protection gap.** If a gap exists on your own worksheet, it is time to start considering additional life insurance coverage.

THE SPECIAL LANGUAGE OF LIFE INSURANCE POLICIES

A life insurance policy is a contract between you and the insurance company. As with all contracts, you should read it carefully and understand it fully before you sign. This may require some tenacity on your part, since many companies provide sample policies only with great reluctance. Furthermore, to understand the agreement you must first master the special language of the life insurance industry. However, the efforts are worth the trouble. Purchasing the wrong kind of insurance or the wrong type of policy can prove costly.

The Basic Policy

In return for amounts paid to the insurance company while you are living, the life insurance agreement obligates the company to pay out a stated amount at the time of your death. Although policies differ widely in language and coverage, this basic agreement should contain some common terminology.

Face amount: The dollar amount of life insurance protection stated on the face of the policy.

FACE AMOUNT The dollar amount stated on the face of the policy is the **face amount.** In the absence of special provisions or additions, the face amount minus any outstanding loans on the policy is the amount paid out at death. Special provisions, such as an accidental death clause, which increases the payout when death is due to accidental circumstances, may affect the actual payout at death.

Single life policy: Covers a single life and is payable at the end of that life.

LIVES COVERED Most policies are taken out on the life of one person and are called **single life policies.** There are, however, policies with more complicated

Joint life policy: Covers more than one life but pays out at the death of the first.

coverage. A **joint life policy** covers more than one person. With this policy coverage, the face amount is paid out at the first death. This may be important to a family that desires to replace the income lost at the death of either the husband or the wife. In this case, a $100,000 joint life policy can be considerably less expensive than a single life policy of $100,000 on the husband and a single life policy of $100,000 on the wife.

Survivorship joint life: Covers more than one life and pays out on the death of the last.

A **survivorship joint life** policy operates in the reverse manner. It pays out on the death of the last individual in the group. This policy is particularly useful in estate planning, when taxes must be paid at the death of the surviving spouse.

Family policy: Covers several family members in one contract.

Many insurance companies issue what is commonly called a **family policy** or family rider. It provides coverage for several family members in one policy. The coverage provided generally consists of whole life insurance on the primary breadwinner and small amounts of term protection on the children, including those born after the policy is issued. Coverage on the children is usually convertible into whole life insurance when the term protection ends at some stated age.

Premium: The periodic payment made to the insurance company.

PREMIUM The periodic payment made to the insurance company is called the **premium.** Depending on the particular policy, this payment may be made on an annual, semiannual, monthly, or even weekly basis. A service charge is usually added for premiums that are paid other than annually.

Nonparticipating insurance: Future net premiums are not dependent upon the earnings and mortality experience of the insurer.

Participating insurance: Policy holders participate in the earnings and mortality experience of the insurer through dividend adjustments.

Dividend: A partial return of premium dependent upon the earnings of the insurer.

DIVIDEND Insurance may be purchased from either mutual insurance companies or stock insurance companies. Typically, the mutual insurance companies issue participating policies, and the stock insurance companies issue **nonparticipating insurance.** A few stock companies do write policies with limited participation, however.

Participating insurance gets its name from the fact that policy holders participate in the earnings and mortality experience of the insurer. If the mutual insurance company pays out less in claims than it expected, the policy holders participate in this good fortune by receiving back the surplus funds in the form of what is called a **dividend.** This dividend is considered a partial return of your initial premium and is therefore nontaxable.

If the company had only unexpected gains, participating insurance would be a great buy. However, policy holders may participate in both unexpected gains and losses. Mutual insurance companies tend to charge higher premiums than stock insurance companies in order to create a fund to cover any unexpected costs. Should these costs occur, dividends need not be paid out. A dividend payment is not guaranteed, and payments will fluctuate with the earnings experience of the mutual insurance company.

Cash value: An amount equal to the savings accumulated during the existence of the policy contract.

Surrender value: The amount returned to the policy holder when coverage is terminated.

CASH AND SURRENDER VALUE The **cash value** of a life insurance policy is equal to the savings accumulated during the existence of the policy contract. Not all insurance policies have a cash value; only those that allocate a part of each year's premium to savings do. In many insurance policies the insured may borrow against the policy's cash value at an interest rate either specified in the policy or set periodically by the insurance company. Closely related to the policy's cash value is its **surrender value.** This is the amount returned to the policy holder when coverage is terminated. Typically, the surrender value of the policy is equal to the cash value plus surrender dividends, minus outstanding loans and surrender charges.

Beneficiary: The individual who receives the proceeds from the life insurance policy.

Contingent beneficiary: The one who receives the proceeds if the primary beneficiary dies first.

BENEFICIARY The person or instrument (e.g., a trust fund) that receives the proceeds of the policy when you die is the **beneficiary.** If two or more individuals are to share the proceeds, then they are known as *co-beneficiaries*. You may also specify a primary beneficiary and a contingent beneficiary. The **contingent beneficiary,** also termed the *secondary beneficiary,* receives the proceeds if the primary beneficiary dies before you do. You may name more than one person as either a primary or a contingent beneficiary. For example, suppose Arnold Steele takes out a policy naming his wife, Sharon, as primary beneficiary and their two children, Nancy and John, as contingent beneficiaries. If Sharon dies before Arnold, the children, or more likely a trust fund for the children, will receive the insurance proceeds.

Special Provisions

Rider: A specialized provision meant to modify or extend coverage in an insurance contract.

The worth of a life insurance policy will depend upon more than just the policy's face amount or cash value. It will also be influenced by the various specialized provisions contained in the policy and the addition of any options, also called **riders,** to the insurance contract. The features you are most likely to encounter are described in Figure 6.6. Some of these provisions are determined by state law, and others can be added by the insured.

Box 6.1 PERSONAL FINANCE NEWS *Late Edition*

Living Benefit Insurance

The availability of living benefit provisions, also called accelerated death benefits, has expanded rapidly over the last few years. More than 18 million Americans now have these provisions in their policies. Playing on the fear of the high cost of long-term health care, living benefit insurance is meant to allay that concern by either providing for your survivors in case of sudden death or providing for you in case of a protracted illness. Custodial nursing home care is not covered under traditional health care insurance, and the government will not pick up the tab unless you have substantially depleted your assets. Obviously, the cost of such care, which can range from $25,000 to $50,000 a year, worries a lot of people.

Living benefit insurance, which is usually available only on cash value policies, can take several forms. Some policies prepay a portion of the face amount in the event of a serious illness; others contain a long-term care rider. Long-term care riders typically pay out a portion of the policy's face amount for each month you are in a nursing home.

In most cases the payment of living benefits reduces potential death benefits, but not necessarily on a dollar-for-dollar basis. A partial prepayment of benefits while living may entail the elimination of potentially larger future death benefits. On one such policy, patients given 18 to 24 months to live can get from 50 to 75 percent of the policy's face value. However, acceptance of this partial sum wipes out all death benefits, in effect placing a very high opportunity cost on the prepayment of death benefits.

Critics of living benefit insurance argue that the prepayment of death benefits subverts the original intent of life insurance and needlessly complicates estate planning. They also point to the uncertain tax status of living benefits. If the predeath payouts are considered health insurance benefits then they are nontaxable. On the other hand, if they are considered a distribution of the policy's cash value, then any taxes deferred on cash value would then become due.

In fact, even for those who need predeath benefits, living benefit insurance may be unnecessary. Owners of cash value policies can receive the cash value through surrendering the policy or borrowing against it with a policy loan. Some companies, such as Prudential of America, will accelerate benefits to any cash value policy holder whom they determine to be terminally ill and nearing death.

There are also viatical companies that purchase the insurance policies directly from the policy holders. (The word *viatical* comes from the Latin word *viaticum,* meaning provisions for a journey.) They typically pay the dying only about 50 to 80 cents on the dollar. Such high discounts on future payments might be avoided by arranging private loans from relatives in return for naming them as beneficiaries on the policy.

Provision	Description
Accelerated death benefits	Also known as living benefits. Predeath benefits that may be triggered by catastrophic illness or terminal illness.
Accidental death benefit	This option provides that, if the death of the insured is accidental, the death benefit will be some multiple of the face amount of the policy. If it doubles the face amount, it is sometimes known as a *double indemnity* provision.
Convertibility	You can exchange one kind of insurance for another without a medical examination. For example, your term insurance policy might be convertible to a specified amount of whole life at each age.
Cost-of-living adjustment	Automatically increases both the face amount of the policy and the premium. You have the right to reject this inflation-adjusted coverage, but if you do so, you may forfeit your right to all future cost-of-living adjustments in the face value of the policy.
Disability waiver of premium	If you become disabled, this rider requires the insurance company to take over premium payments on the policy. It usually takes effect six months after the beginning of the disability period.
Grace period	If you stop making payments and the cash value of your policy is depleted, coverage must cease, but not until the specified grace period ends. This period is usually 31 days.
Guaranteed insurability	Allows you to increase the face amount of the policy, by stated amounts and at specified dates, without a medical examination. A worthwhile option for those who expect a future increase in insurance protection needs.
Incontestability	Prohibits the insurance company, after some period of time, from challenging your unintentional mistakes and omissions on the insurance application.
Nonforfeiture clause	This clause ensures that you will not lose the cash value of your policy if you cease making payments. The cash value may be disposed of in one of three ways: You may receive it in cash; you may use it to extend premium payments on the life insurance coverage; or you may use it to purchase a reduced amount of paid-up life insurance.
Renewability	Allows you to renew your coverage without a medical examination. However, your premiums for subsequent periods may be higher.
Settlement option	This provision determines how the face amount of the policy will be paid out. The choice of settlement option can also be left to the beneficiary.

Figure 6.6
Special provisions of life insurance policies.

KINDS OF INSURANCE PROTECTION

Life insurance can be grouped into two basic categories: term and cash value. Most policies can be easily classified under one of these headings. A few, however, such as universal life, discussed later in this chapter, have the characteristics of both term insurance and cash value insurance.

Term Insurance

Term insurance: Has no cash value buildup; provides only death protection.

Term insurance provides only death protection. A term policy does not build up a cash value. If the insured discontinues premium payments, the coverage simply lapses after a specified grace period. Life insurance agents sometimes attempt to discourage people from purchasing term insurance by suggesting that if they survive the period of coverage, they have in effect paid for nothing, since the policy has no residual value. This is not true. They have paid for and received a reduction in the financial risks associated with the possibility of dying. Such risk reduction is not costless, nor is it valueless.

As we will see, there are many kinds of term insurance. Some are sold under the name term insurance and others are not. In addition, some policies that are sold under the *term* label are not true term policies. The distinguishing feature of a term policy is that it does not have a savings component. Under a true term policy, the entire premium pays for death protection. Therefore, term provides the greatest amount of death protection for each premium dollar.

Because of tax advantages extended to employer-provided term life insurance, this is the type of group life insurance that is typically furnished to employees. The Bureau of Labor Statistics reports that 92 percent of all employees in medium-sized and large firms receive term life protection. The face amount of the employer-supplied insurance is on average equal to about one-and-a-half times the employee's annual salary. This coverage is particularly attractive to older workers. Current law prohibits employers from providing such workers with less insurance protection than younger workers, even though the cost of a given face amount of term protection may be much greater for this group.

Renewable term: Term insurance that may be periodically renewed over some defined term without a medical examination.

INCREASING-PREMIUM TERM Each year as you age, you experience a greater risk of mortality. Therefore, a pure term policy that provides a level death benefit must have increasing premiums in order to offset age-related risks. Yearly **renewable term** is the most common type of increasing-premium term. Figure 6.7 illustrates annual premiums on a representative policy. Renewability indicates that a policy may be ex-

Figure 6.7 Annual renewable term life policy: premium illustration.

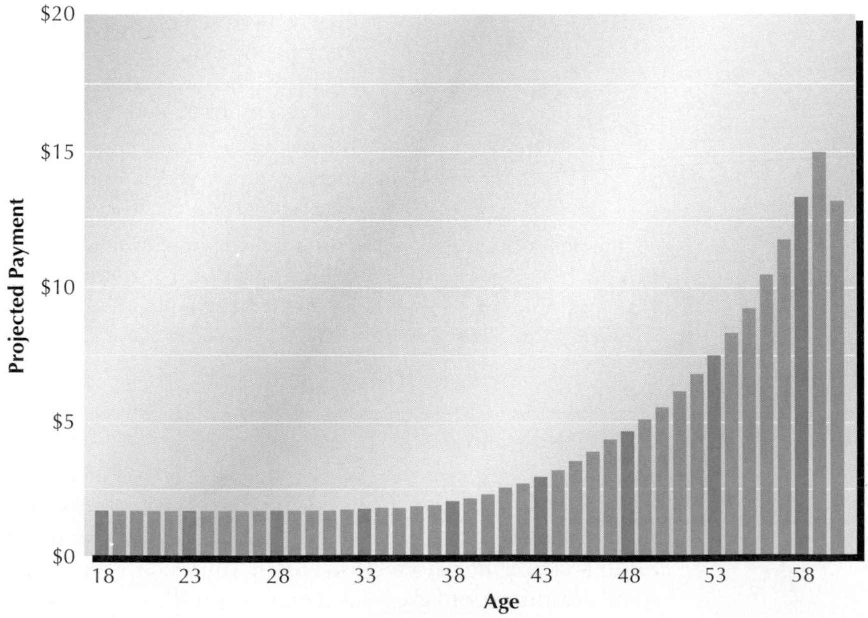

Annual Cost Per $1,000 Of Insurance

STANDARD				
		RENEWALS		
AGE	GUARANTEED FIRST-YEAR PREMIUM	PROJECTED PAYMENT†	GUARANTEED PREMIUM	PROJECTED DIVIDEND†
18	$ 1.88	$ 1.88	$ 2.94	$ 1.06
19	1.88	1.88	3.04	1.16
20	1.88	1.88	3.08	1.20
21	1.88	1.88	3.10	1.22
22-30	1.88	1.88	3.11	1.23
31	1.88	1.88	3.12	1.24
32	1.88	1.88	3.22	1.34
33	1.89	1.89	3.40	1.51
34	1.89	1.89	3.60	1.71
35	1.89	1.89	3.83	1.94
36	1.95	1.95	4.12	2.17
37	2.03	2.03	4.49	2.46
38	2.12	2.12	4.89	2.77
39	2.25	2.25	5.36	3.11
40	2.39	2.39	5.89	3.50
41	2.58	2.58	6.46	3.88
42	2.79	2.79	7.09	4.30
43	3.03	3.03	7.78	4.75
44	3.31	3.31	8.51	5.20
45	3.59	3.59	9.30	5.71
46‡	3.98	3.93	10.12	6.19
47	4.40	4.26	11.01	6.75
48	4.85	4.64	11.98	7.34
49	5.43	5.12	13.03	7.91
50	6.06	5.61	14.23	8.62
51	6.75	6.17	15.60	9.43
52	7.56	6.82	17.17	10.35
53	8.47	7.54	18.98	11.44
54	9.50	8.35	20.96	12.61
55	10.66	9.27	23.14	13.87
56	10.32	10.50	25.54	15.04
57	11.40	11.81	27.97	16.16
58	12.60	13.32	30.57	17.25
59	13.94	14.99	33.41	18.42
60	15.38	13.23	31.97	18.74

NOTES:
Unisex policy. The minimum policy amount is $100,000; the minimum age is 18, and the maximum issue age is 60.
†Projected payments for renewals are equal to the guaranteed premium less the projected dividend. Projected dividends cannot be guaranteed for the future.
‡Increased dividends, due to projected improvements in mortality experience at older ages, caused the projected renewal payments at age 46 and older to be lower than the guaranteed first-year premiums at these ages.

Figure 6.7 Continued.

tended without proof of insurability such as a medical exam. The renewability provision may last for some specified number of years or until you reach some specified age, typically age 65. Since the premium covers only death protection, it is lowest in the early years. Consequently, it is ideal for families with young children who need large amounts of insurance protection at minimal cost. After age 65, term protection may be nonexistent or prohibitively expensive.

LEVEL-PREMIUM TERM There are also *level-premium term* policies for 5-, 10-, and 15-year periods that may be renewable for subsequent periods. The level-term policies hold the premium constant over the specified period by requiring a higher premium than yearly term in the early years and a lower premium than yearly term in the later years. The lower premiums at the end of the policy's term are paid for by the overcharges in the earlier years.

Policies that hold the premium level over a large number of years may actually build up a cash value in the early years. *Life-expectancy term* provides level benefits over the insured's life expectancy. The leveling of the premium over this extended period creates a cash value that increases and then declines to zero at the termination of the policy. The same holds for *term-to-age-65* (or 70), which provides a shorter period of protection than life-expectancy term.

Decreasing term: A term policy with level premiums but decreasing death protection.

DECREASING TERM **Decreasing term** is usually packaged as a one-year renewable policy. Its premium remains constant over time. The increased risk of mortality is reflected in a declining amount of death protection, so your insurance coverage automatically decreases as you age. It is useful for those who can anticipate a declining need for insurance protection.

Group mortgage life: A policy designed to pay off the remaining balance on the mortgage at death.

GROUP MORTGAGE LIFE A form of decreasing term insurance, **group mortgage life** is designed to pay off the remaining balance on a mortgage. The death benefit declines as the remaining balance on the mortgage falls. As with traditional decreasing term insurance, the premium remains level over the term of the mortgage. The face amount at any time may not exactly equal the remaining balance, so, if you die, the beneficiary will receive an amount only approximately equal to the remaining balance.

Group mortgage life is sold through the bank that holds your mortgage. The bank collects a commission from the insurance company for functioning as a sales agent. The bank also benefits in another way: It is the beneficiary on the insurance policy. This arrangement insures that the mortgage is paid off at your death. Your family will have no say in how the proceeds are spent. If you have a low-interest mortgage, paying it off may not be the wisest use of insurance proceeds.

Deposit term insurance: Returns a lump-sum amount at the end of the term of protection; not true term insurance.

DEPOSIT TERM What has been advertised as **deposit term insurance** is not true term insurance, because it has a savings component. With a typical deposit term policy, you are supposedly purchasing something similar to 10- or 15-year renewable term. Each year you pay a term premium on the policy. However, during the first year of coverage you pay an extra premium, which is the deposit. At the end of the coverage period you may get back an amount equal to double the extra premium paid during the first year. This represents the saving component. In reality, however, the deposit you made in the first year may be going to pay the sales commission received by the agent. The insurance company is able to pay you back a lump-sum amount after 10 years because over the 10 years you have paid a higher-than-standard premium on the term protection. When these excessive premiums are taken into account, the rate of return on the first year's deposit is much less than it at first appears. Also, if you terminate the policy before a specified number of years, you may lose the deposit. Most insurance analysts have been highly critical of deposit term and suggest you avoid purchasing this type of policy.

Cash Value Insurance

Cash value insurance: Insurance that provides both death protection and cash value buildup.

Cash value insurance functions both as death protection and as a savings vehicle. There are many reasons why people purchase cash value insurance: The periodic premium payments provide a convenient method for accumulating savings; the cash value may be a comparatively attractive investment; And, for most insurance products, the cash buildup is relatively safe. In some states the cash values and death benefits may even be protected from creditors.

If a cash value policy is terminated, you receive the cash value buildup less any surrender charges. Such payouts may trigger tax liabilities; however, these may be conveniently handled by transferring the funds into retirement annuities. Also significant for your later years is the fact that cash value insurance can continue to provide death protection after term insurance has expired. Consequently, cash value insurance is an important tool in death estate planning, supplying needed funds to pay estate taxes and an efficient method for transferring wealth to your heirs. Furthermore, under recently introduced policy options some insureds may receive benefits before death in order to offset the unexpected cost of catastrophic illness.

One characteristic that often attracts people to cash value policies is that the insured may borrow from the insurance company an amount equal to the cash value at an attractive rate of interest. If the insured should die while owing money on the policy, the amount paid to beneficiaries will be reduced by the amount of the loan.

Whole life, or straight or ordinary life: Cash value insurance with level lifetime payments.

WHOLE LIFE With **whole life,** also called **straight** or **ordinary life,** premium payments are level over the lifetime of the insured. On a cash value policy the amount of death protection is equal to the difference between the policy's face value and its cash value. Figure 6.8 indicates how the cash value and the death protection vary over the term of the policy. In the early years, much of the premium must go toward purchasing the death protection component. As the cash value builds up, and the required death protection declines, more of the premium can be added to the cash value. Thus, the buildup in cash value will be more rapid in the later years. At age 100 the cash value of the policy equals the face amount and the insured receives the face amount if he or she is still living. The rise in the cash value is predetermined, and the insured is often presented with a schedule indicating what the cash value of the policy will be at each year of age.

Limited payment life: Cash value insurance with level premiums over a limited number of years that provides insurance protection over an entire lifetime.

LIMITED PAYMENT LIFE Under a **limited payment life** policy, premium payments remain level up to a certain age, usually 65, and then cease. However, the insurance protection remains effective over the entire life span. This protection is accomplished by charging higher premiums than on a comparable straight life policy over the payment years in order to provide a more rapid buildup in cash value. The insurance company then uses part of the interest earned on the cash value to provide continued protection after premium payments terminate. The allocation of death protection and cash value is illustrated in Figure 6.9.

Endowment life: Rapid buildup of cash value, with payoff of face value after a set number of years.

ENDOWMENT LIFE An **endowment life** policy pays off its face value after a set number of years, thus providing rapid cash value buildup with death protection. With past changes in the tax law, the cash value buildup on most traditional endowment policies no longer qualifies for tax deferral. Consequently, such policies are rarely sold any more.

Figure 6.8 Level-premium whole life.

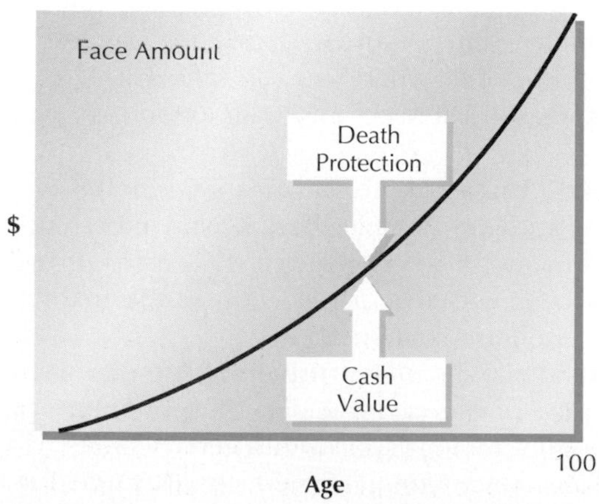

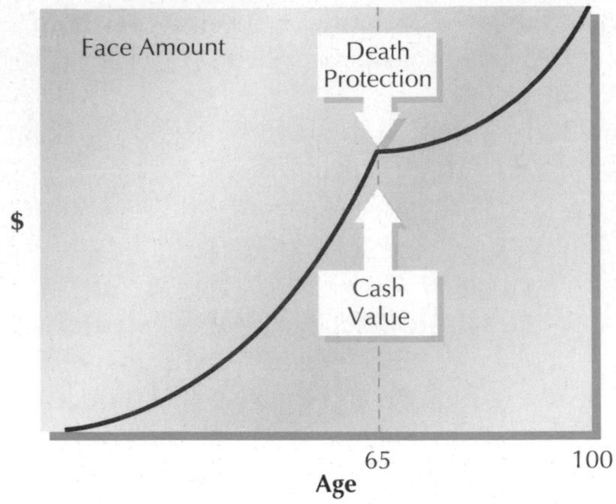

Figure 6.9
Limited payment life.

Modified whole life: Level premiums with varying death protection tied to life-cycle needs.

MODIFIED WHOLE LIFE Most families require less insurance protection in later years. **Modified whole life** attempts to fit the needs of the family throughout the life cycle by automatically reducing the death benefit as the insured ages. As in a whole life policy, the premium payments remain level for life. However, premium payments on a modified life plan will be lower than those on a whole life policy providing identical protection in the early years.

Adjustable life: The face amount of this policy may be adjusted by specified amounts at defined time intervals.

ADJUSTABLE LIFE Under an **adjustable life** plan, both the premium payments and the face amount of the policy are adjustable. The insured is allowed to change coverage as need varies and to change premium payments as income varies. The basic idea seems to be a good one, but this plan has some characteristics you should be wary of.

The face amount of the policy may be increased only by specified amounts at specified time intervals. Unless the policy contains a guaranteed insurability rider, you may have to take another medical exam when you desire to increase the face amount. In addition, a sales charge may be built in to pay the insurance agent a second commission when you increase the insurance coverage. With the added sales charge and the medical exam, increasing the face amount of an adjustable life policy may cost about as much as taking out a new whole life policy.

The premiums are adjusted by allowing the insured to move between term protection and cash value protection. When the insured's income increases, higher premiums can be paid in order to build up cash value. During periods of financial distress, premiums can be cut by opting for lower-cost term protection. The implicit assumption is that when you can afford it, you should purchase cash value insurance. As we will later see, this assumption may be unwarranted.

UNIVERSAL LIFE Universal life was first sold in 1981. Today, universal life and related products such as variable life and variable-universal life control about one-quarter of the market for new policies. This rapid growth in the new life insurance packages has been offset by a reduction in the market share of traditional whole life insurance and term insurance.

Universal life: Permits flexible premium payments, affecting the size of the cash buildup.

Unlike traditional whole life, **universal life** permits flexible premium payments, affecting the size of the cash buildup. The premium payment on universal life is often called a contribution and, within certain limits, is voluntary. Out of this contribution the insurance company deducts a charge for term insurance protection

Box 6.2 SIMPLIFYING FINANCIAL PLANNING
Borrowing Your Cash Value

The cash value on your life insurance can represent a convenient source of liquidity. In most cases, you can promptly tap the cash value with a policy loan. Since the loan is 100 percent collateralized by the policy's cash value, there is no need for a credit check or other financial inquiries that can delay a typical bank loan.

To your advantage, policy loans need never be repaid, and policy loan rates are often substantially below those on other consumer financing. On the negative side, loans will reduce the death benefits, which is probably the primary reason you purchased life insurance in the first place. Moreover, since most of the beginning premiums go to pay sales commissions, there may not be much cash value to borrow against unless the policy has been in effect for a number of years.

When deciding on a policy loan, you should be sure to look at the true opportunity cost of borrowing, which may exceed the policy loan rate. The cash value on your life insurance will earn interest and grow over time. However, if you borrow against the policy, the cash value is used as collateral for the loan. Because the loan may be made at an interest rate that is below what the insurance company can earn on its invested assets, this may reduce the rate earned on the policy's cash value. This practice is called "direct recognition."

For example, suppose you have a universal life policy currently earning 11 percent on cash value, on which you may obtain a policy loan for 8 percent. If you decide to borrow against the policy, the insurance company may reduce the rate earned on the collateralized portion of the cash value to only 5 percent, thus forcing you to give up an additional 6 percent return on the cash value. The true opportunity cost of borrowing is, therefore, equal to 14 percent, the policy loan rate of 8 percent plus the reduced interest rate on the cash value of 6 percent.

When deciding whether to borrow in order to invest your funds elsewhere or when deciding whether to borrow here or elsewhere, the true opportunity cost of 14 percent, and not the policy loan rate of 8 percent, is the starting point for comparison purposes. Tax considerations, of course, can make comparative valuations much more complicated. Interest earned on the cash value is tax-deferred until the policy is surrendered. If the policy is never surrendered, income taxes need never be paid on the death benefits.

and the cost of management. The remainder is deposited in an interest-bearing account. The interest earned either is determined periodically by the insurance company or is tied to an agreed-upon index.

You receive periodic reports on a universal life policy indicating the cost of the term protection, the management expenses, and the earned return on cash value. This provides a significant advantage over traditional whole life, where you may have no idea how much you are really paying for death protection or how much you are really earning on the policy's cash value. Given the more detailed information on a universal life policy, you are in a better position to judge the relative merits of purchasing term insurance separately and investing the difference.

Those who have compared universal life with traditional whole life have concluded that universal life does generally provide a better return on the invested cash value. Indeed, the primary reason for consumer interest in universal life has been the high advertised rate on the investment account. However, there are additional attractions. Within limits set by the company and the government, the insured may borrow against the accumulated cash value. Furthermore, most universal life policies allow the insured to increase the death protection, although another medical examination may be required.

On all policies that have an interest-sensitive cash buildup you should critically evaluate seller illustrations of future benefits. These may be based upon assumed rates of return that never materialize. Through the 1980s and into the 1990s interest rates have generally been on the decline. Therefore, illustrations using historically high rates may not prove true.

Variable life: Permits selective investment of cash value in a market portfolio that determines the cash value in the policy.

VARIABLE LIFE In many ways, **variable life** is similar to universal life. Like universal life, it has a term insurance component and an investment component. A minimum death benefit is guaranteed by the term insurance, while the cash value buildup and additional death benefit protection depend on the performance of selected market portfolios of stocks, bonds, or money market funds. You may be permitted to decide how the cash value will be allocated among the available portfolios and when funds should be switched between portfolios.

If your market portfolio does poorly, the cash value buildup will be less than with either whole or universal life. The speculative risk associated with variable life reduces its ability to secure the financial future of your survivors. Variable life should be compared with other tax-advantageous investments and only secondarily looked upon as death benefit protection. The government recognizes its speculative characteristics by requiring that only registered security dealers be permitted to sell this policy. As on universal life policies, management fees and early withdrawal penalties should be examined closely.

Variable life has not experienced the phenomenal growth of universal life. Its lackluster performance may be due partly to the restrictions on who may sell the policy and partly to the fact that variable life provides less flexibility than universal life. With variable life policies, annual premiums are fixed by the insurer. Regardless of how the market may look, you must contribute to at least one of the policy's portfolios to keep the policy in force. In contrast, universal life permits you to vary the amount you contribute each year and even to skip payments when there is sufficient cash value to cover the cost of insurance protection.

Variable-universal life: Combines the flexible premiums of universal life with the investment selection of variable life.

VARIABLE-UNIVERSAL LIFE **Variable-universal life** is also sold under various other names, such as universal life II. It combines the flexible premiums permitted under universal life with the investment selection permitted by variable life. Depending on your outlook, you can say it blends the best or the worst of each. By allowing both contributions and investments to vary, it becomes a more flexible speculative investment. However, like a traditional variable life policy, if your cash value falls far enough, you may be required to contribute additional funds or lose your family's insurance protection. Furthermore, a forced payout of cash value will require the immediate payment of all deferred tax. This may present a severe hardship for those who have borrowed against the policy's cash value. After repaying those loans, they may have nothing left with which to pay the tax bill.

SELECTING THE RIGHT POLICY

Policy selection may be looked upon as a three-step process.

1. Determine your life insurance needs.
2. Select the type of policy that best fits those needs.
3. Comparison shop specific policies and companies.

By now you should have an understanding as to how much insurance you need and information on the various types of policies that may satisfy your needs. You should be in a good position to select the appropriate insurance vehicle and comparison shop the best price.

Selecting the Type of Policy

Once you have determined your death protection needs, it may be easy to decide on the type of insurance protection you need. Young families with small children are going to need large amounts of death protection. Unfortunately, it is these same families who are on tight budgets and can ill afford to pay high premiums for life insurance. They need to get the greatest amount of insurance protection per dollar spent, and that means purchasing term insurance. It is a mistake to settle for less than needed protection today, in the expectation of some investment return in the future.

Figure 6.10 illustrates market purchases of life insurance by percentage of policies and face amount of protection. Only about one-fifth of the policies issued are for term insurance. However, these same policies cover about two-fifths of insurance protection, the face amount of policies issued. Given the relatively lower cost of term insurance, individuals who buy term acquire greater amounts of death protection. On the other side of the market is relatively expensive limited payment whole life. This occupies 10 percent of the market, but only 2 percent of the face amount on all policies sold.

Cash value insurance should be looked upon as an alternative to term insurance for those who can comfortably afford it. If you can, then you may want to consider purchasing cash value insurance as a supplement to your investment portfolio or as part of your estate plan. As part of your investment portfolio, it should be evaluated like any other investment. Investments are covered in Part 3 of this text, and you probably should review those chapters before you decide upon life insurance for its investment potential. Likewise, you should read Chapter 18 on estate planning, if you are considering purchasing life insurance for that reason.

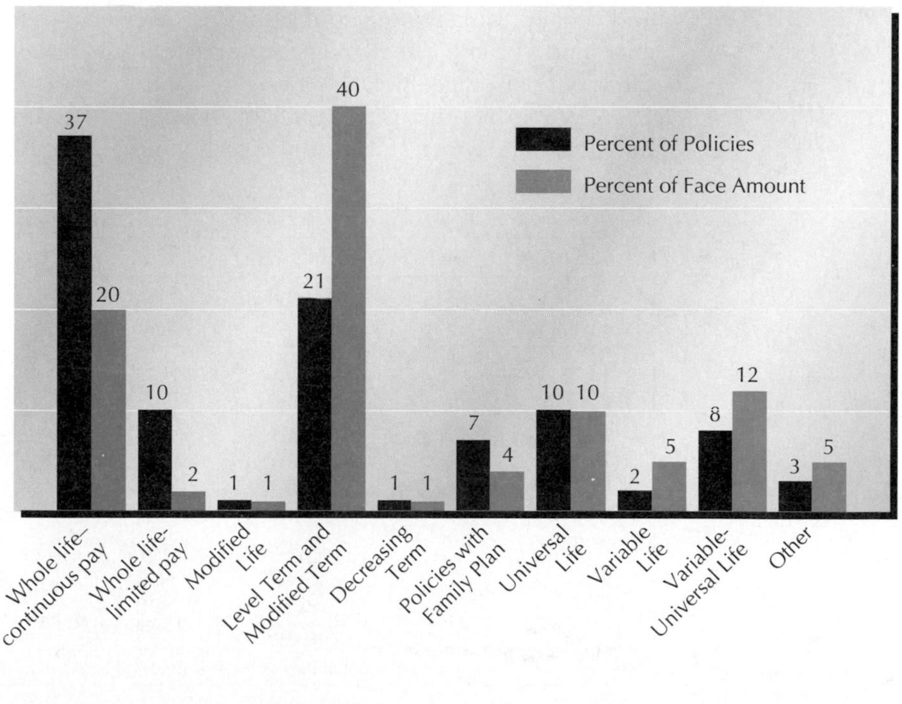

Figure 6.10 Life insurance purchases, 1993.

SOURCE: *1994 Life Insurance Fact Book* (Washington, D.C.: American Council on Life Insurance, 1994).

Term or Cash Value Insurance?

Commissions are significantly higher on cash value insurance than on term insurance. Consequently, insurance agents have stronger incentives for selling cash value insurance. This may lead them to exaggerate the benefits of cash value policies and understate the benefits of term insurance. The unique benefit of cash value insurance is the savings feature. It is often promoted as a method of forced savings for retirement. By paying the premiums when due, you are assured of saving a certain amount each period. But who needs to be forced? Any time we are forced to do something, it means we don't have the right to make a decision. Efficient personal finance requires decisions and not force. Cash value insurance is also promoted as a can't-lose proposition. If you die, you have the insurance protection; if you live, you have the savings. Unfortunately, the savings have often accumulated at unattractive rates of interest.

TERM PLUS A SAVING PLAN For many years Consumers Union has suggested that individuals would be better off purchasing lower-cost term and investing the difference. One such plan is illustrated in Table 6.2. You would have $25,000 worth of death protection if the face amount of the term policy plus the amount in the savings account averaged $25,000 over each year. This is the way payments are allocated in Table 6.2. Assuming the side savings fund earned a 5 percent annual return after taxes, the amount in the side savings fund would equal $5,677.44 after 10 years.

If the amount in the side savings fund after the specified time period is greater than the after-tax surrender value on the cash value policy, then purchasing term and investing the difference should be the preferred option.

UNBUNDLED WHOLE LIFE Consumers apparently followed the suggestion of Consumers Union during the 1970s by increasingly purchasing term rather than cash value insurance. The industry responded by introducing universal life, variable life and, finally, variable-universal life. This reversed the trend in sales of term insurance and cut into the market for traditional whole life. Figure 6.10 indicates that these new insurance policies presently control about one-quarter of the market.

As previously discussed, each of these products unbundles the insurance premium into a payment for death protection and a contribution to savings; thus, they

TABLE 6.2 • BUYING TERM AND INVESTING THE DIFFERENCE AT 5% AFTER TAXES

Year	Term Rate per $1,000	Term Expenditures	Annual Deposit	Term Protection*	End-of-Year Side Savings
1	$2.57	$63.12	$482.38	$24,517.62	$ 506.50
2	2.75	65.93	479.57	24,013.93	1,035.37
3	3.00	70.62	439.63	23,525.00	1,548.75
4	3.15	72.60	432.40	23,018.85	2,080.21
5	3.31	74.37	425.38	22,494.41	2,630.87
6	3.51	77.16	417.34	21,951.79	3,200.62
7	3.79	81.08	408.17	21,391.22	3,789.22
8	4.05	84.22	399.78	20,811.00	4,398.45
9	4.35	88.13	390.62	20,210.93	5,028.53
10	4.75	92.69	378.56	19,592.92	5,677.44

*The term protection plus the amount in the side savings fund will equal about $25,000 each year.

Box 6.3 SAVING MONEY
Taking the Load Off Life Insurance

You want to buy life insurance, but you're put off by the high commission. Don't fret. Many companies now sell no-load or low-commission versions of their major selling policies. No-load means there is no commission on the sales.

No-load polices may not be widely advertised, nor are you likely to find out about them through a life insurance agent. To get information on who sells no-load insurance you can contact life insurance companies directly, or you can consult *The Individual Investors Guide to Low-Load Insurance Products* by Glenn Daily (International Publishing Corp., Chicago, Ill.).

The companies can afford to sell these products for less because they are sold directly to the consumer, eliminating the life insurance agent as middleperson. This is ideal for consumers who don't need the financial planning offered by an agent or who want to avoid high-pressure sales tactics. The no-load policies are sold through the companies own employees, known as "direct writers." They don't earn a commission, so you save money. The one problem is that when you call, you have to know what you want.

The greatest saving is typically on those products having the highest commission, and that means cash value insurance. No-load products are a big advantage for those who might have to surrender their insurance in the early years, when commissions would have eaten up most of the cash value. Even over the long run, however, the cash value buildup can be significantly greater because more of the premium goes into savings.

Low-commission versions of term, whole life, and universal life have been offered for several years. However, it is only recently that low-commission variable life has been sold.

Among all policy types, variable life generally has the largest commission. Sales commissions, insurance charges, administrative costs, and money management fees can take a large bite out of returns on these policies. James B. Hunt, director of the National Insurance Consumer Organization in Alexandria, Virginia, warns that, typically, "a projected return of 12 percent over a period of 20 years turns into 8 percent once the expenses are paid." Obviously, anything that lowers this expense should be a welcome change for consumers.

But consumers still have to be careful. Just because it's no-load or low-commission insurance, doesn't mean it's a good buy. High charges for death protection and administrative expenses can more than eliminate any benefit from low commission. You still have to comparison shop. Get quotes from several companies, and use quote search services (see Helpful Contacts).

do exactly what the critics of whole life have suggested. They combine term and a side savings account into one convenient package. The important benefit is that you know how much you are paying for term protection and how much of a return you are earning on your investment. This is a significant benefit over traditional whole life, where it may be difficult to understand what you are paying for and what you are getting in return.

It appears that the information provided by unbundled insurance premiums has benefited consumers. The consensus is that these new products have on average provided higher investment returns than traditional whole life. However, there are several things you should realize before you jump at high advertised rates on policies such as universal life.

On all policies, such as universal, variable, and variable-universal, that have an interest-sensitive cash buildup it is important to examine the historical returns of the companies' market portfolios. These returns should be compared with returns on other investments, such as mutual funds, that have similar levels of risk. But remember, past returns are no guarantee of similar future returns. Illustrations of future premiums and cash buildup based upon historically high returns may be overly optimistic.

The quality of the coverage will depend upon both the cost of the underlying term insurance and the return on the cash value. If you are paying for expensive term coverage, a high return on the cash value may be no bargain. The insurance company will subtract from each premium the cost of insurance protection and a sales commission; what is left goes to build cash value. If you consider the sales commission on the savings component, your actual return may be much less than the advertised rates. Commissions on universal life policies vary from 5 percent to 90 percent of the first year's premium. Moreover, there may be significant charges if you surrender your policy in the early years.

WEIGHING THE TAX ADVANTAGE OF CASH VALUE INSURANCE A major selling point for cash value insurance has been the tax advantage for individuals in high tax brackets. The interest earned on the policy's cash value avoids taxes at the time it is credited to the savings component. A 9 percent tax-sheltered yield on the cash value is equivalent to a 12.5 percent taxable yield for someone in the 28 percent marginal tax bracket. However, if you decide to surrender the policy, you will have to pay tax on the interest earnings at that time. One alternative is to borrow against the cash value instead of surrendering the policy. But, again, you may run into problems. Both the company and the government can limit the amount you may be permitted to borrow.

The basic tax rule is that if you surrender a policy, you must pay taxes on the difference between the value of savings and the cost of the policy. The cost of the policy is equal to the sum of premiums paid less the sum of dividends received. However, the immediate tax impact may be avoided if you engage in an IRC Section 1035 exchange. To qualify for a nontaxable exchange, you must roll over the cash value into another life insurance policy or an annuity contract. The exchange of life insurance for a retirement annuity can provide supplementary income if you no longer need insurance protection in your later years.

For those interested in maximizing the tax advantage of cash value insurance *single-premium whole life* previously offered the best alternative. With a single premium and in effect, the tax-free returns earned on that premium, you prepay all of the future premiums on a whole life policy. However, Congress felt that this and other policies such as universal life that had significant cash buildup looked more like investments than life insurance. They, therefore, passed rules placing limits on the relationship between a policy's cash value and the death protection it provides. The effect has been to eliminate single-premium whole life from the market.

All life insurance, whether it be whole life or term, provides certain tax benefits at death. Beneficiaries can receive a tax-free payout. In addition, if the insurance contract is properly structured so that the insured gives up all rights of ownership, the proceeds can avoid estate taxes.

Comparison Shopping

In the past, the life insurance industry has not been noted for price competition. A Federal Trade Commission study indicated that high-cost policies often competed successfully with low-cost policies. Apparently, consumers have had difficulty comparing relative costs. Traditional whole life policies have been particularly difficult to compare, because insurance companies have not supplied information on the rate of return for the savings component. Also, life insurance agents have been known to misrepresent the actual cost of the policy. The agent would add up the premiums paid over the 20-year period and subtract from this amount the dividends received and the cash value at the end of the 20 years. The result would often be negative, erroneously indicating to the buyer that the insurance did not "cost" anything. Of course, this calculation ignores the time value of money. Had the consumer been depositing the net premiums into an account paying a competitive market rate of interest over the same period, the total amount in the account at the end of 20 years would have been much greater than the cash value of the policy at that time. The difference between the value in this imaginary account and the cash value of the policy at the end of the 20-year period represents the real cost of the life insurance policy.

Interest-adjusted net cost index: A useful industry-provided index for comparing the relative costs of similar life insurance policies.

COMPARISON INDEXES From the previous discussion, it should be apparent that when policies differ in premiums, cash buildup, and expected dividends, comparing their relative value is no easy task. Comparison indexes provide you with a single statistic for ranking the worth of different insurance illustrations. The National Association of Insurance Commissioners (NAIC) has promoted the use of the 10-year and 20-year **interest-adjusted net cost index,** sometimes called the surrender cost index. About three-quarters of the states now require that the insurance company provide you this information. The index takes into account annual premiums, annual dividends, and the cash accumulation at the end of a 10- and a 20-year period. Assuming you can earn a 5 percent return on alternative investments, the index calculates the annual cost for a given dollar amount of insurance protection. The formula for the index is quite complex. However, all you really need to know is that the higher the index, the greater the cost of the insurance protection.

You must be careful not to use the index for comparing the relative cost of dissimilar policies. Most important, don't use the index to compare the cost of term insurance with the cost of cash value insurance. The cash value insurance will always appear cheaper if you do. The reason for this is simple. The interest-adjusted net cost index measures the cost of a given face amount of life insurance and not a given amount of death protection. If you purchase a term policy with a $10,000 face amount, you are receiving a full $10,000 of death protection over the period of coverage. On the other hand, when you purchase a $10,000 cash value policy the amount of death protection is equal to the face amount of the policy less the policy's cash value. Thus, the death protection declines as the cash value builds. Over time, the cash value insurance provides less pure insurance protection than a term policy with an identical face value. Therefore, per $1,000 of face value, the term policy will likely have a higher interest-adjusted net cost index.

The interest-adjusted net cost index also has another shortcoming. It is based upon an assumed rate of return on savings of 5 percent. When market rates are above this amount, the net cost index will not perfectly reflect the relative value of two dissimilar policies. It will tend to understate the relative cost of policies that have higher current premiums but lower future premiums and higher future dividends.

In California, the Department of Insurance has replaced the interest-adjusted net cost index with the *net payment cost index* and the *yield comparison index* (*YCI*). These indexes take into account the interest credited, the estimated value of the death protection, and the expenses charged. The net payment cost index allows the consumer to rank policies in terms of cost per $1,000 of coverage. The YCI, which is a measure of cash value growth over the index period, is expressed as a percentage. A higher YCI indicates a better buy; however, it should not be confused with the rate of return on cash value.

The problem with all of these indexes is that they are dependent on policy illustrations. In most cases, illustrations are based on assumptions about interest rates, mortality rates, and policy lapses that are not guaranteed. Therefore, even though one policy might have a better index value than another, it may actually turn out to be more costly. Even with a comparison index, you must still examine the underlying assumptions.

THE INSURANCE COMPANY Over the past few years the insured public has been as much concerned over the health of their insurance company as they have been with their own. The bankruptcies of a few large and several small insurers have stimulated these concerns. Although most people who were insured by those companies will eventually get most of their funds back, in the interim they will not be able to get at their assets or receive the high returns they had anticipated.

Providing the consumer with help on this matter are firms that rate the financial soundness of an insurance company. The five major rating services are A.M. Best Company, Duff & Phelps, Moody's Investors Service, Standard & Poor's Insurance Rating Services, and the Weiss Group. Publications issued by some of these services can be found at most university and public libraries.

You should check the rating of the insurance company before you buy a policy. If you have cash value insurance, you should continue to monitor the financial health of the company for as long as you hold the policy. The top solvency rating given by each of these firms is shown in Figure 6.11. There has been much bickering among company representatives as to which firm does the best job of rating the insurance companies. Because ratings often differ by rating agency, it is a good idea to monitor several services.

Recent insurer failures have been blamed on three principal reasons: one, competition among insurers to attract customers by offering products with a high return; two, investment in high-yield but risky instruments such as junk bonds and real estate in order to pay high returns to customers; and three, "runs" by insureds to withdraw funds when it appears that the insurer may be in financial trouble. Unfortunately, monitoring the rating agencies may not provide complete protection. Some insurers received very high ratings for financial soundness just before they failed. This may be especially so if there is a run by insureds to withdraw their cash values. Even a perfectly solid company, which could meet all of its obligations over a longer period of time, may be forced into insolvency today if all the insureds demand their cash back at the same time. In response to this threat, A.M. Best now claims to have revised its rating analysis to take this "run on the bank" potential into account.

Figure 6.11
Top insurance industry ratings.

Rater	Highest Rating	Criteria
A.M. Best Company	A++	Superior ability to meet policy holder and other contractual obligations
Duff & Phelps	AAA	Highest claims-paying ability; negligible risk
Moody's Investors Service	Aaa	Best quality and smallest degree of credit risk. The financial strength of these companies is likely to change, but changes are unlikely to impair their fundamentally strong position.
Standard & Poor's Insurance Rating Services	AAA	Superior financial security on both an absolute and relative basis; they possess the highest safety and have an overwhelming capacity to meet policy holder obligations.
Weiss Group	A+	Excellent financial security; strong ability to deal with economic adversity

Action Plan for the Steeles: Life Insurance

Background Arnold earns a gross annual income of about $60,200 as a chemist. Sharon, working part time as an accountant, grosses about $15,400 per year. They have two dependent children: Nancy, age 9, and John, age 7. They do not intend to have any more children. When John reaches age 16, Sharon plans to work full time. This additional income will help the family finance a college education for both Nancy and John.

Only Arnold has life insurance. His coverage consists of a term policy with a face amount of $50,000 and a straight, nonparticipating cash value policy with a face amount of $50,000. The term policy is part of the group protection provided by his employer. The straight life policy was purchased when he graduated from college. It now has a cash value of about $4,000, of which he has borrowed $2,000. The guaranteed insurability rider on this policy allows him to purchase an additional $25,000 of protection at age 37, his present age.

The Problem The Steeles want to know whether they might need additional life insurance protection. Should they need additional protection, they would like to know how they might go about providing it. Arnold could take advantage of the guaranteed insurability rider on the straight life policy and up the face amount to $75,000. However, he has been attracted to the advertisements for universal life policies and wonders if he is passing up a good thing by not purchasing such a policy.

The Plan The Steeles should first calculate their life insurance protection needs following the procedure outlined in this chapter. In estimating the family maintenance fund they should avoid the multiple-of-salary approach, since this may overstate the insurance needs for a two-income family. They definitely must estimate Arnold's insurance needs, because he is the primary earner. However, they may also consider insurance protection for Sharon. Her death would reduce family income and no doubt increase homemaking expenses. Even more important is the fact that they seem to be relying on her return to full-time employment to help finance college educations. Should she die, the family might not have a sufficient college fund.

When they calculate Arnold's protection needs, they are likely to find a significant life insurance protection gap. A family with two dependent children will need, in most circumstances, more than $100,000 of protection for the primary earner. Also, it does not seem likely the $25,000 guaranteed insurability rider will close that gap. Arnold is probably going to need large amounts of additional death protection over the next 14 years, until John graduates from college. Both Arnold and Sharon can most inexpensively finance these needs with term protection.

Since Arnold and Sharon are not currently taking full advantage of retirement accounts that can shelter both income and interest returns from taxes, they shouldn't be considering additional cash value insurance. Instead, they can either add term protection to their existing coverage or convert completely to term insurance.

Arnold's straight life policy should be surrendered only after careful consideration of all factors. There may be severe penalties on the early withdrawal of cash value. If so, it may be worthwhile to hold on to the policy a little longer to avoid the penalties. In addition, a new policy may be loaded with sales commissions, making it an unattractive alternative. Unfortunately, Arnold's straight life policy was taken out when interest rates were much lower and premiums higher. The same nonparticipating policy written today would carry a lower premium. One solution to this problem is for Arnold to contact the insurance company to find out what alternatives they might be willing to offer him. It is possible that they will lower the premiums in order to be more competitive. They may also allow him to convert to term or universal insurance without penalties and sales commissions. The insurance company is not likely to provide these options unless Arnold asks.

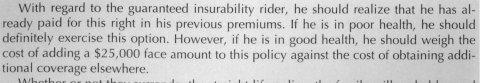

With regard to the guaranteed insurability rider, he should realize that he has already paid for this right in his previous premiums. If he is in poor health, he should definitely exercise this option. However, if he is in good health, he should weigh the cost of adding a $25,000 face amount to this policy against the cost of obtaining additional coverage elsewhere.

Whether or not they surrender the straight life policy, the family will probably need additional term protection on both Arnold and Sharon. They should shop around for this additional coverage and purchase the policy, all other things equal, with the lowest interest-adjusted net cost index. In searching for low-cost protection, Arnold should contact the group insurer where he works. He might find that he can increase the face amount on the group policy at a moderate cost. In addition, both Arnold and Sharon should inspect group plans offered by professional and fraternal organizations of which they are members. Such organizations often sponsor group insurance plans at attractive rates.

When dealing with life insurance agents, the Steeles should seek out those agents that are Chartered Life Underwriters (CLU). This designation indicates that the agent has both the experience and knowledge necessary to adequately explain the product. It also provides some assurance the agent has made life insurance his or her primary career and is likely to still be around if they later need additional help.

SWITCHING POLICIES The general feeling among industry analysts is that the industry is basically sound, and that policy holders should be wary of insurance agents who exaggerate the difficulties faced by some insurers. This may be merely an unjustified attempt at "churning," replacing an existing policy with a new one simply to generate commissions. However, if your insurance company is downrated, you should consider the associated benefits and costs of changing insurers. This is not an easy decision. If you surrender your policy, you may incur substantial surrender penalties and tax liabilities. The tax liabilities can be eliminated or deferred if you decide to switch your investment earnings into another policy and fill out a "1035 exchange form" with the new company. But there may be no way of avoiding additional high first-year commissions and another medical exam to prove insurability on a new policy. One intermediate step between doing nothing and switching insurers is to take out a policy loan. By borrowing against the policy instead of surrendering it, you at least enhance your own liquidity while avoiding surrender charges and protecting death benefits. If the company fails, you have gotten part of your money out; and if it recovers, you can always repay the loan.

PARTICIPATING VERSUS NONPARTICIPATING INSURANCE Historically, policy holders with participating insurance have done better than those with nonparticipating insurance. The major reason was the unexpectedly high interest rates during the late 1970s and early 1980s. Those with participating insurance received some of the benefits of the higher interest rates because mutual insurance companies passed on part of the higher return on their investment portfolios as dividends to policy holders. On the other hand, those with nonparticipating insurance often had cash values accumulating at a historically low rate set at the time coverage was initiated. In an effort to compete, stock insurance companies have been offering policies with a type of participation. Universal life and variable life are two such policies, because the policy holder participates in current market returns.

There is no assurance that policy holders with participating insurance will continue to do better in the future. In fact, during a period of unexpectedly low interest rates, nonparticipating insurance could outperform the other. Little guidance can be offered in this selection except to suggest that if you want certain payments, opt for the nonparticipating policy. If, on the other hand, your budgeting is flexible enough, and you are willing to participate in the earnings experience of the industry, then purchase the participating insurance.

Some policy illustrations for participating life policies show *vanishing premiums* at a point in the future. The premium vanishes when the interest or dividend earnings become large enough to cover the premium. If dividends fall below those anticipated in the illustration, then the premium may not vanish. This fact was learned the hard way by many policy holders who purchased insurance in the 1980s when interest rates were higher. For a significant number, their expectations of vanishing premiums did not materialize, and some whose premiums had vanished found them reinstated as interest rates dropped.

OTHER FACTORS You should recognize that life insurance will differ in cost because of policy riders. The riders attached to a contract play an important role in determining the worth of the policy to you and should be weighed carefully when making comparisons. The first step is to make sure you are not comparing apples and oranges. The second step is to take a close look at the apples. The same company may sell a high-commission and low-commission version of the same policy with identical riders. At times, unethical insurance agents have pointed to an independent survey indicating that their company's product was rated favorably, while forgetting to tell the prospective buyer that the rated policy was different from the higher-cost policy being offered.

Once you have decided what type of protection you want, there are rate-screening services that claim to help you find a low-cost policy. The three most often cited in the press are Insurance Information, Inc., Insurance Quote, and Select Quote. Each can be contacted through an 800 number. Insurance Information provides you with a survey of policies for a fee. The other two services do not charge for information, but they do represent insurers and they will offer to sell you a policy. In addition, there are several services on the Internet that provide free quotes.

If you deal through an independent life insurance agent, choose one who is a Chartered Life Underwriter. It will indicate that this individual has a minimum of three years' experience, has met basic educational requirements, and agrees to abide by a code of ethics. Ask the agent how much of each year's premium goes toward commissions. You may then inquire as to whether you might receive part of that commission as a rebate. This is a hot issue in the industry. Some insurance agents feel that commission rebates are unethical or illegal; others believe that rebates simply signal a competitive market. In any case, there is nothing to prevent you from asking.

Make sure you understand all of the assumptions that the company's illustration is based upon. The agent should explain how sensitive the illustration is to the underlying assumptions. In particular, you should request alternative illustrations of future dividends, premiums, and cash value based on guaranteed rates of return.

Before you buy, carefully read the policy and be sure you understand every term. Also, find out the length of the cooling-off period during which you may change your mind and have your premiums returned without penalty. Finally, after you have decided to keep the policy, you should make copies for your beneficiaries. It is important that they understand the benefits they are entitled to and how the proceeds will be paid. Most policies offer settlement options consisting of either a lump-sum payment at death or an annuity for survivors. You may choose the settlement option or leave the choice to your beneficiaries.

SUMMARY

Life insurance is a key element in a well-formulated personal financial plan. Its primary purpose is to provide a financial safety net for dependent family members at the premature death of the insured. To make sure this safety net is adequate, the death protection needs of the potential survivors must be estimated. If there is an insurance protection gap, it can be closed with additional life insurance. The life insurance can consist of either cash value insurance or term insurance. Each category includes many different kinds of policies. Each policy has a unique variation in premium payment, or death protection, or cash value buildup. The discussion in the chapter should help you evaluate each and choose wisely.

KEY TERMS

adjustable life (p. 178)
adverse selection (p. 160)
beneficiary (p. 172)
cash value (p. 171)
cash value insurance (p. 176)
clean-up fund (p. 163)
contingent beneficiary (p. 172)
decreasing term (p. 176)
deposit term insurance (p. 176)
dividend (p. 171)
endowment life (p. 177)
face amount (p. 170)
family maintenance fund (p. 164)
family policy (p. 171)
gambling (p. 161)
group mortgage life (p. 176)
indemnification (p. 161)
insurable interest (p. 161)
interest-adjusted net cost index (p. 185)
joint life policy (p. 171)
life insurance protection gap (p. 170)
limited payment life (p .177)
modified whole life (p. 178)
nonparticipating insurance (p. 171)
offset method (p. 168)
ordinary life (p. 177)
participating insurance (p. 171)
premium (p. 171)
pure risk (p. 160)
renewable term (p. 174)
rider (p. 172)
risk avoidance (p. 162)
risk management (p. 161)
risk reduction (p. 161)
risk retention (p. 162)
risk transfer (p. 162)
single life policy (p. 170)
speculative risk (p. 159)
straight life (p. 177)
surrender value (p. 171)
survivorship joint life (p. 171)
term insurance (p. 174)
underwriting (p. 160)
universal life (p. 178)
variable life (p. 180)
variable-universal life (p. 180)
whole life (p. 177)

PROBLEMS AND REVIEW QUESTIONS

1. Explain the primary reason for having insurance. For what other reasons might people hold life insurance?
2. What three funding categories are used to estimate life insurance needs? Explain the purpose of each.
3. Why would a two-income family more accurately estimate the family maintenance fund with the needs approach? Discuss other family characteristics that would cause one to prefer the needs approach over the multiple-of-salary approach.
4. What types of family assets might be used to satisfy death protection funding requirements?

5. What is the difference between joint life and survivorship joint life?
6. One life insurance expert suggests that people should never buy participating life insurance, because the purpose of life insurance is to reduce risk not to increase it. Discuss.
7. Renewability and guaranteed insurability are not the same. Explain the difference.
8. If a young family expects that its life insurance needs will increase in the near future, what policy options might they find desirable?
9. What is the distinguishing characteristic of term insurance? Why isn't deposit term true term insurance?
10. What kinds of insurance might offer the best protection against unexpected inflation? Explain why.
11. Suppose you wanted to leave your dependents with enough funds to pay off the home mortgage. Under what conditions would you prefer decreasing term insurance over group mortgage life, and vice versa?
12. If you perceive a need for insurance protection in your retirement years, might you prefer whole life over term life today? Why? Can you think of situations in which you might need insurance protection in your later years?
13. Suppose you took out a universal life insurance policy that charges a 20 percent sales commission on each dollar paid into the policy and pays a 10 percent annual return on the policy's cash value. What is the actual percentage return at the end of one year on each premium dollar placed in the savings component?
14. How does universal life differ from variable life? Which one entails greater risk?
15. What are the pros and cons of life insurance comparison indexes?

Case 6.1 The Wright Family Maintenance Fund

Sue and Tom Wright are both assistant professors at the local university. They each take home about $40,000 per year after taxes. Sue is 37 years of age, and Tom is 35. Their two children, Mike and Karen, are 13 and 11.

Were either one to die, they estimate that the remaining family members would need about 75 percent of the present combined take-home pay to retain their current standard of living while the children are still dependent. This does not include an extra $50 per month in child-care expenses that would be required in a single-parent household. They estimate that Social Security benefits would total about $1,000 per month in child support.

Both Tom and Sue are knowledgeable investors. In the past, average after-tax returns on their investment portfolio have equaled or exceeded the rate of inflation.

QUESTIONS

1. Were Sue Wright to die today, how much would the Wrights need in the family maintenance fund? Explain the reasons behind your calculations.
2. Suppose the Wrights found that both Tom and Sue had a life insurance protection gap of $50,000. How might they go about searching for protection to close that gap?

Case 6.2 Costing a Cash Value Policy

David Lombard is considering the purchase of a $10,000 face amount, nonparticipating, whole life policy. The life insurance agent tells David that the $10,000 insurance protection really won't cost him anything. The annual premiums on the policy are $500, and at the end of 10 years the surrender value after taxes will be $5,000. Therefore, David can get back all of his premium payments at the end of the 10 years.

David decides to make some calculations on his own. He figures that if he deposited $500 annually in a savings account that had a 5 percent annual return after taxes, he would have $6,603.39 after 10 years. He wonders if the insurance policy is really the great deal the agent says it is.

QUESTIONS

1. How much is the death protection provided by the whole life policy really costing David?
2. How might David figure out whether term protection would be cheaper?
3. What other factors might David take into consideration when deciding between term and whole life?

HELPFUL CONTACTS

Consumer Federation of America
1424 16th Street NW, Suite 604, Washington, DC 20036
Provides an insurance rate of return service that analyzes life insurance illustrations. 202-387-6121

Insurance Forum Inc.
P.O. Box 245, Ellettsville, IN 47429
Publishes an industry newsletter that contains changes in ratings of insurance companies and a watch list of companies that are financially vulnerable.

Life insurance quotes from companies that receive a commission if you purchase the policy:
Insurance Quote: 800-972-1104
Life Quote: 800-521-7873
Select Quote: 800-343-1985
Term Quote: 800-444-TERM

National Insurance Consumer Organization
121 North Payne Street, Alexandria, VA 22314
Provides guidance on selection of insurance policies. Publishes comparable rates of return for different policies.

INTERNET ADDRESSES

Insurance Information Institute (industry trade association providing consumer information)
http://www.iii.org/

Insurance News Network (online magazine covering all lines of insurance)
http://www.insure.com/

Insurance Quote (a life insurance quote service)
http://www.iquote.com

National Association of Insurance Commissioners (national organization of state insurance commissioners)
http://www.naic.org/

RISKWeb (links to academic and professional sites and information on risk and insurance)
http://www.riskweb.com/

Social Security Online (publications, forms, and a program for calculating your benefits)
http://www.ssa.gov/

State insurance departments:

Florida
http://www.doi.state.fl.us/index.htm

Idaho
http://www.doi.state.id.us/

Missouri
http://services.state.mo.us/insurance/mohmepg.htm

Texas
http://www.texas.gov/agency/454.html

Viatical Settlements: A Guide for People with Terminal Illnesses (prepared by the Federal Trade Commission)
http://www.ftc.gov/bcp/conline/viatical.htm

Chapter 7

Health Care and Disability Insurance: Protecting Your Earning Capacity

Objectives

1. To describe the separate components of basic health care coverage
2. To discuss the need for major medical insurance
3. To list the important providers and insurers of health care
4. To compare and evaluate health care insurance plans
5. To list sources of disability income
6. To estimate your disability insurance needs

In terms of financial burdens nothing is more devastating than a catastrophic illness. Serious illness or injury is difficult enough to deal with, even without the stress that medical bills and lost income can create. Having quality health and disability coverage can at least lessen if not eliminate the increasing financial hardship that accompanies injury and illness.

Today, national health expenditures average about $3,000 per individual annually, or about 13 percent of total national expenditures. This is up from only 5.3 percent in 1960. Part of the reason for the increase is that as we become wealthier we demand more and better health care. It is also true that the cost of medical care has far outpaced the rest of the economy. Since 1983 the cost of medical care has risen by twice as much as all other prices.

Given these rapid increases in cost, it is no wonder that health insurance, both private and government, has become a significant participant in the health care market. As a percent of total payments for personal health care, third-party payments have risen from a 44.1 percent share in 1960 to almost 80 percent today. Currently, only $1 in $5 represents a direct out-of-pocket expenditure on health care.

Some industry observers see the increase in third-party payments, and the decrease in direct expenditures, as both a consequence and cause of spiraling health care costs. Insurers have responded by expanding personal incentives to hold costs down through co-insurance payments and larger deductibles and by taking more control of health care delivery through managed care plans. This approach places greater financial importance on your choice of health care and health care insurance.

The Bureau of the Census reports that more than 254 million Americans, or 85 percent of all Americans, have some type of private or public health insurance coverage. Unfortunately, that leaves over 37 million without any health insurance protection. Most of the private coverage, about 82 percent, is group coverage related to the past or current employment of a family member. Because health insurance coverage is primarily work related, young adults aged 18 to 24, who are more likely than other age groups to be unemployed, are also more likely to be without health insurance protection. About 28 percent of young adults are without either private or government health insurance; whereas, among those over 65, this statistic drops to only 1.2 percent. Equally important is the fact that many young adults experience a break in coverage. Over one-half of those with coverage were without health insurance for at least one month during the last year.

Many people with insurance are inadequately covered because they have the wrong kind or amount of protection; they either incorrectly believe that their current protection is sufficient, or they simply do not give the subject the attention it deserves. Adequate protection includes reimbursement for major medical expenses through health care insurance and compensation for lost income through disability income insurance.

Protection against loss of income due to illness or injury is even less adequate than health care coverage (see Figure 7.1). Only 40 percent of the work force has private long-term disability income insurance. Apparently, most people feel either that the chances of becoming disabled are too small to require protection or that government programs will prove sufficient. As we will see, both assumptions are incorrect.

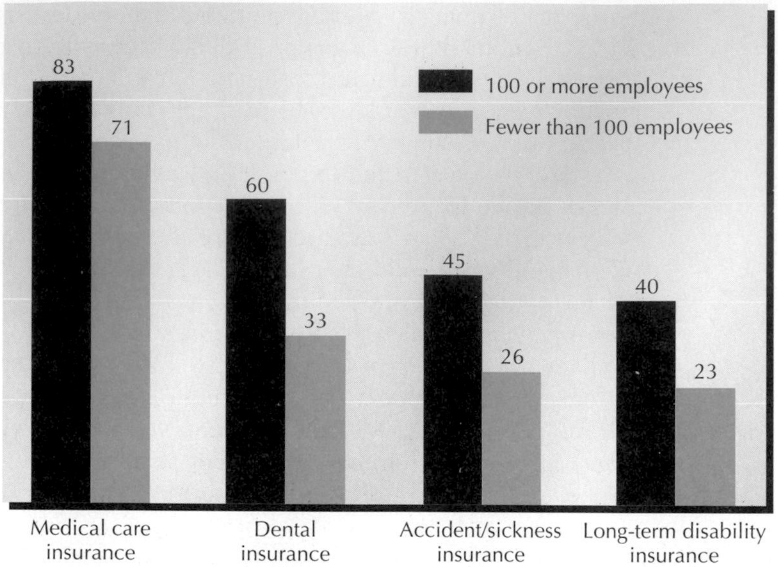

Figure 7.1
Percent of full-time employees participating in employee medical benefits program, 1991–1992.

SOURCE: U.S. Bureau of the Census, *Statistical Abstract of the United States, 1994,* Table 673.

HEALTH CARE INSURANCE

As stated previously, the overwhelming majority of those with private health insurance obtained it through a group insurance plan offered at the workplace. For several reasons, this insurance is often a very attractive deal. First, because of lower administrative costs and because of lower health risks than exist for the population as a whole, insurance companies will on average charge lower premiums for employer-sponsored health insurance. Second, approximately two-fifths of these plans are entirely paid for by the employer, with the rest requiring an average monthly contribution of about $30 for individual coverage and $100 for family coverage. Finally, you and your family are probably eligible regardless of your physical condition.

You might think that most of us have little need to consider health insurance. You simply accept what the employer is offering. This assumption is incorrect. Today, many companies will offer their employees a choice among two or more health care plans with differing employee premiums and differing schedules of benefits. And, in families where both the husband and wife are employed outside the home, these choices are greatly compounded. Not only must each compare the plans offered by their individual employers, they must also consider whether it is better for them to join their respective group plans separately or to participate in only one, listing the spouse as a dependent. No doubt the company personnel officer will help you compare and contrast the available options, but the final decision on what is best for you and your family must be yours. Furthermore, you alone can determine the adequacy of your group coverage and select a supplemental individual or family nongroup policy if you find a serious gap in your health care protection.

Types of Coverage

Unlike auto and homeowners' policies examined in the next chapter, there are no standard formats for most health care policies. This means that most plans will not provide an explanation of coverage that is broken down into the discrete components discussed below. However, after you read the policies closely and discuss them with insurers' representatives, you should be able to reorganize the benefits provided into a more comparable format.

Comprehensive health insurance: Provides both basic health care benefits and major medical protection.

Most policies include **comprehensive health insurance** coverage providing both basic health care benefits and major medical protection. Figure 7.2 contains a worksheet that was used to compare comprehensive benefits offered by a typical fee-for-service plan, such as might be offered by Blue Cross/Blue Shield, and a local health maintenance organization (HMO). This or a similarly styled worksheet can prove extremely helpful when comparing many-faceted health care insurance plans.

Basic health care insurance: Consists of hospital, surgical, and medical coverage.

Hospital insurance: Provides coverage for room and board and other medical expenses while in the hospital.

BASIC HEALTH CARE COVERAGE Three components—hospital insurance, surgical insurance, and medical insurance—make up **basic health care insurance.** Each can be purchased separately, but they are usually combined and sold as a basic health care package.

Hospital insurance will help pay for room and board and other medical expenses while in the hospital. It can take the form of indemnity coverage, expense coverage, or service benefit coverage. *Indemnity insurance* provides for specific dollar payments made directly to you for each day you are in the hospital, regardless of your actual expenses. *Expense insurance* provides for cash reimbursement either to you or to the provider of health care, based upon expenses actually incurred. *Service benefit* insurance guarantees the provision of certain medical services and makes payments only to the provider of health care.

Indemnity insurance: Provides a specified dollar benefit regardless of actual cost.

Hospital **indemnity insurance** typically ranks at least preferable. This is the type of hospital insurance most often sold on television and in newspapers. Although receiving $100 to $150 a day for each day you are in the hospital may sound attractive, it is not likely to cover even your room and board. In addition, many of these policies do not begin payments until you have been in the hospital a set number of days. With the average hospital stay a little over seven days at an average charge of about $6,000, don't plan on collecting much from an indemnity policy that commences payments after the fifth day.

Hospital expense insurance: Pays actual cost up to a daily maximum.

More adequate benefits are generally provided by **hospital expense insurance,** which pays for room and board up to a set daily maximum. In addition, hospital expense insurance should pay for other hospital-related expenses, such as laboratory procedures, surgical materials, and X-rays, typically stating payments for these items as a percentage of the maximum payment for room and board. This is not a trivial supplemental benefit. On average, such items can double the cost of a hospital stay. However, if unique tests and procedures are involved, the total hospital bill could easily run four times the amount actually paid for room and board.

Service benefit coverage: Provides full reimbursement for covered services as long as costs are usual, customary, and reasonable.

Service benefit coverage is the preferred approach to reimbursement. This type is provided by Blue Cross and many HMOs. For qualified and participating hospitals, full reimbursement for covered services is made directly to the health care provider, so long as the charges are less than the specified policy limit defined in dollar terms or days of stay. With service benefit insurance you don't have to constantly keep track of hospital costs in order to ensure adequate coverage. The one drawback is that you may have to stay in a qualifying hospital to receive 100 percent reimbursement.

Surgical insurance: Covers the fees charged by the operating surgeon and anesthesiologist.

Surgical insurance should cover the fees of the operating surgeon and the anesthesiologist. (For the surgical costs of selected operations, see Table 7.1.) An expense-type policy might provide a list of covered operations along with the max-

Type of Benefit	Fee-for-Service Plan Coverage	HMO Plan Coverage
Basic Health Care		
Hospital stay	Semiprivate rate for 120 days per confinement; covers illness, injury, psychiatric care, and alcohol/chemical dependency (excess covered under major medical provision)	Unlimited days paid in full for illness and injury; 20% co-insurance and maximum 30 days per year for psychiatric care and alcohol/chemical dependency
Diagnostic X-rays and lab	UCR (usual, customary, and reasonable) charge	Paid in full
Emergency services	In area: Hospital charges paid in full, doctors' fees at UCR, ambulance not covered Out of area: same as in area	In area: $25 co-payment, ambulance paid in full Out of area: UCR charge
Physician Services		
Surgery	UCR charge	Paid in full
Hospital visits	UCR charge	Paid in full
Office visits	Not covered with exception of 50% UCR for psychiatric care Major medical coverage	$15 co-payment for psychiatric care and 20% co-insurance for alcohol/ chemical dependency
Home visits	Major medical coverage	$15 co-payment
Maternity care	Same as for illness and injury	Paid in full
Prescription drugs	Major medical coverage	$5 co-payment per prescription
Major Medical		
Lifetime max./person	$250,000	Unlimited
Deductible/yr./person	$100	None
Deductible/yr./family	$300	None
Coinsurance/yr./person	20% co-insurance 2,000 maximum expense	20% co-insurance where indicated
Supplemental Benefits		
Accident dental services	Major medical coverage	Paid in full
Adult periodic exam	Not covered	Paid in full
Blood	Major medical after first two pints	Paid in full
Complete hearing exam	Not covered	Paid in full
Immunization and preventive injections	Not covered	Paid in full
Pediatric routine	Not covered	Paid in full
Physical therapy	Major medical coverage	20% co-insurance
Private-duty nursing	Major medical coverage	Paid in full
Routine dental services	Not covered	Not covered
Routine eye exam	Not covered	$15 co-payment
Skilled nursing facility	Not covered	Paid in full with prior approval

Figure 7.2 Plan comparison worksheet with representative benefits listed.

TABLE 7.1 • SAMPLE CHARGES FOR MEDICAL SERVICES, 1993

Office Visits	
Family practice, general practice	$ 59
Internal medicine	116
Pediatrics	71
OB/GYN	93
Surgical specialists	85
Surgical Procedures	
Appendectomy	1,000
Breast augmentation (bilateral)	3,000
Cholecystectomy	1,503
Complete rhinoplasty	3,000
Complete obstetrical care	2,000
Coronary artery bypass with three autogenous grafts	5,486
Diagnostic knee arthoscopy	844
Dilation and curettage	600
Implant pacemaker	1,550
Hospital Expenses	
Average cost to hospital per day	820
Average cost to hospital per stay (7.2 days)	5,794

SOURCE: Data of fees for medical services from *Source Book of Health Insurance Data* (New York, N.Y., Health Insurance Institute, 1994), Tables 4.12 and 4.17. Data on hospital costs from U.S. Bureau of the Census, *Statistical Abstract of the United States, 1994,* Table 182.

Usual, customary, and reasonable (UCR): The typical fee charged in your region for a specific good or service. Insurers will generally not provide reimbursement for expenses in excess of this amount.

Medical insurance: Insurance coverage for general nonsurgical physician care at the office or hospital.

imum amount to be paid for each. A preferred policy, such as one offered by Blue Shield, agrees to pay all surgical costs, as long as these are **usual, customary, and reasonable (UCR)** for your geographic area. If you have a policy with this provision, be sure to find out whether your physician will accept this amount as payment in full. If the doctor will not, find out how much extra he or she is planning to charge you. Don't be embarrassed to discuss fees. If you are going to be charged more than UCR, it is the physician who is making money an issue, not you.

Medical insurance provides payments for general nonsurgical physician care at the office or in the hospital. Average fees for office visits are also shown in Table 7.1. Traditional insurance has used an indemnity approach, paying you so much for each visit. Because you are likely to go to a doctor during the year, as indicated in Table 7.2, such insurance is relatively expensive. It has proved efficient, however, as one component of a comprehensive health care plan offered by a health maintenance organization (HMO). Under an HMO, office visits may be fully cov-

TABLE 7.2 • NUMBER OF YEARLY PHYSICIAN AND DENTAL VISITS PER PERSON IN THE UNITED STATES, 1994

	Age					
Type of Visit	Under 5	5–17	18–24	25–44	45–64	65 and Older
Physician visits	6.9	3.5	4.1	5.4	7.2	10.6
Dental visits	.5	2.4	1.6	2.0	2.4	2.0

SOURCE: U.S. Bureau of the Census, *Statistical Abstract of the United States, 1994,* Table 174.

Co-payment: A payment by the insured covering less than the full cost of the service; the remainder is paid by the insurer.

Major medical insurance: Provides protection after limits on basic health care coverage have been exceeded.

Co-insurance: A requirement that the insured pay a certain percentage of the medical expenses incurred.

ered, or you may be required to make a small co-payment. A **co-payment** is a dollar fee covering less than the full cost of the service. Its purpose is to limit unnecessary use.

MAJOR MEDICAL COVERAGE The one component of health care insurance you should not do without is **major medical insurance,** because it eliminates the greatest risk to your financial health. Basic health care coverage may not pay all of your health care expenses, either because particular services are not covered or because you have exceeded the limits on coverage. Major medical is the backup you need when catastrophic illness strikes. If, after reimbursement under basic health care insurance, your health care expenses exceed a stated deductible, major medical will pick up part of the overage. Most policies have a **co-insurance** clause under which the insurer pays 80 percent of the overage and you pay the other 20 percent. The better policies put a dollar limit, perhaps $2,000, on your out-of-pocket expenses. The illustration in Figure 7.3 is based on the major medical provisions for the fee-for-service policy in Figure 7.2. In this example, health care costs total $9,200, of which basic health coverage pays $4,900, leaving a total overage of $4,300. After a deductible of $100 and a co-insurance payment of $840, your total out-of-pocket expenses would be $940. According to the terms of this policy, the amount you pay normally cannot exceed $2,000 per year.

LONG-TERM CARE COVERAGE With recent attempts by government, hospitals, and insurers to reduce the average hospital stay, nursing or rehabilitative care at home or in a skilled nursing facility is becoming increasingly important. Where coverage for such services does exist, it applies only to services absolutely required by the illness or injury. Most nursing homes are not skilled nursing facilities, and insurers will not typically pay for care that is primarily personal or custodial.

Medicare and most traditional health care insurance limits nursing care to a fixed number of days in a skilled care facility. But policies designed to specifically cover long-term care are sold by insurance companies. These are typically indemnity policies that pay up to a set daily limit for nursing home expenses and home health care. To qualify for custodial care under these policies you must demonstrate that you can no longer care for yourself.

Figure 7.3
Sample illustration of major medical coverage.

	Cost	Basic Health Payment	Overage
Hospital bill	$5,200	$3,000	$2,200
Physician services (office visits)	840	—	840
Surgical services	2,400	1,900	500
Prescription drugs	760	—	760
Total	$9,200	$4,900	$4,300
		Minus individual deductible	−100
			$4,200
			× .20
		Co-insurance	$ 840

You pay the lesser of the deductible ($100) plus the co-insurance ($840) or $2,000.

Long-term care policies are expensive, especially for the aged. The older you are when you first purchase long-term care coverage, the more the policy usually costs. This is because your chances of needing benefits are greater as you age. Moreover, even high premiums are no guarantee that you will get the anticipated benefits. Some insureds have mistakenly thought their policies covered custodial care, whereas the contracts covered only the more restrictive skilled or intermediate care. Others were denied benefits because they did not reveal preexisting conditions on ambiguous forms, or their entry into a nursing home was not preceded by a required three-day hospital stay. Under this last requirement, about half the people in nursing homes would be denied coverage.

Dental insurance: Primarily covers the cost of preventive care, with co-insurance on nonroutine dental work.

DENTAL INSURANCE **Dental insurance** is a nice fringe benefit if it is included in your group plan and paid by your employer. One of the fastest-growing forms of insurance, dental insurance is similar to other kinds of health insurance. Many plans require a deductible, have maximum reimbursement limits, or have co-payments. One major difference is that dental insurance covers the cost of preventive care, usually paying all of the fees for routine checkups and cleanings, 20 percent or more of the cost of fillings and other dental treatment, and 50 percent or so of the cost of orthodontia, bridges, and crowns. If your dental insurance is not part of your overall health insurance plan, it may not be cost-effective to buy the insurance on your own. You should be able to plan for these expenses in your yearly budget. Moreover, expensive dental surgery to correct birth deformities or injuries is in most cases already covered under the surgical expense component of the basic health care package.

SPECIFIC DISEASE AND ACCIDENT INSURANCE Widely sold through the media, specific disease insurance is one policy you should definitely not purchase. Not only is it likely to be a poor bargain, it also makes no financial sense. Why would you want a policy that covers you if you have cancer but pays nothing if you have a heart attack? You need broader coverage that pays out no matter what the cause of illness. Companies offering such policies are playing on our fears of a dreaded disease.

Although accident insurance is often sold by reputable major insurers, the reasons against purchasing it are much the same as those for not purchasing specific disease insurance. The purpose of health care insurance is to reduce your financial risks. Gambling on the cause of future illnesses and injuries does not serve that purpose.

Important Provisions

No matter what type of health care coverage you may have, certain provisions will indicate the quality of your insurance coverage. In general, those with shorter waiting periods, fewer exclusions, and higher policy limits offer better protection.

Preexisting conditions clause: Excludes from coverage certain medical conditions that existed before the policy was initiated.

Waiting period: Preexisting conditions may be covered after this period of time.

WAITING PERIOD UNDER PREEXISTING CONDITIONS CLAUSE All individual policies and some group policies will contain a **preexisting conditions clause,** which excludes from coverage certain types of injuries and illnesses that began before the policy was issued. These conditions may later be covered after a specified **waiting period.**

Be sure you understand how you and your family might be affected by this clause. It is a common means of denying payment. You may be better off keeping

Box 7.1

PERSONAL FINANCE NEWS

Late Edition

Congress Passes the Family and Medical Leave Act

You need to take off work for a family emergency, but you are afraid of losing your job. The Family and Medical Leave Act (FMLA) of 1993 might provide the help you need. Under the act, employers are required to grant employees up to 12 weeks of unpaid leave a year for family emergencies. Moreover, some state laws require even more generous leaves.

The law covers only firms with 50 or more workers, but this includes about half of the labor force. To be eligible you must have spent at least 1,250 hours on the job over the last 12 months. However, you can't be a key person in the enterprise. Employers can exclude the top-paid 10 percent of their employees.

Your leave request may be based upon:

- your own serious health condition
- the birth or adoption of a child
- the need to care for a child, spouse, or parent with a serious health condition

The tricky part is determining a "serious health condition." Your employer can require that a health care provider certify that you or your family member has a "serious health condition" as defined by the FMLA. But because of protections under the Americans with Disabilities Act, your employer can't ask a health care provider for a diagnosis.

It is clear that the common cold, the flu, or a stomachache does not qualify as a serious medical condition. The medical problem typically must require in-patient care, at least two visits to a health care provider, or at a minimum three days absence from work. However, intermittent absences caused by a chronic disabling medical condition may also qualify. For example, disability resulting from pregnancy such as morning sickness qualifies.

When possible, you must give your employer 30 days' notice that you need the time off from work. If you ask for FMLA leave, your employer must respond to your request in writing before your leave starts. Employers are required to inform employees as to whether the requested leave qualifies as FMLA leave.

Although you don't receive pay under the act, you still retain some important benefits. Your employer must maintain your health insurance benefits and any other benefits (such as life insurance and disability insurance) that are maintained for employees taking non-FMLA leave. And when you return, you are guaranteed your seniority rights and the same or equivalent job.

As of yet, most workers have not taken advantage of FMLA. Private estimates are that about 1 percent have taken an FMLA leave, and most of those were maternity leaves. Possible reasons that people aren't using the leave are that they can't afford the unpaid leave, they think it will hurt their career, or they're simply afraid of angering the boss.

Employers that don't obey the law can get into trouble with the U.S. Department of Labor. It is the Department of Labor's charge to investigate and enforce the regulations. If you run into problems, you should contact them. Complaints that can't be resolved may be pursued in civil actions. Employers that have been found to violate the act can be held liable for back pay, lost fringe benefits, and any other actual monetary loss resulting from the violation. In most cases, however, the damages cannot exceed 12 weeks' compensation plus actual monetary loss.

a less-than-satisfactory policy rather than waiting the necessary time before you are fully covered under a new policy. Also, beware of policies that do not waive the preexisting conditions clause after a given period of time.

Guaranteed renewability: Guarantees coverage up to a specified age upon payment of premiums, although future premiums may increase.

GUARANTEED RENEWABILITY Unless you are purchasing temporary coverage to bridge a gap between group insurance policies, you should consider purchasing insurance that is guaranteed renewable until age 65. **Guaranteed renewability** means that no matter what your health, your coverage will continue so long as you pay the premiums. The company does, however, retain the right to increase rates for a given class of insureds.

POLICY LIMITS The maximum amount the insurance company will pay out is particularly important on the major medical portion of your coverage. The limit may hold for each benefit period, usually a calendar year, over a lifetime, or for each illness or accident. Never purchase a policy with a limit of less than $250,000 on hospitalization payments for a given illness or accident per benefit period, or less than a lifetime maximum of $500,000. The likelihood of huge medical expenses, although small, does exist.

WAIVER OF PREMIUM This clause waives your premium payment should you be unable to work because of illness or injury. If your health insurance policy does not contain this provision, you must plan for these payments under your disability income protection.

EXCLUSIONS Some injuries and illnesses will not be covered even when there is no medical history of them. For example, intentionally self-inflicted injuries, injuries covered by workers' compensation, mental illness, or injuries resulting from war or military service are typically excluded. Such elective procedures as cosmetic surgery and dental treatment may be covered only if the condition being treated results from birth defects or accidental injuries.

Some policies will cover maternity expenses, and others will exclude them. Although a maternity plan may be helpful if you are planning an addition to your family, it is not necessary financial protection. After all, you should be able to budget adequately for these expenses over at least a nine-month period. Of much greater importance is how your policy handles the costs of childbirth complications and the costs of treating birth defects. Families capable of bearing children should have insurance that covers all costs of complications and costs of the newborn. Not having this coverage leaves you open to substantial and unnecessary risk. In the United States, 7.1 percent of infants weigh less than 5½ pounds at birth. Although most of these infants may be normal except for size, many hospitals require that each spends some time in an intensive care unit. The specialized care provided in such units can leave you with a substantial hospital bill. If your policy covers dependents only from age 14 days on, you will not be covered for these current and future expenses. Most states have responded to this situation by requiring that all policies covering dependents begin protection at birth. However, policies excluding newborns are still sold in states that do not have this requirement. If you are of childbearing age, avoid these policies.

Insurers and Providers

Blue Cross/Blue Shield: The nation's largest nonprofit provider of hospital and medical insurance.

Both the government and the private sector supply health care insurance. The federal government, through the Medicare programs, is the primary provider of insurance for those 65 and over. The private sector provides supplemental insurance to those in this age group, and the entire insurance program for the rest of the population. **Blue Cross/Blue Shield,** a nonprofit health care insurer, is the nation's largest private insurer. Next are the commercial insurers, basically companies specializing in life and health insurance. Health maintenance organizations (HMOs), the most recent entrants into the health insurance market, occupy the smallest share. However, with the backing of major companies, such as Blue Cross/Blue Shield, which is also the nation's largest operator of HMOs, their market share is growing rapidly.

BLUE CROSS/BLUE SHIELD Blue Cross and Blue Shield work in conjunction with each other to supply both hospital and medical insurance. Blue Cross is largely sponsored and controlled by hospitals and provides hospital insurance using the service benefit approach. Blue Shield, typically under the control of local medical societies, supplies medical and surgical coverage.

About 90 percent of Blue Shield's benefit expenditures go directly for physicians' services. The traditional insurance sold by Blue Shield pays for specified medical procedures and uses a usual, customary, and reasonable (UCR) fee-reimbursement policy. This policy is based on fees charged in your local area and is typically set at a level that would provide complete reimbursement for bills submitted by most physicians. In other words, if your physician bills you for more than the UCR, the majority of patients in your area have been charged less for the same service. Your physician may require a supplemental fee agreement under which you will pay any excess charges not paid by Blue Shield, but in the event you are billed for excess amounts, refer the bill back to Blue Shield for negotiation.

Because the Blues are exempt from taxation as nonprofit organizations, and because of the economic benefits they derive from their huge size, they can usually provide comprehensive benefits at lower cost than other traditional insurers.

Commercial insurer: Excluding Blue Cross/Blue Shield, any private insurer providing health care insurance.

COMMERCIAL INSURERS As used in the health care industry, the term **commercial insurer** stands for any private company that is not associated with Blue Cross/Blue Shield. A commercial insurer may be either a not-for-profit or a for-profit corporation. These companies control approximately 45 percent of the health care insurance market.

Without a standard format for health care policies, and given the willingness of many of these companies to tailor their policies to meet the specific needs of groups and individuals, general statements regarding the quality and types of plans offered by commercial insurers are impossible. Among their ranks are some highly reputable companies willing to experiment with novel group benefits, including routine dental coverage and alcohol abuse treatment. On the other hand, you will find companies selling dread disease or indemnity policies that pay out little of what is collected in premiums. If you understand the basics of health care insurance discussed in this chapter and you compare the policies of various insurers, you should be able to steer clear of the hucksters to find some attractive insurance alternatives in the commercial market.

Health maintenance organization (HMO): Provides comprehensive health care services on a prepaid basis. It is both an insurer and a provider of health care.

Fee-for-service health insurance: The insured selects a provider of medical care and is then reimbursed for covered medical expenses.

HMOs A **health maintenance organization (HMO)** differs from the other insurers because it is not only the provider of insurance but also the provider of the health care. The HMO premium represents a prepayment for future medical services, which are then provided as needed at little or no out-of-pocket cost. With traditional **fee-for-service health insurance,** you seek out a provider of medical care and are then reimbursed for covered medical expenses. The amount of reimbursement may be based upon a usual, customary, and reasonable rate, or it may be set at some fixed amount. You may be responsible for amounts over and above these set rates.

The Health Maintenance Act of 1973 specified stringent requirements for federally qualified HMOs. In brief, they must provide an extensive list of comprehensive benefits, guarantee open enrollment periods for specific times during the year, and purchase insolvency insurance to protect policy holders in the event the HMO cannot meet its debts. In return, the law relieved the industry from many state laws limiting the formation of HMOs and provided that most employers must offer an HMO alternative when available.

Membership has grown rapidly to over 46 million members in about 550 HMOs and now includes about 20 percent of the population. The reason more workers are not members probably is that the employee contribution required under an HMO plan is higher than regular health insurance premiums. Although they are more expensive, HMOs also tend to be more comprehensive. They typically stress preventive health care by paying for periodic physical examinations and other routine office visits with lower deductibles and co-insurance payments than fee-for-service insurance. In addition, many plans also cover such items as dental services, prescription drugs, and extended nursing care.

Group-staff HMO: Delivers health services at one or more facilities through groups of physicians working on a salaried or contractual basis.

Individual practice arrangement (IPA) HMO: Physicians maintain their own offices and then are reimbursed by the HMO for services performed.

There are two basic types of HMOs: the group-staff arrangement and the individual practice arrangement. The **group-staff HMO** provides services at one or more locations with salaried physicians. The **individual practice arrangement (IPA)** contracts with private physicians who maintain their own offices and then pays them on a fee-for-service schedule. Individuals then choose from among the participating physicians for their needed medical services. IPAs generally offer a greater choice of physicians and more conveniently located medical services. Although slightly more costly than group-staff HMOs, IPAs have proved popular. Over the last few years membership in IPAs has grown much more rapidly than in group-staff HMOs.

If all other factors are equal, your choice between a traditional insurer and an HMO should be based on a comparison of your estimated savings on the direct cost of medical services versus the higher monthly premium. The HMO will often prove the better choice for families with more and younger children, because their direct expenses for routine office visits are likely to be higher under a traditional insurer.

Open-ended enrollment plan: An HMO plan in which members may use providers outside the HMO but incur additional cost in the form of a deductible or co-insurance payment.

Recently, some HMOs have begun to offer an **open-ended enrollment plan,** also called a *POS (point of service) plan.* Under an open-ended plan, you may select non-HMO providers if you are willing to incur additional costs in the form of higher deductibles and co-insurances. This provides a health care alternative for those who find that they are dissatisfied with the HMO's choice of providers.

Preferred provider organization (PPO): Selectively offered health care services providing care to insureds at a lower out-of-pocket cost.

PPOs Virtually nonexistent in the mid-1980s, **preferred provider organizations (PPOs)** currently enroll about 20 percent of the participants in employer-sponsored plans. A PPO is only a provider, not an insurer. It works either directly with an employer or through the employer's insurer to provide medical services at less than customary rates to the company's employees. Those who choose a PPO option may still be able to utilize non-PPO services at increased cost. This is not true for persons who belong to an *EPO (exclusive provider organization).* They must receive care from an affiliated provider or pay the entire cost themselves.

Medicaid: A joint federal-state–sponsored program covering medical expenses for the indigent.

MEDICARE AND MEDICAID **Medicaid** is neither an insurer nor a provider of health care. It is a joint federal-state effort to cover the medical expenses of the indigent. Unless you find yourself in this group, you will not have contact with Medicaid services. The coverage and quality of the services offered differ from state to state. Information can be obtained at your state's welfare office.

Medicare: A federal health insurance program for those age 65 or older, or those with certain sicknesses or disabilities.

In one way or another, **Medicare** concerns us all. We either have a relative who is affected by the program, or we will eventually consider enrolling ourselves. A federal health insurance program for those 65 or older, or those with chronic kidney failure or certain other disabilities, it consists of two parts: Part A is hospital insurance and Part B is medical insurance. Coverage under each part is outlined in Figure 7.4. The hospital insurance is financed through the Social Security taxes you pay while you work. The medical insurance is voluntary and is partly paid by premiums from those who choose to participate. These programs are administered through the Social Security Administration. You should contact a local office for information and applications.

Workers' compensation: State programs providing health and disability income coverage for work-related illnesses and injuries.

WORKERS' COMPENSATION All states have **workers' compensation** programs that help pay for medical expenses and lost income resulting from work-related illnesses or injuries. However, not all workers are covered, nor is coverage required in all states. You should ask your employer whether you are covered. If you are, the type and amount of benefits you may receive are set down in state laws. Your personnel office or the state compensation office can provide you with a schedule of potential benefits.

Selecting Health Care Insurance

For many people, health insurance selection is tied to employment selection. They simply refuse to accept a job unless the employer provides adequate health care

Figure 7.4 Coverage under Medicare Part A and Part B.

SOURCE: U.S. Department of Health and Human Services, *Guide to Health Insurance for People on Medicare.* Updated for 1995 coverage.

MEDICARE HOSPITAL INSURANCE BENEFITS (PART A)

	For Covered Services Each Benefit Period		
Service	Benefit	Medicare Pays	You Pay
Hospitalization: Semiprivate room and board, general nursing, and miscellaneous hospital services and supplies. Includes meals, special care units, drugs, lab tests, diagnostic X-rays, medical supplies, operating and recovery room, anesthesia, and rehabilitation services.	First 60 days 61st to 90th day *91st to 150th day Beyond 150 days A *benefit period* begins on the first day you receive service as an in-patient in a hospital and ends after you have been out of the hospital or skilled nursing facility for 60 days in a row.	All but $716 All but $179 a day All but $358 a day Nothing	$716 $179 a day $358 a day All costs
Posthospital skilled nursing facility care: In a facility approved by Medicare. You must have been in a hospital for at least 3 days and enter the facility within 30 days after hospital discharge.	First 20 days Additional 80 days Beyond 100 days Medicare and private insurance will not pay for most nursing home care. You pay for custodial care and most care in a nursing home.	100% of approved amount All but $89.50 Nothing	Nothing $89.50 All costs
Home health care	Unlimited as medically necessary	Full cost	Nothing
Hospice care: Available to terminally ill.	Unlimited as medically necessary	All but costs of out-patient drugs and in-patient respite care	Limited cost sharing for out-patient drugs and in-patient respite care
Blood	Blood	All but first 3 pints	For first 3 pints

*Sixty reserve days may be used only once in a lifetime; days used are not renewable.

MEDICAL INSURANCE BENEFITS (PART B)			
	For Covered Services Each Calendar Year		
Service	**Benefit**	**Medicare Pays**	**You Pay**
Medical expense: Physician's services, in-patient and out-patient medical services and supplies, physical and speech therapy, ambulance, etc.	Medicare pays for medical services in or out of the hospital. Some insurance policies pay less (or nothing) for hospital out-patient medical services or services in a doctor's office.	80% of approved amount (after $100 deductible)	$100 deductible* plus 20% of balance of approved amount (plus any charge above approved amount)**
Home health care	Unlimited as medically necessary	Full cost	Nothing
Out-patient hospital treatment	Unlimited as medically necessary	80% of approved amount (after $100 deductible)	Subject to deductible plus 20% of balance of approved amount
Blood	Blood	80% of approved amount (after first 3 pints and $100 deductible)	For first 3 pints plus 20% of balance of approved amount after $100 deductible

*Once you have had $100 of expense for covered services in a calendar year, the Part B deductible does not apply to any further covered services you receive in that year.

**YOU PAY FOR charges higher than the amount approved by Medicare unless the doctor or supplier agrees to accept Medicare's approved amount as the total charge for services rendered.

Figure 7.4 Continued.

protection. On the other hand, because of the tie-in between employment and health insurance, a few individuals in ill health may be deterred from looking for a job. They fear that employers, concerned about rising medical costs, may be reluctant to hire them. The Americans with Disabilities Act of 1990 provides some help to these prospective workers by setting down hiring restrictions on businesses that employ more than 15 people. Basically, an employer cannot deny a person a job because that individual's medical condition may cause increased insurance claims or higher insurance premiums. Preexisting conditions, however, can be excluded from coverage as long as these same exclusions are applied to all other workers.

Health insurance is a significant fringe benefit provided to most full-time workers. About 83 percent of full-time employees in medium-sized and large firms receive such employment-related health care benefits. Health care selection for these covered employees may entail no more than choosing among a list of employer-provided options. Unfortunately, employee coverage drops to only 71 percent in smaller firms with fewer than 100 employees, and it is virtually nonexistent for part timers. Those who are not covered will face the difficult task of searching for and paying for appropriate individual coverage. Some helpful hints that might guide that journey are given in Figure 7.5.

GROUP COVERAGE Group coverage is generally less expensive than individual insurance. If you are one of the few who cannot take part in a group plan at work,

HINTS ON SHOPPING FOR PRIVATE HEALTH INSURANCE

Shop Carefully before You Buy Policies differ widely as to coverage and cost, and companies differ as to service. Contact different companies and compare the policies carefully before you buy. If an agent won't help you, don't buy from that agent.

Don't Buy More Policies Than You Need Duplicate coverage is costly and not necessary. A single comprehensive policy is better than several policies with overlapping or duplicate coverages. For comprehensive coverage, consider continuing the group coverage you have at work; joining an HMO; buying a catastrophic or major medical policy or buying a Medicare Supplement policy.

Check for Preexisting Condition Exclusions Many policies exclude coverage for preexisting health conditions.

Don't be misled by the phrase, "no medical examination required." If you have had a health problem, the insurer might not cover you for expenses connected with that problem.

Beware of Replacing Existing Coverage Be suspicious of a suggestion that you give up your policy and buy a replacement. Often the new policy will impose waiting periods or will have exclusions or waiting periods for preexisting conditions your current policy covers.

On the other hand, don't keep inadequate policies simply because you have had them a long time. You don't get credit with a company just because you've paid many years for a policy.

Be Aware of Maximum Benefits Most policies have some type of limit on benefits that may be expressed in terms of dollars payable or the number of days for which payment will be made.

Check Your Right to Renew Beware of policies that let the company refuse to renew your policy on an individual basis. These policies provide the least permanent coverage.

Most policies cannot be canceled by the company unless all policies of that type are canceled in the state. Therefore, these policies cannot be canceled because of claims or disputes. Some policies are guaranteed renewable for life. Policies that can be renewed automatically offer added protection.

Policies to Supplement Medicare Are Neither Sold nor Serviced by State or Federal Government State insurance departments approve policies sold by insurance companies, but approval means only that the company and policy meet requirements of state law. Do not believe statements that insurance to supplement Medicare is a government-sponsored program. If anyone tells you that he or she is from the government and later tries to sell you an insurance policy, report that person to your state insurance department. This type of representation is a violation of federal law.

Know with Whom You're Dealing A company must meet certain qualifications to do business in your state. This is for your protection. Agents also must be licensed by your state and must carry proof of licensing showing their name and the company they represent. If the agent cannot show such proof, do not buy from that person. A business card is not a license.

Keep Agents' and/or Companies' Names, Addresses, and Telephone Numbers Write down the agents' and/or companies' names, addresses, and telephone numbers; or ask for a business card.

Take Your Time Do not let a short-term enrollment period high-pressure you. Professional salespeople will not rush you. If you question whether a program is worthy, ask the salesperson to explain it to a friend or relative whose judgment you respect. Allow yourself time to think through your decision.

Figure 7.5 Shopping for health insurance.

look into group policies offered through fraternal and professional organizations. But be careful. Some insurers advertise their policies as part of a group plan but provide none of the expected cost savings. When the identifiable group is not likely to be in any better health than the population as a whole, there is little reason to believe the policy is a good buy. For example, if the group policy is sold "exclusively" to "any American of any age who ever served in any of the Armed Forces anywhere in the world," you probably can do better elsewhere.

INTERIM COVERAGE Previously, workers who lost their jobs were also likely to lose their health insurance protection. To remedy this doubly disastrous situation, Congress now requires employers with 20 or more workers to provide terminating employees with continued health care coverage under a law called COBRA. This must be made available to those ex-workers who cannot obtain either alternative group insurance or Medicare coverage. The employer may charge you for the insurance, but in most instances the cost to you cannot be more than 102 percent of group insurance rates.

Mandated continuation periods are listed in Figure 7.6. When the continuation period ends, the group coverage must be convertible to an individual policy. Although the individual policy can have a higher price and provide fewer benefits, it still may be wise for you to exercise your conversion rights. An entirely new policy would exclude preexisting conditions and require a waiting period before full coverage began. The continuation and conversion of previous health insurance coverage can be used to eliminate any gaps in coverage due to a change in employment or marital status.

Family members also have a right to request a continuation of benefits for three years with the right of conversion thereafter. The circumstances under which benefits would be continued include death of the covered worker, separation or divorce from the covered spouse, or loss of dependent status by a child of an insured parent. If you are a young worker without coverage in your new job, continuing coverage under a parent's group plan is a good idea. As stated previously, it is this age group that is least likely to have adequate health insurance protection.

INDIVIDUAL COVERAGE Most group insurance plans offer expensive comprehensive health coverage that includes basic health and major medical benefits. Individual policies cost 30 to 40 percent more, with a comprehensive family policy costing over $3,000 a year. You can hold down this expense by purchasing only major medical coverage with large deductibles and making out-of-pocket payments for your basic health needs. Increasing the deductible from $100 to $1,000 can cut your premiums by 40 to 50 percent. If you set aside an emergency fund, you can use those resources to self-insure against unexpected basic health costs. Meanwhile, the major medical insurance provides you with the backup protection you need in case of catastrophic illness or injury.

MAJOR MEDICAL COVERAGE When comparing and evaluating health plans, the first thing you should look at is the major medical coverage. Seriously consider only those that provide adequate major medical protection. Although the basic health coverage will affect your day-to-day expenditure, it is the major medical coverage that pays out in time of greatest need. If the employer's health care plan has a maximum limit on reimbursement of less than $250,000 per illness or per life-

Figure 7.6 Continuation period for group health insurance.

Qualifying Events	Beneficiary	Term of Coverage
Termination Reduced hours	Employee Spouse Dependent child	18 months (For individuals who qualify for Social Security disability benefits, special rules extend coverage an additional 11 months)
Employee entitled to Medicare Divorce or legal separation Death of covered employee	Spouse Dependent child	36 months
Loss of "dependent child" status	Dependent child	36 months

Box 7.2 SAVING MONEY
A Flexible Spending Account for Medical Expenditures

Employer-provided flexible spending accounts generally permit you to allocate a portion of your salary for this purpose. Sometimes employers match employee contributions or contribute a fixed amount. If tax-qualified, the salary dollars paid into this account are tax exempt. These dollars may then be used to pay for expenses that would be deductible from personal income taxes under IRS guidelines.

One popular use of flexible spending accounts is to pay for the deductibles and co-insurance on health insurance plans. The money placed in the flexible spending account can be used to pay the difference between the employee's medical expenses and the amount paid for by the company's health plan. Normally, you would have to early $138.89 in taxable income to pay for a $100 deductible if you were in the 28 percent marginal tax bracket and your total medical expenses for the year did not exceed 7.5 percent of your family's gross income. Using tax-exempt dollars through a flexible spending account would result in savings of $38.89, regardless of your proportional medical expenses.

As employers increase deductibles and co-insurance payments in order to hold down the increasing cost of medical insurance, the tax savings provided by flexible spending accounts becomes greater. There is, however, one significant drawback. At the end of the year, any unused funds you have allocated to this account are forfeited. You either use it or lose it.

For persons engaging in personal financial planning, this should not be a serious problem. If you review previous budgets and your upcoming medical needs in the pro forma budget, you should be in a good position to estimate your flexible account needs conservatively and obtain the maximum tax advantage.

time, you should consider supplementing your employer's coverage with privately purchased major medical insurance.

HMO VERSUS TRADITIONAL INSURANCE Assuming that adequate major medical protection exists, you might then turn to analyzing the basic health benefits. Unless the plan is being offered for the first time, the experiences of your co-workers should prove relevant. Try to find other workers with families having similar characteristics to your own and who are living in an area close to yours.

An HMO is likely to cover more basic health care benefits than a fee-for-service plan. It can do this because it charges a slightly higher premium and is more successful at holding down hospital and diagnostic costs. To find out whether the added expense is worth it, simply add up your family's out-of-pocket medical expenses for each of the last few years. If the HMO would have covered these expenses, and they exceed the additional annual premium on the HMO, then it might be the preferred plan for your family. In general, the larger and the younger the family, the more attractive the basic health coverage of an HMO will appear.

If your family has been reluctant to seek medical care when needed because of the necessary out-of-pocket expenses under traditional insurance, the first-dollar coverage provided by many HMOs may be very attractive. In this situation the benefit-cost analysis based on previous expenses would be irrelevant. You might instead base your decision on the average number of office visits in Table 7.2. For example, a family with both parents and two children might average 17.8 office visits per year. At $59 a visit, an HMO that provided office coverage with a $15 copayment would be worth about $783 more than a plan that did not.

Some advocates of HMOs have suggested that they are better than traditional insurers because they concentrate on preventive rather than curative medicine. Because the physician has a financial interest in seeing you remain healthy, you supposedly receive better preventive care and therefore remain healthier. Critics argue that the physician also has a financial incentive to hold back medical care. There is evidence that hospital stays are shorter for patients of HMOs, but the reasons are unclear. As of now, it is not possible to make any generalizations about the quality of care provided by any particular category of health care plans.

Managed care: A health program that manages the services you receive in an attempt to provide adequate care while containing costs.

MANAGED CARE Both fee-for-service companies and HMOs offer managed care plans. **Managed care** is the current term applied to a health insurance plan that puts together a coherent network of providers. Your primary-care physician usually serves as the gatekeeper to this network. It is the gatekeeper's job to guide you through the network so as to ensure that you receive appropriate medical care in the most efficient and inexpensive way. This will limit your choice of physicians and hospitals. Therefore, when considering a managed care plan, you must analyze both the quality of coverage and the quality and location of the covered services. If you travel a lot or you have children living at school, be sure you understand how you will be reimbursed for medical expenses incurred outside the local area network.

The managed care concept has been introduced by many companies in an effort to hold down the heavy cost of medical care and the rising level of health insurance premiums. The three basic cost-containment features employed by managed care plans are: preadmission certification for hospital stays, utilization review for the appropriateness of care, and second opinions for nonemergency surgical procedures. Each of these features places limits on either your or your doctor's choice of medical care. The hope is that eliminating unnecessary or excessively costly choices will provide you with better health care for each dollar spent.

THE INSURANCE COMPANY Be sure to investigage the financial soundness of the medical insurer. A bankrupt insurer could leave you financially ruined. In 1991 Blue Cross and Blue Shield of West Virginia collapsed and left $50 million of medical bills unpaid. Many doctors and hospitals are now trying to collect those bills from patients.

In many states commercial insurers are covered by a state guarantee fund that protects policy holders if an insurer gets into financial trouble. Technically, however, Blue Cross/Blue Shield companies are not viewed as insurance companies and, thus, are not covered by the guarantee funds in most states. In reaction to the failure of the West Virginia company, regulators are attempting to integrate the Blues into state guarantee funds and to set requirements on financial reserves.

HMOs that are federally qualified by the Health Care Financing Administration must carry insurance to cover the unpaid bills of patients in the event they become insolvent. They are also required to include clauses in all contracts with doctors and patients prohibiting the providers of medical services from collecting directly from patients. Nevertheless, you still may suffer if preexisting conditions prevent you from obtaining insurance elsewhere.

A.M. Best and the other rating agencies mentioned in Chapter 6 can be used to check out the financial stability of the commercial insurers. Physicians in your area should be able to provide some insight on the financial soundness of local and regional insurers such as HMOs and the Blues. Be wary of companies that have been stretching out the payment of physician's fees or hospital expenses. This can indicate impending financial problems.

MEDICARE AND MEDIGAP INSURANCE Both Medicare hospital and medigap insurance are a good buy at the time you become eligible. Medicare will, however, leave some serious gaps in your health care coverage. You can consider closing them with a private supplemental health insurance policy. As Figure 7.4 shows,

Medicare does require substantial deductibles and co-insurance payments. In the event of catastrophic illness, these payments could deplete the investment portfolio generating your retirement income.

Medigap insurance: Private insurance meant to partially or totally cover those health care expenses that are not reimbursed by Medicare.

Medigap insurance is designed to fill this gap between expenses that are covered by Medicare and those that are not. A medigap policy that places a realistic limit on deductibles and co-insurance payments in an excellent choice. Furthermore, if you purchase a medigap policy within six months of turning age 65 and enrolling in Medicare Part B, federal law now states that you cannot be turned down or charged extra because of your health status or medical condition. And once you have coverage, a medigap policy may not be canceled or a renewal refused because of your ill health.

Under directions from the U.S. Congress, the National Association of Insurance Commissioners (NIAC) has developed 10 standardized policies. Medigap insurers can promote only those policies as supplemental medicare insurance; all must sell at least a basic policy that addresses the following gaps in Medicare benefits:

- Either all or none of the Medicare Part A in-patient hospital deductible
- The Part A hospital co-insurance for days 61–150
- The Part A co-insurance amount for each of Medicare's 60 nonrenewable lifetime hospital in-patient reserve days used
- The reasonable cost of the first three pints of blood or equivalent quantities of paced red blood cells per calendar year unless replaced in accordance with federal regulations
- The Part B co-insurance amount after the policy holder pays the $100 annual deductible

Medigap policies do not cover procedures that Medicare would consider unnecessary, nor do they cover custodial nursing care. Furthermore, federal and state permission to sell medigap insurance does not mean that the policies are reasonably priced or that the insurer is financially sound. Therefore, be sure to shop around.

DISABILITY INCOME PROTECTION

Only those workers with dependents need life insurance, but every worker needs disability income protection. Young workers often purchase life insurance while ignoring the much greater risk of disability. This is especially unfortunate because your chances of suffering a serious disability are surprisingly high. The Social Security Administration estimates that a 20-year-old has over a 20 percent probability of experiencing an insured disability before reaching age 65 (see Figure 7.7). Since the requirements for an insured disability are rather strict, it is likely that many more individuals will experience a significant earnings loss at some point in their work life. In fact, over one-fifth of 55- to 64-year-olds state that they have a work disability that limits the kind or amount of work they do.

Long-term disability insurance that bridges at least part of the gap between when short-term benefits end and retirement begins is provided to approximately two-fifths of the work force in firms with over 100 employees. In smaller establishments only about one-fifth of employees are similarly covered. Those without long-term disability protection must rely entirely on Social Security benefits or a de-

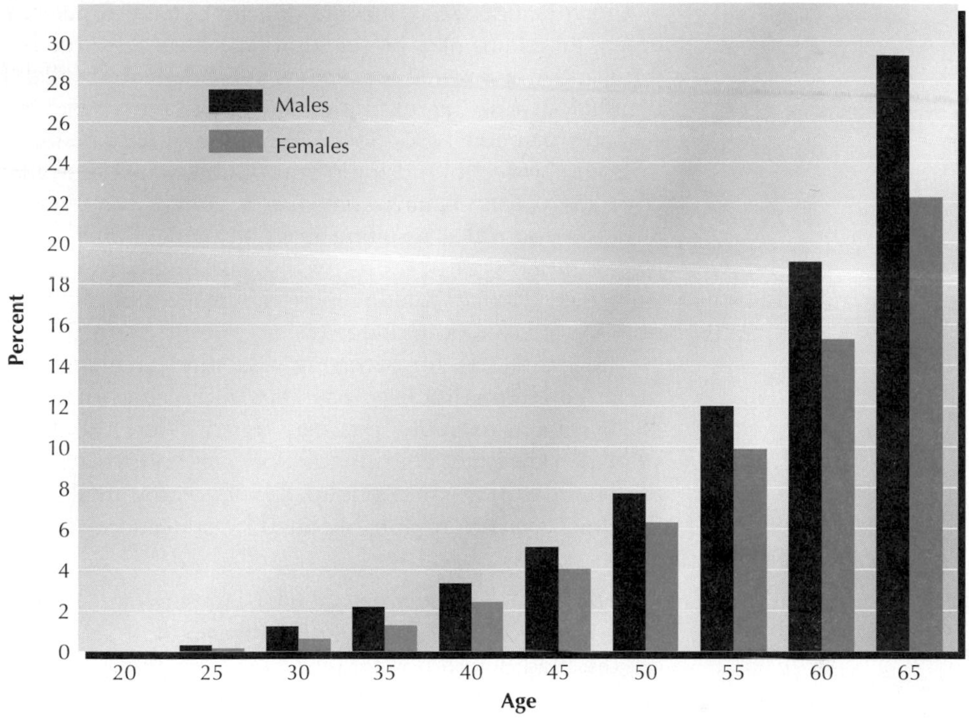

Figure 7.7 Probability of Social Security insured disability from age 20 to given age.

SOURCE: U.S. Department of Health and Human Services, A death and disability life table for the 1966 birth cohort.

clining bank account. Furthermore, few will be able to collect the Social Security benefits they may be depending on. The rules are quite strict. You must be able to prove that the disability is total and will last for at least one year or terminate in death. Nothing is paid out for partial disability unless it is preceded by a period of total disability. And if you do qualify, benefit checks do not begin until at least six months after you become disabled.

Sources of Disability Income

In the event you become disabled, you will probably have to rely on a variety of sources for support. Listed below are some common means of support used by the disabled during periods of reduced market income.

Accident insurance: Pays a set dollar amount in the event of physical dismemberment.

ACCIDENT INSURANCE Also called *dismemberment insurance,* **accident insurance** pays the insured a set dollar amount for the loss of life, limb, or sight. It pays nothing when the physical loss is caused by an illness rather than an accident. Furthermore, the amount paid is unrelated to your actual income loss. Its major selling point is its low price. One company charges $2 a month for $150,000 of accident life, with smaller payments for dismemberment. The price is low because your chances of collecting are small.

Disability income insurance: Partially replaces lost income during a period of defined disability.

DISABILITY INCOME INSURANCE As with health care insurance, the cheapest **disability income insurance** is obtained through group coverage sponsored by employers. Group benefits are typically integrated with Social Security payments and workers' compensation to provide a level of benefits dependent upon current wages. This usually does not exceed 60 percent of salary.

Individual disability income policies usually provide a set dollar amount of coverage. Premiums may be stated in terms of each $100 of monthly disability benefits purchased. Various endorsements and riders are available to tailor the policy to individual needs. For example, the amount of benefits may be dependent upon whether you qualify for Social Security disability benefits.

Both short-term and long-term disability income plans are available. Short-term coverage usually begins immediately after an accident but has a short waiting period for disabilities resulting from sickness. Benefit payments may then continue for six months, or at most, two years. Long-term disability income insurance typically has a longer waiting period, but benefits will continue for either a stated number of years or until age 65.

The conditions for receiving disability payments are generally more stringent under long-term disability insurance and may even change with the duration of the disability. For example, you may be considered disabled over the first two to five years if you cannot perform the duties of your own occupation. Payments after this period, however, will continue only if you are unable to engage in any occupation for which you are reasonably fitted by education, training, or experience.

PENSION PLANS Instead of purchasing separate group disability insurance, some employers will incorporate a disability option into the existing pension plan. If you are disabled before normal retirement age, you may be able to receive an immediate pension under a disability clause in the pension plan. The method for calculating monthly benefits may or may not differ from that used for normal retirement. However, even at reduced benefit levels, this alternative may be desirable.

Also look for a waiver of contributions clause. Under this option the employer will continue to contribute to your pension plan for as long as you are disabled. Thus, at normal retirement age you could collect the full retirement pension even though you had not worked up until normal retirement age.

SOCIAL SECURITY To be considered disabled under the Social Security law, you must have a physical condition that prevents you from doing any substantial gainful work and that is expected to last 12 months or is expected to result in death. In 1996, if you could earn over $500 a month in gross wages, after deductions for medical services and equipment required because of your impairment, you were considered capable of substantial gainful employment. Obviously, these requirements rule out Social Security payments for all but the severely and, apparently, permanently handicapped. Because you and your family could suffer a severe reduction in income and still be ineligible for disability income from Social Security, you will likely have a need for private disability income insurance.

To receive this disability income protection, you must have accumulated a sufficient number of work credits in recent employment. The precise requirements and method for calculating the monthly benefit are explained in Appendix B on Social Security.

WORKERS' COMPENSATION If the disabling injury or illness is work related, you may also be entitled to disability benefits under your state's workers' compensation statutes. These laws hold employers strictly liable for injuries in the workplace. This means that the employer is responsible, regardless of who is at fault. In return for assuming strict liability, compensation paid by employers is limited to mandated amounts. The benefits vary from state to state and are generally set equal to a given percentage of the average weekly wage within the state.

Specific types of injuries, such as loss of an arm, may come under the state's definition of permanent partial disabilities. For such injuries, the worker may receive a lump-sum payment or weekly payments for a limited time.

Many states also provide maintenance and benefits for workers undergoing rehabilitation. Workers' compensation or related programs may handle this coverage. Again, specifics can be provided at your state's workers' compensation office.

WAIVER OF PREMIUM OR PAYMENT CLAUSES Life and health insurance policies should be examined for clauses that waive future premium payments in the event of disability. If you have mortgage life insurance on your home or credit life insurance on a car loan, be sure also to examine these for a disability clause.

Insurance Clauses Affecting Disability Benefits

The quality of your disability insurance protection will depend upon more than just the promised monthly benefits. It will be determined largely by the duration and conditions under which the benefits will be paid.

DEFINITION OF DISABILITY How disabled must you be before you can collect benefits? The answer depends on the exact wording in the insurance contract. A policy that considers you disabled if you cannot perform the main duties of your regular occupation is better than one that considers you disabled if you are unable to engage in any occupation for which you are reasonably suited by education and experience. For example, a surgeon suffering the loss of a hand would be considered disabled under the first definition, but not necessarily under the second, if he or she could practice some other medical specialty. Obviously, both of these are better than a policy that considers you disabled only when you cannot engage in any type of paid work.

Most policies provide for some compensation in case of partial disability. Some definitions of partial disability are related to income loss, while others are defined in terms of the physical handicap. In many policies, however, you must experience a period of total disability before you collect partial benefits. The level of partial benefits may be equal to a set percentage of total disability benefits or geared to the income loss created by the partial disability. For example, if you earned $2,000 a month before the disability and now earn $500 a month, you have suffered a 75 percent reduction in income. If the maximum monthly benefit under the insurance policy is $1,000, you will receive a partial benefit equal to 75 percent of the $1,000 maximum monthly benefit. In this situation, partial disability benefits are $750 per month.

Disability elimination or waiting period: The time between the onset of the disability and the beginning of disability benefits.

ELIMINATION OR WAITING PERIOD The time between the onset of the disability and the beginning of disability payments is the **disability elimination or waiting period.** The longer the elimination period, the less likely you are to collect, and therefore, the lower your premium.

A good method of holding down your insurance costs is to opt for the longest elimination period you feel comfortable with. An emergency fund of highly liquid assets would permit you to continue to meet your financial obligations during this time. This is a highly rewarding strategy. Increasing the waiting period from 7 days to 60 days can reduce premiums by more than 50 percent; from 7 days to a year reduces them by more than 65 percent.

Be sure you understand how the policy handles intermittent disabilities. If you are disabled and then return to work after recuperating, must you again go through a waiting period if you have a relapse? Most policies don't require another elimination period if you are disabled by the same cause within six months after returning to work.

Benefit period: The duration of disability benefits.

BENEFIT PERIOD Depending on the policy, benefit payments may last one, five, ten years, or until age 65. Your greatest financial risk is a lifetime disability. The best risk-reduction strategy is to opt for the policy with the longer **benefit period** and to hold down your premiums by choosing a longer elimination period. If this strategy proves too expensive, policies with shorter benefit periods may be used to protect income during a readjustment period or during the financially demanding childrearing years.

Coordination of benefits clause: Ensures that disability benefits received from all sources are not greater than either some defined amount or a maximum percentage of previous earnings.

Social insurance substitute: Provision of private disability income benefits in the event that social insurance benefits are not forthcoming.

COORDINATION OF BENEFITS CLAUSE Many policies use a **coordination of benefits clause** to state the maximum disability income you may receive from all insurance sources, both public and private. The maximum is usually stated as a percentage of your current income. Without this limit, you might be able to earn more by owning multiple policies and not working.

SOCIAL INSURANCE SUBSTITUTE The **social insurance substitute** may be included as a rider or as part of the basic policy. In the event you are disabled but still do not satisfy the strict requirements for Social Security benefits or are not covered by workers' compensation, this provision will replace those benefits with private insurance payments. This is a highly desirable provision because it eliminates an important source of uncertainty regarding your total disability payments, thus permitting you to estimate more accurately potential disability income.

PROVISION FOR REHABILITATION Some policies explicitly provide for the continuation of benefits while you are in a rehabilitation program. This provision ensures that your benefits will not be terminated if you enter a work-related program. Some policies even state that tuition and equipment expenses for such programs will be covered. If you are disabled, and your policy does not contain this provision, you should check with the insurance company anyway. They may be more than willing to cover these expenses. After all, they have an incentive in seeing you return to gainful employment.

RENEWABILITY The disability policy should be renewable without evidence of insurability; however, renewability provisions do vary.

Class cancelable: The insurer can cancel policies for an entire class of insureds.

The most unfavorable provision is found in policies that are **class cancelable.** This means the insurance company has the right to cancel an entire class of policies. For example, it can cancel all policies written before a specific date or within a specific state. If you are in poor health, this action can leave you in the position of finding expensive alternative coverage.

Next best are policies that are guaranteed renewable. These cannot be canceled as long as you pay your premiums; however, the premiums can increase. Better yet are policies that are *guaranteed renewable and noncancelable.* Such a provision gives you the right to renew your policy at the same premium.

Action Plan for the Steeles: Selecting a Group Plan

Background Arnold's employer offers a choice of health care insurance plans, including a local HMO operated under an IPA, and traditional fee-for-service insurance. Principal coverage under both health care plans is outlined in Figure 7.2.

Over the last few years, the Steeles have been members of the HMO. They have been generally satisfied with the service, although in a few instances they had to go out of their way to find a specialist who was a participating physician. Except for a small co-payment on prescription drugs, the comprehensive benefits offered by the HMO have eliminated almost all of their out-of-pocket expenses. This saving has more than paid for any locational inconvenience in the delivery of medical services.

The Problem Previously, both health care plans have been fully paid for by the employer. However, the HMO has recently increased its membership fee substantially. In an effort to get workers to sign up for the less expensive fee-for-service plan, the company is requiring employee contributions of $39 a month from families that join the HMO.

Arnold and Sharon reviewed the family use of basic health care services for the previous year and estimated that health care expenditure would have been about $600 under the fee-for-service plan. Their actual out-of-pocket expenses in the HMO were $190. This amount plus the monthly fees for the HMO means that if next year is like last year, the HMO will cost them about $658 ($190 + $468). They wonder whether it is worth switching insurance plans to save $58. If they do nothing, they will be automatically enrolled in the HMO.

The Plan The Steeles should begin their comparison with an examination of major medical benefits. The fee-for-service plan certainly provides barely adequate protection for most families, with a policy limit of $250,000 and 20 percent co-insurance up to a $2,000 out-of-pocket maximum. However, the HMO provides for unlimited covered expenses without co-insurance payments for all injuries and most illnesses. Given these provisions, the HMO provides superior protection in the event of catastrophic illness or injury.

The Steeles should be especially aware of the major medical provision, since Arnold has above-average health risks as a chemist. He is covered by workers' compensation for job-related illnesses and injuries. But he handles many hazardous chemicals each day, and it may be difficult to prove that an illness was caused by any one of these products. Thus, there is a chance that, should he become ill, he will be denied benefits under workers' compensation.

The HMO also provides superior basic health coverage, paying for office visits and prescription drugs, with a small co-payment, and all surgical fees. The fee-for-service plan does cover physician fees, but it pays only the UCR charge, which may leave the Steeles with some additional uncovered expenses. Moreover, should their usage of basic health services increase by even a small amount, the HMO would have the financial advantage.

With so little difference in cost, the Steeles should base their decision on nonmonetary factors. Are they pleased with their present plan? Have they received superior service? Have they been denied treatment or found it difficult to get appointments with participating doctors?

One thing the Steeles should consider is making use of the flexible spending account that is provided by their employer. So far, they have been making their copayments with after-tax dollars. By placing funds in the flexible spending account at the beginning of the year, they can use tax-free dollars to pay their medical expenses. This strategy can proportionately cut their out-of-pocket medical expenses by about the size of their marginal tax rate. The major drawback is that any funds left in the account at the end of the year are permanently lost. But, by relying on records of past expenses and conservatively allocating monies to this account, they should come out ahead. After all, in a 28 percent marginal tax bracket, if they use up more than 72 percent of funds in the account they are still better off than if they didn't have one.

One last point: Had the analysis indicated that a switch appeared favorable, the Steeles would also have to examine the preexisting conditions clause in the fee-for-service plan. It may be better to remain with less-favorable coverage than to be uninsured because of a preexisting condition.

INFLATION PROTECTION A policy written to cover a certain percentage of your salary will provide some inflation protection. That is, as your salary increases, your insurance protection will increase correspondingly. If you are instead purchasing insurance that provides fixed-dollar payments, an *option to purchase* rider should be considered. It permits you to purchase additional protection in the future without evidence of insurability.

Ensuring that you have the appropriate level of protection at the beginning of the disability provides only partial protection against inflation. If your dollar benefits are unchanged during the period of disability, then inflation will erode the real worth of these payments. Social Security benefit payments are normally adjusted for increases in the cost of living, so that at least a portion of your disability payments may receive inflation protection. However, some disability policies provide for a dollar-for-dollar reduction in benefits to offset increases in Social Security payments, thus leaving your total compensation from Social Security and private disability insurance unchanged. A policy that establishes the company's dollar payments at the beginning of the disability and that does not permit future reductions in these payments is preferred. Better yet is one with a cost-of-living rider that automatically adjusts dollar payments during the disability period for inflation.

Determining Disability Income Insurance Requirements

Your disability income requirements will depend on the duration and severity of the disability. For disabilities lasting six months or less, you may have to rely on sick leave, short-term group disability benefits provided by an employer, or workers' compensation if the disability is work related. Lacking those, an emergency fund equal to six months' wages can provide the needed support through this interim period. For disabilities lasting longer than six months, you will have to consider your income needs until, typically, age 65, when retirement benefits begin. A good rule of thumb is that you should plan to replace about 60 to 70 percent of your lost gross income. This figure is based on the assumptions that some of your disability benefits will be nontaxable and that you will no longer incur work-related expenses. (Employer-provided benefits will be largely taxed, but privately purchased disability benefits will be tax free.) In any case, you may find it difficult to replace a larger percentage of your income through private insurance, since most insurers do not want to provide an incentive for not working.

Starting with your income replacement requirements on line 1 of Figure 7.8, you can then reduce this amount by your current sources of disability income. Include income benefits from existing group and individual policies. Be sure to examine your pension plan for an early retirement option in case of disability, and list this income source on line 4. You can obtain an estimate of your potential Social Security disability benefits from the local office. Don't include potential payments from

Box 7.3 SIMPLIFYING FINANCIAL PLANNING
Having a Living Will

Breakthroughs in medical science now make it possible to extend life far beyond what we had thought likely only a few decades ago. But advances in the extension of life do not always go hand in hand with improvements in the quality of life. For those who worry about being kept alive in a vegetative state with little or no chance of recovery, the "living will" can be the answer.

A living will is really not a will at all. It is a medical directive indicating the type of life support you are willing or unwilling to receive in the event you are unconscious or in a coma and unable to speak for yourself. In most states it is a legal document and, therefore, the state you live in may specify the precise form it must take.

In order for a living will to be effective, it must state your wishes precisely, so that your intent is clear. The Harvard Medical School's Health Letter, called the Medical Directive, distributes a living will that lists 12 standard medical procedures and treatments. For each you can make your wishes very clear by indicating the type of life-prolonging treatment you are willing to accept. (For a small fee, copies can be obtained by contacting Harvard Health-Medical Directive, P.O. Box 380, Boston, MA 02116.)

The Patient Self-Determination Act of 1991 requires that all institutions receiving Medicare or Medicaid funds inform patients upon admission of their right to sign an "advance directive." This includes a living will in which you have the right to refuse life-sustaining treatment and a health care power of attorney in which you appoint someone to make health care decisions for you if you are unable to. You don't have to sign an advance directive, but if you do, a record of it should be kept in your medical file.

The time to make these decisions, however, is not upon entry into a health care facility. By that point you may be incapacitated and your family may be in crisis. It is better to plan for such emergencies well in advance, when both your health care and financial concerns can be combined into a fully integrated plan. In addition to a living will and a health care power of attorney, this plan should include a last will and testament and a durable power of attorney. Similar to the health care power of attorney, the durable power of attorney enables a designated guardian to manage your financial and legal matters if you are unable to. After all, who is going to cash your checks and pay your bills when you cannot? If you fail to specify your choice in advance, the court may appoint someone who is not of your own choosing.

You should review these documents periodically to ensure that they still conform with your wishes. As you get older or your family situation changes, the kind of medical care you desire may also change. You can then revise or revoke old documents so as to conform to your changing desires.

workers' compensation. You want to have adequate coverage whether or not the disability is work related.

If you just want a rough estimate of what Social Security disability benefits would be, you can use the estimates in Table 7.3. The basic disability benefit would be received by the disabled worker. In addition, you can assume that mothers caring for dependent children under age 16 and earning no more than $500 a month would

Figure 7.8 Estimating your disability insurance needs.

DISABILITY INSURANCE		
1. Income replacement requirements (60%–70% of gross income lost)		______
2. Group insurance benefits	______	
3. Individual insurance benefits	______	
4. Early retirement benefits	______	
5. Social Security benefits	______	
6. Total integrated benefits		(______)
7. Additional disability income insurance needed		______

TABLE 7.3 • ESTIMATES OF MONTHLY SOCIAL SECURITY DISABILITY BENEFITS PAID, BY WAGE LEVEL

	Average Annual Social Security–Covered Wages				
Beneficiary	Less than $10,000	$10,000–$20,000	$20,000–$30,000	$30,000–$50,000	$50,000 and over
Worker alone	620	800	970	1,250	1,440
Worker, spouse, and 1 child (family maximum)	900	1,200	1,460	1,880	2,160

additionally receive 50 percent of the basic monthly disability benefit. Children under 18 years of age would also get 50 percent of the basic benefit. In all cases, however, you should assume that total payments to the disabled worker, dependent children, and caring mother do not exceed the maximum family benefit.

Your total integrated benefits are listed on line 6. This is not necessarily equal to the sum of lines 2 to 5. You must examine each of your policies for coordination of benefits clauses and social insurance substitute riders. Participation limits set down in these sections of the disability policies may limit your total integrated benefits to less than the summed total of lines 2 to 5.

If you subtract your total integrated benefits from your total income replacement requirements on line 1, you will have determined your need for additional income insurance protection on line 7. You may be able to satisfy this need through additional individual or group insurance. If you do purchase additional insurance, make sure its benefits will not be offset by a reduction in prospective payments under your present policies.

SUMMARY

Protection against the financial consequences of illness or injury is provided by health care insurance and disability insurance. Health care insurance is meant to cover the cost of medical treatment. It consists of basic health care coverage and major medical coverage. Many workers choose from among group plans, including both traditional insurance and health maintenance organizations, offered by their employers. Disability insurance is meant to replace a portion of income lost because of illness or injury. It is provided publicly through Social Security and workers' compensation programs and privately by insurance companies. A good financial plan should include protection against all the major financial consequences of a serious illness or injury.

KEY TERMS

- accident insurance (p. 213)
- basic health care insurance (p. 197)
- benefit period (p. 216)
- Blue Cross/Blue Shield (p. 203)
- class cancelable (p. 216)
- co-insurance (p. 200)
- commercial insurer (p. 204)
- comprehensive health insurance (p. 197)
- coordination of benefits clause (p. 216)
- co-payment (p. 200)
- dental insurance (p. 201)
- disability elimination period (p. 215)
- disability income insurance (p. 213)
- fee-for-service health insurance (p. 204)
- group-staff HMO (p. 205)
- guaranteed renewability (p. 202)
- health maintenance organization (HMO) (p. 204)

hospital expense insurance (p. 197)

hospital insurance (p. 197)

indemnity insurance (p. 197)

individual practice arrangement (IPA) HMO (p. 205)

major medical insurance (p. 200)

managed care (p. 211)

Medicaid (p. 205)

medical insurance (p. 199)

Medicare (p. 205)

medigap insurance (p. 212)

open-ended enrollment plan (p. 205)

preexisting conditions clause (p. 201)

preferred provider organization (PPO) (p. 205)

service benefit coverage (p. 197)

social insurance substitute (p. 216)

surgical insurance (p. 197)

usual, customary, and reasonable (UCR) (p. 199)

waiting period (disability) (p. 215)

waiting period (health care) (p. 201)

workers' compensation (p. 206)

PROBLEMS AND REVIEW QUESTIONS

1. What kinds of insurance provide protection against the financial consequences of illness and injury?
2. Discuss the three forms of reimbursement undertaken by hospital insurance policies. Which is the preferred coverage? Explain why.
3. What is the difference between medical insurance and major medical insurance? Which is more important? Why?
4. Suppose you have $5,000 of health care expenses that are not covered by your basic health insurance. You have a major medical policy with $500 deductible and 20 percent co-insurance. What are your out-of-pocket expenses?
5. What is the nation's largest insurer of health care? Which branch of this organization supplies the hospital insurance?
6. For certain procedures, Blue Shield agrees to pay the physician a UCR fee. How is this fee determined? What should you do if you are charged in excess of this amount?
7. How does an HMO differ from traditional insurance provided by Blue Cross/Blue Shield and most commercial insurers? How would you go about comparing the relative benefits of purchasing traditional insurance or joining an HMO?
8. How does an HMO differ from a PPO?
9. Name the two government programs that provide health care benefits. Which one is run entirely by the federal government?
10. Why should group coverage cost less than individual coverage?
11. A family with two adults and three children under 17 is considering purchasing medical insurance to cover doctors' fees for office visits. Estimate the expected value of this protection. Why is this health care insurance necessary or not necessary?
12. How does Social Security define "substantial gainful employment"? Explain how definitions of disability contained in private insurance policies can determine the quality of the insurance protection.
13. It is impossible to purchase disability insurance covering 100 percent of lost income. Why?
14. What part does the elimination period play when planning for adequate disability income protection?
15. Discuss some disability income protection strategies that can help you cope with the erosion of benefits due to inflation.
16. What type of nursing home care is traditionally not reimbursed under health insurance plans?
17. What is the purpose of a living will?
18. What should comprehensive health insurance cover?
19. How can an employer-sponsored flexible spending plan help save you tax dollars?
20. What is meant by managed care?

Case 7.1 The Hurleys Compare Disability Insurance

The Hurleys have narrowed their choice of disability insurance for Mr. Hurley down to two policies. They cost the same and are identicial except for those differences outlined below. They are guaranteed renewable and have an elimination period of 15 days.

	Policy 1	Policy 2
Monthly benefit	$500	$300
Benefit period	10 years	To age 65
Maximum replacement from all sources	Lesser of $2,000 a month, or 60% of income	60% of income

Mr. Hurley is currently 35 years of age with two children. Over the next 10 years his childrearing responsibilities should end. His current job pays $30,000 a year and is covered by Social Security. He calculates potential family disability benefits from Social Security at about $900 a month while the children are still at home. He is currently in line for an upper-level management position. Should he get it, his salary will increase substantially.

QUESTIONS

1. From the Hurleys' point of view, discuss the relative merits of each policy. Which would you recommend?
2. Which policy provides the better inflation protection? Why?
3. Do these policies provide adequate income replacement for the Hurleys?
4. Suppose the Hurleys must limit the amount spent on disability insurance to the cost of these policies. Are there any changes in coverage that might lower their risk without increasing their premiums? Explain.

Case 7.2 Walter and Ella Sisak Examine Their Health Care Insurance

Walter and Ella have decided that the time has come for them to consider expanding the family unit. In preparation, they examine their health care insurance for maternity coverage. The policy was written by a commercial insurer and is identical to the fee-for-service plan in Figure 7.2. Benefits for maternity care are the same as for illness or injury. Their insurance agent informs them that for an extra $500 a year in premiums, they can purchase first-dollar coverage on all maternity-related expenses. This would include prenatal and postnatal office visits for Ella. They expect that maternity care will consist of about $3,000 in hospital charges and $2,000 in physician fees.

QUESTIONS

1. Is the $500 maternity care endorsement worth the cost? Without this endorsement, how much is a typical pregnancy likely to cost the Sisaks?
2. What other provisions should the Sisaks look for? What coverage is essential at childbirth?

HELPFUL CONTACTS

Society for the Right to Die
250 West 57th Street, New York, NY 10107
Provides information and forms for living wills in 41 states and the District of Columbia.

United Seniors Health Cooperative
1331 H St. N.W., Suite 500, Washington, DC 20005 (telephone 202-393-6222)
Provides information on new open-enrollment provisions for medigap policies.

INTERNET ADDRESSES

Blue Cross and Blue Shield of Massachusetts (health tips and review of benefits)
http://www.bcbsma.com/

Cornell Law (excerpts from *New York Medicaid Eligibility*)
http://www.law.cornell.edu:80/medicaid/ma.table.html

Senior Health Insurance Benefits Advisors (free information, counseling, and assistance for seniors)
http://www.doi.state.id.us/shiba/shiba.htm

Social Security Online (explanation of social security benefits and eligibility)
http://www.ssa.gov/

State of California Disability Insurance (eligibility and plan benefits)
http://wwwedd.cahwnet.gov/diind.htm

Chapter

8

Property and Liability Insurance: Protecting Your Lifestyle Assets

Objectives

1. To understand the basic components of the homeowners' and auto insurance packages
2. To list and explain the standard formats for homeowners' insurance policies
3. To learn how to evaluate your auto and home insurance needs
4. To be able to find and fill any gaps in your homeowners' and auto coverage
5. To know how to handle insurance claims for the home and auto efficiently

Property loss insurance: Reimburses you for damage to your property due to accidental or natural circumstances or due to the negligence of others or yourself.
Negligence: The failure to exercise due care, the care expected of a prudent person.
Personal liability insurance: Protects you against claims resulting from the financial harm your negligence may cause others.

It is unfortunate that many people wait until after an accident or catastrophe to closely read the provisions in their property and casualty insurance coverage. Some will find that their homeowners' or auto policy covers more than they expected. Others may feel cheated, having less coverage than they thought or receiving less reimbursement than they expected. With a little forethought and financial planning, you can protect yourself from financial harm due to either the negligence of others or the vagaries of nature.

In this chapter we will examine both homeowners' and auto insurance. Each is a package of component policies covering disasters at home or on the road. Both can provide nonoverlapping protection against property loss and personal liability. **Property loss insurance** reimburses you for damage to your property due to accidental or natural circumstances or due to the negligence of others or yourself. By **negligence** we mean the failure to exercise the care expected of a prudent person. **Personal liability insurance** provides protection from claims against you resulting from the financial harm your negligence may cause others.

HOMEOWNERS' INSURANCE

The homeowners' insurance package usually provides better protection, at a lower cost, than the sum of its parts. Over the years, homeowners' policies have evolved into a few standard formats that seem to serve adequately the needs of the typical homeowner or renter. In order to fully understand the differences among homeowners' policies, you first must know some standard insurance terminology and the basic elements of a homeowners' policy.

The Terminology of Homeowners' Policies

You will find that most homeowners' policies are written in a clear and straightforward style. In fact, if you can't understand your policy and your insurance agent can't provide an adequate explanation of your coverage, you may have sufficient reason for finding another insurer. However, even the best-written policies contain some points that require an explanation to help you fully realize what you have purchased and how you are protected.

All risks coverage: Insurance covers all risks that are not specifically excluded in the policy.
Named perils coverage: Insurance covers only risks that are specifically named.

ALL RISKS VERSUS NAMED PERILS INSURANCE The policy should indicate whether you have **all risks coverage** or **named perils coverage.** The type need not remain the same throughout the policy. You may find that some items come under all risks insurance and others come under named perils insurance. All risks protection doesn't necessarily cover you against all risks. It does protect you against all risks that are not specifically excluded in the policy. Named perils insurance is just what the term implies: It covers only risks that are specifically stated in the policy. Therefore, with all risks protection you should see a list of circumstances not covered, whereas under named perils you should see a list of circumstances that will be covered.

The difference is important, because each places its own obligations on the insurer and the insured. Under all risks coverage, the insurance company is responsible for showing that your loss was not due to one of the specific exemptions stated in the policy. Alternatively, under named perils coverage, it is your responsibility to demonstrate that your loss was due to one of the named perils.

Replacement cost: The amount needed to replace new for old, with no deduction for depreciation.

REPLACEMENT COST VERSUS ACTUAL CASH VALUE The policy should indicate whether you will be reimbursed for losses at replacement cost or actual cash value. When the insurance company agrees to pay **replacement cost** on damaged goods, you receive the amount needed to replace new for old, with no deduction for depreciation. For example, if the roof on your home is destroyed, the insurance company will pay for the construction of a new roof, regardless of the age of the old one.

Box 8.1

PERSONAL FINANCE NEWS

Late Edition

National Flood Insurance Reform Act of 1994

The government and, of course, taxpayers are getting tired of bailing out flood victims. A large percentage of homeowners in floodplains have never bothered to take out flood insurance. But then why should they have? The government has always been there with emergency aid when they needed it. The National Flood Insurance Reform Act of 1994 is supposed to change that by placing additional requirements on who must purchase flood insurance and by imposing penalties on financial institutions that do not enforce the new restrictions.

The National Flood Insurance Program was established under the National Flood Insurance Act of 1968. The government began subsidizing flood insurance because private insurers were unwilling to take on the risk of major losses that could accompany a catastrophe such as a Mississippi flood or a Florida hurricane. From the beginning it has been a joint private and public program. Flood insurance is still sold through private insurance companies but with the backing of the federal government.

The Flood Disaster Protection Act of 1973 dictated mandatory flood insurance requirements on certain properties in communities that participated in federally subsidized flood control programs. Homeowners in flood-prone areas were required to purchase flood insurance on all federal financing, such as that through the Federal National Mortgage Corporation. However, only federally regulated banks and thrifts were charged with ensuring that borrowers complied with the law. Without penalties for those who didn't, enforcement was lax. The American Bankers Association estimated that only about 17 percent of lenders observed the law. This left about 75 percent of mortgaged properties in flood zones uncovered.

The new act forces all financial institutions that are regulated by federal agencies to comply with and help enforce the flood insurance requirements. Before you finance a new mortgage, renew an old mortgage, refinance an existing mortgage, or take out a home equity loan, the lender must first determine whether the property is in a designated flood area.

Only FEMA (Federal Emergency Management Agency) knows whose homes are in Special Flood Hazard Areas. Because it takes an expert to read the flood zone maps prepared by FEMA, you are going to have to pay about $20 to $25 for the privilege of finding out.

Your lender is the one who is going to make sure you sign up for needed flood insurance, because, the way the law is written, they have to pay for the insurance if you don't. Moreover, if they knowingly lend money on a property that does not have the required flood insurance, the government will fine them. Lenders can be fined $350 for each violation or up to $100,000 a year. So if you don't keep up your premium payments, they'll pay and then come after you for reimbursement.

To ensure that you keep paying, the lender can require you to deposit flood insurance premiums in an escrow account. In fact, the law forces the lender to escrow the flood insurance premiums if it retains such an account for any other purpose, such as property taxes, or homeowners' insurance.

Premium payments for flood insurance can vary widely, with premiums depending on the probability of flood damage. Homes built in a Special Flood Hazard Area have at least a 26 percent chance of experiencing a flood during the term of a conventional 30-year mortgage. The flood zone maps are periodically updated to reflect the changing probabilities of flooding. Therefore, even if you need not purchase flood insurance when you originate a loan, it's possible that sometime during the life of the loan you will receive notice that because of changing circumstances you now must have flood insurance.

On the plus side, if your home is in an area no longer rated as a flood hazard region, then you can drop your flood insurance. But you might want to think twice about doing so; one-third of flood claims come from outside special flood-designated areas.

Actual cash value: Market value, which is equal to replacement cost minus depreciation.

Actual cash value is equal to replacement cost minus depreciation. If the typical roof lasts 20 years and yours is destroyed in the tenth year, under actual cash value reimbursement you would receive only 50 percent of the funds needed to replace the roof. This could place you in a very unfortunate position if you did not have the additional funds needed to repair the structural damage to the home. Without a roof over your head, you would need to rent some place to live. In addition, you would still be responsible for the mortgage payments on the home. Failure to pay could wipe out a good portion of your remaining equity in the home. For this reason, most homeowners' policies provide for reimbursement at replacement cost for structural damage and reimbursement at actual cash value for the contents. Moreover, additional living expenses while the structure is being repaired may be partially or totally reimbursed.

Co-insurance: Requires the homeowner to become a co-insurer when the home is insured for less than 80 percent of its replacement value.

REPLACEMENT COST PROVISION Homeowners' policies contain a provision that requires the homeowner to provide **co-insurance** when the dwelling unit is insured for less than 80 percent of replacement value. Replacement value is the cost of rebuilding the home from the foundation up. It should be approximately equal to the price of a similar new home minus the cost of the lot and foundation.

The following example shows how a co-insurance clause works. Suppose the replacement value of your home is $100,000. If your insurance coverage on the dwelling is at least $80,000, the insurer will pay the full cost of repairing covered damages to the dwelling, up to the face amount of the policy. However, if your protection is for less than $80,000, you will receive less than full replacement cost. You would, in effect, become a co-insurer by having to pay the difference when repairing the structure.

Let's look at a specific example. Suppose a fire in the kitchen causes structural damage that would cost you $10,000 to repair. If you carry $50,000 of insurance on a home with $100,000 replacement value, you fall below the 80 percent requirement. In this situation the amount you would receive from the insurance company would be calculated under the following formula:

$$\frac{\text{Amount of dwelling protection}}{80\% \times \text{replacement cost of dwelling}} \times \frac{\text{cost of damage at}}{\text{replacement cost}} = \text{insurance payout}$$

$$\frac{\$50,000}{80\% \times \$100,000} \times \$10,000 = \$6,250$$

The payout is reduced by the ratio of your actual protection to the 80 percent requirement. Thus, you would receive only $6,250, less the deductible on the policy.

There is one important exception to the above analysis. If the actual cash value of the loss were greater than the $6,250 calculated under the co-insurance formula, then the insurer would reimburse at actual cash value up to the policy limits. For example, if the actual cash value of structural damage to the kitchen, equal to replacement cost minus depreciation, is estimated at $8,000, you will receive $8,000 rather than $6,250. Notice that this reimbursement is still less than $10,000 replacement cost, the amount received by a comparable fully insured homeowner.

Co-insurance may seem like a scheme designed to cheat homeowners, but it actually serves a very good purpose. Most losses are for much less than the replacement value of the home. Without the co-insurance clause, some homeowners might be tempted to reduce insurance costs by carrying less than full coverage on the home, leaving them with inadequate coverage in the case of total destruction.

A recent study by Marshall and Swift, a private consulting firm, discovered that underinsurance is a serious problem. They found that 67 percent of all houses nationwide are underinsured by an average of 35 percent.

Inflation guard endorsement: Periodically increases the face amount of dwelling protection to reflect rising market prices.

INFLATION GUARD ENDORSEMENT With rises in the general price level, the cost of replacing your home should also increase. This means that unless you periodically increase the face amount of dwelling protection, your coverage will eventually fall below 80 percent of the replacement cost of the home. To protect against this deficit, you can include an **inflation guard endorsement** that periodically increases the face amount of dwelling protection. The increase may either be set at an agreed-upon percentage or tied to an index of construction costs.

Be careful, because the inflation guard endorsement does not necessarily mean that you have the right amount of coverage. Even with the endorsement, it is still your responsibility to make sure that there is neither too much nor too little dwelling protection.

DEDUCTIBLE CLAUSE A deductible clause limits payments to damages that exceed a given dollar loss. For example, a $100 deductible means that payments will be made only for damages exceeding $100, and then the amount of the payout will be reduced by $100. Under a $100 deductible, you would receive $400 back on a $500 loss. By including a deductible, the insurer eliminates the cost of handling many small claims. This saving can be passed on to the homeowner through lower insurance rates. Including deductibles in your policy is an excellent way of holding down your insurance costs.

Some policies contain a disappearing deductible. For example, the insurer might agree to pay 111 percent of the excess of any loss over $50, up to losses of $500. If you suffer a loss of $150, the insurer will pay you 111 percent of $100, or $111. If your loss is $500 or more, you will receive complete reimbursement.

Mortgage clause: Insurance payments for structural damage are made to the mortgage holder.

MORTGAGE CLAUSE You will discover in the **mortgage clause** that payments for damages to the dwelling and surrounding structures are made to the mortgagee, if the mortgagee is named in the policy. The mortgagee is the lender, not you. The lender may hold the money to pay for repairs or to pay off the loan if the house is not rebuilt.

Apportionment clause: Apportions financial responsibility among multiple insurers so that the insured cannot collect more than 100 percent of the loss.

OTHER INSURANCE AND THE APPORTIONMENT CLAUSE If you have more than one insurance policy, you will find that each will pay only for damages up to their proportionate share of coverage. The **apportionment clause** makes it impossible for you to collect more than 100 percent of your losses by having multiple policies.

Because of the significant cost advantage of having all your homeowners' protection under one policy, you are not likely to want dual coverage. This clause is important, however, when you have additional coverage on a business conducted in the home. In this situation it may be unclear whether a particular loss is to be covered under your homeowners' insurance or your business insurance. Whoever pays, the apportionment clause makes sure you will not collect more than 100 percent of the value of the loss.

Subrogation clause: Places your right to sue after the insurer's.

SUBROGATION CLAUSE Most insurance policies, both homeowners' and auto, contain a **subrogation clause** that places your right to sue for recovery after the insurer's. If the insurer pays you for a loss, it can then seek to recover its payments from the party who caused the harm. You are entitled to sue for and collect only amounts that exceed those you have received from the insurer. Likewise, the insurer cannot sue for or collect more than you were paid under the insurance coverage.

Property Coverage

Homeowners' policies contain two sections: Section I on property coverage and Section II on liability protection. The first section includes a discussion of your coverage for losses to the dwelling unit and your personal belongings. It states the method for determining reimbursement and the types of losses covered. Subsections A, B, C, and D in Section I are organized by type of property loss and typically begin with a discussion of coverage on the dwelling.

Dwelling protection: Protects against structural damage to the home.

COVERAGE A—DWELLING PROTECTION **Dwelling protection** generally protects you against damage to the structure resulting from fire, lightning, civil commotion, smoke, hail, vehicle damage, aircraft damage, riot, and explosion. Unless the dwelling has been unoccupied for the previous 30 days, you may also be covered for damage resulting from vandalism and malicious mischief. Loss from earthquake, flood, nuclear accident, and war will be specifically excluded.

The face amount of your dwelling protection is the most important number in the homeowners' policy. As stated previously, to avoid co-insurance payments, you should set the face amount at or above 80 percent of the cost of rebuilding. The amount of dwelling protection is also important because most of your other property loss limits will be stated as a percentage of the amount of insurance carried on the dwelling.

Appurtenant structures: Structures other than the dwelling unit.

COVERAGE B—APPURTENANT STRUCTURES Structures other than the dwelling unit are called **appurtenant structures.** They include the garage, the storage shed, and even the mailbox. These will usually be covered for losses up to 10 percent of the amount on the dwelling unit.

Unscheduled personal property: Items not specifically listed as insured on the policy.

COVERAGE C—CONTENTS The loss of **unscheduled personal property**—items that are not specifically listed in the policy—from theft or damage at the home will generally be covered for about 50 percent of the dwelling coverage. This coverage is not as generous as it sounds. First, reimbursement is usually set at actual cash value, and second, there are much lower limits on specific valuables. Typical examples of coverage limits are $200 on money, coins, and numismatic property, and $1,000 on boats and boating equipment resulting from any loss. For loss or theft, the limits are $1,000 on jewelry, watches, and fur; $2,500 on silverware, goldware, pewterware, and $2,500 on guns. If your valuables exceed these limits, you can take out additional insurance coverage by attaching a personal property floater to your homeowners' policy.

Many policies cover computer equipment for up to $5,000 damage, regardless of whether it is used for business. Some companies, however, may refuse to pay for damage to business-related property such as computers, fax machines, and printers unless they are covered by an optional rider insuring a home business.

One aspect of a homeowners' policy that most people overlook is the protection it provides away from home. If you read this subsection, you will likely find that your personal property away from home is covered for at least 10 percent of the value of the personal property on the premises.

COVERAGE D—LOSS OF USE This often-unnoticed subsection on additional living expenses can prove extremely helpful in event of serious loss. If a covered loss leaves your home uninhabitable, it will pay for the additional expenses necessary to retain your normal living standards. The limit on this might be expressed as 10 to 20 percent of dwelling protection prorated for the amount of time spent out of the house, or the limit might be stated as a period of time over which additional expenses will be paid.

TOTALING UP THE COVERAGE It is unlikely that a single catastrophe would permit you to collect up to each of the previously stated limits. However, if such a disaster did occur, the total reimbursement could be considerably greater than the face amount of the homeowners' policy. On a policy with a face amount of $100,000 in dwelling protection, the maximum payout is as follows:

Dwelling	$100,000
Appurtenant structures (10%)	10,000
Unscheduled property on premises (50%)	50,000
Unscheduled property off premises (5%)	5,000
Additional living expenses (20%)	20,000
Total coverage	$185,000

In addition, you might also receive payment for the following incidentals.

Theft of items from cars. Surprisingly, your homeowners' policy provides an incentive for locking your car. Property taken from your car is covered only if there are signs of forced entry.

Credit card and check forgery. Assuming you promptly notify the credit card company when you lose your card, you may be covered up to $1,000 against misuse of that card. Moreover, in addition to reimbursement for losses suffered through credit card or check forgery, the insurance company may also defend you in any suit demanding payment under these circumstances.

Debris removal. The insurance company may pay the cost of removing property damaged under a covered loss.

Emergency removal. If your property is damaged while you are removing it from the premises in order to avoid a covered peril, you may still be reimbursed. For example, suppose your roof is damaged by a covered loss, and you temporarily move your belongings to a storage garage to avoid damage to your personal property while the roof is being repaired. If, in the interim, the storage garage burns down and you lose your belongings, they will be covered the same as if they had been at your home.

Fire department charges. If your fire department charges for a service call, the insurance company will probably pay up to $500 of service charges.

Necessary repairs after loss. You have an obligation to protect your property from further damage after a loss. Reasonable expenses for temporary repairs, such as boarding up a broken window until it can be replaced, will probably be compensated.

Trees, shrubs, plants, and lawns. When the covered loss causes damage to your landscaping, you may be reimbursed for up to 5 percent of the dwelling protection.

EXCLUSIONS ON PROPERTY LOSS COVERAGE The following classes of property are specifically excluded from contents coverage, either because they are nonpersonal in character or because they are more appropriately covered by other types of policies:

1. Articles described separately in a personal articles floater or insured elsewhere
2. Animals, birds, or fish
3. Motorized land vehicles and electronic communication and sound devices attached to them
4. Aircraft and parts
5. Property of roomers, boarders, and tenants
6. Property in an apartment regularly rented to others
7. Property rented or held for rental to others
8. Business records
9. Credit cards and fund transfer cards, except as provided under additional coverages

Liability Coverage

Liability coverage: Protects you and your family from the financial harm your negligence causes others.

Liability coverage, explained in Section II of the homeowners' policy, protects you and your family from the financial harm your negligence causes others. The three components to this protection consist of personal liability insurance, medical payments insurance, and insurance against physical damage to the property of others.

COVERAGE E—PERSONAL LIABILITY The insurer will pay, up to the limits of protection, all legally obligated expenses for bodily injury or property damage, assuming you did not intentionally inflict them. In addition, the insurer will also pay defense and settlement costs if it decides to fight the payment in court. However, once the insurance company has paid up to the policy limits, it is no longer legally responsible for further damage payments or for the legal defense.

The generally recommended minimum is $300,000, but the standard limit under this section is $100,000. This is not much protection when your actions result in serious physical harm. For example, if you are sued for $150,000 and your liability coverage is for $100,000, the insurer might decide to pay $100,000 to the injured party, leaving you with the cost of defending against a potential $50,000 award.

COVERAGE F—MEDICAL PAYMENTS COVERAGE Minor injuries that occur on your property are covered by medical payments insurance, regardless of who is at fault. Off your premises it pays for minor injuries that are caused by you. It doesn't pay the medical bills for you or your family, only the medical bills of others.

Most policies limit payments to a relatively small amount, $500 to $1,000 per person. While this is not major dollar protection, it nevertheless serves a useful purpose by providing the means and incentive for timely medical treatment. This protects both you and the insurer. Immediate inspection and documentation of the injury may prevent the filing of larger claims resulting from exaggeration or delayed medical action.

DAMAGE TO THE PROPERTY OF OTHERS Similar to medical payments coverage, property liability insurance pays for minor property damage, regardless of who is at fault. The limits are $250 to $500 per occurrence.

EXCLUSIONS ON LIABILITY COVERAGE The homeowners' policy doesn't cover slander or libel, nor does it protect you against business-related liabilities. Professional practices need special malpractice insurance, and this need is generally recognized. Where problems occur, they usually have to do with defining a business. For example, if you take on an occasional babysitting job, you may or may not be covered under your homeowners' policy. However, if you regularly take in the neighbor's children for a fee, you probably will not be covered. If there is any question that your activities might constitute a business, you should check with your insurance agent.

If your child works part time delivering papers or mowing lawns, be sure your policy covers those activities. Most homeowners' policies will state that the business exclusion does not apply to occasional and part-time business activities of an insured person who is under 21 years of age.

In general, your liability coverage will not extend to accidents in your automobile or aircraft. It will cover boating accidents on boats having less than a stated horsepower and less than a given length. For these exclusions you will need specialized insurance.

Box 8.2 SIMPLIFYING FINANCIAL PLANNING
A Property Insurance Protection Checklist for College Students

When you headed off to school did you check to see if you had everything you needed? It's likely that you overlooked an important item: your property insurance protection. You can remedy that oversight by answering a few simple questions.

✔ 1. Is your personal property protected under your parents homeowners' policy?

Most homeowners' policies cover the property of students away at college, but the coverage may not extend to off-campus housing. The easiest way to find out whether you are adequately covered is to discuss the matter with your family's insurance agent. If you are not covered under your parents homeowners' policy, consider purchasing a separate renters' insurance.

✔ 2. Do you have adequate overall property protection?

Personal property coverage is typically 50 percent of dwelling coverage. However, the limit on property away from home may only be 10 percent of personal property coverage. On a home insured for $200,000, personal property coverage would be $100,000, and coverage of property away from home would be $10,000. In most cases, this should be adequate. However, if more protection is needed an endorsement could be added to your family's homeowners' policy.

✔ 3. Have you taken a personal inventory?

A descriptive list of the important items in your apartment, along with approximate values, should be compiled. Keep the list somewhere other than at school; typically, the family home is the best place. If the apartment is broken into while you are not at school, you will be able to supply the authorities with an accurate list of property that may be missing.

✔ 4. Do you exceed the limits on specific classes of property?

Valuable property is more likely to be lost or stolen when it is away from home than when it is at home. Coverage for computers and related equipment is probably limited to $5,000. Jewelry typically has a lower limit of $1,000. Property that exceeds policy limits can be insured with a personal articles floater.

Policy Format

The present homeowners' policy took its standard form in the 1950s. Today there are established formats into which almost all policies can be categorized. The coverage under each is outlined in Figure 8.1.

Basic Format (HO-1) provides the least coverage, insuring against the 11 most common perils on a named peril basis. Only a few of these policies are sold, because most homeowners correctly demand more adequate protection.

Broad Form (HO-2) also provides named perils coverage for both dwelling and personal property. However, it is broader than HO-1, including seven additional named perils. It is the second most popular homeowners' insurance package.

Special Form (HO-3) is now the most widely purchased form and is highly recommended for most homeowners. It provides all risks coverage on the dwelling and named perils coverage on the personal property. The typical excepted perils on the all risks coverage are flood, earthquake, war, and nuclear accident.

Contents Broad Form (HO-4) is for renters. The dwelling is not covered because it is the landlord's responsibility. Coverage on personal property is for the same named perils as under HO-2. There are also additional living expense coverage equal to 20 percent of the limit on personal property and protection on tenant improvements to the property equal to 10 percent of the personal property coverage.

Comprehensive Form (HO-5) provides all risks coverage on both the dwelling and personal property. It differs from HO-3 in that HO-3 includes only named perils coverage for personal property. The Comprehensive Form has the most protection and is the most expensive of all policies. In place of HO-5, some insurance companies provide HO-3 with Comprehensive Endorsement HO-15.

Condominium Form (HO-6) is similar to renters' form HO-4. Like the landlord, the condominium association usually provides insurance for the building and other structures. This may not cover, however, the condominium owners' additions and improvements to the dwelling unit. Therefore, the Condominium Form covers the owners' interest in additions to the dwelling unit at replacement cost up to a set limit. Furthermore, additional living expenses are paid for up to 40 percent of the coverage on personal property, instead of 20 percent. The policy also provides for endorsements in the event the owner is assessed for property or liability losses not covered under the association's insurance.

Older Home Form (HO-8) is for homes with actual cash value substantially below their replacement cost. For many older homes, the cost of replacement may be many times current actual cash value. All other forms require dwelling protection at 80 percent of replacement cost in order to avoid problems under the co-insurance clause. This would require owners of certain older homes to carry exorbitant amounts of dwelling protection. In addition, the insurance companies would have to charge high rates, because whenever the potential payout on the policy is substantially above actual cash value, there is a tremendous incentive for arson.

With Older Home insurance, the dwelling is insured for its market value. With the potential for arson reduced, owners of older homes can obtain reasonably priced insurance. The idea is to be able to return the dwelling to a serviceable condition, but not necessarily with materials of like kind and quality.

Comprehensive Endorsement Form (HO-15) This provision extends the coverage offered under HO-3 by providing all risks coverage on contents. In combination with HO-3, it provides the same coverage as HO-5.

Figure 8.1 Insured perils under homeowners' policies.

Peril	Basic Format (HO-1)	Broad Form (HO-2)	Special Form (HO-3)	Contents Broad Form (HO-4)	Compre-hensive Form (HO-5)	Condo-minium Form (HO-6)	Older Home Form (HO-8)
1. Fire or lightning							
2. Loss of property removed from premises endangered by fire or other perils							
3. Windstorm or hail							
4. Explosion							
5. Riot or civil commotion							
6. Aircraft							
7. Vehicles							
8. Smoke							
9. Vandalism and malicious mischief							
10. Theft							
11. Breakage of glass constituting a part of the building							
12. Falling objects							
13. Weight of ice, snow, sleet							
14. Collapse of building(s) or any part thereof							
15. Sudden and accidental tearing asunder, cracking, burning, or bulging of a steam or hot water heating system or of appliances for heating water							
16. Accidental discharge, leaking, or overflow of water or steam from within a plumbing, heating, or air-conditioning system or domestic appliance							
17. Freezing of plumbing, heating, and air-conditioning systems and domestic appliances							
18. Sudden and accidental injury from artificially generated currents to electrical appliances, devices, fixtures, and wiring (TV and radio tubes not included)							
All perils except flood, earthquake, war, nuclear accident, and others specified in your policy. Check your policy for a complete listing of perils excluded.			Dwelling Only				

Specialized Insurance

To close a gap in protection from either a standard exclusion or an insurance liability limit, you might consider some of the following additions to your homeowners' policy.

Endorsement: An amendment to the basic policy extending or changing the type of insurance coverage.

ENDORSEMENT An **endorsement** is a paragraph that amends the original policy. It is added to make the standard policy more closely fit your individual needs. For example, coverage on personal property is often stated as a percentage of dwelling protection. If the standard policy states that personal property is covered up to 50 percent of dwelling protection, and you feel that your belongings need greater protection, you may increase the percentage with an endorsement.

Endorsements may also be used to change the kind of coverage. Most policies agree to pay actual cash value on personal property damage. With an endorsement for "replacement cost coverage," you could change that. The perils insured against may also be changed with an endorsement. As previously mentioned, the standard policy excludes damage resulting from earthquakes. At additional cost, an endorsement can provide financial protection from this calamity.

A small business in your home might also be covered by business pursuits endorsement. However, for anything substantial you will need a separate business insurance policy to cover all business-related risks.

Of interest to most homeowners is an "inflation guard" endorsement. As housing values rise, this endorsement automatically increases your coverage. It is a worthwhile addition, ensuring that you will not get caught short under the co-insurance clause.

Floater: Schedules property for specific coverage.

FLOATERS The term **floater** is left over from the industry's early days, when it specialized in marine insurance. Like the cargo on a ship, your valuables can be insured with a *personal articles floater*. This can take the form of a separate policy or an endorsement to the original policy. Under the unscheduled property coverage, fairly low limits are set on payments for damaged or stolen valuables. If you need coverage beyond these limits, you can acquire it with a floater.

In a floater, the property is *scheduled*. This means it is described in terms of type and quality, and its value is supported by a report from a professional appraiser or bill of sale. Personal articles floaters usually cover all risks with no deductible.

Umbrella coverage: Provides catastrophic protection that begins where basic coverage ends.

AN UMBRELLA POLICY **Umbrella coverage** is written over an underlying homeowners' policy and a family auto policy. It takes over when the liability limits on these policies are reached. For example, if your homeowners' policy covers liability losses up to $100,000, an umbrella policy can protect you from losses in excess of $100,000, up to $1 million or more.

An umbrella policy is often written on a "following form" basis, meaning it will follow the form of the underlying coverage on which it was written. Consequently, you will be insured for the same perils as in the underlying policy. Some umbrella policies, however, will provide for extended perils coverage along with increased limits.

EARTHQUAKE INSURANCE Earthquake insurance may be purchased as an endorsement to the homeowners' policy. In earthquake-prone areas such as California, this insurance carries a high premium and a high deductible. A typical earthquake deductible equal to 10 percent of total coverage on the home would leave the first $15,000 of damage uncovered on a $150,000 home. Because of the high premiums and attempts by insurers to cut back their exposure in this market, fewer firms than you might expect carry earthquake protection. At most, only about one in four California homes is covered.

In California, where insurers have been reluctant to sell earthquake insurance, the legislature passed a law requiring insurers to offer earthquake insurance along with normal homeowners' policies. In response, some insurers have been withdrawing from the homeowners' insurance market. Persons who can't find normal coverage can apply for the state's FAIR (Fair Access to Insurance Requirements) plan, a joint venture of private insurers. Similar FAIR plans that provide access to auto and property coverage for high-risk insureds are available in about half the states.

National Flood Insurance Program: A federal program that insures homeowners against flood damage.

FLOOD INSURANCE Because flood damage is an excluded peril under homeowners' policies, you will have to rely on the federal government's **National Flood Insurance Program** (see Box 8.1). Your community must participate in this program before individual homeowners are able to purchase government flood insurance. The federally guaranteed insurance is sold by participating private insurance companies. You can locate an insurer through your agent or by contacting the FEMA (Federal Emergency Management Agency).

When you apply for a home mortgage, a second mortgage, or a home equity loan it is likely that your lender will require certification as to whether your home is in a Special Flood Hazard Area. If it is, you must acquire flood insurance before the loan can be closed.

Selecting Homeowners' Insurance

Now that you understand the basics of homeowners' coverage, you should be able to compare policies and select an insurer using the following steps.

STEP 1 You can start the selection process by first determining what and how much insurance you need. An insurance agent will help you determine replacement cost based upon type of construction and building costs in your locality. You can arrive at a similar cost figure yourself by calling the local builders' association for current construction costs per square foot and then multiplying this number by your square footage. However, if your home is nonstandard or has a potential market price of over $200,000, you might want a more reliable estimate of replacement cost. For this you should hire a professional appraiser. Two organizations providing competent appraisers are the American Institute of Real Estate Appraisers and the Society of Real Estate Appraisers.

STEP 2 Decide on the type of coverage and the required additions to that coverage. For most owners of single-family homes, Special Form HO-3 is probably the most appropriate. However, those with unique older homes, or with especially valuable personal property, should respectively consider HO-8 and HO-5.

Your analysis of required additional coverage can begin with an inventory of your personal property. Review the sample limits in the section on unscheduled property coverage. If it appears that you own valuables exceeding those limits, you will need an appraisal of current actual cash value in order to take out a scheduled property floater. Next, review the discussion of specialized insurance, and make a list of what endorsements or special coverage you feel are necessary.

STEP 3 Contact an agent from a major insurer. Explain to the agent how much insurance you think you need, what format you find most desirable, and what additions you think are necessary. No doubt the agent will have some recommended changes or additions. You should consider these and accept the ones you believe are worthwhile. Finally, get a price on the total package, including endorsements and floaters.

You don't want to purchase the policy at this point. Market studies have found significant differences in the cost of similar policies. It is recommended you talk to at least two other insurers and get a price on the same policy you discussed with the first agent. This shouldn't be too difficult. As stated previously, homeowners' policies are fairly standard, so an HO-3 from one company will be almost identical to an HO-3 from another company.

STEP 4 The last step before purchasing is to check out the insurance company and the insurance agent. You want the company to be there when you need help, and you want to be justly paid when you have a covered loss. The financial condition of the insurer can be checked out in *Best Key's Rating Guide on Property and Casualty Insurers* or *Standard & Poor's Insurance Ratings Services* available in most public libraries. These guides summarize each insurer's financial stability with a simple letter grade. Preferably, you should avoid any company with less than a top rating. You are purchasing insurance to lower your risks; you don't want to gamble on the insurer's continued existence.

Checking out how well a company deals with its clients is a more difficult task. You should consider the experience of any friends who have applied for reimbursement on covered losses within the last few years. In addition, you should contact your state's insurance commission to see if they have any information on the companies in which you are interested. In some states the insurance commission will supply you with the number of customer complaints by company.

Direct writer: An insurance agent who is an employee of an insurance company and who works exclusively for that company.

Independent agent: An insurance agent who works on commission for two or more insurance companies.

Some companies sell their policies through company employees called **direct writers.** Other companies use **independent agents,** who work on commission and sell policies for two or more companies. If you buy from an independent agent, this individual will handle your claim. A company with direct writers will have a separate claims department. Obviously, the character and reliability of the particular agent who sells you the policy are more important when you are dealing with an independent. Therefore, check out the independent with the Better Business Bureau and with previous clients.

Companies that use direct writers save on selling costs, a saving that can be passed on to you in lower premiums. In addition, survey results from *Consumer Reports* indicate that consumer satisfaction was not appreciably different for companies using direct writers and companies using independent agents. This suggests you might do better purchasing through a direct writer. However, these surveys test satisfaction, not expectations. Consumers using independent agents may have expected and received better service. If you value personalized service and have found an independent agent who is considerate of your needs, he or she may be worth a few dollars more in premiums.

STEP 5 After you purchase the policy, be sure to conduct an annual review of your insurance needs, updating your personal inventory and dwelling protection and acquiring new appraisals as market prices change. If the insurance company needlessly increases your rates, try comparison shopping again.

Making Sure You Collect on a Loss

Having adequate insurance coverage is not enough to ensure that you will receive appropriate compensation in the event of property loss. Policy holders with identical losses and identical coverage may receive different levels of reimbursement simply because they approach the claim process differently. Making good on a claim requires documentation, notification, and evaluation.

DOCUMENTATION The first step in filing a claim should be taken before the loss occurs. The loss must be documented. Of course, doing so is a lot easier while you still have your property in good condition.

When you apply for scheduled property coverage with a floater, you will be required to document the property's actual cash value. Be sure to update the appraisals whenever market prices change, including both upward and downward movements. During periods of rising prices, an outdated appraisal will provide you with less-than-adequate insurance coverage. Alternatively, during falling prices, you may be paying for too much protection. The insurer is unlikely to pay more than replacement cost; therefore, too much insurance is a waste of money. It is also a good idea to photograph your valuables, with closeups of any identifying characteristics, such as trademarks, copyrights, and signatures.

On unscheduled property coverage, evidence of worth need be supplied only after the loss. You are entirely responsible for documenting and describing your loss to the insurance company. To do this, you should keep an inventory of your belongings, including a description of each item that indicates all identifying marks, the original purchase price, and the date of purchase. For the more expensive items you should include a copy of the bill of sale in your records. While taking inventory, you should check for items that might exceed the recovery limits on your homeowners' policy. Consider scheduling these goods with a floater. Take photos of every room in your house, or better yet, make a videotape tour of your home. Now take all of this documentation and store it in a safe place away from the home. If your house burns down, you don't want this destroyed with it.

NOTIFICATION When a property loss occurs, you should first contact the relevant civil authority, then take whatever steps are needed to protect your property from further damage. Your failure to notify the police or a credit card company in the event of theft may invalidate your coverage. Next, contact your insurer. Your agent should be able to inform you immediately whether you are covered, in addition to supplying information on what you should do next. Insurance agents are used to dealing with tragedies. At a time like this, the support they can provide in seeking alternative shelter or assistance with repairs and debris removal can be invaluable.

Next, before anything is repaired or removed, be sure you have fully documented the loss. Take photos of the damage. If you followed the previous advice, you will now have a set of before and after snapshots. Also, request copies of any police or fire reports on the damage, and get the names and addresses of any witnesses to the mishap.

EVALUATION If the insurer feels your claim may be covered, an adjuster will be sent to verify the claim and determine the amount of loss. You should supply the adjuster with copies of all the evidence of loss you have collected. Under most circumstances, a settlement offer will be made promptly. Don't be too hasty to accept. The insurance company's objective in making a prompt settlement offer is probably honorable and good business practice. They believe that the client needs immediate help and will judge the company by how quickly the representatives respond to that need. But it may be a while before you fully realize all that you have lost. Take the time to review your inventory of damaged items and to search out the replacement cost on these goods. Because actual cash value is equal to replacement cost minus depreciation, the current market price of a similar good will play an important part in determining the insurance payout under either replacement cost reimbursement or actual cash value reimbursement.

Let the adjuster make the first settlement offer, and request an explanation of how the amount was determined. If you feel the offer is too low or you are denied payment on what you believe is a covered loss, you may state your case to the adjuster and ask that the settlement offer be reconsidered. If you still can't agree, you can demand that the settlement be submitted to arbitration. However, this is not costless. You and the insurer will be required to split the cost of the arbitrators' fees. Obviously, you should demand this only if the prospective benefits from arbitration exceed your share of the cost.

One less costly but potentially less effective action is to write your state's insurance commission. They are not likely to take action on an individual complaint. But if yours is one of many, the state commission may decide to look into the problem.

You may be able to deduct any unreimbursed casualty losses on your personal income tax return. Only sizable losses, however, are likely to lead to any significant tax savings. The rules for reducing your taxable income by the amount of the loss are quite strict. First, you can reduce your taxable income only by the amount by which the loss exceeds 10 percent of your adjusted gross income. Second, the loss must be assessed at market value and not replacement cost.

AUTOMOBILE INSURANCE

Automobile insurance is meant to protect you against three risks: (1) bodily harm and property damage to others from negligent operation of the vehicle; (2) personal injury to you, your family, and guests riding in your car; and (3) damage or loss of your car due to fire, theft, or collision. Of the three, the first has the potential for the greatest financial loss.

Who Needs Auto Insurance Coverage?

The simple answer is that if you drive a car, you do. Your chances of being involved in a fatal accident are less than 1 percent (see Figure 8.2). But you have about a 75 percent chance of being in some kind of car accident over the next five years, and if you are an unmarried male driver under age 25, the odds are even higher. In most states, liability insurance is mandatory. However, regardless of state requirements, it is just downright foolish to take a car on the road without adequate coverage. One accident can result in hundreds of thousands of dollars in claims against you and your estate.

Coverage under the Family Auto Policy

The standard policy covers you and other family members living with you. It also protects others when driving one of your covered cars and you and your family when driving someone else's auto.

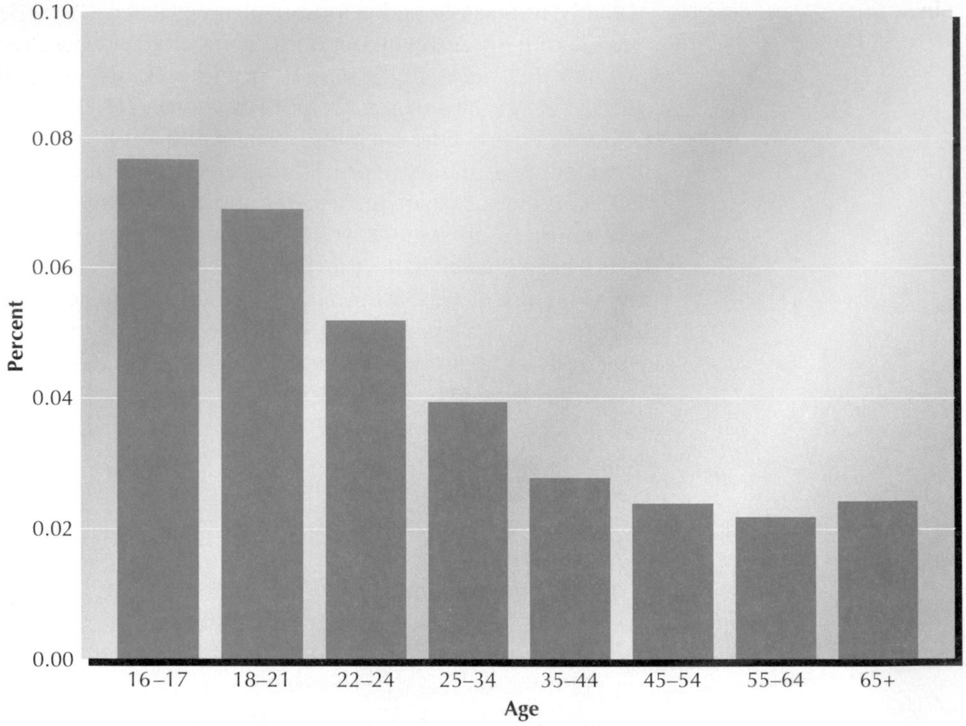

Figure 8.2 Probability of licensed driver's being involved in a fatal accident.

SOURCE: U.S. Bureau of the Census, *Statistical Abstract of the United States, 1994,* Table 1022.

Family Auto Policy and **Personal Auto Policy:** Auto policies providing standardized coverage for families and individuals.

The **Family Auto Policy** and the more recently introduced **Personal Auto Policy** follow a standard format used by most insurers. Policy comparisons are fairly easy, because coverage is usually divided into identical parts listed in the same order. However, auto policies tend to be written in stilted language and are difficult to read. If your policy contains the terms *first party, second party,* and *third party,* just remember that the first party is you and the second party is the insurer. If you collide with another car, the driver of that car becomes the third party. Claims by you or your passengers are first-party claims. Those by the driver or passengers in the other vehicle are third-party claims.

PART A—LIABILITY The most important component of your auto insurance is liability coverage. It operates much the same as liability coverage under the homeowners' policy, except that it applies only to damages resulting from an auto accident.

Split liability limit: Provides specific limits on liability coverage for a single individual, a single accident, and property damage.

The Family Auto Policy has a **split liability limit.** If your policy has one, you will see the liability limits presented in the following format: 100/300/10. The first number indicates the maximum amount the insurer will pay for bodily injury to a single person. The second number is the maximum amount the insurer will pay for all injuries sustained in a single accident, and the last is the insurer's liability limit for property damage in a given accident. For example, suppose there were two riders in the other car. One sustained $210,000 in bodily injury and the other $80,000 in bodily injury. The insurer would reimburse the first rider for $100,000 and the second rider for the full $80,000 sought, since total payments are under the $300,000 limit for a single accident. In addition, the insurer would pay for damage to the other vehicle up to $10,000. You would be responsible for the excess liability, which would include $110,000 to the first rider and any property damage exceeding $10,000.

Single liability limit: Provides a single limit that covers all bodily and property losses incurred in a single accident.

The Personal Auto Policy has a **single liability limit.** This means the insurer will pay up to this limit for each accident, regardless of how this amount may be divided among the injured and for property damage. When the single liability limit on one policy is the same as the limit per accident on a split liability policy, the single liability limit provides the better coverage. In the previous example, a single liability limit of $300,000 would have left you with little or no excess liability.

You may find that the limits on your policy will depend on which state you happen to be driving in. Where state laws require higher limits than those shown on your policy, the state requirements should apply. However, you may be required to pay the insurer the difference between your liability limits and the amount the company pays out under a given state's liability laws.

In addition to damages up to your policy limits, the insurer will also cover the cost of defending you in a lawsuit. This coverage will include such supplementary costs as legal and defense fees, premiums on appeal bonds, and the cost of bail bonds up to about $250. When in court, you may receive payments for up to about $50 a day in lost earnings. However, you can collect these payments only so long as the insurer has not paid out damages up to the liability limits. Once the company has reached that point, perhaps through an out-of-court settlement with the injured party, then further legal costs are all yours.

Don't try to skimp on this area of auto coverage. Many states require you to have at least 10/20/5. This level is much too low to serve as a standard for your own needs. Middle-income families should have at least 100/300/25, or preferably 300/500/25. You will find that a relatively small percentage increase in your annual premium can substantially increase the liability limits. Those in an upper-income bracket are especially vulnerable to lawsuits and should consider an umbrella policy raising liability protection on both the homeowners' and auto policy to $1 million or more.

A liability limit of $300,000 may sound like a lot of protection. It actually isn't. The damages suffered by a severely injured person who is unable to work can easily exceed this figure. You might suggest you don't need this much insurance because you don't have $300,000 in assets to protect. But the higher your protection, the less likely it is that you will have any excess liability above your insurance cov-

Box 8.3 SAVING MONEY
Holding Down Insurance Costs for Young Drivers

Away at School
If students attend school far from home (more than 100 miles) and drive the family auto only on vacations and holidays, most insurance companies will lower the premiums on student drivers by 12 to 33 percent.

Good Grades
Students with good grades have fewer accidents. Insurers recognize that fact by offering a discount of from 5 to 25 percent for students with at least a B average.

Sporty Car
Insurers target certain makes and models for higher premiums because these are more likely to be stolen or damaged. You can find out which autos carry higher premiums by contacting your insurer. Unfortunately, these are most often the same cars favored by younger drivers.

Family Auto Policy
Individual coverage is more expensive than insuring all the drivers in the home under a single family auto policy. New drivers purchasing an individual policy may be placed in an "assigned risk" pool, for which rates are much higher than on ordinary policies.

Young Driver, Old Car
In a multicar family, assign the youngest driver to the oldest car in the family. If the high-risk driver doesn't drive the luxury sedan, premiums should be lower.

erage. Moreover, court awards can be based on more than just your present assets; they can also be based upon your future earning potential. With inadequate liability coverage, you could be forced to sell everything you own and to make continuing payments out of your future income.

Medical payments coverage: Covers minor medical expenses for those riding in your car during an accident.

PART B—MEDICAL PAYMENTS Injuries to you, your family, and guests riding in your car are insured under **medical payments coverage,** regardless of who is at fault. The coverage also applies when you or your family are riding in other vehicles or when one of your family members is hit by a car while walking. The typical limits on payments are low, between $500 to $5,000 per person. It is not meant to take the place of a good health insurance plan. In fact, if you have good health insurance, you should consider holding limits in this part to a minimum. The only situation your health insurance does not cover is injury to a guest rider. However, your liability insurance, or that of the other driver, may cover the guest's injuries.

Some companies will include death and disability insurance under the medical payments section. A special life insurance or disability policy would take care of these contingencies with broader coverage than would a policy that covers only auto accidents.

Uninsured motorists coverage: Covers bodily injury to you or your family members from either an uninsured driver or a hit-and-run driver.

PART C—UNINSURED MOTORISTS **Uninsured motorists coverage** is worthwhile low-cost protection, about $11 per year for a policy with 25/50/10 limits. In most states, damage to your auto is not covered under uninsured motorists. It primarily covers bodily injury to you or your family members from either an uninsured driver or a hit-and-run driver. The coverage also applies when riding in other cars or walking. However, for the policy to pay off, the other driver must be at fault.

You may want to carry this protection even if your state requires auto liability insurance, since there is no way the state can ensure that every driver is financially responsible. The need for this coverage is apparent when you consider that over 15 percent of drivers do not carry auto insurance. However, some financial planners advise clients do without uninsured motorist coverage if they have adequate health and disability insurance.

Underinsured motorists coverage: Protects you when the at-fault motorist is insured for less than the damages incurred.

In many areas you may purchase supplementary **underinsured motorists coverage.** This operates in the same manner as uninsured motorists, except that when the other motorist is insured for less than the damages, your policy pays for the difference up to specified limits.

Collision coverage: Pays for damage to your car in a collision, regardless of who is at fault.

Other than collision coverage: All risks coverage on your car.

PART D—DAMAGE TO YOUR AUTO Part D consists of two separate components, collision and other than collision. **Collision coverage** pays for damage to your car in a collision, regardless of who is at fault. If the other driver is responsible for damages, your insurer will seek reimbursement and refund the deductible if it is successful. **Other than collision coverage,** previously called comprehensive auto coverage, provides all risks coverage on your car. Specifically included are such perils as fire, theft, falling objects, windstorm, flood, earthquake, and collision with an animal. Both coverages carry deductibles, and under either, the insurer has the option of paying for repairs or paying you for the actual cash value of a similar auto.

Because the actual cash value on older cars is small, it is generally recommended that you not purchase property damage insurance on cars five years or older. The premiums do not justify the minimal benefits in case of loss. With newer cars, you can hold down your premiums by including higher deductibles. Again, the optimal strategy is to take on the small risks yourself and use the savings to transfer the big risks.

EXCLUSIONS Most policies will exclude noninstalled sound and CB equipment from theft coverage. The chances of such accessories being stolen are just too high. You might consider covering these with a floater on your homeowners' policy.

A few other common exceptions are important to your personal liability coverage. Some are clear-cut, and others are not so obvious. If you think you might be subject to any of the following exclusions, you should discuss the matter with your insurance agent.

- You are not covered if the accident was intentional.
- You are not covered when you are driving someone else's car without permission.
- You are not covered when driving a car you own if it is not listed on your policy. However, when you trade in a listed car for another, your old insurance will cover the new car for a 30-day grace period, during which the insurance company should be notified of the purchase.
- You are not covered when you are carrying passengers or property for a fee, except in the case of carpools.
- You are not covered under your family auto policy when driving a motorcycle.
- You are not covered if you are driving a car that is not yours but is made available to you on a "furnished and available" basis, such as a company car.
- You are not covered when driving a noninsured car of a live-in relative.
- You are not covered by the family auto policy when driving a rental car unless you are a "named insured." Both the individual whose name appears on the declaration page and the resident spouse are named insureds. The standard family auto policy covers the named insured when driving any "owned or nonowned automobile." Resident relatives are covered only when driving an "owned or nonowned private passenger automobile."

No-fault insurance: Allows policy holders to recover financial losses from their own insurer, regardless of who is at fault.
Verbal threshold: Injured individuals may sue for reimbursement for physical injuries that satisfy this definition.
Monetary threshold: Injured individuals may sue for medical expenses that exceed this amount.

NO-FAULT INSURANCE Several states have attempted to hold down the cost of insurance by introducing no-fault plans. A **no-fault insurance** plan is one that allows policy holders to recover financial losses from their own insurer, regardless of who is at fault. In return for receiving reimbursement from your own insurer, there may be restrictions placed upon your right to sue. You retain the right to sue only when your physical injuries are severe according to a **verbal threshold** or your medical expenses exceed a **monetary threshold.** By eliminating the costly and timely determination of who is at fault in most accidents, no-fault insurance is meant to provide lower insurance premiums.

No-fault insurance has not always worked as intended. Twenty-five states and Puerto Rico have now adopted no-fault laws. But in only 13 of these states are there thresholds that limit the right to sue. Nonexisting or low monetary thresholds can result in widespread first-party payments for small claims and costly legal suits on all others. New Jersey, a no-fault state, led the nation in auto premiums in 1993, with an average premium of $1,095 per car.

Nevada, Pennsylvania, and Georgia have all abandoned the no-fault experiment after drivers in those states experienced sharp increases in premiums. Insurance companies, however, continue to believe that no-fault insurance can be a success if properly written. They are generally lobbying for changes in no-fault laws to set verbal thresholds that restrict all but the severely injured from entering the courtroom. A study conducted by the Insurance Research Council found that states with a high threshold (Florida, Hawaii, Minnesota, and New York) were more successful in holding down increases in auto injury costs.

Personal injury protection (PIP): Mandatory coverage in no-fault states that allows you to collect expenses for personal injury from your own insurer, regardless of fault.

Although the required minimum amount of coverage varies, in all no-fault states you are required to carry **personal injury protection (PIP).** This permits you to recover medical and hospital expenses, lost wages, and other injury-related expenses up to your policy limits from your own insurer, regardless of fault. However, because lawsuits are still possible, in most of these same states you also must carry personal liability protection.

A sometimes confusing point is that in all but one state, Michigan, no-fault does not cover property damage. Consequently, you will be able to collect only for damage to your car if either you collect from the driver at fault or you collect under your collision insurance.

OTHER COVERAGE There are several supplemental coverages that some insurance companies make available. These are generally considered high-cost add-ons, and most consumer groups advise against their purchase. The most common is *rental reimbursement,* which covers a rental vehicle if your car is damaged or stolen. Insurance for *towing and labor* charges for road repairs can also be added. And if you really love your car, there is *auto replacement coverage* that insures that your car will be either repaired or replaced.

Collision damage waiver (CDW): A waiver of the rental firm's right to charge you for damage to the rental.

Your policy may cover damage to a rental car. About 70 percent of auto policies do. Similar coverage may also be provided by your credit card company when you use that card to pay for the rental. With this coverage you can avoid purchasing a **collision damage waiver (CDW)** when you rent a car. CDW looks like insurance, but it isn't. It is actually a waiver of the rental firm's right to charge you for damage to the rental. The cost of this limited protection can be very high, from $9 to $15 dollars a day, which totals from $3,285 to $5,475 over a 365-day year. A number of states have passed laws that either regulate or curtail the sale of this high-priced item.

The Cost of Auto Insurance

The average cost of auto insurance in 1993 was $730 per car: $412 for liability, $206 for collision, and $112 for comprehensive coverage. But the actual range of cost varied greatly across the nation. The average auto premium was higher in the densely populated states such as New York ($985) and lower in the sparsely populated states such as South Dakota ($485).

The cost of auto insurance can also vary widely from one company to another. Progressive Insurance conducted rate comparison studies in Ohio and Florida. They found that the difference between the highest and the lowest quote for a six-month premium was on average $447 in Ohio and $396 in Florida. Obviously, comparison shopping for auto insurance can be highly rewarding.

Talk over your need with several different insurance agents. As with homeowners' policies, most auto companies sell a standardized policy, making it easy to compare features and price. Moreover, it may be wise to shop for both homeowners' and auto insurance at the same time, since some companies provide a multiple-policy discount when both are purchased. Be sure to request the applicable discounts listed in Table 8.1. To help with your shopping, you should fill out a worksheet like that in Figure 8.3, listing the kind, amount, and cost of each coverage.

Check with you state's Department of Insurance. Several states provide buyers guides and rate reporting services. They should also be able to provide some background information on insurers in your state. Moreover, before you buy, be sure to review the financial stability of the insurer with one of the rating services such as Best's or Standard & Poor's.

TABLE 8.1 • TYPICAL DISCOUNTS OFFERED BY AUTO INSURERS

Discounts Offered for Cars with the Following Features	Discounts Offered for Insureds with the Following Characteristics
Antilocking brake system	Away-at-school driver
Antitheft devices	Carpool driver
Automatic seat belts or air bags	Driver training
High-level brake light	Good driving record
	Good student record
	Mature driver
	Multicar household
	Multipolicy household
	Nonsmoking driver
	Retired driver

THE RATE BASE The cost of your insurance policy will depend on your risk class. It is based on factors over which you have some control, such as your driving record, and others over which you have no control, such as your age. If other drivers in your age group are accident prone, you are going to be charged more for insurance, independently of how good or bad a driver you happen to be. This may sound discriminatory, and in a sense it is. However, an efficient system of insurance requires the assignment of probabilities to groups of events. The insurance company must be able to discriminate, on the basis of experience, between apparent high-risk groups and low-risk groups.

Individual auto insurance premiums are determined in a two-stage process. First, each state is divided into territories, and each territory is assigned a base rate dependent on risk factors and costs within that region. Next, the base rate is multiplied by a value that is based on the risks associated with the personal characteris-

Figure 8.3
Auto insurance comparison worksheet.

Company ____________________

	Limits	Deductible	Annual Rate	
Liability	______		______	
Medical payments	______		______	
Personal injury protection (no-fault states)	______		______	
Uninsured motorists	______		______	
Underinsured motorists	______		______	
Collision		______	______	
Other than collision		______	______	
Total Cost				______

Discounts (see Table 8.1)

Type	Percentage Discount	Dollar Discount	
1. ____________	______	______	
2. ____________	______	______	
3. ____________	______	______	
etc. ____________	______	______	
Total Dollar Discount			(______)
Total Cost after Discount			______

tics of the insured. Your risk classification will take into account each of the following factors: your age, sex, marital status, educational level, driving record, and even the kind of car you drive.

When discounts are offered (see Table 8.1), they are figured from the base rate, not from the individual auto insurance premium. A young male driver, for example, might receive a 10 percent discount for having taken driver education. If his base rate is $200 and his annual premium is $760, his discount will be $20, not $152.

DRIVING RECORD One factor over which you definitely do have some control is your driving record. A chargeable accident (basically, one that is your fault) or a serious driving violation will increase your premiums by 40 percent or more. A history of such behavior can cause your rates to double and may result in cancellation of your policy. You will then have to purchase very expensive insurance from a company specializing in high-risk drivers or from the *shared* market in your state. In this market, which is also called the *assigned risk* market, your policy is placed in a pool with those of other high-risk drivers. The insurance companies agree to jointly share the cost and risk of providing for the insurance needs of these drivers. In about half the states, these are known as FAIR (Fair Access to Insurance Requirements) plans.

CAR MAKE AND MODEL It is obvious that a car requiring more expensive repairs will carry higher rates for property damage coverage than other vehicles. What is not so obvious is that certain cars will carry higher rates for liability coverage and collision because the chances of you, your passengers, and others being seriously injured in this particular car are greater.

The relative mix of age groups driving a particular car should affect that car's risk exposure. However, even after we consider that factor, some cars are just more accident prone than others. The insurance companies have responded by providing discounts for cars in low-risk groups and surcharges for cars in high-risk groups. The next time you think about buying a car, it is probably wise to check with your insurance agent to find out how your planned purchase ranks. The insurance saving on an alternative purchase might more than outweigh any saving on purchase price.

Before, At, and After the Accident

The odds are overwhelming that you will be involved in at least one auto accident. Accordingly, having the correct coverage and understanding what you should and should not do can prove extremely rewarding.

BEFORE THE ACCIDENT Adequate liability protection is a must. You should periodically review your policy to make sure that your family has the right kind and amount of coverage. Auto insurance information, including your policy number, agent, and telephone number, should be kept in the glove compartment. Any preprinted insurance forms allowing you tō report the particulars of any accident, including a sketch of the scene should also be placed there.

AT THE ACCIDENT If you are driving a car involved in a collision, you must stop the vehicle immediately. Do not, however, leave it in a position that creates a traffic hazard and causes another accident. Give your name and address, insurance in-

Auto Accident Checklist

1. Stop the vehicle immediately and remain at the scene until a police officer arrives.
2. Give your name and address, those of the vehicle's owner, and the registration number of the vehicle to:
   (a) Any injured person.
   (b) The owner, operator, or attendant of any damaged vehicle.
   (c) Any police officer at the scene of the accident.
3. Obtain the name and address of the driver of the other vehicle, all passengers, and witnesses.
4. Obtain license numbers of all vehicles involved.
5. Make notes of all significant circumstances surrounding the accident.
6. If there are serious injuries, make the injured person comfortable and phone for medical aid immediately. Under no circumstances should you move the injured person.
7. If you or any passenger in your car is injured, consult with your doctor immediately and encourage others to do so.
8. Obtain a copy of the police officer's accident report.
9. File all accident report forms required by the state or local government.
10. Report the accident to your insurance company as soon as possible.

Figure 8.4
Auto accident checklist.

formation, and the registration number of the vehicle involved, to the other driver, any injured persons, and the arriving police officer. Obtain similar information of all persons involved in the accident and witnesses to the accident. Furthermore, get the name of the arriving police officer, and request a copy of the officer's accident report (see Figure 8.4).

Make notes of the circumstances concerning the accident, including the position of the cars before and after the accident, traffic signs, road and weather conditions, and road obstacles. Step off the skid points to measure them, and locate the point of collision. If you have a camera with you, photograph the damage and the accident scene.

Assist the investigating officer by providing all factual information when requested. Do not offer any opinion on the cause of the accident or admit any guilt or blame. If others are injured, your first reaction may be to feel responsible. On calmer reflection, you might realize the fault was not yours. If you are arrested, ask to meet with your attorney before offering any explanation.

Action Plan for the Steeles: Holding Down the Cost of Auto Insurance

Background The Steeles have received a renewal notice on their auto insurance. They were surprised to find that their auto premiums had increased substantially. An accompanying letter from the insurance agent assured them they were favored customers receiving both a good driver's discount and a multiple-car discount. Most of the increase was due to a rise in the cost of property damage coverage. This increase was deemed necessary after new data indicated that accidents and thefts had risen dramatically in their locality.

The coverages and premiums for next year are shown in the table following.

The Problem The Steeles are not sure whether they should pay these premiums without first doing some comparison shopping. They also would like to know if they might be better off reducing either the breadth or limits of their auto coverage.

The Plan The Steeles should get insurance cost estimates from other companies. Given the wide range in auto premiums, comparison shopping is recommended when in doubt. Some companies specialize in insuring good drivers by providing these drivers with larger than usual discounts. With their good driving records, the Steeles should seek out a few of these companies. When comparison shopping, they should be sure they are getting prices on identical coverage. Therefore, they should first review the appropriateness of their present insurance.

The current liability limits are the lowest a family with their financial resources should have. They should consider raising these ceilings now. If they don't raise them now, they should definitely do so when Sharon takes on a full-time accounting position. If they want to save on auto insurance, they ought to consider changes in property damage coverage. It is probably too soon to drop these coverages on the Honda, but they should consider doing so in a year or two. They may now, however, decide on increasing the deductibles. Their present coverage, with deductibles of $100/$50, is costing $820. After checking with their agent, they will find that deductibles of $250/$100 will reduce the cost of this coverage to about $500.

The Steeles may have overlooked a gap in their present coverage. The trailer camper is not listed on their auto policy. Should the trailer be damaged in an accident or stolen, their auto insurance will not cover this loss. However, their liability protection will still apply. Should the trailer come loose and cause damage, they would be protected against the claims of others under their auto insurance. The Steeles' homeowners' policy specifically states that coverage on trailers is limited to $500. In addition, it does not cover theft when the trailer is away from the resident premises. For about $50 a year, the trailer could be covered for property damage on the auto policy. Given the relatively low market value of this item, $2,100, the Steeles will have to decide themselves whether they really need this additional protection.

Coverages and Limits of Liability	1995 Van	1993 Honda
Bodily injury and property damage ($100,000/$300,000/$50,000)	$316	$316
Uninsured and underinsured motorists ($100,000/$300,000)	70	70
Collision ($100 deductible)	290	300
Other than collision ($50 deductible)	110	120
Total premium by vehicle	$786	$806

Do not make any payments, or accept any payments, at the scene of the accident. A settlement offer should be considered only after you have discussed the matter with your agent and, possibly, an attorney.

If there are serious injuries, your first obligation is to seek medical aid. You may make the injured person more comfortable, but do not move the injured in any way that might aggravate a serious injury. Even if the accident was not your fault, if your actions contribute to the other person's injuries, you may be liable. If you think that you or anyone in your car might be injured, be sure to seek treatment immediately. You will be reimbursed under your medical payments coverage.

AFTER THE ACCIDENT Be sure to report the accident to your insurance agent as soon as possible and to file any written reports required under your state's motor vehicle statutes. Most policies require that you notify the company within one day of the accident. If you fail to satisfy this requirement, the insurer can later refuse to honor any claim resulting from the accident.

Keep track of all your accident-related expenses, including medical payments, lost wages, and additional traveling costs. These are all collectible damages when the other driver is at fault. If you think these losses may be sizable, you should seek the advice of an attorney. You may find that, in addition to the economic damages, you may also be able to collect for pain and suffering.

In a suit for damages, the plaintiff's attorney usually recovers a contingency fee. A few lawyers may be willing to work on an hourly basis, however. The contingency fee is normally 30 percent of the awarded damages, but the exact percentage is negotiable. This pays only for the lawyer. Whether you use an hourly basis or a contingency fee, there will be added expenses for such things as expert witnesses. These additional expenses must be paid whether you win or lose the case. Be sure to request that the lawyer first seek your approval before incurring any of these extra costs.

If the accident was your fault and it appears the damages awarded may exceed the liability limits on your policy, the insurer should inform you of this likelihood. You must then independently hire an attorney to take over when the insurer's participation ends and to make sure the insurance company has operated in your best interests.

SUMMARY

Homeowners' and auto insurance are your principal defenses against major risks to your property from damage and liability. Adequate protection is an essential component of every financial plan. Homeowners' and auto insurance are sold in standard formats covering the important needs of most insureds. Homeowners' insurance protects your dwelling and its contents from most common disasters. It also protects you from liability exposure that is not related to your business or auto. The auto insurance package protects you and your family from liability and property damage resulting from auto accidents.

KEY TERMS

actual cash value (p. 227)
all risks coverage (p. 225)
apportionment clause (p. 228)
appurtenant structures (p. 229)
co-insurance (p. 227)
collision coverage (p. 242)
collision damage waiver (CDW) (p. 244)
direct writer (p. 237)
dwelling protection (p. 229)
endorsement (p. 235)
Family Auto Policy (p. 240)
floater (p. 235)
independent agent (p. 237)
inflation guard endorsement (p. 228)
liability coverage (p. 231)
medical payments coverage (p. 242)
monetary threshold (p. 243)
mortgage clause (p. 228)
named perils coverage (p. 225)
National Flood Insurance Program (p. 236)
negligence (p. 225)
no-fault insurance (p. 243)
other than collision coverage (p. 242)
Personal Auto Policy (p. 240)
personal injury protection (PIP) (p. 244)
personal liability insurance (p. 225)
property loss insurance (p. 225)
replacement cost (p. 226)
single liability limit (p. 241)
split liability limit (p. 240)
subrogation clause (p. 228)
umbrella coverage (p. 235)
underinsured motorists coverage (p. 242)
uninsured motorists coverage (p. 242)
unscheduled personal property (p. 229)
verbal threshold (p. 243)

PROBLEMS AND REVIEW QUESTIONS

1. Explain the difference between all risks insurance and named perils insurance. List three perils not ordinarily covered under the basic homeowners' policy.
2. Which cost is greater, replacement cost or actual cash value? Why?
3. What is the difference between unscheduled property and scheduled property? How is scheduled property insured?
4. Julie's employer provides her with a portable computer for use at home so she can finish a marketing report she has been working on. During a break-in at her home, the $2,000 machine is taken. Might she be covered under her homeowners' policy?
5. Larry recently started operating a mail-order business in the basement of his home. Unfortunately, a fire put an end to his dreams of success by destroying about $10,000 worth of goods that had been temporarily stored in his basement. Will his homeowners' policy cover the loss? Why or why not?
6. While on her newspaper route, Jane's daughter tosses a paper through a subscriber's front window, causing $300 in damages. Might Jane be covered by her homeowners' insurance?
7. List seven standard formats for homeowners' policies. Which policy best serves your own needs? Why?
8. Why is it important to insure your dwelling for at least 80 percent of its replacement cost? How does the co-insurance clause operate?
9. What is the most important component of your auto insurance coverage? Why?
10. Who is covered under the Family Auto Policy? List several situations in which this policy would not protect you from personal liability.
11. Ruth had stopped for breakfast during a long morning drive to the ski slopes. While she was inside eating, someone broke into her car and made off with over $500 in ski equipment. What should she do? Under what policy might she be covered?
12. Last week Fred traded in his old junker for a new sports car. Not used to the fast response of a sports car, he accidentally drove it off a country road into a field, killing a cow. The car suffered extensive damage, and the farmer is demanding compensation for the dead cow. Fred had insurance on his old car. But he hadn't yet gotten around to informing his insurer of the trade-in. Will his old policy still cover him?
13. While riding to school on her bicycle, Ruth was run off the road by a hit-and-run driver. Except for a broken arm that is healing nicely, she was unhurt. Under which insurance policy, and under what section of that insurance policy, might her parents apply for reimbursement of medical expenses?
14. While stopped for a red light on Main Street, Ralph's car was hit from behind by a negligent driver. Because he was in a state with no-fault insurance, and since nobody was injured, he didn't think it was necessary to get the other driver's name and license number. Under what section of his auto policy is he covered?
15. Name several factors insurers consider when setting auto insurance rates. How might you hold down your auto insurance costs?
16. Why do auto insurers prefer a high monetary threshold?
17. Where would a homeowner obtain flood insurance?
18. Peter is away at college and drives the family car only when he comes home on special occasions. How might Peter's family hold down the cost of their auto insurance?
19. Why is it wise to review your auto policy before you rent a car?
20. Why is uninsured motorists coverage sold in states that have laws requiring compulsory auto insurance?

Case 8.1 A Fire at the Pages

It was around midnight when the smoke alarm woke Peter and Barbara Page. The fire had started in the attached garage and was already flaming when the fire department arrived. By the time it was put out, the Pages' home had sustained damages that would take $20,000 to repair. In addition, their Honda, with a market value of $8,000, was totally destroyed.

When the Pages purchased their home, they took out a homeowners' policy with $60,000 worth of dwelling protection. Since then they have received several letters from the insurance company suggesting they increase the dwelling coverage. For one reason or another they just never got around to responding. Now the insurer tells them that because their coverage was for less than 80 percent of the home's replacement value, as determined by the replacement cost provision, the insurance company probably will not pay the full cost of repairs. To avoid co-insurance payments, they should have been carrying at least $90,000 in dwelling protection.

QUESTIONS

1. Given the position of the insurance company, what is the smallest reimbursement the Pages can expect?
2. Is there any chance they can collect for the destroyed auto? How much and from whom?
3. Suppose the Pages disagree with the insurer's cost estimates. What course of action should they follow?

Case 8.2 After the Accident

Bob Brown was recently involved in a minor auto accident. His car was hit from behind, and he in turn slammed into the car in front of him. He would like someone to explain his coverage and show him where in his auto policy each of his losses might be covered. Help him out by doing that for each of the following items:

1. The cost of a medical checkup for his passenger, Ruth
2. The front and rear damage to his car
3. The damage to the car in front of him
4. The damage to the car behind him
5. The total amount of liability protection for bodily harm and property damage

HELPFUL CONTACTS

Insurance Information Institute
110 William Street, New York, NY 10038 (telephone 800-942-4242)
Offers numerous publications on property and casualty insurance. Will answer insurance questions on hotline.

INTERNET ADDRESSES

Earthquake Home Preparedness Guide (from EQE, an engineering consulting firm)
http://www.eqe.com/publications/homeprep/index.html

Federal Emergency Management Agency (frequently asked questions about flood insurance)
http://www.fema.gov/fema/finifp.html

Insurance News Network (homeowners' insurance rates across the country and a comparison cost index for new car insurance)
http://www.insure.com/index.html

U.S. Dept. of Agriculture (disaster preparedness and subsequent financial relief)
gopher://gopher.reeusda.gov:70/11/disasters

Part 3

INVESTING FOR THE FUTURE: Growing Your Financial Resources

The next six chapters deal with investments. They explain different investment alternatives, discuss investment strategies, and describe important aspects of the investment process. Above all, they continuously alert you to the trade-off between the return you can expect from an investment and the degree of risk you must take to earn it. According to many financial advisers, failure to understand this trade-off is the single most important reason investors lose with their investments—and these losses are often catastrophic in relation to the investors' net worths. To succeed as an investor, you need an understanding of investment risk and realistic expectations of investment return.

Along with considering investment risk and return, you must also ask whether or not you should be investing in the first place. Of course, the answer depends on how broadly we define *investment.* If it includes assets held for liquidity or to accommodate your lifestyle, the answer is you should be investing immediately and constantly. On the other hand, if we follow a narrower definition and include only those assets we hold for the specific purpose of increasing our net worths, then investment should come *only after* we have provided for adequate liquidity and have enough insurance to protect us against unexpected losses.

A key to successful investing is to understand *why* you are investing. Is it to provide for retirement? Educate your children? Buy a new car three years in the future? Or are you simply looking for a way to lower your income taxes? Your answers to these questions help determine the type of investment vehicles you should choose. This notion of linking specific investments to specific savings goals was introduced in Chapter 2 in the discussion of planned savings. Throughout Part 3, we will continue to stress the importance of having clearly defined investment objectives.

Chapter 9

Financial Markets and Institutions: Learning the Investment Environment

Objectives

1. To identify the basic investment alternatives
2. To understand the nature of securities markets, distinguishing between organized exchanges and the over-the-counter market
3. To recognize important legislation that protects investors
4. To learn how to select a stockbroker and how to choose an investment account
5. To know how to take an investment position and how to place investment orders
6. To recognize and use various sources of investment information

If you are a first-time investor, you might find the investment process bewildering and fearsome. Reading news items in the *Wall Street Journal* or watching *CNBC News* on cable convinces us that finance people speak a foreign language. Worse yet, there seems to be no logic in their stories. For example, a reporter announces, "The government's most recent employment figures hint strongly that a recession is coming." This must be bad news, right? Wrong, she then goes on, "Encouraged by the recent data, the stock and bond markets soared to new highs."

Fear not. The language isn't that hard to learn, and, believe it or not, there really is some sense in most investment news. This chapter will get you started by describing investment alternatives and by explaining important investment markets and institutions. Although you won't be an investment professional five chapters later, you certainly will know enough to make sound investment decisions.

GOALS AND INVESTMENT ALTERNATIVES

Our investment goals differ. If you are a young person starting a career, you may want to achieve a goal different from that of people preparing for retirement. You are concerned with building an estate; they are concerned with preserving what they have. You may be willing to sacrifice current income; they might depend upon it to meet living expenses. Obviously, an investment that's good for you may be totally inappropriate for them. Before starting an investment program, define your goals as clearly as you can, then indicate specifically how an individual investment is related to those goals. Goal definition is made easier when you understand yourself better: that is, when you are aware of your investment needs. Then you can look at the basic investment alternatives.

What Are Your Needs?

Surprisingly, perhaps, earning a return on an investment is not the only need many people try to satisfy from investing. The pleasure associated with many investments derives from your using them (your home) or simply owning them (your antiques). Also, if you are looking for a dollar return, this goal has to be further defined to state whether you want more now or more later: that is, a current versus a future return. And people are quite different in their tax situations and attitudes toward risks.

Tangible investments: Investments that can provide enjoyment in use as well as an investment return.

TANGIBLE AND INTANGIBLE INVESTMENTS The first major classification of investments is based on whether an asset is tangible or intangible. Tangible assets, also called hard assets, are things you can (but don't necessarily) use or enjoy while owning them. Houses, antiques, gold coins or bullion, diamonds and other precious stones, land, and even certain automobiles are examples of **tangible investments.** Some people might object to referring to some of these as investments, since your main reason for buying them is not to earn a return, but that's not an important distinction. Anything that has the potential to increase in value over time is an investment, regardless of its other characteristics. If you can sleep on it, drive it, and enjoy looking at it, all the better. If fact, many American have found over the years that their most profitable investments were the tangible ones, particularly their homes. During the 1970s, you would have done much better owning the average home than the average common stock, but in the 1980s, the situation was exactly the reverse. Another factor important to some people is the greater personal control they have with tangible investments. If you invest in an apartment complex, for example, you can decide what the rents will be or how much upkeep to provide. If you invest in an apartment complex indirectly, say, through a limited partnership or a corporation, someone else makes those decisions for you. If you like to control things, you have a mental disposition for tangible investments.

Intangible investments: Financial assets that provide claims to tangible assets or the earnings they provide.

Intangible investments, also called financial or paper assets, are actually claims to tangible assets or the earnings those assets produce. For example, a share of common stock is a claim against the issuing corporation's assets and an entitlement to any divided or other distributions the corporation might make.

CURRENT VERSUS FUTURE RETURN Some investments offer a return the moment you invest in them—a savings account, for example. Others pay a return less frequently. Most bonds pay interest twice a year, and most stocks that pay dividends usually do so four times a year. Dividends, interest, or any other type of asset income you receive on a regular basis during a year is called a **current return.** Many people prefer owning investments that offer current return, since it supplements their other income. Retirees, for example, often depend upon current investment income to meet living expenses.

Current return: Dividends, interest, or other types of asset income received on a regular basis.

Some investments, however, offer no current return whatsoever. Your only return comes about if you can sell the investment to someone else (or have it redeemed by the issuer) at a price greater than what you paid for it. Since this exchange takes place in the future, it is called a **future return,** or simply a capital gain. The common stocks of many growth companies have never paid dividends and probably will not for some time in the future. Investors buying these stocks realize that their only return will be from price appreciation over time. These kinds of investments appeal to investors who do not want or need current return but instead are investing to achieve future goals. The Steeles fall into this category (see the accompanying action plan).

Future return: A return expected in the future resulting from the potential sale of an asset that has appreciated in value.

Some investments offer both current and future returns. For example, if you buy a share of IBM common stock for, say, \$100, you will receive a yearly dividend of \$1.00, giving you a 1.0 percent current return on your investment. Obviously, you would be looking for a better return than this in buying IBM, and you would hope to get it through price appreciation. Your target might be 14 percent a year. An investment's **total return** is the sum of its current and future returns, and, in the IBM example, this would be 15.0 percent. Before making an investment, then, you should decide what proportion of total return you want as current return and what proportion as future return.

Total return: Sum of current return and future return.

YOUR INCOME TAX SITUATION Having read Chapter 5, you know the importance of income taxes in overall financial planning. As you move into higher tax brackets, you have a greater incentive to choose investments that avoid or defer taxes. For example, interest on municipal bonds is not subject to federal income tax, but interest on a U.S. Treasury bond is. Suppose for a \$1,000 investment you could earn \$60 a year in the municipal bond or \$80 in the Treasury bond. Which do you prefer? With no taxes to consider, your answer should be out in an instant—the Treasury bond. But suppose you are in a 28 percent tax bracket; now your choice is less clear. The Treasury bond would yield \$57.60 after taxes, but the municipal bond would yield \$60, clearly making it a better pick.

Risk averters: Investors who prefer to avoid risk or at least expect adequate compensation for undertaking risky investments.

YOUR ATTITUDE TOWARD RISK Your attitude toward risk will also shape your investment horizons. Some of us are by nature **risk averters.** We feel extremely uncomfortable in risky situations and prefer to avoid them or at least expect adequate compensation for undertaking them. Going back to the choice between the two bonds above, it could be that an investor in a 28 percent tax bracket would still prefer the Treasury bond to the municipal, not on the basis of after-tax return, but simply because it is a less risky investment. He reasons that an issuing municipality has a far greater chance of defaulting on its interest or redemption obligation than does the U.S. Treasury, and to him, the after-tax greater return is not worth the added risk.

Risk seekers: Investors who will undertake risky investments for less compensation than that demanded by risk averters.

Just as there are risk averters, there are also **risk seekers**—but these aren't foolish people. Risk seekers also expect additional return for undertaking risky investments, although they don't demand as much as risk averters. To them, a marginally better return of 1 percent might be enough to buy the municipal bond. Both risk-seeking and risk-averting approaches can be satisfied in investment markets. In fact, investor differences help make these markets function as smoothly as they do.

Basic Investment Alternatives

There are many different kinds of investments, and Table 9.1 summarizes their return and risk characteristics by five categories. The rankings assigned to each (A++ is the best and F– the worst) reflect your authors' opinions. Your instructor might have different rankings. Reaching a ranking everyone agrees with is impossible; for one thing, it depends on the period of time you use to measure risk or return, and for another, the techniques one uses to measure each can differ. Table 9.1 simply provides a rough idea of these two characteristics. Also, the ranking is for a typical investment within the class, but there are many variations within each class. For example, a typical common stock is riskier than a typical corporate bond, but not every common stock is riskier than every corporate bond. A share of AT&T common stock might be far less risky than a bond issued by Fly-by-Night Airlines. A detailed discussion of each of these kinds of investments is presented in the next five chapters, but a brief overview of all is a helpful start.

INVESTMENTS HELD FOR LIQUIDITY Chapter 3 explained investments that satisfy your liquidity needs. Remember from that discussion that there are degrees of liquidity, ranging from checking and savings accounts that are almost perfectly liquid to certificates of deposit that have penalties for early withdrawal. Also, while we give these investments a return rank of only a C, bear in mind that they frequently have done far better than some of the other investments with higher ranks, particularly during high-inflation periods.

SECURITIES WITH LONG OR NO MATURITIES By maturity, we mean the length of time you must wait before the issuer agrees to redeem the security. Corporate and government bonds, which represent creditorship claims—that is, the issuer borrows money from you and promises to repay it in the future—have maturities ranging from one to over 30 years. Common stock and most preferred stock, which represent ownership claims—that is, you are a part owner of the business—have no maturities. The issuing corporations never redeem them, and the only way you can recover your cost is by selling them to someone else. Of course, there is no guarantee you will sell at the same price you paid for them; you might get more, you might get less. When we say in Table 9.1 that there is no appreciation with

TABLE 9.1 • INVESTMENT ALTERNATIVES

Investment	Dividends, Interest, Rents (Current Return)	Potential Price Appreciation (Future Return)[a]	Rank[b]	
			Total Return	Total Risk
I Investments held primarily for liquidity: savings accounts, money market deposit accounts and mutual funds, U.S. Series EE and HH bonds, and certificates of deposit	Yes	No	C	A+
II Securities with long or no maturity				
Bonds and notes:				
U.S. Treasury issues	Yes	No	C+	A
Municipal and state government issues	Yes	No	B–	A–
Corporate issues	Yes	No	B	A–
Preferred stock	Yes	No	B–	B+
Common stock	Some	Yes	A–	B–
III Pooling arrangements				
Mutual funds:				
Income funds	Yes	No	B	A
Growth funds	Some	Yes	A	C
Balanced funds	Yes	Yes	B+	B
Investment trusts	Yes	Yes	B+	B
Limited partnerships	Some	Yes	B	C–
IV Contractual claims				
Warrants and rights	No	Yes	A+	D
Put and call options	No	Yes	A+	D
Commodity and financial futures	No	Yes	A++	F–
V Tangible assets				
Real estate:				
Personal residence	No	Yes	A	A
Others	Usually	Yes	B+	D
Gold and other metals	No	Yes	B+	D
Jewelry and collectibles	No	Yes	A–	F

[a]This does not consider price appreciation that is embedded in the investment, such as that sold on a discount basis: e.g., U.S. Treasury bills, U.S. Series EE bonds, and zero coupon bonds. Nor does it include cyclical price variation arising from interest rate changes.

[b]Rank is based on a typical investment, but there are many variations within each class. Returns are ranked from low (C) to high (A), and risks are ranked in opposite order—low (A) to high (F).

bonds and preferred stock, we mean that such appreciation is not what investors *expect* from these securities *when they are issued,* since the interest or dividends they pay are fixed and cannot grow. However, their prices do fluctuate with respect to changes in interest rates overall. Therefore, it is possible to have capital gains—or capital losses—with them.

Because of price volatility, bonds, preferred stocks, and common stocks are all considered risky, but common stocks are the riskiest of the three, and all can be very risky during unsettled economic times. None of these are suitable investments if there is a possibility you may need to sell them to raise cash. They are more appropriate for long-term investment.

POOLING ARRANGEMENTS A pooling arrangement allows you to achieve greater diversification for your investment dollar than if you attempt to buy individual securities. For example, one share of a mutual fund gives an ownership interest in perhaps as many as 100 different common stocks. Pooling arrangements also provide professional investment management. Not only do you reduce risk through diversification, you might also improve your return.

CONTRACTUAL CLAIMS A contractual claim gives you a legal right or obligation to buy or sell something at a given price within a given period of time. Warrants and rights are issued by corporations, and they usually entitle you to buy a certain number of shares of the issuing corporation's common stock. Put and call options are similar to warrants and rights except that they are issued (written) by individuals. A *call* entitles buyers to buy, and a *put* entitles them to sell, shares of a corporation's common stock. People who buy options pay a price for them, since they are actually privileges, not obligations. If you buy an option entitling you to buy, say, 100 shares of General Motors stock at $60 a share, you are not forced to make the purchase; and if GM's stock price fell below $60, you would choose not to. So the most you can lose is what you paid to buy the option.

Commodity and financial futures are like options, but they differ in one important aspect. Rather than being a privilege to buy or sell something, they are an obligation to do so. If you enter into a futures contract on, say, 5,000 bushels of corn at a price of $3.00 per bushel, you are obligated to comply with that agreement regardless of what happens to the price of corn. Even if it falls to $2.00 a bushel, you must buy it at $3.00; thus, your losses with futures contracts are not limited as they are with options. Your potential future return with options and futures is extremely high—but so are your losses, and that is why we rank them highest in risk.

TANGIBLE ASSETS Only a few of the many tangible assets are listed in Table 9.1. We have singled out the personal residence from other real estate because it has been such a good investment for so many people. Perhaps our risk assessment is too favorable, but in many cases the prices of homes have not been as volatile as prices of common stocks or even U.S Treasury bonds. Other real estate, particularly raw land, is another story.

The demand for gold, other metals, and jewelry and collectibles is highly erratic over time. All these kinds of investments are exceptionally risky. With some, such as collectibles, you need specialized knowledge to compete in their markets.

SECURITIES MARKETS

On a normal day about 450 million shares of stock are traded on the New York Stock Exchange. Assuming an average price of $40 a share means that about $12 billion worth of securities change hands on just this one exchange and just for common and preferred stocks and warrants. Add to this the combined total values of options, commodity futures, bonds, notes, and all short-term debt securities, and you begin to see the magnitude of the securities industry.

Organized Exchanges

Organized exchange: A physical place where securities are traded.

Facilitating the exchange process is the **organized exchange,** which is usually understood as a physical place where buyers and sellers—or their representatives—face each other in making transactions. Each exchange has a floor that is arranged to trade specific securities at specific locations. Only members of an exchange are authorized to make trades, and only securities listed on the exchange are traded.

New York Stock Exchange (NYSE): Largest organized exchange in the world.

THE NEW YORK STOCK EXCHANGE The **New York Stock Exchange (NYSE)** is the largest organized exchange in the world. Practically all the large corporations in America have their securities listed there. In total, over 1,800 firms are listed, with over 2,500 different stocks. To be listed on the NYSE, a business must meet certain requirements, such as having at least 2,000 stockholders owning 100 or more shares and a minimum of 1,100,000 shares of stock held by the public. Many firms appreciate having their securities listed on the NYSE, since it is often taken as a sign of financial strength and maturity. However, it certainly is no guarantee of success; many listed companies have gone into bankruptcy over the years.

ORDER EXECUTION ON THE NYSE Organized exchanges are fascinating places to visit. What appears to be utter chaos is actually an efficient system for transferring billions of dollars' worth of securities each trading day. Figure 9.1 shows order execution on the NYSE and introduces its members who may be involved in the process. To be a member, you must buy or lease a "seat." Seat prices are determined by the demand for them, and they have varied considerably over time. For example, they hit a high of $515,000 in 1969, fell to $35,000 in 1977, and then rebounded to $1.1 million in 1987, right before the big crash on October 19, 1987. The price slumped to $575,000 in a sale in early 1993.

Figure 9.1 A trade on the New York Stock Exchange (NYSE).

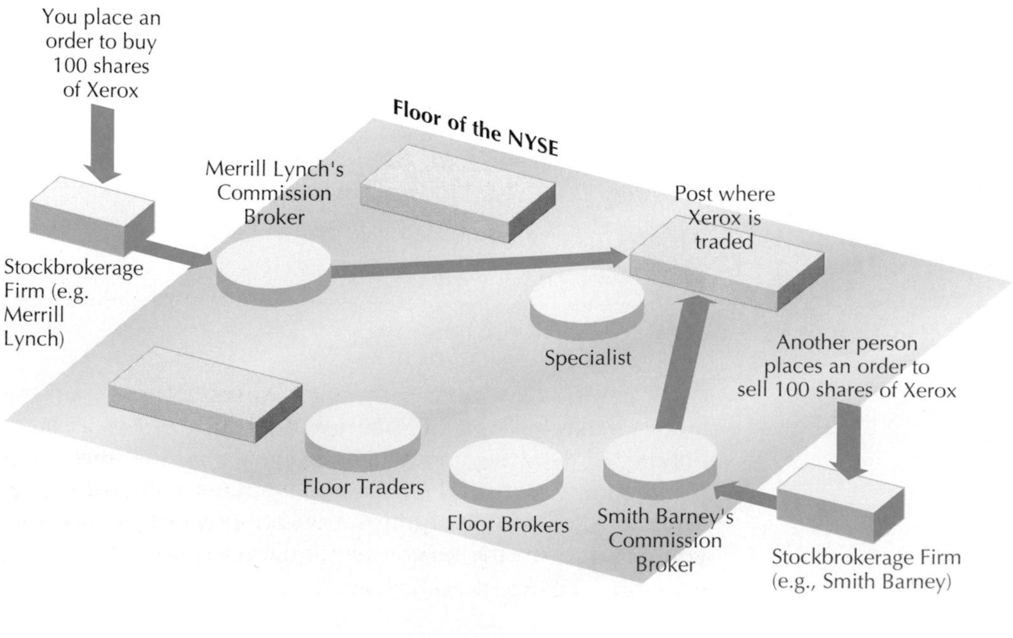

Commission brokers. Commission brokers are employed by stockbrokerage firms. Assuming you deal with Merrill Lynch and have placed a market order to buy 100 shares of Xerox, your representative will transmit the order to one of Merrill Lynch's commission brokers on the floor of the exchange. Suppose that, at the same time, someone else places an order to sell 100 shares of Xerox through her broker, Smith Barney. Both commission brokers would then go to the post where Xerox is traded. For an actively traded issue, such as Xerox, there will be a number of brokers and traders bidding to buy or sell shares. All of them will try to get the best possible price, either for their customers or for themselves. In effect, shares are auctioned to the highest bidders. (The NYSE and similar markets are thus called *auction markets.*) Perhaps the Merrill Lynch and Smith Barney brokers settle a trade at $50 a share. The entire transaction may be completed in less than two minutes.

Specialists: Members of organized exchanges responsible for maintaining orderly and continuous markets.

Specialists. **Specialists** play a number of critical roles in the trading process. They are expected to maintain an orderly and continuous market in the six or seven stocks assigned to them. To keep wide swings in price from occurring, they must buy or sell for their own accounts. For example, assume that when your commission broker arrives at Xerox's trading post, no other broker or trader is there to trade Xerox. Then it is the specialist's responsibility to trade. Another responsibility for the specialist is to maintain the limit books, which contain all limit orders clients have placed with their brokers. (Limit orders will be explained shortly.) Because of the inside information specialists have, it is possible for them to profit handsomely at the expense of outside investors. The NYSE, however, insists that customers' interests come first and specialists' second. This rule is monitored constantly for compliance and enforced rigorously because the integrity of the specialist is critical to maintaining customer confidence in the system.

Floor brokers and floor traders. Floor brokers are not associated with any particular stockbrokerage firm but serve as independent operators. They assist commission brokers by executing orders on their behalf, for a fee. They also serve stockbrokerage firms that do not own seats on the floor. Floor traders operate strictly for themselves, hoping their position on the floor will help them trade stocks profitably.

American Stock Exchange (Amex): Another (smaller) organized exchange in New York City.

THE AMERICAN STOCK EXCHANGE The **American Stock Exchange (Amex)** is very similar to the NYSE in terms of physical layout and trading details, but it has easier listing requirements. Often called the "junior board," the Amex is younger than the NYSE and has less prestige. A good number of its listed securities are from relatively unknown companies nationally, and a fairly large percentage are energy oriented. As you probably guess, on balance the volatility of Amex securities is higher than that of NYSE securities. The Amex also has a bond-trading area, and bond transactions on the Amex are conducted in the same way as those on the NYSE.

REGIONAL STOCK EXCHANGES Along with the two major exchanges, there are 14 regional stock exchanges, such as the Cincinnati Stock Exchange and the Pacific Coast Stock Exchange. Regional exchanges list securities of companies within their geographic areas, but very often these securities also are traded on the NYSE or Amex. In this respect they are duplicates, and it is hard to justify their existence. Together, all the regional exchanges account for a little less than 10 percent of all trading on organized exchanges.

ORGANIZED OPTIONS AND FUTURES EXCHANGES Options are traded on five organized exchanges: the Chicago Board Options Exchange, the American Option Exchange (part of the Amex), the Philadelphia Option Exchange, the Pacific Coast Exchange, and the New York Stock Exchange. Options are traded in a manner similar to stock trading.

There are over a dozen organized commodity exchanges in the United States and Canada, and others throughout the world. Trading on commodity exchanges differs somewhat from trading on stock exchanges. It takes place by public outcry and through a complicated series of hand signals. You might have seen pictures of commodity trading and wondered how anything is ever accomplished in what appears to be bedlam. If you have an opportunity to visit any organized exchange—but particularly the commodity exchanges—don't pass it up; although free, they are sufficiently entertaining to be worth an admission charge.

Over-the-Counter Markets

Over-the-counter (OTC) market: Securities trading via electronic communications.

NASDAQ: Name of the electronic communications system used in the OTC market.

Trading over the counter sounds like an illegal activity—but it's not. In fact, in terms of the number of different stocks traded, it is the largest securities market, surpassing the NYSE and Amex combined. In contrast to an organized exchange, the **over-the-counter (OTC) market** consists of a network of securities dealers who trade securities through an extensive communication system called **NASDAQ** (National Association of Securities Dealers Automated Quotations System). You may have heard the NASD's commercials: "NASDAQ, the stockmarket for the next 100 years." In addition to common and preferred stocks and warrants, all government and many corporate bonds are traded in the OTC market. Any securities

Box 9.1 **PERSONAL FINANCE NEWS** *Late Edition*

NASDAQ: The Stock Market for the Next 100 Years—Well, Maybe

A few years ago, the people who run NASDAQ wanted to increase the public's awareness of its market. They ran a TV ad proclaiming NASDAQ as the stock market for the next 100 years. It was a clever piece with considerable impact. Pretty soon, people who never invested a dime in their lives were asking, "What the heck is NASDAQ?" Put simply, NASDAQ is an electronic marketplace where buyers and sellers trade over their computers, rather than face to face as they do on an organized exchange.

Unfortunately for NASDAQ, right when the ad was at its popularity peak, a study by two finance professors revealed that maybe NASDAQ trading wasn't so great for investors. The problem they uncovered was that bid-asked spreads on many stocks seemed excessive. (A bid price is what you receive when you sell a stock; the asked price is what you pay to buy it. At any point in time for a given stock its asked price is higher than its bid price.) The finance profs felt that the excessive disparity resulted from a lack of competition among the investment firms that trade through NASDAQ.

The study had a powerful impact within the investment community. The SEC (Securities and Exchange Commission, an independent agency of the U.S. government) was impressed and initiated its own investigation. Naturally, NASDAQ officials denied any wrongdoing, but they also started a study. The issue hasn't been fully resolved, but spreads on certain actively traded stocks, such as Microsoft, seem to have declined. Regardless of the ultimate resolution, it was a "black eye" and an embarrassment to NASDAQ.

Meanwhile, the old guard at the New York Stock Exchange could hardly contain itself for joy. They always maintained that face-to-face contact between buyer and seller in an open forum gives investors the most competitive prices. Interestingly, the Big Board is in the process of developing its own computerized trading system. We might wonder how it will differ from NASDAQ's and how face-to-face contact will be preserved.

dealer can buy or sell through NASDAQ, and many stockbrokerage houses make their own portfolio rather than acting as an agent of a customer. Most OTC stocks are of relatively small and unknown companies.

Many of these eventually become large, prosperous businesses, and promoters of small companies often tout that tomorrow's IBMs are found today in the OTC market. Of course, that's true, but it is also true that many of tomorrow's bankrupts are found there. The point is, trading some OTC stocks is very risky. Don't be fooled into thinking that if it is an OTC company with an exotic name, it must be a big money maker in the future. Actually, where a security is traded should be the least important consideration in judging whether it is worth buying.

REGULATION OF THE SECURITIES INDUSTRY

The nature of the securities industry has offered disreputable people considerable opportunities to defraud investors. Since 1933, important laws have been passed to protect investors; in addition, the industry has initiated reform through self-policing efforts. You have much greater protection now than in the past, but it would be a mistake to think fraud no longer exists or to believe losses you might suffer are the fault of your broker. It is important to know your rights and your obligations before you invest.

Federal Legislation

Federal laws form the backbone of investor protection. The important federal acts are explained in the following sections.

THE SECURITIES ACT OF 1933 The Securities Act of 1933 calls for full disclosure of new securities to be traded in interstate commerce. Such securities must be registered with the Securities and Exchange Commission (SEC, an independent agency of the Federal government), which approves their sale. To receive approval, the applicant must provide the SEC with economic and financial data relevant to the firm and the new offering. It does so in the form of a **prospectus.** After the SEC has determined that the prospectus represents adequate disclosure of all material information affecting the company's value and after the SEC has approved the registration, the company must provide the prospectus to any potential investor. Misrepresentation or fraud in preparing the prospectus can be the basis for lawsuits by investors and the SEC against the issuing corporation, its directors, stockbrokers handling the issue, and even public accountants who assisted in its preparation.

Prospectus: Document describing a new security issue.

Stiff penalties and possible jail sentences have done much to provide investors with reliable and relevant prospectuses. However, SEC approval in no way assures the issues will be successful. Many new firms have prepared impeccably clean prospectuses and then gone into bankruptcy. The message is clear if you are considering investing: Obtain a prospectus; read it thoroughly, particularly the section explaining risk factors; and believe what it says. Some investors seem to think a prospectus is a mere formality; it isn't. It is a helpful document and should be regarded as such.

THE SECURITIES EXCHANGE ACT OF 1934 The Securities Exchange Act of 1934 extended regulation to securities that had already been issued. With this provision, it brought under government regulation almost all aspects of the security markets. It required all securities traded on organized exchanges and the exchanges themselves to be registered with the SEC (which it established). It outlawed fraud and misrepresentation by anyone engaged in the sale of securities, including stockbrokers and their representatives. It forbade price manipulation, and it required registered firms to file with the SEC both a detailed annual report (called a **10-K Report**) and quarterly financial statements. It also stipulated that annual reports be provided to shareholders.

10-K Report: Detailed financial report that must be filed with the Securities and Exchange Commission; also available to shareholders.

The act also established guidelines for security trading by insiders, the intent being to prevent them from taking advantage of their privileged information. Initially, insiders were considered a firm's officers, employees, directors, or relatives of each. In recent years, the SEC has broadened its definition of *insider* to include practically anyone with information not available to the general public. In a noted case, a newspaper reporter was convicted under the law for providing advance information about news items subsequently printed in the paper.

THE MALONEY ACT OF 1938 The Maloney Act of 1938 required trade associations in the securities industry to register with the SEC. Only one—the National Association of Securities Dealers (NASD)—has been formed and registered. The NASD is the self-regulating arm of the securities industry. It establishes and enforces a professional code of ethics and is responsible for testing and licensing dealers.

THE INVESTMENT COMPANY ACT OF 1940 The Investment Company Act of 1940 brought regulation to investment companies, which we more frequently call mutual funds. Such companies are required to register with the SEC and provide shareholders with adequate information about the company's activities. A subsequent amendment to the act forbade paying excessive fees to fund advisers.

THE INVESTMENT ADVISORS ACT OF 1940 The Investment Advisors Act of 1940 requires anyone providing advice to investors (for a fee or other compensation) to register with the SEC and indicate his methods of investment analysis. The determination of who is an investment adviser has come under scrutiny in recent years because many products and services not usually thought of as investment-related are now being tailored in that direction. Two good cases in point deal with financial advisers and insurance agents. The former advise clients on a wide range of financial activities, including investments; the latter sell policies that look like and pay out like investments. Should these professionals register as advisers? The trend in court cases seems to answer Yes. As an investor, keep in mind that registration does not improve the quality of advice offered or in some other manner guarantee its usefulness. Some advisers advertise their registration, perhaps with the intent of impressing potential clients. Do not be impressed—virtually anyone with about $250 to pay the fee can register.

THE SECURITIES INVESTOR PROTECTION ACT OF 1970 The Securities Investor Protection Act protects investors from financial losses that might result from the failure of their broker. It created the Securities Investor Protection Corporation (SIPC), which insures an investor's account up to $500,000 for securities held and up to $100,000 in cash holdings. Most brokerage firms are members of the SIPC and contribute to its funding. It has been particularly helpful to discounters in their efforts to overcome investor reluctance to deal with out-of-town brokers.

Some investors believe that the SIPC protection extends to any losses on securities they hold while a broker is in financial difficulty. This is not true. SIPC guarantees only that your securities eventually will be delivered to you or to another broker. Losses or gains during the time the failing firm's arrangements are being sorted out are the investor's. For example, SIPC only guarantees delivery of 100 shares of GM, if that is what you held with a failing broker; it does not guarantee a price for those shares. GM might have been worth $80 a share when your broker ceased to operate but be worth only $50 a share when you eventually have access to the shares.

State Law and Self-Regulation

State security laws actually predate federal law. Kansas passed the first "blue sky" law in 1911, and all states now have similar legislation. These laws attempt to keep investors from being defrauded by promoters selling securities worth no more than a piece of blue sky. State laws (patterned after the federal laws) apply to *intrastate* securities sales. Although federal laws apply to *interstate* sales, the SEC can be contacted for any expected fraudulent activity in securities trading.

In addition to federal and state regulation, the securities industry has its own internal regulatory process. Most of this is found in the National Association of Securities Dealers' Rules of Fair Practice, Code of Procedure, and Uniform Practice Code. These three documents cover a wide range of trading activities, specifying rules and appropriate conduct guidelines for NASD members.

Binding arbitration: A method of resolving disputes among stockbrokers and customers.

An extremely important part of self-regulation is the process of **binding arbitration.** If you have a complaint against your broker for not handling a transaction

Box 9.2 SAVING MONEY
Using Arbitration to Resolve Disputes with Your Broker

On the advice of a registered representative of a large brokerage company, an elderly couple invests most of their life savings—about $30,000—in bonds issued by a now-defunct energy company. They lose everything and appeal to the broker for compensation on the grounds that the representative put them in an unsuitable investment. The company declines to make restitution. Now what? In a growing number of cases, the answer is *binding arbitration.*

Investors with gripes such as the elderly couple's or those involving excessive trading (called "churning"), unauthorized transactions, or other misconduct can file a claim to have the dispute settled through binding arbitration. The process is quite simple and relatively inexpensive, with filing fees ranging from $25 to $1,000 (for disputes in excess of $500,000).

If a claim is less than $10,000, it is settled by one arbitrator, who rules on the evidence provided by each side. Larger claims are heard by three-person panels in a formal hearing that is similar to a trial. Each side can be represented by an attorney, issue subpoenas, and cross-examine witnesses. If your claim goes to a hearing, expect to be on the "hot seat," with the opposing attorney trying to show that you were an intelligent investor, making your own investment decisions drawn from alternatives suggested by the representative. You must show that your losses were caused by the representative.

Establishing such evidence might be difficult if you do not keep accurate records of your communications with the representative. As usual, the best evidence is in written form; but you should keep a careful diary of verbal communications, such as tips or other forms of advice. Note the time and date and carefully record the nature of the conversation. In the past, punitive damages were not permitted in arbitration cases; however, that is no longer true, and large punitive awards were made in several high-visibility cases.

The alternative to arbitration is litigation. This route is expensive, and it is usually not advised if a claim is less than $200,000. Moreover, it may not be available to you since most brokerage firms require you to agree to use binding arbitration to resolve disputes.

properly, or for pressuring you to invest in securities totally inappropriate for your investment objectives, or for any suspected misconduct, you can appeal to any of the organized exchanges, the NASD, or the American Arbitration Association, for binding arbitration to resolve the problem.

Claims less than $10,000 are usually resolved quickly by one arbitrator, but claims above the amount involve more-complicated procedures. As its name implies, decisions are final. When considered against the only alternative for seeking a resolution—hiring your own attorney and filing a suit—binding arbitration makes a great deal of sense, since it is much cheaper and faster.

USING THE SERVICES OF A STOCKBROKER

Most financial investments are bought and sold with the assistance of a securities dealer, usually called a stockbroker, or broker for short. (A major exception are mutual fund shares, which are discussed in Chapter 13.) The first step is to select a broker and to choose either a cash or a margin account. Then you must know whether to take a long or a short position. Finally, you need to distinguish among various types of orders.

Selecting a Stockbroker

Finding a stockbroker is not difficult. The number of brokers available has grown considerably since the industry was deregulated in 1974. In recent years, even commercial banks and savings and loans have entered the stockbrokerage business, and the chances are good that some of these institutions, along with traditional stockbrokers, are located in your community. The major distinction between stockbrokers is whether they are considered a full-service or a limited-service (usually called a discount broker) firm.

Full-service stockbroker: A stockbroker who provides a wide range of services, including research and advice, but generally charges high commissions.

FULL-SERVICE STOCKBROKERS As the name implies, a **full-service stockbroker** provides a wide range of investment products—usually any you can think of—along with recommendations from its research department on which securities to buy or sell. Full-service firms, such as Merrill Lynch or Smith Barney, are probably the ones you recognize.

The full-service broker is often involved in selling stocks of companies that have their first public offerings, and being one of their customers allows you to participate in these offerings. Sometimes these are profitable; other times they are not. But the greatest benefit a full-service broker can offer you is advice on selecting stocks and managing your portfolio. As we shall soon see, you pay for these services through substantially higher commissions. If you fail to use them, you are in effect wasting your money.

You should know that a broker's sales representative (the person you probably call your "broker") is a salesperson first and an investment adviser second. This person may call you frequently to inquire about your investment needs. Of course, frequent calls can lead to frequently buying and selling, which in turn reduces your investment profits or adds to your losses. A conscientious full-service broker will discourage frequent transactions (called "churning the account") and will, instead, become familiar with your investment objectives and help you arrange a portfolio to achieve them.

TABLE 9.2 • ILLUSTRATIVE STOCKBROKERAGE COMMISSIONS: COMMON STOCK TRANSACTIONS

Transaction	Value of the Transaction	Commissions: Cost and Percentage of Value — Full-Service Broker $	%	Well-Known Discounter $	%	Smaller Discounter $	%
10 shares @ $35	$ 350	18	5.1	35	10.0	25	7.1
200 shares @ $25	5,000	130	2.6	89	1.8	35	0.7
500 shares @ $18	9,000	225	2.5	107	1.2	58	0.6

SOURCE: Advertised rates and telephone inquiry.

Discount broker: A stockbroker who provides most services except research and advice and offers low commissions.

DISCOUNT BROKERS The advent of the **discount broker** after deregulation introduced important changes in the stockbrokerage business. The discounter emphasizes only one thing—low commissions. And, as Table 9.2 shows, these can be substantially below commissions charged by full-service brokers, although they are less expensive on small trades. As you can see, brokers' commissions vary widely, and you should ask for a commission schedule before opening an account. You should see from Table 9.2 why small investors who trade frequently find it difficult to show any gains. With the 10-share transaction, even the lowest percentage of 5.1 means that if you bought and sold the 10 shares only once in a year, you must show price appreciation of 10.2 percent simply to cover commissions. Very few investors are good enough to overcome this burden.

Action Plan for the Steeles: Selecting a Stockbroker

Background The Steeles realize that achieving their future goals will depend greatly upon earning a reasonable return on their investment assets. With this in mind, Arnold and Sharon have begun investing in common stocks. They are using a full-service broker, although they have given her specific guidelines as to the types of stocks they like—safe ones with good dividend yields. Their broker provides a menu of stocks meeting this criterion, and the Steeles then make their selections. They do very little trading, probably averaging three transactions a year. Their intention is to accumulate a portfolio of 15 or so good stocks, which they will hold until retirement. Of course, in some cases they may sell one holding and replace it with another.

The Problem Arnold and Sharon question the need for a full-service broker, since they are doing most of the investment selection work. They estimate a commission savings of $100 to $150 a year by switching to a discount broker. This broker provides a monthly newsletter with recommended stocks but does not employ representatives who help clients with specific needs.

The Plan The Steeles are not using their full-service broker effectively by merely asking her to provide an investment menu. This person should be trained to advise the Steeles on which stocks are right for them, given their investment objectives, and she should be able to help the Steeles with their overall portfolio plan. The two parties probably have not communicated well, and, without placing blame on one or the other, the Steeles should meet with the broker and discuss clearly their risk-tolerance level and investment objectives (why they are investing in the first place and what they hope to accomplish). They should ask the broker for a detailed plan with her specific stock recommendations.

Rationale for the Plan The Steeles choice of a discount broker would be appealing if they had more-extensive training and background in investment analysis. Until they reach that stage, the extra commissions each year do not seem a high price to pay for professional help. Of course, the Steeles still must monitor their portfolio periodically to determine that the broker's advice is indeed professional and worthwhile.

Round lots: Orders for 100 shares or multiples of 100 shares.

Odd lots: Orders for less than 100 shares.

ROUND LOTS AND ODD LOTS The basic trading unit when placing orders is 100 shares. Orders for 100 shares, or multiples of 100 shares (e.g.: 300 shares) are called **round lots;** orders for a fraction of 100 shares are called **odd lots.** So an order for 250 shares involves one round lot of 200 shares and an odd lot of 50 shares. There is no specific disadvantage in dealing in odd lots, although you should realize that most stockbrokers have a minimum commission amount, regardless of order size. So a trade with a low dollar amount will lead to a high commission as a percentage of the trade amount. As we have just illustrated, this erodes your potential return considerably.

Kinds of Accounts

Having picked a stockbroker, you should next open an account. This doesn't take much time. If you are married, it's a good idea to open a joint account, with each spouse having authority to initiate orders. Your account can be either a cash account or a margin account.

Cash account: A stockbrokerage account similar to a regular charge account.

CASH ACCOUNT A **cash account** is similar to a regular charge account used by many retailers, except you must pay for securities you purchase within three working days after the purchase is made. So, if you buy on Monday, you have three days to come up with the cash. The same time frame applies when you sell securities; that is, you must deliver shares sold within three working days. Some brokers will ask for an initial deposit before executing orders; others will not. If you wish, the broker can have your shares mailed to you, or you can choose to let the broker hold them. Holding your own shares prevents problems that might arise if the broker goes bankrupt or experiences other difficulties, but you must take steps to safeguard them, and a safe-deposit box is the only really safe place.

Actually, holding shares may not be possible in the future. Plans are currently in progress to do away with stock certificates, and your ownership interest would be shown only in so-called book-entry form.

Margin account: A stockbrokerage account that allows borrowing from a stockbroker, using securities as collateral.

Initial margin requirement: An amount that must be deposited when buying securities on margin; the current rate is 50 percent.

MARGIN ACCOUNT A **margin account** sounds mysterious to the uninformed. Actually, it is nothing more than a loan the broker makes to you using your securities as collateral to support the loan. Here's how it works.

Say you open a margin account by depositing \$3,000. (All brokers require a minimum deposit for a margin account, and the Board of Governors of the Federal Reserve System requires an **initial margin requirement** of 50 percent of the value of securities purchased.) Then, you buy 100 shares of ABC stock at \$50 a share. Thus, you bought \$5,000 worth of stock, ignoring commissions, with a \$3,000 deposit; obviously, the other \$2,000 came from your broker. Now, what happens if the stock goes up or down in value? No problem, if it goes up. You can sell whenever you like and repay the \$2,000 loan *plus interest* and pocket the difference. If it goes down, keep one simple fact in mind—the loss is all yours. You don't share it with the broker. So if ABC goes down to \$30 a share and you then sell, the broker still gets $2,000, *plus interest* and you still pocket the difference—$1,000 in this case. You lose $2,000 which is $20 ($50 – $30) a share times the 100 shares.

Perhaps the mystique surrounding margin trading is the possibility of getting a margin call (this means your broker calls and asks for more money) if the price of a security falls below a certain level, called the **maintenance margin requirement.** This requirement varies among firms but cannot be less than the minimum of 25 percent of the market value of your securities set by the Board of Governors of the Federal Reserve System. If a broker had, say, a 30 percent requirement, this means the security in our previous example could go no lower than $28.57 a share before you would get a margin call. The way you get the above number is as follows:

Maintenance margin requirement: A minimum equity required in an account to continue using a broker's loan.

Step 1. Divide the broker's loan by 1.0 minus the maintenance margin requirement; that is $2,000.00 (1.0 – 0.3) = $2,000.00/0.7 = $2,857.14.

Step 2. Divide your answer by the number of shares held: $2,857.14/100 = $28.57.

Since you still owe the broker $2,000, your equity in the account is $857.14 ($2,857.14 – $2,000.00). As a check on your math, your equity should be 30 percent of the market value of your securities. In this example, 30 percent of $2,857.14 is $857.14, so our math is correct.

Using a margin account magnifies your gains or losses, as would any loan you use to buy securities. In the previous example, if you had used your own funds, you could have purchased only 60 ($3,000/$50) rather than 100. Thus, if the price of the stock had gone up or down by $10, for example, your gain or loss would have been $600 rather than $1,000. A loan allows you to **leverage** your investment, which automatically increases the range of possible returns, which in turn is synonymous with more risk. Keep that in mind: Leverage always increases risk.

Leverage: Using borrowed funds, such as with a margin account, to buy securities.

Kinds of Positions

After you open an account with a broker, the next step is to begin trading. Brokers refer to this as opening a position, and there are two kinds you can take: a **long position,** meaning you buy securities, and a **short position,** meaning you sell securities (that you don't own).

Long position: A purchase of securities.

Short position: Sale of securities you don't own.

A long position is what you typically associate with investing: You buy, and then own, securities. A long position can be viewed as buying now and selling later. In contrast, with a short position, you sell now and buy later. This seems confusing, and certainly more mysterious than a margin account. How can you possibly sell securities you don't own? The broker helps you accomplish this by lending the securities to you. Here's how it works.

MECHANICS OF A SHORT POSITION Suppose you think KLM stock is overvalued at $40 a share and sure to go down in price over the next year. Your strategy is to sell 100 shares now at their high price and then buy them a year later after their price has fallen. You call the broker and tell him you wish to short-sell 100 shares of KLM. He will execute your order in exactly the same fashion as if you already owned the shares, and the buyer will receive 100 shares from your broker. Where did your broker get the shares? He probably borrowed them from other clients who own KLM shares and hold them in margin accounts. Is the broker adding risks to these clients by lending their shares? No, because the broker will insist that you deposit sufficient margin to cover potentially adverse price movements. In the above example, you would have to deposit at least 50 percent, or $2,000. You could deposit more if you wanted to, but it would be foolish to do so, since your deposit does not earn interest.

If you guessed correctly about KLM's price and it declines to $30 a share, you close out your short position by buying the stock and returning the borrowed shares to your broker. Your account was credited $4,000 when you sold them, and you need only $3,000 to buy them back. The $1,000 difference is your gain. If you deposited $2,000 to initiate the short sale, your account would now have $3,000 in it. If you guessed incorrectly about KLM and its price went up to $50 when you decided to close your position, you would lose $1,000 and your account would have only $1,000 left in it.

SHORT POSITION RISKS Is a short position any riskier than a long one? Probably so, because the long-run trend of stock prices has been upward, and you're betting against the trend with a short sale. Moreover, you lose all earnings potential on your margin deposit, and you also must pay any dividends declared on stocks sold short. If KLM declared a $1.00 per share dividend while you were short, you would have to pay $100. (You probably are wondering if this means that two dividends are paid on the same stock—one by you and one by KLM. Yes, because the person who loaned the shares expects to receive a dividend, as does the person who bought them from you.)

Kinds of Orders

You place an order when you wish to buy or sell securities. Your order will be executed either on the floor of an organized exchange, such as the New York Stock Exchange, or between brokers in the over-the-counter market. You can place three kinds of orders: a market order, a limit order, and a stop order.

Market order: An order to buy or sell securities at the market price prevailing when the order is executed.

MARKET ORDER A **market order** instructs your broker to buy or sell securities at the best possible price. At the time you make a transaction, the broker will give you an up-to-the-minute price of a security. For example, you might call wishing to buy 100 shares of Alcoa. The broker will use his quotation terminal to find the last price paid for a share of Alcoa; assume it was $50. If you then instruct the broker to buy or sell Alcoa "at the market," you are placing a market order. Are you guaranteed a price of $50? No, even though your order may be executed in less than two minutes, Alcoa's price could change during that time.

Limit order: An order to buy or sell securities at a specific price.

LIMIT ORDER A **limit order** sets the price that you are willing to pay for a security. For example, if Alcoa's price is very volatile, you may fear that it could increase during the time it takes to execute a market order. If $50 a share is the top price you want to pay, you would use a limit order specifying that price. Limit orders remain in effect until they are either canceled or executed. Some investors do not want limit orders to remain "alive," so they place day orders, which are limit orders that are automatically canceled at the end of the day they are placed. Limit orders are not that important for actively traded issues such as Alcoa, since the large number of buyers and sellers usually keeps the stock's price from fluctuating widely within a short period of time. However, shares of less actively traded stocks are different. Perhaps as few as 200 or 300 shares trade each day, and substantial price changes are then possible. Limit orders are more appropriate here.

Box 9.3 SIMPLIFYING FINANCIAL PLANNING
Your Broker—Your Banker

Let's suppose a minor financial emergency arises and you need to raise cash rather quickly. Should you see your local banker? You might, but a quicker route might be to tap into a margin account you establish with a stockbrokerage firm.

Many people are hesitant to have a margin account, since such accounts are used typically by aggressive investors as a source of funds to buy more securities. Used in this fashion, a margin account clearly adds risk to a portfolio. However, there is nothing preventing you from having a margin account without borrowing. Used this way, you establish a reservoir of readily available credit.

Suppose you have securities worth $5,000 in the account and no broker's loan against them. With a phone call you could arrange to borrow up to $2,500 and have the money almost immediately. Furthermore, the interest charged by the broker is usually at the prime rate plus 1 or 2 percent. Compared with other sources of consumer credit, that can be a steal. At this writing, the broker's loan cost about 9.5 percent versus about 19 percent on a bank credit card.

There are two problems to consider. Since you never have to pay off the principal on a broker's loan (barring a margin call), theoretically you can finance forever whatever it is that prompted the loan. If this is an item that decreases in value and needs to be replaced periodically, obviously, not reducing the loan in proportion to the depreciation value will keep you from accumulating enough funds to finance an eventual replacement. And there is the problem of a margin call. If the value of your securities falls appreciably, the broker will require a deposit of additional funds. As a hedge here, you should consider borrowing less than the maximum allowable—for example, never more than 30 percent of the total value ($1,500 in the above example).

Stop order: An order that is triggered by the market price of a security; often used to stop losses.

STOP ORDER A **stop order** (often called a stop-loss order) is a market order that is triggered by the market price of a security. It is used to protect profits or limit losses. Suppose you bought Alcoa at $50 and its price subsequently increased to $80. You would have a nice profit but might not wish to sell, because Alcoa's price could go still higher. You could then place a stop-loss order on Alcoa at a price of, say, $75. If its price continued to rise, the order would be meaningless; but if its price fell to $75 (the trigger), the stop-loss order would become a market order. Again, you would not be guaranteed a $75 price, but only the best price your broker could get, which might be higher or lower, as is the case with all market orders. Stop orders are used by investors who do not wish to watch their securities closely or make frequent selling or buying decisions. (Stop orders can also be used to buy securities.) Also, some investors use such orders because they feel they lack adequate discipline to make correct decisions during emotionally charged periods. As a security's price falls, you are often tempted not to sell because you convince yourself it's bound to increase again. Consequently, you sit and watch as the price falls—perhaps back to the original purchase price, eliminating your entire gain. With a stop order, you make the selling decision without the emotional atmosphere created by a falling price.

Do Things on Paper First

Now that you have information about accounts, positions, and orders, should you begin investing immediately? We don't think so. It is often a good idea to have a trial period in which you make investments on paper. This is especially true if you plan to pick your own securities. This trial period, if you do it seriously, will familiarize you with the mechanics of investing and will give you firsthand experience with price volatility. Of course, you can always mimic a trial period by going back in time and selecting securities and then seeing how your selections would have fared, but this experience is often not the same as investing for future periods. In general, we have some background on the general market or specific securities, which is bound to influence our investment decisions. (Most of us like to cheat by picking known winners!)

KEEP HONEST RECORDS The whole experience will be useless if you fail to keep honest records. It's surprising how much we wish to avoid admitting—even to ourselves—the mistakes we make. If you pick a stock and its price goes down, then measure your loss as carefully as you might measure a price increase. If the stock or bond pays dividends or interest, note that too, along with the date it's received. In this dry run you would buy all the risky securities you might want to buy later. Include options and futures contracts in your portfolio if you are thinking of buying them. It is better to understand their enormous risks now rather than later, when it can cost you dearly.

Figure 9.2 A portfolio summary sheet.

NAME: *Cindy Lipton*

REPORTING PERIOD: *1/1/96 – 3/31/96 (13 weeks)*

Securities	(1) No. of Shares, Bonds, etc.	(2) Purchase Price per Unit	(3) Total (1) × (2)	(4) Commissions	(5) Total Invested (3) + (4)	(6) Closing Prices	(7) Total Closing Market Value (6) × (1)	(8) Gain or (Loss) (7) – (5)	(9) Dividends or Interest	(10) Total Gain or Loss (8) + (9)
1. *Apple Computer*	*23 shares*	*$42.75*	*$ 983.25*	*$ 35.00*	*$1018.25*	*$49.00*	*$1127.00*	*$ 108.75*		*$ 108.75*
2. *Armco Steel*	*190 shares*	*5.25*	*997.50*	*35.00*	*1032.50*	*4.25*	*807.50*	*(225.00)*		*(225.00)*
3. *Tandem*	*60 shares*	*16.50*	*990.00*	*35.00*	*1025.00*	*16.00*	*960.00*	*(65.00)*		*(65.00)*
4. *Exxon*	*22 shares*	*45.50*	*1001.00*	*36.00*	*1037.00*	*49.50*	*1078.00*	*41.00*	*11.00*	*52.00*
5. *IBM*	*8 shares*	*105.00*	*840.00*	*31.00*	*871.00*	*98.00*	*784.00*	*(87.00)*	*9.68*	*(77.32)*
6.										
7.										
8.										
9.										
10. Money Market Fund										
			$ *4811.75*	$ *172.00*	$ *4983.75*		$ *4756.50*	$ *(227.25)*	$ *20.68*	$ *(206.57)*

Supplementary Information:

A Interest on margin balance = $ — (amount borrowed × margin rate)

B Dividends on stock sold short = $ —

Gain (Loss) This Period:

1 Dollar return = Column (10) – (A) – (B) = $ *(206.57)*

2 Rate of return = dollar return ÷ Column (5) = *–0.0415 (4.2%)*

3 Rate of return annualized = rate of return for the period × 52/*N* (*N* = number of weeks held) = *–16.8%*

EVALUATE YOUR PERFORMANCE After a time, say, three months, you should designate a cutoff date and measure your performance for the period. A form, such as the one illustrated in Figure 9.2, is helpful in doing this.

As you see, the investor (Cindy Lipton) narrowed her investment choices to five common stocks. Cindy assumed she had about $5,000 to invest and planned investing about $1,000 in each security. When the quarter ended, she was somewhat surprised with the results and very glad she started investing with a dry run. As you see, she lost $206.57 for the quarter, and this figure doesn't include commissions she would incur if she actually wanted to sell out on March 31. Cindy was woefully underdiversified. Even though she bought five securities, three are in the computer industry—Apple, Tandem, and IBM.

Notice the relatively high total commissions in relation to the total amount invested: about 3.5 percent ($172/$4,983.75). This wouldn't be too bad if Cindy planned to hold the portfolio for some time, but it is very high if she plans to turn it over every quarter. If she did, the commissions alone would probably consume all her gains.

Cindy's quarterly rate of return of −4.2 percent indicates that if her performance remained the same, she would lose 16.8 percent (about 1/6) of her original investment in one year. Needless to say, this loss is considerable, and Cindy concluded that she needed more experience before investing on her own.

FINDING INVESTMENT INFORMATION

Most investment decisions require some research. Even if you decide to limit your investing to mutual funds or other pooling arrangements, you still must evaluate the alternative funds available. And if you make your own investment decisions, your research must be ambitious. Information is the key to good research, and the sections to follow provide an overview of available sources.

Company Sources

As noted earlier, companies are required by the SEC to provide shareholders with annual and quarterly financial reports. Companies must also provide 10-K Reports if they are requested. A 10-K Report is a detailed compilation of a company's financial performance for the previous year. It presents the same data found in a company's annual financial report but may include other information not found there, such as asset depreciation methods or officer compensation levels.

Considerable information can be found in company reports. In addition to financial data, these documents contain discussions of past results and plans for the future. The corporate officers who provide these statements want to present their company in its most favorable light. Thus, caution is necessary.

To gain information more quickly, you might ask that your name be placed on a company's mailing list for press releases to financial analysts and other interested parties. Moreover, some investors call or write companies, requesting information or clarification of certain topics that appear in financial reports. The success of this approach depends on the nature of your request and willingness of management to respond to it. You cannot expect that management will release privileged or sensitive information.

Investment Advisory Services

There are thousands of individuals registered with the Securities and Exchange Commission (the SEC). These people have licenses to offer (for a fee, usually) investment advice. But don't assume that their government licenses guarantee good advice. Some is good, but much isn't; or at least, it's no better than what you can find free at the library.

LIBRARY SOURCES Most libraries contain three excellent investment services: *Moody's, Standard & Poor's,* and *Value Line*. Of course, you can also subscribe to each and have it delivered to your home, but they are relatively expensive. Among other things, each offers a manual containing financial data for several thousand companies and a weekly newsletter that reports on economic trends and specific industries and companies. Each also recommends stocks to purchase or avoid. To become familiar with all their publications, you should visit your local or school library and ask the reference librarian to show them to you. Certainly, if you are doing any research on an individual company's securities or on an industry, start with one of these publications.

ADVISORY SERVICES YOU PAY FOR When you read *Barron's* for the first time, you probably will be surprised at the number of advertisements by investment advisers appearing there. These advisers usually offer a weekly or monthly newsletter. Some also offer "hotline" connections that allow you to call for their up-to-the-minute advice, or they might call you if there is an important change in their opinions. You pay handsomely for these services, and the logical question is, Are they worth it? It is difficult to answer that question. To begin with, you have to evaluate them on a risk-adjusted basis. Many tout that they beat the market, but it isn't clear that they do so, after considering risk. They tend to do well in bull markets (an expression meaning rising prices), but not so well in bear (falling-price) markets. Moreover, some will have you buying and selling securities very frequently, which substantially increases commissions costs. After these are deducted from your gains, your net return might not be any better than if you simply put together a random portfolio and held it for the entire period. Finally, unless you have sufficient funds to offset their advisory fees—which can be as high as $500 a year—their cost is simply too high in relation to the amount you invest.

Newspapers and Magazines

Many investors find a considerable amount of information in newspapers and magazines. This information includes investment stories and articles that might stimulate your interest as well as financial data. Most of the newspapers and magazines mentioned below are available at libraries.

THE *WALL STREET JOURNAL* The *Wall Street Journal* is a newspaper published each work day. Many investors subscribe to the *Journal* or read it at their offices or libraries. It is not exclusively investment-oriented but rather covers a wide range of business and economic topics. Practically every issue has at least one story of relevance to most investors along with extensive price and trading information on a wide range of securities. It would be fruitless to attempt to describe this publication in detail; you simply must read an issue to appreciate its comprehensive coverage of investments. An interesting part of the *Journal* is its daily report on various market indicators, such as the Dow Jones Industrial Average (DJIA). The DJIA is perhaps the most widely watched market index in the United States because of its historical significance. Because it covers only 30 individual stocks, it is not considered a comprehensive market index. The S&P 500 Stock Index also has wide appeal, and it is far more representative of the overall market and differs in its method of computation.

BARRON'S *Barron's,* a sister newspaper to the *Journal,* is published weekly and is exclusively investment-oriented. It has regular columns dealing with different aspects of investing and a market laboratory section in each issue. In addition, it features stories on different companies, reports interviews with security analysts and other investment advisers, and offers refresher articles on different aspects of investing.

INVESTOR'S BUSINESS DAILY *Investor's Business Daily (IBD)* is a daily newspaper devoted exclusively to investment news. It provides full coverage of trading activity of stocks, bonds, options, futures, and mutual funds. *IBD* is similar to Section C of the *Journal* except that its coverage, in some respects, is more thorough. For example, it provides graphic displays of 30 stocks of interest on the NYSE, Amex, and OTC market each day; in addition, it highlights one company for extensive analysis, both graphic and in terms of the company's underlying fundamentals. If you are interested exclusively in investment news, you might consider *IBD* as an alternative to the *Journal.*

MAGAZINES A number of good magazines provide investment information and ideas. *Forbes* is exclusively investment-oriented. Its stories and regular features usually are realistic in outlook, often forewarning investors of potential problems with various investments. Its annual survey of mutual funds is well worth the price of that issue.

Financial World is similar to *Forbes* but less extensive and perhaps less conservative in outlook. Although not a get-rich-quick magazine, it takes a more positive view than does *Forbes.*

Fortune magazine usually features in-depth articles on different companies or industries. These articles provide excellent background material but are not geared directly toward investing. Nevertheless, the articles are timely, as are the regular monthly columns.

Money magazine covers a wide range of financial planning topics, including investing. Its investment articles often provide personal investment stories—almost always of success—that are interesting and thought-provoking. After reading *Money,* you get the impression that becoming wealthy through investing is a simple task, involving little risk. More articles on investment failures would help temper that impression.

Computer Data Sources

Many investors are using personal computers (PCs) to assist them in making investment decisions or in managing and evaluating their portfolios. There are a number of data sources. For example, the Dow Jones News/Retrieval system is a vast source of information, ranging from 10-K extracts to transcripts of *Wall Street Week,* the popular PBS weekly investment program.

Practically all investment advisory services, such as Value Line and S&P, offer investment information on diskette or over a telephone line. Indeed, so many sources are available that if you plan to use the computer in investing, you should consider subscribing to *Computerized Investing*. This bimonthly newsletter is published by the American Association of Individual Investors (AAII), a nonprofit organization of more than 130,000 members dedicated to helping people make better investment decisions (call 312-280-0170 for information). The newsletter covers a wide range of computer data sources and investment applications; one issue during the year exceeds 600 pages and covers software and data bases exclusively.

Last, but not least, considerable information is available on the Internet. This area is so vast that we cannot do justice to the topic here. If you know how to "cruise the net," you should be able to locate many excellent web sites. America Online and CompuServe provide financial information through your computer and access to the Internet, both at a relatively modest monthly fee.

SUMMARY

People have different investment goals because their investment needs are different. After you determine your own needs, you can evaluate basic investment alternatives, which range from perfectly safe bank deposits to extremely risky commodity futures contracts.

Securities are traded on organized exchanges, such as the New York Stock Exchange, and in the over-the-counter market. Federal and state regulation of the securities industry is extensive; in addition, the industry is self-regulated through the NASD.

When you are ready to invest, you must select a stockbroker, who can be a full-service or a discount broker. Once you have a broker, you must decide whether to open a cash or a margin account, and then place orders to buy or sell securities. The three basic orders you can place are a market order, a limit order, and a stop order.

Getting information is essential to a sound investment program. Companies provide financial data about themselves, and investment advisory services provide similar information. Newspapers, magazines, and computer sources, such as the Internet, are also useful sources of information.

KEY TERMS

American Stock Exchange (Amex) (p. 261)

binding arbitration (p. 265)

cash account (p. 268)

current return (p. 256)

discount broker (p. 267)

full-service stockbroker (p. 266)

future return (p. 256)

initial margin requirement (p. 268)

intangible investments (p. 256)

leverage (p. 269)

limit order (p. 270)

long position (p. 269)

maintenance margin requirement (p. 269)

margin account (p. 268)

market order (p. 270)

NASDAQ (p. 262)

New York Stock Exchange (NYSE) (p. 260)

odd lots (p. 268)

organized exchange (p. 260)

over-the-counter (OTC) market (p. 262)

prospectus (p. 263)

risk averters (p. 257)

risk seekers (p. 257)

round lots (p. 268)

short position (p. 269)

specialists (p. 261)

stop order (p. 271)

tangible investments (p. 255)

10-K Report (p. 264)

total return (p. 256)

PROBLEMS AND REVIEW QUESTIONS

1. How do tangible and intangible investments differ, and what investor needs can be satisfied with tangible investments?
2. What is an investment's total return? What type of investors prefer a current return? Who might prefer a future return?
3. Compare an organized exchange with the over-the-counter market.
4. Distinguish among commission brokers, floor brokers, and floor traders. Explain a critical role played by specialists on the floor of an organized exchange.
5. What is NASDAQ?
6. Very briefly highlight the six federal laws (discussed in this chapter) regulating the securities industry.
7. Explain a prospectus and a 10-K Report.
8. What are the differences between a full-service broker and a discount broker? Identify a round lot and an odd lot.
9. How does a cash account differ from a margin account?
10. What is an initial margin requirement? If its value is 0.50, and if you have $10,000 to invest, you can buy securities with a total market value of $________.
11. What is a maintenance margin requirement? Assume that you bought 100 shares of Acme, Inc., at $100 a share. If the maintenance margin requirement is 0.30, at what price would your broker give you a margin call? What does a margin call mean?
12. Allen Gold thought Exxon's common stock was far overpriced at $45 a share; therefore, he executed a short sale on 100 shares. How did his stockbroker assist in arranging this short sale, and how much profit (ignore commissions) will Al make (or lose) if: (*a*) Exxon goes down to $40 a share, or (*b*) it goes up to $50 a share? Does Al have to put up any money for this short sale? Would you recommend short selling as a routine practice over the long run? Explain.
13. Explain market, limit, and stop orders. In what situations would investors use stop orders? Explain.
14. Identify three investment advisory services usually available at most libraries.
15. Identify three financial newspapers and four financial magazines.

Case 9.1 Rose Geisler's Investment Plan

Rose Geisler, a college graduate in electrical engineering, has a good position with a major electronics firm. Her current annual salary is $65,000, and, since Rose is single with no financial obligations, she plans to invest all her savings (around $11,000) in common stocks. Rose has done some research on security selection, and she feels capable of picking her own stocks. At present, she likes the technology sector and also thinks companies in the auto industry will do well.

At the advice of her former personal finance instructor, Rose has decided to have a trial run before she actually invests. So she has selected three stocks—Intel, Microsoft, and GM—and has tracked their performances for six months. The results appear below:

	Intel	Microsoft	GM
1. Purchase price per share	$60	$80	$40
2. Number of shares purchased	50	50	100
3. Commission	$85	$85	$80
4. Closing prices	$50	$65	$50

QUESTIONS

1. Using a format similar to the one illustrated in this chapter, show the results of Rose's experiment.
2. Calculate the following: (*a*) the portfolio's dollar gain or loss, (*b*) the rate of return for the six-month period, (*c*) the annualized rate of return. Evaluate the portfolio's performance. Do you have any advice for Rose? Explain.

Case 9.2 Should the Delaneys Open a Margin Account?

Pat and Ed Delaney are a married couple with two children. Both have professional positions, and their joint income is over $70,000 a year. Their net worth is well over $100,000, and they have excellent liquidity with very little short-term debt.

The Delaneys want to start an investment program by investing in growth stocks. They believe their situation calls for the services of a full-service broker who will guide their selections. One of the brokers they interviewed urged them to open a margin account, since the amount they wanted to invest initially—$10,000—was not enough, in her opinion, to achieve adequate diversification. She put together a list of 10 stocks and urged the Delaneys to invest $2,000 in each one.

QUESTIONS

1. Assuming the Delaneys would pay 12 percent a year on the broker's loan associated with the margin account, determine their net annual return (expressed as a percentage of the amount they invest) if their stocks paid a current dividend of 5 percent and increased in market value by 20 percent. Make a similar calculation assuming a current dividend of 5 percent and a decrease in market value of 20 percent. (Ignore commissions in both your calculations.) What advice do you have for the Delaneys about leverage?
2. Suppose the broker has a maintenance margin requirement of 30 percent. Ignoring dividends and commissions, how low could the market value of the Delaneys' holdings go before they would get a margin call? For simplicity in calculations, assume they bought 2,000 shares of only one stock at $10 a share.
3. What other advantage(s) might the Delaneys have with a margin account? Given their particular situation, do you recommend one for them? Explain.

HELPFUL CONTACTS

U.S. Securities and Exchange Commission
Washington, DC 20549
A very useful publication is *What Every Investor Should Know.*
Investor complaints: Office of Consumer Affairs (telephone 202-272-7440).
Copies of filed documents: Public Reference Room (telephone 202-272-7450).
Locator for other telephone numbers: 202-272-3100.

To obtain a background check on a securities dealer, including past and pending legal problems, contact your state's securities agency and request a report through the North American Securities Administrators Association's Central Registration Depository.

INTERNET ADDRESSES

American Stock Exchange
http://www.amex.com/

Bank of America (questions that determine your attitude toward risk and an asset allocation strategy)
http://www.bankamerica.com/tools/sri_assetall.html

Federal Trade Commission (articles on investment fraud)
gopher://gopher.ftc.gov:70/11/ConsumerLine/publications/investments

Information for Investors (compiled by the Dept. of Finance at Ohio State University)
http://www.cob.ohio-state.edu/dept/fin/cern/

Nasdaq Financial Executive Journal (articles of interest to investors)
http://www.law.cornell.edu/nasdaq/nasdtoc.html

National Association of Investors Corporation (services for individual investors and investment clubs)
http://www.better-investing.org/index.html

Yahoo: Markets and Investments (use this site as a springboard to many excellent sources of investment information)
http://www.yahoo.com/Business_and_Economy/marketsandInvestments/

The *Wall Street Journal,* Money and Investing Update (a truly great site that provides financial information throughout the day)
http://update.wsj.com/update/edit/frontpg.html

Chapter 10

Investment Basics: Understanding Risk and Return

Objectives

1. To grasp the nature of risk and its sources and to relate risk to investment return
2. To see the importance of diversification and to understand how it reduces investment risk
3. To understand how to accomplish adequate diversification, both among asset groups and within an asset group
4. To grasp the concepts of required return and expected return and to see how they are used in security selection
5. To become familiar with important methods and issues involved in establishing a portfolio and making changes over time

Beginning investors often find it difficult to select securities that are appropriate for them. Inexperience is partly to blame, but the core problem is an inability to recognize how much potential return a particular investment offers and the kind and degree of risk they must take to earn the return. You often hear people say, "Oh, I wouldn't put my money in common stocks—they're far too risky. I'll stick to conservative savings accounts." Keeping your money in a safe place might provide short-run security, but what do you give up in the long run? In 30 or 40 years, will these people accumulate a sufficient nest egg for retirement?

Investing is very serious business. It is not an activity that you should begin without preparation or with preconceived notions such as "stocks are too risky." Your goal is not to avoid risk altogether or to bet your life savings on one investment's performance; rather, you should attempt to create a portfolio of investments that connect suitably to all your investment goals and to your individual risk-tolerance level.

RISK AND RETURN

Our review of investment alternatives in Table 9.1 reveals that investments with higher returns also have higher risks. Economists tell us there is no such thing as a free lunch, and in the investments arena that is certainly true. This positive direct relationship between risk and return can be called the **iron law of risk and return,** and it serves as a good forewarning: If you are seeking high returns, be prepared to undertake high risks.

Iron law of risk and return: The strong positive correlation between higher investment return and greater risk.

What Is Risk?

You probably have an intuitive understanding of **risk** as the possibility of losing some or all of your investment. Games of chance are considered very risky because you can lose your entire bet. Most stocks and bonds are risky because their prices might decline after you buy them, and some may even go into bankruptcy, costing you practically your entire investment. This is the dismal side of risk, but there is also a bright side. You wouldn't invest in a risky venture unless you anticipated a high return. Therefore, an evaluation of risk must consider these high returns as well as losses, and it is actually better to view risk as a range of possible returns—positive and negative. The greater this range, the greater an investment's risk.

Risk: Often thought of as a possibility of loss; but a better definition is variability of return.

AN EXAMPLE OF RETURN VARIABILITY The concept of risk as return variability is illustrated in Figure 10.1, which shows three hypothetical $1,000 investments. Investment *A* is a deposit in a savings account promising to pay 10 percent interest for the upcoming year. Assuming the deposit is FDIC insured, you are virtually certain of getting back $1,100 at the end of the year and earning a return of $100. Investment *B* is a U.S. Treasury bond that pays interest of $120. If you bought the bond for $1,000 and sold it for the same amount a year later, you would get back $1,120. But this result is not assured. Suppose instead that the bond's price could go up or down by $50 during the year. In the first case, your total return would be $170 ($120 + $50); in the second it would be $70 ($120 − $50). Investment *C* is a speculative common stock that pays no dividends. Your only return is through price appreciation. If its price increased by 30 percent over the year, you would make $300 on your $1,000 investment. If the price decreased by 10 percent, you would lose $100.

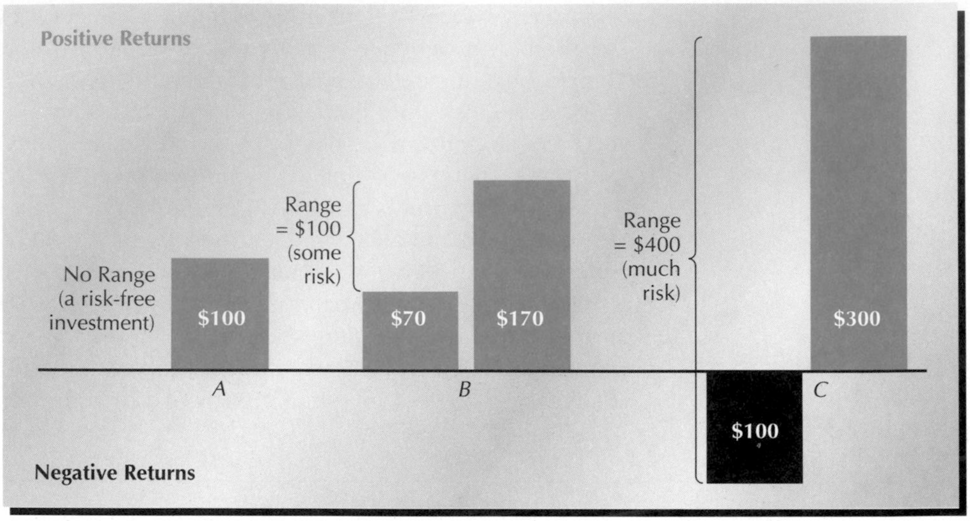

Figure 10.1
Range of possible returns for three $1,000 investments: *A*, *B*, and *C*.

A is a risk-free investment since it has no range; that is, it has only one outcome. *C* is the riskiest investment, since it has the widest range of possible returns ($400). *B* has some risk, since its range of returns is $100. Estimating the range of possible returns provides a good approximation of risk, and it is often used for that purpose.

RISK AND TIME It is often felt that investment risk is influenced by the passage of time, and there are two perspectives on the issue. First, the greater the time before an investment's return is expected, the riskier the investment—all things considered. The rationale is simple: We never know what the future holds, and the further we extend our projections, the more likely they are to be wrong. This principle implies greater variation in returns on long-term investments than on short-term ones.

The second perspective is somewhat different. Here, we ask the question, Are we more likely to achieve an investment goal by holding an asset for a shorter or a longer period of time? Of course, the answer depends very much upon the type of asset held. Consider a risky one, such as common stocks. Suppose we learn (as we soon shall) that common stocks have shown an average yearly return of about 12 percent over the past 70 years or so. We would like to invest in them and hope to earn the average yearly rate in the future. Are we most likely to achieve this goal by holding stocks for one week, one year, or 10 years? You probably guessed the last choice—and you are right. The longer the investment horizon, the greater the odds of earning the annual rate. This is why we realize that holding stocks for short periods of time is risky. This message was driven home very forcefully by "Black Monday"—October 19, 1987—when the stock market fell about 23 percent. The prospect of losing 23 percent of your portfolio in *one* day is indeed evidence of considerable risk, which is why financial planners urge us to hold common stocks only if we have relatively long investment horizons.

Sources of Risk

What factors make an investment risky, that is, widen its range of possible returns? The various sources of risk can be placed into two groups: those associated with changing conditions of the overall economy and those related to changing conditions of the issuers of the securities.

Inflation risk: The risk that an investment's return may fall short of the inflation rate.

Business cycle risk: Fluctuations in an investment's return resulting from fluctuations in the business cycle.

Interest rate risk: The risk that the price of a fixed-return asset will decline if interest rates rise.

CHANGING ECONOMIC CONDITIONS Practically every investment's return is influenced by changes in economic conditions. First, many investments have **inflation risk,** which means that their returns may not keep pace with the rate of inflation. Any investment that pays a fixed number of dollars of return is subject to inflation risk because the purchasing power of your fixed return declines during inflation. Most government and corporate bonds fall in this group, explaining why investment advisers suggest not buying them if you expect inflation to increase.

Second, many investments are subject to **business cycle risk.** Economic growth seldom takes place in an even-keel manner. Usually, there is a period of rapid expansion followed by a period of recession. The profits of most businesses tend to follow these cycles, and so do the prices of their common stocks. The prices of real estate and other tangible assets also move in step with the economy, and their returns are similarly influenced by it.

Closely related to both inflation risk and business cycle risk is **interest rate risk.** This risk has to do with the relationship between the price of a fixed-return security that has already been issued and returns available on newly issued, similar securities. For example, suppose you bought a government bond for $1,000 that paid $100 a year in interest, a yield of 10 percent. What would happen, though, if a month later, because of tightened credit conditions, the government began issuing new bonds that yielded 12 percent? The bond you bought would still yield only 10 percent, but if you tried to sell it, nobody would be willing to give you $1,000 for it, since they could just as easily buy newly issued bonds paying $120 interest on $1,000. The buyer would expect the same percentage return on yours as he or she could get with any other bond of that type, so you would have to sell yours at a loss. At a price of $833, for example, your bond would also have a current yield of 12 percent, as calculated below:

$$0.12 = \frac{\$100}{\$833}$$

Thus, you would lose $167 ($1,000 – $833) by holding the bond during a period of rising interest rates. Interest rate risk has become increasingly important in recent years because interest rates have been so volatile.

Management risk: Poor earnings performance of a firm associated with poor management.
Business risk: Risk associated with a company's product or service lines.
Financial risk: Risk associated with the use of considerable debt in a company's financing arrangement.

CHANGING CONDITIONS OF THE ISSUER Even in very good economic times, some firms go bankrupt; and in bad times, many do. You may buy the stock of a promising growth company anticipating a high return over time but then find that, because of poor management, the firm does not do well. In addition to this **management risk,** other sources of risk have to do with the issuer's condition. First, the company's line of business presents certain risks, usually called **business risk.** Making personal computers in the 1990s is inherently riskier than selling consumer perishables such as food. (Osborne Computer—an eventual bankrupt—was riskier than General Mills.) Another source of risk has to do with the way a company raises capital. Firms that borrow heavily are inherently riskier than those that issue mostly common stock. During periods of economic stress, the firm with a large amount of interest due its bondholders will be more vulnerable to bankruptcy than a firm without such payments. This risk is often called **financial risk,** and corporate financial managers attempt to minimize its impact, considering the firm's need for expansion capital.

How Much Return Do You Need?

Having looked at risk, let us turn our attention to return. Suppose you are willing to undertake risk. How much return should you realistically expect to receive for doing so? The answer to that question for a specific investment is called the invest-

Box 10.1

PERSONAL FINANCE NEWS

Late Edition

Do Small Investors Have a Chance?

Do small investors have a chance? The answer is an emphatic Yes. In this age of insider information, computerized investment strategy, and megabuck trading, you might think the small investor ought to call it quits and look for a comfortable mutual fund. Although many have taken that route, an equal number—if not more—have hung in there and are doing quite well, thank you.

Evidence of the small investor's success is usually hard to come by, but one indication is the performance of investment clubs who are affiliated with the NAIC (National Association of Investment Clubs). As the graph shows, in relation to the overall market, the clubs' performance was quite good for the period indicated: They beat the market in 11 of the 18 years—a performance many professional money managers did not achieve. Moreover, the average performance of the clubs has been pulled down in recent years by the large increase in new clubs, who do not perform as well as the established clubs.

Why are the clubs, and the small investors who are their members, successful? There probably are a number of reasons, but the most important seem to be that they do considerable research before investing in specific securities, and they then hold them for the long run, which avoids frequent trading and high commissions. Moreover, they often act on instincts or plain common sense. For example, a club in a rural Ohio community, called the Farmerette Investment Club, has been remarkably successful by sticking to companies with products and services its members know well. Not surprisingly, you find Bob Evans Restaurants (an Ohio-based company) and Ralston Purina (a company serving the agricultural industry) in the club's portfolio.

So, if you are investing $200 instead of $200,000, you can take heart that investment ante is less important than investment skill and hard work. As usual, doing your homework often leads to the higher grade. And, if you want the companionship of friends while doing homework, join an investment club. (You can get information from NAIC: phone 810-583-6242.)

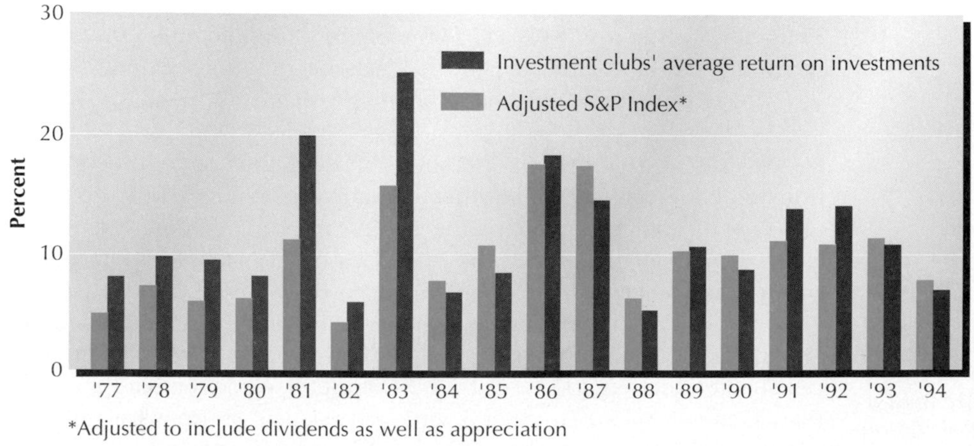

Performance of investment clubs. SOURCE: National Association of Investment Clubs, Royal Oak, MI.

Required rate of return: A realistic estimate of the minimum return an investment must offer to be attractive, given its degree of risk.

Real rate of return: Inflation-adjusted nominal return.

ment's **required rate of return.** It is important to understand that all investments are influenced by expected inflation. Investors are interested in a real—rather than nominal—rates of return. A **real rate of return** takes inflation into consideration, whereas a nominal rate of return does not. If a given investment offers a nominal 10 percent annual rate of return, its real rate is only 4 percent if annual inflation over its life is expected to be 6 percent. Thus, it is always advisable to express historical rates of return in real terms, or at least to have both inflation rates and nominal rates handy. If you can get 10 percent on an investment today while your parents could get only 4 percent on the same kind of investment 20 years ago, the probable explanation is higher expected rates of inflation today, which has nothing to do with the investment itself.

ALMOST SEVEN DECADES OF EVIDENCE Investment analysts have been examining rates of return for some time. The results of one such study are summarized in Table 10.1. The first part of the table shows how much $1,000 would have increased if it had been invested in the four kinds of securities indicated. (Also shown is the CPI.) It is presumed that all interest or dividend earnings were reinvested in the security as they became available. The common stocks are a broad index of such stocks called the Standard & Poor 500 Stock Index (the S&P 500), which is a comprehensive measurement of stock prices of the largest and most important corporations in the United States. The years shown in the table were selected to illustrate the risks inherent in the various securities. As you can see, although you would have done considerably better in common stocks over the 69-year period, the road was quite bumpy along the way. Your $1,000 in 1925 was up to $2,204 in 1928, but if you held on until 1932, you were down to $789. Notice

TABLE 10.1 • RETURNS FROM FOUR INVESTMENTS AND CHANGES IN THE CONSUMER PRICE INDEX (SELECTED YEARS)

	Selected Years	Common Stocks	Long-Term Government Bonds	Long-Term Corporate Bonds	U.S. Treasury Bills	Consumer Price Index
Year-end values of $1,000 invested in each	1925	$ 1,000	$ 1,000	$ 1,000	$ 1,000	$1,000
	1928	2,204	1,175	1,186	1,099	955
	1932	789	1,407	1,439	1,204	730
	1936	2,367	1,746	2,116	1,213	780
	1937	1,538	1,750	2,174	1,217	804
	1945	3,965	2,513	2,930	1,233	1,015
	1955	18,561	2,868	3,527	1,381	1,497
	1965	53,008	3,460	4,552	1,823	1,777
	1972	84,956	4,136	5,760	2,577	2,371
	1974	53,311	4,268	5,647	2,976	2,894
	1978	89,592	5,342	7,807	3,728	3,778
	1985	279,117	11,037	16,546	7,496	6,097
	1994	810,538	25,856	38,012	12,186	8,351
Rates of return:						
Average annual, 1926–1994		12.2%	4.8%	5.4%	3.7%	3.1%
Highest return, single year		+54% (1933)	+40% (1982)	+44% (1982)	+15% (1981)	+18% (1946)
Lowest return, single year		–43% (1931)	–9% (1967)	–9% (1969)	0% (1938)	–10% (1932)
Range		97%	49%	53%	15%	28%

SOURCE: © *Stocks, Bonds, Bills, and Inflation 1996 Yearbook*™, Ibbotson Associates, Chicago (annually updates work by Roger G. Ibbotson and Rex A. Sinquefield). Used with permission.

the reversal in common stocks from 1936 to 1937 and from 1972 to 1974, illustrating again that you can lose a considerable amount of money in common stocks in a rather short period of time.

RETURNS AND INFLATION Looking at rates of return provides additional insights on the alternative investments. First, notice that Treasury bills and inflation were fairly close over the entire period. Assuming this relationship will continue, if you invest in one of the most liquid and safest of securities—Treasury bills—you can expect to earn a return slightly higher than the inflation rate. Going into other securities should provide a greater real return. The historical average with common stocks was 9.1 percent (12.2 – 3.1); with government and corporate bonds, it was 1.7 (4.8 – 3.1) and 2.3 (5.4 – 3.1) percent, respectively.

Risk premium: The difference between an investment's required return and the return on U.S. Treasury bills.

RISK PREMIUM The difference between an investment's required return and the return on Treasury bills is often called the investment's **risk premium.** In other words, the bill rate is considered a risk-free rate of return; you can earn this without taking any risks. Any investment with risk must offer a return greater than this risk-free rate. Otherwise, you would not invest in it. For example, the risk premium on common stocks is 8.5 percent (12.2 – 3.7). You might notice the relative risk of each investment by looking at the range of returns between the highest and the lowest. This range goes from 97 percent for common stocks (the highest) to 15 percent for Treasury bills (the lowest).

THE ACCUMULATION OF WEALTH It seems almost unbelievable that a $1,000 investment could grow to $810,538 over 69 years. If accumulating wealth is that easy, we should all be worth millions. Unfortunately, few people would have been so fortunate to have earned this accumulation, nor should you expect to earn it in the future. First, remember that the calculation assumes the reinvestment of all dividends and other cash distributions. At some point in time, most people begin to withdraw cash rather than reinvest it. Second, the effect of paying federal income taxes is ignored; if considered, it would certainly lower the accumulation.

Despite these shortcomings, the data in Table 10.1 clearly make a strong case for owning common stocks, particularly if you are a young person. Put simply, common stocks are the only financial asset capable of growing in value over the long term. Even if you assume that in a real-world setting you would have accumulated only about half of the $810,538 (say $405,000), you still would be enormously better off than if you had invested exclusively in bonds or Treasury bills.

THE REWARDS OF DIVERSIFICATION

Portfolio: A group of assets held at the same time.

Diversification: A portfolio attribute that can reduce investment risk.

The advice "Don't put all your eggs in one basket" is particularly applicable in the area of investments. By holding a **portfolio,** which is simply a group of assets held at the same time, certain risks can be avoided. In the short run, you might be lucky and do very well with one or two investments; but eventually luck reverses itself, and profits turn to losses. Unquestionably, an important part of a sound investment program is adequate **diversification.** Below, we explain diversification and show how it applies to investing in common stocks.

Why Diversification Works

Diversification creates a synergistic quality in a portfolio in the sense that the portfolio's risk can be much less than the sum of the risks associated with all the securities it holds. In other words, you might hold two assets that by themselves are very risky but when held together create a very low-risk portfolio. The key to risk reduction is the correlation of returns between the two assets. We need an example.

AN EXAMPLE OF RETURN CORRELATION Figure 10.2 shows the returns from two hypothetical assets—A and B—over time. In each case, the return varies from 5 percent to 15 percent, and each asset has an average return of 10 percent. If you held either A or B, you would have a fairly risky asset since the range of returns (5 to 15 percent) is quite large. But look what would happen if, rather than investing all your money in one or the other, you allocated it evenly between the two.

You should see that whenever A's return is decreasing, B's return is increasing, and vice versa. Under the ideal arrangement assumed in our example, your return in the portfolio of A and B would always equal 10 percent. For example, when A's return is 15 percent, B's is 5 percent, and the average of the two is 10 percent. In effect, you have a no-risk asset—the portfolio—that provides as good a return as the average return over time from either A or B, individually. If you are a rational investor, you should prefer holding the portfolio as opposed to holding only one of the assets.

Returns from assets A and B are perfectly, negatively correlated; that is why you can eliminate risk by holding the two together. Perfect negative correlation seldom, if ever, exists in the real investment world; nevertheless, significant risk reduction is achievable even if asset returns are simply *poorly* correlated. There are many examples of poor correlation.

WHEN DIVERSIFICATION IS LESS EFFECTIVE You probably already grasp the situation when diversification may not work effectively—when asset returns are highly, positively correlated. Indeed, if returns are perfectly, positively correlated, they are clones of each other and there is nothing to be gained by holding both. For example, suppose that every time gold's price increases, silver's price increases by a proportionate equal amount; and, the same correlation holds for price decreases. (Silver and gold returns are highly positively correlated, but not perfectly so.) In

Figure 10.2 Returns over time from two hypothetical investments.

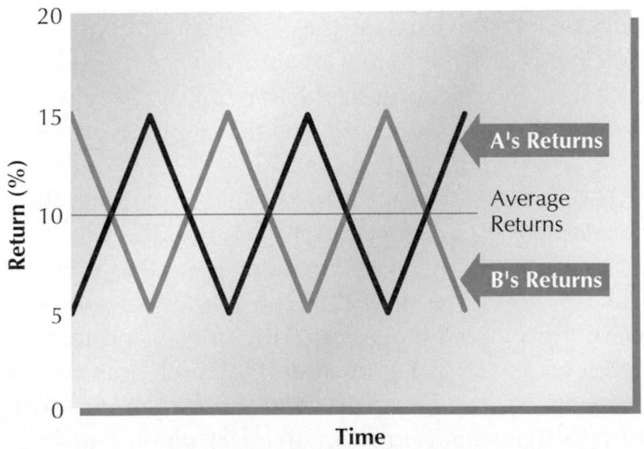

this situation, if your interest in the metals is strictly one of investing for price appreciation, then there is no benefit to investing in both. Select gold or silver and look for another commodity with returns that correlate poorly with theirs.

RETURN CORRELATIONS AMONG KEY FINANCIAL ASSETS Statistical correlation studies have measured the degree of return correlation among the key financial assets—stocks, bonds, and Treasury bills. Their findings indicate rather poor correlations among the major groups, particularly between stocks and Treasury bills. These findings lend support to the conventional recommendations of financial planners that you should diversify among stocks, bonds, and bills (or other highly liquid assets). Although, compared with an all-stocks portfolio, such diversification lowers your average return over time and reduces your wealth accumulation, it adds far greater return stability.

The major asset groups' returns are poorly correlated, but there is high positive correlation within a group. Corporate and Treasury bond returns are very highly correlated; so much so that it makes little sense to hold both in the same portfolio.

Diversification Guidelines

Diversification is so critical to successful investing that certain guidelines should be followed. The objective is to achieve a reasonable portfolio return while simultaneously reducing return variability as much as possible.

DIVERSIFY AMONG INTANGIBLES AND TANGIBLES Not only should you diversify among the key financial assets, you should further diversify between financial and tangible assets, such as real estate or commodities. For example, during the inflationary 1970s, common stocks did very poorly while gold showed excellent returns. Its price appreciated from around $35 an ounce early in the decade to over $850 in 1980. Since the early 1980s, the situation has reversed: Stocks have boomed while gold has busted.

DIVERSIFY GLOBALLY Recent investment studies clearly demonstrate the importance of investing on a global basis. Cross-country diversification reduces portfolio risk and frequently *increases* portfolio return. This is the best of both worlds. The explanation is that economies throughout the world do not expand and contract together. So there may be hard times in the United States while Europe and Asia are booming. This mix sets up the poor return correlations needed to reduce risk.

Moreover, certain parts of the world are growing much more rapidly than others: for example, South America and the Pacific Basin region compared with the United States. By investing in these parts of the world, you not only diversify but you also pick up the higher returns that typically accompany rapid growth.

DIVERSIFY WITHIN ASSET GROUPS This is perhaps the most important rule. Some people take the view that you should "Put all your eggs in one basket and watch the basket very closely," but for most of us that is a prescription for poverty. Few investors are so clever that they can identify the specific assets that will boom in the upcoming period. Indeed, the majority of professional money managers fail to do as well as an unmanaged stock index such as the S&P 500. An old market pro was once asked how much diversification should an investor have. His answer: Keep diversifying until you can sleep at night. Not bad advice, but we'll be more precise in the next section.

APPLYING A RISK-RETURN MODEL

Although it's interesting (and sometimes even fun) to study financial theory and investment returns, it's far more profitable to be able to apply what we learn. In this regard, theorists have developed certain techniques that many practitioners have used successfully. One approach is derived from the so-called capital asset pricing model (CAPM, for short). The CAPM can be applied to investing in any type of asset, but it has been used most extensively in common stock investment. Our discussion will be limited to that area.

Eliminating Random Risk

When you hold a limited number of stocks, you open yourself to all the risk factors discussed above; that is, you are taking on risks associated with the overall economy as well as those associated with individual firms. A portfolio eliminates these latter risks. If you like the personal computer industry and put all your "apples" into Apple Computer, you rise or fall with this one stock. By putting half your money into Apple and the other half into, say, Tandem, you divide the risks associated with these two firms. If Apple fails in market acceptance, Tandem might prosper. Of course, both might prosper or both might fail, but the probabilities are greater for one prospering or failing.

Studies have shown what happens to risk as you increase the number of stocks in a portfolio. A fairly typical outcome is shown in Figure 10.3. This is a hypothetical, randomly constructed portfolio with individual securities drawn by chance from the S&P 500 Stock Index. What do you find interesting in the figure?

Box 10.2 SIMPLIFYING FINANCIAL PLANNING
Are You Losing Sleep over Underdiversification?

If you have been losing sleep over underdiversification, there is a good explanation. Investment advisers constantly beat the drum for diversification, so there's no shortage of news stories in the popular investment media extolling its advantages. But you might find it comforting to know that you probably are better diversified than you think.

Many investors hear that, to hedge inflation, their portfolios should include tangibles, such as gold or silver. They worry, then, because they don't own any. But other tangibles are also good inflation hedges; one of the best is a home. If you own (or plan to own) a home, stop worrying about adding tangibles. If anything, your portfolio is probably too heavily weighted in tangibles and you need more in financial assets.

Another concern is global investing. We hear how important this is as a means of reducing wide swings in our portfolio's value. Again, sleep is lost because investors do not own foreign stocks. Although it is helpful to invest in foreign-based companies, you might be surprised to learn that many U.S. companies, such as Coca-Cola, Boeing, and Gillette, do as much or more business abroad as they do at home. There are many truly multinational companies, and owning their shares automatically diversifies your portfolio globally.

Rather than worrying needlessly about global or tangibles diversification, investors should focus more on diversifying within their common stock holdings. Studies of individual investor accounts reveal the sad fact that most investors hold five or fewer stocks, often all in the same industry. This approach offers virtually no diversification benefits and frequently leads to disaster.

To keep things simple, follow this guideline: Invest in 20 companies, with 15 having foreign sales of at least 40 percent of total sales. (You can find this information in a company's annual report or in investment references such as *Value Line*.) Do not have more than two companies in the same industry. If you do not own a home, select five companies involved with natural resources (examples: Exxon, Barrick Gold, Phelps Dodge, and Georgia-Pacific). Finally, never try to time buying or selling the shares. Use the company's dividend reinvestment plan (DRIP) to acquire more shares. Indeed, if a company doesn't have a DRIP, drop it and look for one that does.

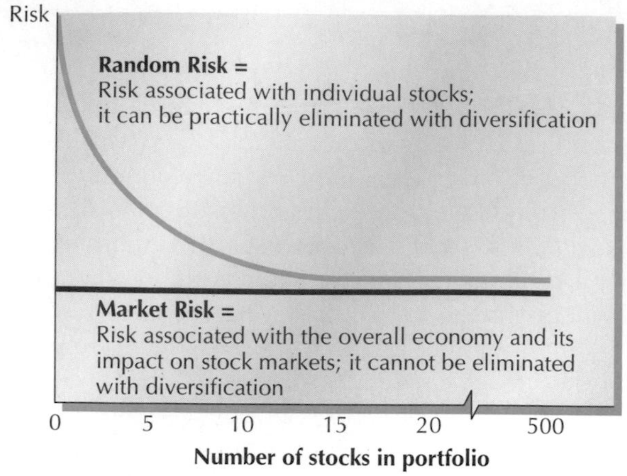
Risk
Random Risk =
Risk associated with individual stocks;
it can be practically eliminated with diversification
Market Risk =
Risk associated with the overall economy and its
impact on stock markets; it cannot be eliminated
with diversification
0
5
10
15
20
500
Number of stocks in portfolio

Figure 10.3
Risk reduction in relation to the number of stocks (randomly selected) in the S&P 500 Stock Index.

Random risk: Risk associated with any single asset; it can be reduced by holding the asset in a portfolio.
Market risk: Risk associated with unpredictable movements of the overall market; it cannot be reduced by a portfolio.

First, notice the extent to which risk can be reduced by holding only a few stocks in a portfolio. With only five, you can cut your risk almost in half. After 20, you have virtually eliminated all the risk that can be eliminated, which is called **random risk.** Second, no matter how much you diversify, you cannot eliminate all risk, (individual stock returns are poorly, but not negatively, correlated) and that which remains is called **market risk.** In other words, even if you owned all the stocks in the S&P 500, you still could expect considerable return variation over time, as we have discussed.

Managing Market Risk

Since you cannot eliminate market risk, the next best step is to manage it. By managing risk, we simply mean that you receive sufficient return over time to compensate you for undertaking it. A general but very, very important first rule is: *If you invest in stocks as risky as the overall market, you should receive a risk premium equal to that of the overall market.* Recall our discussion earlier about risk premiums, and how the overall market has averaged about an 8.5 percent risk premium over a long period of time. Now we put that information to use. Suppose you are contemplating investing in the overall market (either by selecting 20 stocks randomly or by buying a mutual fund that approximates the market). What is your required return for one year? Step 1: Determine what the rate will be on risk-free, one-year U.S. Treasury securities. Step 2: Add the risk premium, and you have your answer. For example, if the U.S. Treasury securities rate is 3.5 percent, the required market return is 12.0 percent (3.5 + 8.5). Although simple, it is nevertheless a sound approach for estimating a required return. Assuming you invest, are you guaranteed the 12.0 percent return? Of course not. It could be much higher or much lower, as we saw in Table 10.1.

A second, and equally important, rule in investment risk management is: *If you invest in stocks more or less risky than the overall market, you should expect a risk premium greater or less than the overall market premium in direct proportion to the greater or lesser risk taken.* Common sense tells us we should receive a higher return if we take greater risks, but, unfortunately, it doesn't tell us *how much* higher. More sophisticated—but not difficult to understand—techniques are needed to answer that question.

TABLE 10.2 • WHAT BETA VALUES MEAN

Range of Beta Values for a Stock	What It Means
Less than zero; that is, a negative beta	The stock's price moves in the opposite direction from the market; very few stocks have negative betas over extended periods of time.
Zero	The stock's return is independent of the market; this could be a risk-free U.S. Treasury security, where return is guaranteed regardless of the market's performance.
Zero to +1.0	The stock's price moves in the same direction as the market but not as much; stocks with betas less than 1.0 are considered conservative investments.
Equal to +1.0	The stock has the same risk as the market; if you bought all beta 1.0 stocks, your portfolio's return and risk would be the same as if you bought the overall market.
Greater than +1.0	The stock's price moves in the same direction as the market but by a greater percentage amount; buying these stocks increases your risk relative to the market.

Beta: A statistic that measures the responsiveness of an asset's return in relation to changes in the overall market return.

ESTIMATING A STOCK'S RISK The first step now is to determine the risk of an individual stock in relation to the overall market. This is done with a statistical figure called **beta.** A stock's beta measures the responsiveness of its return over time to that of the overall market. For example, if Apple Computer's beta is +1.5, it means that if the stock market goes up 10 percent, Apple's common stock goes up 15 percent; if the market goes down 10 percent, Apple goes down 15 percent. A beta value indicates relative risk, with higher betas meaning greater risk. Table 10.2 summarizes ranges of beta values and their meanings, and Table 10.3 shows examples of betas of companies that might be familiar to you.

TABLE 10.3 • BETA VALUES FOR VARIOUS COMPANIES

Company	Major Business	Beta Value
America Online	PC communications; Internet link	2.50
AT&T	Long distance telephone	0.90
Avon	Cosmetics	1.25
Barrick Gold	Gold mining	0.45
Battle Mountain	Gold mining	0.25
Detroit Edison	Electric utility	0.70
Gillette	Razor blades	1.25
Intel	Computer memory chips	1.35
MCI	Long distance telephone	1.25
Micron Technology	Computer memory chips	1.75
Phillips Petroleum	Oil refinery	0.80
Southwest Airlines	Major airline	1.50
Texaco	Oil refinery	0.65

SOURCE: *Value Line Investment Survey Summary and Index,* June 16, 1995 (various pages).

Betas are not difficult to calculate, although the method involves a type of statistical analysis that may not be familiar to you. Fortunately, betas are available from a number of sources, such as the one cited in Table 10.3.

ESTIMATING A STOCK'S REQUIRED RETURN After determining a stock's beta value, you can then estimate its required return. Considerable historical evidence shows that stock returns over time are related to their beta values; specifically, risk premiums are shown to be directly proportional to beta values. The following equation expresses this relationship:

$$\text{Stock risk premium (\%)} = \text{stock's beta value} \times \text{market risk premium (\%)}$$

If a stock has a beta of +1.5, its risk premium should be 12.8 percent:

$$12.8\% = 1.5 \times 8.5\%$$

The total required return on a stock consists of the risk premium plus the expected return on risk-free Treasury securities. If this latter rate is 3.5 percent, the stock's total required return is 16.3 percent (3.5 + 12.8). The diagram in Figure 10.4, which incorporates the figures we have just used, is a convenient way to express and summarize the important relationship between required return and risk.

THE IMPORTANCE OF THE RISK-FREE RATE OF RETURN You should understand the important role played by the rate of return on U.S. Treasury securities. All required rates of return depend upon it, and if it changes, so will these rates. For example, if this rate went up to 8.5 percent, all other rates would similarly increase by 5 percent; the market return will now be 17.0 percent, and a 1.5 beta stock will be 21.3 percent. The market risk premium, of course, is an estimate, and it might change if investors become more or less enthusiastic about potential profits in the market. However, for someone investing on a long-term basis, it is not unrealistic to look upon the premium as being relatively constant. A current "ballpark" figure often used is 8 percent, based upon the very long-run returns discussed in this chapter.

Figure 10.4
Required rates of return in relation to beta values.

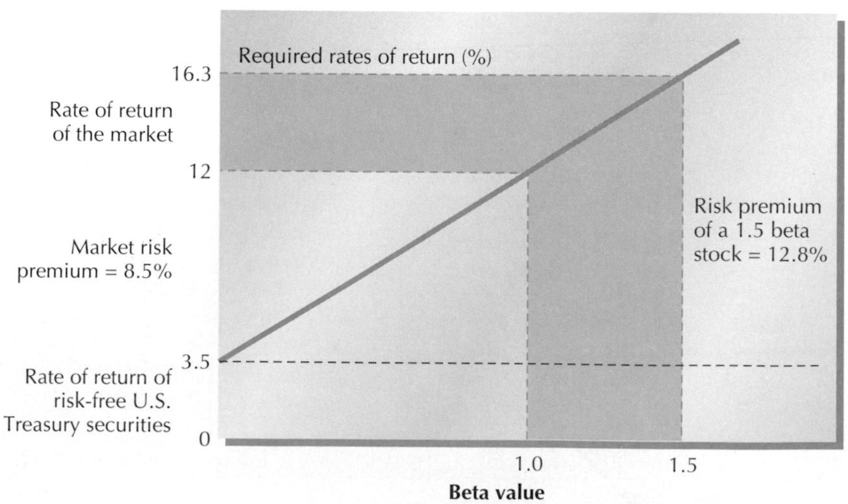

Making Stock Selections

Expected total return: An actual return that investors expect to earn on a stock in an upcoming period.

Finding a stock's required return does not answer the question of whether the stock should be bought or sold. To make these decisions we need a stock's **expected total return.** This is a return that investors believe they will actually earn with the stock in the upcoming investment period. We will discuss this return in detail in the next chapter; for now, let's work with it as a given.

Consider three investments—A, B, and C—shown in Table 10.4. They differ substantially in risk, as measured by their beta values, and in expected returns. How would you rank them in terms of appeal? Would you take C because it offers the highest return? Some investors might, but it would be a mistake.

Alpha: A measure of a stock's appeal, calculated by subtracting required return from expected return.

LOOK FOR A STOCK'S EXCESS RETURN Actually, A is the best investment. Why? Because it offers the highest **alpha** value, which is the difference between expected return and required return; that is,

$$\text{Alpha} = \text{expected return} - \text{required return}$$

Alpha values can be positive, as they are with investments A and C, or negative, as with investment B. Any stock with a negative alpha value should not be bought, and you might consider selling if you already own it. Stocks with positive alpha values are buying opportunities, with greater alphas indicating greater investment appeal.

Stock A with its 2.2 percent alpha value seems a good investment. Stock C's situation is not so overwhelming, since a 0.5 percent alpha value is quite small. As noted in the table, you might flip a coin to make a choice here.

IS SELECTING STOCKS THIS EASY? The answer to this question is a resounding No. The CAPM technique is very simple, which makes it appealing; but there are several problems to consider. First, beta may not always measure a stock's risk appropriately, particularly when a company is undergoing dramatic changes in business or financial risk. A beta calculated from historical data may not reflect the riskiness of the new firm. Second, as we shall see in the next chapter, estimating a stock's expected total return is very difficult.

Despite all the criticisms, though, the technique is useful if it does nothing more than force us to consider both risk and return in the investment selection process. Equally important, it highlights the need to earn higher returns if you take greater risks. If you invest your money in roller-coaster (high beta) stocks, you should at least get the thrill of the ride (a high return).

TABLE 10.4 • SELECTING STOCKS BY COMPARING REQUIRED RATES OF RETURN WITH EXPECTED RATES OF RETURN

Stock	Beta Value	Required Rate of Return	Expected Rate of Return	Alpha Value	Decision
A	0.5	7.8%	10.0	+ 2.2%	Definitely accept; expected rate well exceeds required rate
B	1.5	16.3%	14.0	− 2.3%	Definitely reject; expected rate is far below required rate
C	2.0	20.5%	21.0	+ 0.5%	A borderline case; flip a coin to make your choice

Action Plan for the Steeles: Stock Portfolio Management

Background In late December 1996, the Steeles had invested $22,800 in common stocks—$6,800 in a mutual fund and $16,000 in five different companies. They found the mutual fund on their own; the stocks were recommended to them by their stockbroker. Arnold and Sharon told the broker that they wanted safe stocks that offered a yield (current return) about the same as they might earn on one-year certificates of deposit. Earning this amount would leave them no worse off than if they invested in CDs; if the stock prices appreciated, they would be in a better position. Since making their initial five investments they have met with the broker and asked her for more guidance in selecting securities.

The Problem The Steeles' stock investments (shown in the accompanying table) are earmarked for retirement. If they perform well, Arnie may retire at an earlier age. The key to success is selecting stocks that fit well with the Steeles' objective. Equally important is achieving a high degree of safety—the Steeles do not wish to invest in highly speculative situations. The broker feels that the Steeles' portfolio should be repositioned to reflect their long-run investment goal and to create greater diversification.

The Plan Sell 100 shares of InChemCo, the 50 shares of Dow Chemical, and the 100 shares of Consolidated Edison. This will provide $8,400 that should be invested in stocks with greater growth potential. She recommends 70 shares of Intel at $65 a share and 70 shares of Gillette at $55 a share. Commissions will total about $400 for the trades; while not trivial, this cost should be recovered quickly with better growth.

Rationale for the Plan Although the Steeles' portfolio includes high-quality stocks, it has a number of serious weaknesses. First, too much (26 percent) is invested in InChemCo (Arnie's employer). The company has a stock purchase plan, which is appealing, since shares can be purchased at a discount; however, this does not justify a continual holding, and 100 shares should be sold.

Second, combining Dow Chemical with InChemCo places too much emphasis upon the chemical industry. The Dow shares should also be sold.

Third, the Steeles' investment approach seems sensible, but it does not fit well with their long-range goal. In effect they are investing in high-yield stocks rather than high-growth stocks. Not only is this approach contrary to their objective, it means they must pay income taxes on dividends received. It would be much better to invest in stocks that offer higher future returns as opposed to higher yields. Intel and Gillette should provide such growth.

THE STEELES' STOCK PORTFOLIO

Stock	Number of Shares	Current Price	Total Value	Amount Invested	Expected Yield
Fidelity Fund	400	$17.00	$ 6,800	$ 3,000	3.2%
InChemCo	200	30.00	6,000	3,800	2.0
Dow Chemical	50	50.00	2,500	3,000	3.2
Consolidated Edison	100	29.00	2,900	3,100	6.6
Xerox	50	48.00	2,400	1,500	4.3
Ameritech	40	55.00	2,200	1,800	4.5
			$22,800	$16,200	

BUILDING AND CHANGING A PORTFOLIO

Although the need to diversify in building a portfolio is important, there are other issues to also consider. First, assets selected must be suitable to meet the investor's objectives. You will understand this topic better after you have become more familiar with the wide variety of investments available; so our discussion of selecting assets is deferred to Chapter 13. But other issues can be addressed now. In the following sections, we discuss the topics of acquiring and selling securities over time.

Acquiring Securities

As funds become available to acquire securities, how should we do it? Two methods are often advised by financial planners—dollar cost averaging and routine investment plans.

Dollar cost averaging (DCA): A method of investing that calls for a constant amount investment at regular time intervals.

DOLLAR COST AVERAGING **Dollar cost averaging (DCA)** is a mechanical method of investing in securities. Table 10.5 shows how it works. As you see, the idea is quite simple. You establish an investment plan calling for equal dollar investments at regular intervals. By following the plan, you then buy securities at a wide range of prices, and, over time, you will have an average cost somewhere between the highs and the lows. In this example, the average cost after six months is $8.89 per share. The mechanical nature of the plan keeps investors from using their own judgment to determine buying points or from buying a given number of shares (rather than investing a given number of dollars) at regular intervals.

A supporter of this plan believes that investors' judgments usually are wrong, because they are guided by emotions or incorrect assessments of the market situation. In the enthusiasm of a bull market (rising prices), we tend to invest too heavily; in the gloom of a bear market (falling prices) we don't invest at all. Following this approach, the average cost of purchased shares is much higher than the average with DCA.

Dividend reinvestment plans (DRIPs): Plans offered by corporations that allow shareholders to reinvest cash dividends.

ROUTINE INVESTMENT PLANS There are a number of ways to make investments on a regular basis. Many companies have **dividend reinvestment plans (DRIPs)** that enable investors to reinvest dividends they receive from a company's stock to buy more of the company's shares. Since dividends are paid at regular quarterly intervals, a DRIP accomplishes the same end as dollar cost averaging on a quarterly

TABLE 10.5 • ILLUSTRATION OF DCA, ASSUMING $1,000 INVESTED EACH MONTH

(1) Date	(2) Shares Purchased	(3) Price per Share	(4) Total Shares Held	(5) Total Cost	(6) Average Cost (5)/(4)	(7) Cumulative Profit (Loss) [(3) × (4)] − (5)
1/1	100.00	$10	100.00	$1,000	$10.00	$ -0-
2/1	83.33	12	183.33	2,000	10.91	200
3/1	125.00	8	308.33	3,000	9.73	(533)
4/1	100.00	10	408.33	4,000	9.80	83
5/1	166.67	6	575.00	5,000	8.70	(1,550)
6/1	100.00	10	675.00	6,000	8.89	750

basis. A similar routine investment process arises if you own mutual fund shares and choose to reinvest dividends and capital distributions rather than receiving them in cash. Many mutual funds also encourage routine investing by offering plans that automatically transfer a certain amount of funds each week (or other period) from your checking account to the mutual fund.

All the above plans are effective primarily because they put savings and investment first, rather than last, in your budget. But, they are not substitutes for sound investment selection in the first place. You don't want to dollar cost average with a poor stock or use the DRIP of a company with no future. The downside of regularity in investing is that we might not review our holdings as often as we should.

Selling Securities

The decision to sell securities may be as difficult to make as the decision to buy them. There are a number of factors to consider. They are discussed below.

THE SECURITY BECOMES OVERVALUED Let's suppose that you bought stock A, which we discussed previously and showed to be a good value within the CAPM framework. Suppose that its price was $20 a share when you bought it, but it's

Box 10.3 SAVING MONEY
Periodic Investment Plans: A Good Idea Gone Bad?

Some years ago, stockbrokerage firms began offering periodic investment plans (PIPs), the idea of which was to help small investors establish a routine investment approach. You pick the stocks and tell the broker how much you wish to invest in them each period (say, every three months). That's it. Make out your check each quarter and watch your portfolio grow.

The idea is good, but it seems that over the years the brokers have increased commissions and fees to a point where you are probably better off investing in a mutual fund. One large brokerage house, for example, charges 4 percent on dividend reinvestments up to $100. Reinvestments above $100 are subject to diminishing rates that decline to 1.5 percent on amounts over $500. On top of these charges, you pay commissions on an initial investment and periodic reinvestments. These commissions range between 10 percent and 1.15 percent. And, of course, when you sell and begin withdrawing funds, there are additional commissions.

The accompanying table shows dollar accumulations with a PIP versus two no-load mutual funds. The first is assumed to have operating costs of 1 percent of assets—about average for all equity funds. The second is an index fund with an operating cost ratio of 0.25 percent of assets. Other assumptions in each case are: (1) a 12 percent total annual return consisting of a 4 percent dividend return and 8 percent price appreciation, (2) quarterly investments, and (3) withdrawal of funds after the years indicated.

The PIP does worse in every case, although the differences versus the average fund might not be described as enormous. However, that seems an appropriate description when the PIP is compared with the index fund. It also describes the differences between the average fund and the index fund—a point mutual fund investors should take to heart.

Of course, a PIP allows you to select your own investments. You might do better than a mutual fund; but then, you might do worse.

	Accumulation		
Plan	PIP	Avg. Fund	Index Fund
$1,000 initial investment plus $100 each quarter:			
10 years	$ 9,275	$ 9,930	$10,452
20 years	35,676	35,778	39,881
$100 initial investment plus $100 each quarter:			
10 years	6,570	7,325	7,650
20 years	27,077	28,238	31,156

now $50 a share. The CAPM might now indicate that it's overvalued and should be sold. Surely, one important reason to sell a security is if we believe that it is no longer attractive relative to other securities that could be purchased.

SELLING FOR TAX REASONS The tax law often encourages security sales. For example, suppose that you bought shares of GM stock, which subsequently declined in value. You now have a $3,000 loss. Should you sell? If you do, you establish a loss that can be used to offset other income on your tax return, saving you taxes. The amount depends on your marginal tax rate: At a 28 percent rate, you save $840 ($0.28 \times 3{,}000$).

Investment advisers say that you should not sell securities *simply* to save taxes; nevertheless, in certain situations it makes good sense. For example, you may think that Ford and Chrysler are just as attractive as General Motors; by selling the latter and buying one of the former, you will save enough in taxes to allow you to buy more shares. Changing investments for tax reasons is referred to as a **tax swap.** Swaps are very popular, but more so with bonds than with stocks.

Tax swap: Selling a security to establish a tax loss and then reinvesting funds in a similar security.

YOUR INVESTMENT OBJECTIVES CHANGE Over time, it is likely that your investment objectives will change. You might want more current income as opposed to price appreciation, or you might want less portfolio risk. Clearly, changing objectives require the sale of certain securities and the purchase of others.

Economic Changes and the Portfolio

A frequently debated issue in portfolio management is whether your investment activities should ignore economic conditions or be managed in ways to exploit expected changes. The argument is referred to as buy-and-hold versus market timing.

Buy-and-hold strategy: A method of portfolio management that does not attempt to trade securities over economic cycles.

BUY-AND-HOLD STRATEGIES As the name implies, a **buy-and-hold strategy** means you do not attempt to enhance your portfolio return by "trading with the investment cycle." People advocating the buy-and-hold approach argue that economic cycles cannot be forecasted. Since you can't forecast cycles, there is no way you can consistently benefit by trading in anticipation of them, and all you do is make your stockbroker wealthy by trying. Buy-and-hold advocates stress the importance of *carefully constructing* a well-diversified portfolio to begin with rather than continually *changing* one to improve performance.

The growing evidence that economic cycles cannot be forecasted certainly supports this view. Even the so-called experts have been consistently off their forecast targets, often by so much that any random forecasting device forecasted as well. If you like the idea of simply building and then holding a portfolio, there is no reason to be defensive about its simplicity.

Market timing: A method of portfolio management that changes a portfolio's composition in relation to expected market changes.

MARKET-TIMING STRATEGIES **Market timing** attempts to change a portfolio's composition in anticipation of expected changes in returns among different investments. Timing strategies range from the complex to some that are very simple. A simple one usually involves going back and forth between a common stock mutual fund and a money market fund. The simpler versions are growing in popularity, and certain advisers now specialize in offering timing advice or in managing portfolios based upon their timing methods.

Since no evidence overwhelmingly supports even professional market timers, you should think twice before attempting your own timing techniques. If a formula

TABLE 10.6 • HYPOTHETICAL RETURNS AND MARKET TIMING

(1) Period	(2) Return on U.S. Treasury Bills	(3) Return on Common Stocks	(4) Return If You Guess Correctly Each Period	(5) Return If You Guess Incorrectly Each Period
1	+10%	+40%	+40%	+10%
2	+ 8	−20	+ 8	−20
3	+12	+50	+50	+12
4	+ 6	−10	+ 6	−10
Total	+36%	+60%	+104%	−8%
Average return	+9%	+15%	+26%	−2%

appeals to you, our advice again is to try it on paper first and evaluate it critically. If it seems to work, then consider investing in a mutual fund family that allows you to switch among individual funds at little or no cost. (Fund switching is explained in Chapter 14.)

MARKET TIMING CAN INCREASE INVESTMENT RISK You must realize, however, that market timing can increase investment risk. This is illustrated best with an example. Columns 2 and 3 in Table 10.6 show hypothetical returns available with U.S. Treasury bills and common stocks over four periods of time. If you had invested in bills at the beginning and held them, your average return would have been 9 percent. Similarly, if you had bought and held stocks, your average return would have been 15 percent. But what would have been your average return had you sold at the end of each period and reinvested in the other asset? The answer depends, of course, on how accurately you guessed which asset would give the better return. Column 4 in Table 10.6 assumes you always held the higher-yielding asset: that is, you guessed perfectly each period. With this clairvoyance your average return would have been the most possible—26 percent. Column 5, though, shows what would have happened had you forecasted perfectly incorrectly—a negative 2 percent return. If you were partially correct in your forecasts, the average return would have been somewhere between these extremes. Recalling that risk is associated with variation in returns, you should see why timing is riskier than buy and hold. Sure, there is a possibility of a greater average return over time, but there is also the possibility of a lower average return. And remember, the nature of risk is precisely this *greater variation* in expected return.

SUMMARY

Risk is understood as the variability of return over time. Investors compare expected risks and returns in making asset selections. The "iron law of risk and return" states that to achieve higher rates of return, investors almost always must take greater risks. Historical data show that common stocks have much higher rates of return than bonds and U.S. Treasury bills, but they also have more risk.

Risk is reduced by diversifying. Diversification works best when asset returns are perfectly, negatively correlated, but it can be very effective if asset returns are simply poorly correlated. Diversification should take place between tangibles and intangibles; it should be global (cross-country) in nature; and, it should be undertaken within asset groups.

Investment theory provides a technique for selecting common stocks. A stock's required return is determined on the basis of its beta value and a risk premium for the overall market.

The required return is then subtracted from a stock's expected return to determine its alpha value; stocks with high positive alpha value are good stocks to buy.

Portfolios are usually built over time, and assets should be acquired by employing routine acquisition methods, such as dollar cost averaging or dividend reinvestment plans. Selling securities is done for income tax reasons, or because they are overvalued, or because the investor's objectives change. Some investors attempt to enhance their returns by engaging in market-timing techniques. The success of such activities is questionable.

KEY TERMS

alpha (p. 293)
beta (p. 291)
business cycle risk (p. 283)
business risk (p. 283)
buy-and-hold strategy (p. 297)
diversification (p. 286)
dividend reinvestment plans (DRIPs) (p. 295)
dollar cost averaging (DCA) (p. 295)
expected total return (p. 293)
financial risk (p. 283)
inflation risk (p. 283)
interest rate risk (p. 283)
iron law of risk and return (p. 281)
management risk (p. 283)
market risk (p. 290)
market timing (p. 297)
portfolio (p. 286)
random risk (p. 290)
real rate of return (p. 285)
required rate of return (p. 285)
risk (p. 281)
risk premium (p. 286)
tax swap (p. 297)

PROBLEMS AND REVIEW QUESTIONS

1. How would you define risk to someone who doesn't have a grasp of investment fundamentals? Do you think the best definition is "Risk is the chance of losing money"? Explain.
2. Explain two views that you might take relating risk to time. Which is the more appropriate if you are a long-term (over 10 years) investor?
3. Drew Dugan is considering investing in one of three securities listed in the following table. Drew isn't familiar with return or risk and would like you to explain the data. Also, he would like your opinion on which security to invest in; he generally considers himself a risk-seeking individual.

	Securities		
	A	B	C
Highest expected return	50%	15%	30%
Lowest expected return	–30%	10%	–20%
Most likely return	20%	12%	22%

4. What sources of risk are associated with the overall economy? What sources are associated with individual issuers of securities? Explain two perspectives of the relationship of risk to time.
5. From 1925 through 1994, which financial investments were the most and the least risky? Explain and provide evidence for your answer.
6. Referring to Table 10.1, indicate the best- and poorest-performing securities over the period 1965–1978. (*Hint:* Calculate *percentage* increases.) What does your answer suggest about investment risk? Explain.
7. People often understand through common sense that diversification reduces risk. But, explain *why* diversification works and when it works most effectively. Also, indicate when it may not be effective.
8. Briefly explain three diversification guidelines.

9. How many securities must you hold for adequate diversification? Does diversification eliminate all risk, or does some remain? Explain.
10. What is meant by managing risk, and how is the beta concept used in this effort?
11. Dan Stramm thinks if you invest in common stocks, you ought to get three times as much return as you would if you invest in Treasury bills. Do you agree with Dan? If not, explain how you would estimate a required return for common stocks.
12. How do you calculate a stock's alpha value? How do you use it to select stocks?
13. Explain dollar cost averaging and why it may be helpful for certain investors. What is a dividend reinvestment plan, and what advantage does it offer? Also, briefly explain several other routine investment techniques.
14. Briefly explain three reasons for selling securities.
15. Explain a market-timing strategy, comparing it with a buy-and-hold strategy. Does a market-timing strategy increase or decrease investment risk? Explain.

Case 10.1 Selecting Stocks for Bart Parks

Bart Parks is a bachelor, 33 years old, with a good income and a reasonable net worth. Bart has about $20,000 invested in individual common stocks, most of them recommended by his broker, Buzz Bushkin. He's done well with Bushkin over the years, and he is particularly pleased that Bushkin always gives him a list of several stocks to choose from, instead of just one. Bart has saved another $3,000 for the market and has asked Bushkin for a new list, which appears below. Bushkin recommends Alpha Dynamics, but Bart is concerned with this selection because he has heard that Alpha's latest product—an automatic envelope opener—has not met huge market acceptance.

Bart has turned to you for help, and in response you have gathered data on expected returns and betas (shown below).

Security	Current Price	Expected Return	Beta
Bushkin's alternatives:			
Alpha Dynamics	$10	30%	2.0
Beta Depressants	18	10%	0.3
Gamma Globulins	6	32%	3.1
U.S. Treasury bills	—	10%	0.0
A market mutual fund	16	18%	1.0

Bart doesn't consider himself either excessively risk averting or risk seeking, but he does expect a return commensurate with the degree of risk inherent in a security. Also, Bart's current holdings give him adequate diversification, so that need not concern him in selecting a stock now.

QUESTIONS

1. Calculating alpha values, explain if you agree or disagree with Bushkin's selection.
2. Should the information Bart has heard about Alpha's new product be a concern in his selection? Explain.
3. Assuming that Bart takes Bushkin's advice, calculate the commission he will pay and compare this with the commission he probably would pay to a discount broker.

Case 10.2 Arlene Elton Considers Dollar Cost Averaging

Arlene Elton has been investing in LKV Aeronautics common stock over the past six months. She bought 300 shares initially at $25 a share. A month later, after a nice move by LKV, she bought another 300 shares at $35 a share. LKV then went into a tailspin over the next three months, and at the end Arlene considered selling all her shares at $15 a share. She's glad she didn't, though, because the stock rebounded in the last month and is currently selling at $30 a share. Arlene has saved some more money and is now thinking of buying 200 more shares. Before buying them, she has decided to talk to a friend, Mark Hatfield, who also invests in stocks. Mark uses dollar cost averaging. He thinks Arlene should also consider this technique. Indeed, he is convinced that dollar cost averaging almost guarantees successful investment results over time.

QUESTIONS

1. Assuming that Arlene goes ahead with her plan to buy 200 more shares of LKV, she will have invested $24,000 to buy 800 shares. Suppose that instead she had invested $4,000 each month over the six months and purchased shares at the following prices: $25, $35, $30, $20, $15, and $30. Set up a table that shows the number of shares purchased each month, the total value of her holdings, and her profit or loss after the purchase.
2. Compare Arlene's actual performance with the performance from dollar cost averaging. Calculate the average share cost each way, and use the values in your discussion.
3. Do you think Arlene is the type of person who should use dollar cost averaging? Explain.
4. Do you agree with Mark that dollar cost averaging guarantees good investment results? Explain.

HELPFUL CONTACTS

See Chapter 9.

INTERNET ADDRESSES

Federal Reserve Bank of Minneapolis (covers an array of economic conditions)
http://woodrow.mpls.frb.fed.us/economy/

Federal Reserve Bank of St. Louis (provides historical yields on many U.S. Treasury securities)
http://www.stls.frb.org./fred/

Chapter 11

Common Stock: Your Most Common Investment

Objectives

1. To identify basic shareholder rights and the means by which corporations make distributions to shareholders
2. To recognize the investment opportunities in various types of stocks, such as growth stocks or income stocks
3. To understand how to determine the investment appeal of a stock using the CAPM-application approach and the price-to-earnings approach
4. To become familiar with the methods of technical analysis, including price graphs
5. To recognize certain pressure indicators and to interpret their changes over time
6. To identify and interpret certain patterns in price graphs

Common stock: Shares that give you an ownership interest in a company.

Everybody likes to get in on the ground floor of an emerging growth company, such as Intel or Microsoft. To do this you must buy a company's **common stock.** Although it is riskier than bonds or preferred stock, it gives you a stake in the company's future—for better or worse. A $100 investment in Microsoft's shares in 1986 was worth about $7,200 in mid-1995—not bad work for a decade! And it is safe to say that, with few exceptions, you should buy common stock only when you are willing to risk that its future price will exceed its current price; if you don't think that will happen, then you should invest in something else. Essentially, most common stocks are for the future, but in varying degrees; some are completely growth oriented, others are far less so. This chapter explains common stock investing. Perhaps it will help you find the Microsofts of the future; but even if it doesn't, it should make you a more informed investor.

CHARACTERISTICS OF COMMON STOCK

Becoming an informed investor begins by learning common stock's basic characteristics. The important ones are explained in the following sections.

Shareholders' Rights

Suppose you were thinking of buying 100 shares of Mead Corporation (a paper and forest products company with other diversified interests) at $56 a share in mid-June 1995. Along with receiving a stock certificate evidencing your ownership, illustrated in Figure 11.1, you would have become one of about 17,000 people or institutions owning Mead common stock, and you would have an interest of 0.0000017 (100/60,000,000) in the company. Although your holding is a minuscule one, you are nevertheless an owner of Mead. And, although you have far less power than someone owning a million shares, you have identical privileges. You have the right to vote for members of the board of directors or in other matters affecting the company; you have the right to maintain your proportionate interest in the company; and, you have the right to share in its distribution of earnings or assets.

Proxy: An assignment of your voting rights to someone else.

THE RIGHT TO VOTE In most cases your voting right gives you one vote for each share of common stock you own, although some stock is classified as nonvoting. In contrast to voting in political elections, in a corporation you can assign your vote to someone else through a **proxy.** So if you can't make the annual stockholders' meeting where voting takes place, you can return it with your signature, either giving or not giving authority to vote your shares. It is hard to get excited over a voting right if you own 0.0000017 of a company. However, if you and several friends are contemplating going into business and forming a corporation to do so, then be very careful about who owns how many shares and how these shares might be voted in controversial decisions. Hardly anything is more powerless than a minority interest in a corporation, even if that minority is 49 percent. Make sure in these situations to have an attorney's advice before the corporation is formed and shares are distributed.

Preemptive right: A right to maintain your proportionate interest in a company.

THE PREEMPTIVE RIGHT Your right to maintain a proportionate interest in a company is called the **preemptive right.** If Mead wanted to sell 10 million more

Figure 11.1 A sample common stock of the Mead Corporation. (Courtesy of the Mead Corporation.)

shares of common stock to raise capital, you would have the right to buy 17 (0.0000017 × 10,000,000) more shares. You probably guess the preemptive right is about as important as the voting right with most stocks you will buy. But again, you should see that it can be important in small, closely held corporations. It is possible to have a corporation organized in such a way that you give up your preemptive right, so again, it pays to be careful if you are about to get into such an arrangement.

THE RIGHT TO SHARE IN EARNINGS OR ASSET DISTRIBUTIONS Your obvious intent for investing in a company is to receive a return. With common stock you have the right to participate (in proportion to the number of shares you own) in any distribution of earnings or assets. This right is limited, however. For example, most states prohibit any distributions that would impair the firm's capital and subject its creditors (usually bondholders) to greater risk. In addition, if the corporation has any preferred stock outstanding, any current or past unpaid dividends must be paid on it before any distributions are made to common stockholders. This means that, as a common stockholder, you come last in line, behind bondholders and preferred stockholders. You are said to have a **residual claim;** that is, you get what is left. Although this sounds dismal, actually, getting what is left is why you buy common stock in the first place. Bondholders and preferred stockholders have

Residual claim: The claim against assets or earnings of common stockholders; the claim comes after the claims of bondholders and preferred stockholders.

prior claims, but the amounts they are entitled to are fixed each year; that is, regardless of how well (or poorly) the company does, the amount they get is the same. In contrast, the amounts available to common stockholders vary in direct proportion to the company's profits. Figure 11.2 illustrates this relationship.

The hypothetical company has bonds outstanding requiring $5,000,000 a year in interest and preferred stock requiring $3,000,000 a year in dividends. This represents $8,000,000 of fixed obligations that must be paid before any earnings are available to common stockholders. If the corporation has a bad year and earnings are only $9,000,000, common stockholders' claims will be $1,000,000. If the corporation has a good year and earnings are $19,000,000, the bondholders' and preferred stockholders' distributions will still total $8,000,000, but common stockholders' claims will now be $11,000,000. It should be noted that the corporation might not pay out all the common stockholders' claims in dividends. In fact, most companies retain a portion of the earnings and reinvest them in the business. For example, in the good year just described, perhaps $5,000,000 would be paid in dividends and $6,000,000 retained. In the bad year, it is possible that no dividends would be paid. However, many companies continue paying common stock dividends, even in very poor years. Mead, for example, had earnings of $2.61 a share in 1990 and paid a dividend of $0.97 per share. Although its earnings fell to $1.21 per share in 1991, it actually increased the dividend to $1.00 a share.

Distributions to Shareholders

Although shareholders have a right to share earnings, this does not mean that the corporation pays its shareholders each year a cash amount equal to the annual

Figure 11.2
Sharing a company's earnings.

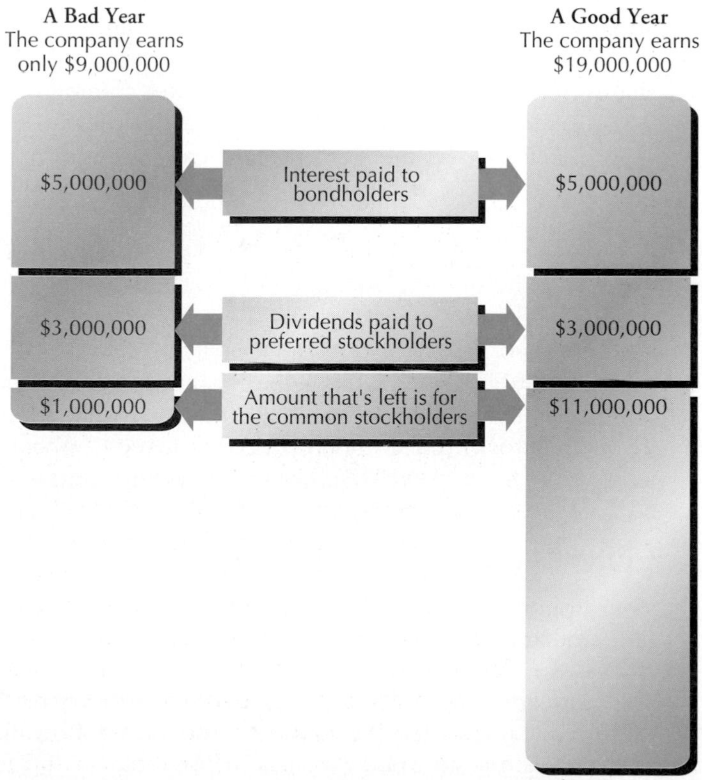

earnings. Actually, there are various types of distributions corporations make, some in cash and some in shares of the company's stock.

Regular dividend: Cash distribution made to shareholders on a regular basis, usually each quarter.

Periodic share repurchases: Corporate repurchase of shares having a similar effect as cash dividends.

CASH DISTRIBUTIONS As the name implies, cash distributions are cash payments the corporation makes to its shareholders. By far the most common type of cash distribution is the **regular dividend.** Many corporations pay dividends on a regular basis. For example, Mead Corporation paid an annual dividend of $1.00 per share from 1991 through mid-1995, when it increased the amount to $1.12. After this increase, Mead shareholders most likely expected to receive $1.12 for several years in the future, when they hope it will be increased again.

Although far less popular, many companies have begun **periodic share repurchases** as a way of distributing cash to shareholders. These plans offer shareholders the right to sell shares back to the corporation at a set price, which is higher than the market price at the time the repurchase offer is made. In effect, regular repurchases offer the same cash advantage to shareholders as regular cash dividends as long as they don't mind reducing their holdings in the company. (You have the option of selling shares or not.) There can be tax advantages as well with share repurchase. Mead, by the way, was aggressively buying back some of its shares in mid-1995, although it was buying them in the open market rather than through a formal repurchase plan.

Stock dividend: A dividend paid by issuing additional shares of a company's stock.

Stock split: Giving additional shares of stock to current stockholders.

NONCASH DISTRIBUTIONS In many cases, corporations' managements want to reward shareholders but cannot do so because the business does not have sufficient cash. Frequently, noncash distributions are made, which include stock dividends and stock splits. With a **stock dividend,** you don't receive cash; instead, you receive shares of the company's stock. For example, if you owned 100 shares of Mead and the company declared a 10 percent stock dividend, you would get an additional 10 shares. Are stock dividends attractive? Not really, because every stockholder gets a proportionate increase in shares. All you then have are more shares of stock but no more assets or greater earning potential for the company. As a result, the day a stock dividend is paid, the price of the stock goes down by the same percentage as the percentage increase in the number of shares. Instead of having 100 shares of Mead at, say, $56 a share, you would have 110 shares at $50.91 a share.

Closely related to a stock dividend is a **stock split.** Here, a company simply gives you and all other stockholders more shares of stock. Two-for-one splits are the most common, which means the number of shares you own doubles. (Mead accomplished a two-for-one stock split in May 1987.) Are stock splits by themselves desirable? No, for the same reasons stock dividends aren't. Granted, many companies that have done well, such as Microsoft, sometimes split their shares to lower the stock's price and broaden its market appeal. But it's not the split that adds value, it is the underlying strengths of the company.

Opportunities in Common Stocks

Your opportunities to earn a return with common stocks are as varied as the many different kinds of corporations that issue them. You can buy very conservative stocks with low risk, or you can find those that are extremely risky. The total return you can expect over the long run should reflect your willingness to assume risk—the more you take, the higher your return. The following are the different kinds of stocks most investors buy.

Box 11.1

PERSONAL FINANCE NEWS

Late Edition

Watch the Super Bowl and Be a Super Forecaster

Want to get your portfolio started right each year? Forget technical analysis, fundamental analysis, expert advice, and anything else that takes a lot of work and might have some connection to the stock market. Instead, enjoy a football game. Specifically, watch the Super Bowl each January and if one of the old NFL teams wins, buy; if one of the expansion AFL teams wins, don't buy (for even better results, go short). Sounds crazy, right? Well, the accompanying table shows how you would have done with this strategy since the Super Bowl began. You would have missed the market direction in only 4 of 29 years, which is remarkable. (And several misses were so close that a few points' change at year's end could have given a perfect record.) Indeed, the chances of doing this well by luck are about 10 in 1,000. With performance this good, why use anything else?

Let's be serious. Stock market performance and the Super Bowl are definitely independent events. The fact that they appear not to be is a coincidence. But if you look at an endless number of independent events, you should find one eventually that forecasts the market as well as or better than the Super Bowl. If you understand the point here, you should also understand why some supposedly sophisticated forecasters show remarkable forecasting results. Keep this in mind: With thousands of professionals forecasting, the odds are excellent that we can find one or two who do it almost perfectly. Are they lucky, or are they good? You make the decision.

SUPER BOWL FORECAST RESULTS

Year	Winner	League	Change in the Market
1967	Green Bay Packers	NFL	+20.09%
1968	Green Bay Packers	NFL	+ 7.66
1969	New York Jets	AFL	−11.42
1970	Kansas City Chiefs	AFL	+ 0.16*
1971	Baltimore Colts	NFL	+10.79
1972	Dallas Cowboys	NFL	+15.63
1973	Miami Dolphins	AFL	−17.37
1974	Miami Dolphins	AFL	−29.72
1975	Pittsburgh Steelers	NFL	+31.55
1976	Pittsburgh Steelers	NFL	+19.15
1977	Oakland Raiders	AFL	−11.50
1978	Dallas Cowboys	NFL	+ 1.06
1979	Pittsburgh Steelers	NFL	+12.31
1980	Pittsburgh Steelers	NFL	+25.77
1981	Oakland Raiders	AFL	− 9.72
1982	San Francisco 49ers	NFL	+14.76
1983	Washington Redskins	NFL	+17.27
1984	Los Angeles Raiders	AFL	+ 1.39*
1985	San Francisco 49ers	NFL	+26.34
1986	Chicago Bears	NFL	+14.33
1987	New York Giants	NFL	+ 2.03
1988	Washington Redskins	NFL	+12.41
1989	San Francisco 49ers	NFL	+27.50
1990	San Francisco 49ers	NFL	− 6.56*
1991	New York Giants	NFL	+26.31
1992	Washington Redskins	NFL	+ 4.46
1993	Dallas Cowboys	NFL	+ 7.06
1994	Dallas Cowboys	NFL	− 1.54*
1995	San Francisco 49ers	NFL	+34.11

*Shows incorrect forecast.

Growth company: A company with expected earnings growth greater than the growth of the overall economy.

GROWTH COMPANIES The earnings and dividend-paying potential of a **growth company** are expected to grow at a rate faster than the growth rate of the overall economy. The price of its common stock should also grow rapidly in the future. Of course, there are all sorts of growth companies. Microsoft is one, Sybase is another. Microsoft represents less risk than Sybase, because it has a good history of achieving growth, and its chances of continuing to do so in the future are very good. Sybase, on the other hand, is a relative newcomer to the computer software industry, but it may have the more rapid growth. If you are interested in buying growth stocks, get as many recommendations as you can from brokers or other advisers, and narrow down the field to 10 or 15 companies that appeal to you.

Income stocks: Stocks that pay high dividends in relation to their market prices.

INCOME STOCKS As their name suggests, **income stocks** pay high dividends in relation to their market prices and offer good current rates of return. However, they vary considerably in risk, so be sure to review that characteristic before investing. Because of their capabilities for paying regular cash dividends, public utilities are often considered the best income stocks. In recent years, their dividend yields have been in excess of 7 percent, and some also offer reasonable growth prospects. They are not without risks, though, as investors learned with public utilities that have not been permitted to use nuclear reactors.

Blue chip: A low-risk stock that reliably provides investors with the expected dividend or growth.

BLUE CHIPS The popular expression **blue chip** really doesn't tell you much about a stock. It usually refers to low-risk stocks—those you can count on to deliver the dividend or growth you expected when you bought them. It also usually refers to what is called *high-capitalization stocks,* which means the issuing corporations are very large companies with many millions of shares outstanding. Being a blue chip doesn't guarantee success, however. The New York Central Railroad was the bluest of the blue in the 1920s and bankrupt in the 1960s.

Cyclical stocks: Stocks that are highly responsive to changes in the business cycle.

CYCLICAL STOCKS **Cyclical stocks** are more responsive to changes in the business cycle than are other stocks. Companies in the capital goods industries, such as the Mead Corporation, are good examples of cyclical stocks. Investors like to "play" cyclical stocks by buying them in recession periods and then selling out as the economy improves. Sounds easy, but it isn't, because it is almost impossible to know when the stock's price is at the bottom of its cycle.

Special situation: Any potentially profitable investment opportunity, but often referring to a possible takeover.

SPECIAL SITUATIONS Anything can be a **special situation,** but the most common is when one company is expected to take over another. Almost always these takeovers result in a substantially higher price for the stock of the company taken over. For example, Lotus Development's price was about $30 a share in 1995, when IBM announced it would offer $65 a share. If you can get in on a takeover shortly before the event takes place, the profit opportunity is enormous. Naturally, the trick is to know if and when a takeover will occur. If you don't have inside information, you must rely upon opinions of so-called experts in identifying takeover situations. Very often these opinions are no better than random guesses. Other special situations could involve changes in key managers, favorable or unfavorable legal opinions, granting of a license or patent, a new and unexpected invention, and many others. All these events can change a company's financial outlook dramatically and its stock price accordingly.

How to Read Stock Quotations

Considerable financial information about many companies is published every day in both hometown newspapers and the important financial newspapers, such as the *Wall Street Journal.* Unfortunately, some people cannot use this information because they have not learned how to read stock quotations. Actually, it's very simple once you understand the symbols. Figure 11.3 shows a typical day's quotations as they appear in the financial pages. The format applies to stocks traded on the New York Stock Exchange, the American Stock Exchange, and the NASDAQ

52 Weeks High	52 Weeks Low	Stock	Div.	Yld %	P-E Ratio	Sales 100s	High	Low	Close	Net Chg.
				– A –	A –	A –				
17¾	7⅞	AAR	.44	3.1	18	12	14⅝	14¼	14⅜	+⅛
52⅜	29½	ACF	1.40	2.8	64	262	49⅞	49½	49¾	...
20	14¾	AMF	.50	2.9	...	380	17½	17⅛	17½	+⅛
51	39½	McKess	2.40	6.2	11	201	39½	38⅞	39	–½
24½	13¼	McNeil	.60	3.5	...	251	17⅜	17¼	17¼	–¼
58	42	Mead	1.12	2.0	24.7	519	56⅜	55¼	56⅜	+1⅛
90	47⅝	Mea	pfA2.10	3.1	...		90	90	90	...
36⅞	14½	Measix	...	...	30	107	39⅝	32⅛	32⅜	–½
59⅞	41	Medtrn	.72	1.5	14	1126	47¼	46¼	47	...
56½	36¾	Melion	2.44	5.9	6	2707	42	41⅛	41½	–1⅛
28	25½	Melion	pf2.60	1.1		22	26¾	26½	26⅝	

58	42	Mead	1.12	2.0	24.7	519	56⅜	55¼	56⅜	+1⅛
1	2	3	4	5	6	7	8	9	10	11

1. The highest price per share paid in the past year, prices are quoted in dollars and eighths of dollars, so a price of 10⅛ = $10.125 a share. Mead's highest price was $58.
2. The lowest price per share paid in the last year. Mead's lowest price was $42.
3. The company's name, which is usually abbreviated. For example, McKess is McKesson and Robbins, a pharmaceutical company.
4. The indicated regular dividend in the current year based on what the company has paid in the last quarter or six months. Some companies also pay extra dividends in good earnings years, but these are not shown. Mead's regular dividend was estimated at $1.12 a share.
5. The current yield, which is found by dividing the current year regular dividends by the closing price of the stock. Mead's current yield is 2.0 percent.
6. The price-earnings ratio, which is the company's earnings over it's last fiscal year divided into the closing price of the stock. Mead's ratio is 24.7.
7. The number of shares sold on that day, in hundreds. For example, 519 means 51,900 shares of Mead stock.
8. The highest price paid for the stock that day. Mead's was 56⅜ (56.375).
9. The lowest price paid for the stock that day. Mead's was 55¼ (55.25).
10. The last price paid that day. Mead's was 56⅜.
11. The difference between the closing price that day and the closing price of the previous day. For example, Mead's closing price on the previous day was 1⅛ ($1.125) lower than its closing price on the reported day.

Figure 11.3 How to read stock quotations.

National Market Issues. An abbreviated format, which shows only volume, last price, and price change, is used for smaller over-the-counter stocks. This listing is called NASDAQ Small-Cap Issues.

FUNDAMENTAL ANALYSIS OF COMMON STOCKS

What is a stock worth? In mid-1995, Mead was selling in the $55–$60 price range. Was it worth that much, or was it worth more, or less? These are very difficult questions to answer, but investors must at least try; otherwise, securities could sell at any set of prices. You may choose not to undertake value analysis on your own, but even if you rely on professional analysts' opinions, you should be familiar with their techniques. We will consider two basic approaches—application of the CAPM (introduced in the previous chapter) and a price-to-earnings analysis. The section concludes with a discussion of book value.

Application of the CAPM

In the previous chapter we learned that a stock offer has two pertinent returns: (1) a required return, which reflects its individual risk and a risk premium for the overall stock market, and (2) an expected return, which reflects what you as an investor believe the stock will offer in terms of a cash dividend or potential price appreciation. The required return concept was developed thoroughly in the previous chapter; now let's turn our attention to the expected return.

Recall from Chapter 10 that the expected total return, *TR,* is the sum of current return, *CR,* and future return, *FR;* that is,

$$TR = CR + FR$$

Current return can be expressed in ratio or percentage form. For example, if you expected to receive a $1.12 dividend on a share of Mead in 1995, and if you paid $56 a share, your expected current return would be 2.0 percent, calculated as follows:

$$CR\% = \frac{\$1.12}{\$56.00} = 0.02, \text{ or } 2.0\%$$

EARNINGS AS A SOURCE OF DIVIDENDS All dividends must come eventually from earnings. If a corporation's dividends exceed the sum of its current earnings and earnings it has accumulated in the past, then it is actually liquidating itself. It is relatively easy for potential investors to estimate a current dividend, because it is also relatively easy to estimate both a company's current earnings and the proportion of those earnings it is likely to distribute. Moreover, many companies indicate what the current dividend will be. But it is not so easy to estimate future earnings and future dividends. How much Mead will earn per share in 1997 or 2001 is not an easily answered question. Nor is it easy to know the company's future policy with respect to dividend distributions. Mead might undergo a complete change in the nature of its business, and this change might demand more cash, forcing Mead to cut the proportion of its earnings it pays in dividends.

EXPRESSING FUTURE RETURN IN THE TOTAL RETURN EQUATION Bringing future return into the total return equation is done most easily by expressing it as a percentage return, and the most commonly used percentage is the company's expected *annual growth* in dividends (or earnings) in the future. So, if you thought Mead's dividends would grow at a 15 percent annual rate each year in the future, this is its future return percentage. Add this to the current return percentage to arrive at the total return percentage; that is,

$$TR\% = CR\% + FR\% = 2.0\% + 15.0\% = 17.0\%$$

It makes sense to include the dividend growth factor since a stock with a growing dividend should be worth more than one without growth. Moreover, the growth factor allows you to make return comparisons among different stocks with different current return characteristics. For example, suppose another stock was available at $56 a share that was similar to Mead in risk but with a different dividend. Say it paid $2.24 a share—twice as much as Mead. Is it a better buy? Looking only at current return, you might say yes: Its current return percentage is 4.0, also twice Mead's. But if its expected growth rate were only 6 percent, then Mead would be the better choice because the other stock's total return would be only 10.0 percent (6.0 + 4.0). A comparison of future dividends with each stock, as shown in Figure 11.4, indicates that for about nine years after purchase, dividends are higher with the other stock, but then Mead takes the advantage and keeps it thereafter. After 20 years, Mead's dividend is over twice that of the other company.

WAS MEAD WORTH $56 A SHARE? To answer this question, recall from the previous chapter the concept of alpha, which is calculated as follows:

$$\text{Alpha} = \text{expected return} - \text{required return}$$

Greater positive values of alpha signal greater investment appeal; conversely, negative alpha values indicate stocks that should not be bought and perhaps should be sold, if you already own them.

Figure 11.5 summarizes the evaluation of Mead. Short-term Treasury securities yielded about 5.5 percent when the analysis was undertaken. Also, Mead's 15 percent growth rate was taken from an advisory service's report on Mead (see Figure 11.6, page 313). The *Value Line Investment Survey* is widely used by both amateur and professional investors. It is highly regarded but, of course, not infallible in valuing stocks. As a beginning investor, you should review the *Survey* for stocks that you like. Notice in Figure 11.6 that we use Mead's expected growth in earnings (rather than expected dividend growth), because it generally is the best estimate of future dividend-paying capacity.

Figure 11.5 shows that Mead has a positive alpha value of 1.1 percent. Mead, then, represented a *moderately* attractive stock at the time the analysis was done. However, the alpha value is not so large that we classify Mead as a "strong buy." Investment analysis is not rocket science, and it's quite possible that Value Line's estimate of Mead's 15 percent growth rate is too optimistic. Notice in the upper left-hand corner of the report that Value Line gave Mead a ranking of 3 in both safety and timeliness. The latter ranking reflects that Mead will be an average per-

Figure 11.4
Future dividends per share (DPS) with Mead and another company.

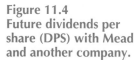

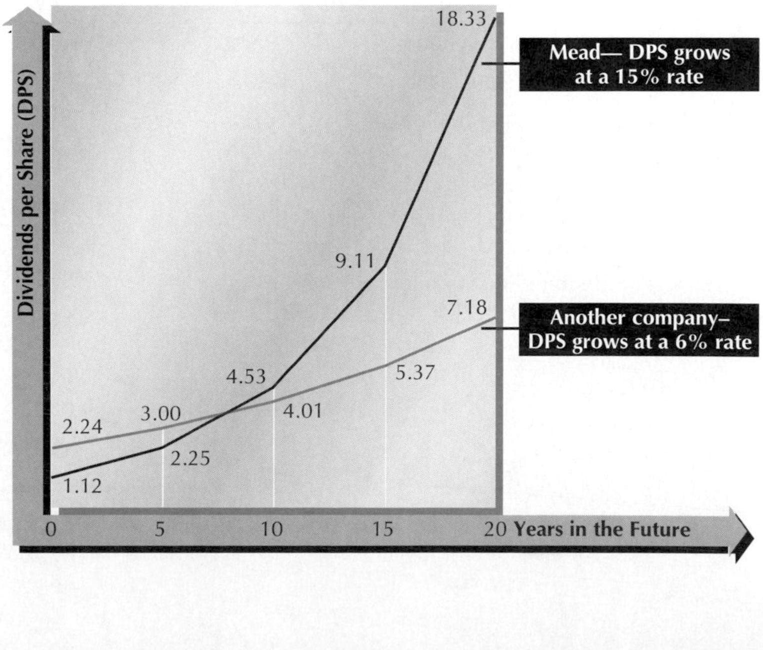

former over the investment horizon shown (to the year 2000). Value Line's method of ranking stocks indicates that stocks with rankings of 1 are the most attractive buying opportunities and those with rankings of 5 are the least attractive.

Price-to-Earnings Analysis

Price-to-earnings analysis: A method of valuing common stocks based on a company's expected future earnings.
Earnings per share (EPS): A company's total earnings divided by the total number of shares of common stock outstanding.
Price-earnings (P/E) ratio: The price of a company's stock divided by the company's earnings per share.

A **price-to-earnings analysis** is a somewhat simpler and more direct approach than the CAPM method. Basically, analysts who follow this approach feel that the price of a share of a company's stock depends entirely on the company's future **earnings per share (EPS).** EPS is simply the company's total earnings divided by the total number of shares of common stock outstanding.

Analysts also use a **price-earnings (P/E) ratio,** which reflects how much a stock is worth in relation to its EPS; that is,

$$\text{P/E ratio} = \frac{\text{stock's price}}{\text{EPS}}$$

So if a stock earns \$1.50 per share and if a P/E ratio of 12.0 seems appropriate for valuation purposes, rearranging the above equation shows that the stock's price should be \$18.00 a share:

$$\begin{aligned}\text{Stock's price} &= \text{EPS} \times \text{P/E ratio}\\ &= \$1.50 \times 12\end{aligned}$$

A price-to-earnings analysis is only as good as the analyst's estimates of EPS and the P/E ratio. Further discussion of each is needed.

Figure 11.5 Comparing Mead's required rate of return with its expected rate of return, mid-June 1995.

Required Rate of Return		Expected Rate of Return	
1. Market risk premium	8.0%	1. Current market price of stock per share	\$56.00
2. Mead's beta weight	1.30	2. Expected 1995 dividend	\$ 1.12
3. Mead's risk premium = Line 1 × Line 2 = 8.0% × 1.30 =	10.4%	3. Current yield = Line 2 ÷ Line 1 = \$0.65 ÷ 36 =	2.0%
4. Risk-free rate on U.S. Treasury securities =	5.5%	4. Expected annual growth in earnings	15.0%
5. Required rate of return = Line 3 + Line 4 =	15.9%	5. Expected rate of return = Line 3 + Line 4 =	17.0%

Difference (alpha) equals 1.1%: The decision is to buy Mead since its required rate of return is lower than its expected rate of return.

MEAD CORP. NYSE-MEA

RECENT PRICE	53	P/E RATIO	12.1 (Trailing: 23.2 / Median: 15.0)	RELATIVE P/E RATIO	0.85	DIV'D YLD	1.9%	VALUE LINE	927

TIMELINESS (Relative Price Performance Next 12 Mos.) **3** Average

SAFETY **3** Average

(Scale: 1 Highest to 5 Lowest)

BETA 1.30 (1.00 = Market)

1998-00 PROJECTIONS

	Price	Gain	Ann'l Total Return
High	80	(+50%)	12%
Low	50	(-5%)	1%

Insider Decisions

	J	J	A	S	O	N	D	J	F
to Buy	0	0	0	0	0	0	0	1	1
Options	0	0	0	0	0	0	0	2	1
to Sell	0	0	0	0	0	0	0	0	1

Institutional Decisions

	2Q'94	3Q'94	4Q'94
to Buy	56	81	61
to Sell	77	77	93
Hld's(000)	43531	44824	41954

High:	20.6	22.4	30.4	48.4	49.5	46.6	39.5	37.3	41.6	48.5	53.3	55.5
Low:	13.6	16.8	21.3	21.0	29.0	34.3	19.5	24.5	33.3	37.5	39.3	48.6

Target Price Range 1998 1999 2000

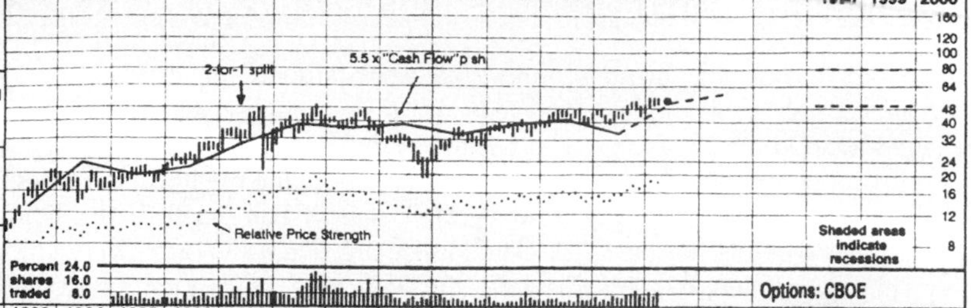

Options: CBOE

1979	1980	1981	1982	1983	1984	1985	1986	1987	1988	1989	1990	1991	1992	1993	1994	1995	1996	© VALUE LINE PUB., INC.	98-00
49.48	51.42	55.18	50.65	39.35	44.06	44.10	51.39	67.04	70.69	72.86	81.90	78.50	80.08	80.94	78.66	*95.30*	*101.90*	Sales per sh	*113.20*
3.91	3.71	3.47	1.39	2.37	4.21	3.59	4.02	5.47	6.97	6.66	7.04	6.16	7.05	7.57	6.27	*9.40*	*10.60*	"Cash Flow" per sh	*10.10*
2.60	2.36	1.96	d.70	.52	2.26	1.51	1.75	2.79	3.70	3.10	2.61	1.21	1.93	2.20	2.28	*4.80*	*6.10*	Earnings per sh B F	*5.00*
.83	.92	.97	.88	.50	.53	.60	.60	.65	.74	.85	.97	1.00	1.00	1.00	1.00	*1.00*	*1.08*	Div'ds Decl'd per sh C■	*1.35*
2.48	4.83	6.01	2.61	1.37	2.85	4.81	2.83	2.79	5.55	9.73	7.80	4.55	4.51	5.86	5.45	*6.60*	*6.15*	Cap'l Spending per sh	*7.10*
14.51	15.95	16.60	13.91	14.11	15.72	16.63	16.91	19.85	24.82	26.55	26.28	25.34	25.46	26.66	37.67	*39.45*	*44.80*	Book Value per sh D	*57.65*
51.93	52.64	52.55	52.65	60.14	61.74	62.15	62.61	62.78	63.15	63.30	58.27	58.34	58.73	59.19	57.94	*53.00*	*53.00*	Common Shs Outst'g E	*53.00*
5.1	5.4	6.9	--	29.1	7.7	13.1	14.8	12.6	10.5	12.8	11.2	26.0	19.4	19.6	20.1	*Bold figures are Value Line estimates*		Avg Ann'l P/E Ratio	*13.0*
.74	.72	.84	--	2.46	.72	1.06	1.00	.84	.87	.97	.83	1.66	1.18	1.16	1.32			Relative P/E Ratio	*1.00*
6.2%	7.2%	7.1%	9.3%	3.3%	3.0%	3.0%	2.3%	1.8%	1.9%	2.1%	3.3%	3.2%	2.7%	2.3%	2.2%			Avg Ann'l Div'd Yield	*2.2%*
						2740.4	3217.7	4208.8	4463.9	4612.1	4772.4	4579.3	4703.2	4790.3	4557.5	*5050*	*5400*	Sales ($mill) F	*6000*
						11.2%	11.9%	12.0%	12.9%	11.3%	11.6%	11.4%	11.7%	12.2%	10.2%	*12.5%*	*13.5%*	Operating Margin	*12.0%*
						129.8	142.5	168.2	199.8	221.2	247.5	288.4	299.6	316.1	225.5	*230*	*240*	Depreciation ($mill)	*270*
						93.5	109.3	175.3	240.3	200.3	162.6	70.8	114.2	131.7	138.0	*270*	*325*	Net Profit ($mill)	*265*
						31.8%	51.6%	44.1%	36.7%	36.2%	35.9%	35.8%	37.5%	38.4%	39.9%	*39.0%*	*39.0%*	Income Tax Rate	*40.0%*
						3.4%	3.4%	4.2%	5.4%	4.3%	3.4%	1.5%	2.4%	2.7%	3.0%	*5.3%*	*6.0%*	Net Profit Margin	*4.4%*
						49.2	185.8	330.9	286.3	284.7	288.8	346.6	399.5	419.8	806.5	*530*	*625*	Working Cap'l ($mill)	*1200*
						505.2	803.7	764.6	924.3	949.8	1256.6	1315.7	1332.3	1368.8	957.7	*830*	*730*	Long-Term Debt ($mill)	*950*
						1033.6	1058.9	1246.0	1567.5	1680.8	1531.3	1478.4	1495.4	1578.0	2182.6	*2090*	*2375*	Net Worth ($mill) D	*3050*
						7.6%	7.7%	10.8%	11.1%	9.3%	7.5%	4.1%	5.5%	5.9%	6.0%	*10.5%*	*11.5%*	% Earned Total Cap'l	*7.5%*
						9.0%	10.3%	14.1%	15.3%	11.9%	10.6%	4.8%	7.6%	8.3%	6.3%	*13.0%*	*13.5%*	% Earned Net Worth	*8.5%*
						5.4%	6.8%	10.8%	12.4%	8.7%	6.7%	.8%	3.7%	4.6%	3.6%	*10.5%*	*11.0%*	% Retained to Comm Eq	*6.5%*
						40%	34%	23%	19%	27%	37%	82%	51%	45%	43%	*20%*	*18%*	% All Div'ds to Net Prof	*27%*

CAPITAL STRUCTURE as of 12/31/94
Total Debt $973.8 mill. **Due in 5 Yrs** $149.6 mill.
LT Debt $957.7 mill. **LT Interest** $75.0 mill.

(LT int. earned: 3.0x; total int. cov.: 2.8x)
(30% of Cap'l)

Leases, Uncapitalized Annual rentals $27.2 mill.

Pension Liability None

Pfd Stock None

Common Stock 57,941,093 shs. (70% of Cap'l)

CURRENT POSITION ($MILL.)	1992	1993	12/31/94
Cash Assets	18.4	9.3	484.0
Receivables	582.1	598.2	606.6
Inventory (LIFO)	425.9	446.8	382.4
Other	103.0	77.0	421.0
Current Assets	1129.4	1131.3	1894.0
Accts Payable	364.7	350.3	245.6
Debt Due	10.7	12.5	16.1
Other	354.5	348.7	825.8
Current Liab.	729.9	711.5	1087.5

ANNUAL RATES of change (per sh)	Past 10 Yrs.	Past 5 Yrs.	Est'd '92-'94 to '98-'00
Sales	6.0%	2.5%	*6.0%*
"Cash Flow"	10.0%	2.0%	*6.5%*
Earnings	12.0%	-7.5%	*15.0%*
Dividends	4.5%	6.0%	*5.0%*
Book Value	7.5%	4.5%	*11.5%*

Calendar	QUARTERLY SALES ($ mill.) A B F Mar.Per	Jun.Per	Sep.Per	Dec.31	Full Year
1992	1088	1225	1254	1135	4703.2
1993	1135	1263	1261	1129	4790.3
1994	1007	1165	1208	1175	4557.5
1995	*1200*	*1350*	*1275*	*1225*	*5050*
1996	*1300*	*1450*	*1350*	*1300*	*5400*

Calendar	EARNINGS PER SHARE A B F Mar.Per	Jun.Per	Sep.Per	Dec.31	Full Year
1992	.31	.71	.63	.28	1.93
1993	.43	.78	.62	.37	2.20
1994	.27	.74	.68	.59	2.28
1995	*1.05*	*1.40*	*1.35*	*1.00*	*4.80*
1996	*1.30*	*1.85*	*1.70*	*1.25*	*6.10*

Calendar	QUARTERLY DIVIDENDS PAID C■ Mar.31	Jun.30	Sep.30	Dec.31	Full Year
1991	.25	.25	.25	.25	1.00
1992	.25	.25	.25	.25	1.00
1993	.25	.25	.25	.25	1.00
1994	.25	.25	.25	.25	1.00
1995	.25				

BUSINESS: Mead Corp. produces printing, writing, and specialty papers, paperboard, corrugated containers, and packaging products; distributes paper, plastic products, packaging equipment and supplies, school and office supplies. Sold Mead Data Central (MDC) in October, 1994. Sold Kingsport, TN paper mill in March, 1995. Owns/controls 1.4 mill. acres of U.S. timberlands. Has 50% interest in Northwood Forest Ind. (produces lumber and pulp). Labor costs: 19% of sales. Has 16,100 employees; 16,700 shareholders. Officers & Directors own 2.8% of stock; Oppenheimer Group, Inc., 6.8%; (3/95 proxy). Chairman, President & Chief Executive Officer: Steven C. Mason. Incorporated: Ohio. Address: Courthouse Plaza N.E., Dayton, Ohio 45463. Telephone: 513-495-6323.

Mead has significantly enhanced its earnings potential . . . Last fall's sale of the Data Central business left the company with $1.05 billion in proceeds. Rather than acquire additional capacity, management chose to reduce debt with two thirds of the receipts, and will buy back $350 million worth of shares by June. Earnings will also get a boost from the recent sale of the Kingsport uncoated paper mill, whose losses approximated $10 million in each of the past two years. These moves to boost share earnings are complementing the ongoing cost reduction plans initiated in 1992. Marked improvements in productivity, resulting from tighter cost controls, reduced headcount, and more efficient manufacturing processes, masked the pricing weakness experienced until last fall.

. . . which will help it take advantage of paper price hikes. With the sale of the Kingsport mill, coated paper now provides about 75% of paper sales. Mead's leverage in coated paper will provide a big boost to earnings in 1995 and 1996. Prices began firming last fall. And we think realizations will rise higher for these late-cycle grades, given the year-long strength of uncoated and lightweight paper prices.

The packaging businesses will also likely see improved profits. Stronger worldwide economic growth has led to better demand for Mead's coated board, container board, and packaging products. Despite higher freight costs and stiffer competition, profits should rise by 15%-20% this year thanks to price increases already announced for most grades and entrance into higher-margined markets.

Other businesses should show modest improvement as well. We estimate that Mead's 50% equity stake in Northwoods, a pulp and lumber producer, will contribute $55-$60 million in earnings, versus the $50 million received last year. And the sluggish distribution and school supplies businesses should report modest earnings growth after three years of flat profits, thanks to a restructuring and purchase of a $100 million Canadian supply firm.

These shares are ranked to perform at least as well as the market averages in the coming year. However, share net may peak as soon as next year, resulting in subpar returns over the long haul.

Charles C. Moran *April 21, 1995*

(A) Qtrs. 1-3 end on 13th Sun. (B) Excl. net gains(loss) from extra./nonrec. items: '86, ($1.16); '87, 66¢; '88, $1.67; '89, 23¢; '90, ($2.09); '91, ($1.09); '92, (72¢); '93, (12¢). '94 $9.11. Next egs. report due late Jul. (C) Next div'd meeting about May 4th. Goes ex-div'd about May 2nd. Apprx. div'd paymnt. dates: 1st of Mar., Jun., Sep., and Dec.■ Div'd reinvestm't plan avail. (D) Incl. intang.: '94, $80 mill., $1.36/sh. (E) In mill., adjusted for stk. split. (F) 1994 restated for MDC sale.

Company's Financial Strength	B++
Stock's Price Stability	65
Price Growth Persistence	65
Earnings Predictability	55

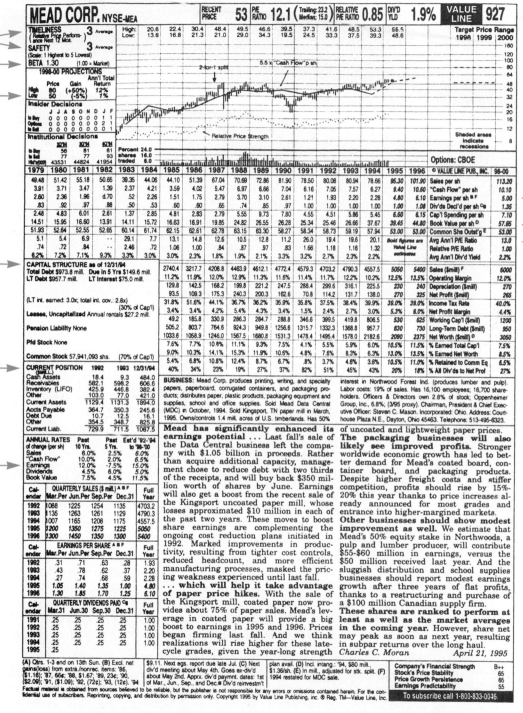

Figure 11.6 Value Line's research report on the Mead Corporation.

SOURCE: *Value Line Investment Survey,* April 21, 1995, p. 927. Copyright 1995 by Value Line Publishing, Inc. All rights reserved. Reprinted by permission.

Box 11.2 SIMPLIFYING FINANCIAL PLANNING
Using the High-Yield Method to Beat the Market

Beating the market is not easy—just ask over half of all professional money managers who come up short each year. Surprisingly, one very simple method has an excellent track record and a rapidly growing number of converts. There are even mutual funds that offer the method, if you prefer to avoid even the slight details of investing on your own.

What do you need to do? At the beginning of each year find the 10 (of 30) stocks in the Dow Jones Industrial Average (DJIA) with the highest dividend yield. The dividend yield is simply a stock's annual dividend divided by its current market price. If Exxon's market price is $60.75 and its annual dividend is $3.00, its dividend yield is 0.049 ($3.00/$60.75), or 4.9 percent. Dividend yields are reported in each issue of the *Wall Street Journal,* where you also can find a listing of the 30 stocks in the DJIA. If you want to avoid the aggravation of finding 30 yields, read the *Journal* or *Barron's* or *Money Magazine* around the first of the year and they probably will give you the list of the 10 highest-yielding stocks in a story about the method.

Regardless of how you get the 10 stocks, invest an equal amount in each at the start of a year, then sit back and reap. From 1972 through 1994, this method has scored an average annualized return of 17.1 percent versus only 10.9 percent for the overall DJIA. Why does it do so well?

High-yielding stocks often represent so-called turnaround situations. A company, such as Sears at one time, may fail to keep up with its competitors in terms of market share or production efficiencies. As a result the stock price plummets; but the company has ample cash and continues paying a decent dividend. So the dividend yield rises, and the company makes the top 10 list. Often, these companies solve their problems—as Sears did—and their stock prices rebound sharply.

Would the high-yield method work in pinpointing other potential turnarounds? Sure, but be careful: Stocks in the DJIA are large blue chips who have the resources to make drastic operational changes. If you find a small company with a high yield, it may never turn around; instead, it may lower or cut its dividend altogether. Now, your high-yielder is a no-yielder, and its price might fall sharply. It is much simpler to limit your choices to the DJIA.

Finally, although it's tempting to find ways to beat the market, a sound investment program usually focuses on a long-term horizon and stresses the suitability of investment vehicles to the investor's objectives and risk-tolerance level. If you're investing for the long run and not looking for short-run turnarounds, growth stocks seem a better choice than high-yielding stocks.

USE FUTURE (NOT PAST) EPS AMOUNTS A company's past earnings might have historical interest and perhaps might help us forecast its future earnings, but you should understand that it is indeed the future earnings that matter in valuing stocks. As you can see in Figure 11.6, Value Line provides data for a long period of time—actual amounts from 1979 through 1994 and forecasts for 1995, 1996, and the 1998–2000 period.

Looking at EPS amounts (third line under year), you should see that Mead's earnings are quite volatile, which is typical of a cyclical company. The company earned $3.70 in 1988, but earned only $1.21 in 1991 (a recession year). Earnings rebounded to $2.28 in 1994 and were forecasted at $4.80 in 1995 and $6.10 in 1996. Notice, though, that they are expected to decline to $5.00 in the 1998–2000 period.

Action Plan for the Steeles: Investing in Growth Stocks

Background The Steeles met with their broker recently and had a thorough discussion of their investment goals. The broker advised them to reposition their stock investments more toward growth and less toward current yield. She recommended the sale of Consolidated Edison and Dow Chemical and the purchase of Gillette and Intel.

The Problem The Steeles understand the difference between growth and income stocks, but they cannot grasp *how much* of a difference there might be between the two types in terms of accumulating funds at a future point in time. As a follow-up, they asked the broker to compare the four stocks, clearly demonstrating their financial differences.

The Plan The Steeles will follow their broker's advice if she can defend it with meaningful comparisons. The broker prepared the data in the accompanying table. Item 1 clearly shows the superior past earnings growth of Gillette and Intel, and item 2 confirms the high dividend yields of Con Ed and Dow. Items 3 and 4 indicate significantly better price appreciation with Gillette and Intel, particularly the latter, and item 5 dramatically underscores the ability of growth stocks to accumulate value over time. Clearly, past performance does not ensure a comparable future performance. However, the broker feels that each company holds a dominant position in a growing industry and has excellent international exposure.

Rationale for the Plan The Steeles are convinced that the plan is sound. The only drawback is the safety rating of Intel, which indicates about average safety. Gillette's safety is on a par with Dow's, and Con Ed is clearly the safest. The Steeles recognize that Intel (and other growth stocks) carry higher risk. However, their long-term investment horizon can accommodate such risk, and the Steeles have decided to follow their broker's advice.

COMPARING THE FOUR COMPANIES

Item	Con Ed	Dow	Gillette	Intel
1. Average annual rate of growth in EPS (through 1994):				
a. Last 10 years	3.0%	7.5%	16.5%	30.5%
b. Last 5 years	2.5	−13.0	18.0	36.0
c. Forecasted 1998	2.0	16.0	17.0	15.5
2. Average annual dividend yield for the past 5 years	6.9	4.6	1.6	0.2
3. Stock price:				
a. 10 years ago	$ 18	$ 25	$ 3	$ 4
b. 5 years ago	25	60	16	12
c. Recent (mid-1995)	30	70	45	63
4. Percentage price increase:				
a. Over past 10 years	67%	180%	1400%	1475%
b. Over past 5 years	20	17	181	425
5. Accumulated value of $1,000 invested 5 years ago	$1,650	$1,450	$2,900	$5,300
6. Safety rating (1 = safest)	1	2	2	3

a. Data taken or derived from *Value Line Investment Survey*, July 1995, pages 170, 827, 1062, and 1242.
b. Adjusted for stock splits and stock dividends.
c. Assumes reinvestment of annual dividends at a 10 percent rate.

FINDING P/E RATIOS Various approaches are used to determine appropriate P/E ratios, but none are completely satisfactory, and in the final analysis good judgment may be the best guide. On the Value Line report, notice at the top of the page the 12.1 P/E ratio. This value reflected Mead's price at the time of the report (April 21, 1995) and its EPS over the previous four quarters. A second choice is Value Line's estimate of 13.0 for the 1998–2000 period (see the eighth row of data under 98–00). A third method that is widely used is to equate the P/E ratio with the company's expected EPS growth rate. Value Line estimates Mead's growth at 15 percent (see Earnings), so use 15 (forget the "percent") as Mead's P/E ratio.

Each of the above P/E amounts seems fairly low in relation to recent-year P/E values (see the eighth row of data): 26.0, 19.4, 19.6, and 20.1 for the years 1991–1994. However, this period reflected a rebound from the 1990–1991 recession, when Mead's earnings were somewhat depressed. Investors were paying high prices, relative to earnings, in those years because they expected future earnings to be much better. As it turned out, they were correct. But if the earnings growth is expected to be moderate, it would be a mistake to continue using high P/E ratios. All things considered, a range of P/E values from 12 to 15 seems reasonable and perhaps a bit conservative. Let's take the average of the two—13.5.

DETERMINING MEAD'S VALUE, AGAIN Working with Value Line's EPS estimate of $4.80 for 1995 and using 13.5 for the P/E ratio, we can calculate that a share of Mead stock is worth $64.80 (13.5 × $4.80). We refer to this amount as Mead's **fundamental value,** which is a value based on a company's underlying strengths, usually its capacity to generate future earnings. Mead was selling at about $56 a share when the analysis was undertaken, and since its fundamental value is a bit higher than its price, we conclude that Mead is a bit undervalued and a moderately "good buy." This is the same conclusion that the CAPM application gave us; of course, a partial explanation for this agreement is that Value Line's data were used in both approaches. However, that isn't the complete answer, and often the two methods have conflicting conclusions, regardless of the data sources.

Fundamental value: A stock value based on the underlying strengths of a company.

Fundamental Value and Book Value

Investors often refer to a company's **book value,** which is determined by dividing a company's net worth by the number of shares of common stock outstanding. The net worth of a business is measured in the same way that someone's personal net worth is measured; that is, net worth equals total assets minus total liabilities. (Refer to Chapter 2 if you need to review the concept.) Figure 11.6 shows Mead's book values in row 6 of the yearly tabular data. As you see, Mead had a book value of $37.67 at the end of 1994. Value Line estimated that the number would grow to $44.80 by the end of 1996. If Mead was "worth" only about $39.00 in mid-1995, why should anyone be willing to pay $56 or more for a share?

Book value: A company's net worth divided by the number of common stock shares outstanding.

BOOK VALUE'S LIMITATIONS The answer is that book value often is a poor estimate of fundamental value. Book value reflects the historical costs of a company's assets, which may be poor indicators of the current or replacement costs of those assets. Moreover, what a company paid for an asset may have little connection to the asset's ability to generate future cash inflows to the company. Also, perhaps the most valuable of all assets—a company's goodwill—is not even shown on its balance sheet. What is the brand name Coca-Cola worth? If you guess, "a lot," you are correct; it's probably worth far more than all of Coke's other assets combined. Yet it is not listed on Coke's balance sheet. These limitations make book value a poor estimate of fundamental value in most cases.

MARKET-TO-BOOK RATIOS However, it would be a mistake to conclude that book value has no use whatsoever. If, over time, the price of a company's stock increases (or decreases) more rapidly than its book value increases (or decreases), we might want to know why. If there is no underlying explanation, then perhaps

Market-to-book ratio: The market price of a common stock divided by its book value.

the stock is being overvalued (or undervalued) in the market. So analysts often examine a company's **market-to-book ratio,** which is simply market price divided by book value. Mead's ratio in 1995 is 1.42, using $56 as the price and $39.45 as an estimate of book value.

Most stocks have market-to-book ratios greater than 1.0, and these values change considerably over time. For example, since 1960, the average ratio for the 500 stocks in the Standard & Poor 500 Stock Average (the S&P 500) has varied from 1.13 (1982) to 3.93 (1993). In mid-1995, Mead's value of 1.42 was low in relation to the S&P 500 average of around 3.6. The ratio also varies widely among different types of companies. For example, at mid-1995, Microsoft's ratio was about 10.0, which is typical for firms in the software industry.

All other things equal, analysts prefer low market-to-book values rather than high values. Indeed, some analysts feel that you will find more undervalued stocks if you limit your analyses to companies with low ratios. If you follow their advice you might be attracted to Mead and you probably would ignore Microsoft. Many other analysts argue that could be a big mistake. Their view is probably the correct one, since there is no reason to limit your perspective in searching for good investments. Try to apply the CAPM or price-to-earnings method to any company. Be careful, though, if a company seems terribly undervalued. Our introductory treatment of valuation cannot cover all possible problems. If you are going to make your own stock selections, you really should learn more about investments. We'll cover an alternative approach—technical analysis—in the next section, but taking an investments course at a university would be very helpful.

TECHNICAL ANALYSIS

Technical analysis: A method of security analysis based on factors other than underlying fundamentals.

There is no satisfactory definition of **technical analysis** except to say it is not based on underlying fundamentals of a company or the overall economy and that it relies heavily on graphical presentations (see Figure 11.7) and analyses. Most professional technical analysts also use fundamental analysis, but they feel that technical analysis helps if it reinforces their initial findings. We can take two perspectives on technical analysis: the use of pressure indicators and the interpretation of price graphs.

Pressure Indicators

Pressure indicator: A comparison of two market values expressed as a ratio of one to the other.

A **pressure indicator** is simply a comparison between two market values, which presumably measure a particular force or sentiment in the market. The comparison often is made in a ratio format; that is, the value of one variable is divided by the value of another. There probably are as many different pressure indicators as there are technical analysts following the market. Our discussion below explains three indicators that are watched widely, but you should realize there are others that are equally popular.

Advance/decline line: A line showing the ratio of the number of stocks increasing in price relative to the number decreasing.

THE ADVANCE/DECLINE LINE The **advance/decline line** shows for a particular time period the number of stocks increasing in price relative to the number decreasing. Many analysts calculate the A/D ratio—advances divided by declines. A reading of 4.2, for example, indicates that 4.2 stocks advanced in price for each 1.0 stock that declined. Stocks with unchanged prices are not considered in calculating the ratio.

The advance/decline line for stocks traded on the American Stock Exchange is shown in Figure 11.7. We don't know specific values for the line since they are not shown in the graph; however, the trend is shown, and that is the most important perspective for technical analysts. A rising trend is considered "good" (in terms of continued rising prices), and a falling one is "bad" (continued falling prices).

As you should see, the A/D trend was downward until the end of March, when it reversed and started upward. A relative peak was reached around the middle of May, and the line was then flat (no apparent trend) until the end of June. The rather sharp drop toward the end of June certainly would be a concern, but it is not conclusive evidence that a new downturn may have started.

Relative strength line: A line comparing the price movements of two variables.

RELATIVE STRENGTH LINE A **relative strength line** compares the price movements of two variables. It can be calculated using individual stocks, or using a stock and an index, or using two stock indexes. For example, if both the Amex Index and the S&P 500 Index have a value of 400, a relative strength value is 1.0 (400/400). If the Amex then rises to 450 while the S&P stays flat, a second value is

Figure 11.7
Chart of financial data for stocks traded on the American Stock Exchange.

SOURCE: Reprinted with the permission of *Investor's Business Daily,* June 29, 1995, p. A24.

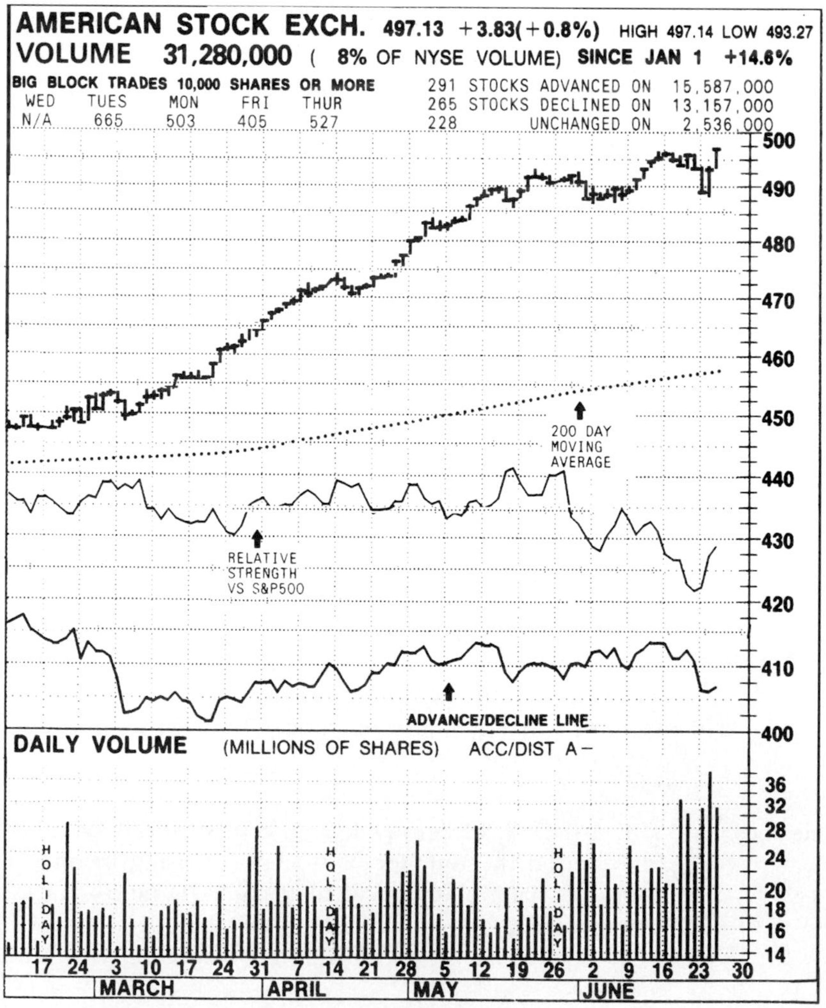

1.125 (450/400). This example shows rising relative strength, which is considered desirable in the sense that once an uptrend starts, it is likely to continue. Of course, downtrends have the opposite interpretation.

In Figure 11.7, values of the American Stock Exchange Index are compared with values of the S&P 500 Stock Index. Again, the trend is of key importance; this trend was flat until the end of May, when it then began to decline. If you felt that this trend would continue, you would be hesitant to invest in the smaller, more speculative stocks that trade on the Amex as opposed to the larger stocks that constitute the S&P 500.

New highs–new lows indicator: A ratio between the number of stocks recording their highest prices for the past year and the number recording their lowest prices.

NEW HIGHS–NEW LOWS A **new highs–new lows indicator** compares the number of stocks reaching their highest prices of the past 12 months relative to those reaching their lowest prices. Analysts often construct the ratio of new highs to new lows and again place emphasis upon the trend. Also, once again, a rising trend is desirable. The data source (*Investor's Business Daily*) for Figure 11.7 does not show a new highs–new lows index in its graphic, but it does provide numerical data as shown in Figure 11.8. As you see, on the reported day 23 stocks on the Amex reached new highs and three recorded new lows. Similar data for the NYSE and NASDAQ are also provided.

Figure 11.8
New highs–new lows data.

SOURCE: Reprinted with the permission of *Investor's Business Daily*, July 3, 1995, p. A28.

New Price Highs
288 Common Stocks

NYSE (n) – 112 New Highs, 4 New Lows
NASDAQ – 153 New Highs, 18 New Lows
AMEX (a) – 23 New Highs, 3 New Lows

Stocks listed within each group,
are in order of greatest increase in volume.
Closing price and EPS Rank are also shown.
(NASDAQ NMS common stocks over $2 only)
†See Graphs in NYSE, NASDAQ or AMEX "Stocks In The News"

Name / Exch.	Symbol	Close	EPS	Name / Exch.	Symbol	Close	EPS
COMPUTERS (33)				Dionex Corp	DNEX	45¾	84 †
ConcComp	CCUR	2½	40	Siliconix	SILI	19⅜	72
Group 1 Sftwr	GSOF	12½	72	Keithley Instr (a)	KEI	22	35
Boca Rsrch	BOCI	27	90	G T I Corp	GGTI	19⅜	32
BachmanInfo	BACH	7⅞	48	Flextronics	FLEXF	21⅞	88
Geoworks	GWRX	12½	45	ASMLthgrpy	ASMLF	35⅞	69
ComputrTask (n)	TSK	14	72	Varian Assoc (n)	VAR	56	92
Computervis (n)	CVN	6⅝	76	KulickeSoffa	KLIC	66[illegible]	75
AuspexSys	ASPX	12½	68	Sier SemiC	SERA	31⅜	76
TrinitechSys (a)	TSI	8	25	Motorola (n)	MOT	67⅜	90 †
Cambex	CBEX	10⅝	53	Tektronix Inc (n)	TEK	49⅛	79 †
ComshareInc	CSRE	20⅝	73	AppliedMatl	AMAT	86⅝	97
Stormedia	STMD	31½	76	UnitrodeCorp (n)	UTR	28⅛	69
Humingbird	HUMCF	29¼	68	BMC Inds (n)	BMC	25⅛	93
Jetform	FORMF	16¼	76	ZilogInc (n)	ZLG	49⅞	93
IntSilSys	ISSS	37¾	40	MISC (18)			
JHnryAssoc	JKHY	14⅝	94	Insilco	INSL	35¾	31
RtnlSoftware	RATL	13⅝	76 †	CentrlSprnklr	CNSP	24½	79
SierraOline	SIER	25	47	Boise Cascde (n)	BCC	40½	76
Synopsys Inc	SNPS	62⅝	98 †	Alliedsgnl (n)	ALD	44½	81 †
HBO & Co	HBOC	54½	97	Intl Paper (n)	IP	85¾	77
CompaqCmp (n)	CPQ	45¼	71	SnapOnInc (n)	SNA	38¾	56
Cognex Corp	CGNX	40¼	[illegible]	[illegible]rline Tch (n)	ESL	22⅝	74
Wonderware	WNDR	[illegible]	[illegible]	[illegible]amp (n)	UCC	57⅞	76
Peak Tech	PEAK	[illegible]	[illegible]	[illegible]ts (n)	TG	[illegible]	[illegible] †
Informix	IF[illegible]	[illegible]	[illegible]	[illegible]	[illegible]	[illegible]	[illegible]

INTERPRETING PRESSURE INDICATORS We should not place too much emphasis on the movement of any single indicator; rather, we should examine a group of similar indicators that might reveal a particular market attribute. For example, the three indicators discussed above reflect a condition of the market that analysts call **breadth.** If the majority of relevant indicators are rising, breadth is considered strong and an upward movement in stock prices should continue. Conversely, weak breadth might point to an eventual weak market.

Breadth: A condition of the stock market revealed by various technical indicators; strong breadth implies a strong market.

For example, many market technicians probably would not regard the increase in the Amex Index from early March to late June as a strong market, even though the index value increased from about 450 to almost 500. Why? Because the advance/decline line may have peaked and is starting down and the relative strength line seems clearly in a downward direction. Breadth is described as "weak," and a negative factor for the market.

Along with the breadth attribute, analysts look at other market attributes. For example, they consider psychological factors to determine if investors are becoming excessively optimistic or pessimistic. So you can read in *Barron's* "Market Watch" section each week investor sentiment readings provided by various data-collection firms. Indeed, *Barron's* is an excellent starting point to increase your familiarity with many technical indicators. You often find graphic analysis there as well.

Graphic Analysis

The expression "A picture is worth a thousand words" is certainly taken to heart by many technical analysts who use graphic analysis in their search for investment opportunities. Actually, to them the graph is far more than a picture; it is a puzzle, and the trick is to find clues for solving the puzzle. We'll discuss several techniques of technical analysis, but we begin with an explanation of graphing methods. Graphs can be constructed in various ways. Today, many technical analysts use computer models to prepare numerous types of graphs. We focus on two relatively simple methods that require nothing more than pencil and paper.

Time graph: A graph showing the price of a stock over time.

TIME GRAPH A **time graph** simply records the price of a stock for each selected period, with daily and weekly recordings being the most popular. Figure 11.9 shows a stock chart for the KFP Company. It is typical of many charts prepared by technical analysts. The top frame shows a time graph using weekly prices over 1995 and 1996, and, as you see, the price ranged from $30 to almost $50. For now, ignore any interpretation of the time graph. The bottom frame in Figure 11.9 shows each period's volume—the number of shares traded. Volume is an important factor to most technical analysts, and most price charts include it. As you see, time graphs are easy to construct. So are point-and-figure graphs, but they need to be explained.

Point-and-figure graph: A graphing method that records only significant price changes.

POINT-AND-FIGURE GRAPH A **point-and-figure graph** is a graphing technique that records only *significant* price changes and ignores trivial changes. The analyst must set the value to determine what is a significant price change, and this value depends upon the price of the stock. You might consider a $1 change significant for a $20 stock but regard it as trivial for a $100 stock; in this case, a $5 change might be considered significant. After determining the significant amount, you then record a change on the graph only when it equals or exceeds that amount.

For example, suppose you select a $15 stock and regard $1 change as significant. The stock may trade from $15 to $16 for several weeks and nothing would be

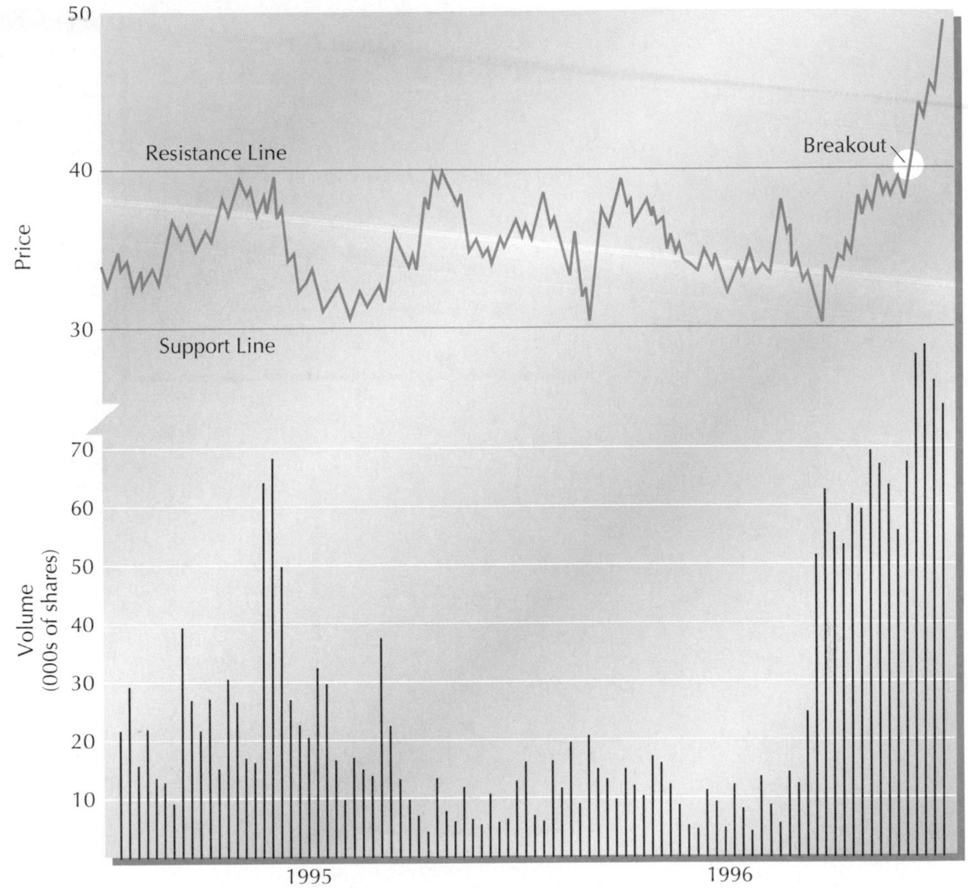

Figure 11.9
A stock chart for KFP Company.

recorded. Suppose then it closes one day at $16.25. You record an *X*, as shown by the illustration in Figure 11.10. *X*s are used to show price increases, and *O*s reflect price decreases. The stock's price continued increasing to $20 a share, requiring four more *X*s. Then it reversed and closed under $19 and continued downward to $17, then rebounded to $21, and so forth. Notice that time is not important in this graph. All the recorded *X*s and *O*s may have taken place over five months or five years.

A point-and-figure graph has the advantage of saving time since you do not record price each period. However, if you set the figure for significance too low, you will make more recordings than are necessary. Finally, most methods of interpreting graphs are the same for both time and point-and-figure graphs.

INTERPRETING GRAPHS Graphic presentations by themselves mean very little, other than being a convenient way to display price data. It's the interpretation of a graph that distinguishes technical analysis from other analytical methods that merely use graphs as pictorial devices. Although there are a variety of interpretation approaches, we consider two popular methods—support and resistance lines and moving averages.

Support and resistance lines. The price time graph in Figure 11.9 features a support line and a resistance line. Notice that KFP's price on several occasions reached

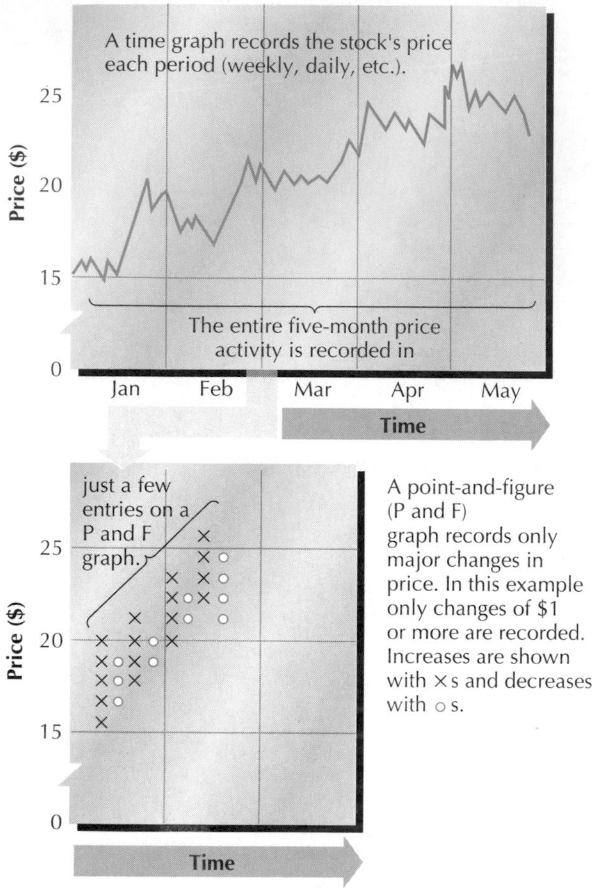
A time graph records the stock's price each period (weekly, daily, etc.).
Price ($)
25
20
15
0
The entire five-month price activity is recorded in
Jan
Feb
Mar
Apr
May
Time
just a few entries on a P and F graph.
Price ($)
25
20
15
0
Time
A point-and-figure (P and F) graph records only major changes in price. In this example only changes of $1 or more are recorded. Increases are shown with ×s and decreases with ○s.

Figure 11.10
Price graphs.

$40 but did not go higher. The analyst then regards $40 as a resistance barrier. Note also that on three occasions the price retreated to $30 a share but went no lower. It is described as "having support" at the $30 price.

After the analysts develop support and resistance lines, they then consider any breakout through a line as being very important. As you see, KFP's price broke the resistance line in late 1996. From a technical perspective, price should continue rising until it reaches a new resistance level. Breaking a resistance line is considered a strong pattern, particularly when it is accompanied by rising volume as is the case for KFP. Conversely, penetrating a support line shows weakness.

It appears relatively simple to do, but construction of support and resistance lines is sometimes not feasible because there are no clear support or resistance prices. There also may be a problem in interpretation if a breakout has occurred. For example, suppose that when KFP's price reached $40 in mid-1996 that instead it went as high as $42 and then pulled back under $40. Would you have known at that time, when it broke through $40, that it was a false breakout? Probably not, and you may have purchased the stock.

Moving average: An averaging technique that is updated by adding a most current value and deleting a least current value.

Moving averages. Perhaps the most popular technical tool is a **moving average,** which is a form of trend line. If you look again at Figure 11.7, you see an example—a 200-day moving average for the Amex Price Index. Constructing a moving average is simple, as shown in Table 11.1, where the daily price of a stock is

Box 11.3 SAVING MONEY
Inexpensive Data Sources

Researching your own stock selections requires data. To avoid the problem of obtaining timely data, many investors rely on newsletters and other advisory services. Apart from the issue of how good these services are, inexpensive they are not. Many cost between $250 and $500 a year. Spread over a $100,000 portfolio, this cost might be insignificant, but many investors have $20,000 or less invested. Now you need to watch your pennies.

There are many excellent data sources available at no or low cost. Most libraries have publications from Value Line, Standard & Poor's, and Moody's, which provide ample financial data for thousands of companies. The only problem is that not all the data are as current as you might like. No problem; ask the reference librarian if *Compact Disclosure* is available on the library's computer system. This source is very easy to use and provides tons of financial information, including earnings-per-share estimates by professional financial analysts and recent trades by company insiders. Although some information from *Disclosure* is very current, it too is not up-to-the-minute in some critical areas.

To have information provided to you as quickly as it is to professional analysts, you need to surf the Net; that is, you must connect to the Internet. Many companies are establishing Web sites (an Internet location—like a phone number) where they make all sorts of information available to the public, including earnings and other financial data. You can read the material on screen, print it, or download it to your computer for any analysis you care to undertake. This area is bound to grow in the future, and the day may come when the SEC requires that all companies provide financial information readily to anyone, not simply to professional financial analysts. The SEC *Edgar System* already provides on the Net data supplied by companies in compliance with securities legislation (10-Ks, 10-Qs, and other documents).

If you can get on the Net, you can access an almost endless number of financial data providers, much of it free. For example, MIT provides price and volume charts for over 600 companies. Several brokerage firms have Net locations that not only provide data but also allow you to trade securities through the Net. Again, this trend is likely to explode in the future. As of now, the Internet appears destined to be the individual investor's best tool. It's important to learn how to use it.

recorded for 14 days. We will construct a five-day moving average, so no average can be calculated for the first four days. On day 5, we add the first five prices for a total of $136, then divide by 5 to get the average price of $27.2. Now, day 6's price of $19 is added to the previous total and day one 1's price of $30 is dropped from it. This gives a new total of $125 and a new average of $25.

TABLE 11.1 • CALCULATING A FIVE-DAY MOVING AVERAGE OF A STOCK'S PRICE

Day	Price	Calculation	Moving Average
1	$30	—	
2	28	—	
3	29	—	
4	27	—	
5	22	(30 + 28 + 29 + 27 + 22)/5 = 136/5 =	$27.2
6	19	(136 – 30 + 19)/5 = 125/5 =	25.0
7	16	(125 – 28 + 16)/5 = 113/5 =	22.6
8	17	(113 – 29 + 17)/5 = 101/5 =	20.2
9	20	(101 – 27 + 20)/5 = 94/5 =	18.8
10	25	(94 – 22 + 25)/5 = 97/5 =	19.4
11	27	(97 – 19 + 27)/5 = 105/5 =	21.0
12	22	(105 – 16 + 22)/5 = 111/5 =	22.2
13	16	(111 – 17 + 16)/5 = 110/5 =	22.0
14	22	(110 – 20 + 22)/5 = 112/5 =	22.4

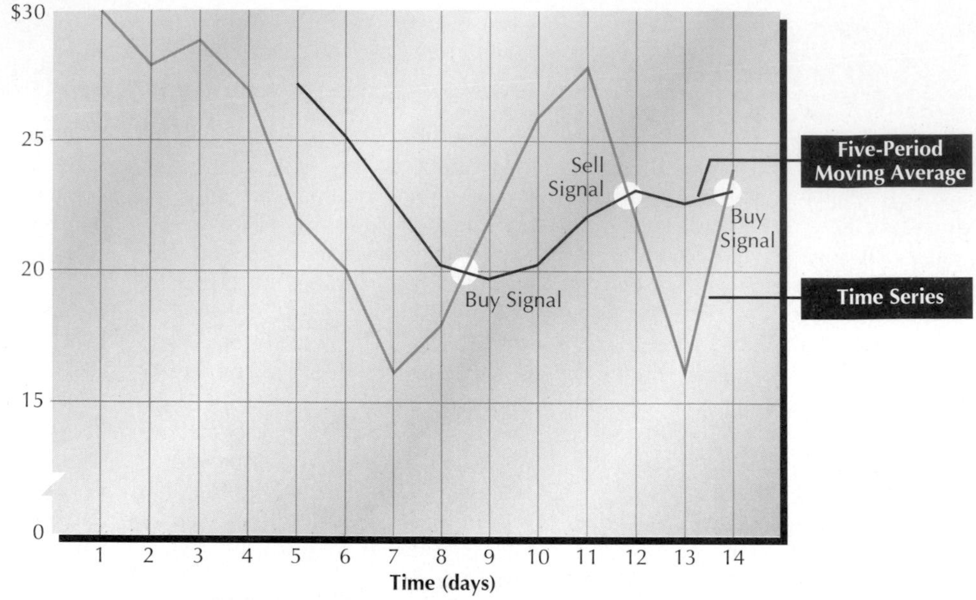

Figure 11.11
Buy and sell signals using a moving average.

The process of dropping the least recent price and adding the most recent is continued each day, so we have a moving average. As you see in Table 11.1, the moving average declines to $18.8 as the stock's price drops and then rebounds when the price rises. When a stock's price is above its moving average, it is in an uptrend, which is considered a strong pattern. The reverse situation is a weak pattern.

Buy and sell signals with moving averages. Many technical analysts compare a stock's price movements with a moving average to determine buy and sell points. An illustration is provided in Figure 11.11, which uses the data from Table 11.1. There are two rules. First, a buy signal is given when the stock's price graph crosses a moving average from below; this occurred twice: at day 8 and at day 14. Second, a sell signal is given when the stock's price graph crosses the moving average from above, which occurred once, at day 12. Following these signals, then, you bought (say, 100 shares) at $20 a share, sold them at $22 a share three days later, and after two days repurchased them at $22 a share.

You made a profit of $200 after 14 days, but commissions will consume most of it. A five-day moving average is too short a time period and it leads to excessive trading, called whiplash. On the other hand, a very long moving average will give signals only after the price of the stock has moved a considerable amount. Most analysts use a variety of moving averages, ranging over various periods of time. Whether they lead to better returns than simply buying and holding a stock is highly debatable, which leads us to a final evaluation of technical analysis.

How Useful Is Technical Analysis?

Can technical analysis pinpoint stocks that might score major price gains in the future? On the surface, the techniques seem impressive, and academic researchers have probed the question for decades. Unfortunately, the consensus conclusion is that they cannot. To be fair, however, we must state that some studies have shown that technical analysis does provide an edge over picking stocks randomly. But, after allowing for commissions, as we suggested above, the edge disappears.

Perhaps the major problem with most technical approaches is that they do not foster a long-run view of investing. Most people have neither the time nor the endurance to "play" the market. Wealth building is much more efficiently accomplished by simply buying an adequately diversified portfolio and holding it. If you prefer to select your own stocks, fundamental analysis should be the more helpful of the two broad methods. But even with it, you should avoid excessive trading. Finally, by all means avoid the hype that many technical newsletters and promoters put forth. Their advertisements are simply outrageous and erroneous. No method will provide the returns they tout; remember, the overall stock market has shown a long-run average return of 10 to 12 percent a year. It's highly unlikely that you will earn 50 to 100 percent in a year, as some ads tout.

SUMMARY

Common stocks represent ownership interests in a company. As an owner, you have the right to vote, a preemptive right, and a right to share in earnings or asset distributions; however, your right to share ranks after similar rights of bondholders and preferred stockholders. The primary type of cash distribution is the regular dividend, but periodic share repurchases also provide cash distributions to common shareholders. Noncash distributions are made in shares of the company's stock and are referred to as stock dividends or stock splits. There are different opportunities with common stock investing, including growth stocks, income stocks, blue chips, cyclical stocks, and special situations.

Fundamental analysis of common stocks determines value by analyzing a company's fundamental strengths and weaknesses. Two widely used analytical methods are the application of the CAPM and a price-to-earnings approach. Fundamental analysis produces a fundamental value for a company's stock, and if this value exceeds the stock's market price the stock is a good buy. Analysts also compare a company's market value with its book value; all things equal, a lower ratio of market to book is preferred to a higher ratio.

Technical analysis uses pressure indicators and graphical analysis to value stocks. Three widely used pressure indicators are the advance/decline line, the relative strength line, and a new highs–new lows ratio. Graphic analysis uses time graphs and point-and-figure graphs. Two methods of graphic interpretation are support and resistance lines and moving averages. Although technical analysis is widely used, there is some question as to its ability to generate returns any better than those with a simple buy-and-hold approach.

KEY TERMS

advance/decline line (p. 317)

blue chip (p. 308)

book value (p. 316)

breadth (p. 320)

common stock (p. 303)

cyclical stocks (p. 308)

earnings per share (EPS) (p. 312)

fundamental value (p. 316)

growth company (p. 307)

income stocks (p. 308)

market-to-book ratio (p. 317)

moving average (p. 322)

new highs–new lows indicator (p. 319)

periodic share repurchases (p. 306)

point-and-figure graph (p. 320)

preemptive right (p. 303)

pressure indicator (p. 317)

price-earnings (P/E) ratio (p. 312)

price-to-earnings analysis (p. 312)

proxy (p. 303)

regular dividend (p. 306)

relative strength line (p. 318)

residual claim (p. 304)

special situation (p. 308)

stock dividend (p. 306)

stock split (p. 306)

technical analysis (p. 317)

time graph (p. 320)

PROBLEMS AND REVIEW QUESTIONS

1. Explain your rights and return potential as a common stockholder, bondholder, or preferred stockholder. Discuss whether one of these is better than the other two.
2. Suppose you and two friends are considering forming a corporation to produce and market computer software programs that each partner has written. Explain whether you think you should be concerned about voting rights and the preemptive right, assuming each shareholder receives 1,000 shares.
3. Magna Corporation has the following securities outstanding: 1,000,000 shares of common stock, 200,000 shares of $2.50 (annual dividend) preferred stock, and $10,000,000 of 15 percent bonds. Calculate earnings per share available to common stockholders if Magna earns:
   (*a*) $5,000,000
   (*b*) $2,200,000
   (*c*) $1,000,000
4. Compare a regular cash dividend with a periodic share repurchase. Which has greater appeal to you? Explain.
5. Explain a stock dividend and further explain if you would prefer it to a cash dividend. What are stock splits, and how desirable are they?
6. Bartholomew Industries' common stock indicates a dividend of $2 a share next year, and its dividend has been growing at an annual rate of 15 percent. If its stock has a current market price of $40 a share, calculate your total expected return on the stock.
7. Bartholomew Industries' (see Question 6) common stock has an estimated beta of 2.2. Assuming you could earn 9 percent on U.S. Treasury securities and the market risk premium is 8 percent, should you buy the stock? Explain, using your answer from Question 6 here.
8. Tartan Corporation has the following 10-year data:

Number of common shares outstanding	1,000,000
Average annual earnings	$2,635,000
Average market price of the common stock	$20/share

   (*a*) Securities analysts think Tartan will earn $5 million next year and have 1,200,000 common shares outstanding. What price do you expect for its common stock next year? Begin your answer by calculating a P/E ratio.
   (*b*) Calculate the market-to-book ratio using your answer to part *a* and assuming a book value of $10 a share.
   (*c*) If the price of Tartan's stock is currently $30 a share, explain if you think it's a good buy.
9. Define the following: pressure indicator, advance/decline line, relative strength line, and new highs–new lows indicator.
10. Suppose that you are following the market and observe that the advance/decline line has been rising, the relative strength line is flat, and the new highs–new lows ratio is falling. How would you rate market breadth, and what is your outlook for the market in the future? Explain.
11. Compare a time graph with a point-and-figure graph.
12. What are support and resistance lines? Explain how they are used to determine when a stock should be bought or sold. What role does volume play in the analysis?
13. Prices for XYZ stock had the following sequence of values beginning with day 1 and ending with day 6: $10, $15, $18, $25, $20, $12. Construct a three-day moving average with values for days 3, 4, and 5. Indicate sell or buy points, if there are any.
14. You heard the following news commentary on television last night: "Milt Davis, Morrel-Lunch's chief technical analyst, noted that IBM broke through its two-year resistance line and could be headed for the $170–$180 area." What do you think Milt is talking about? Explain.
15. The following listing appeared in the financial pages of a local newspaper; explain what it means.

52 weeks									Net
High	Low	Stock	Div	Yld.	P/E	High	Low	Close	Chg.
17¾	7⅛	AAR	.44	3.1	18	14⅛	14	14⅛	+¼

Case 11.1 Ed Driessen's Stock Pick

Ed Driessen is in a management trainee program at Leyton and Leyton Company, a manufacturer of business forms and accounting systems. During his first month on the job (January 1997), Ed was assigned to the sales department to become familiar with its operations. In reviewing customer accounts, Ed happened to notice a substantial increase in orders from Antogen, Inc., a hospital supplies company with diverse interests in that area. Since most of these orders were for invoices, purchase orders, and other forms related to sales, Ed reasoned that Antogen might be on the verge of increasing its sales and profits rapidly. If this were to happen, its common stock might be a very good buy.

Before buying, however, Ed thought it would be a good idea to research the stock at the local library. One day during his lunch hour, he stopped there and gathered some data and made a photocopy of Antogen's price chart. (The data and the chart are shown here.) Ed isn't quite sure how to use all this information, but a friend of his indicated that it shows fairly good performance and that Ed's investment should work out well for him. Ed is ready to buy

DATA FOR ANTOGEN, INC.

Current market price per share: $50
Earnings per share (EPS):
Average annual growth 1987–96: 10%

1996 actual	$3.60
1997 estimated	$4.30
1998 estimated	$5.20

Dividends per share:
Average annual growth 1987–96: 10%

1996 actual	$1.00
1997 estimated	$1.20
1998 estimated	$1.44

Average price/earnings (P/E) ratio:

1987–96	10
1996	12

Current beta estimate: 1.5

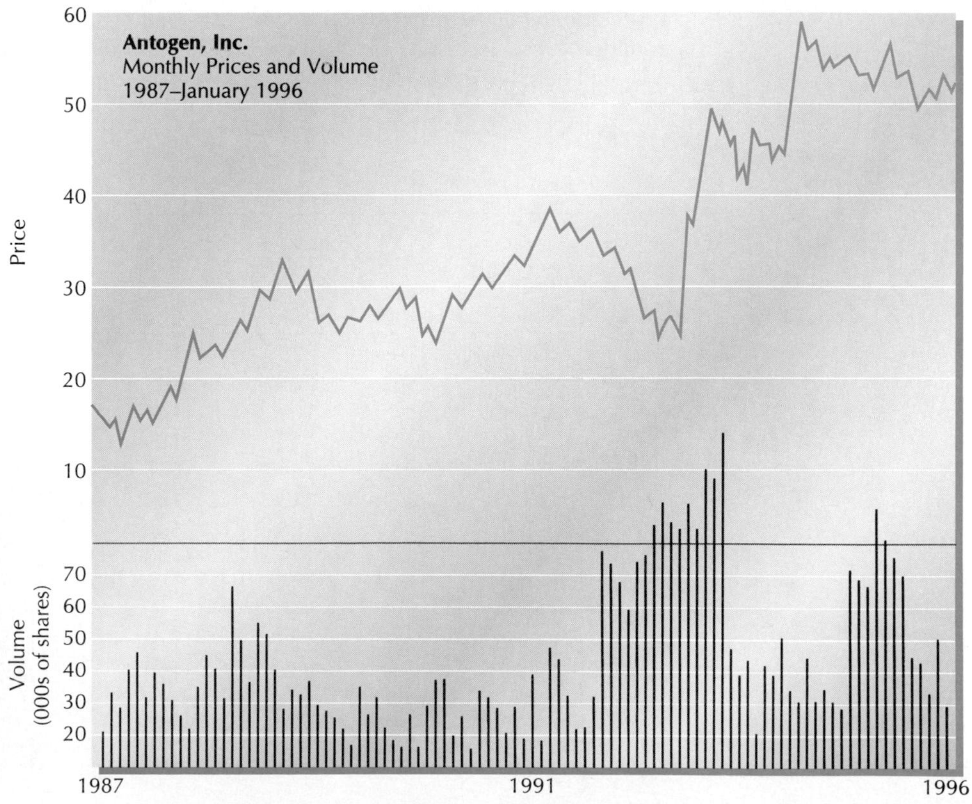

the stock, but would first like your opinion. He is single and has good insurance coverage, and his position with Leyton and Leyton seems very secure and promising for the future.

QUESTIONS

1. Assume that at the time Ed asks your advice, the rate of return on U.S. Treasury securities is 9 percent and that a market risk premium of 8 percent seems appropriate. Using the 1987–1996 dividend growth rate, do you think Ed should buy the stock? Explain your answer. Suppose you use the dividend growth rate indicated for 1997 and 1998 instead of the 1987–1996 rate; what is your answer then? Which rate do you feel is the more appropriate? Explain.
2. Rather than using a dividend approach, suppose you prefer to judge a stock's value by using a price-to-earnings analysis. Based on the available data, does this approach indicate the stock is a good buy? Explain your answer.
3. Does the stock's price chart help you in making a decision? Explain.
4. What do you think of Ed's hunch? Do you feel he has information that might not be available to investors in general? Does the information given suggest that other investors are not aware of Antogen's prospects for growth? Explain.
5. All things considered, do you think Ed should buy the stock? Defend your answer. (Assume that Ed already has adequate diversification.)

Case 11.2 Madge Feeney Wants to Get Technical

Madge Feeney has accumulated about $20,000 and has invested it in various federally insured savings accounts. Her average return last year was 6 percent, an amount that Madge feels is too low to help achieve her goal of having $40,000 in five years. Madge is considering investing in several stocks, and she is particularly interested in WJT Electronics. Madge watches CNBC News regularly and is intrigued by the comments of technical analysts who often appear on the shows. She notes their frequent references to technical indicators, moving averages, support and resistance lines, and others. Lacking any training in the area, she has come to you for help. At your request, she gathered the data appearing below (all values rounded to the nearest whole number), but she has no idea what to make of the information. You will help her by responding to the following questions.

S&P 500 STOCK INDEX DATA

		Number of Stocks with Prices					WJT Data	
					At Yearly			
Day	Index Value	Higher	Lower	No Change	High	Low	Price	Volume (000s)
1	505	110	225	165	12	22	$56	88
2	507	146	205	149	14	15	54	37
3	510	187	169	144	9	14	53	98
4	509	172	143	185	16	9	49	76
5	513	201	144	155	26	9	51	128
6	519	287	113	100	43	8	50	63
7	523	276	88	136	76	7	51	233
8	521	234	133	133	65	9	49	101
9	524	188	155	157	45	10	55	128
10	526	228	233	39	12	13	58	357
11	532	197	193	110	26	18	62	289
12	530	103	281	116	18	26	64	103
13	531	135	304	61	9	45	58	221
14	523	67	341	82	2	87	53	89
15	514	29	303	168	8	56	57	431

QUESTIONS

1. Calculate the ratio of advancing to declining stocks each day and then construct the advance/decline line.
2. Calculate the ratio of the new highs to new lows each day and then construct a new highs–new lows line.
3. Using your work from Questions 1 and 2, discuss how market breadth changed over the period. Also, explain if the indicators helped predict the market's rise and fall over the period.
4. Construct a time graph for WJT, showing both price and volume.
5. Construct a relative strength line, using WJT prices and values for the S&P 500 Index. Discuss WJT's relative strength.
6. Construct a five-day moving average for days 5 through 15. Pinpoint any buy or sell signals. Discuss if "whiplash" is a problem.
7. What is your feeling as to how the market *and* WJT might perform for day 16 and the near future? Discuss, clearly indicating if you think WJT is a good buy.

HELPFUL CONTACTS

Many investors use public or university libraries to access information about specific companies and industries. The advisory services listed below have numerous publications and are particularly useful data sources. Ask a reference librarian for the specific publications carried by the library. Since the publications are expensive, you should try library copies (before considering a purchase) to determine their value to you.

Moody's Investors Service, Inc.
99 Church Street, New York, NY 10007
Comprehensive information for bond and stock investments.

National Association of Securities Dealers
Finance Dept., 9513 Key West Avenue, Rockville, MD 20850
Ask for the *NASDAQ Fact Book and Company Directory,* which provides address, phone number, stock symbol, and one-year price history for many smaller companies.

Standard & Poor's Corporation
825 Broadway, New York, NY 10004
Similar to Moody's; its *Monthly Stock Guide* covers over 5,000 firms. If you use a full-service broker, he or she might give you a copy.

Value Line Publishing, Inc.
711 Third Avenue, New York, NY 10017
Its *Investment Survey* is very popular because of its successful stock ranking system. It also has an excellent publication covering options, warrants, and convertibles.

You can receive a company's annual report by contacting the company directly. Usually, reports are provided by the corporate treasurer's office.

INTERNET ADDRESSES

CompuTEL Securities: The Investor's Internet Toolbox (a really great site, supplying fundamental data and stock charts for many companies; also does option pricing)
http://www.rapidtrade.com/ctframes.htm

MIT StockMaster Stock Charts (provides price and volume charts on 450 stocks)
http://www.ai.mit.edu/stocks/graphs.html

PAWWS: Security APL Quote Server (provides stock quotes and other market information)
http://www.secap/.com/cgi-bin/qs

SEC EDGAR Data Bases (access to all forms that companies must file with the SEC; includes 10-K and 10-Q forms)
http://edgar.stern.myu.edu/tools.shtml

Chapter

12

Fixed-Income Securities: An Important Alternative to Common Stocks

Objectives

1. To understand corporate bondholders' rights and the payment characteristics of corporate bonds
2. To become familiar with bond trading costs and price quotations published in the financial pages of newspapers
3. To identify different types and payment characteristics of U.S. Treasury and U.S. agency securities
4. To recognize different types of municipal bonds and to understand their income tax advantage
5. To know how to calculate a bond's current yield, yield to maturity, and present value
6. To understand default risk and interest rate risk associated with bond investments
7. To become familiar with preferred stock, recognizing its characteristics and investment quality

Fixed-income securities, consisting primarily of bonds and preferred stock, are a popular investment alternative to common stocks. The expression *fixed income* refers to the fact that many bonds pay a fixed amount of interest each year over their entire lives. In contrast, the dividend amount a common stock pays usually depends on the corporation's profits; and, although investors hope the dividend grows over time, very often it remains unchanged or even declines. Fixed-income securities, though, may be just as risky as common stocks in terms of market price volatility—a fact you must learn and respect as a fixed-income investor.

We explain the characteristics of bonds and preferred stocks in this chapter, highlighting the importance of return opportunities and risk drawbacks. Even though you may never invest directly in bonds or preferred stocks, you may have the opportunity to do so through your retirement plan or some other pooling arrangement. That is why it's important to know what you are buying. Bonds usually have a place in investors' portfolios, but knowing what that place is requires serious study.

CORPORATE-ISSUED BONDS

Corporations raise far more money selling bonds to investors than they do selling common stocks. Think of a bond as an IOU: that is, as a piece of paper proclaiming the fact that its issuer acknowledges owing you money and agreeing to repay your loan at some future date along with interest at periodic intervals. This idea seems simple enough, but there are numerous details that must be addressed, particularly with corporate bonds. Figure 12.1 shows an announcement of a bond offering made by Showboat, Inc. We will use it as an example periodically in our discussion.

Your Rights as a Bondholder

Bond indenture: Document accompanying a bond issue—a contract between the issuer and bondholders.

Just as stockholders have certain rights, so do bondholders. Bondholders' rights are described clearly in a document that accompanies each bond issue—the **bond indenture.** The indenture is actually a contract between the issuing institution and the bondholders. In some respects it is similar to a loan agreement you sign when you borrow from a bank. Since it is impossible for the issuer to have an individual contract with each bondholder, the indenture acts as a comprehensive contract covering all bondholders. To see that the issuer lives up to its agreements in the indenture, a trustee (which is usually a large commercial bank) is appointed to represent bondholders.

Protective covenants: Restrictions placed upon a bond issuer designed to strengthen the bondholders' position.

Mortgage bonds: Bonds secured by collateral.

Because of the risk of bankruptcy, many bond indentures contain **protective covenants** (restrictions) to strengthen the bondholders' position. Perhaps the best protection is provided by **mortgage bonds,** which are secured by collateral. In the event of bankruptcy, the bondholders' interest is protected by the pledged property, which does not have to be shared with other creditors or stockholders. Notice in Figure 12.1 that Showboat's bonds are mortgage bonds. Although the announcement doesn't tell us the collateral securing the mortgage, we might guess that it is a steamboat (or steamboats). So, if Showboat goes bankrupt, the bondholders get the boat(s), but what they may be worth is anybody's guess. The bondholders hope they would be worth at least $275 million, the amount they paid for the bonds.

This announcement is neither an offer to sell, nor a solicitation of an offer to buy, any of these securities. The offer is made only by the Prospectus.

New Issue

May 14, 1993

$275,000,000

SHOWBOAT.

Showboat, Inc.

9¼% First Mortgage Bonds due 2008

Price 100%

Copies of the Prospectus may be obtained in any State from such of the undersigned as may legally offer these securities in compliance with the securities laws of such State.

Donaldson, Lufkin & Jenrette
Securities Corporation

Lehman Brothers

Figure 12.1 Announcement of a mortgage bond issue.

Debentures: Bonds not secured by collateral.
Subordinated debentures: Bonds with claims given to other bond issues.

Bonds without supporting collateral are called **debentures,** and there are still other bonds that offer even less protection. These are called **subordinated debentures.** If you buy this kind of bond, your claim to assets in liquidation are subordinated to (meaning they come after) the claims of another issue.

Payment Characteristics of Bonds

Fixed return: A return of a specific dollar amount each year, characteristic of bonds and preferred stock.
Face value: An amount for which a bond is redeemed at maturity.

Regardless of who issues them, bonds have many similar characteristics. The most important of these is the **fixed return.** Let's look at the return components in greater detail.

FACE VALUE The **face value** of a bond is the amount for which the issuer agrees to redeem the bond at its maturity. When a bond is issued, it has a set life; for example, a 25-year bond means the bond will not be redeemed by its issuer until 25 years after the date it is issued. Showboat's bonds had a 15-year life when they were issued in May 1993. In effect, bondholders lent money to Showboat and are not asking for repayment of the loan until 15 years later. This probably seems like a long time to you, and it is; but many bonds are issued with maturities this long and longer. However, many have shorter maturities, and issuers frequently stagger bond maturities to accommodate the many different needs of potential investors.

Practically all corporate bonds sold to the public have the same face value—$1,000—although some (mostly those issued by various governments) have higher face values. When a bond series is issued, the issuer attempts to adjust its interest rate so that it can be sold *at par,* which means it is sold at the face value. However, bonds issued in the past and currently traded on bond markets may have market prices completely different from their face values, because interest rates may have increased or decreased since their issuance.

Coupon bonds: Bonds that pay periodic interest.

Coupon rate: Stated interest rate on a bond.

SEMIANNUAL INTEREST PAYMENTS Most bonds pay interest twice a year and are referred to as **coupon bonds.** The amount of interest you receive is stated on the bond and expressed as a percentage of par value. For example, a 12 percent bond pays $120 a year ($1,000 × 0.12) in interest, or $60 each six months. Showboat's bond pays 9.25 percent interest, or $92.50 a year. This rate is often called the **coupon rate.** This term is a carry-over from the past, when most bonds were coupon bonds and you received interest by clipping coupons from the bond and presenting them to a bank for payment. Since all corporate bonds now are registered, rather than coupon bonds, the interest checks come directly to you, or to your broker if your certificates are held at a firm.

Box 12.1

PERSONAL FINANCE NEWS

Late Edition

Making a Strong Case for Bonds

Traditionally, investors bought bonds because they were safer than stocks and offered a steady income—just what you want for retirement. Those are good reasons and they still apply. But, many investors don't fully appreciate that bonds have other qualities enhancing their appeal. They're not just for old folks anymore.

First, recently bond returns have been very good, often matching stock returns. Most investors know that stocks really boomed from 1982 through 1991, offering an average annual return of almost 15 percent; few realize that corporate bonds did practically as well, with a return of 13.7 percent. Indeed, the difference in returns—the "spread"—has averaged around 2.5 percent in recent years, a figure much lower than its very long-run average of 5 percent.

Second, bond returns are poorly correlated to stock returns. The correlation was strong during the 1980s, when inflation was being wrenched out of the economy, helping both stocks and bonds, but over a longer sweep of history return correlations have been quite low. That's good, because a portfolio invested in both stocks and bonds will show less value volatility than if all your money is in one or the other.

Third, and most important, bonds are unquestionably the investment of choice in a deflating economy because bond returns thrive on recessions and falling prices. During the 1930s, the average annual return on bonds was 5 percent, while stocks averaged 0 percent. Earning 5 percent a year with no inflation is very good. We're hearing more talk these days that our economy is gradually deflating and that persistent high inflation, a major fear of the 40–60-year-old generation, is a thing of the past.

Finally, your bond investments should not be short term, or you are simply speculating on interest rate movements. Holding bonds, though, can often try your patience and stimulate an overproduction of stomach acid. Bond losses were extensive in 1994—the second worst year for long-term Treasury bonds over the 1926–1994 period (loss of 7.6 percent)—but by mid-1995 all the losses were recouped and bonds were on their way to an excellent year. If you invest in bonds, stay the course.

Zero coupon bond: A bond that pays no periodic interest; all interest is earned at the bond's redemption.

ZERO COUPON BONDS A **zero coupon bond** (zero, for short) is a bond that pays no semiannual interest; you earn interest by buying the bond at less than face value and receiving face value at redemption. For example, you buy a bond for $940 today and have it redeemed for $1,000 one year later. The interest earned is $60 in this case, and the percentage return (yield) is 6.383 percent ([$60/$940] × 100). Zero coupon bonds have increased considerably in popularity in recent years, primarily because investors like to hold them for retirement funds.

Zeros are issued in a wide array of maturities, some as long as 40 years. For any given yield, the longer a bond's maturity the bigger the difference between its price and its redemption value, called the *discount*. So, a two-year zero with a 6.38 percent yield would have a price of $883.60 and a discount of $116.40 ($1,000.00 – $883.60). We'll discuss valuation methods for both coupon bonds and zeros more fully later in this chapter.

Retirement Methods

Although many bond issues have long maturities, in reality most such bonds are retired (terminated) long before their maturity dates. There are three retirement methods: redemption at maturity or by a call from the issuer, through the operation of a sinking fund, or with a conversion of the bond into shares of the issuer's common stock.

REDEMPTION AT MATURITY OR EARLIER As mentioned above, the issuer agrees to redeem your bond at its maturity. However, many corporate bonds (and some government bonds) can be redeemed earlier at the discretion of the issuer. These **callable bonds** allow the issuer an earlier redemption, and such redemption usually takes place at a price above face value. For example, a bond may be callable at $1,100. Corporations attach calls to bonds to give them greater flexibility in future financing. It might be necessary to raise capital even in periods when interest rates are very high; therefore, a corporation might sell bonds yielding, say, 12 percent. Interest rates might then fall, and the corporation could sell similar bonds and pay interest of only 8 percent. Naturally, it would like to do this, and the call feature allows it to. It issues 8 percent bonds and uses the proceeds to redeem the 12 percent bonds. What's good for the corporation, though, isn't good for you. You may have thought that you would receive 12 percent for 20 years, but the bond is redeemed at the end of two years. That is why callable bonds yield more than noncallable bonds and why you should look closely for a call feature on any bond you are considering buying.

Callable bonds: Bonds that can be redeemed before their maturities.

Sinking fund: A system for gradual retirement of a bond issue.

SINKING FUNDS Another retirement method involves the use of a **sinking fund,** which consists of reserving funds for the purpose of gradually retiring bonds before their maturity. Most sinking funds operate through a plan stipulating that a portion of the bonds in a bond issue be retired each year. For example, Showboat's bonds have a 15-year life (issued in 1993 and redeemable in 2008); so, a sinking fund might require that 1/15 of the issue be retired annually. This gradual retirement of an issue provides greater safety to bondholders as opposed to having all the bonds redeemable at one time. Finally, in retiring each year's portion of the bond issue, sinking funds' managers may use the call provision explained above or they might simply buy the bonds in the bond market.

Convertible bond: Bond that can be converted into shares of the issuer's common stock.

Conversion value: The value of a bond as determined by the value of the common stock into which the bond can be converted.

THE CONVERTIBLE FEATURE A particularly attractive bond to potential common stock investors is the convertible bond. A **convertible bond** may be redeemed, but it may also be converted into shares of the issuing corporation's common stock. For example, Ashland Oil (an integrated energy company) has a convertible bond that allows you to exchange one bond for 19.5 shares of its common stock. The bond pays 6.75 percent annual interest on its face value. Suppose you paid $1,000 for this bond; is it a good investment? It could be, but much depends upon the price of Ashland's common stock. Suppose the stock is selling for $40 a share; then the bond's value as common stock—its **conversion value**—is $780 ($40 × 19.5), which is less than the $1,000 you paid for it. And since you could get a 7 percent yield on Treasury bonds at the time you were getting 6.75 percent on the Ashland bond, you might think it is a poor investment. But suppose Ashland's common stock increases to $80 a share: Now the bond is worth at least $1,560 ($80 × 19.5). You should see from this example that convertible bonds are quite different from conventional bonds. They offer potentially higher returns by virtue of their conversion privilege, but they are also riskier. Also, it takes a specialized skill to determine the investment quality of convertibles, so it is a good idea to work with a professional if you are interested in buying them.

Investing in Corporate Bonds

After you have a reasonable understanding of bond valuation techniques, you might decide to be a corporate bond investor. At this point, you must become familiar with the mechanics of making your investments. Having the skill to read bond quotations is a must, and understanding the commission setup is important.

READING CORPORATE BOND PRICE QUOTATIONS Figure 12.2 illustrates three bond price quotations as they often appear in the financial section of many newspapers. The explanations in Figure 12.2 should not need more comment here; however, notice that, on the Office Depot bond, there is a substantial discount of $490 ($1,000 – $510), which is explainable by its rather distant redemption date in the year 2007. Notice too, for the Navistar bond, the rather large increase in price ($16.25), based on its closing price of $875; the percentage change in price is almost 1.9 percent ([$16.25/$875] × 10). This matches the daily price volatility of many common stocks and illustrates the potential price risk of bond investments.

TRADING COSTS The cost to trade corporate bonds can be quite high. First, you typically buy bonds through a stockbrokerage firm and, of course, pay a commission. The amount varies from one firm to the next, but expect to pay a cost of $25 to $40 per bond if you buy one bond. The cost per bond goes down substantially if you increase the size of your order. An order to buy five of the Navistar bonds shown in Figure 12.2 might involve a commission of $100, or $20 a bond. On the basis of the bond's closing price of $875, the commission rate is 2.29 percent ([$25/$875] × 100). This might not seem too high, but there is another cost to consider.

Most securities, including bonds, are traded in the market at bid and asked prices. A bid price is the highest price a buyer is willing to pay to buy a bond; the asked price is the lowest price a seller will take to sell it. The asked price is always higher than the bid price, and the difference is called the *spread*. So if you buy a bond, you will pay the asked price, but you receive only the bid price when you

Corporate bond prices are reported in the financial pages of many newspapers. Typical listings and explanations are shown below. Quotations were in mid-April 1993.

Bond			Cur Yld	Vol	Close	Net Chg
Mead	6¾	12	cv.	51	100½	−½
Nav Str	9	04	10.3	245	87½	+1⅝
Off Dep	Zr	07	—	40	51	+⅛
(1)	(2)	(3)	(4)	(5)	(6)	(7)

(1) Name of the issuer: Nav Str is Navistar and Off Dep is Office Depot.
(2) Coupon rate of interest: 6¾ tells us the bond pays $67.50 a year interest. Zr means a zero coupon bond.
(3) The year the bond matures: Mead's bond matures in 2012.
(4) *Cur Yld* means the bond's current yield: Navistar's current yield of 10.3% is determined by dividing the annual interest of $90 by the bond's closing price of $875. The symbol *cv.* in the Cur Yld column tells us the bond is a convertible, and current yields are not calculated for convertibles.
(5) *Vol* means the number of bonds traded: 51 Mead bonds traded on the day being reported.
(6) *Close* is the last price the bond traded at during the day: Mead's closing price is 100½. This reported price is 1/10 the actual price; to get the actual price, you must multiply the reported price by 10:

$$\begin{aligned} \text{actual price} &= 10 \times \text{reported price} \\ &= 10 \times 100\tfrac{1}{2} \\ &= 10 \times 100.5 \\ &= 1{,}005 \end{aligned}$$

(7) *Net Chg* means the difference between the closing price of the day being reported and the closing price of the previous day: Navistar's price increased (+) by 1⅝, which means the price was up $16.25 (10 × 1⅝ = 10 × 1.625 = 16.25) for the day.

Figure 12.2 Reading corporate bond price quotations.

sell. The trouble with bonds is that the spread often is large, sometimes as much as $50 per bond. Obviously, the spread adds to your trading cost and certainly discourages frequent trading. As with common stocks, if you invest in bonds you should have a long investment horizon.

POOLING ARRANGEMENTS MAY BE BEST Along with the potential for high trading costs, bond investors must constantly be on guard to determine if their bonds have been called. Failing to meet a call does not mean you lose the value of your bond but it does mean that you lose any interest payments that were scheduled to be made after the call date. For example, suppose Navistar called its bonds on June 30, 1997. Suppose further that the interest payment dates were June 15 and December 15. For whatever reason, you missed the call on June 30 and did not realize it until January 5, 1998. Navistar will still redeem your bond at the call price, but it will not make the December 15, 1997, interest payment that you thought was owed you. This oversight problem is even more serious with zero coupon bonds because there is no periodic interest payment whose omission might alert us to a call.

All things considered, investing in bonds should perhaps be left to investment professionals. Not only can they operate with much smaller trading costs and follow individual bond issues more closely, but they also are able to diversify far more effectively. We are better off by simply investing in a mutual fund, or other pooling arrangement, that invests in bonds. We'll cover these investment vehicles in the next chapter.

GOVERNMENT-ISSUED BONDS

As noted earlier, corporations raise huge sums of money each year by selling bonds, but government units raise even more. You have heard of the national debt, which as of this writing stands at about $3.6 trillion (about $15,000 for every U.S. citizen!) and which grows by about $200 billion each year. On top of this huge amount, state and local governments add about $150 billion of new debt each year. As a citizen, you might oppose these annual deficits, but as an investor you might feel very comfortable owning the debt instruments the deficits create. We discuss the variety of government-issued bonds in the following sections.

U.S. Treasury Securities

U.S. Treasury securities are the most popular investment vehicles in the world. They are owned by investors throughout all parts of the world and are actively traded 24 hours a day. Treasury securities are issued in three forms: Treasury bills, with maturities of one year or less; Treasury notes, with maturities from 2 to 10

Box 12.2 SIMPLIFYING FINANCIAL PLANNING
Buy Treasuries Directly

Investors throughout the world consider U.S. Treasury-issued securities the bedrock of safety. Actually, from a safety perspective a Treasury security is the same as currency itself; the major difference is that one pays interest and the other does not. Despite the advantages, unfortunately, small investors seldom buy Treasuries, primarily because they are unaware of how easy it is.

That might change in the future, though, since buying Treasuries now can be done directly through the Treasury, eliminating the middleman and the usual buy/sell commissions. Over 1 million Americans are currently using the Treasury Direct program, and the number is growing rapidly.

It's simple to sign up: Get an application form from the nearest Federal Reserve Bank or one of its branches. Fill out the form, being careful to include your Social Security number and your bank's nine-digit "routing transit" number (call your bank if you aren't sure of the number).

Treasuries are sold at auctions, and you must be sure to submit the application before the auction day. Information about upcoming auctions will be available at the Federal Reserve bank. Your application is referred to as a "noncompetitive tender," which means that you agree to accept the average yield that arises from competitive bidding at the auction.

After the purchase you now have a Treasury Direct account. Interest paid on the securities each six months will be forwarded to your bank, as will the redemption of the securities at their maturity. What could be easier? Finally, a brief summary of Treasury securities is shown below.

Security Name	Maturity	Minimum Investment	Interest Information
U.S. Treasury bills	Up to 1 year	$10,000 (cashier's check)	Interest is earned via a discount from $10,000
U.S. Treasury notes	2–10 years	$1,000–$5,000 (personal check)	Interest is paid semiannually
U.S. Treasury bonds	10–30 years	$1,000 (personal check)	Interest is paid semiannually

years; and Treasury bonds, with maturities from 10 to 30 years. Treasury bills are held for liquidity purposes as discussed in Chapter 3, so we will focus on bonds and notes. Also, the term *Treasury bonds* (T-bonds, for short, or simply Treasuries) is often used to describe both notes and bonds, and we will make no distinction between the two in our discussion. With the exception of maturity, notes and bonds are identical.

T-BOND PAYMENTS T-bonds are issued only in coupon form and they pay semiannual interest. As with corporate bonds, par value is $1,000 and interest payments depend on the coupon rate. For example, an 8 percent bond pays $40 interest each six-month period. Since T-bonds have no default risk, their yields always are lower than all other comparable-maturity bonds. Table 12.1 shows a variety of bond yields in 1995 and 1994 and, as you see, Treasuries' yields are the lowest in each year with the exception of municipal bond yields. An income tax advantage explains this oddity, and we'll discuss it later.

The yield disadvantage with T-bonds is usually not trivial. For example, the difference at mid-1995 between high-quality corporate bonds and Treasuries was 0.74 percent (7.24 percent – 6.50 percent). Each 1/100 of a percentage point is called a **basis point (bp),** so the difference was 74 bp. That may not seem like much, but many bond investors often have huge sums invested. On $1 million—a moderate-sized investment for many investors—a difference of 74 bp is $7,400. Since high-quality corporate bonds have very little default risk, this differential is like "found money." Why, then, does anyone invest in Treasuries? Actually, they appeal to investors with extremely low risk tolerances who want the Treasuries' safety. These investors look at the $7,400 as rather inexpensive insurance guaranteeing their $1 million investment, rather than as "lost money."

Basis point (bp): 1/100 of a percentage point.

U.S. TREASURY STRIPS Although the Treasury does not issue zero coupon bonds, it provides a mechanism that allows large brokerage firms to create such bonds, and these are called **U.S. Treasury Strips** (STRIPS, for short). The creation process is somewhat involved and of little concern to investors; however, they are indeed concerned that STRIPS also be free of default risk. And they are. As with zero coupon corporate bonds, but to a much greater extent, Treasury Strips are an appealing vehicle for retirement investments.

U.S. Treasury Strips: Zero coupon bonds derived from U.S. Treasury coupon bonds.

U.S. TREASURY INFLATION-INDEXED BONDS In mid-May 1996, the Treasury announced that it intended to issue a new class of bonds, called **inflation-indexed Treasury bonds,** with the first issue coming to market by year end. This new bond is truly unique in that its redemption value will be adjusted each year to keep pace with inflation. For example, assume that on January 2, 1997, you bought one of the new bonds at its face value of $1,000. Suppose, then, that inflation for 1997

Inflation-indexed Treasury bonds: Bonds issued by the U.S. Treasury with redemption values that are adjusted each year for inflation.

TABLE 12.1 • VARIOUS BOND YIELDS AT MID-JULY 1995 AND 1994

Type of Bond	1995	1994
Corporate bonds: best quality	7.24%	8.03%
medium quality	7.44	8.72
U.S. Treasury bonds	6.50	7.80
Mortgage-backed agency bonds	7.40	8.40
General obligation municipal bonds	5.91	6.27

is determined to be 3 percent; then the redemption value of the bond is adjusted upwards to $1,030. Such an adjustment would occur each year until the bond's maturity. So, if inflation was 10 percent in 1998, the bond's redemption value would be increased to $1,133 (1.10 × $1,030).

The final details on the new bonds were not available as of this writing, but many analysts believe the bonds will be extremely popular with long-term investors. The assurance that your investment's value will not be ravaged by inflation over time is clearly an advantage over traditional bonds with fixed redemption amounts. But, of course, there is a catch: The inflation-indexed bonds will certainly offer lower coupon interest payments than conventional Treasuries. The extent of the difference cannot be determined until the new bonds begin trading in the bond market, but analysts believe the differential could be as much as 1.0 to 1.5 percent. So, if a conventional Treasury offers 7 percent, an inflation-indexed Treasury with the same maturity might yield 5.5 to 6.0 percent.

READING TREASURIES' QUOTATIONS Treasuries, including STRIPS, are reported in the financial pages of many newspapers, and quotations of coupon bonds are illustrated in Figure 12.3. Although Treasuries are free of default risk, they certainly are *not* free of price risk. Indeed, the price volatility of many T-bonds equals and exceeds that of corporate bonds.

Notice the yield figure provided for each bond: 5.23 percent for the first bond, for example. This yield—called yield to maturity—is different from the current yield reported for corporate bonds. Each will be explained shortly.

Figure 12.3 does not show a STRIP. STRIP prices are reported in the same fashion, but they may be much smaller. For example, a STRIP with the same maturity and yield as the third bond in Figure 12.3 (Aug 22) would have a quoted price of 12:28, which equals $128.75 ([28/32 + 12] × 10). So you get $1,000 back for each $128.75

Figure 12.3 Reading Treasury notes and bonds quotations.

Rate	Maturity	Bid	Asked	Bid Change	Yield
9	May 98n	106:30	106:32	+6	5.23
15 3/4	Nov 01	161:10	161:14	+4	6.48
7 1/4	Aug 22	98:29	98:31	+2	7.34
(1)	(2)	(3)	(4)	(5)	(6)

(1) *Rate* refers to the coupon rate. Notice the high coupon rate of 15 3/4 percent for the second bond; this bond was issued many years ago when interest rates were high.

(2) *Maturity* refers to the month and year when the bond matures; the first bond matures in May 1998. The symbol *n* indicates a note rather than a bond.

(3) *Bid* is the highest price bond dealers were offering to buy the bond. Fractional parts are thirty-seconds, and actual prices are 10 times the quotation. Thus, the second bond's bid price is $1,613.13 ([161 + 10/32] × 10).

(4) *Asked* is the lowest price dealers were accepting.

(5) *Bid Change* shows the difference between the bid price on the quotation day and the bid price of the previous day. The change of +6 points for the first bond means its bid price was up $1.88 (6/32 × 10).

(6) *Yield* means yield to maturity. Notice that the first two securities have coupon rates higher than their yields, so they are selling at premiums to face value. In contrast, the third security is selling at a yield slightly higher than its coupon rate, so it is selling at a discount.

you invest (the discount is $871.25), if you hold the bond until its maturity in the year 2022.

U.S. Agency Bonds

Agency bonds: Bonds issued by agencies of the federal government other than the Treasury.

Agencies of the federal government besides the Treasury also issue notes and bonds, which are referred to as **agency bonds.** There are two types of agency bonds—those that are virtually identical to Treasury bonds and those related to mortgage and other forms of lending. The former are referred to as conventional agency bonds, and the latter are called mortgage-backed bonds.

CONVENTIONAL AGENCY BONDS Conventional agency bonds have the same features as coupon Treasury bonds, and their prices are also reported in the financial pages. Although considered by most investors to be also free of default risk, these bonds usually offer a slightly higher yield. The difference is explained by poorer liquidity in the sense that there is less trading of agency bonds and greater bid-asked price spreads. Investors who do not trade bonds frequently perhaps can ignore this lack of liquidity and go for agencies' better yields.

MORTGAGE-BACKED BONDS Certain agencies of the federal government are involved in the credit industry. For example, you may buy a home and finance it with a mortgage loan from a local bank. Although you may never know it, the bank might sell the mortgage to the Government National Mortgage Association (GNMA), which buys many similar loans and holds them in what is called a "pool." GNMA then issues bonds to investors on the basis of the payments being collected in the pool. The cash collected by the pool is distributed (said to be "passed through") to the investors; in this fashion, the bonds are supported by the mortgages and so are called **mortgage-backed bonds.** Such bonds issued by the GNMA are called "Ginnie Maes." Although not a mortgage loan, your student loan has probably been sold by the lending bank to the Student Loan Marketing Association, which creates bonds (called "Sallie Maes") that are supported by pools of student loans.

Mortgage-backed bonds: Agency bonds that "pass through" interest and principal payments from a pool of mortgages.

Ginnie Maes and other similar mortgage-backed bonds are quite different from Treasury and conventional agency bonds. First, you are paid monthly, rather than semiannually, and the payment consists of both interest and principal, rather than interest alone. Remember, the agency is passing through payments made by mortgage borrowers. Second and much more important, your investment is greatly influenced by changes in mortgage rates. For example, when these rates decline substantially, homeowners who owe money on their mortgages refinance their homes. This means that the old mortgage, the one you own indirectly, is paid off, which is undesirable, because you had hoped your Ginnie Mae would pay a good rate of interest for a long time; unfortunately, it will not because of the refinancing.

The potential of an early payoff adds an element of risk that investors expect compensation for carrying when they buy such bonds. As Table 12.1 shows, they are rewarded with higher yields. As you see, mortgage-backed securities offered 90 basis points more than Treasuries in 1995 (7.4 percent – 6.5 percent) and 60 basis points more in 1994 (8.4 percent – 7.8 percent). The complexities of mortgage-backed bonds offer a strong incentive to invest in them through a mutual fund rather than on your own.

Municipal Bonds

Municipal bonds: Bonds issued by state and local governments.

Municipal bonds (referred to as munis) are bonds issued by state and local governmental units to finance their capital spending programs. An average of about $200 billion of municipal bonds are issued each year, and they are very popular with investors in high tax brackets.

General obligation (GO) bond: A municipal bond supported by the full taxing authority of the issuing governmental unit.

Revenue bond: A municipal bond supported by the revenues of a particular project.

TYPES OF MUNICIPAL BONDS If a muni bond issue is supported by the full taxing authority of the issuing governmental unit, it is a **general obligation (GO) bond;** if it is supported only by the revenues that a particular capital project generates, it is a **revenue bond.** In general, GO bonds offer better protection than revenue bonds and therefore are safer investments. As you might guess, GO bond yields, such as those shown in Table 12.1, are a bit lower than revenue bonds.

Munis are issued in coupon and zero coupon form with face values usually $5,000. You should realize that munis can have default risk even though they are issued by a government. At this writing, the government of Orange County, California (one of the richest counties in the United States), is in effect bankrupt and might default on its bond obligations. Diversification is a must, providing yet another strong case for bond investing through mutual funds.

Pre-tax equivalent yield: A pre-tax yield a taxable bond must offer to have the same after-tax yield as a municipal bond.

THE INCOME TAX ADVANTAGE Any interest received from a municipal bond is free of federal income tax. This is a major advantage for munis versus taxable bonds. The muni yields in Table 12.1 are the lowest of all shown. However, to put them on a comparable footing with the other bond yields, you need to adjust for the income tax differential. To do this, we calculate a muni's **pre-tax equivalent yield,** which is the yield a taxable bond must offer before taxes to have the same after-tax yield as the muni. The pre-tax equivalent yield (*PTEY*), considering an investor's marginal tax rate (*MTR*), is calculated as follows:

$$PTEY = \frac{\text{muni yield}}{1.0 - MTR}$$

So the 5.91 percent muni yield in 1995 has the pre-tax equivalent yield of 8.21 percent (5.91%/[1.0 − 0.28] = 5.91%/0.72). A similar calculation for 1994 provides 8.71 percent (6.27%/0.72). When adjusted for taxes, the muni yields in Table 12.1 are the highest each year.

The advantage is even better for investors in higher tax brackets. For example, someone in the 39.6 percent bracket had a PTEY of 9.79 percent (5.91%/[1.0 − 0.396] = 5.91/0.604) in 1995. This yield is so good in comparison with the others in Table 12.1 that you might wonder why investors in the top tax bracket invest anywhere else. Your curiosity is well founded, and, indeed, many wealthy investors confine much of their investing to municipal bonds. There is a risk, though; Congress may pass new tax laws that reduce marginal tax rates on income or may seek a whole new tax base such as a national sales tax. Discussions in Congress of both of these topics in 1995 put a damper on the muni bond market.

RETURN AND RISK CHARACTERISTICS OF BONDS

Clearly, there are reasons why bond investment is so popular. Although young people tend to favor common stocks, seeking their long-term growth, other investors are drawn to the more certain cash payments bonds offer. But there is substantial risk in bond investing, and informed investors of all ages must understand its sources and how it operates. The sections below explain both return and risk characteristics of bonds.

Expected Return from Bonds

If you bought a bond at its face value when it was issued and eventually redeemed it at its face value, then your return would consist exclusively of the semiannual interest payments you would receive each year. The above situation may not happen, however. You may buy the bond for more or less than its face value; doing that leads to a capital loss or gain if you hold it to maturity. Or you may sell the bond before maturity, and the price you receive will probably be different—perhaps quite different—from your purchase price. Therefore, just as with common stocks, a bond's return may consist of both a current return and a future return. Each must be considered in evaluating investment performance.

Current yield: A bond's annual interest divided by its market price.

CURRENT RETURN OR CURRENT YIELD The current return with a bond comes from the semiannual interest payments. This is often expressed in percentage form and is called the **current yield.** To calculate the current yield, all you need to do is divide the annual interest by the current market price of the bond. Suppose you have a bond that pays \$120 a year interest: If its current market price is \$1,000, then its current yield is 12 percent (\$120/\$1,000). If its price if \$900, its current yield will be 13.3 percent (\$120/\$900). The formula is

$$\text{Current yield} = \frac{\$I}{\$P}$$

where

I = annual interest
P = current market price

If you refer to Figure 12.2 you will notice that current yields are reported for corporate bonds. Although that information is helpful, you usually want to know more about a bond's return than the current yield. You also want to determine its yield to maturity.

Yield to maturity: A yield measurement that considers a bond's annual interest plus price appreciation or depreciation if the bond is held to maturity.

YIELD TO MATURITY In addition to current yield, bond investors often are interested in a bond's **yield to maturity,** which may differ from current yield. A yield to maturity is the return you would earn by buying a bond today and holding it until it is redeemed by the issuer. A precise calculation of yield to maturity requires the use of a financial calculator, but a close approximation is possible using the following formula:

$$\text{Yield to maturity} = \frac{\$I + (\$1,000 - \$P)/N}{(\$P + \$1,000)/2}$$

where

I = annual interest
P = current market price
N = number of years remaining to maturity

It is assumed that the bond has a face value of $1,000. Let us return to the bond mentioned above and assume that its market price is $900 and that it has five years to maturity. Its yield to maturity is 14.7 percent, as calculated below:

$$\frac{\$120 + (\$1{,}000 - \$900)/5}{(\$900 + \$1{,}000)/2} = \frac{\$140}{\$950} = 0.147, \text{ or } 14.7\%$$

PRESENT VALUE OF A COUPON BOND Bond investors often determine a bond's present value. This task is performed quickly with a financial calculator, but it can also be accomplished with present value tables. Recall from Chapter 1 that a present value is simply a discounted future value. To review, if you expected to receive $1,000 one year from today, and if you felt you could earn 10 percent interest on your money, then the $1,000 has a present value of $909.10. You find this amount by multiplying the future value by the present-value-of-$1 factor from Table A.3 in Appendix A. Referring to that table, go to the 10 percent column and the period 1 row; you read 0.9091, and 0.9091 × $1,000 = $909.10.

Remember that discounting is simply the opposite of compounding. So if you invested $909.10 today to earn 10 percent for one year, your accumulation (compounded value) is $1,000 ($909.10 × 1.10 = $1,000).

Table 12.2 shows the present value calculation for the five-year coupon bond we are discussing, using a 15 percent interest rate. The bond has a present value of $899.46, which is approximately its price of $900. Notice that the bond provides two sources of cash inflow: (1) the annual interest of $120 for five years and (2) the $1,000 redemption value at the end of the fifth year. For simplicity, we assume that the bond pays annual, rather than semiannual, interest. Also, interest is assumed to be paid at the end of each year.

A QUICKER METHOD FOR FINDING PRESENT VALUE Table 12.2 is used to illustrate the process of finding a coupon bond's present value. However, there is a quicker solution that uses the present-value-of-$1-annuity table (Table A.4 in Appendix A). There are two operations. First, from Table A.4 find the present value of $1 annuity for 15 percent and 5 years; it is 3.3522. Multiply this number by the annual interest to find the present value of the coupon interest cash inflows—$402.26 (3.3522 × $120). Second, find the present value of the future redemption value, which has already been done in Table 12.2. The value is $497.20. Add the two present values to

TABLE 12.2 • FINDING THE PRESENT VALUE OF A BOND

Year	Cash Inflow to Investor		PV of $1 Factor ($i$ = 15%)*	Present Value of the Cash Inflow
1	Interest	$ 120	0.8696	$104.35
2	Interest	120	0.7561	90.73
3	Interest	120	0.6575	78.90
4	Interest	120	0.5718	68.62
5	Interest	120	0.4972	59.66
5	Redemption	1,000	0.4972	497.20
			Bond's present value = total =	$899.46

*PV of $1 factors are found in Table A.3 in Appendix A. Look in the 15 percent column.

arrive at the total present value of $899.46. This quicker method is very desirable if you are examining bonds with long maturities.

PRESENT VALUE OF A ZERO COUPON BOND Finding the present value of a zero coupon bond is very simple since there are no coupon interest payments to consider. The only cash inflow to discount is the future redemption value of $1,000. For example, the present value of a five-year zero discounted at 15 percent is $497.20. Once again, you find this value in Table 12.2.

PRESENT VALUE AND YIELD TO MATURITY If the bond's cash inflows are discounted by the bond's yield to maturity, the present value is the same as the bond's price. Indeed, the yield to maturity should be viewed as the precise discount rate that equates a bond's price to the sum of its discounted future cash flows. For most practical purposes, 15 percent can be considered the true yield to maturity on the coupon bond since $899.46 is almost $900. Also, we can see that the 14.7 percent estimate using the approximation method is a fairly close estimate.

However, a bond's future cash inflows can be discounted using any rate that the investor feels is relevant. For example, suppose that you are convinced that interest rates will fall in the future and that very shortly our example coupon bond will have a yield to maturity of only 9 percent. What will be its new present value? To find the answer, simply consult Table A.3 in Appendix A and obtain PV of $1 factors from the 9 percent column. Substitute these values for those in Table 12.2 and calculate the new present value. Your answer should be $1,116.65. So, if you are right in your assessment of future interest rates, this bond's price will increase by $216.75 ($1,116.75 − $900.00). But if you are wrong, its price will fall. This potential price volatility is unquestionably a serious risk element that deserves more attention.

Risks of Bond Investment

If you buy a bond, there are two major sources of risk facing you. First, unless you are investing in Treasury or agency bonds, there is the possibility that the bond's issuer will default on paying interest or redeeming the bond at maturity. Second, all bond prices, regardless of issuer, are sensitive to changes in the overall level of interest rates.

Default risk: Probability of receiving bond interest and redemption payments.

DEFAULT RISK **Default risk** has to do with the probability of actually receiving the promised interest and redeeming the bond at face value. If the probabilities of both of these happening are high, the bond is considered low risk; if the probabilities are low, the bond is risky. As we saw earlier in the chapter, default risk depends in large measure on the protections provided in the indenture. All things considered, a subordinated debenture is much riskier than a mortgage bond. But default risk also depends upon the financial strength of the issuer. You probably would be safer with a Sears or Du Pont subordinated debenture than a mortgage bond issued by Fly-by-Night Airlines using a dilapidated hangar or vintage airplane as collateral.

Very frankly, very few investors are sufficiently skilled to do their own bond safety analysis; it is far better to rely upon professional rating services. The major sources—Standard & Poor's and Moody's—are shown in Figure 12.4 (page 346). Of

Box 12.3 SAVING MONEY
No Reason to Settle for 85 Percent

Recent changes by Congress to the Series EE (savings) bond should cause some investors to rethink their bond investments. There no longer is a floor to your return, such as 4 percent; instead, you receive 85 percent of the yield on either six-month Treasury securities (if you hold the bonds less than five years) or 85 percent of the yield on five-year Treasuries (if you hold five years or longer). Taking away the floor diminishes the appeal of savings bonds as short-term investments, but the bigger problem is that your long-term return is not so great.

To begin with, the return on five-year Treasuries is likely to average 1 to 2 percent less than the return on 20- or 30-year Treasuries; then, you receive only 85 percent of that return. So the return that you finally receive is about the equivalent, on average, of what you might earn in very short-term Treasury bills. We shouldn't complain about receiving the Treasury bill yield if we are holding savings bonds for liquidity purposes, but this yield is not adequate for long-term bond investment.

Unfortunately, many families *do* hold savings bonds for long periods of time. For example, parents and relatives like to give them as gifts to small children with the usual feeling that the bonds can help much later in the recipients' lives. Then, too, the convenience of buying savings bonds leads many people to buy them for their retirement. Sadly, these long-term holdings will not produce the accumulations that other bonds could.

True, savings bonds have other appealing features, such as federal income tax avoidance if they are used for certain educational purposes and if the owners meet certain conditions. But these other features do not apply to many investors, so they are worth nothing. If you want to hold Treasury bonds as a long-term investment, and if there are no unique advantages applicable in your case, then go after all the yield—not just 85 percent.

It's relatively easy to buy bonds directly from the Treasury without a commission, and your broker can buy them for you in a flash. The broker's commission will be insignificant in the long run when it's compared with savings bonds' smaller yields. Also, there are a number of very good mutual funds specializing in Treasury bonds. Tell Grandma and Grandpa and aunts and uncles that opening a custodial mutual fund account for the kids (a five-minute task) will be as warmly appreciated as savings bonds.

course, you can expect bond yields to vary by each rating class, with the lowest yield on AAA-rated bonds.

Interest rate risk: Price volatility of a bond in relation to changes in market rates of interest.

INTEREST RATE RISK After you purchase a bond, your investment will be subject to **interest rate risk.** This risk results from the fact that if credit conditions tighten or loosen after your purchase, interest rates in general will go up or go down. Along with these changes, the market price for your bond will also change, as we have already demonstrated. The primary factor determining how risky a bond is in relation to interest rate changes is its maturity; the longer the maturity, the greater the price volatility and risk. This is seen best through the use of an example.

Let us assume that you are considering three different bonds each with a 12 percent coupon rate: One matures in one year, another in five years (our previous example bond), and the third in 20 years. Assume further that each is currently selling for $1,000, meaning each has a yield to maturity of 12 percent. Now assume that after you purchase each one, yields to maturity on identical new bonds (1) increase to 15 percent or (2) decrease to 9 percent. Let us see what would happen to the market prices of the three bonds. The new market prices can be calculated using the discounting techniques for finding present values that we just explained. Table 12.3 shows the results. As you see, if yields to maturity rise to 15 percent, your loss is greatest with the 20-year bond and least with the one-year bond; but if interest rates fall, you enjoy the biggest gain with the 20-year bond and, again, the least with the one-year bond. It should be clear that your greatest exposure to risk is with long-maturity bonds.

Standard & Poor's (S&P)	Moody's	Description
AAA	Aaa	The highest quality, carrying the smallest degree of investment risk and generally referred to as "gilt edge."
AA	Aa	Also of high quality, differing in only small degree from the highest rating in ability to repay the debt.
A	A	Possesses many favorable investment attributes and considered upper medium grade obligation; a strong capacity to pay interest and repay principal, but somewhat more susceptible to adverse effects of changes in circumstances and economic conditions.
BBB	Baa	A medium grade obligation; has adequate capacity to pay off debt, but adverse economic conditions or changing circumstances are likely to lead to a weakened capacity to pay interest and repay principal. Moody's, in addition, considers the rating to have some speculative characteristics.
BB	Ba	The highest of the purely "speculative" ratings; protection of interest and principal payments is considered very moderate and not well safeguarded during both good and bad times over the future.
B	B	Generally lacking characteristics of the desirable investment; assurance of interest and principal payments over any long period may be small.
CCC	Caa	Considered in poor standing; elements of danger to payment of principal or interest may be present. Moody's includes some issues in default in this category; S&P does not.
CC	Ca	Speculative in a high degree; having other marked shortcomings. Moody's also uses for some issues in default.
C	C	S&P reserves the rating for bonds that are not paying interest; Moody's denotes issues with extremely poor prospects of ever attaining any real investment standing.
D		S&P only; reserved for issues in default, with interest and/or principal payments in arrears.

Figure 12.4
What the bond ratings mean.

PREFERRED STOCK

Preferred stock: A hybrid security with characteristics of both common stock and bonds.

Preferred stock represents another type of fixed-income investment. It is often called a hybrid security because it has characteristics of both common stock and bonds. It is unfortunate the word *preferred* is used to describe this type of security, for it suggests that in some way it must be superior to common stock. Although preferred stock is certainly different from common stock, it isn't necessarily preferable.

Characteristics of Preferred Stock

Most of preferred stock's characteristics make it similar to bonds, except one: By law it is considered a form of equity ownership. Therefore, preferred stockholders

TABLE 12.3 • CHANGES IN MARKET PRICES OF THREE BONDS IN RESPONSE TO CHANGES IN INTEREST RATES

	Market Prices		
Yield to Maturity	1-Year Bond	5-Year Bond	20-Year Bond
9%	$1,028	$1,117	$1,274
12%	1,000	1,000	1,000
15%	974	900	812
Change in Yield to Maturity	Change in Market Prices		
Down by 3%	$+28	$+117	$+274
Up by 3%	−26	−100	−188

rank behind bondholders in terms of asset distributions in the event of liquidation. If a corporation files bankruptcy, all its creditors' claims must be settled before any payments can be made to preferred stockholders.

DIVIDEND FEATURES Like common stock, preferred stock is paid a dividend, not interest. However, the dividend is usually a fixed amount, and it is often expressed as a percentage of par value (which is usually $100), similar to how interest is paid on bonds. For example, an 8 percent preferred stock would mean that an $8 a year dividend is paid on each share of stock. Even though a preferred stock has a par (or face) value of $100, its price in the marketplace could be quite different, depending again upon the overall level of interest rates. Some preferred stocks do not have par values; they simply state the dollar amount of dividend.

Cumulative, noncumulative: Feature of preferred stock indicating if nondeclared dividends will (cumulative) or will not (noncumulative) carry forward to future years.

Preferred dividends can be **cumulative** or **noncumulative.** Cumulative means that if a dividend is not declared in one year, it accumulates and must be paid in a future year before any dividend can be paid on the common stock. With noncumulative stock, a missed dividend is lost forever. It is important to know that a corporation is not required legally to pay preferred dividends. In contrast to bond interest, which becomes a legal liability of a corporation the moment it is due, preferred dividends are not liabilities until they are declared. You can find some preferred stocks with many years' dividends in arrears, and some speculators frequently buy these stocks, anticipating an improvement in the company's earnings and knowing that all the accumulated dividends must be paid before management can resume regular dividend payments on the common stock.

Participating dividends: Dividends in excess of the basic stated amount.

A few preferred stocks have **participating dividends,** which means that after common stockholders have received a stated dividend, any distribution above this amount must be shared with the preferred stockholders. This is an extremely attractive feature to attach to preferred stock. A corporation that does so usually has financial weaknesses and must offer this bonus to make its preferred stock salable.

PREFERRED STOCKHOLDERS' RIGHTS As mentioned previously, preferred stockholders do not enjoy the same legal protections as bondholders do. However, there are similarities. For example, preferred stock is issued under an offering agreement, and many protective covenants are written into it. Some agreements go so far as to give voting rights to preferred stockholders (which they almost never have) if the common stockholders fail to live up to the terms of the agreement or are unable to manage the business profitably. However, these restrictions are rare.

You are better advised to think of preferred stock as a considerably weaker instrument than a bond with respect to your protections in bankruptcy.

Convertible preferred stock: Preferred stock that converts into shares of the issuers' common stock.

THE CONVERTIBLE FEATURE A growing number of new preferred stocks are convertible. Just as in the case of convertible bonds, **convertible preferred stock** converts into a given number of shares of the company's common stock. In recent years, the convertible feature has replaced the participating feature as a "sweetener" to help sell the preferred.

Expected Return from Preferred Stock

The expected return from nonconvertible preferred stock is calculated in the same way as the expected return on bonds. You receive a fixed annual dividend (usually paid quarterly), which is the current return, and you may have a future capital gain or loss if you sell the preferred for a price more or less than your purchase price. It must be noted, though, that most preferred stock does not have a maturity date when the corporation must redeem it. It is said to be issued in perpetuity. Therefore, you cannot calculate a yield to maturity, but you can calculate a current yield in the following way:

$$\text{Current yield} = \frac{\$D}{\$P}$$

where

D = annual dividend
P = market price of the preferred stock

A preferred stock paying $2 a year in dividends and having a market price of $18 would have a current yield of 11.11 percent ($2/$18). This is the same calculation we made to find a bond's current yield. Although the preferred stock may not have a redemption date, it may have a call option attached, allowing a corporation the right to call the shares if it wishes to.

If they are listed on the organized exchanges, preferred stocks are reported in the same sections as common stock in the *Wall Street Journal* or other newspapers. The symbol *pf* appears after the name of the company, designating the issue as preferred. Many companies have issued preferred stock (particularly public utilities), but many more have not. Companies often view preferred stock as a poor substitute for bonds in raising capital, since bond interest can be deducted in figuring the corporation's income tax, but preferred dividends cannot be deducted. At tax rates most corporations pay, this amounts to a substantial difference in tax dollars.

Action Plan for the Steeles: Investing for the Children's Education

Background As a first step in financial planning, the Steeles have set forth specific investment goals. The most important is providing a college education for John and Nancy. College expenditures will begin in about 10 years, and Arnie and Sharon must start investing now, and continuously over the next 10 years, to accumulate sufficient funds. The Steeles have estimated college expenses in nominal dollars (see Chapter 2), but now they must adjust these amounts to take into consideration the expected annual inflation rate for college expenses, which they estimate at 6 percent. The accompanying table indicates the inflation-adjusted amounts the Steeles must accumulate.

Year (from Now) Expenses Begin	Nominal Amount	Inflation-Considered Amount (6% Rate)
10	$12,000	$ 21,490
11	12,000	22,780
12	24,000	48,293
13	24,000	51,190
14	12,000	27,131
15	12,000	28,759
Total	$96,000	$199,643

The Problem The Steeles must earn no less than 6 percent after taxes on their investments *each year* to accumulate the needed amounts. Their pretax rate of return must be 8.6 percent (6%/[1 – 0.30]), assuming a marginal tax rate of 30 percent. Yield is very important if the Steeles are to stay within their savings budget, but they regard safety as even more important.

The Plan The Steeles should limit their investments to either U.S. Treasury bonds or highest-quality municipal bonds. When the Steeles were developing their plan, yields on 10-year Treasuries and 10-year municipals ("munis") were around 8.5 and 6.3 percent, respectively. Each type of bond can be purchased in zero coupon form with a maturity matched to the date funds are needed in the future. Since the after-tax yields of the munis and Treasuries were fairly close, the Steeles will select the Treasuries for the first-year investment. But this might change in the future if yield differences favor munis.

Specifically, they will buy "Treasury Strips" with a 10-year maturity. Suppose the Steeles wanted to invest a sum now that would be sufficient to cover the $21,490 needed in 10 years. Since each bond has a $1,000 redemption value, they would need to buy 21.49 bonds (round to 21). Ten-year STRIPS were quoted at a price of $429 per bond. So the Steeles would have had to invest $9,009 (21 × $429) in year 1 to accumulate the needed $21,490 10 years later.

The Steeles can buy the STRIPS directly or through a mutual fund (e.g., Benham Target Maturity Trust). They will use the Benham Trust to avoid commission, although their yield will be slightly less because of the fund's operating costs.

Rationale for the Plan Zero coupon bonds are the only investment that guarantees a future sum of money. If the Steeles selected interest-bearing bonds, they would face the problem of reinvesting the periodic interest payments. If these subsequent investments must be made at lower rates, their target accumulations will not be achieved.

If rates do decline in the future, the Steeles will have a problem if they continue investing in zero coupon bonds. However, they have decided to stick with safety, which means they must revise their savings plans to reflect larger savings requirements; unless, of course, the annual inflation rate of college costs declines. Falling interest rates often accompany falling inflation rates, but there is no assurance that this correlation will continue in the future.

Investment Quality of Preferred Stock

Another aspect of the tax law also makes preferred stock a less desirable investment from the individual investor's point of view. A provision in the tax law allows corporations to exclude from their taxable incomes up to 70 percent of dividends they receive from stocks of domestic corporations. For example, if General Motors

Corporation received $1,000 in dividends from shares of IBM stock it owned, only $200 would be subject to GM's corporate income tax. This provision encourages corporations to invest in both common and preferred stocks, but particularly in the latter. As a result, current yields on preferred stocks are reduced relative to bonds, because corporate buying in the marketplace bids up the prices of preferred shares. This is why you usually find preferred yields less than long-term bond yields, even though they are riskier investments. Although they may be attractive to a corporate investor, preferred stocks are not attractive to individual investors. Unless you are investing in convertible preferreds it would be better to avoid preferreds and stick to bonds.

SUMMARY

Corporate issued bonds are favored by many investors, who have certain rights detailed in the bond indenture. Coupon bonds pay periodic interest determined by the coupon rate and a bond's face value. Zero coupon bonds do not pay periodic interest but offer a return through a price discount from par value. Bonds are retired, either through redemption at maturity or earlier or by being converted into shares of common stock. Investing in all bonds, corporate bonds in particular, involves complex issues and is probably done most effectively by individuals through mutual funds.

U.S. Treasury securities are the most popular investments in the world. Their payment characteristics are similar to corporate bonds, including the availability of zero coupon issues. Conventional agency bonds are virtually identical to Treasury bonds, but mortgage-backed agency bonds are quite different. These bonds are related to the mortgage-lending industry and "pass through" mortgage payments to the bond investors. Municipal bonds are issued by state and local governmental units. They may be supported by the unit's full taxing authority (general obligation bonds) or by the revenues of a specific capital project (revenue bonds). Each bond type is free of federal income tax, which makes them very appealing to investors in high marginal tax brackets.

Preferred stock is issued by corporations. Although it is stock, its payment characteristics make it comparable to bonds. Preferred stockholders enjoy certain rights defined in the offering agreement. Most preferred stock has a perpetual life and a cumulative, but not participating, dividend feature. Because preferred stock is favored by corporate investors, unfortunately, its investment quality to individual investors, is diminished.

KEY TERMS

agency bonds (p. 340)
basis point (bp) (p. 338)
bond indenture (p. 331)
callable bonds (p. 334)
conversion value (p. 335)
convertible bond (p. 335)
convertible preferred stock (p. 348)
coupon bonds (p. 333)
coupon rate (p. 333)
cumulative (p. 347)
current yield (p. 342)
debentures (p. 332)
default risk (p. 344)
face value (p. 332)
fixed return (p. 332)
general obligation (GO) bond (p. 341)
inflation-indexed Treasury bonds (p. 338)
interest rate risk (p. 345)
mortgage-backed bonds (p. 340)
mortgage bonds (p. 331)
municipal bonds (p. 341)
noncumulative (p. 347)
participating dividends (p. 347)
preferred stock (p. 346)
pre-tax equivalent yield (p. 341)
protective covenants (p. 331)
revenue bond (p. 341)
sinking fund (p. 334)
subordinated debentures (p. 332)
U.S. Treasury Strips (p. 338)
yield to maturity (p. 342)
zero coupon bond (p. 334)

PROBLEMS AND REVIEW QUESTIONS

1. Is a bond a loan? If it is, who is the borrower and who are the lenders?
2. What is a corporate bond indenture? Differentiate among a mortgage bond, a debenture, and a subordinated debenture.
3. Using a bond's face value and coupon rate, explain how the amount of semiannual interest is determined.
4. Indicate three ways that a bond may be retired.
5. Explain a convertible bond. Would you be inclined to buy such a bond if it was issued by a growth company? Discuss.
6. Interpret the following corporate bond price quotation, clearly indicating its closing price and the price change.

Bond			Cur Yld	Vol	Close	Net Chg
GM	8½	15	8.8	23	96½	+⅜

7. Why do U.S. Treasury bonds have the lowest yields of all bonds?
8. What is a U.S. Treasury Strip?
9. Interpret the following Treasury bond price quotation, clearly indicating its bid price and change in bid price:

Rate	Maturity	Bid	Asked	Bid Change	Yield
6¾	Jun 26	109:14	109.18	+12	6.12

10. The quotation indicated in Question 9 indicates a "yield." What type of yield is this?
11. Calculate the yield to maturity for the following bonds (each has a par value and redemption value of $1,000):
    (*a*) 8 percent coupon rate, 10-year maturity, $1,200 price
    (*b*) 12 percent coupon rate, 20-year maturity, $800 price
12. Using appropriate tables found in Appendix A, determine the present value of the following bonds (each has a redemption value of $1,000):

Bond	Annual Coupon Interest	Maturity (Years)	Yield to Maturity
A	$120	10	8%
B	60	20	8
C	zero	20	10

13. Suppose the yields to maturity for bonds A and B increase to 10 percent. Calculate the new present value of each and, comparing it with your answer to Question 12, discuss which bond has the greater interest rate risk.
14. What is meant by default risk, and how do investors usually determine how much a bond might have?
15. The five bonds listed below all have the same maturity and coupon rate. Also shown are five yields. Match the yield to the bond.
    (*a*) Municipal 10%
    (*b*) Treasury 8%
    (*c*) Ginnie Mae 7%
    (*d*) Corporate, best quality 9%
    (*e*) Corporate, medium quality 6%
16. What feature of a municipal bond is particularly appealing? Suppose you have a marginal tax rate of 28 percent, and a municipal bond offers a yield of 5 percent. Would you prefer this bond to a similar quality corporate bond with a yield of 6.5 percent? Show why or why not.

17. What is a cumulative, nonparticipating preferred stock?
18. If a preferred stock (issued in perpetuity) has a price of $20 a share and pays an annual dividend of $1.50 a share, what is its current yield? Can you calculate its yield to maturity? Explain. Could you experience a capital gain or loss with this stock? Explain.
19. Why is preferred stock normally not an attractive investment to individual investors?

Case 12.1 Brendan Hoyt Speculates about Bonds

Brendan Hoyt has been fortunate to accumulate about $50,000 of savings, currently held in a money market fund. Brendan is single and has a good position that pays over $80,000 a year. He has no serious financial obligations. He is reluctant to speculate in the stock market because he has a poor background in security analysis, but he believes he can forecast future interest rates with moderate success.

Brendan is convinced that interest rates will fall two percentage points very shortly. His friend, Tina Tobe, has told Brendan that if he really can forecast interest rates, he should speculate in the bond market. He can limit his bond selections to Treasuries, so he doesn't have to worry about possible defaults. Tina says that he should buy Treasury Strips with a 20-year maturity and a yield to maturity of 10 percent. Brendan likes the idea but fails to see why STRIPS are Tina's choice. He thinks he should select bonds with the highest yields to maturity, and right now those are 10-year bonds with a 14 percent coupon rate (coupon interest of $140 annually) and with a yield to maturity of 12 percent.

QUESTIONS

1. Brendan needs your help. Calculate the present value of the zero coupon bond and of the 14 percent coupon bond.
2. Assuming a $50,000 investment, how many of each bond type could he buy if he invested the entire amount in one or the other?
3. Assume that Brendan forecasts correctly and that each bond's yield to maturity declines by two percentage points. Determine the new present value for each bond and then further determine which bond provides the greatest profit opportunity.
4. Assume that Brendan guesses incorrectly and each bond's yield to maturity increases by two percentage points. Again, determine new present values and indicate which bond suffers the largest loss. What advice can you offer Brendan?

Case 12.2 The DuBays' Preference for Bonds

Nelson and Claire DuBay are in their early fifties. Their two children are both grown and living in their own households. Nelson and Claire have reasonably good positions, and their combined income in 1992 was over $75,000. Their net worth of about $150,000 is mostly in their house and furnishings, but they do have adequate liquid resources. The DuBays are concerned about retirement. Neither has a particularly good retirement plan, and their savings were depleted substantially by college costs for their children. However, they live on a rather modest budget and believe they can save about $10,000 a year for the next 10 years or so. Nelson and Claire would both like to retire at age 62. Therefore, considering the reinvestment of earnings at even modest rates, such as 7 to 10 percent, they should have between $140,000 and $160,000 at retirement time. Of course, they would like to have much more than this, if that would be possible.

However, the DuBays are very concerned about risks associated with the investments they might make to achieve their objective. In discussing the situation with their stockbroker, Edith Klune, they conclude that common stocks simply have too much risk and possibly not enough return to achieve their goal in only 10 years. Klune has suggested they limit their investments to corporate and government bonds. To help them, she prepared the accompanying list and suggested they purchase $2,000 of each bond each year, beginning January 1, 1993.

Issuer	Coupon Rate	Par Value	Year of Maturity	Current Market Price	S&P Rating
1. U.S. Treasury	9%	$1,000	2017	$1,200	—
2. BIM Corporation	7%	1,000	1997	900	AA
3. City of Oakland, California—General Revenue Bonds	7%	1,000	2007	1,000	BBB
4. Vaga Foods	14%	1,000	2002	1,100	B
5. AT&T	6%	1,000	2002	900	AAA

QUESTIONS

1. Assuming the DuBays are in a 28 percent tax bracket, and following Klune's advice, calculate the *current yield* and *yield to maturity* on each bond. Express the municipal bond's yields in pretax yield equivalent form.
2. Consider now the issue of price appreciation with the bonds, and explain how this might influence the DuBays' selection. For example, how does the U.S. Treasury bond compare with the AT&T bond in this respect? Since the DuBays do not apparently need high current return, which of the two do you recommend?
3. Discuss *interest rate risk* and *default risk* of the U.S. Treasury bond relative to the AT&T bond.
4. Do you agree with Klune's advice for the DuBays? Do you think default risk has been considered adequately? Explain.

HELPFUL CONTACTS

Corporate and municipal bond investors must be concerned with bond safety. Bond ratings are provided by Moody's Investors Service, Inc. and by Standard & Poor's Corporation. Their addresses are provided at the end of Chapter 11.

INTERNET ADDRESSES

Bonds and Fixed Income Securities (links provided by the University of Göttingen)
http://www.wiso.gwdg.de/ifbg/finbond.html

Department of the Treasury, Bureau of Public Debt (full explanation of all Treasury Securities and how to buy them in the Treasury Direct System)
gopher://gopher.gsa.gov/00/staff/pa/cic/money/t-bills.txt

The Vanguard Group of Investment Companies—Vanguard Fixed-Income Securities Fund (excellent discussion of the risks in fixed-income investing)
http://www.vanguard.com/funds/prospect/p028.html

Yahoo Directory on Bonds
http://www.yahoo.com/Economy/Markets_and_Investments/Bonds/

Chapter 13

Mutual Funds and Other Pooling Arrangements: Simplifying and (Maybe) Improving Your Investment Performance

Objectives

1. To understand why pooling arrangements are important alternatives to direct investment
2. To identify the important characteristics of open-end and closed-end mutual funds
3. To be able to evaluate a mutual fund within a risk and return framework
4. To recognize the characteristics of unit investment trusts and real estate investment trusts and how each differs from mutual funds
5. To understand the basic framework of limited partnerships and why they appeal only to a limited number of investors
6. To learn the basics of portfolio construction and maintenance and appreciate why mutual funds simplify the process

The previous two chapters explained the potential rewards and risks of investing in stocks and bonds. They should help you get started in finding, evaluating, and choosing these securities for your portfolio, and, if you follow this path, be ready to spend a considerable amount of time and effort. An alternative path is to use mutual funds. In truth, many investment advisers feel that this approach is much more appropriate for most investors. We agree. But your efforts in studying the past two chapters have not been wasted. Mutual funds invest in the same securities that you might invest in directly. As such, the funds have reward-risk profiles similar to those of the securities they own. Knowing what stocks and bonds are all about will definitely help you make better mutual fund choices.

The important characteristics of mutual funds and other pooling arrangements are explained in this chapter. Actually, the term *mutual fund,* or simply *fund,* is often used in a generic sense to describe any pooling arrangement. There are legal distinctions among the different arrangements, but our focus is upon their investment differences.

MUTUAL FUNDS

Mutual fund: An investment company that invests in securities issued by corporations or governmental units.

Net asset value (NAV): The net value of one mutual fund share determined by the net market value of the shares the fund owns.

A **mutual fund** is an investment company that invests its funds in securities issued by corporations or governmental units. When you buy shares of a mutual fund, you are buying a proportionate interest in the fund's securities. As a simple example, if a fund owns 100 shares each of IBM, Xerox, and General Motors, and if you own 10 percent of the fund's outstanding shares, then you effectively own 10 shares in each of those corporations. The value of a mutual fund share—called its **net asset value (NAV)**—depends on the values of its underlying securities; in the above example, those are IBM, Xerox, and General Motors. Suppose that, on a particular day, the market values below existed; then NAV is calculated as follows, assuming the fund has no liabilities:

(1)	IBM—$120/share × 100 shares	= $12,000
(2)	Xerox—$80/share × 100 shares	= 8,000
(3)	GM—$70/share × 100 shares	= 7,000
(4)	Value of the fund's portfolio	= $27,000
(5)	Number of shares outstanding in the fund	= 1,000
(6)	Net asset value (NAV) per share = (4) divided by (5)	= $ 27

Owning 10 percent of the shares outstanding means you own 100 shares and the value of your investment is $2,700 ($27 × 100). Surely, the first bit of information you want when considering a mutual fund's shares is its NAV per share.

Characteristics of Mutual Funds

To many investors, the single biggest advantage of a mutual fund—after diversification—is its professional management. As discussed in Chapters 11 and 12, determining which securities to buy and when to buy and sell them are very difficult decisions—and time consuming if you take them seriously. By investing in a mutual fund, you transfer these problems to someone else, who may have better training to handle them. Mutual funds charge for these services, but the charges are quite minimal and usually worth it. Before looking more closely at mutual fund selection, you should first understand some characteristics of mutual funds.

Load fund: A mutual fund that charges commissions on share purchases.
No-load fund: A mutual fund with no purchase commissions.

LOAD VERSUS NO-LOAD FUNDS A **load fund** is one that charges commissions on the shares you buy; a **no-load fund** does not charge commissions. In a load fund, the price you pay for a share is called the offer price, and it is higher than NAV, the difference being commission. In a no-load fund the price you pay is NAV. (We should point out that mutual funds typically have some liabilities outstanding at any point, and these are deducted from the funds' assets to arrive at *net* assets; however, these liabilities are inconsequential in comparison with assets.) Mutual funds' NAVs are reported in most newspapers, and some also show offer prices, as indicated in Figure 13.1. Notice that Trend Fund is a no-load fund, but the Blue Chip Fund has a load. The size of the load (or commission) varies among funds and is often expressed as a percentage of the offer price. As you see, Blue Chip had a load of $0.56 ($18.77 – $18.21), and expressing this as a percentage of its price gives 2.89 percent ($0.56/$18.77). The figure is fairly common among load funds, although some are much higher.

Obviously, with commissions, you should be concerned with whether load funds outperform no-loads. On balance they do not. There have been spectacular performers on each side—but there also have been dreadful losers, and most studies show their average performances to be about the same, on a risk-adjusted basis. So why buy a load fund? There is no compelling reason to do so, unless you receive other advantages, such as investment advice. If you invest regularly, saving commissions gives you that much more money invested, and over the long run these extra amounts will produce a substantial addition to the value of your holdings.

Box 13.1 SIMPLIFYING FINANCIAL PLANNING
Want to Invest in a Mutual Fund? Just Do It!

The most popular investment vehicle over the past 10 years must be the mutual fund. From $135 billion invested in 1981, there was over $2.0 trillion invested in 1995. This is remarkable. Equally remarkable, though, is the number of people who feel that mutual funds are good investments but, for one reason or another, do not invest in them, or who do so only through a broker. Why?

In a recent survey, some respondents indicated that they didn't know where to look to find a fund. Others didn't think the "hassle" of investing in a fund on their own was worth it, so they let their brokers find one for them. Many felt nervous about venturing into an unknown situation and therefore left their money in bank savings accounts.

What these people need desperately is more confidence in themselves and a "power of positive thinking" attitude. In short: just do it, and here are four simple steps to get started.

1. Two large fund families are Fidelity and Vanguard; their phone numbers are 800-544-8888 and 800-662-7447, respectively. Use either to get started; when you become more knowledgeable, you might use the many other fund families that are available. If you want to start with a very small investment, use 20th Century Ultra (800-345-2021), which has no minimum investment requirement.

2. Call and ask for information on any three or four of their most popular funds (either no-load or loads less than 5 percent) that match your investment goal. Review them as well as you can and pick one. The application takes about three minutes to complete.

3. Regardless of how much money you have to invest, make a small initial commitment. The idea is simply to get in the game, not to find the ideal fund right at the start.

4. Invest regularly, which you can do in two ways. First, check the automatic reinvestment boxes on the application form, both for dividend and capital gain distributions. Second, arrange to have an amount automatically deducted from your checking or savings account and invested in the fund each month. Most fund families provide this service.

A fund family–you have the advantage of free switching within this family.

Example of a load fund.

r means a redemption fee is charged.

Within this grouping, Fidelity offered 57 different funds; it offered 115 funds in total.

NL means no-load fund.

	NAV	Offer Price	NAV Chg.
Fidelity Invest:			
AgTF r	11.57	11.57	+.02
A Mgr	12.57	NL	-.01
Balanc	12.05	NL	-.04
BluCh	18.21	18.77	-.02
CA TF	11.37	NL	. . .
CA In	9.80	NL	. . .
Canad	16.17	16.67	-.02
CapAp	16.21	16.71	+.06
CpInc r	7.10	NL	+.01
CngS	129.53	. . .	-.22
Contra	22.81	23.52	-.11
CnvSc	12.80	NL	-.02
Destl	15.71	. . .	-.06
Destll	24.32	. . .	-.13
DisEq r	15.61	NL	-.03
EmGr r	13.65	NL	-.03
Eq Inc	24.85	25.36	-.06
EQll	13.17	NL	-.04
Eqldx	14.43	NL	-.03
Europ	15.54	16.02	+.05
Exch	86.70	. . .	-.19
Fidel	19.00	NL	-.08
Trend	45.90	NL	-.18
USBI	10.32	10.32	+.03
UtilInc	11.98	NL	+.01
Value	28.90	NL	-.21
Wrldw	9.18	NL	. . .

Figure 13.1 Typical listing of mutual funds.

In addition to the commission, or front-end load, some funds also have a redemption charge, or rear-end load. The Emerging Growth Fund illustrated in Figure 13.1 has a 1 percent redemption charge. The increasing popularity of funds, coupled with their apparent success, prompted many funds to begin front- and rear-end loads.

Open-end fund: A fund that issues or redeems shares at their NAVs.

Closed-end fund: A fund with a relatively fixed number of shares outstanding that are purchased (or sold) in the open market rather than from (or to) the fund.

OPEN-END VERSUS CLOSED-END FUNDS An **open-end fund** issues shares at their NAV to anyone caring to buy them and, equally important, is also willing to redeem shares at their NAV. For example, if you held shares in any of Fidelity's funds, you could have sold them back to the funds at any time. You generally buy or sell shares directly from or to the fund, rather than through a stockbroker. Of approximately 3,500 total mutual funds in existence, about 3,000 are open-end funds, and their greater popularity is due in part to the assurance investors have in always being able to sell their shares at NAV. They are also widely advertised, and the load funds are promoted by sales representatives. If you want information about open-end funds, including a free directory giving addresses and phone numbers for practically all of them, write the Investment Company Institute, 1600 M Street, NW, Washington, DC 20036. The Institute's *Mutual Fund Fact Book* is also a good buy.

A **closed-end fund** is different in a number of respects. First, it has a relatively fixed number of shares outstanding. Second, you buy these shares as you would buy shares of any other corporation; that is, its shares are traded on organized exchanges or in the over-the-counter market. Third, because the fund neither buys nor sells shares to the public, you must buy or sell them from or to another party, which further means you are not guaranteed their NAV, as either a seller or a buyer. Finally, these funds are seldom promoted, so chances are good you won't know much about them unless you do research on your own. However, quite a few closed-end funds are available with a variety of investment objectives, and Figure 13.2 shows just a few.

DISCOUNTS ON CLOSED-END FUNDS ENHANCE THEIR APPEAL A major point of interest about closed-end funds is the size of premium or discount, which is the difference between their market prices and their NAVs. As you see in Figure 13.2, some of the funds were selling at premiums while others were selling at discounts. More often than not, these funds sell at discounts, which enhances their investment appeal. For example, suppose you can buy Adams Express at an 8 percent discount. To keep things simple, suppose Adams Express held securities that offered a 10 percent current return. If you invested $100 in these securities directly, you would get $10 in dividends or interest. But you need to invest only $92 in Adams Express to get a $10 return. Rather than a 10 percent rate of return, your rate is 10.87 percent ($10/$92). This is a sizable increase in return for no increase in intrinsic risk. You should realize, though, that the size of the discount varies over time, and it could increase after you invest. This means the market price of your shares declines relative to NAV, and if you then sell, you do so at a loss, or at a relatively smaller gain than would have been the case had the discount remained the same.

Prospectus: A document describing a fund in considerable detail.
Shareholder report: A statement showing how a fund has performed in the past and the securities it currently owns.

THE FUND'S OBJECTIVES It is obviously important to select a fund that is attempting to achieve the same investment goal you are. If you call or write a fund, you will be sent a **prospectus** and a **shareholder report.** The prospectus describes

Figure 13.2
Typical partial listing of closed-end funds.

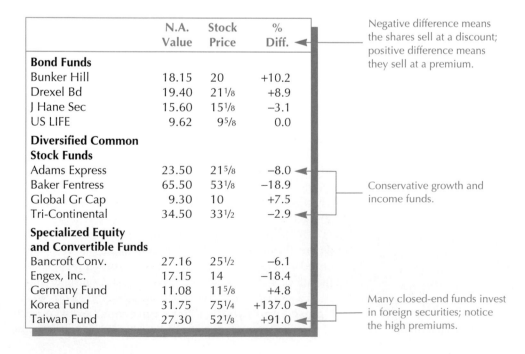

	N.A. Value	Stock Price	% Diff.
Bond Funds			
Bunker Hill	18.15	20	+10.2
Drexel Bd	19.40	21 1/8	+8.9
J Hane Sec	15.60	15 1/8	−3.1
US LIFE	9.62	9 5/8	0.0
Diversified Common Stock Funds			
Adams Express	23.50	21 5/8	−8.0
Baker Fentress	65.50	53 1/8	−18.9
Global Gr Cap	9.30	10	+7.5
Tri-Continental	34.50	33 1/2	−2.9
Specialized Equity and Convertible Funds			
Bancroft Conv.	27.16	25 1/2	−6.1
Engex, Inc.	17.15	14	−18.4
Germany Fund	11.08	11 5/8	+4.8
Korea Fund	31.75	75 1/4	+137.0
Taiwan Fund	27.30	52 1/8	+91.0

Negative difference means the shares sell at a discount; positive difference means they sell at a premium.

Conservative growth and income funds.

Many closed-end funds invest in foreign securities; notice the high premiums.

the fund in detail, and the shareholder report indicates how the fund has performed in the past and the securities it currently holds. Risks associated with investing in the fund are also discussed, and they should be read as thoroughly as material describing the fund's objective and its past performance.

International fund, global fund: A fund that invests in foreign securities.
Sector fund: A fund that invests in only one industry.
Maximum capital appreciation fund: A fund that uses a variety of strategies in an effort to earn high returns.
Index fund: A fund that attempts to match the return on a market index.

Figure 13.3 indicates the more common fund objectives. As you see, there are a number from which to choose. While growth, income, and balanced funds are the most popular, many investors use the other funds also. **International funds** and **global funds** allow you to invest in foreign countries where returns have often been higher than in the United States. **Sector funds** make it possible to invest in one industry if you think that industry will do better than the overall economy. **Maximum capital appreciation funds** use a number of investment strategies in an effort to earn high returns. For example, some look for companies that might be acquired (at high prices) through takeovers. Some invest in distressed companies (even bankrupts) that are expected to recover.

A particularly interesting fund is an **index fund.** It invests in securities that constitute a market index, such as the S&P 500 Stock Index. Its sole objective is to earn the return the index earns. Beginning investors often feel they can do better than a simple index, which has no investment strategy or approach. In actuality, however, many investment professionals do not perform as well as an index. Studies indicate, for example, that fully two-thirds of equity mutual funds underperform the S&P 500 on a risk-adjusted basis.

Money market fund: A fund that invests in money market instruments issued in large denominations.

A particularly popular fund is the **money market fund.** There are several reasons for this popularity. For one thing, these funds are known as dollar funds, which means you always buy or sell shares at $1.00 each. Actually, the fund is a form of checking account, allowing you to write checks against your balance in the account. You earn interest daily and can withdraw all funds credited to your account at any time. Withdrawals can be made by telephone or wire, but are more

Figure 13.3 Types of mutual funds.

Type of Fund	Objective	Primary Investment Securities
Growth	Price appreciation over time	Common stocks
Income	High current return	Bonds, preferred stocks
Balanced	Moderate growth plus moderate current return	Bonds, preferred and common stocks
Money market	High liquidity plus higher current return than bank savings accounts	Money market securities
Maximum capital appreciation	Exploit opportunities to earn high returns	Varies, depending upon strategy
Sector	Invest in one industry	Common stocks
International	Earn returns in countries outside the U.S.	Common stocks
Global	Earn returns in both the U.S. and foreign countries	Common stocks
Index	Earn returns equal to a market index, such as the S&P 500	Common stocks or bonds; depends on the index

frequently made by checks. The usual minimum withdrawal is $500, but some accounts allow checks for any amount. The big appeal is the earnings on the account. In contrast to some checking accounts that pay no or low interest, these funds usually offer rates that are about the same as those earned on liquid money market instruments.

Important Mutual Fund Services

Along with a professionally managed and well-diversified portfolio, mutual funds offer other appealing features. Some of the more important services are described below.

Reinvestment plan: An option a fund investor can choose to have cash distributions used to acquire more fund shares.

REINVESTMENT PLANS A **reinvestment plan** allows you to automatically reinvest the fund's dividends and capital gain distributions into additional shares of the fund. You choose the amount you wish to reinvest: It can be all or only a fraction of the total distributed. Many investors like to receive dividends in cash but prefer having capital gain distributions reinvested. When you fill out an application to buy shares, you indicate how you wish to handle reinvestment.

TRANSACTIONS BY TELEPHONE Once you have completed an application, you can buy or sell shares by calling a toll-free telephone number. You can also arrange to have funds wired to your bank, which eliminates delays with checks in transit. If you sell shares and have the funds wired, they can be in your interest-earning bank account the next day.

Fund switching: An option allowing fund investors to switch among funds within a fund family.

FUND SWITCHING **Fund switching** allows you to withdraw money from one fund to reinvest in another, so long as the two funds are members of the same family (Fidelity, for example). If the fund is a no-load, this feature is particularly attractive for investors trying market-timing techniques. In general, switches up to a certain number can be made without charges; however, you will pay commissions on a load fund. Be sure to determine your fund's policy before you begin making switches.

Recently, some fund families have agreed to allow investors to switch from one family to another; e.g., a Fidelity fund to a Vanguard fund. This is a big advantage to investors holding funds in both families.

ADAPTABILITY TO IRAs Most mutual funds make attractive IRAs (the IRA is discussed in Chapters 5 and 17). This is so because of the wide range of investment objectives available and their relatively low administrative costs, which usually are less than $20 a year (some funds offer them free). To open an IRA, all you need to do is indicate your intent to the fund and you will be sent a simple document for your signature. This document, along with the completed application form to the fund, automatically makes your investment an IRA.

Selecting a Mutual Fund

Once you have defined clearly your investment objective, you will find many funds available for your choice. Picking one or two is a difficult task. You can get started by looking at a fund's historical performance and comparing it with its risk. Use a beta value (if one is available) in this effort. Other steps to take include reviewing the fund's current holdings, comparing its expenses in relation to its earnings or to the market value of its securities, and seeing how often it buys and sell securities (called the fund's portfolio turnover).

EVALUATE PERFORMANCE A fund must indicate its past performance in its financial reports to shareholders. Figure 13.4 shows such a report for Fidelity Fund, a very large, open-end growth and income fund that is part of the Fidelity family. This report is typical of reports all mutual funds provide investors, although Fidelity's report is particularly useful in that it discusses how to evaluate performance.

Growth of a $1,000 investment and cumulative total return. The cumulative total return is the return a fund earned over a given period of time. For example, the cumulative total return for 10 years is 259.45 percent for Fidelity. If you invested $1,000, held it for 10 years, and reinvested all distributions in Fidelity as they were received, you would have earned $2,594.50 and the $1,000 would have grown to $3,594.50. You should see that a $1,000 investment in the S&P 500 would have grown to $3,835.80 at the end of 10 years.

Average annual total return (AATR). The average annual total return (AATR) is a difficult calculation and cannot be solved accurately without time-value-of-money techniques. Fortunately, fund reports provide the values. Fidelity's 13.65 percent average annual total return for 10 years is the rate you would have earned by investing $1,000 10 years ago and having that grow to $3,594.50 today. This is a good return but, as you see, the S&P 500 did better for the 10-year period. However, Fidelity outperformed the S&P 500 for the other two periods indicated.

The reinvestment assumption. A key input in determining both the average annual total return and the cumulative total return is the assumption of immediate reinvestment of fund distributions. To illustrate the situation, let's look at an example. Although funds actually make quarterly distributions, we will assume that all distributions were made at midyear and then reinvested at the average NAV for the year. We also assume that one share was owned at the beginning of each year.

	Year 1	Year 2
(1) NAV, beginning of year	$15.42	$17.93
(2) NAV, end of year	$17.93	$16.30
(3) Average NAV = [(1) + (2)]/2	$16.68	$17.12
(4) Distributions during the year	$ 1.85	$ 0.74
(5) Shares acquired during the year = (4)/(3)	0.111	0.043
(6) Shares owned at year end	1.111	1.043
(7) Value of shares owned at year end = (2) × (6)	$19.92	$17.00
(8) Change in value during the year = (7) − (1)	$ 4.50	−$ 0.93
(9) Average annual total return = (8)/(1)	+29.2%	− 5.2%

The cumulative total return can also be determined from the above data. You had 1.043 shares of the fund at the end of year 2 for each share that you owned at the beginning of that year. Since you actually owned 1.111 shares at the year's beginning, you would have owned 1.158773 (1.043 × 1.111) shares at year-end. And the total value of those shares is $19.70 (1.158773 × $17.00). Your initial investment at

Performance: The Bottom Line

There are several ways to evaluate a fund's historical performance. You can look at the total percentage change in value, the average annual percentage change, or the growth of a hypothetical $10,000 investment. Each performance figure includes changes in a fund's share price, plus reinvestment of any dividends (or income) and capital gains (the profits the fund earns when it sells stocks that have grown in value).

Cumulative Total Returns

Periods ended December 31, 1994	Past 6 months	Past 1 year	Past 5 years	Past 10 years
Fidelity Fund	5.30%	2.58%	55.15%	259.45%
S&P 500®	4.87%	1.32%	51.77%	283.58%
Average Growth & Income Fund	2.64%	–0.94%	49.80%	224.96%

Cumulative total returns show the fund's performance in percentage terms over a set period — in this case, six months, one, five, or 10 years. For example, if you had invested $1,000 in a fund that had a 5% return over the past year, you would have $1,050. You can compare these figures to the performance of the Standard & Poor's Composite Index of 500 Stocks — a common proxy for the U.S. stock market. You can also compare them to the average growth & income fund, which currently reflects the performance of 375 growth & income funds tracked by Lipper Analytical Services. Both benchmarks include reinvested dividends and capital gains, if any.

Average Annual Total Returns

Periods ended December 31, 1994	Past 1 year	Past 5 years	Past 10 years
Fidelity Fund	2.58%	9.18%	13.65%
S&P 500®	1.32%	8.70%	14.39%
Average Growth & Income Fund	–0.94%	8.29%	12.38%

Average annual total returns take the fund's actual (or cumulative) return and show you what would have happened if the fund had performed at a constant rate each year.

Figure 13.4 Data from Fidelity's 1994 Semiannual Report.
SOURCE: *Fidelity Fund Semiannual Report,* December 31, 1994.

the beginning of year 1 was $15.42, so your gain is $4.28 ($19.70 – $15.42). The cumulative total return over the two-year period is 27.76 percent ([$4.28/$15.42] × 100).

The year-to-year changes in returns reveal the riskiness of investing in a fund. In the table on page 361, going from a +29.2 percent return to a –5.2 percent return suggests quite a bit of risk. Risk is often incorporated into an analysis by determining a fund's beta value and using it to adjust the average annual total return (*AATR*), as shown in the following examples.

Risk-adjusted return. Professionals who evaluate mutual fund performance often make comparisons among funds using the risk-adjusted rate of return (*RAROR*). One very simple way to calculate this follows:

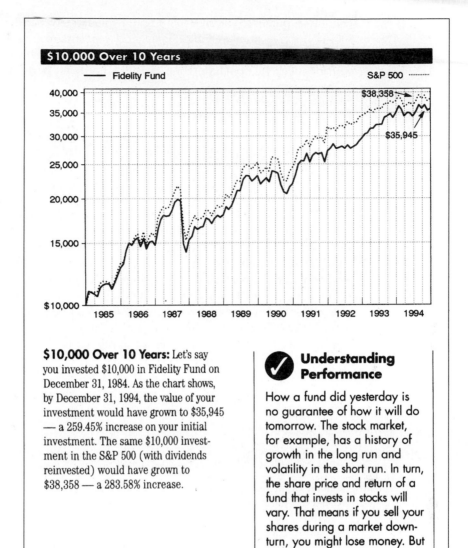

$10,000 Over 10 Years: Let's say you invested $10,000 in Fidelity Fund on December 31, 1984. As the chart shows, by December 31, 1994, the value of your investment would have grown to $35,945 — a 259.45% increase on your initial investment. The same $10,000 investment in the S&P 500 (with dividends reinvested) would have grown to $38,358 — a 283.58% increase.

✓ Understanding Performance

How a fund did yesterday is no guarantee of how it will do tomorrow. The stock market, for example, has a history of growth in the long run and volatility in the short run. In turn, the share price and return of a fund that invests in stocks will vary. That means if you sell your shares during a market downturn, you might lose money. But if you can ride out the market's ups and downs, you may have a gain.

Figure 13.4 Continued.

$$RAROR = \frac{AATR}{\text{fund's beta weight}} - \text{S\&P 500 return}$$

One investment advisory service estimated Fidelity Fund's beta at 0.86, which means it is less risky than the overall market. Using Fidelity Fund's 10-year AATR and the S&P 500 10-year AATR, we have

$$\text{Fidelity's } RAROR = \frac{13.65}{0.86} - 14.39 = 15.87 - 14.39 = +1.48\%$$

The +1.48 percent indicates the amount the Fidelity Fund overperformed the S&P 500. A positive number indicates a good performance; and the larger the positive number, the better the performance. Of course, a negative number indicates poor performance. We conclude, then, that Fidelity Fund performed rather well over the 10-year period.

REVIEW THE FUND'S CURRENT PORTFOLIO At this point, you should look at each fund's current holdings. Space prevents a listing of all the securities held by Fidelity, but a summary shows that the fund held stocks and bonds of over 240 different companies in 18 basic industry groupings. Unquestionably, Fidelity was well diversified.

EXAMINE EXPENSES AND PORTFOLIO TURNOVER Managing a mutual fund involves certain administrative expenses. The greater these expenses, the fewer resources the fund has to invest or make shareholder distributions. These expenses are usually related to the size of the portfolio and the frequency of security purchases and sales. This frequency is measured by a turnover percentage. (For example, if a fund replaced 10 percent of its holdings with new holdings, its turnover would be 10 percent.) Table 13.1 shows Fidelity's data for three years: 1992 through 1994. It is important, by the way, to express expenses as percentages of average net assets because funds are quite different in size, and a large fund naturally has higher expenses than a small one. The ratio of expenses to average net assets for most eq-

Box 13.2 SAVING MONEY
Focus on Loads and Annual Expenses

You have $1,000 to invest and are considering mutual funds. Two have come to your attention: Fund A has an 8.5 percent load and typically incurs operating expenses at 2 percent of net assets; Fund B is a no-load fund with an expense ratio of 0.25 percent. If each fund manager earns, say, 12 percent each year before expenses, how much better off are you with Fund B? Answers are in the table below.

B's advantage is anything but trivial, but you probably think this example is stretched to make a point. It is somewhat, but not completely. There are funds with loads as high as 8.5 percent, and you certainly can find two funds with that much difference in expense ratios.

Saving money, then, is simple: First, ignore all load funds; second, select only those no-load funds with low operating expense ratios. But, as with all simple plans, there are a few hitches. First, by eliminating all load funds you cut out a few super performers, such as Fidelity's Magellan Fund—the best performer of all funds over the past 15 years. By relaxing the rule to exclude only high-load funds (loads over 5 percent), you keep most of the better performers, including Magellan.

Second, many load funds are sold by stockbrokers who also provide investment and portfolio management advice. Notice in the table that the load has far less importance with long holding periods. Paying $820 over 20 years may not be an excessive amount if the broker provides useful advice.

The table clearly shows that operating costs are the real villain in the long run. Indeed, some studies have shown that selecting funds with low cost ratios is the most consistent method of selecting funds that are likely to perform well in the future. One mutual fund family, Vanguard, emphasizes low costs, and its funds typically have the lowest ratios in the industry. Not surprisingly, its funds—particularly its index funds—are consistently among the better performers.

Years after Investment	Accumulation:		B's Advantage	Advantage due to:	
	Fund A	Fund B		No Load	Low Costs
1	$1,007	$1,120	$ 113	$ 95	$ 18
10	2,373	3,106	733	265	468
20	6,156	9,646	3,490	820	2,670

TABLE 13.1 • FIDELITY FUND MANAGEMENT EXPENSES AND PORTFOLIO TURNOVER

	1992	1993	1994
Ratio of expenses to average net assets	0.67	0.66	0.65
Portfolio turnover	151%	261%	207%

SOURCES: Fidelity Fund financial reports for 1994.

uity funds is around 1.0 percent. Fidelity's ratios are well below that figure, indicating that management controls expenses rather well.

MUTUAL FUND RATINGS IN THE POPULAR PRESS You can get help in selecting mutual funds from a number of sources, including financial advisory services that charge fees. More readily available sources, though, include the *Wall Street Journal, Barron's, Money, Business Week,* and *Forbes*. *Money* has a "Fund Watch" column appearing in each monthly issue. In addition, it ranks a large number twice a year, reporting each fund's one-, five-, and 10-year performance along with a risk rating. It also gives each fund's address and phone number, making it easy for you to get information.

Specialized Fund-Rating Services

Although considerable information and useful advice are available from popular-press sources, several specialized services provide more-thorough reports on many funds, along with their rankings in a return-risk rating system. A report on Fidelity Fund from one such source, Morningstar, is shown in Figure 13.5 (page 336). As you can see it is quite detailed.

Much of the information in the report should be familiar to you from material presented earlier. Notice in the middle of the page (under the heading "Risk Analysis") the fund's alpha and beta values. Use these terms in the same fashion that we used them in previous chapters. Ideally, you want high alphas and low betas. Notice too the attention given to comparing the fund with the S&P 500 (third row of tabular "History" data), and particularly note Morningstar's four-star rating (small box at the top middle of the page). Five-star is the best, but a four-star rating indicates an above-average performance when a fund is compared with other funds having similar investment objectives.

Morningstar's reports are very helpful in finding top-performing funds. Indeed, its research is so good that many investors rely upon it, rather than doing their own research, to select funds. Your library may carry the service, or you may want to subscribe on your own. The telephone number in the copyright notice at the bottom of the report is a starting point.

INVESTMENT TRUSTS

Investment trusts are another type of pooling arrangement. They have been formed to achieve a variety of investment objectives, ranging from investing in risk-free Treasury securities to speculating in the precious gems market. The two most pop-

Volume 25, Issue Number 4, June 23, 1995. Reprinted with permission.

Fidelity

Ticker	Load	NAV	Yield	SEC Yield	Assets	Objective
FFIDX	None	$20.49	1.6%	N/A	$2249.8 mil	Growth/Inc.

Fidelity Fund seeks long-term capital growth. Current return is also a consideration.

The fund invests primarily in common stocks and convertible securities. It may also purchase debt securities for current income. The percentage of its assets in any one type of security may vary. The fund diversifies in two ways: by investing in several types of securities at the same time and by investing in different industries. The fund may invest up to 5% of assets in lower-quality debt and may also purchase restricted securities. It may also make foreign investments, and engage in options and futures contracts.

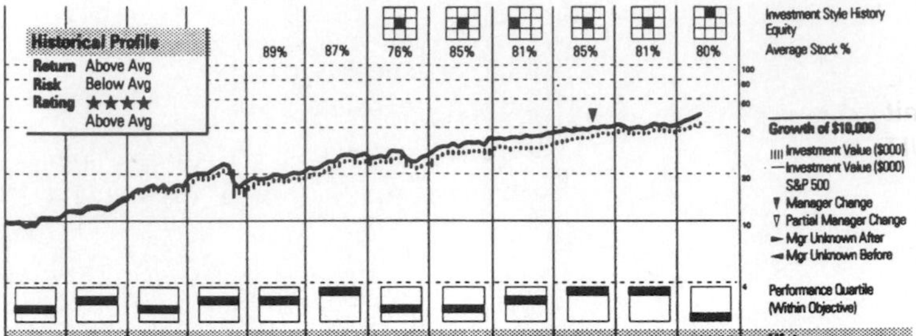

Portfolio Manager(s)

Beth F. Terrana, CFA. Since 8-93. BS'77 SUNY-Binghamton; MBA'83 Harvard. Terrana began her financial career in 1978 as an assistant portfolio manager with Morgan Guaranty Trust Co. She worked as assistant vice president of Putnam Mgmt. until she joined Fidelity Investments in 1983. She is currently a vice president and portfolio manager with Fidelity.

History	1984	1985	1986	1987	1988	1989	1990	1991	1992	1993	1994	05-95
NAV	14.82	18.08	16.05	13.58	15.42	17.93	16.29	18.46	18.94	19.27	18.48	20.49
Total Return %	1.61	27.66	15.76	3.28	17.85	28.80	-5.10	24.15	8.46	18.36	2.58	11.45
+/- S&P 500	-4.66	-4.08	-2.92	-1.98	1.24	-2.88	-1.98	-6.34	0.84	8.31	1.27	-6.01
+/- Wilshire 5000	-1.44	-4.90	-0.33	0.92	-0.09	-0.37	1.09	-10.06	-0.51	7.08	2.65	-4.06
Income Return %	5.15	5.22	3.86	2.87	4.30	4.22	4.05	2.88	2.63	2.30	1.76	0.57
Capital Return %	-3.55	22.44	11.91	0.41	13.55	24.58	-9.15	21.26	5.83	16.06	0.82	10.88
Total Rtn %Rank All	62	35	50	34	19	16	71	38	40	20	9	30
Total Rtn %Rank Obj	67	47	55	42	32	25	62	75	41	10	11	86
Income $	0.72	0.72	0.66	0.48	0.56	0.68	0.74	0.50	0.48	0.44	0.33	0.10
Capital Gains $	4.40	0.05	4.08	2.72	0.00	1.17	0.00	1.15	0.58	2.55	0.94	0.00
Expense Ratio %	0.66	0.66	0.60	0.67	0.67	0.64	0.66	0.68	0.67	0.66	0.65	---
Income Ratio %	5.06	4.25	3.48	2.75	3.69	3.76	4.04	2.84	2.37	2.94	1.85	---
Turnover Rate %	200	215	214	211	175	191	259	267	151	261	207	---
Net Assets ($mil)	618.5	761.5	782.4	873.1	895.2	1085.5	1065.9	1309.7	1353.2	1546.2	1886.1	2249.8

Performance 05-31-95

	1st Qtr	2nd Qtr	3rd Qtr	4th Qtr	Total
1991	16.03	-0.66	5.29	2.30	24.15
1992	1.28	0.22	1.08	5.72	8.46
1993	6.61	2.61	5.71	2.36	18.36
1994	-2.47	-0.12	5.51	-0.19	2.58
1995	6.99	---	---	---	---

Trailing	Total Return %	+/- S&P 500	+/- Wil 5000	% Rank All	% Rank Obj	Growth of $10,000
3 Mo	7.94	-2.26	-0.80	25	70	10,794
6 Mo	12.87	-6.33	-4.20	36	83	11,287
1 Yr	14.64	-5.51	-2.97	16	59	11,464
3 Yr Avg	12.56	0.75	0.92	13	16	14,261
5 Yr Avg	10.90	-0.52	-0.61	25	37	16,771
10 Yr Avg	13.56	-1.03	-0.21	20	26	35,656
15 Yr Avg	15.19	-0.13	0.46	18	21	83,361

Most Similar Funds in MMF

T. Rowe Price Spectrum Grth	Strong Fit
Dreyfus Core Value Inv	Strong Fit
Scudder Growth & Income	Strong Fit

Tax Analysis	Tax-Adj Return %	% Pretax Return
3 Yr Avg	9.56	76.2
5 Yr Avg	8.25	75.7
10 Yr Avg	10.15	74.9
Potential Capital Gain Exposure		10% of assets

Risk Analysis

Time Period	Load-Adj Return %	Risk %Rank[1] All	Risk %Rank[1] Obj	Morningstar[2] Return	Morningstar[2] Risk	Morningstar Risk-Adj Rating
1 Yr	14.64					
3 Yr	12.56	59	23	1.47	0.64	★★★★
5 Yr	10.90	63	39	1.21	0.73	★★★★
10 Yr	13.56	56	45	1.22	0.81	★★★★
Average Historical Rating (114 months)						3.9 ★s

[1] 1=low, 100=high [2] 1.00 = Equity Avg

Other Measures			Standard Index S&P 500	Best Fit Index SPMid400
Standard Deviation	8.01	Alpha	1.8	2.8
Mean	12.21	Beta	0.86	0.72
Sharpe Ratio	1.05	R-Squared	77	77

Portfolio Analysis 12-31-94

Share Chg (06-94) 000	Amount 000	Total Stocks: 209 / Total Fixed-Income: 37	Value $000	% Net Assets
	62680	US Treasury Bond 8.125%	63512	3.37
85	609	British Petroleum (ADR)	48648	2.58
267	575	IBM	42292	2.24
259	295	Hercules	34082	1.81
407	444	Scott Paper	30712	1.63
86	516	Philip Morris	29670	1.57
175	295	Mobil	24854	1.32
486	486	Tyco International	23081	1.22
151	358	Caterpillar	19728	1.05
-169	187	Xerox	18523	0.98
	19960	US Treasury Note 5.75%	17346	0.92
420	420	Viacom Cl B	17046	0.90
147	366	Sears Roebuck	16850	0.89
293	478	AlliedSignal	16259	0.86
372	394	Southwestern Bell	15904	0.84
355	392	Ameritech	15843	0.84
151	533	Union Carbide	15658	0.83
603	603	Sunbeam-Oster	15535	0.82
113	196	Pfizer	15141	0.80
	110	Chrysler Cl A Cv Pfd $4.625	14959	0.79
29	205	FNMA	14939	0.79
	14670	US Treasury Note 7.875%	14711	0.78
232	232	American Home Products	14533	0.77
	15800	US Treasury Note 6.25%	14291	0.76
306	724	Federated Department Stores	13939	0.74

Investment Style

Style: Value Blend Growth; Size: Large Med Small

	Stock Portfolio Avg	Rel S&P 500	Rel Objective
Price/Earnings Ratio	20.0	1.06	1.11
Price/Book Ratio	3.7	0.93	1.07
5 Yr Earnings Gr %	8.4	0.80	0.86
Return on Assets %	7.6	0.94	1.02
Debt % Total Cap	32.2	1.12	1.10
Med Mkt Cap ($mil)	5578	0.37	0.60

Analysis by Erik Laughlin 06-09-95

Investors shouldn't be too put off by Fidelity Fund's recent underperformance.

Through May 1995, the fund is lagging far behind its peers. Although it has made more than 11%, that's pocket change compared with what some funds have pulled in during the recent rally. A couple of factors have held the fund back: One is its light position in financials, which manager Beth Terrana cut in 1994's second half because she feared interest-rate increases would cut their profits. In addition, Terrana, who looks for out-of-favor stocks with improving fundamentals, has naturally held a lot of beaten-down retail and cyclical issues. These have remained beaten-down in 1995, though.

An investor might make the mistake of doubting Terrana's management abilities–after all, the fund's recently poor results are a large portion of her short one-and-a-half-year tenure at the fund. Her record, however, is not limited to this fund: From 1985 to 1990, she built consistently strong results at Fidelity Growth and Income, and from 1990 to 1993, she did a fine job turning around Fidelity Equity-Income. Also, this fund's strength in 1994 owed to some adroit moves Terrana made after taking over.

For the most part, Terrana remains devoted to out-of-favor cyclicals, including a number of restructured global manufacturers. Even though she expects the economy to slow, she believes the streamlined operations of her holdings will allow them to exceed analyst estimates. Terrana isn't a complete contrarian, though, as she is also overweighting rallying technology. She has even added to financials again recently, because she thinks their prospects now look better than they once did.

Given Terrana's long record of success, it's hard not to be confident in her current tactics. Investors certainly shouldn't flee just because of the fund's year-to-date returns.

Special Securities	% of assets
● Private/Illiquid Securities	1.5
○ Structured Notes	0.0
● Emerging-Markets Secs	0.1
○ Options/Futures/Warrants	No

Composition % of assets 03-31-95		Index Allocation % of stocks	
Cash	9.0	S&P 500	63.0
Stocks	84.1	S&P Mid	6.6
Bonds	4.2	US Sm Cap	21.3
Other	2.7	Foreign	12.1

Sector Weightings	% of Stocks	Rel S&P
Utilities	4.3	0.36
Energy	10.7	1.05
Financials	7.5	0.67
Industrial Cyclicals	16.7	1.02
Consumer Durables	9.1	1.56
Consumer Staples	9.5	0.76
Services	10.5	1.32
Retail	8.1	1.49
Health	9.9	1.13
Technology	13.6	1.37

Address	82 Devonshire Street, Boston, MA 02109
Telephone	800-544-8888
Advisor	Fidelity Management & Research
Subadvisor	FMR (U.K.)/FMR (Far East)
Distributor	Fidelity Distributors
States Available	All
Report Grade	A
Income Distrib	Quarterly

Minimum Purchase	$2500	Add: $250	IRA: $500	
Min Auto Inv Plan	$2500	Systematic Inv: $100		
Date of Inception	04-30-30			

Expenses & Fees

Sales Fees	No-load		
Management Fee	0.09% flat fee+0.52%G		
Actual Fees	Mgt: 0.51%	Dist: 0.25%	
Expense Projections	3Yr: $21	5Yr: $36	10Yr: $81
Annual Brokerage Cost	0.42%		

MORNINGSTAR Mutual Funds

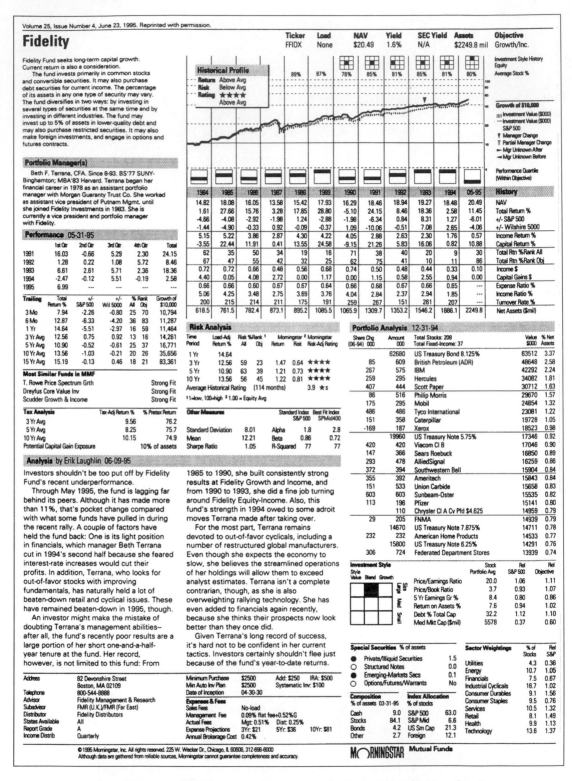

Figure 13.5 A page from Morningstar's *1995 Mutual Fund Sourcebook.*

ular investment trusts are the unit investment trust (UIT) and the real estate investment trust (REIT). Each is explained in the following sections.

Unit Investment Trusts (UITs)

Unit investment trust (UIT): A pooling arrangement similar to an open-end fund; however, the investment portfolio is relatively fixed (unmanaged) over the fund's life.

A **unit investment trust (UIT)** is similar in some respects to an open-end mutual fund, but there are important differences. As Figure 13.6 shows, a UIT is formed when an originator, a large financial firm (such as John Nuveen and Company) creates a portfolio of assets and then sells trust units to individual investors. In most cases you can sell your units back to the trust at their NAVs, which may be quite different—higher or lower—from their original cost to you. Basically, this is how an open-end mutual fund works. The big difference is that the original portfolio of securities remains intact until they are redeemed or the trust is dissolved. The trust is thus an unmanaged fund, reducing administrative expenses considerably; but you do pay a commission (usually 4 percent) to the trust originators.

Municipal (muni) bond trust: A UIT that invests in municipal bonds.*

MUNICIPAL BOND TRUSTS The **municipal (muni) bond trust** is probably the most popular of all UITs. Muni trusts appeal to investors in the highest federal income tax brackets. Some of these trusts have been formed to offer both state and local tax exemption as well, but these often have lower yields than nationally invested trusts and may not offer a significant after-tax advantage. Moreover, because their portfolios are limited to narrow geographic and taxing regions, they typically involve higher risk because of the shortage of suitable securities available for an adequately diversified portfolio.

The default risk with a trust usually is low. Some originators have taken greater risks recently, however, so it is important to review a trust's prospectus to examine the quality of the portfolio it will hold. If more than, say, 20 percent of the issues are rated below BBB (Standard & Poor's minimum investment grade) or Baa (Moody's), there is potential for default losses, and you must decide whether you will be comfortable with this situation. About one-half of the trusts being formed in recent years offer default insurance. While reducing risk, insurance also reduces yield by as much as 40 basis points.

Figure 13.6 Formation of a municipal bond unit investment trust.

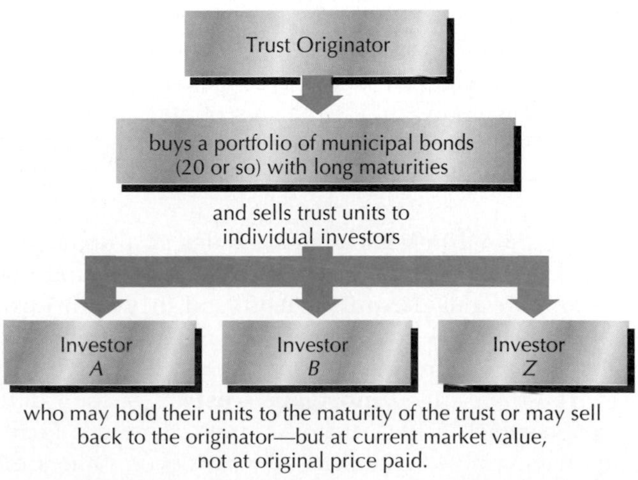

Box 13.3

PERSONAL FINANCE NEWS

Late Edition

Want to Index the Market? Get a Spider.

Investing in stock indexes has become very popular, and there are a number of good mutual funds that make this investment approach available to individual investors. The Vanguard Group pioneered the concept and is today's unquestioned leader in index investing. Recently, though, another investment has been created that also provides an indexing opportunity. The new entrant is a unit investment trust (UIT) created by the American Stock Exchange.

This UIT is called Standard & Poor's Depository Receipts (SPDRs), often referred to as "spiders." Each unit issued by the trust represents a 1/10 interest in the S&P 500 Stock Index. So, if the S&P 500 Index has a value of 550, each unit has an intrinsic value of $55. Actual trading prices of the units on the Amex are very close to intrinsic values, with only slight differences. The trust itself has invested millions of dollars in the shares of companies that make up the index; in effect, the trust's investments support the units held by investors. Buying the S&P 500 Stock Index, then, is no more difficult than buying shares of any actively traded stock. And, if you buy the units, your price gains or losses over time and quarterly dividends will almost perfectly mimic the index.

Spiders have been popular with investors, leading the Amex to consider developing other index-based UITs. But are they a better way to index than using mutual funds? The trust's operating costs are very low, which is favorable for investors, but so are Vanguard's. Moreover, Vanguard does not have a commission on its S&P 500 Index fund, but you will pay a broker's commission to buy spiders. On balance, each approach seems a cost effective way to index, and the final choice might depend on whether you invest primarily through mutual funds or directly in stocks with the assistance of a broker. It's a matter of personal preference.

GNMA trusts: UITs that invest in agency passthrough bonds.

GNMA TRUSTS Most large stockbrokerage houses have formed **GNMA trusts** that invest in Ginnie Mae and other agency passthrough securities. These UITs have also been popular because investing directly involves difficulties, primarily the $25,000 face value of a single security. Most trusts pass both interest and principal payments to trustholders each month, thus providing a steady cash flow.

Real Estate Investment Trusts (REITs)

Real estate investment trust (REIT): A pooling arrangement (similar to a closed-end mutual fund) that invests in real estate and real estate mortgages.

A **real estate investment trust (REIT)** is a type of closed-end investment company similar to closed-end mutual funds explained earlier. To be considered an investment company for tax purposes, the REIT must derive 70 percent of its income from real estate and distribute no less than 90 percent of its income as cash dividends. Many REITs are publicly held, which means that their shares are traded on organized exchanges or in the over-the-counter market. In effect, you buy or sell their shares as you would the shares of any other public corporation. This feature makes REIT shares very marketable, but not necessarily liquid, since their prices are often as volatile as those of other stocks.

Equity trusts: REITs specializing in investing in real estate.

Mortgage trusts: REITs specializing in mortgage lending.

DIFFERENCES AMONG REITs REITs differ in a number of respects. First, some invest in buildings, shopping centers, warehouses, and many other kinds of properties. These are called **equity trusts,** and they earn income from renting space to tenants. Other REITs do not invest in properties but instead invest by lending funds to others; that is, they make loans (usually mortgage loans) to builders and developers. These are called **mortgage trusts.** A second difference has to do with the manner in which a REIT finances itself. Some are financed entirely with owners' equity, having no long-term debt whatsoever. Others make extensive use of borrowed funds, which increases their leverage.

Since REITs differ so much in both the kinds of investments they make and how they are financed, they also differ considerably in their expected return and risk characteristics. Some are extremely safe, while others are very risky. Before investing, you should research their underlying fundamentals, by either doing the work yourself or asking your broker for a research report and an opinion on which ones seem appropriate for your investment objectives.

THE RETURN FROM A REIT As noted earlier, 90 percent of a REIT's earnings must be distributed as dividends. The current return on many REITs is therefore fairly high but also volatile, a factor you should not overlook if a stable return is important to you. Similar to the NAV of a mutual fund, the equity per share (*EqPS*) of a REIT can be determined by dividing assets minus liabilities by the number of shares outstanding; that is,

$$EqPS = \frac{\text{(REIT assets} - \text{liabilities)}}{\text{REIT shares outstanding}}$$

EqPS is an important figure to investors who want to know if the market price of a REIT share is selling at a discount or premium to it. You should understand, however, that assets are measured at their book—rather than appraised—values. If a REIT acquired properties some years ago, there is a good possibility that book value will be substantially below appraised value. So it is important not to attach excessive importance to the EqPS figure.

INVESTMENT APPEAL OF REITs Many financial planners feel that a portion of your portfolio should be invested in certain types of assets to hedge against inflation. Real estate has been particularly effective in this capacity, and people who buy homes not only achieve living space but also add an important asset to their portfolios.

Unfortunately, not all investors are homeowners. REITs (of the equity trust variety) should be even more appealing to them. If you are a renter, consider seriously a REIT investment. A good place to begin your search for information is the National Association of REITs, 1129 20th Street NW, Suite 705, Washington, D.C. 20036 (telephone 202-785-8717).

LIMITED PARTNERSHIPS AND INVESTMENT CLUBS

Two other popular pooling arrangements are limited partnerships and investment clubs. These are quite different organizational forms; you are likely to be fairly active in the latter, but have little input in the former.

Limited Partnerships

Limited partnership: A pooling arrangement that combines features of a corporation and a general partnership.

A **limited partnership** is a legal arrangement that combines features of a corporation and a general partnership. The formation of a limited partnership is illustrated in Figure 13.7; as you see, limited partnerships engage in a wide variety of business activities. However, owning and managing real estate is the most important.

A limited partnership is similar to a corporation in that most investors (called *limited partners*) are inactive in management of the business, preferring instead to

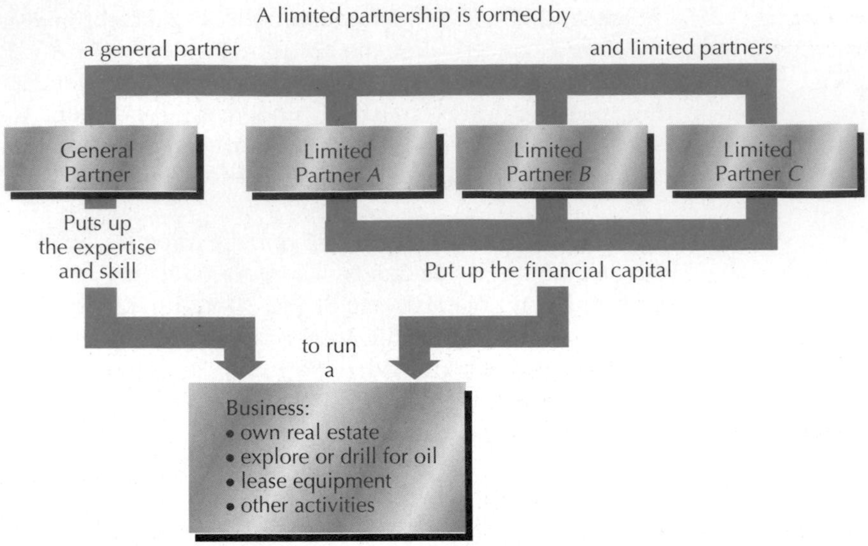

Figure 13.7 Formation of a limited partnership.

turn over these responsibilities to a person called the *general partner*. It resembles a partnership in that profits or losses from the business are passed directly to the partners rather than being profits or losses of the business itself. It is the federal income tax implications of this last feature that makes limited partnerships appealing. For example, suppose you invested $1,000 in a corporation and owned 10 percent of the shares. Suppose further that the business did poorly and showed a $20,000 net loss for the year. This corporate loss would have no personal income tax implication. In a limited partnership, however, you would take your share of the business loss on your individual tax return. In the above example, you could deduct $2,000 (10 percent of $20,000) in the year of the loss. If you were in a 28 percent tax bracket, you would have reduced your taxes by $560. Limited partnerships are often called **tax shelters,** and you can see why; however, limited partnerships are also used even when tax advantages are not the most important goal.

Tax shelters: A term used to describe limited partnerships.

LIQUIDITY WITH LIMITED PARTNERSHIPS Unlike mutual funds and unit investment trusts, limited partnership interests cannot be sold in any readily available markets. If partnership interests are held by the public and if the promoter is a large stockbrokerage firm, they might be able to find a buyer, but there is no guarantee. If the partnership is privately held, selling your interest may be extremely difficult. You might wait until the partnership is dissolved to recover your original investment plus any capital appreciation. Obviously, if liquidity is an important concern, then a limited partnership interest is not a suitable investment.

THE TAX SITUATION WITH LIMITED PARTNERSHIPS The 1986 Tax Reform Act eliminated many of the tax advantages previously associated with limited partnerships. The act's loss limitation rules stipulate that any loss from a limited partnership can be used to offset gains from other limited partnerships, but any combined net loss cannot be used to offset other forms of income, such as earned income or portfolio income. (See Chapter 5 for a review of the loss limitation rules.)

INVESTMENT POTENTIAL The income tax situation seriously limits the investment quality of many real estate limited partnerships. Without any particular tax advantages to consider, you should evaluate this investment no differently than you would all other passive investments, such as stocks or bonds. However, evaluation might be more difficult since cash flows from the business, including its eventual liquidation, are difficult to estimate. In today's environment it is probably good advice to avoid all limited partnerships unless you are skilled at interpreting the materials they provide.

You can, of course, rely upon a financial adviser; but be careful if that person receives a commission from the partnership in which you invest. At the very least, have the adviser explain (in writing) the return and risks you can expect and why the partnership is suitable for your investment objectives. Investment scams frequently take on the appearance of legitimate business activities, many cloaked in the mystique of the limited partnership. Put simply, you can't be too cautious. All things considered, small investors are well advised to simply avoid limited partnerships altogether.

Investment Clubs

Investment club: A pooling arrangement characterized usually by a small number of members, monthly meetings and dues, and regular investment (and social) activities.

For many people, an **investment club** is the ideal way to achieve diversification: It gives them an opportunity for fun and fellowship, along with a possibility of profit. Most investment clubs invest in common stocks, although you can find a range of investment objectives. Some of the clubs have excellent performance records, and their members take a most serious attitude toward finding good investments.

You invest in a club by paying monthly dues, usually in the $25 range, which are then used to buy securities selected by the membership. Most clubs reinvest dividends and capital gains. Securities are often recommended for purchase by members given the task of researching a specific company or industry, and this is perhaps the most enjoyable part of being a member. You can expect divergent opinions and robust discussion in any club in which members take their investments seriously. If you would like to join an investment club but don't know how, you can write the NAIC at Department B, 1515 E. Eleven Mile Road, Royal Oak, Michigan 48067.

CONSTRUCTING AND MAINTAINING YOUR PERSONAL PORTFOLIO

Now that we have examined the two most popular direct investments—stocks and bonds—and the popular pooling arrangements, it is time to put it all together by considering your personal portfolio. Investors share many common characteristics, but in a sense each investor is unique in terms of his or her risk attitude and financial goals. A portfolio suitable for you may be totally inappropriate for your parents.

Portfolio Construction

A portfolio should begin with a plan that considers your risk-tolerance level and your investment objectives. Then, specific investments are selected and combined to achieve the objectives within the risk tolerance specified. An important reason why many investors have so little success is that they do not specify concrete investment objectives. General goals, such as "making a lot of money," are too ambiguous to be of much help. We all want to make money—but over what period of time and subject to what degree of risk?

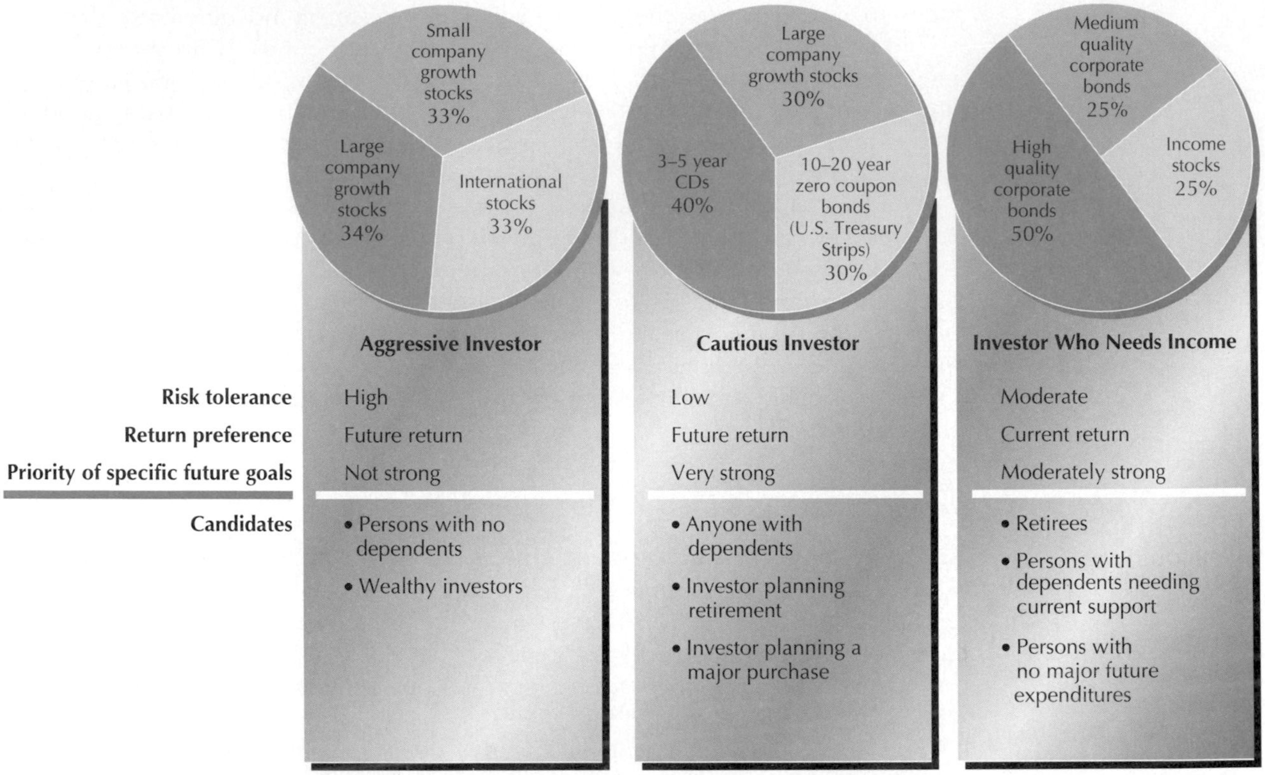

Figure 13.8 Portfolios are designed to meet specific investment objectives. These differ, depending upon circumstances and the investor's risk tolerance. Three cases are shown. The asset weights in each portfolio should be considered as broad approximations, since more exact amounts would require detailed information about specific investors. Also, it is assumed that the investor owns a home, has sufficient funds to meet liquidity needs, and has adequate life insurance.

Figure 13.8 illustrates the portfolio construction process for three different types of investors. (Of course, other types are possible.) It is assumed that each investor owns a home and has adequate liquid assets and insurance. If any of these conditions are not met, then a different asset portfolio would be recommended. For example, if a home was not owned, then it would be desirable to allocate 30 to 40 percent to real estate (or some other form of investment with inflation-hedging capacity), possibly REITs, and cut back proportionately in the other asset categories.

AGGRESSIVE INVESTORS As an aggressive investor, you are likely to have a high risk-tolerance level and generally prefer future return to current return. We assume in this example that you have no specific future goals with high priorities; although that assumption could be relaxed with respect to a retirement goal. As you see, the recommended asset mix is one-third each for large company growth stocks, small company growth stocks, and international stocks. Many excellent mutual funds offer these kinds of stocks, and you should diversify by owning two or three funds in each category. It is very important to make sure of the fund's investment objective. For example, the Fidelity Fund we have been reviewing would not be a good choice even though it has a good performance history. It is a growth *and income* fund, not simply a growth fund.

Although the recommended mix of assets will provide some degree of diversification, particularly with the international stocks, your portfolio still will have a high degree of market value volatility. However, if you hold the portfolio for a reasonably long period of time (say, 10 years or longer), you should show a good accumulation of value.

CAUTIOUS INVESTORS A cautious investor generally has a low risk-tolerance level but, more important, also attaches a high priority to accumulating sufficient sums of money to achieve certain future goals. If you are planning for a major expenditure in five years, or retirement in 10 years, and you want to be sure that sufficient

Action Plan for the Steeles: Considering Income Taxes in Constructing Their Portfolio for Retirement

Background The Steeles have been working diligently to construct a portfolio that meets their investment objectives and risk-tolerance levels. A good portion of their investment assets will be dedicated to accumulating a retirement nest egg. They plan to accomplish this by investing in common stocks, mutual funds, or both.

The Problem Each investment method can be effective, but the Steeles need to consider how the federal income tax will influence their potential accumulation amount. Mutual funds are required by law to distribute to shareholders the income they receive and any realized capital gains. Shareholders receive this information each year and, of course, include the items on their income tax returns. The Steeles are paying taxes—at a 28 percent marginal rate—on the distributions they receive from the Fidelity Fund. So, if the fund shows a return of 20 percent, the after-tax return to the Steeles will be 14.4 percent ($[1.0 - 0.28] \times 20\%$). A 28 percent reduction in return is a serious matter.

The Plan The income tax also applies to direct investments in stocks or bonds, but, by investing directly rather than through mutual funds, the Steeles have greater control of its impact. For example, selecting growth stocks minimizes taxable dividends, and, by not selling the stocks, the Steeles avoid capital gains. The Steeles should continue with their plan of accumulating 15–20 different stocks diversified widely among different industries. To gain international diversification, the Steeles should include companies with considerable foreign sales and profits—Coca-Cola, for example. Since the Steeles presently own shares in only five different companies, they should continue holding at least one mutual fund until they achieve greater diversification. The Fidelity Fund they currently own has a good performance history, but it does not focus exclusively on growth. It will take some time for the Steeles to achieve adequate diversification, so they should switch into one of Fidelity's growth funds. Although there may be no tax advantage, because a fund's capital gains are taxable, its investment approach more closely matches the Steele's investment objective.

Rationale for the Plan The plan rests on the assumption that the Steeles have no opportunities to invest through tax deferral plans such as IRAs or 401(k)s. Should these arrangements become available, then the Steeles could consider holding mutual funds in them. At that point, Arnie and Sharon must determine whether they can invest as effectively as the top-performing mutual funds and whether they want to continue doing all the investment-related work.

funds are available to meet that target, then your portfolio must be constructed accordingly.

In our example, 70 percent of your funds are invested in assets with predetermined accumulation amounts—bank-issued certificates of deposit (CDs) and U.S. Treasury Strips. (Of course, the maturities of these investments would match the horizon dates of your goals, which may not be the same as those in the example.) You could use mutual funds to acquire the Treasury Strips, or you could purchase them directly through a broker.

Even though you have a strong priority for achieving future goals, it often makes sense to put some of your funds into a growing asset, such as large company growth stocks, since you do not need current return. Clearly, this move adds an element of risk to your future accumulation amount, and you should not make it if your future plans are in a sense "set in stone." But such rigidity is not common with many investment goals. You might plan $10,000 for a nice vacation in four years, although any amount between $8,000 and $12,000 will do; adding a growth asset gives you a good shot at the higher amount but also brings a possibility for the smaller one.

INVESTORS WHO NEED INCOME If you need income from your investments, you must select vehicles that provide high current returns. Our example assumes that you have a moderate risk-tolerance level. So you could place half your funds in high-quality corporate bonds and divide the other half between two moderately riskier investments—medium-quality corporate bonds and income stocks. This mix should provide a return of one to two percentage points more than if you invested in very safe bonds, such as U.S. Treasuries. Of course, if you have a very low risk-tolerance level, then the Treasuries would be more appropriate.

Mutual funds are definitely the best route for the recommended investments here. As we noted in Chapter 12, bond investment is somewhat complex and can be expensive for small amounts invested. You will have no trouble finding very good bond funds. Those offered by the Vanguard Group are particularly appealing because Vanguard features low operating costs and no front-end loads. Several studies have shown that performance differences among fixed-income funds are explained mostly by variations in fund expenses. So find funds with low expenses and you are likely also to find funds with good performance potential.

Maintaining Your Portfolio

Over time, the values of assets in your portfolio are likely to change; some assets will increase in value while others decline, or increase less rapidly. Of the three investor types discussed above, fluctuations would be most likely for the aggressive investor. As the investment values change, the portfolio weights will also change. For example, the aggressive investor's small company growth stocks might show substantial increases over several years and become, say, 50 percent of the portfolio's total value. Clearly, it may be necessary to rebalance the portfolio. Several rebalancing approaches are used—a constant ratio plan and a variable ratio plan.

Constant ratio plan: A method of rebalancing a portfolio that restores each component to a preset percentage.

CONSTANT RATIO PLAN As the name implies, a **constant ratio plan** adjusts the portfolio back to its target weights—a third in each asset category for the aggressive investor example. So you would sell some of the small company growth stocks and reinvest in the large company growth stocks and the international stocks, assuming that each was under 33 percent. To avoid excessive trading, you might do rebalancing only once a year or when one asset exceeds a predetermined limit, say 40 percent. Rebalancing might be done more often with mutual funds if switches among funds are free.

Some investment advisers feel that rebalancing your portfolio not only keeps the portfolio in line with your investment goals but also has the advantage of selling some assets that have appreciated (perhaps excessively) in value and buying those that have not fared well (but are hoped to do so in the future). If you like this idea, then why not carry it to a higher level?

Variable ratio plan: A method of rebalancing a portfolio that places greater weight on underperforming assets in a restoration.

VARIABLE RATIO PLAN A **variable ratio plan** does just that; it rebalances, but it stacks the proportions in favor of assets that have performed poorly in recent periods. For example, you would reduce small company growth stocks to, say, 25 percent while increasing large company growth stocks and international stocks to, say, 37.5 percent each. You should see that this plan not only departs from your original plan but is also a form of market timing. Our discussion of market timing in Chapter 10 was not encouraging, and neither is our opinion of variable ratio plans.

Asset Allocation Mutual Funds

Asset allocation mutual funds: Mutual funds that operate with certain portfolio component weight guidelines.

If you dislike the idea of constructing and maintaining a portfolio, you could consider investing in **asset allocation mutual funds** and let the fund managers make such decisions for you. These funds operate within certain guidelines as to component weights of their portfolios. For instance, Fidelity has three such funds, each having a different objective. Its Asset Manager fund, for example, seeks high total return with relatively low risk. Its target asset weights are 40 percent common stocks, 40 percent bonds, and 20 percent short-term securities, and it adjusts its portfolio to fluctuate around those weights. Although we don't know its actual strategy, it is likely to be a version of a constant or variable ratio plan.

Asset allocation funds are appropriate for investors with broadly defined investment objectives, such as our above aggressive investor. Unfortunately, there is some evidence suggesting that their returns are not very good, when measured in a risk-return setting. Much of their poor performance arises from poor market-timing results, the very area in which they supposedly are better than the average small investor.

SUMMARY

Mutual funds are the most popular form of pooling arrangement. Some have loads (a buying commission), others do not; some are open-end funds (shares are bought from and redeemed by the fund), others are closed-end funds (shares are traded in securities markets). Investors should seek funds with objectives similar to their own and should consider the services the funds provide. After determining a fund's objective, investors should evaluate the fund's performance, considering both its past returns and its risks. Reviewing the fund's operating expenses and portfolio turnover rate may also help identify above-average funds.

Investment trusts are another popular pooling arrangement. Unit investment trusts (UITs) typically acquire municipal bonds or mortgage passthrough securities. UITs do not manage their portfolios but, rather, hold securities until they mature. Real estate investment trusts (REITs) invest in real property or mortgages related to property financing. REIT portfolios are managed, and their performance can be evaluated in a manner similar to that used for evaluating closed-end funds.

A limited partnership differs substantially from mutual funds and trusts insofar as it is governed by different income tax regulations, which may or may not appeal to investors. In general, limited partnerships have little appeal to smaller investors. In contrast, investment clubs—another pooling arrangement—have considerable appeal.

Pooling arrangements are ideal investment vehicles for constructing and maintaining a personal portfolio. A portfolio is constructed to achieve investor objectives within a risk-tolerance framework. Aggressive, cautious, and income-seeking investors will seek very different asset mixes. After portfolio component weights are established, investors may need to rebalance their portfolios periodically as component market values change. Constant and variable ratio plans are often used to rebalance. Investors who wish to minimize all portfolio work might invest in asset allocation mutual funds.

KEY TERMS

asset allocation mutual funds (p. 375)
closed-end fund (p. 357)
constant ratio plan (p. 374)
equity trusts (p. 368)
fund switching (p. 360)
global fund (p. 359)
GNMA trusts (p. 368)
index fund (p. 359)
international fund (p. 359)
investment club (p. 371)
limited partnership (p. 369)
load fund (p. 356)
maximum capital appreciation fund (p. 359)
money market fund (p. 359)
mortgage trusts (p. 368)
municipal (muni) bond trust (p. 367)
mutual fund (p. 355)
net asset value (NAV) (p. 355)
no-load fund (p. 356)
open-end fund (p. 357)
prospectus (p. 358)
real estate investment trust (REIT) (p. 368)
reinvestment plan (p. 360)
sector fund (p. 359)
shareholder report (p. 358)
tax shelters (p. 370)
unit investment trust (UIT) (p. 367)
variable ratio plan (p. 375)

PROBLEMS AND REVIEW QUESTIONS

1. What is a mutual fund? Define NAV, and explain how it is calculated.
2. What is the difference between a load and a no-load fund? Is one a better performer than the other?
3. What is the difference between an open-end and a closed-end fund? Which type might show a discount? Is a discount an advantage or disadvantage? Explain.
4. Kim Karnes is thinking of buying the three mutual funds listed below:

	NAV	Offer Price	Closing Price on NYSE
Alpha	10.50	N.L.	—
Beta	21.00	22.90	—
Gamma	30.75	—	$26.25

   But Kim doesn't know what any of the above means. Help Kim by explaining the difference in the three funds.
5. Identify nine different fund objectives. Explain which appeals most to you.
6. Briefly explain four important services provided by mutual funds.
7. Distinguish between a fund's cumulative total return and its average annual total return over a given time period, say five years.
8. Metro Fund had a cumulative total return of 150 percent over the past four years. If you invested $1,000 in the fund four years ago, how much is your investment worth today?
9. What roles do a fund's operating costs and portfolio turnover rate play in terms of fund evaluation? Explain.

10. You bought 100 shares of an open-end mutual fund one year ago at $10 a share. You received a $0.50 per share distribution six months ago when the fund's NAV was $12.50 a share. If the fund's NAV at the end of the year was $12 a share, calculate your rate of return on the fund for the year.
11. Provide a brief explanation of the following, indicating their advantages and disadvantages:
    (*a*) a unit investment trust,
    (*b*) a real estate investment trust,
    (*c*) a limited partnership,
    (*d*) an investment club.
12. Explain how your risk-tolerance level and investment objectives influence the construction of your personal portfolio.
13. Indicate the type of securities or mutual funds that you believe are suitable for an aggressive investor whose primary investment goal is capital accumulation over the long term. Contrast your advice in that case to the advice you would give a person with a low risk-tolerance level who seeks current income.
14. Explain constant and variable ratio plans. Which is actually a form of market timing? Explain.
15. Describe an asset allocation fund. What type of investor might be interested in such funds?

Case 13.1 The Byrons' Search for a Mutual Fund

Lorrie and Dave Byron are saving for their children's education. They estimate they will need about $10,000 a year for a six-year period beginning nine years from now. The Byrons have sufficient liquidity and will not need these investment funds until then. They have decided that mutual funds represent the best investment vehicle for them, and they are currently trying to select one for their first investment of $3,000.

Lorrie is impressed with the Sun Income Fund, which invests mainly in fixed-income securities. Lorrie notes that it has a good history of making distributions and that its rate of return last year (1996) was 17.0 percent. Dave disagrees with Lorrie's selection; instead, he favors the Ambrux Capital Appreciation Fund. It invests heavily in the common stock of growth companies, and it distributes very little each year, preferring rather to reinvest capital gains. He argues that since they will not need distributions, it doesn't make sense to invest in a fund that features them. He also notes that Ambrux's rate of return last year was 33.4 percent, a much better performance than Sun's.

Lorrie agrees that growth might be a better investment goal than high current income, but she thinks it doesn't matter how much a fund distributes, since they will elect to have all distributions reinvested in the fund anyway. Her preference for the Sun Fund rests mostly with her feeling that it is less risky—and she thinks the beta values for each support this view.

QUESTIONS

1. Using the data on page 378, calculate the rates of return for each fund for 1995 and 1996. Your figures for 1996 should agree with the values given in the case. Calculate the average rate of return for the two-year period for each fund.
2. Show how much their $3,000 investment would be worth as of December 31, 1996, assuming it was invested in one or the other fund. Assume that distributions during the year were used to acquire additional shares at the average NAV for the year.
3. Assuming that each fund is no-load and that the two funds are similar in other important respects, which do you recommend for the Byrons? Explain the reason(s) for your choice. Be sure to comment on the issue of distributions from the funds.
4. Explain whether you think it might be a good idea for the Byrons to divide their investments between the two funds.

	Sun Income Fund	Ambrux Capital Appreciation Fund
NAV:		
December 31, 1994	$16.50	$12.50
December 31, 1995	15.00	11.00
December 31, 1996	16.00	14.00
Distributions per share:		
1995	$ 3.00	$ 0.50
1996	1.50	0.60
Current beta value	0.60	1.20

Case 13.2 Evaluating Cliff Swatner's Portfolio

Cliff Swatner is single, 33 years old, and owns a condominium in New York City worth $250,000. Cliff is an attorney and doing well financially. His income last year exceeded $90,000, and he has sufficient liquid assets to supplement his condominium and other tangible assets. Several years ago, Cliff began investing in stocks and bonds. He made his selections on the basis of articles he read describing good investment opportunities. Some have worked well for Cliff, but others have not. Cliff has never taken the time to evaluate his portfolio performance, but he feels it isn't very good. Cliff currently has about $90,000 invested. He has been dating a woman lately and hopes to marry her in three years, at which time he will need $20,000 for marriage expenses and a honeymoon. Cliff's only other objective is to accumulate funds for retirement, but he does not have a specific dollar target for this goal. Cliff feels that he has a moderate risk-tolerance level.

QUESTIONS

1. Explain some disadvantages of Cliff's current investment approach.
2. Construct a portfolio for Cliff, limiting your selections to mutual funds (assume that he sells his current stock and bond holdings). Make sure your plan indicates specific dollar amounts for each portfolio component.
3. Explain how Cliff should rebalance his portfolio periodically, indicating how frequently rebalancing should be done.

HELPFUL CONTACTS

National Association of Investment Clubs
1515 East 11 Mile Road, Royal Oak, MI 48067

Filing an arbitration claim:

American Arbitration Association
140 West 51 Street, New York, NY (telephone 212-484-4000)

American Stock Exchange, 86 Trinity Place, New York, NY 10006

National Association of Securities Dealers
Two World Trade Center, New York, NY 10048 (telephone 212-858-4400)

New York Stock Exchange, 11 Wall Street, New York, NY 10005

U.S. Securities and Exchange Commission
Washington, DC 20549
Office of Consumer Affairs: 202-272-7440

Investment Company Institute
1600 M Street, Washington, DC 20036 (telephone 202-293-7700)
The Institute has a number of useful free publications concerning mutual funds.

Two excellent sources of mutual fund evaluations and beta values (for use in your own evaluation work) are:

Morningstar, Inc.
225 W. Wacker Dr., Chicago, IL 60606 (312-696-6000)

CDA/Wiesenberger Investment Company Services
CDA Investment Technologies, Inc.
Rockville, MD 20850 (301-975-9600)

INTERNET ADDRESSES

Fidelity Investments Online Center (information on the Fidelity family of funds)
http://www.fid-inv.com/

Internet Closed-End Investor
http://www.icefi.com/

Mutual Funds Magazine
http://www.mfmag.com

NetWorth (mutual funds)
http://networth.galt.com/

No Load Mutual Fund Guide (information on no-load funds supporting this web site)
http://networth.galt.com/www/home/mutual/100/100guide.htm

Vanguard Mutual Funds (prices and performance for this fund group)
http://www.vanguard.com/

Chapter 14

Other Investments: Expanding the Investment Menu

Objectives

1. To understand what is meant by an income-producing property and how one should be evaluated for investment purposes
2. To recognize why land investment is usually considered risky and suitable primarily for wealthy investors
3. To see why vacation homes can be good investments and how the federal income tax law affects their potential returns
4. To identify different methods for holding gold or silver as investments
5. To appreciate the inherent risks in precious metals, gems, hobbies and collectibles, and commodity future contracts
6. To understand the nature of a derivative security and why such securities are extremely risky
7. To know the important characteristics of call and put option contracts and futures contracts

Most investors limit their portfolios to stocks, bonds, and mutual funds; however, not a small number look for profits elsewhere. Fortunes have been made (and lost) in real estate or speculating on the price of gold. If you have an aggressive investment nature and a high risk tolerance, you might find some of these investments very appealing. But be forewarned: You are venturing into potential high-risk areas. Learn the risks well before you take a plunge, and consider this chapter as merely an introduction. As a serious investor, you need to know much more.

REAL ESTATE

Real estate appeals to people who like to be active in managing their investments. If you buy shares of General Motors stock, GM's managers—not you—run the business, but if you buy an apartment complex, you are the boss. Another major appeal is that most (perhaps all) of your investment is financed with borrowed funds—the property mortgage. Banks put up the money, and you put in your know-how and hard work—it's an offer many investors can't refuse, although, many times they should.

Income-Producing Property

Income-producing property: A real estate investment that provides periodic rentals.

Net operating income (NOI): A profit measurement—the difference between gross rentals and the costs of providing tenants' services.

An **income-producing property** is one that provides periodic rentals. As the owner, you receive these rents each period (usually each month), and it is your responsibility to provide tenants all the services specified in the rental agreement. These services can range from virtually nothing—all you provide is the land—to practically everything, such as heat and air conditioning, painting and repairs, water and sewerage, and possibly other services. From gross rentals you must deduct costs of providing tenants' services; the difference is your **net operating income (NOI),** which is one source of return. Another is a gain if you happen to sell the property for more than you have invested in it; and a third source is any tax savings you might enjoy because of deductions allowed by the IRS.

ALTERNATIVES AVAILABLE The three sources of return vary considerably depending upon the type of property you are considering. For example, an apartment unit in a deteriorated part of town may not show capital appreciation over time; in fact, its market value may decline. In order to be economically viable, this investment would have to show a high NOI or have special tax deductions. Alternatively, another property might show a poor NOI but be located in a growing part of town where property values are rising rapidly. In this case, you might accept the lower current return in favor of the higher expected future return. As you see, property investment is very much like common stock investment, where you also must decide between current and future return.

Another factor to consider is the property's physical condition, and there is usually a trade-off here too. The real estate market is not perfect in the sense that property prices always reflect their true economic value; nevertheless, they are extremely efficient in this respect. This implies that the poorer the condition of a property, the lower its price. Such situations offer opportunities to first-time buyers without much cash: They can buy lower-priced properties and invest their own time and efforts to improve them. This is called using **"sweat equity"** as a replace-

"Sweat equity": Use of your own labor to enhance a property's value.

ment for financial equity, and it has helped many ambitious people launch successful endeavors in real estate. Naturally, you shouldn't think that every neglected property can be improved by sweat equity; in fact, many are so considerably overpriced, given their poor physical conditions, that they are better left alone. And it would be foolish to jump into this investment arena without proper training and, possibly, guidance from someone experienced in the area.

Along this line, many real estate professionals will tell you to stick to properties familiar to you at the start and gradually undertake more ambitious projects as your knowledge and experience grow. This strategy applies particularly to finding potentially profitable properties and arranging suitable financing to buy them. We can't help you with finding properties, but we can show you how to calculate a return on property investment and how to evaluate it. And, by all means, do calculate a return for each property you are thinking of buying. It forces you to look critically at the economics of the investment and to avoid emotional factors that often are present in buying real estate.

Finally, after you buy a property, you must manage it professionally and in a businesslike manner. Prompt collection of rents and payment of bills are musts, and so is routine maintenance. All this takes time and effort that should be considered before investing. Contrary to what some realtors may tell you, there are very few properties that manage themselves.

MEASURING RETURN Measuring the return from a real estate investment is somewhat involved—primarily because of income tax complexities—but the techniques are not difficult to understand. An example will help clarify them. In 1996, Arnold and Sharon Steele were considering a number of investment opportunities. One property particularly appealed to them. It was a duplex situated in a good neighborhood that was mostly residential, but with some service and retail businesses. It was not far from their home, making it convenient to manage. Property values in the neighborhood did not fluctuate much and had been increasing at about 5 percent a year. The duplex was in sound physical condition, featuring brick construction, and it had been improved within the past 10 years by the addition of separate heating and air-conditioning units for each apartment. Each tenant paid $400 a month rent and all utilities except water and sewerage. Lawn service and snow removal were provided by the owner.

The seller's asking price was $80,000, but she most likely would have accepted $75,000 from a buyer with financing in hand. Arnold and Sharon discussed the property with a loan officer from a savings and loan, who indicated that a $60,000, 9 percent (fixed rate), 30-year loan would be available to them. This means the Steeles needed a $15,000 down payment. Details of the loan appear in Table 14.1.

TABLE 14.1 • DETAILS OF THE STEELES' MORTGAGE LOAN

Year	Total Payments	Annual Payoff		Loan Balance
		Interest	Principal	
1	$5,793	$5,383	$410	$59,590
2	5,793	5,345	448	59,142
3	5,793	5,303	490	58,651

Amount: $60,000.
Term: 30 years.
Monthly Payment: $482.77.
Rate: 9%, fixed.

To evaluate this investment, Arnold and Sharon followed standard guidelines used by most realtors and property appraisers. These guidelines involve a series of steps.

Step 1. Calculate the first year's net operating income (NOI) and cash flow before taxes. This is done in Figure 14.1. It is important to make these estimates of NOI as accurate as possible because subsequent years' NOIs are based on it. In the Steeles' case, licenses and permits, insurance, property taxes, and sewer and water are obtained readily from existing records; but vacancy losses and repairs and maintenance are not so easily determined and require careful estimating. Even though tenants pay their own utilities, keeping the heating and air-conditioning units in good shape is the Steeles' responsibility. In addition, they must allow for periodic painting as well as plumbing or electrical repairs.

The $1,200 allowance for these latter items should be adequate but may not be in the event of a major problem. If everything goes according to plan, the property will show a negative cash flow of $203 in the first year, which doesn't sound good. As you see in Figure 14.1, **cash flow before taxes** is simply NOI minus total payments on the mortgage.

Cash flow before taxes: A profit measurement—NOI minus debt service outlays.

Step 2. Calculate cash flows before taxes for the remaining number of years the property will be held. In order to do this, two estimates are needed. First, you must estimate how much NOI will grow (or decline) over time, and second, you must determine how long the property will be held. Of course, each of these estimates is often difficult to make. The Steeles feel that they will hold the property at least six years and maybe longer, but to simplify our calculations we will assume that they will sell it after three years. As for growth in NOI, the Steeles feel that a 5 percent annual rate is reasonable. Given these assumptions, the NOIs and before-tax cash flows can be calculated. They are shown in Table 14.2 and, as you see, the picture is still bleak.

Step 3. Determine the impact of income taxes. If a property shows a profit, it is, of course, taxable. Equally important, if the property shows a loss, it can offset other

Figure 14.1 Calculating the annual net operating income (NOI).

1. Estimated annual gross rentals (fully rented: $400 per unit × 2 units × 12 months)	$9,600
2. Less allowance for vacancies (10%)	960
3. Gross operating income	$8,640
4. Less operating expenses:	
a. Licenses and permits	$ 60
b. Property and liability insurance	440
c. Property taxes	900
d. Repairs and maintenance	1,200
e. Water and sewer	450
5. Total operating expenses	$3,050
6. Net operating income	$5,590
7. Less mortgage payments	5,793
8. Cash flow (negative) before taxes	$ (203)

TABLE 14.2 • CALCULATION OF CASH FLOW BEFORE TAXES			
	Year 1	Year 2	Year 3
NOI (expected to grow at 5% each year)	$5,090	$5,870	$6,163
Less debt service	(5,793)	(5,793)	(5,793)
Cash flow before taxes	$ (203)	$ 77	$ 370

taxable income you might have and thereby reduce your income tax liability. (Offsets are subject to the loss limitation rules, explained in Chapter 5. To earn the maximum offset of $25,000, the taxpayer must be active in managing the property and have an adjusted gross income of less than $100,000. The Steeles meet each restriction.) Table 14.3 shows the income tax impacts for each of the three years. As you see, the property shows a loss in each year. Since these losses would reduce the Steeles' other taxable income, they have value, the amount of which depends upon the Steeles' marginal tax rate. Assuming a 28 percent marginal tax rate, the Steeles would reduce their tax liability each year by the amount shown in Table 14.3. You have probably noticed that the higher your marginal tax rate, the greater the value of a tax loss. Since many properties show losses—at least in their early years—you can understand why property investment is particularly appealing to investors in high tax brackets. For the same reason, it might not be profitable to low-bracket investors.

Depreciation: An income tax deduction that allows you to recover the cost of an asset.

Depreciation basis: The allowable value of an asset upon which depreciation is based.

After-tax cash flow: A profit measurement—before tax cash flow adjusted for income tax flows, which can be positive if a property shows tax losses.

To understand **depreciation,** you need to know that it is an income tax deduction that allows you to recover the cost of an asset as it wears out over time. In the Steeles' case, it is allowed on the building but not on the land on which the building sits. Therefore, the Steeles must estimate the land's value and subtract it from the purchase price. Assuming the land's value is $10,000 and subtracting it from $75,000 gives $65,000, which is called the property's **depreciation basis.** Now you can write off a portion of this basis each year using several allowable methods. We show the easiest, called straight line depreciation. You divide the basis by the number of years the IRS allows as its estimated life to arrive at an annual depreciation expense. The current tax law sets this write-off period at 27.5 years (regardless of how long the building actually lasts); therefore, the Steeles will have a $2,364 ($65,000/27.5) deduction each year.

Step 4. Calculate the **after-tax cash flow.** Bringing together the before-tax cash flow from Table 14.2 with the value of the taxable losses from Table 14.3 gives us the after-tax cash flow in Table 14.4. As you see, the investment is looking better, and had your analysis stopped at Table 14.2, your evaluation of the property

TABLE 14.3 • CALCULATION OF INCOME TAX IMPACTS			
	Year 1	Year 2	Year 3
Cash flow before taxes, from Table 14.2	$ (203)	$ 77	$ 370
Add principal payments, from Table 14.1*	410	448	490
Deduct depreciation	(2,364)	(2,364)	(2,364)
Taxable income (loss) from the property	(2,157)	(1,839)	(1,504)
Steeles' marginal income tax rate	× 0.28	× 0.28	× 0.28
Value of the taxable losses	$ 604	$ 515	$ 421

*Principal payments are not tax deductible; interest payments are, however.

TABLE 14.4 • CALCULATION OF AFTER-TAX CASH FLOW

	Year 1	Year 2	Year 3
Cash flow before taxes—Table 14.2	$(203)	$ 77	$370
Value of taxable losses—Table 14.3	604	515	421
After-tax cash flow	$ 401	$592	$791

would have been far poorer than it is now. But is it a good investment? To answer this question we need additional steps.

Step 5. Estimate the property's resale value at the end of the holding period and calculate the after-tax amount of cash you would receive from selling it. These are also difficult figures to estimate, but let's assume the property's market value increases at the same rate as the increase in its NOI (a fairly common assumption), which was 5 percent a year. Then its value at the end of three years will be $86,822 ($75,000 × 1.05 × 1.05 × 1.05). But when it's sold, the Steeles probably will pay a realtor's commission of, say, $6,078 (this is a 7 percent commission, which is fairly common: $86,822 × 0.07 = $6,078). So, they will net $80,744 ($86,822 – $6,078) from the sale. However, the IRS will want a portion of their gain and also a portion of the depreciation deductions they have taken. In IRS jargon, this latter item is called **recapture.** The taxes the Steeles will owe—$3,594—from sale of the property are calculated in Figure 14.2. Subtracting the $3,594 from the net proceeds from sale of the property—$80,744—leaves the Steeles with $77,150; and after they pay off their mortgage balance of $58,651 (see Table 14.1), they can pocket the difference of $18,499 ($77,150 – $58,651).

Recapture: A taxable gain resulting from the sale of an asset that has been depreciated.

Step 6. Determine the investment's net present value and estimate the annual rate of return. Using the cash flows in Table 14.4 along with the initial investment of $15,000 and the ending value of $18,499, we can determine the property's net present value (NPV) by using the discounting process introduced in Chapter 1. The technique is illustrated in Figure 14.3, using two discount rates—12 percent and 10 percent. These numbers were not pulled out of the air.

The 12 percent rate was used initially, since the Steeles felt an investment of this type should provide an after-tax return at least this high to be worthwhile. As Figure 14.3 shows, however, the property has a negative NPV of $439 when a 12 percent discount rate is used. A negative NPV means that the property's actual rate of return is less than 12 percent. So a second discount rate—10 percent—was then used. It resulted in a positive NPV of $347, telling us that the actual rate is greater than 10 percent. The difference between the two NPVs is $786 ($347 – [–$439]), so we estimate the actual return at 10.9 percent: 0.10 + [($347/$786) × 0.02].

Rates of return are used frequently in real estate investment, making it important for you to understand them. You should see that a property's actual return is a *spe-*

Figure 14.2 Calculation of taxes due from sale of the property.

Net gain on the sale = $80,744 – $75,000 =	$ 5,744
Plus three years' depreciation = 3 × $2,364 =	7,092
Total	$12,836
Steeles' marginal income tax rate	× .28
Taxes due from the sale	$ 3,594

Year (1)	Cash Flows (2)	Present Value Interest Factors (i = 12%) (3)	(i = 10%) (4)	Discounted Cash Flows (i = 12%) (5) = (2) × (3)	(i = 10%) (6) = (2) × (4)
1	$ 401	0.8929	0.9091	$ 358	$ 365
2	592	0.7972	0.8264	472	489
3	791 + 18,499 19,290	0.7118	0.7513	13,731	14,493
1. Gross present value (GPV)				$14,561	$15,347
2. Less initial investment (downpayment)				15,000	15,000
3. Net present value (NPV)				$ (439)	$ 347

Figure 14.3 Determining the property's net present value (NPV).

cific discount rate that discounts its future cash flows to an amount that equals its initial investment. So, if we discounted the cash flows in column 2 of Figure 14.3 with present value factors for a 10.9 percent rate, the gross present value will be $15,000. However, present value tables usually are not sufficiently comprehensive to include fractional rates, such as 10.9 percent, which explains why many investors use calculators or computers. Unfortunately, not all who use these devices understand how rates are calculated, or what they mean. Actually, the electronic devices go through the same procedures shown in Figure 14.3 and explained above; but they execute them in the blink of an eye. Speed is helpful, but understanding is far more critical.

Step 7. Take risk into consideration. Measuring risk in property investment is exceptionally difficult. Surely, you have noticed that practically all of the gain came from selling the property and not from the annual cash flow. This situation is characteristic of many—if not most—property deals. This means the rate of return is very sensitive to a few critical factors, which are the assumed future selling price of the property and the amount of the down payment. To illustrate the first factor, assume that the selling price increases by 8 percent a year, instead of 5 percent, the rate of return jumps to about 19 percent. Now the investment looks very good. However, getting an 8 percent increase each year might be extremely difficult, and the annual increase could just as easily be 2 percent. The point is that this property is a very risky investment, and it should be recognized as such. The Steeles must make the best and most realistic estimates they can to evaluate the property, and they shouldn't fool themselves, or let a realtor fool them, with overly optimistic guesses of future prices.

Action Plan for the Steeles: Investing in a Rental Property

Background The Steeles have read that real estate is an excellent investment, and they have located a rental duplex that requires a $15,000 down payment. Financing the down payment would require selling some of their stocks or mutual fund shares.

The Problem Arnold and Sharon like the idea of managing a property. They have very basic household-repair skills, but they are not discouraged by the work commitment accompanying such an investment. They would enjoy upgrading the property through landscaping and painting and then keeping it in good shape.

The Plan The property must offer no less than a 12 percent annual after-tax return to compensate the Steeles adequately for the risk they would assume with an additional $60,000 in mortgage debt. Although Arnie and Sharon feel that a 5 percent appreciation factor is realistic; they recognize that even real estate prices do not always increase. Indeed, when they were looking at the property, prices locally and nationally had weakened and the real estate outlook was anything but excellent.

The Steeles' analysis (presented in this chapter) indicates a return of only 10.9 percent. They also did some "what if" analysis on their home computer and determined that if tenants' rents could be raised from $800 to $900 a month, everything else unchanged, the return would increase substantially above the cutoff rate of 12 percent. The Steeles believe that tenants would not resist a rent increase, since rents have not been raised for several years and since they intend to improve the physical appearance of the property. If their assumption is correct, the property return looks attractive.

It is impossible to tell the Steeles that they should or should not buy the duplex. They are aware of the risks and have prepared a good analysis. The decision now is theirs. Some financial planners, though, would urge a more cautious plan.

Rationale for the Plan Apart from the added risk associated with more debt, investing in the duplex creates an excessive reliance on real estate in the Steeles' portfolio. At the end of 1996, real estate represented about 63 percent of the Steeles' total assets (see Chapter 2). If they acquire the duplex, the amount rises to 86 percent ($280,000/$325,540). Even if we look only at investment assets, real estate's share goes from 0 to 70 percent ($75,000/$107,800). The Steeles should do more "what if" planning, this time focusing on what could happen to their family if worst-case possibilities occurred. Suppose Sharon works fewer hours, or Arnold's raise is much smaller, or an apartment is vacant all year? The fixed mortgage obligations do not change, and the family must sacrifice other goals.

LEVERAGE ALSO MAGNIFIES RATE OF RETURN AND RISK Real estate investment often involves substantial amounts of borrowed funds. This provides leverage in exactly the same way as using a margin account to buy common stocks. Many of the popular get-rich-quick books focus on real estate investment where high rates of leverage are possible. In the Steeles' case, these promoters would argue that the Steeles should offer a down payment of only $10,000 or even $5,000, borrowing the balance on a second mortgage arrangement or through a land contract. As you might guess, with a smaller down payment their rate of return increases, even after allowing for additional interest on the additional funds borrowed.

Leverage seems almost like magic—put in a little less money and get out a little more return. Of course, it isn't magic, and it works to your advantage only as long as property prices are increasing; but if they remain constant or decline, then leverage works against you. Many unfortunate real estate investors learned this lesson the hard way when real estate prices peaked in the early 1990s. Some lost every dollar they had invested, including in some cases a substantial amount of equity in their personal residences, which they used to start the credit pyramid. Don't be fooled by such schemes—they're all risky. Instead, take a realistic view of real estate as a possible addition to your portfolio. A property such as the one the Steeles examined will not make you rich no matter how much you leverage it; but it can be a decent investment, particularly if you don't mind dealing with tenants and doing the necessary maintenance to keep the property in shape.

Investing in Land

The advice to "buy land because they're not making any more of it" has appealed to many investors. Some have become very wealthy by holding a key piece of land in a rapidly developing community or in an area where major deposits of natural resources have been found. Apart from these sensational ventures, more modest—but certainly not poor—returns have been found in land investment.

The risks associated with land depend directly on the kind of land you buy. The price of farmland, for example, usually reflects the prices of crops that can be grown on it, and this explains why farmland did so well in the inflationary 1970s, when commodity prices were rising. It also explains why its return fell in the 1980s when commodity prices fell. Commodity price volatility is likely in the future, so you can expect farmland prices to be volatile as well. Natural resource land, such as coal land in eastern Kentucky or West Virginia, also shows this pattern, but land held for residential or commercial development represents a different set of risks. Usually, such land is unproductive until development is finished, meaning there is no income from crop or mineral sales to help offset costs of holding the land. And these costs can be considerable, particularly during periods of high interest rates, or if the property's zoning leads to high property taxes. Moreover, the future value of such land is determined greatly by future population and business trends that are not easily predicted.

Most land investments are characterized by poor cash flows during their holding periods; poor tax-sheltering opportunities, since land is not depreciable; and a high future payoff when the land is finally developed or sold. All this adds up to considerable risk, which increases many times if you also cannot diversify. As a result, land investment is usually appropriate only for the very wealthy.

The Vacation Home

There was a time when only the very wealthy could consider owning a vacation home. Today, millions of Americans do. True, most of these people have incomes far in excess of the national average, but not all of them are "super rich." A number of factors explain the growing popularity of vacation homes. First, we have more leisure time and are looking for ways to enjoy it. Second, it is easier and more commonplace to rent a vacation home during periods when it is not used; in many instances, rental managers take care of all rental details and simply mail a check to the owner. Third, the federal income tax law might allow certain deductions that increase your after-tax income, making the vacation home more affordable. Finally, in some cases the vacation home has shown an excellent return on investment.

As you would probably expect, persons or families most interested in vacation homes are those in their middle ages who are planning retirement. Their goal is to have a place to enjoy occasionally during their remaining work years and then to serve as a principal residence in retirement. Popular areas for these people are the Sun Belt states, particularly Florida, Arizona, Georgia, and North and South Carolina. Surprisingly, even many young people are considering vacation homes. Retirement may be the last thing on their minds; instead, they are looking for current enjoyment and a good investment.

WHERE TO LOOK Only you can judge what vacation area and kind of home appeal to you. If you like photographing alligators in the Louisiana swamps, you probably won't be happy in a condo at Cape Cod. But you should think twice before buying a vacation home in the swamps, particularly if you might want to sell it some day. This is a stretched example, but it should make the point that the market value of a vacation home depends very much on its appeal to other people. Locating in an area of strong demand improves the financial side of your investment by making renting much easier and by allowing the property's market value to keep in step with inflation. However, there is another aspect to the location issue: If you buy in an area that is already very popular, you usually pay a premium price for the home. Vacation home advisers often tell you to look instead for areas that are not current hot spots but have good growth prospects. It isn't easy determining today where tomorrow's vacation spots will be, but it may be worth a try.

In recent years the vacation home market has been hit very hard by the overall recession. In some areas, particularly in the Northeast and certain parts of Florida, prices have fallen as much as 40 percent. This sharp decline should indicate two factors of importance: First, this type of investment can be very risky; second, there may be some good values for potential investors.

WHAT KIND OF HOME TO BUY After you find a location, the next question is what kind of home to buy. Buying one requiring frequent care and maintenance will cut into your vacation time. (Do you really want a weekend getaway that needs weekly lawn mowing and regular painting?) On the other hand, if you are used to living in a conventional home, you might feel very uncomfortable in a condo where you ride the elevator each time you go out. Also consider whether you intend to rent the place. If so, who will make the arrangements? If you own an isolated cabin in the woods, these are your responsibilities; but with a condo in a major development, all these services can be provided—for a fee, of course.

Because buying a vacation home is such a major purchase, you should take considerable time researching alternatives. Listing each important factor on paper along with an importance rating to family members is an excellent idea. Try to get a family consensus on location and type of dwelling. Then you must see if it fits within the family budget. In this respect you should now be able to understand most of the cash flows related to the investment, with the possible exception of the federal income tax situation. As usual, it is extremely important and often makes the difference between buying and not buying.

FEDERAL INCOME TAX IMPLICATIONS The tax law is complex in this area, and to make matters worse, it seems to change constantly. At present, the tax treatment depends on how frequently you use the home personally and how frequently it is rented. There are three possible situations.

Situation 1. You rent it for 14 days or less. In this case the IRS is not concerned with your property as an investment. This means you need not report any rental income, but you cannot take any expenses other than those you normally take as itemized deductions. For example, you cannot deduct operating expenses such as utility bills, depreciation, or maintenance costs; but you can deduct mortgage interest and property taxes if you file an itemized return.

Situation 2. You use the property for 14 days or less (or not more than 10 percent of the total days it is rented, whichever is greater). In this situation, the property is treated like any other real estate investment, with one exception: A portion of mortgage interest—determined by the percentage of personal-use days to total-use days—cannot be deducted either as a business or as a personal itemized expense.

It is again important to recognize that any business loss is subject to the loss limitation rules discussed previously and in Chapter 5. To deduct losses, you must be active in managing the property. Unfortunately, that is not the case with many vacation home complexes.

Situation 3. You use the property 15 days or more (or for more than 10 percent of the total days it is rented, whichever is greater) and also rent it for 15 or more days. Now, the property is a combination of personal residence and business, and its tax treatment is similar to that of hobbies. In short, this means you cannot have a business loss for tax purposes. It sounds simple, but there is a complication having to do with the amount of total expenses you can deduct. The IRS insists that you allocate expenses on the basis of the property's use as a business and as a personal residence. An example is shown in Table 14.5. In this case the taxpayer used the property 15 days and rented it 30 days, for a total of 45 days. The personal percentage then is $1/3$ ($15/45$), and the business percentage is $2/3$ ($30/45$). All expenses are allocated on the basis of these percentages. Notice that the loss of $200 resulting from the business cannot be used to offset other income.

Notice in particular how much tax difference one day can make. Had the taxpayer stayed one fewer day, he or she would have been in situation 2, and total deductions would have been $1,800 (the total net loss) less allocated personal mortgage interest. For purposes of an example, if we assume this amount is $200, the deduction would have been $1,600, which is far more than the $900 with situation 3. It is extremely important that you estimate as carefully as possible how often you will use and rent the vacation home so that you can evaluate the tax situation correctly before you buy a place; and it is just as important after a place is bought so that you can take full advantage of tax provisions. You need to review the law before you buy a place or, if you already own one, before you decide how

Box 14.1 SIMPLIFYING FINANCIAL PLANNING
Avoiding Investment Scams

It is estimated that investment scams cost Americans over $40 billion a year; and no one, regardless of their education, moral character, or ability to fend off shysters, is immune from being victimized. If you ever have had even the slightest notion that wealth *can* come without risk, you are ripe for a fleecing. Consider the following suggestions that may make your financial planning easier and perhaps save you money at the same time.

- Never invest through a telephone solicitation. In fact, learn to hang up (forcefully, perhaps) as soon as you suspect the caller is pitching something.
- Never be impressed by the appearance of a presenter or the decor of his or her office. Most scamsters look very successful.
- Never assume that a deal is legitimate if it is associated with a "name" company, such as one with shares traded on the New York Stock Exchange. The connection may be weak, or it may not be true, or the company may indeed be listed *and* crooked.
- Never invest in anything you cannot understand. If you need help, hire a professional. Consider engaging the services of a professor of investments or financial planning. They usually are unbiased and not overly expensive.
- Never invest with a person who is playing to your psychological needs. A sure tipoff is a statement such as, "I can see that you are an intelligent person who . . ."
- Do investigate the credentials of a presenter, by consulting either the Better Business Bureau or your state's securities agency. The latter can provide a dossier (prepared by the Central Registration Depository) on the presenter if he or she is a securities salesperson. Moreover, tell presenters of your intention to do this; it might be the last time you see them.
- Absolutely never make an exception to the above six rules.

TABLE 14.5 • DETERMINING FEDERAL INCOME TAX DEDUCTIONS ON A VACATION HOME			
	Allocations		
	Personal 1/3	Business 2/3	Total
Rentals	$ —	$ 3,000	$ 3,000
Less: Taxes and interest	(900)	(1,800)	(2,700)
Operating expenses	(400)	(800)	(1,200)
Depreciation	(300)	(600)	(900)
Net income (loss)	$(1,600)	$(200)	$(1,800)
Amount deductible for tax purposes	$ 900	-0-	$ 900

to use it for the year. Also, keep in mind that the test for days of personal use includes only those days you actually use the home. Days spent there fixing up or remodeling don't count in this test. Therefore, if one of the personal-use days in the above example was a "fix-up" day, it wouldn't have counted. As usual, you must keep good records to support the residency test, as well as all deductions you claim. Finally, you should realize the example illustrated in Table 14.5 is a fairly simple one that does not address all the possible complications that might arise.

OTHER TANGIBLE ASSETS

Although many people prefer investing in tangible assets, they are not content investing only in real estate. As alternatives, these investors have looked toward precious metals and gems, and some have found their most profitable investments right in activities they most enjoy doing—building their hobbies and adding to their collectibles.

Precious Metals and Gems

Precious metals and gems have appealed to people throughout the ages. Gold and silver are extremely durable and easily fashioned into jewelry or other objects. In addition, their ability to reflect light creates a beauty unmatched by other commodities. Gold is valued for this reason much more than silver, but silver also has many applications in industrial uses. Like gold and silver, gems, such as diamonds, emeralds, and rubies, are much sought after throughout the world. In some respects, precious metals and gems are the all-purpose investments: You can enjoy wearing them, you have a chance of earning a return if their prices increase, and your friends can see how wealthy you are.

GOLD Gold mania swept the world throughout the late 1970s and early 1980s. Much of it had to do with buying by Middle East nations made rich by steep increases in the price of oil, but even the average person was caught up in it. Almost overnight, every shopping center had a gold store where you could sell coins, jewelry, and anything else that had a trace of gold or silver. Before the bubble finally broke, the price of gold had gone from $36 an ounce in 1970 to $875 an ounce in 1980, but its price has fallen substantially since then and has been in the $380–$420 range in recent years. Gold is an extremely risky investment, and this must be understood and appreciated before you invest.

Gold bullion: Gold ingots, most weighing 32.15 ounces.

You can invest in gold in a number of ways. One is to own **gold bullion,** but most of this comes in ingots weighing 32.15 ounces. If the price of gold is, say, $400 an ounce, each ingot would be worth $12,860. This puts it out of reach for most investors, and you must also be concerned with storing it and having it certified if you sell it. You can own gold indirectly by buying the common stock of companies that mine gold. Campbell Red Lake Mine is one such company, but there are others. (To achieve adequate diversification, you also can invest in mutual funds that buy the stocks of gold-mining companies. One such fund is Fidelity's Precious Metals and Minerals Portfolio.) Changes in the market prices of the stocks of these companies are closely correlated to changes in the price of gold. Buying gold indirectly by investing in such companies is called a **play on gold.** It has an advantage over owning gold directly in that many of these stocks pay annual dividends, thereby providing a current return.

Play on gold: Investing in gold indirectly, such as buying shares of gold-mining companies.

Although the above approaches have relative advantages and disadvantages, the most common approaches are either owning gold coins, such as the Canadian Maple Leaf, or buying gold certificates issued by commercial banks and other financial institutions.

Gold coins: A popular gold investment medium; most are one ounce in weight.

Gold coins. The most popular of the **gold coins** are the one-ounce South African Kruggerand and one-ounce Canadian Maple Leaf. These can be purchased almost anywhere, and they store nicely in bank safe deposit boxes. (Remember, though, these boxes are not insured against fire and theft.) Because they are coins, their weight and purity are standardized, making them easily transferable. Moreover, because they contain only one ounce of gold, you can determine conveniently the amount you wish to hold in your portfolio. (You can also get them in $1/2$, $1/4$, and $1/10$ ounce sizes.) Gold coins have two big disadvantages: They offer no current income that might be available with gold-mining stocks, and they sell at a premium over their intrinsic gold value. The premium means you buy less actual gold for your investment dollar. The premium varies and tends to decline as the price of gold rises. In effect, it is the price you pay to get the advantages just cited. Commissions to buy coins are typically 3 to 8 percent of the amount purchased, depending on how much you buy and where you buy it. Advisers recommend shopping around, since these costs vary considerably. Also, many states charge a sales tax on each purchase.

Gold certificates: Issued by commercial banks and other financial institutions and backed by a specific gold holding.

Gold certificates. Buying **gold certificates** may be the way to own gold if you don't want current income and don't care to handle or look at the metal itself. Many commercial banks sell gold certificates for any amount of gold you care to purchase. The certificate itself merely documents your ownership claim; the actual gold is owned or controlled by the selling institution. You should insist that your gold be stored in an independent warehouse or bank and that it not be lumped together with the seller's other assets. If it is, you run the risk of having no better position than that of a general creditor if the seller fails and goes into bankruptcy. Storage costs usually consist of a one-time charge of $1/2$ percent (or less) of the amount purchased, up to a maximum of around $60. Also, commissions or markups are lower with certificates than with bullion or coins, particularly on large orders.

Some financial institutions allow you to buy a form of gold certificate in much the same manner as you would buy a gold futures contract (futures contracts will be explained shortly). Since these institutions offer a variety of ways to own gold, make sure you understand clearly the type of ownership plan you are using. Also, make sure the institution is a reputable one.

SILVER In general, silver is very similar to gold as an investment. It can be owned in the same ways, and its risk is certainly as great. While gold's price was rising, silver went from $2 an ounce to over $50 an ounce. Its price has been in the $4.50–$6.00 range in recent years. Silver is in far greater supply than gold, but much more of it is lost in its industrial uses. Someone has estimated that over 90 percent of all the gold ever mined is still in existence; for silver, the same figure is less than 10 percent. Having industrial applications is both a good and bad feature—good because it increases silver's demand, but bad because substitutes can be found for it. On balance, these applications probably increase its price volatility.

Box 14.2 SAVING MONEY Gold versus Gold Stocks

So you're convinced that gold is ready to make a move. Fine. Now, how do you play your hunch? There are a number of choices, but an important one is whether you care to invest directly in the metal or indirectly by buying an intangible whose value is correlated closely to that of gold. Among the more popular intangibles are the common stocks of gold-mining companies. As the graph below shows, their returns and gold's often move in a lockstep manner. Notice, though, that variations in the stock returns are more pronounced than variations in gold's price. So with the stocks you get a bigger play for your buck. If you guess correctly, you will magnify your return by buying stocks rather than gold itself, such as gold coins or bullion. If you guess wrong, your losses also will be magnified. An advantage to owning gold-mining stocks is the possibility of earning dividends. Gold itself pays no current return and in fact involves holding costs.

Finally, over the entire period shown in the graph, the average return on gold was around 1 percent, while the fund's average return was 5 percent. So you were compensated for taking the greater risks with the funds, although you would have been better off had you invested in risk-free U.S. Treasury bills.

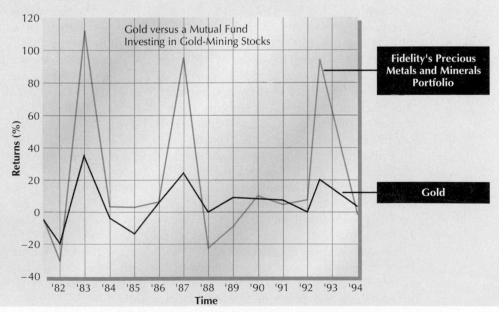

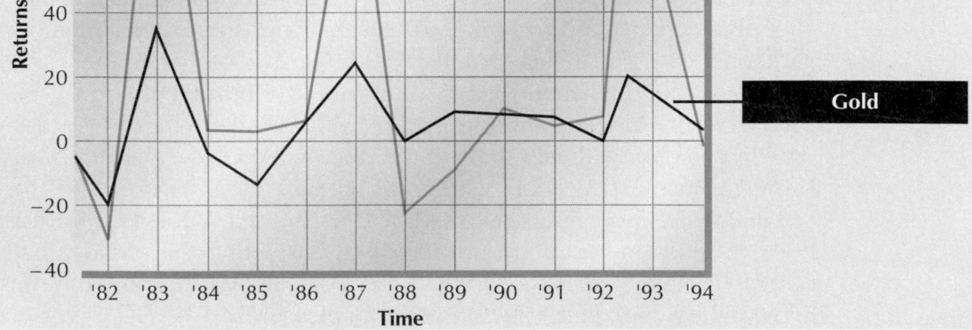

GEMS Diamonds (and other gems) seem to be everybody's best friends—boys' as well as girls'. If the soaring prices of gold and silver didn't impress you, consider this: The wholesale price of a one-carat, highest-quality diamond (called "D flawless") went from $1,800 in 1970 to $53,000 in 1980. And how's this for risk: By 1982, its price was down to $14,000!

It is far beyond the scope of this text to discuss the skills one needs to be an active investor in the gems markets. Simply be forewarned that unless you are appropriately trained, don't be one. If you are convinced that precious gems are the best investments for you, then find a reputable dealer and participate in plans that he or she might have to accommodate your interest. For a start, you can consider subscribing to a magazine called *Precious Gem Investor* (P.O. Box 1367, Lafayette, California 94549). You can also get a free pamphlet from the government, *Gemstone Investing,* by writing to the Federal Trade Commission, Room 1301, Sixth St. and Washington Ave., N.W., Washington, D.C. 20580.

Hobbies and Collectibles

Have you inherited a U.S. stamp or U.S. coin collection? And, if so, have you priced it recently? If not, you may be in for a pleasant surprise. Markets for all types of collectibles have developed over the years. In addition to coin and stamp collections, people have become interested in antiques of all types. Persian rugs, dolls, railroad sets, beer cans, ceramics, and many more.

Hobbies and collectibles: Popular tangible investments, but with considerable risk and a need for specialized knowledge.

Hobbies and collectibles can be the riskiest of all your investments, particularly if your knowledge of the items is inadequate. Collections often include one-of-a-kind items, and establishing their value may be impossible. And even if you are successful and buy an item that appreciates, say, 50 percent in value in one year, you may find that your transaction costs—commissions and others—will be 30 percent or more. If you have a collection of some type and enjoy buying and selling to improve it, there isn't a great deal of danger of losing much; but if you find yourself buying things simply because you think prices are going up, then your hobby has become an investment, and one that could prove very unprofitable.

Knowledgeable collectors insist you should always buy the very best items you can afford, even if these are small pieces such as a set of china or a fine museum print. As little as $500 can get you started if you follow this approach, but even at this level it is important to know what you are doing. You are unlikely to gain enough background in a wide range of collectibles, so it makes sense to specialize in one or a few areas. Find your "thing" and then visit libraries, museums, galleries, flea markets, garage sales, and any other place that can help you. Understand, though, that the markets for hobbies and collectibles often follow fads and a boom–bust cycle. Today, the baseball card dealer has replaced the gold shop in shopping centers, and the prices of baseball cards and other memorabilia are skyrocketing. A 1952 Mickey Mantle rookie card goes for $6,000, and even rookie cards have been hawked for $25 on a cable shopping network. It is impossible to predict when such a euphoric market will end, but you can be assured that this one, in common with all others in the past, will come to an end. And when it does, losses for many speculators will be substantial.

Finally, the federal income tax law does not allow losses from hobby activities, but you must pay taxes on any profits. Considering this disadvantage along with others discussed above, hobbies and collectibles are probably investments to avoid, unless they give you considerable pleasure.

DERIVATIVE SECURITIES

Derivative securities have increased enormously in popularity in recent years, and you may have heard the term *derivatives* on the evening news. The news story was probably not a favorable one, because derivative securities have been misused in some notable cases that involved huge losses (Orange County, California, being the best known). Despite this "bad press," investors are still attracted to derivatives because of their potential for large gains in short periods of time.

Derivative security: A security whose value depends on the value of another asset.

A **derivative security** receives its name because its value is derived from the value of another asset, referred to as the *underlying asset*. As that asset's value changes, so does the value of the derivative. A big appeal with derivatives is that their changes in value are usually far greater, percentage-wise, than the value changes of their underlying assets. In this sense, they are said to have "built-in" leverage.

There are various types of derivatives, but you are most likely to encounter option contracts and futures contracts. Each is explained in the following sections.

Option Contracts

An option contract is based upon one party's (the seller's) agreeing to sell an underlying asset to another party (the buyer) at an agreed-upon price before the expiration of a certain date. For example, assume that it is March 31, 1997, and a contract between Jane Roe and John Doe is executed, specifying that Jane agrees to sell 100 shares of IBM stock to John for $100 a share any time before June 30, 1997.

Be sure to differentiate between the option contract itself and the asset underlying the contract. Jane sells the option contract to John at some price, say $500. If the price of IBM stock goes above $100 a share, John might then exercise his option to buy 100 shares of IBM at $100 a share. At that point, Jane then must sell the underlying asset—the 100 IBM shares.

Call option: A security that gives its owner the right to *buy* an underlying asset.

Put option: A security that gives its owner the right to *sell* an underlying asset.

CALL AND PUT OPTIONS Jane and John have entered into a **call option** contract, or simply a call. A call gives its holder (John) the right to *buy* the underlying asset. In contrast, a **put option** contract, a put, gives its holder the right to sell the underlying asset. Both types of contracts are very popular and are used in a variety of trading strategies. They are standardized contracts that trade on organized exchanges, such as the CBOE (the Chicago Board Options Exchange), and option prices appear every day in financial newspapers, such as the *Wall Street Journal*.

The exchanges have very strict trading rules to minimize fraud and protect traders from buying a contract where the other party might not be able to deliver the underlying asset. Indeed, trading options is as easy and quick as trading stocks, particularly from the option buyer's perspective.

CALL OPTION BUYERS People who buy options often do so for speculative reasons. You may be convinced that IBM's price will go up to $120 before June 30. So you buy the above-mentioned option for $500. Suppose you are right, and it's now June 29. Your call option will be worth at least $2,000, since the contract allows you to buy 100 shares of IBM at $100 a share, which you could immediately sell in the stock market for $120 a share. Because you paid only $500 for the contract, you quadrupled your money in three months!

But suppose IBM's price falls below $100 at the end of the trading day on June 29; now the option is worthless, and you lose your entire $500. Clearly, option trading is extremely risky and should be viewed by most people as outright gambling.

CALL OPTION SELLERS If you were lucky enough to make a $2,000 profit, as in our example, who do you think lost $2,000? If you guessed the person who sold the option contract, you are correct. But why would anyone be so foolish as to sell options, a practice that is called **option writing?** Sellers may have several reasons.

Option writing: A term referring to the selling of option contracts.

First, they may be speculating, guessing that IBM's price will go under $100 a share. So they sell the contract to earn a quick $500, hoping the option expires worthless. Or they may currently own 100 shares of IBM and are thinking of selling them at $100 a share. But why do that? Why not sell a call contract, and if IBM's price goes above $100 they have nothing to lose since they own 100 shares that can be delivered to satisfy the option contract. In short, they "squeeze" another $5 a share ($500/100) out of the stock by writing the contract. This strategy (which has several variations) is called **covered option writing**—it's fairly popular with sophisticated investors.

Covered option writing: Selling call options on stocks an investor owns.

PUT OPTION BUYERS AND SELLERS Buyers and sellers of put options are also motivated by speculative trading. If you thought IBM would go down in price, you would buy a put. Puts work the same way as calls, except in the opposite direction. If a put on IBM also had a contract exercise price of $100 a share, and if IBM went down to $80, you also would make $2,000 on the contract; the put would be worthless if IBM's price was above $100 at the contract's maturity.

Sometimes puts are bought to protect the value of stocks that you currently own; this strategy is called a **put insurance hedge.** Suppose that you owned 100 shares of IBM and you do not want their aggregate value to fall below $10,000. What to do? Simple: Buy a put contract with a $100 exercise price, which gives you the right to sell your 100 shares at $100 a share. Buying a put in this situation is actually no different from buying an insurance policy that underwrites the value of your stock. It's expensive insurance, though. In our example, one put contract would likely cost about $500, and, remember, it provides only three months of protection.

Put insurance hedge: Buying a put option on stocks an investor owns.

Futures Contracts

Futures contracts are based on the future delivery of commodities (such as corn) or financial instruments (such as U.S. Treasury bonds). One party in such a contract agrees to accept delivery of a standardized quantity of an item at a future date. The second party agrees to make such delivery, and both parties agree on the price at which the exchange will take place. The person taking delivery is called the buyer; with the contract, he or she has a guaranteed price on the particular item for the life of the contract. If the market price of the item goes above this contract price, the buyer will make a profit; but if the price goes below it, the buyer suffers a loss. It is important to note that the contract is a legal obligation to perform. This is important from the buyer's perspective. In contrast to buying an option, in which case the most you can lose is the cost of the option ($500 in our previous example), if you buy a futures contract your losses are virtually unlimited; that is, they continue to mount as long as the commodity's price falls. The situation works in reverse if you are the seller of a futures contract. You lose when prices go above the contract price and gain when it goes below it.

Futures contracts: Contracts that involve future deliveries of commodities and financial instruments but at prices negotiated today.

Box 14.3 PERSONAL FINANCE NEWS *Late Edition*

Wouldn't Touch a Derivative with a 10-Foot Pole? You May Already Own One

With so much bad news lately about risky derivative securities, many people shake their heads and wonder why any investor would get involved with them. Surprise: They may already be involved in a big way, through their mutual funds, banks, insurance companies, and other financial institutions. Of course, the people who run these places will tell you that their activities are designed to lower your risks. That's a good idea; but, unfortunately, a profit (greed?) motive may also be at work.

Take the case of market-indexed CDs, which are offered by commercial banks. These CDs have returns linked to the performance of the stock market, and their big appeal is that they are guaranteed to *never* lose money. The catch? Well, you won't lose money, but you give up any interest that you could have earned by investing in a conventional CD. Still, how can the bank guarantee no losses? Hasn't the market occasionally taken some huge declines? Indeed, the market has, but the bank insures against such losses by hedging with, you guessed it, derivatives.

In effect, when you buy a market-indexed CD you are indirectly buying a conventional CD and then using its interest to buy options on the stock market. There is nothing wrong with this activity unless the bank isn't very good at managing risk with options and creates losses for other depositors to bear. Banks have actually done a pretty good job in this area, but other institutions have not. The treasurer of Orange County, California, Robert L. Citron, got involved with a derivative-based security and lost $1.7 billion for that county's taxpayers (about $3,500 for each one!)

Is there anything you can do to avoid such risks? Many institutions, such as mutual funds, now report their derivative activities in annual financial reports and other documents. So you might be alerted if you find excessive activity; unfortunately, it may be difficult to determine whether the derivatives help the institution manage risk or are used to earn potentially higher returns.

Perhaps the best way to avoid derivatives-related risks is to avoid any investments that offer higher returns than similar-risk investments. If a money market fund, for example, offers a 6 percent return while other funds are offering 5 percent, you can bet it's adding risk somewhere, and there is a good chance that derivatives are involved. Also, stay clear of so-called hedge funds. These funds do little hedging, and they typically have huge and very risky derivative positions.

You aren't likely to get burned in market-indexed CDs, but don't think you aren't paying for the no-loss guarantee. The options the bank buys to cover their potential losses are not cheap insurance. In the long run, you are far better off investing directly in the market or in conventional CDs. If risk bothers you, hold a portfolio of the two, tilting as much to the market share as your risk tolerance allows.

USE OF MARGIN Most commodity futures speculators use margin accounts in their trading activities. Table 14.6 shows only a partial list of the large number of commodities available for purchase or sale. The margin requirement is set by the organized commodity exchanges, and the required amount depends on the commodity in question. The more volatile the commodity's price, the greater the required margin. In general, margins are extremely thin. For example, to trade corn you would need only $675, about 5 percent of its market value in Table 14.6. Notice that if corn increased only $0.14 a bushel, you would double your investment ($0.14 × 5,000 bushels); and if it decreased by $0.14, you would be wiped out, assuming you were the buyer in each case. A price change of $0.14 per bushel of corn often takes place over two or three trading days, which should alert you to the risks of trading futures contracts.

INVESTMENT SUITABILITY Considering the risks involved, with both leverage and price volatility, futures contracts are, in our view, not suitable investments unless you have considerable investment funds (probably over $100,000) and are willing

TABLE 14.6 • SOME COMMODITIES TRADED ON MAJOR COMMODITY EXCHANGES

(1) Commodity	(2) Contract Size	(3) Unit Price[a]	(4) Market Value (Money at Risk) (2) × (3)	(5) Margin Required[b]
Grains:				
Corn	5,000 bushels	$ 2.86	$ 14,300	$ 675
Soybeans	5,000 bushels	5.97	29,850	1,500
Canola	20 metric tons	394.50	7,890	500
Livestock:				
Feeder cattle	50,000 pounds	0.65	32,500	750
Pork bellies	40,000 pounds	0.47	18,800	1,350
Metals:				
Gold	100 troy ounces	383.40	38,340	1,555
Silver	5,000 troy ounces	5.58	27,900	2,465
Financial:				
British pound	62,500 pounds	1.54	96,250	2,025
U.S. Treasury bonds	8%, $100,000 face value	110, 875.00	110,875	2,700
S&P 500 Stock Index	500 times Index	559.10	279,550	11,250

[a]Approximate prices at mid-August 1995. Contracts selected are those with closest delivery month.
[b]Margin requirements as of August 8, 1995.

to assume such risks. Even then, you must be willing to put in a reasonable amount of time to understand the mechanics of commodity trading, not to mention understanding trading strategies. Moreover, you should be cautious of any pooling arrangement that trades futures or option contracts. Do not presume that so-called professional investors can consistently trade these securities profitably. Their track record isn't much better than that of individual investors.

SUMMARY

Along with stocks, bonds, and mutual funds, many investors hold other assets. Real estate is the most popular tangible asset. An income-producing property provides a net operating income (NOI), which is one source of return. Other sources are capital gains and tax savings. Most real estate deals involve considerable borrowing that acts as leverage, which magnifies both risk and return. Investing in real estate also includes investing in land. Because of its risks, land investment is usually most suitable to wealthy investors. Vacation homes have also become popular investments; however, the tax law should be considered in buying or using the vacation home.

In addition to real estate, tangible assets include precious metals and gems and hobbies and collectibles. Gold is by far the most popular precious metal. Silver's price parallels gold's in volatility, and it can be owned in the same ways. Gem investment is a highly specialized area, requiring considerable expertise, which is also true for hobbies and collectibles.

Derivative securities derive their value from the values of other assets. Call and put option contracts and futures contracts are widely traded within a variety of strategies. They are extremely risky securities, generally not suitable for small investors.

KEY TERMS

after-tax cash flow (p. 384)
call option (p. 395)
cash flow before taxes (p. 383)
covered option writing (p. 396)
depreciation (p. 384)
depreciation basis (p. 384)
derivative security (p. 395)
futures contracts (p. 396)
gold bullion (p. 392)
gold certificates (p. 392)
gold coins (p. 392)
hobbies and collectibles (p. 394)
income-producing property (p. 381)
net operating income (NOI) (p. 381)
option writing (p. 396)
play on gold (p. 392)
put insurance hedge (p. 396)
put option (p. 395)
recapture (p. 385)
"sweat equity" (p. 381)

PROBLEMS AND REVIEW QUESTIONS

1. Explain potential sources of return from an income-producing property, and discuss important topics to consider when you are looking at alternative income-producing properties.
2. Define the following terms:
   (*a*) net operating income (NOI)
   (*b*) cash flow before taxes
   (*c*) tax shelter
   (*d*) depreciation
   (*e*) after-tax cash flow
3. Matilda Blakesley is thinking of buying a duplex in an area close to the university she is attending. It is in very run-down condition, but she is sure the seller will assist with financing, allowing her to buy it with only $3,000 as a down payment. Matilda is a sophomore and a hard worker; she plans to fix up the place and resell it at the end of her senior year. Discuss Matilda's plan, focusing on potential problems and advantages.
4. Explain various factors that make land investment risky.
5. Why is the location of a vacation home an important factor in your buying decision? Should you buy only in areas that appeal to you personally, or in areas that appeal to other people? Discuss. Also, briefly explain three different residency situations that will affect the federal income tax treatment of a vacation home.
6. Would you describe the price of gold as stable or volatile? Explain. In what ways can you own gold? Which way do you consider best in your own case?
7. What factors should you consider before you invest in gems or hobbies and collectibles?
8. Define a derivative security, and explain why it is said to have built-in leverage.
9. Explain how a call contract works, creating an example, say Microsoft stock, to help with your explanation. Assume that a call on the stock could be bought that has a one-month maturity and a $60 exercise price; the call costs $400 to buy. Make sure that your answer shows why someone might want to buy a call and why that purchase might be very risky.
10. Explain option writing; further, explain covered option writing. Why would anyone engage in covered option writing?
11. Explain several reasons why you might buy put options.
12. Define a futures contract, and explain why trading futures is a very risky endeavor. Make sure that you include a brief discussion of margin in your answer.

Case 14.1 The Pettys' Real Estate Venture

Wilma and Norman Petty are a married couple in their late twenties. They have two young children who will both be in school next year, and Wilma expects to have much more time available to help with the family's income. However, because she cannot work full time, she is having trouble finding a decent position. She and Norm have saved about $10,000 (in total) and have it invested in a money market mutual fund where it currently earns 6 percent before taxes. They are thinking very seriously of using $7,000 of it as a deposit on a fourplex located close to their home. The property is structurally sound but in a somewhat run-down condition. The Pettys think that all it really needs is lots of paint and elbow grease, but there is a chance the heating, plumbing, or electrical system might require a major improvement. The property is owned by the savings and loan that repossessed it when the previous owner could not make the monthly payments of $720. The S&L would let the Pettys assume the loan of $70,000 at the same interest rate (12 percent), maturity (30 years), and monthly payments. The Pettys are in favor of this loan because it has a fixed rate.

Three of the four apartments are now rented at $200 a month. Wilma is confident that the fourth apartment will rent shortly—also at $200 a month—if it is advertised in the newspaper. All utilities, including water and sewerage, are paid by tenants. Wilma will manage and maintain the property, eliminating those expenses, but they expect the following outlays in the first year: (*a*) potential vacancy losses = 10 percent of gross rentals; (*b*) advertising, licenses, and permits = $50; (*c*) insurance = $600; (*d*) property taxes = $900; (*e*) allowance for repairs and major maintenance = 5 percent of gross rentals.

If Wilma and Norm go ahead with the deal, the purchase price of the property will be $77,000—their down payment plus the loan assumption. A reasonable estimate of the land's value is $17,000. They think they will hold the property about three years and then try to sell it for $90,000, working through a realtor who will charge 7 percent commission. They also think the property's NOI will increase 5 percent a year, and they estimate that 97 percent of their monthly mortgage payments is interest and 3 percent is principal. The Pettys are in a 28 percent tax bracket and will probably continue to be in the future. They will depreciate the building over 27.5 years using straight-line depreciation. Finally, the loss limitation rules will not apply in the Pettys' case.

QUESTIONS

1. Going through the steps detailed in this chapter, calculate an approximate average rate of return on the property to the Pettys.
2. Calculate approximate average rates of return, assuming the property is eventually sold for: (*a*) $95,000, (*b*) $85,000.
3. Given your answers to Questions 1 and 2 and considering other facts in the case, do you feel this is a good investment for Wilma and Norm? Explain, making sure you include risk in the discussion.

Case 14.2 Should Francine Buy a Vacation Condominium?

Francine Lester has been quite successful as a free-lance author in New York. Along with success, though, comes a high tax bracket (28 percent), and Francine thinks she should do something to soften her tax situation. At a recent party, she discussed the problem with one of her friends—Lou Cimino—from whom she usually rents a vacation condo for two weeks each year. Lou felt she ought to buy a condo like his and, as a matter of fact, one right next to his was on the market for $65,000. Lou said that he rented his 60 days last year at $70 a day (this is what Francine paid) and his only expense was a flat fee of 20 percent of rentals that he paid to the rental agent. (This included utilities, association dues, laundry and linen service, and all others.) He was sure this same arrangement would be available on Francine's unit, if she were to buy it. Financing is available on the property (assume it is identical to the data shown in Table 14.1), but Francine would need a down payment of $5,000.

She is very excited about the deal but thinks she should temper her enthusiasm by looking at some cash flow figures. That's where you come into the picture, since Francine knows absolutely nothing about real estate investment. She does not plan to sell the place for some time—if ever—so she is not concerned about growth or fluctuations in the property's market value. She will continue to take her usual two weeks of vacation and feels she can rent it in the same way Lou does; also, she would be active enough in managing the condo that loss limitation rules would not apply. Lou also explained that his unit had a depreciation basis of $45,000 for federal income tax purposes, and that he depreciated it over a 27.5-year period using straight-line depreciation.

QUESTIONS

1. Calculate the appropriate cash flows and then explain if the condo investment seems a good deal in Francine's case. (Ignore any allocation of mortgage interest for personal-use days.)
2. Assume Francine decided to spend one extra day at her condo. How much would this day cost? Show your calculations.
3. Francine said she was not concerned about changes in the market value of the condo, but suppose it increased 3 percent in value each year for three years after her purchase. Assuming she could sell it at the end of three years without a realtor's commission, calculate her average annual rate of return on the property. Show your work and discuss your conclusion.

HELPFUL CONTACTS

Commodity Futures Trading Commission (telephone 202-254-3067)

Boards of Trade (some will provide free educational materials):
Chicago Board of Trade: 312-435-3758
Chicago Mercantile Exchange: 312-930-1000
New York Mercantile Exchange: 212-938-2973
Kansas City Board of Trade: 816-753-7500

Information and materials on real estate investment may be available from the Board of Realtors in your local area. Check the Yellow Pages of your telephone directory.

INTERNET ADDRESSES

Chicago Board of Trade (this is an excellent site for information and futures prices)
http://www.cbot.com/mplex.htm

Chicago Mercantile Exchange (this site equals that of the Chicago Board of Trade)
http://www.cme.com/

Part 4

LONG-TERM PLANNING: Enjoying Your Financial Resources Now and Later

All financial planning must take into consideration both the short-term impacts and the long-term consequences of our decisions. In these last chapters we examine topics in which long-term considerations are of paramount importance. Chapters 15 and 16 review decisions that have an ongoing influence on expenditures. These include the housing decision and the decision to purchase consumer durables. Chapters 17 and 18 have to do with decisions that have a major effect at the end of the life planning cycle. These consist of retirement planning and estate planning.

Purchases of homes and consumer durables involve a significant commitment of both present and future resources. Each of these purchases will generate a long-term stream of benefits and a long-term stream of costs. In many cases, these purchases involve borrowing and the use of credit. Knowledge of financial markets, the time value of money, and market rates of interest is needed. All these topics have been dealt with in earlier chapters. The next chapters expand upon the previous analysis by examining the special characteristics of credit markets that finance major purchases.

Retirement and estate planning require a long-term commitment to saving and a long-term plan for transferring those savings for the benefit of ourselves and others. Both retirement and estate planning must be approached early in the life cycle. Adequate retirement plans take many years to implement. Furthermore, retirement and estate planning should complement your current investment and tax strategies.

None of your plans and goals, particularly those pertaining to major financial decisions should be considered separate from all others. A book must be read one chapter at a time, but that isn't the way to implement your financial planning. What you need is an integrated approach, in which major financial decisions are part of a personal financial plan that leads to financial independence for you and your family.

In the last few decades, people have tended to retire earlier and live longer, increasing the importance of long-term planning. You probably already recognize the need for retirement planning but not the need for estate planning. You might even think of skipping the final chapter because you believe that this topic concerns only the very rich. That would be a mistake. Estate planning can have a tax impact on families with moderate income as well. More important, estate planning will determine how your wealth will be shared by your beneficiaries. This is an important concern for every family, especially those with dependent children.

Chapter 15

Housing: The Cost of Shelter

Objectives

1. To determine how much you can afford to spend on housing
2. To describe the several types of home ownership
3. To explain the real estate transaction from appraisal to closing
4. To understand the many kinds of home mortgages
5. To estimate whether it is financially more attractive to buy or to rent
6. To know how to handle a potential foreclosure

The most prized piece of real estate is a single-family home on its own lot with a lawn. This was and still is the American Dream. The average first-time home buyer is about 30 years of age, and the buyer moving up to a larger home is approximately 8 years older. At the end of the 1970s, the leading edge of the baby boom entered the home-buying market, significantly increasing the demand for housing. Given this aging wave of baby boomers and the currently more favorable financial conditions, it is not surprising that the demand now appears to be shifting to larger and more expensive homes. Alternatively, with the shrinking 25-to-34 age population, buying a starter home may not be as difficult as it was in previous decades.

Housing Affordability Index: Published by the National Association of Realtors, it is related directly to the ability of a median-income family to purchase a median-priced home.

The National Association of Realtors publishes the **Housing Affordability Index** presented in Figure 15.1. When the median family income is enough to qualify for a conventional loan on an existing median-priced home, the index assumes a value of 100. When the index rises, more families find it easier to purchase and finance the typical home. For example, when the index rises to 110, those earning about 90 percent of the median family income will now qualify for a loan on a median-priced home.

During the 1970s and the beginning of the 1980s, housing became less affordable because of increases in both the cost of a home and the cost of finance. Consumer prices were rising rapidly, but housing prices were rising faster, creating substantial gains for those who were wise (or lucky) enough to purchase a home at the beginning of the 1970s. Along with rising inflation came rising interest rates. Those who were fortunate enough to beat high prices and high interest rates by purchasing a home in the early 1970s made a very wise investment.

The boom in the housing market ended in 1979 when home mortgage rates began to soar. With the exceptionally high cost of finance, homes became so much less affordable that housing prices finally began to fall behind the rapid rise in the general price level.

After the beginning of the 1980s the trend has been generally in the opposite direction. Inflation has been brought under control, and interest rates have taken a significant drop. Figure 15.2 illustrates the fall in mortgage rates from double-digit levels in the early 1980s. The decline in interest rates combined with the slower rise in house prices has made housing significantly more affordable for the typical home buyer. In the mid-1990s the Housing Affordability Index is now at a high of around 130.

Figure 15.1 Composite housing affordability index.

SOURCE: National Association of Realtors®.

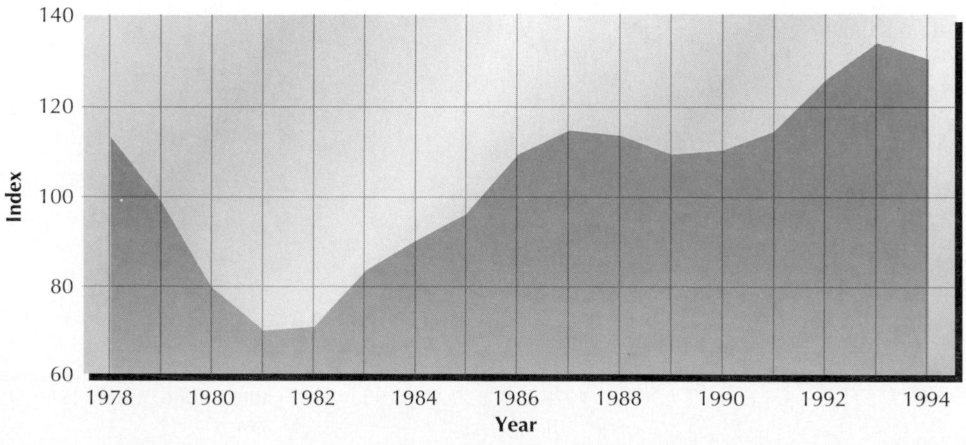

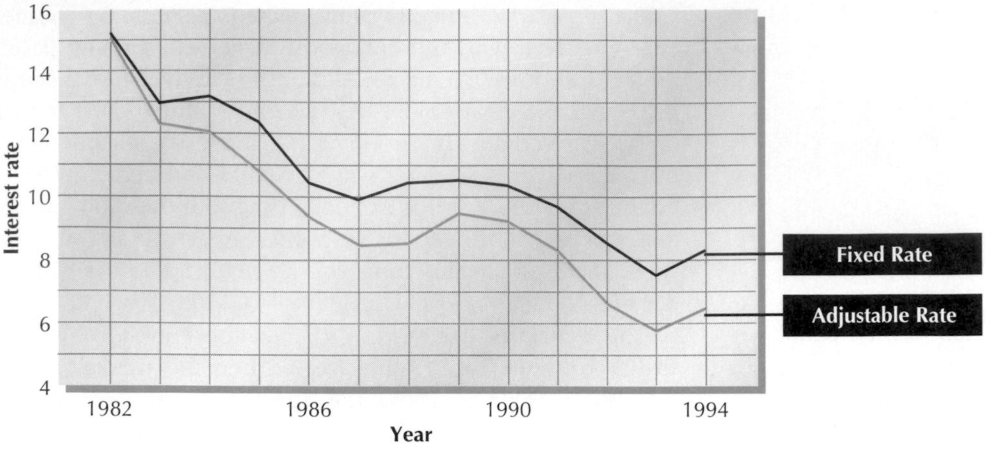

Figure 15.2 Effective mortgage rates on conventional home loans.
SOURCE: Federal Housing Finance Board.

While becoming more affordable, housing has also become less of the investment vehicle it once was. As Figure 15.3 indicates, the price of existing housing after adjustment for the declining value of the dollar has remained relatively stable. Nationwide statistics, however, do not reveal the variability in regional and local markets. From 1989 to 1994, the median sale price of an existing home rose by 13.6 percent in the Midwest but fell by 4.2 percent in the Northeast. Purchasing a home may still be a wise decision, but prospective home buyers should carefully examine the local market conditions. In today's market, consumers must fully weight the benefits, costs, and risks of home ownership.

RENT OR BUY?

You have little choice in the matter: You need shelter. However, the ways in which you may satisfy that need are practically unlimited. Like most decisions, this one must take into account your preferred lifestyle and your financial constraints. You

Figure 15.3 Median sales price of existing one-family homes.
SOURCE: National Association of Realtors®. Inflation-adjusted values were calculated by others.

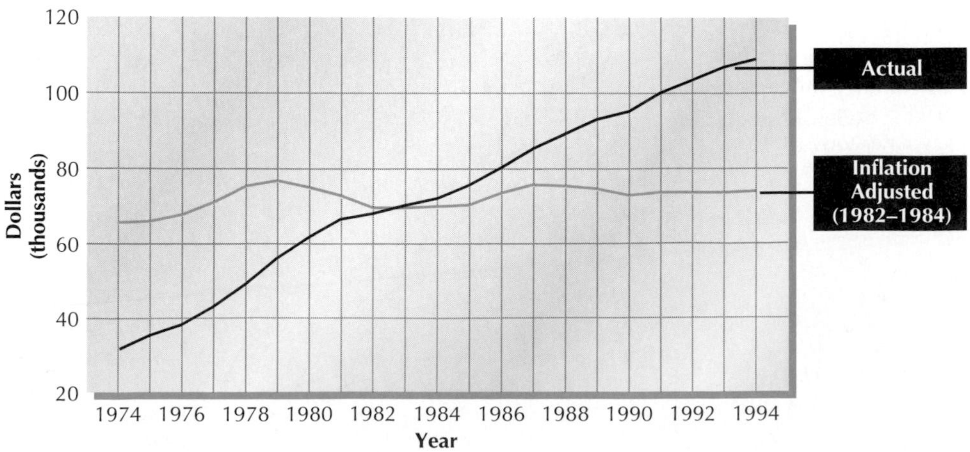

can decide on a rental that places minimal demands on your time or finances. You can purchase a single-family home, thus taking on all the responsibilities of maintenance and of carrying a home mortgage. Or you may prefer to purchase a condominium or a cooperative, with characteristics falling somewhere between those of a rental unit and those of a single-family home. Obviously, your choice will, and should, depend on what makes you feel most comfortable. All we can do is point out the various advantages and disadvantages concerning your choice of shelter.

Figure 15.4 outlines some of the lifestyle considerations surrounding the choice. The following discussion will be concerned with the financial considerations. We do not mean to imply that the financial decision is the most important one. The financial decision is an objective one that we can help you analyze. Your preferred living arrangement is a personal choice.

To find out whether you are a candidate for home ownership, you should first estimate how much you can afford. Given this information, you can then examine housing within your price range. Once you understand what the market has to offer, you can decide whether it is financially more advantageous to buy or to rent.

Figure 15.4
Rent versus buy: personal considerations.

Renting	Buying
Lifestyle Choices	
Landlord may place restrictions on pets, guests, and children. There also may be restrictions on how you may redecorate your rental unit.	For condos and co-ops, similar restrictions may exist in the bylaws. The single-family home provides the most freedom in choice of lifestyle. You need only abide by city zoning ordinances.
Privacy	
You may be bothered by both other tenants and the landlord. The landlord will have rights to inspect the premises and to show the unit to prospective tenants.	You can have as much or as little privacy as you want, depending on the type of home ownership you choose.
Maintenance	
Maintenance costs will be included in your rental payments. With a responsible landlord you will be free of maintenance concerns. With an irresponsible landlord your only remedy may be to move.	You alone are responsible. You must budget for maintenance expenses and be prepared to do it yourself or hire a capable person.
Mobility	
At the end of the leasing period you simply pack up and leave. If you must move before the lease is up for renewal, you usually can negotiate a mutually agreeable termination.	Selling costs may be considerable, including sales commissions and fixing-up expenses. You are at the mercy of the marketplace. If home demand is down, you must either accept a lower price or incur carrying costs until the market improves.
Financial Risk	
The only risk you face is the possible loss of your personal property in the rental unit. This risk can be covered by renter's insurance.	Your home is also an investment. You can insure it against natural disasters and most other risks. However, you cannot insure against a forced sale at below market price resulting from the loss of your job.

Determining What You Can Afford

The general rule of thumb for determining how much you can afford either to rent or purchase is that you spend no more than 25 percent of your after-tax income on housing expenses. For buyers, this usually implies a home purchase price of about two and one-half times after-tax income. Unfortunately, this is only a rule of thumb; the actual guidelines used by lending institutions can be a lot more complicated.

A worksheet incorporating the housing expense and repayment test set down by Freddie Mac is contained in Figure 15.5. You begin by entering your annual and monthly gross income on lines 1 and 2. This includes all before-tax income from normal and regular sources.

Figure 15.5
How much house can you afford?

	Sample Data	Your Data
1. Annual gross income	$35,000	______
2. Monthly gross income (divide line 1 by 12)	$ 2,917	______
Housing Expense Test		
3. Housing expense-to-income ratio	× 0.28	×
4. Allowable housing expenditure (multiply line 2 by line 3)	$ 817	______
5. Estimated nonmortgage housing expenses	200	______
6. Affordable monthly mortgage payment under housing expense test (subtract line 5 from line 4)	$ 617	______
Debt Repayment Test		
7. Debt repayment-to-income ratio	0.36	×
8. Allowable debt payment (multiply line 2 by line 7)	$ 1,050	______
9. Monthly installment debt and alimony	$ 120	______
10. Total nonmortgage expense and installment debt repayment (add line 5 and line 9)	$ 320	______
11. Affordable monthly mortgage payment under debt repayment test (subtract line 10 from line 8)	$ 730	______
Your Affordable Home Purchase		
12. Affordable monthly mortgage (enter the lesser value on line 11 and line 6)	$ 617	______
13. Monthly payment per $1,000 mortgage (see Table 15.1)	$ 8.05	______
14. Your affordable mortgage (divide line 12 by line 13 and multiply by $1,000)	$76,646	______
15. Fractional amount borrowed	0.80	______
16. Your affordable home purchase (divide line 14 by line 15)	$95,807	______

Next, multiply the housing expense-to-income ratio on line 3 by your monthly gross income on line 2, and enter the result on line 4. This indicates the total amount you may devote to housing expenses. A maximum housing expense-to-income ratio of 0.28 is used in the example.

The Federal Home Loan Mortgage Corporation (popularly called Freddie Mac) recommends that your monthly housing expenses not exceed 28 percent of gross monthly income. Furthermore, it suggests that your total monthly debt payments, including housing expenses, not exceed 33 to 36 percent of your gross monthly income. Most lenders will attempt to abide by these ratios. However, you may find a few who are willing to surpass the recommended ratios if you have proven yourself creditworthy.

Line 5 includes all your nonmortgage housing expenses. These will consist of mortgage insurance premiums, property insurance, real estate taxes, and, when applicable, homeowners association or condominium maintenance fees. Subtracting nonmortgage housing expenses (line 5) from line 4 indicates your affordable monthly mortgage payment under the housing expenses test (line 6).

The debt repayment test is used to ensure that other claims on your paycheck do not interfere with your ability to meet your mortgage payment. An allowable debt-to-income ratio of 0.36 is used in the example. If you plan to place 10 percent or less down on the purchase price, use the lower limit of 0.33. On line 9 include all installment debt with more than 10 payments remaining, in addition to any other regular claims on your income, such as alimony payments. Adding in nonmortgage expenses and subtracting the total from the allowable debt payment on line 8 provides your affordable monthly mortgage payment under the debt repayment test.

You must satisfy both the home expense and debt repayment test, therefore your affordable monthly mortgage will be the equal to the lower of the values on line 6 and line 11. The next step is to determine how much you can borrow, given your ability to cover the monthly mortgage payments on line 12. To estimate this, you first need to know the current initial interest rates on home mortgages. You will find that interest rates differ by lending institution, type of mortgage, and size of down payment. However, after a few calls to local financial institutions, you should have some idea what the going market rate is. You then can use this rate to find your monthly payment per $1,000 of mortgage loan in Table 15.1. Enter this value on line 13. In the example, it is assumed that the annual interest rate on an expected 30-year loan with a 20 percent down payment is 9 percent. This produces the monthly payment per $1,000 of $8.05 on line 13. Divide line 12 by line 13, and then multiply the result by $1,000 to obtain an estimate of your affordable mortgage on line 14.

The home purchase price will be equal to the amount borrowed plus the down payment. Given a 20 percent down payment, the mortgage will equal 80 percent of the selling price, and the affordable home purchase price is $95,807 shown on line 16.

Types of Housing

Current data on the housing market can be found in Figure 15.6. Since World War II the U.S. Congress has pursued a policy of fostering home ownership through subsidies and tax breaks. That policy has largely succeeded, as demonstrated by the increase in owner-occupied housing. In 1940, only about 44 percent of housing units were owner occupied. This percentage rose to a high of 65.6 percent in 1980, but has since stabilized at about 64 percent.

TABLE 15.1 • MONTHLY PAYMENT PER $1,000 OF MORTGAGE LOAN

Contract Interest Rate (%)	Duration of Loan (Years)					
	5	10	15	20	25	30
16	$24.32	$16.75	$14.69	$13.91	$13.59	$13.45
15	23.79	16.13	14.00	13.17	12.81	12.64
14	23.27	15.53	13.31	12.44	12.04	11.85
13½	23.01	15.23	12.98	12.07	11.66	11.45
13	22.75	14.93	12.65	11.72	11.28	11.06
12½	22.50	14.64	12.33	11.36	10.90	10.67
12	22.24	14.35	12.00	11.01	10.53	10.29
11½	21.99	14.06	11.68	10.66	10.16	9.90
11	21.74	13.78	11.37	10.32	9.80	9.52
10½	21.49	13.49	11.05	9.98	9.44	9.15
10	21.25	13.22	10.75	9.65	9.09	8.78
9½	21.00	12.94	10.44	9.32	8.74	8.41
9	20.76	12.67	10.14	9.00	8.39	8.05
8	20.28	12.13	9.56	8.36	7.72	7.34
7	19.80	11.61	8.99	7.75	7.07	6.65
6	19.33	11.10	8.44	7.16	6.44	6.00
5	18.87	10.61	7.91	6.60	5.85	5.37

The 1980s exhibited the first decade-long reduction in the home ownership rate since the 1930s. Largely responsible for this decline were those in the less-than-35-years-old age group. A large percentage of these young adults have lately decided to rent rather than buy. Since housing affordability generally increased during the 1980s, this change in behavior cannot be explained by financial factors. The Bureau of the Census suggests that the decline in home ownership is most likely due to changing lifestyles. Nonmarried-couple households increased during the 1980s, and such nonfamily households are less likely to own homes than traditional married-couple families.

As you might expect, the home ownership rate for specific groups of households can diverge widely from this overall percentage. Home ownership varies directly with age, income, and net worth. Under age 35, only 39 percent of households own the home they are living in. By age 55 to 64, ownership has risen to 79 percent. Household income and net worth both increase with age, so housing becomes both more affordable and more tax advantageous, because of federal income tax deductions for mortgage interest and property taxes.

The data suggest that the typical household starts out in a rental unit. With an increase in income and the accumulation of the necessary down payment, families tend to purchase their first home when the head of the household is around age 30. And when they do purchase, the overwhelming choice is the traditional single-family home. Your household, however, need not be typical. Choose the types of housing and the type of occupancy that best fits your lifestyle and financial plan. To do that you must first familiarize yourself with the available types of housing and then analyze the financial benefits of buying versus renting.

APARTMENT HOUSING Although any style of living unit can be rented, it is usually the apartment we think of first. The census data indicate a movement toward build-

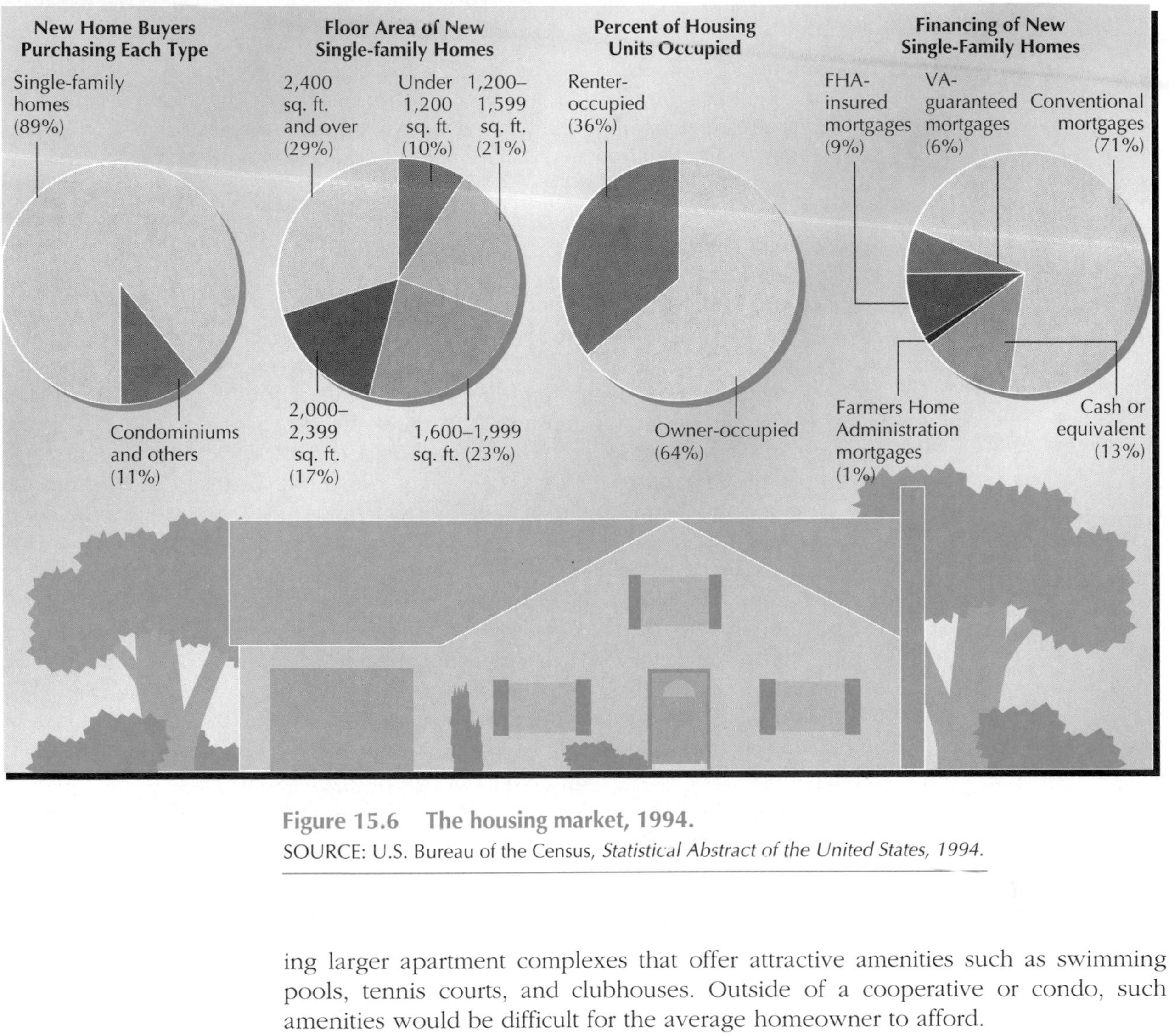

Figure 15.6 The housing market, 1994.
SOURCE: U.S. Bureau of the Census, *Statistical Abstract of the United States, 1994.*

ing larger apartment complexes that offer attractive amenities such as swimming pools, tennis courts, and clubhouses. Outside of a cooperative or condo, such amenities would be difficult for the average homeowner to afford.

For mobile individuals demanding minimal responsibilities and an environment in which social relationships are nurtured, a large apartment complex may be desirable. This group seems to be the one to which new apartment construction is designed to appeal.

Condominium: A form of ownership in which there is an individual ownership interest in the living unit but a shared ownership unit in the common areas.

CONDOMINIUM HOUSING Condominium housing can offer the extras of apartment living along with the rewards of home ownership. However, strictly defined, **condominium** does not refer to a particular type of housing. It stands for a unique type of ownership where part of the property is individually owned and part is owned in common with other members of the condominium complex. You own your living unit and have a shared interest in other areas of the condominium site, such as recreational and maintenance areas. This means you will be responsible not only for the financing and upkeep of your individual unit, but you will also be assessed charges for the financing and upkeep of the common areas. Before you purchase, you should fully understand what these charges are and how they will be determined in the future.

As an owner, you are a member of the condominium association and will be able to vote for directors in whom most of the governing powers will be vested. Condominiums are created by the laws of the state where they are located. The laws provide a legal framework for the operations of the directors and for the conditions and restrictions imposed on a property. Although this framework will differ from state to state, in all states you have a right to receive copies of the basic documents in which the legal and economic bases of the condominium are set out. This information will be contained in the declaration, bylaws, operating budget, and management agreement for the condominium.

Cooperative: A corporate form of ownership in which individuals own stock giving them exclusive use of a dwelling unit.

COOPERATIVE HOUSING As in a condominium, several owners share an undivided interest in cooperative housing. However, a **cooperative** has a corporate form. Instead of purchasing the individual living unit, you purchase stock in the corporation and then lease the living unit from the corporation. The corporation owns the living units and carries the mortgage on them. Its expenses are covered by the rents set in the lease agreements. As a stockholder, you can vote for the board of directors. One major problem associated with cooperatives is that you must receive the consent of the board of directors before you can transfer your stock and lease.

SINGLE-FAMILY HOUSING Single-family homes can be found to fit almost every need, if not every price range. The typical new home will contain about 2,000 square feet in two stories on a slab, with three bedrooms, two baths, and a garage. If you can't find one that satisfies you, you can always consider having one built.

When you purchase a single-family home, you take on all the responsibilities of finance and maintenance that go with it. You are your own landlord and maintenance person and must budget your money and time accordingly. When something needs to be fixed, you must be ready to do it yourself or have the funds to hire someone else.

MULTIFAMILY HOUSING If you are considering purchasing a multifamily dwelling, you are looking for an investment that also satisfies your own need for shelter. The financial considerations concerning investment in real estate are not covered in this chapter. It is suggested that you read the sections in this chapter on real estate transactions and mortgage financing, and then turn to Chapter 13 for a discussion on investing in tangibles.

MOBILE HOMES Over 90 percent of mobile homes are not very mobile. They travel only from the manufacturer to the dealer and finally to a housing site, where they usually remain permanently affixed. For this reason, the industry prefers the term *manufactured home*. Because the homes are constructed at the factory, the cost per square foot of living space is considerably less than for on-site construction.

The mobile home may be placed on a solitary plot or within a mobile home park. Parks often have common recreational areas and offer many of the conveniences of large apartment complexes. Typically, mobile home parks rent sites using long-term lease agreements. However, there are a few condominium mobile home developments, where you purchase the site and then pay a monthly maintenance fee to cover the cost of the common areas.

The construction of new mobile homes must satisfy safety requirements specified in the National Mobile Home Construction Act and must display a permanent label stating so. This label does not certify that the home will be approved for government-insured financing provided by the Department of Housing and Urban Development.

Because the market price of mobile homes has typically depreciated with age, financing has been a problem. Mobile homes are usually financed with a 20 percent down payment, a personal property loan of 10 to 15 years duration, and an interest rate a few percentage points above that on conventional home mortgages. For those who qualify, federally insured mortgages for longer durations and with lower down payments are available through the Federal Housing Administration (FHA) and the Veterans Administration (VA).

A Cost Comparison

When you purchase a home, you are undertaking a sizable investment of your own money. The financial question is, Would you be better off renting and investing your funds elsewhere? The answer will depend upon expected future housing prices, the expected return on financial investments, the length of time you expect to stay in one location, and the expected tax advantage from home ownership.

THE TAX ADVANTAGE Several immediate and long-term tax advantages are associated with buying a home. If you itemize deductions—and you probably should if you have a home mortgage—both the state and local taxes you pay on the property and the interest you pay on the mortgage may be deductible from your adjusted gross income when you calculate your federal taxable income. This means that if you are in the 28 percent marginal tax bracket, each dollar you pay in property taxes and interest saves you 28 cents in federal income taxes. Naturally, the higher your marginal tax rate, the greater is the income tax advantage. As a renter, you may find these items included in the price of the rent, but you as a renter cannot take them as a deduction on your income tax return. It is true that the landlord can deduct these expenses, and this tax advantage to the landlord may be reflected in a lower rental price, but don't plan on it. Rental prices in most areas are set by supply and demand. During periods when rental units are scarce, it is unlikely that any of the landlord's tax advantage will show up in favorable rental prices.

Federal tax law changes enacted in 1986 and 1987 placed a few restrictions on the deduction of home mortgage interest. Mortgage interest is now fully deductible only on first and second homes, if total home mortgages do not exceed $1 million. In addition, for all interest on a second mortgage, such as a home equity loan, to be deductible, total mortgages must be both less than the market value of the home and less than $100,000 plus the cost of improvements and your remaining acquisition indebtedness.

Home ownership provides more than the immediate tax benefit. Special tax treatment accorded capital gains provides an additional long-term tax advantage. If you sell a home for more than you paid for it, you can defer paying taxes on the gain if you purchase another home within a two-year period. To qualify for the tax deferral you must file IRS Form 2119, *Sale or Exchange of Principal Residence,* to indicate the details of the sale and purchase. As an added bonus, after you reach 55, you need not pay taxes on $125,000 of these accumulated gains.

Finally, there is a hidden tax advantage that is often overlooked. Suppose you could rent your present home for $500 a month; this is the market worth of the shelter, which you are receiving. This value is part of the return from the investment in the home and may be thought of as an implicit rent paid to and received

Box 15.1 SIMPLIFYING FINANCIAL PLANNING
Keeping Track of Your Housing Capital Gains

You have a capital gain whenever you sell something for more than it cost you. The IRS is interested in your capital gains because it collects taxes on such gains at the same rate as on your other earnings. In order to make sure it doesn't miss any of those taxes, it requires the settlement agent at the closing on the home to report the details of the transaction to the IRS on a Form 1099B.

Congress has attempted to encourage home ownership by providing for special tax treatment. Paying taxes on your home ownership capital gains can be delayed as long as you purchase another home of equal or greater value within two years of selling the previous one and file a Form 2119 with your personal income tax return. Additional favorable treatment includes a one-time tax exclusion on $125,000 of your gains if you are over 55 and cannot delay the taxes due by purchasing another home. Given these tax breaks, it is important to keep adequate records to ensure that you are not paying too much or too little in taxes.

For each home that you have owned, you should permanently retain records on:

- All documents relating to the financial circumstances of the purchase and sale of the home
- All costs incurred in preparing the home for sale and selling the home
- Form 2119
- The cost of all home improvements

The retention of these records will simplify the task of substantiating your cost basis and qualifying for your capital gains exemption.

Your capital gain is equal to the net sales price (selling price minus selling expenses) less the cost of the home and the cost of any improvements you have made on the home. While home owners usually do retain adequate records on the purchase and sale of a home, they often neglect to keep track of their home improvement costs. In order to reduce your potential capital gain, such improvements must consist of expenses other than for normal maintenance and repair. In addition, your expenses must be adequately documented. It is not the responsibility of the IRS to prove that you didn't make the improvements; rather, it is your responsibility to prove that you did. To substantiate these expenses, you should maintain a file labeled "home improvements," and simply place copies of any receipts or bills for home improvement expenditures along with a short explanation of what was done whenever these improvements occur.

When the tax on your capital gains is no longer delayed by the purchase of another home, you will have to pay taxes on all of your accumulated gains. In effect, you will have to total up the capital gains on each of the several homes you may have owned. The home owners capital gain exclusion of $125,000 may sound like a lot of money, but 20 or 30 years from now it may be worth a lot less. Above that exclusion, each dollar of documented home improvement costs will make you very glad that you have kept a file labeled "home improvements."

by yourself. However, payments to yourself are not considered income for tax purposes. Thus, the implicit rental income accompanying home ownership remains tax free.

BUYING VERSUS RENTING Figure 15.7 shows a worksheet for comparing the relative costs of buying and renting a home. The worksheet contains entries for a one-year comparison and a five-year comparison. Both periods are considered because it is most likely that the best choice depends on the length of time spent at one location. The sample data are based on a home that could be purchased for $110,000 or rented for $780 per month plus utilities. If purchased, it is assumed the buyer would place 20 percent down and borrow $88,000, to be paid back over 30 years at an annual percentage rate of 9 percent. It is also assumed that all prices, including the market price of the home, will rise at 4 percent a year.

The gross gain from buying is equal to the appreciation in the market value of the house. Looking first at the one-year comparison, the assumed appreciation rate of 4 percent is equal to $4,400 on the $110,000 house. This is not reduced by taxes, since it is assumed the gain can be postponed until age 55, at which time it is tax

Givens: Home: $110,000 Purchase Price
4% annual inflation
Mortgage: $88,000 loan
9% annual interest on outstanding balance with $22,000 down payment; monthly payment $708.07 for 30 years
Rent: $780 per month plus utilities
Marginal Tax Rate: 28%

	One-Year Comparison			
	Buying		Renting	
	Sample Estimates	Your Estimates	Sample Estimates	Your Estimates
Gross gain				
Appreciation	$ 4,400	______		
Interest earned after taxes paid			$ 1,426	______
Expenses				
Mortgage interest after taxes saved	$ 5,685	______		
Property taxes after taxes saved	$ 1,512	______		
Fuel and utilities	1,800	______	1,800	______
Insurance	500	______	200	______
Rent			9,360	______
Repair and maintenance	1,200	______		
Closing costs after taxes saved	2,000	______		
Sales commission	6,864	______	______	______
Total expenses	$19,561	______	$11,360	______
Net gain or loss (gross gain – total expenses)	($15,161)	______	($ 9,934)	______
Net savings from renting = $5,227				

	Five-Year Comparison			
	Buying		Renting	
	Sample Estimates	Your Estimates	Sample Estimates	Your Estimates
Gross gain				
Appreciation	$23,832	______		
Interest earned after taxes paid			$ 8,114	______
Expenses				
Mortgage interest after taxes saved	$27,978	______		
Property taxes after taxes saved	$ 8,189	______		
Fuel and utilities	9,749	______	$ 9,749	______
Insurance	2,708	______	1,083	______
Rent			50,697	______
Repair and maintenance	6,500	______		
Closing costs after taxes saved	2,000	______		
Sales commission	8,030	______	______	______
Total expenses	$65,154	______	$61,529	______
Net gain or loss (gross gain – total expenses)	($41,322)	______	($53,415)	______
Net savings from buying = $12,093				

Figure 15.7
Buy versus rent: cost comparison.

free. Of course, this assumption commits you to purchasing another house when this one is sold.

The gross gain from renting is based on the assumption that if you did not buy, the $22,000 downpayment would remain in an investment fund paying an annual interest rate of 9 percent. This investment would provide interest income of $1,980 before taxes. However, with an assumed marginal tax rate of 28 percent, interest earned after taxes is $1,426 = $1,980 × (1 − 0.28).

The related expenses of home ownership and renting are listed next. Mortgage interest payments can be taken from an amortization schedule prepared by your lender. This schedule will specify your yearly repayments on the loan and your yearly interest payments (for an example, see Table 15.2). On the present loan, mortgage interest payments for the first year are $7,896. Assuming you itemize de-

TABLE 15.2 • AMORTIZATION SCHEDULE FOR A FIXED RATE MORTGAGE

Loan amount: $88,000.00
Monthly payment: $708.07
Annual contract rate: 9%
Term (years): 30

Year	Principal Repayment	Interest Payment	Ending Principal Outstanding
1	$ 601.21	$ 7,895.60	$87,398.79
2	657.61	7,839.20	86,741.18
3	719.30	7,777.51	86,021.88
4	786.78	7,710.04	85,235.10
5	860.58	7,636.23	84,374.52
6	941.31	7,555.51	83,433.21
7	1,029.61	7,467.21	82,403.60
8	1,126.19	7,370.62	81,277.41
9	1,231.84	7,264.98	80,045.57
10	1,347.39	7,149.42	78,698.17
11	1,473.79	7,023.03	77,224.39
12	1,612.04	6,884.77	75,612.35
13	1,763.26	6,733.55	73,849.08
14	1,928.67	6,568.15	71,920.42
15	2,109.59	6,387.23	69,810.83
16	2,307.48	6,189.33	67,503.35
17	2,523.94	5,972.87	64,979.40
18	2,760.70	5,736.11	62,218.70
19	3,019.68	5,477.14	59,199.02
20	3,302.94	5,193.87	55,896.08
21	3,612.78	4,884.03	52,283.30
22	3,951.69	4,545.13	48,331.61
23	4,322.38	4,174.43	44,009.23
24	4,727.85	3,768.96	39,281.38
25	5,171.36	3,325.46	34,110.02
26	5,656.47	2,840.35	28,453.55
27	6,187.08	2,309.73	22,266.47
28	6,767.47	1,729.34	15,499.00
29	7,402.31	1,094.51	8,096.69
30	8,096.69	400.12	0.00
Total	$88,000.00	$166,904.45	

ductions, the actual interest expense after taxes is $5,685 = $7,896 × (1 − 0.28). Similar tax adjustment should be made for property taxes and points, the prepaid interest component of closing costs.

All of the other expenses, except for the sales commission, are self-explanatory. The sales commission has been set equal to 6 percent of the expected market value of the home at the end of the holding period. Given an initial cost of $110,000, a one-year holding period, and an expected increase in value of 4 percent, the sales commission will be $6,864. Since this expense is postponed until the home is sold, it is an often-overlooked cost of home ownership.

The five-year comparison employs the same basic assumptions as the one-year comparison. The annual interest rate is 9 percent, and all prices, including fuel, insurance, maintenance, taxes, and rent are assumed to rise at a 4 percent annual rate.

Such analyses, including this example, commonly show that renting appears the better alternative over the short run, whereas ownership is cheaper over the long run. The high turnover cost of buying and selling a home makes renting the better short-term choice. On the other hand, the inflation protection of home ownership makes it the optimal long-term choice.

THE REAL ESTATE TRANSACTION

A home is most likely the largest single purchase you will make. Because it is so costly, and because few of us buy and sell homes often enough to become experts on the subject, you should seek the advice of experienced professionals. You may want to rely on an appraiser, a real estate agent, a home inspector, and an attorney.

The Appraisal

As a buyer or a seller, you need information on market price. Housing prices depend on myriad factors, the principal ones being size, construction, age, and location. The last factor is often overlooked by first-time home buyers. There may be a wide spread in the selling price of identical houses in two different locations. Remember, you are really buying more than a home. You are buying into a neighborhood, a score of community services, and a school system. Only someone very familiar with the local housing market may be able to appraise all these and other relevant factors.

Professional appraisers may be located in the Yellow Pages under *Real Estate Appraisers*. Look for the listing American Institute of Real Estate Appraisers, National Society of Real Estate Appraisers, or Society of Real Estate Appraisers. Each organization certifies expert appraisers. If there are none listed in your area, contact a lender of home mortgages. Because they also require an appraisal, they should be able to provide you with a list of competent appraisers. In all cases, ask for credentials and references.

If you are a buyer, the mortgage lender will conduct an appraisal, but you should not rely on this procedure to determine the market value of your potential home. The lender's interest and yours are not the same. The lender wants to determine if the value of the house exceeds the amount borrowed by some safety margin. An independent appraisal may be necessary, because, as a buyer or a seller, you need to know that you are paying or receiving the market value.

The Real Estate Agent

Unless you as a buyer have a special agreement with the real estate agent, the agent will be representing the seller. You should keep this in mind. Many people fall into a comfortable relationship with the agent who is showing them homes, and in the course of casual conversation reveal too much about what they are willing to pay. Because the agent's interest must be with the seller, this information may be later used to undermine the buyer's negotiating position.

As a seller you can choose to use a real estate agent or not. Only about 15 percent of all house sales are made without an agent. However, with an agent's commission at about 6 to 7 percent of the sale price, selling the home yourself can appear to be an attractive alternative. To make the best decision, you must think in terms of earning the commission, rather than saving it. You will have to take on the work of advertising and showing the home and dealing directly with potential buyers. This work can be both time consuming and, for some people, emotionally draining.

Before selecting a real estate agent to buy or sell a home, talk to several home owners and discover their personal experiences. First, ask for an overall assessment of the agent's performance. Then ask them whether their agent had many listings or was mainly showing homes listed by other real estate agencies. An agent with few listings may be in the real estate business only part time, and thus may not provide the publicity or attention you need. Ask homeowners whether they felt pressured by the agent to sell their homes at low prices or buy homes they disliked. The decision to buy or sell is an important and complicated one. Even without an aggressive real estate agent, you will be under enormous pressure. Finally, ask what percentage of the sale price the agent took as a commission on the sale. This is a negotiable item. Many times an agent will agree to a reduction in the percentage charged in order to get a new listing or to see a sale completed. Remember, however, the smaller the commission, the smaller is the agent's incentive to devote time to the selling of your home.

If you are selling a home, you should have several agents appraise its value. Ask for documentation on the sale price of similar homes in the same neighborhood and the highest price at which each agent would be willing to list your home. Do not necessarily go with the agent willing to list your home at the highest price. Some unscrupulous agents may agree to list your home at a noncompetitive price just to get the listing. Their hope is to eventually get the homeowner to lower the listing price after it becomes obvious that there are no buyers in this price range. If you had an independent appraisal before contacting the real estate agents, you now should be in a good position to judge the honesty and knowledge of the agents with whom you are dealing.

Some real estate agencies will offer special inducements in an effort to get your home listing. These may turn out to be less valuable than first appearances would suggest. For example, some agencies will agree to buy your home if it cannot be sold by a specified time. Unfortunately, the price at which they are willing to purchase the home may be substantially below the price at which they are listing it. In addition, you may be still charged a commission, even though the home was purchased by the real estate agency at a low market price. Finally, the agreement may bind you to purchase a new home through this same agency, which will, of course, collect a commission on that transaction.

Be sure that the agent you choose to sell your home is a member of the Multiple Listing Service (MLS). This will provide information on your home to all other real estate agencies in your area who are also members of the MLS. Because of fee-splitting arrangements among MLS members, every agent has an interest in selling your home.

Listing agreement: A contract between the seller and the real estate agent providing the agent with authority to represent the seller in return for a commission on the sale.

After you have selected a particular agent, you will be asked to sign a **listing agreement.** This is a contract between you and the real estate agent. It provides the agent with authority to act as your salesperson in return for a commission on the sale of the home. Important items on the contract will consist of the listing price, the commission, a description of the property, any terms and conditions for sale, duration of the listing, and exclusivity of the listing. The last item will determine whether you have the right to retain other sales agents during the term of the listing agreement.

Exclusive right to sell: Entitles the agent to a commission no matter who sells the property.

Exclusive agency agreement: The agent has an exclusive right to broker the property but may agree to share the commission with other agents. If you locate the buyer yourself, you don't pay a commission.

Open agreement: Any agent can broker your home. The commission goes to the agent who locates a buyer. If you sell your home, you don't pay a commission.

Net listing agreement: Provides the seller with a predetermined amount of money from the sale of a property. The real estate agent receives the difference between the sale price and the amount promised the seller.

There are three basic types of listing arrangements: the exclusive right to sell, the exclusive agency, and the open agreement. The **exclusive right to sell** entitles the agent to a commission regardless of who sells the property. Under an **exclusive agency agreement,** the seller agrees to retain one agent, but the agent collects the commission only if it is sold with the help of the agent. If you locate a buyer yourself, you don't pay a commission. In both of the above agreements the agent can co-broker the property, offering to split the commission with any other agent who can help find a buyer. With an **open agreement** the agent receives a commission only if he or she discovers a buyer. If you or another agent sells the home, you don't owe a commission to the agent who listed your home under an open agreement.

Beware of clauses that automatically extend the listing period, prohibit recording (public notice) of the listing agreement, or contain a net listing agreement. Each of these can result in serious problems for the seller. Automatic extensions beyond the typical 90-day period reduce the agent's incentive to sell your home in a timely manner. Public notice may be required if the contract is misrepresented. A **net listing agreement** provides the seller with a predetermined amount of money from the sale of the property. The real estate agent receives the difference between the sale price and the amount promised the seller.

The Home Inspection

Instead of depending upon a warranty as insurance against defects, get information on potential problems before you purchase. A thorough inspection by a qualified housing inspector should uncover problem areas that would otherwise go unnoticed. A home inspection will cost you between $125 and $250. For this amount, you should receive a written report stating the condition of the home and its component systems.

The American Society of Home Inspectors trains and certifies qualified individuals. They may be found in the Yellow Pages under *Building Inspection Services, Inspection Bureaus, Engineers,* or *Real Estate Inspectors*. Since most of the ASHI membership is in the East, you may not be able to find one in your area. In any case, be sure the inspector you hire has nothing to gain from your purchasing the home. The inspector should not, for example, run a remodeling firm or depend upon a real estate agency for support. Ask for the names of previous customers and insist on being present during the home inspection. The person you hire should be able to answer all questions you may have during the inspection.

The Purchase Contract

The offer to purchase a home is made on a document entitled *Contract to Purchase, Purchase Agreement,* or *Deposit Receipt*. When both the buyer and the seller have agreed to all the conditions in the purchase contract, it becomes a binding agreement that creates rights and obligations for both parties. For this reason, you should consult an attorney before you sign. Most real estate transactions are closed, however, without the aid of an attorney. Unfortunately, too many people consult an attorney only when they want to get out of a disagreeable contract. Such remedial action can be very costly.

You and your attorney should carefully examine the purchase contract to make sure it contains the following:

1. The purchase price, the down payment, and the type of financing. When buying a new home, beware of an "escalator" clause that would permit the builder to increase the price because of future cost increases.
2. Anticipated closing costs and prepaid items and who will pay them.
3. A description of the property and a list of all items being sold with the house. For new construction, plans and specifications should be included, and you should carefully review these with your architect and home inspector.
4. A statement as to who is responsible for the property from the date of the contract to the date the property is conveyed to you.
5. The amount of the deposit and the conditions under which the buyer or the seller might void the contract. For example, failure to buy or sell another house, inadequate financing, an unsatisfactory inspection report, or failure to obtain marketable title may all be good reasons for voiding the purchase contract.
6. A stated date after which the offer lapses if not accepted.

The process leading to the sale of a home begins when the buyer makes an offer to purchase, with a signed purchase contract and a commitment of earnest money. The seller may then accept the offer, reject the offer, or make a counteroffer by altering some or all of the terms on the purchase contract. Likewise, the buyer may then accept the counteroffer, reject it, or make another counteroffer. This process continues until the two sides either terminate negotiations or agree upon a sale.

Earnest money: Money deposited by the buyer, to be kept by the seller if the buyer does not abide by the terms of the offer to purchase. It demonstrates the buyer's good faith in the offer.

Deed: A written instrument transferring title of real estate to the buyer.

Title search: An examination of public records in order to determine who may have enforceable claims on the property.

Marketable title: Legal evidence of a right to property that is free of claims from other parties.

The buyer's deposit of **earnest money** demonstrates that the offer is made in good faith. If the offer to purchase is not accepted or lapses, the earnest money should be returned to the buyer. If the seller accepts the offer to purchase, a third party—either a broker, a title company, or an escrow agent—will hold the money in a trust account until the sale is closed or the contract is broken. Should the buyer fail to purchase the home as indicated in the contract, the seller can keep the earnest money. On the other hand, if the seller breaks the contract, the deposit is returned to the buyer. When the sale goes through, the deposit is applied to the buyer's down payment on the purchase.

The Title Search

The **deed** is a written document that transfers title, or ownership, to the buyer. However, the deed does not show who else might have rights to the property. In the **title search,** an attorney examines the public records to determine if others may have enforceable claims on the property. At the completion of the search, the attorney will render an opinion as to whether **marketable title** exists. A marketable title is free of all claims from other parties.

The mortgage lender will conduct a title search. However, the fact that you are granted a loan does not necessarily mean the title is free of all defects. A loan may be still granted if the lender feels assured that the full value of the loan can be repaid in spite of minor defects in the title. In addition, if the search is deficient, you may have no claim against the attorney. The attorney is financially responsible only to the client. If the lender ordered the search, the lender is the client and not you. For this reason you should have an independent examination.

Title insurance: Protects the insured against defective title.

The mortgage lender will require that you purchase **title insurance.** This insures the bank, not you, against a defective title. To protect your interest in the title, you can obtain owner's title insurance. You will save money by purchasing this coverage at the same time you buy the lender's policy. As with all insurance, coverage can vary. Read the insurance contract carefully to be sure it covers all defects in title, both in and out of the public record.

The Closing

Closing: The meeting at which the sale is finalized and the title is transferred.

Closing, or settlement, costs: Payments due at closing.

Immediately before you are about to complete your home purchase, schedule a final walk-through to ensure that everything is as it should be. The meeting at which the purchase and the mortgage are finalized is called the **closing.** The seller receives payment. The buyer undertakes the mortgage and receives the deed. By mutual agreement between the buyer and the seller, actual possession of the property may take place not at this time but at some later date. Whoever closes the sale is required to report the terms of the sale to the IRS in order to ensure compliance with tax law. Costs due at this time are called **closing,** or **settlement, costs.** A sample list of these costs is given in Figure 15.8.

Figure 15.8
A checklist of potential closing costs.

Government Charges
Prorated taxes
Recording fees
Transfer taxes
Lender Charges
Appraisals
Attorney fees (lender)
Credit report
Document preparation
Hazard (homeowner's) insurance
Inspections (lender)
Land survey
Mortgage insurance
Origination fees
Points
Prepaid interest
Title insurance (lender)
Title search
Other Sale-Related Charges
Attorney fee (buyer)
Inspections (buyer)
Real estate agent sales commission
Title insurance (buyer)

GOVERNMENT CHARGES At the date of the closing, property-based taxes will be prorated to the buyer and seller over the current tax period. In addition, there may be various state and local charges on the transfer and the recording of the transfer. These charges are usually modest, but in some states these fees can run as high as 1 percent of the sale price.

LENDER'S CHARGES The buyer generally pays lender's charges. They include the lender's cost of processing the loan, plus related costs such as property appraisals and inspections. Title charges include the costs of title search, title insurance for the lender, and document preparation. A single premium paid at this time will keep the policy in force until the house is sold again.

The Real Estate Settlement Procedures Act requires that the lender give you a good faith estimate of your closing costs within three days of receiving your loan application. The origination fee to start processing of your loan cannot be more than 1 percent of the mortgage amount. Other fees they may charge include appraisal fees, inspection fees, and attorney fees.

Points: Prepaid interest; one point is equal to 1 percent of the amount borrowed.

Points, also called discount points, may be included. Points are considered prepaid interest and are charged when the interest rate is below the yield required by lenders that buy mortgage securities. One discount point is equal to 1 percent of the amount borrowed. For example, on an $80,000 mortgage, 1½ discount points are equal to $1,200. This has the effect of reducing the amount borrowed from $80,000 to $78,800. You still, however, owe the bank the unpaid balance of $80,000. Consequently, paying points raises the annual percentage rate (APR) on the loan above the **contract rate,** the rate applied to the unpaid balance for calculating your monthly mortgage payments. This difference arises because the APR calculates payments as a percentage of $78,800 (amount borrowed), whereas the contract rate calculates payments as a percentage of the amount owed ($80,000).

Contract rate: The interest rate applied to the unpaid balance on the home mortgage.

If the loan is closed before the last day of the month, the lender will want the borrower to prepay the balance of that month's interest. The lender may also require the borrower to prepay mortgage and hazard insurance. On some loans, particularly those with low down payments, the lender requires the borrower to set up and periodically fund a reserve account for paying insurance and property taxes. This account, called an *escrow account,* ensures that these payments will be made on time.

OTHER SALE-RELATED CHARGES These may include the cost of your attorney, title insurance coverage for the buyer, and any home inspections arranged by the buyer or seller. The seller typically pays the broker's commission on the sale of the home. It currently runs about 6 or 7 percent of the sales price, but the exact percentage is negotiable.

Warranties

Homes, like other goods, will be covered by unwritten implied warranties set down in state law. Written warranties may also accompany the sale. These fall into two categories; the first are builders' warranties on newly constructed homes, and the second are home buyers' warranties on the resale of existing homes. Neither of these warranties relieves you from the duty of conducting a full and adequate home inspection before you buy.

Builders' warranties are meant to assure the buyer that the new home is structurally sound. The buyer receives a 10-year warranty covering a list of defects that decrease in number as the home ages. During the first year almost all defects in workmanship and materials are covered. In the second year the list of guaranteed items is substantially shorter, and in the remaining eight years only major structural defects are covered.

There have been problems with builders' warranties. Consumer groups have been highly critical. They charge that policies have been issued on poorly built homes. Moreover, the claims process may be complicated and lengthy, often forcing the consumer to deal with the original builder who was responsible for the faulty construction.

Such poor risk management forced the nation's largest seller of builders' warranties, Home Owners Warranty Corp. (HOW), into receivership in 1994. Persons who have claims covered by HOW will likely receive only 40 cents for each dollar requested. Other major warranty firms are still in business. However, at least one other has been under financial supervision because of insufficient capital requirements.

The second type of warranty, the warranty on the resale of an existing home, is similar to an extended service contract. Rather than covering the structural integrity of the home, it insures the major home appliances included in the sale. Typically, it last for only six-months to a year. This provides the buyer with some assurance that he or she will not have to incur the cost of a new furnace or water heater soon after purchasing the home. Be warned that most policies include high deductibles on service calls and may even exclude preexisting mechanical problems. There is no standard format for resale warranties; therefore, policy coverage may vary widely.

FINANCING THE PURCHASE

You can shop around for a home mortgage at a variety of financial institutions, including commercial banks, mutual savings banks, mortgage companies, and savings and loan associations. Today's mortgage market is highly competitive. You are likely to find the same lender offering both fixed and adjustable rate loans, in addition to offering several ways in which each of these loans may be structured. You should ask the loan officer to explain each of the loan options and discuss how each might fit your own financial situation. The decision is an important one. A typical mortgage will commit you to interest payments that, over the life of the loan, can equal as much as three times the original amount borrowed.

The larger your down payment, the lower the interest rate, and the longer the term of the loan, the smaller is the monthly mortgage payment. The typical home buyer makes a 20 percent down payment on a 30-year mortgage. However, with mortgage insurance you may obtain a home mortgage with as little as 5 percent down.

Through various government agencies, home loan disclosure requirements are specified and enforced. Generally, you must receive information on all of the items discussed in this section on home mortgages. Furthermore, you should receive this information before you apply for the loan or pay a loan origination fee.

The annual percentage rate (APR), explained in Chapter 4 on consumer credit, is the most important disclosure. It takes into account the interest rate and other credit charges, such as mortgage insurance, points, and loan origination fees, into a uniform measure of cost. Unfortunately, the published APR on adjustable rate loans must be based upon the initial interest rate. Since the future interest rate on the loan may differ from the initial interest rate, the APR in the mortgage contract will not likely reflect the interest costs you will actually incur. Therefore, on adjustable rate loans the lender is also required to describe the circumstances that will lead to rate changes and to give an example of the payment changes that can occur. For such loans, the circumstances under which rates may change are as important to know as the APR.

Realistically, it is impossible to present every repayment scenario for many adjustable rate loans. Loan officers will ordinarily try to be helpful, but time constraints may prohibit them from providing you with a complete examination of the loan being offered. Therefore, some previous knowledge of mortgage instruments may greatly aid you in the search for a home mortgage. The mortgage comparison checklist in Figure 15.9 should prove helpful when reviewing the characteristics of the available mortgages.

Fixed rate mortgages: Home mortgages on which the interest rate and monthly payment remain constant over the life of the loan.

Principal: The remaining balance on the amount borrowed.

Fixed Rate Mortgages

Fixed rate mortgages have an interest rate and monthly payments that remain constant over the life of the loan. For example, if you borrowed $88,000 at 9 percent for 30 years, you would have level monthly payments of $708.07 over the entire 30-year-period. Part of each monthly payment will go to the repayment of **principal**—the amount owed—and part will go toward payment of interest on the principal.

Figure 15.9 Mortgage comparison checklist.

Lender		
Loan type (fixed or adjustable)		________
Annual percentage rate		________
Duration (years)		________
Percentage down payment		________
Application fee		________
Points		________
Title insurance		________
Prepayment penalty		________
Other closing fees		________
Mortgage insurance		________
Initial interest rate		________
Initial monthly mortgage payment		________
Balloon payment		________
Additional Information on Adjustable Rate Loans		
Interest adjustment index		________
Adjustment period		________
Periodic rate cap		________
Aggregate rate cap		________
Periodic payment cap		________
Negative amortization (Y/N)		________
Adjustable duration (Y/N)		________
Additional Information for GEM and GPM Loans		
Mortgage payment schedule:	Year 1	________
	Year 2	________
	etc.	________

Amortize: To satisfy an obligation by periodic payments of interest and principal.

When you repay a loan by periodic payments, you are said to **amortize** your debt. Table 15.2 contains an amortization schedule for a fixed rate loan. During the first years of the loan, most of the mortgage payment will go toward paying interest on the principal. As the amount owed declines, a larger percentage of the mortgage payment will go toward paying off the principal. Near the end of the loan period, almost the entire mortgage payment will serve to reduce the outstanding principal.

Adjustable Rate Mortgages

Adjustable rate loans: Home mortgages on which the interest rate is periodically adjusted over the term of the loan.

The distinguishing feature of **adjustable rate loans** is that the interest rate on the loan is not fixed over the entire life of the loan. This feature is about the only common characteristic of adjustable rate loans; there are almost as many types of them as there are homes. To add to the confusion, they come under various names—such as variable and flexible rate loans.

Adjustable rate mortgages reduce the risk to lending institutions but increase the risk to borrowers. An upward movement in interest rates means that the borrower will now have to pay additional dollars of interest on the remaining loan balance. To compensate the borrower for this future risk, adjustable rate mortgages carry an initial interest rate below the rate offered on a standard fixed rate mortgage. The difference between the initial rate on fixed and variable loans can vary widely as credit market conditions change. As Figure 15.2 indicates the differential has fluctuated between 1½ and 2 percentage points in recent years.

The Federal Trade Commission suggests you examine all of the following when shopping for an adjustable rate mortgage:

- The initial interest rate
- How often the rate may change
- How much the rate may change
- The initial monthly payments
- How often payments may change
- How much payments may change
- The mortgage term
- How often the term may change
- The index to which rate, payment, or term changes are tied
- The limits, if any, on negative amortization

Interest rate adjustment period: The time between potential adjustments in the interest rate applied to the outstanding loan balance.

Interest rate adjustment index: The index to which changes in the mortgage interest rate are related.

INTEREST RATE ADJUSTMENT PERIOD AND THE ADJUSTMENT INDEX The interest rate on the remaining loan balance may be changed after a specified period. The period between one rate change and the next is known as the **interest rate adjustment period.** The majority of adjustable rate loans have an adjustment period of one year. The change in the rate is tied to the change in an **interest rate adjustment index** that tends to mirror the general movement in interest rates throughout the economy. The most common indexes are listed below.

- National Average FHLB Mortgage Contract Rate
- National Average Cost of Funds to FSLIC-Insured Associations
- London Interbank Offering Rate (LIBOR)
- Regional Average Cost of Funds to FSLIC-Insured Associations
- Six-month U.S. Treasury Rate
- Five-year U.S. Treasury Rate

- Three-year U.S. Treasury Rate
- One-year U.S. Treasury Rate
- Three-month U.S. Treasury Rate

Financial analysts tend to favor the use of the National Average FHLB Mortgage Contract Rate as an interest rate index, because it seems to be less volatile than the other indexes.

Margin: The amount added to the index rate in order to calculate the interest rate on the mortgage contract.

To determine the contract interest rate on the outstanding mortgage balance, lenders add a few percentage points, called the **margin,** to the index rate.

Index rate + margin = contract interest rate

For example, suppose an index rate such as the National Average FHLB Mortgage Contract Rate were 7.5 percent at the time of adjustment and the margin were 2 percentage points. The contract rate applied to the outstanding loan balance would be 9.5 percent. The amount of the margin differs from one lender to the other, but it is usually constant over the life of the loan.

At periodic dates specified in the mortgage contract, the contract rate will be recalculated to reflect changes in the indexed rate. Using the current example, suppose the index rate fell from 7.5 percent to 7.25 percent at the next rate adjustment. With a 2 percent margin, the contract rate will decline from 9.5 percent to 9.25 percent. Lenders have been known to incorrectly determine the interest rate readjustment; therefore, you should locate information on the index and check the lender's calculation.

Teaser rate: An abnormally low initial interest rate meant to attract borrowers.

A few lenders offer what have become known in the industry as **teaser rates,** which are a promotional gimmick. Over some initial period a reduced margin is used to calculate the adjustable rate. When this period ends, a higher margin is used to compute the rate over the remaining term of the loan. This produces an upward adjustment in the flexible rate independent of any change in the interest rate adjustment index.

Periodic rate cap: Limits the movement on changes in the interest rate during any one interest rate adjustment period.

Aggregate rate cap: Limits the total change in the interest rate over the entire term of the loan.

RATE CAP Some loans may have rate caps that limit the movement in your interest rate. These typically limit increases but may also limit decreases in the rate. A **periodic rate cap** limits changes during any one adjustment period. Suppose you had a 1½ percent periodic cap, and the underlying index rate rose by 2 percent. The adjustable rate applied to the outstanding loan balance would be limited to a 1½ percent increase during this adjustment period. However, the unused half percent may be applied during the next adjustment period.

An **aggregate rate cap** limits changes over the entire life of the loan. If you had a 5 percent aggregate cap on your mortgage rate, then no matter how high the financial index rose, a mortgage with an initial rate of 9 percent could never go above 14 percent. By federal law, all adjustable rate mortgages must have a lifetime ceiling on the contract rate. There is no federal limit on how high the cap may be, although most states do set limits.

Payment cap: Limits changes in the monthly mortgage payment.

PAYMENT CAP A **payment cap** limits changes in your monthly loan payments. Under a payment cap, it is possible for the interest rate on your adjustable rate loan to increase while your monthly payments either remain unchanged or do not increase as much as required by the interest rate adjustment.

Don't assume you don't have to pay the higher interest, however. For example, suppose you take out a 30-year, $88,000 mortgage at an initial interest rate of 9 percent and an annual adjustment period. At the 9 percent rate your initial monthly payments are $708.07. If, at the end of the first year, the interest rate rises to 11 percent, the monthly payments would ordinarily increase to $838.04. However, if the yearly adjustment under the payment cap is less than $129.97 ($838.04 – $708.07), then the monthly payments will not increase to the level required to completely discharge the loan in the remaining 29 years. The difference between your monthly payment under the cap and the required payment may be made up in one of several ways. The term of the loan can be lengthened beyond the initial 30-year agreement. Alternatively, the term might remain unchanged, but the lending institution might require an additional lump-sum payment at the time the mortgage is to be paid up. Still another method is for future monthly payments to be increased. The lending institution should specify in the mortgage contract the method it plans to use.

In the current example, the amount outstanding on the mortgage at the end of the first year will be $87,398.79. At an annual percentage rate of 11 percent, interest payments alone amount to $803.04 per month. If the payment cap keeps the monthly payment from rising beyond $803.04, **negative amortization** will result. This term simply means that instead of your debt getting smaller over time, it will get larger. You will owe the lending institution more at the end of the year than you did at the beginning. Obviously, this situation can create problems for both you and the lending institution. For this reason, only about 4 percent of mortgage contracts permit negative amortization. In all other cases, the payment cap cannot hold monthly payments to less than the interest owed on the outstanding loan balance.

Negative amortization: The resulting increase in the amount owed when the monthly payment is less than the interest due on the previous balance.

CONVERTIBLE FEATURES Lenders have recently been promoting **convertible mortgages.** These are adjustable rate mortgages that can be converted into fixed rate mortgages during a specified time period, usually between the thirteenth and sixtieth months of the loan. The fixed rate will be determined by rules set down in the mortgage contract. If you elect to make the conversion, the lender will charge a fee that, most likely, will be equal to either a stated dollar amount or a percentage of the outstanding loan balance.

Convertible mortgage: An adjustable rate mortgage contract that permits the borrower to convert to a fixed rate contract at some point during the term of the loan.

The rate on the fixed rate loan may depend on the value of the interest adjustment index at the date of the conversion. If you believe that interest rates will decline, then a convertible mortgage would allow you to get the benefits of an adjustable rate loan today and the expected benefit of a lower rate on a fixed rate loan at a future date.

You should be careful not to place too much value on the conversion feature. Adjustable rate loans rarely carry penalties for paying off a loan before it is due. Therefore, even with an ordinary adjustable rate loan, you always have the choice of paying it off and refinancing with a fixed rate loan. If you refinance, however, you will be charged closing costs and points on the new loan. The real value of the conversion feature is, consequently, the difference between the conversion fee and traditional refinancing charges.

Specialized Mortgage Formats and Creative Financing

Most borrowers will end up with either a basic fixed rate or adjustable rate mortgage. During times of tight credit and high interest rates, however, both lenders and borrowers have demonstrated an increasing willingness to experiment with new financial instruments. Some of these less common mortgage formats are pro-

Box 15.2

PERSONAL FINANCE NEWS

Late Edition

HUD Holds Lenders to Account

The Real Estate Settlement Procedures Act (RESPA) provides HUD (the U.S. Department of Housing and Urban Development) with the authority to monitor mortgage transactions. In 1995, HUD used its rulemaking authority to promulgate new regulations governing escrow accounts. The effect of the changes will be to substantially reduce the amount needed to fund the accounts. HUD estimates that home buyers could save as much as $477 million a year in closing costs needed for escrow accounts. The rules apply to all new mortgages and by October 1997 to all preexisting mortgages.

Escrow accounts into which borrowers make payment for items such as property taxes and homeowners' insurance often represent an important bonus for the banking industry. Homeowners receive little or no interest on these accounts. Consequently, banks have an incentive for borrowers to keep as large an amount as possible in escrow.

The new rules state that lenders cannot keep more than two month's prospective payments in escrow. Some had required a four- or five-month cushion. Moreover, in calculating the size of the cushion, lenders must now use an *aggregate* accounting method, rather than *single* accounting method. In the past, lenders have almost unanimously used the single account method.

Under the single accounting method, there are separate accounts for such items as taxes and insurance. The lender then calculates a separate escrow requirement for each account. Unfortunately, excess funds in one account are not used to offset needed funding in another account. With the aggregate accounting method, the escrow account must be treated as one large pot from which all payments are made. Under this method, the amount needed in the escrow account will always be less than under the single accounting method.

HUD provides a free spreadsheet template for calculating the value of the aggregate account. If you order the program from HUD there is a charge for the disk and shipping. For those who have Internet access, it can be downloaded free from the HUD User gopher (gopher://huduser.aspensys.com:73/11/2/homeown).

In addition to current monthly expenses, RESPA allows the lender to hold two months' of projected increases as a cushion against tax and insurance charges that are higher than expected. To ensure that lenders do not overestimate projected expenses, they must annually balance the account and refund any amount in excess of $50. An amount less than $50 could be applied to next year's account. Previously, lenders simply applied the entire excess to next year's escrow.

Creative financing: Unique mortgage formats provided by sellers in order to satisfy the special needs of a buyer.

Acceleration clause: Allows the lender to require immediate repayment of the loan if the borrower misses a scheduled payment.

Due-on-sale clause: Requires immediate repayment of outstanding balance when the mortgaged property is sold.

Prepayment penalty: A penalty on early repayment of the loan for reasons other than the sale of the home.

vided by financial institutions. In other arrangements, termed **creative financing,** the seller of the home provides some or all of the financing. Details of these innovative forms of home financing are shown in Table 15.3.

Reading the Fine Print

In addition to understanding the economic characteristics of the loan, you must also understand the legal ramifications. This means reading the fine print and carefully examining each clause.

The **acceleration clause** will allow the lender to speed up the rate at which the loan comes due if you miss a payment. Be sure you understand how and when this clause becomes operative. Also, be wary of an acceleration clause that then permits the lender to foreclose on the loan "without notice."

A **due-on-sale clause** requires immediate repayment of the loan when the property changes hands. Such clauses are common and have been enforced by the courts.

The prepayment clause indicates how early payment on the loan will be handled. The loan contract could impose a **prepayment penalty** if you repay the loan early for reasons other than the sale of the home. This clause is generally not permitted on adjustable rate loans.

TABLE 15.3 • THE ESSENTIALS OF CREATIVE MORTGAGE FINANCING

Type	Description	Considerations
Fixed rate mortgage	Fixed interest rate, usually long-term; equal monthly payments of principal and interest until debt is paid in full.	Offers stability and long-term tax advantages; limited availability. Interest rates may be higher than other types of financing. New fixed rates are rarely assumable.
Adjustable rate mortgage (ARM)	Interest rate changes are based on a financial index, resulting in possible changes in your monthly payments, loan terms, and/or principal. Some plans have rate or repayment caps.	Readily available. Starting interest rate is slightly below market, but payments can increase sharply and frequently if index increases. Payment caps prevent wide fluctuations in payments but may cause negative amortization. Rate caps, limit amount total debt can expand.
Renegotiable rate mortgage (rollover)	Interest rate and monthly payments are constant for several years; changes possible thereafter. Long-term mortgage.	Less frequent changes in interest rate offer some stability.
Balloon mortgage	Monthly payments based on fixed interest rate; usually short-term; payments may cover interest only, with principal due in full at term end.	Offers low monthly payments but possibly no equity until loan is fully paid. When due, loan must be paid off or refinanced. Refinancing poses high risk if rates climb.
Graduated payment mortgage (GPM)	Lower monthly payments rise gradually (usually over 5–10 years), then level off for duration of term. With flexible interest rate, additional payment changes possible if index changes.	Easier to qualify for. Buyer's income must be able to keep pace with scheduled payment increases. With a flexible rate, payment increases beyond the graduated payments can result in additional negative amortization.
Price level adjusted mortgage (PLAM)	Monthly payment and outstanding loan balance adjusted for changes in the Consumer Price Index.	Wages increases may match price level changes. Negative amortization is possible; although short-term variability should be less than with an ARM.
Shared appreciation mortgage	Below-market interest rate and lower monthly payments, in exchange for a share of profits when property is sold or on a specified date. Many variations.	If home appreciates greatly, total cost of loan jumps. If home fails to appreciate, projected increase in value may still be due, requiring refinancing at possibly higher rates.
Assumable mortgage	Buyer takes over seller's original, below-market-rate mortgage.	Lowers monthly payments. May be prohibited if "due on sale" clause is in original mortgage. Not permitted on most new fixed rate mortgages.
Seller take-back	Seller provides all or part of financing with a first or second mortgage.	May offer a below-market interest rate; may have a balloon payment requiring full payment in a few years or refinancing at market rates, which could sharply increase debt.
Wraparound	Seller keeps original low rate mortgage. Buyer makes payments to seller, who forwards a portion to the lender holding original mortgage. Offers lower effective interest rate on total transaction.	Lender may call in old mortgage and require higher rate. If buyer defaults, seller must take legal action to collect debt.

(*continued*)

TABLE 15.3 • CONTINUED

Type	Description	Considerations
Growing equity mortgage (rapid payoff mortgage) (GEM)	Fixed interest rate but monthly payments may vary according to agreed-upon schedule or index.	Permits rapid payoff of debt because payment increases reduce principal. Buyer's income must be able to keep up with payment increases.
Land contract	Seller retains original mortgage. No transfer of title until loan is fully paid. Equal monthly payments based on below-market interest rate with unpaid principal due at loan end.	May offer no equity until loan is fully paid. Buyer has few protections if conflict arises during loan.
Buy-down	Developer (or third party) provides an interest subsidy, which lowers monthly payments during the first few years of the loan. Can have fixed or flexible interest rate.	Offers a break from higher payments during early years. Enables buyer with lower income to quality. With adjustable rate mortgage, payments may jump substantially at end of subsidy. Developer may increase selling price.
Rent with option	Renter pays "option fee" for right to purchase property as specified time and agreed-upon price. Rent may or may not be applied to sales price.	Enables renter to buy time to obtain down payment and decide whether to purchase. Locks in price during inflationary times. Failure to take option means loss of option fee and rental payments.
Reverse annuity mortgage (equity conversion)	Borrower owns mortgage-free property and needs income. Lender makes monthly payments to borrower, using property as collateral.	Can provide home owners with needed cash. At end of term, borrower must have money available to avoid selling property or refinancing.
Zero rate and low rate mortgage	Appears to be completely or almost interest free. Large down payment and one-time finance charge, then loan is repaid in fixed monthly payments over short term.	Permits quick ownership. May not lower total cost (because of possibly increased sales price). Doesn't offer long-term tax deductions.

SOURCE: Federal Trade Commission, *The Mortgage Money Guide,* with additions by authors.

Escrow account: Funds held by the lender to ensure payment of housing-related insurance and taxes.

On some loans, the lending institution adds to the monthly mortgage payment an amount to cover home insurance or property taxes. The lender accumulates these funds in what is called an **escrow account.** When the insurance or property taxes become due, the lender will pay these bills out of the funds in the escrow account. By doing so, the lender ensures that these obligations are being met.

An escrow account is required when the mortgage is insured by the Federal Housing Administration or the Veterans Administration or when the loan is for 90 percent or more of the value of the house. In all other situations, the need for an escrow account is negotiable between the borrower and lender.

If possible, you should avoid setting up an escrow account. In most places the lending institution will pay no interest on the funds held. In the 14 states where lenders are required by law to pay interest on escrow accounts the rate paid is typically less than the rate on a passbook savings account. You can do better by holding these funds in your ordinary savings account and paying your taxes and insurance directly. If you have an escrow account, you should contact the lending institution to see if it can be closed.

Insured Mortgages

Conventional financing: Financing that is neither government insured nor guaranteed.

The term **conventional financing** is used for mortgages that are neither government insured nor guaranteed. Conventional mortgages may have private mortgage insurance on high-risk loans to protect the lender in the event you default on the loan. Where such mortgage protection is needed, however, it is normally arranged through either the Federal Housing Administration (FHA) or the Veterans Administration (VA). These programs make nonconventional mortgages available to individuals who might otherwise be considered poor credit risks.

FHA mortgage insurance: Federally backed insurance protecting lenders against nonrepayment of mortgage.

FEDERAL HOUSING ADMINISTRATION (FHA) FHA mortgages are not government loans. **FHA mortgage insurance** protects the lender against loss on the mortgage, thereby permitting the lender to offer more liberal credit terms to families who could not otherwise afford a home.

The FHA insures mortgages when both property and borrower meet certain standards. Information on current requirements can be found by contacting the FHA or lenders that provide FHA-insured loans. If you are eligible, you may borrow up to a government-set maximum with a relatively low down payment of no more than 5 percent of the purchase price. Prior to 1984, the government also set a ceiling on the interest rates that could be charged on FHA-insured loans This ceiling was often below competitive market rates of interest on conventional financing. Lenders made up for the low interest rate on FHA-insured loans by charging additional discount points to be paid by the seller. The government in its wisdom has since decided that it really can't set prices in private markets without causing serious disruptions. Each lender is free to charge whatever it perceives to be a competitive market rate of interest. The insurance is paid for by adding one-half percentage point to the interest charged on the mortgage balance.

VETERANS ADMINISTRATION (VA) All veterans and current members of the Armed Services are entitled to loan guarantees through the Veterans Administration. The stated purpose of the program is to help veterans finance the purchase of reasonably priced homes at favorable rates of interest. The guarantee encourages lenders to make bigger loans with a smaller down payment than they otherwise could, because the government guarantees repayment of up to 50 percent of the loan and a legislatively set dollar maximum. However, the VA requires that borrowers have a debt repayment-to-income ratio of 41 percent or less.

The Veterans Administration still sets an interest rate ceiling on VA-insured loans. When the ceiling is below rates on conventional loans, you can expect lenders to add on discount points to make up for the difference.

Private mortgage insurance: Privately backed insurance protecting lenders against nonpayment of mortgage.

PRIVATE MORTGAGE INSURANCE If you obtain a conventional mortgage with less than a 20 percent down payment, you will probably be required to purchase **private mortgage insurance.** This insures the lender for the difference between the 20 percent usually required and the lower down payment. The up-front premium is about 1 percent of the mortgage amount. There is also an annual charge of about 0.4 percent that is added to the monthly mortgage payment. Annual premiums should be discontinued when your equity in the home reaches 20 percent of the home's market value. However, lenders are slow to remove this charge; therefore, you should request that the insurance be eliminated when you have accumulated the required equity in the home.

Box 15.3 SAVING MONEY
Biweekly Mortgages

Most mortgages require that you repay the loan in monthly installments. You may have the choice, however, of obtaining a biweekly mortgage, on which you make a repayment once every two weeks. If you decide on a biweekly mortgage, you will end up making 26 biweekly payments during the year. When the biweekly payment is set equal to one-half the monthly payment, the total annual value of the biweekly payments will equal 13 monthly payments instead of the traditional 12.

With the extra monthly payment you will reduce the term of the mortgage and eliminate a good chunk of your future interest payments. In the accompanying table it can be seen that the higher the interest rate on the loan, the more interest you save and, therefore, the earlier you pay off the loan. On a 30-year, $100,000 mortgage with an annual contract rate of 8 percent, a biweekly loan with a periodic payment of one-half the monthly mortgage payment would pay off after about 23 years; at a 12 percent rate it would pay off after only about 19 years. The corresponding interest savings range from $46,227 to $115,719. At first glance, a biweekly mortgage looks like an excellent idea.

You should remember, however, that your interest expense is less because you are paying of the mortgage at a faster rate. By using these dollars to pay off your mortgage at an earlier date, you give up the option of either investing these funds elsewhere or using them to pay off higher-cost debt. The optimal strategy will depend upon which alternative provides the greatest after-tax savings or return.

Surprisingly, you don't need a biweekly mortgage to pay off your loan balance at a faster rate. Most traditional mortgage contracts allow you to make partial prepayments of principal at your discretion, thus providing you with greater flexibility than a similar biweekly loan. You probably already have the choice of making or not making a thirteenth monthly payment.

Annual Contract Rate (%)	Monthly Payment*	Biweekly Payment	Term of Biweekly Mortgage (Years)	Total Interest on Monthly Mortgage	Total Interest on Biweekly Mortgage	Total Interest Saved
12	$1,028.61	$514.31	19.04	$270,301	$154,582	$115,719
10	877.57	438.79	20.96	215,926	139,138	76,788
8	733.76	366.88	22.85	164,155	117,928	46,227

*Monthly payments on a 30-year $100,000 mortgage.

Refinancing

If you took out a mortgage at a high interest rate, and rates have since come down, you should consider the possibility of refinancing the loan. Your first step is to contact your current lender concerning refinancing. If you have been a good customer, the lender may be willing to reduce some of the up-front costs associated with refinancing. Your up-front expenses will consist of a possible prepayment penalty on the old loan and points and origination costs on the new loan. Your future savings will consist of lower monthly mortgage payments. To determine whether you should refinance, you must estimate your payback period: that is, the length of time required for your future savings to cover your up-front expenses. With the average family moving once every seven years, you most likely should not refinance if the payback period is longer than seven years.

Because loans may be written in so many ways, the proposed new loan is likely to differ by more than just the interest rate. You must also weigh these additional factors into your decision to refinance. For example, you may be considering giving up a high fixed rate mortgage for a currently low adjustable rate mortgage. This exchange may be profitable if rates stay low. Whether such an ex-

Current Loan		
Amount borrowed	$ 80,000	
Outstanding balance	$ 78,698	
Original term (months)	360	
Remaining term (months)	240	
Annual contract rate	9.00%	
Present Monthly payment		$708.07
New Loan		
Initial balance	$ 78,698	
Term (months)	240	
Annual contract rate	7.00%	
New monthly payment		610.15
Monthly savings		$ 97.92
Initial Cost of Refinancing		
Origination fee	$ 100.00	
Closing costs	1,100.00	
Points (1%)	786.98	
Total initial costs	$1,986.98	
Divided by monthly savings	97.92	
Approximate payback period (months)	20.29	

Figure 15.10 Refinancing: Calculating the approximate payback period.

change is attractive to you depends upon how much risk you are willing to accept.

Figure 15.10 contains a worksheet for calculating the approximate payback period. To calculate your monthly savings at the lower interest rate, the new monthly payment should be based upon the outstanding loan balance and the remaining term on the old loan. Given a refinancing cost of $1,987 and savings on monthly mortgage payments of $97.92, the reduction in mortgage payments would pay for the cost of refinancing in about 20 months. This is only an approximate payback period, because it does not consider the differential tax treatment for mortgage interest and closing costs or the different rates at which low- and high-interest mortgages pay back principal.

You should recognize that the tax treatment of points differs for refinancing. On the initial home mortgage the IRS has decided you can deduct all points representing prepaid interest in the year the loan is taken out. For refinancing, however, the deduction must be spread out over the term of the mortgage. In the current example, you would have an annual itemized deduction of $39.35 = $787/20 years. Of course, if you sell the home before the mortgage is paid off, any remaining non-itemized points may be deduced in the year of the sale.

WHAT IF YOU CAN'T MEET YOUR MORTGAGE PAYMENTS?

Foreclosure: A legal process that terminates your rights to a mortgaged property and forces its sale.

The unexpected can happen. You can lose your job, or your business can enter troubled times. Whenever the possibility exists that you may be unable to meet your future mortgage payments, your first step is to contact the lending institutions. If you do not meet your scheduled payments, the lender probably has the right to demand immediate payment on the remaining loan balance. Failure to meet this demand may result in **foreclosure.** This legal process terminates your rights to the property and forces its sale. You receive any excess of the sale price over the amount needed to discharge the loan. Of course, because of the immediacy surrounding the sale, the price may be relatively low, leaving you with little or nothing in return. Fortunately, this process involves costs and risks for the lending institution, so that you may both benefit by avoiding foreclosure. This is why you should contact the lending institution before you actually have to miss payments. It is possible that, through a renegotiation of the loan, the monthly payments can be reduced. This reduction can be accomplished by stretching out the term of the loan, postponing repayment of principal, or even negative amortization. If you are experiencing a temporary setback in earnings, the lender may provide you with a supportable schedule of payments until you resume your previous financial status. If your problems are more permanent, you may have to consider selling the house and buying down or moving into a rental unit. The loan renegotiation may permit you the time you need to sell the house on your own and avoid a forced sale at a depressed price.

Selling a home in a declining housing market can be a serious problem for borrowers with low down payments. The potential sales price may be less than the outstanding mortgage balance. In this case, the lender may be willing to enter into a *compromise* or *short sale,* in which the lender agrees to receive less than the full value of the mortgage. This permits the mortgagee to sell the house for less than the original loan amount.

When your lending institution appears uncompromising, you may still be entitled to some special help if you have a federally insured FHA or VA loan. To find out if you quality, you should contact, respectively, the U.S. Department of Housing or the Veterans Administration. These agencies can provide free homeowner counseling, and under the Home Mortgage Assignment Program, reduce or suspend mortgage payments for unemployed workers for a period up to three years. The one requirement is that you can show that you kept up with the mortgage payments while you were working.

If a potential foreclosure seems likely, you should consult an attorney. Under the bankruptcy code you may be able to force the lending institution to accept a proposed repayment plan, or at least delay the forced sale until you can sell the property at a favorable price.

Action Plan for the Steeles: Refinancing

Background In 1986 the Steeles purchased their present home. They financed the purchase with a $160,000, 30-year, adjustable rate mortgage from First Federal Savings and Loan. The mortgage has an annual interest adjustment cap of 1 percent, and an aggregate interest rate cap of 16 percent. Annual adjustments on the anniversary of the closing date are based on the most recently published value of the National Average FHLB Mortgage Contract rate. The mortgage is assumable, and there are no prepayment penalties.

The Problem The Steeles recently received notice from First Federal that the adjustable rate on their home mortgage will equal 8 percent over the next year. Accompanying this notice was an offer to exchange their adjustable rate for a fixed rate on the remaining balance and term of their current mortgage. For a renegotiation fee of $500 they could exchange their adjustable rate of 8 percent for a nonassumable fixed rate of 9 percent. They wonder whether they should accept First Federal's offer. If interest rates rise again, their payments on the adjustable might skyrocket. On the other hand, Arnold feels that he might be transferred in another year or two, in which case they would have to sell their current home.

The Plan The first thing the Steeles should do is to contact other lenders to make sure this is the best available offer. Assuming that it is, they might then consider what might happen under different assumptions.

Under the worst-case scenario, inflation could increase, pushing the change in the interest rate on the adjustable mortgage to its limit. The accompanying table indicates what would happen given upper-limit adjustments in the interest rate. The remaining unpaid balance on their home mortgage is about $154,000; at 9 and 8 percent rates of interest, this would mean a monthly payment of $1,307 and $1,236, respectively. In the first year the adjustable rate mortgage would save the Steeles $103 per month. In the third year the monthly payment on the adjustable rate mortgage would rise above the monthly payment on the fixed rate mortgage. But even at the end of the third year, there would still be a slight overall total benefit of $96 from having selected the adjustable rate mortgage.

	Fixed Rate Mortgage		Adjustable Rate Mortgage		Difference	
Year	Rate	Monthly Payment	Rate	Monthly Payment	Monthly	Annual
First	9%	$1,307	8%	$1,204	$103	$1,236
Second	9%	1,307	9%	1,304	3	36
Third	9%	1,307	10%	1,405	−98	−1,176
					Total	$96

Only in the unlikely event that the adjustable rate again rose by the maximum amount in each of these years would the fixed rate mortgage begin to appear more favorable by the beginning of the fourth year. With less than maximum upward adjustments on the adjustable rate mortgage, the fixed rate mortgage looks like an expensive alternative. If interest rates remain flat over the next three years, the fixed rate mortgage will cost the Steeles $3,708 more in monthly payments. The Steeles will have to ask themselves whether the elimination of future interest rate risk and the accompanying uncertainty in mortgage payments is worth this potential cost.

Obviously, this is a very difficult and important decision. The wrong interest rate assumption could commit them to paying thousands of additional dollars should they remain in the present home. Unfortunately, no one can perfectly forecast interest rate movements. Anyone who could would become a millionaire overnight through speculation in financial markets.

Given the strong possibility that the Steeles might move within the next few years, keeping their present adjustable rate mortgage is probably the preferred alternative. Only under the worst-case inflation scenario does the fixed mortgage look better by the fourth year.

Another factor they should consider is that the fixed rate is nonassumable, whereas the adjustable rate is assumable. If inflation does pick up, the government could tighten credit markets in an effort to control inflation. An assumable mortgage with a small margin can help them sell a home in a tight credit market.

SUMMARY

Choosing a place to live is a major financial decision requiring a well-defined strategy. You should estimate the purchase price you can afford, examine housing in this price range, and then calculate the relative gain or loss associated with the buy-rent decision. If you decide that purchasing a home is the better alternative, seek help from professionals, including an appraiser, a home inspector, a real estate agent, and an attorney specializing in real estate. To finance the purchase, you can select from among numerous mortgage formats, including both fixed and adjustable rate loans with a variety of payment options. The discussion in this chapter should provide guidance in that selection.

KEY TERMS

acceleration clause (p. 428)
adjustable rate loans (p. 425)
aggregate rate cap (p. 426)
amortize (p. 425)
closing (p. 421)
closing costs (p. 421)
condominium (p. 411)
contract rate (p. 422)
conventional financing (p. 431)
convertible mortgage (p. 427)
cooperative (p. 412)
creative financing (p. 428)
deed (p. 420)
due-on-sale clause (p. 428)
earnest money (p. 420)
escrow account (p. 430)
exclusive agency agreement (p. 419)
exclusive right to sell (p. 419)
FHA mortgage insurance (p. 431)
fixed rate mortgages (p. 424)
foreclosure (p. 433)
Housing Affordability Index (p. 405)
interest rate adjustment index (p. 425)
interest rate adjustment period (p. 425)
listing agreement (p. 419)
margin (p. 426)
marketable title (p. 420)
negative amortization (p. 427)
net listing agreement (p. 419)
open agreement (p. 419)
payment cap (p. 426)
periodic rate cap (p. 426)
points (p. 422)
prepayment penalty (p. 428)
principal (p. 424)
private mortgage insurance (p. 431)
settlement costs (p. 421)
teaser rate (p. 426)
title insurance (p. 421)
title search (p. 420)

PROBLEMS AND REVIEW QUESTIONS

1. What is the relationship between market rates of interest and affordable housing?
2. If your income after taxes is $28,000 per year, and you expect to pay about $100 per month on utilities, about how much can you afford to spend on monthly rental payments?
3. Given an affordable monthly mortgage payment of $650, and a mortgage interest rate of 12 percent on a 30-year loan, what is the size of the affordable mortgage? Given this affordable mortgage, and a 10 percent down payment, what is the affordable purchase price?
4. How does a cooperative differ from a condominium?
5. Suppose you had $6,000 in mortgage interest payments during the year and you were in the 28 percent marginal tax bracket. What is the real cost of the mortgage interest payments after tax considerations? Suppose you had $6,000 in rental payments during the year and you were in the 33 percent marginal tax bracket. What is the real cost of the rental payments after tax considerations?
6. Suppose housing prices rise at a 5 percent annual rate over the next five years. If a house now costs $100,000, how much will it bring after five years and the payment of a 6 percent sales commission?
7. What are the tax advantages attached to home ownership, and under what conditions will long-term capital gains on the sale of a residence be tax free?
8. What occurs at *closing*? Give three items that would be included in closing costs.
9. A lender is offering an 11 percent fixed rate mortgage, requiring a down payment equal to 20 percent of the home's purchase price. The lender estimates that closing costs should be equal to $500 plus 4 points. How much will closing costs be on a $120,000 home?

10. What are the relative advantages of fixed and adjustable rate loans?
11. What are some important characteristics of adjustable rate loans that you should examine carefully?
12. An adjustable rate mortgage has a yearly interest rate adjustment cap of 1 percent. If the indexed rate moves up by 1½ percent in the first year, and ½ percent in the second year, how much can the interest rate on the remaining loan balance move up after the first year, and after the second year?
13. Suppose you expect your income to increase significantly over the next few years. You would like to purchase a home that more closely fits your future income status rather than your present circumstances, thereby avoiding relocation expenses in a few years. What types of mortgages might be of interest to you?
14. You are thinking of retiring in about 15 years. You would like to purchase a home now but would like to have it paid off before retirement. You plan to live on reduced income during retirement, so the tax deductions on mortgage interest would not be significant at that time. What types of mortgages might be of interest to you?
15. What does the term *conventional financing* mean? What government programs exist for nonconventional financing?
16. Whom does private mortgage insurance protect, and why is it sometimes required?
17. Name two government organizations that can help you obtain a home mortgage with a relatively small down payment.
18. What is a PLAM, and how is it affected by the rate of inflation?
19. What is the distinguishing feature of a convertible home mortgage?
20. What is foreclosure, and how might you avoid an impending foreclosure?

Case 15.1 How Much House Can Kim and Dan Bergholt Afford?

Kim and Dan Bergholt are both government workers. They are considering purchasing a home in the Washington, D.C. area for about $280,000. They estimate monthly expenses for utilities at $220, maintenance at $100, property taxes at $280, and home insurance payments at $50. Their only debt consists of car loans requiring a monthly payment of $350.

Kim's gross income is $45,000 per year and Dan's is $38,000 per year. They have saved about $60,000 in a money market fund on which they earned $5,840 last year. They plan to use most of this for a 20 percent down payment and closing costs. A lender is offering 30-year variable rate loans with an initial interest rate of 8 percent given a 20 percent down payment and closing costs equal to $800 plus 3 points.

Before making a purchase offer and applying for this loan, they would like to have some idea whether they might qualify.

QUESTIONS

1. Estimate the affordable mortgage and the affordable purchase price for the Bergholts.
2. Suppose they do qualify; what other factors might they consider before purchasing and taking out a home mortgage?
3. What future changes might present problems for the Bergholts?

Case 15.2 Should the Bergholts Choose the Rental Option?

The real estate agent tells the Bergholts that if they don't care to purchase, they might consider renting. The rental option would cost $1,400 per month plus utilities estimated at $220 and renter's insurance of $25 per month.

The Bergholts believe that neither of them is likely to be transferred to another location within the next five years. After that, Dan perceives that he might move out of government service into the private sector. Assuming they remain in the same place for the next five years, the Bergholts would like to know if it is better to buy or rent the home. They expect that the price of housing and rents will rise at an annual rate of 5 percent over the next five years, the same rate they expect to earn on the money market fund. All other prices, including utilities, maintenance, and taxes are expected to increase at a 3 percent annual rate. After federal, state, and local taxes, they get to keep only 55 percent of a marginal dollar of earnings.

QUESTIONS

1. Given the information in this and the previous case, estimate whether it is financially more attractive for the Bergholts to rent or to purchase the home over a five-year holding period. (Assuming the initial interest rate of 8 percent, interest payments over the five-year period would equal $87,574.)
2. Suppose it turns out that they have to relocate after one year. Which is the preferred alternative after one year? (Interest payments over the first year would equal $17,852.)

HELPFUL CONTACTS

Division of Consumer Affairs, Board of Governors of the Federal Reserve System
20th and C Streets, NW, Washington, DC 20551 (telephone 202-452-3946)
For complaints dealing with financial institutions.

HSH Associates
1200 Route 23, Butler, NJ 07405
For a small fee, they provide information on mortgage rates in your area or, if you already have a loan, an ARM Check Kit to guide you through recalculation of your adjustable rate mortgage.

Office of Fair Housing and Equal Opportunity
U.S. Department of Housing and Urban Development
Room 5204, Washington, DC 20410 (telephone 800-424-8590)
For housing discrimination complaints.

INTERNET ADDRESSES

American Society of Home Inspectors (membership locator)
http://www1.mhv.net/~dfriedman/ashihome.htm

Federal Trade Commission (articles on home mortgages)
gopher://gopher.ftc.gov:70/11/ConsumerLine/publications/homesrealestate

Homebuyer's Fair (information on housing price, mortgage rates, and much more)
http://www.homefair.com/homepage.html

HSH Associates, Financial Publishers (latest information on adjustable rate indexes)
http://www.hsh.com/

Mortgage Guaranty Insurance Corporation (information on private mortgage insurance and home buyers checklist)
http://www.mgic.com/

Partners Mortgage Loan Qualification Software (through FRB-Minneapolis)
http://woodrow.mpls.frb.fed.us/banking/develop/partners.html

U.S. Census, Housing News (short articles with recent housing data)
http://www.census.gov/hhes/housing/

U.S. Dept. of Housing and Urban Development (federal assistance for homeownership)
http://www.hud.gov:80/

Chapter 16

Consumer Durables: Satisfying Your Continuing Needs

Objectives

1. To estimate the replacement cost for consumer durables
2. To describe the characteristics of warranties
3. To obtain information on new and used car prices
4. To calculate the cost of owning and operating an automobile
5. To evaluate the lease-buy decision
6. To explain the complaint process for correcting auto defects
7. To state your rights under lemon laws

Consumer durables: Consumer goods that provide benefits that extend over a period of at least one year.

In this chapter we will examine those major family purchases called **consumer durables,** which may be strictly defined as goods that provide consumer benefits over a period of at least one year. Such goods make possible our high standard of living; however, they also make significant demands on both our financial resources and our available time.

CONSUMER DURABLES AND THE HOUSEHOLD BUDGET

About 10 percent of consumer expenditures are devoted to household furnishings, appliances, and automobiles. However, when we consider the ongoing costs of operations and maintenance for these same items, their proportionate impact on the household budget is much greater. In one way or another, one dollar out of every four dollars that consumers spend is somehow related to the purchase of consumer durables or the operation and maintenance of consumer durables.

Budgeting Considerations

Given both the lumpiness of expenditures on consumer durables and their interrelatedness with other household expenditures, it is easy to see that consumer durables create special budgeting problems. Without adequate planning, repair or replacement is likely to be an unexpected event that creates havoc with the household budget. In addition, replacement cost tends to be inadequately anticipated. Since most of us purchase a car or a major home appliance only once every few years, we don't keep track of changing prices. *Sticker shock* results when we realize how much we must now spend for replacement. An associated effect is called **savings illusion.** As our savings accumulate, we feel wealthier. But when the time comes to replace a major purchase, we find out that we are not really any better off. All we actually have been doing is accumulating funds to replace those consumer goods that have worn out.

Savings illusion: The failure to take recent price increases into account, thus creating an overestimate of our real wealth.

Another unique characteristic of a consumer durable is that it gives rise to multiple entries on the household budget. A product that is purchased with savings is listed as an expense at the time of purchase. If it is financed through borrowing, however, it will create inflexible future expenses until the loan is repaid. The continuing outflow required for maintenance and operations must also be budgeted. Moreover, additional expenses will most likely show up in separate household accounts for utilities and fuels.

Replacement Cost

The cost of replacing a consumer durable can be financed either through accumulated savings or through borrowing. In Chapter 4, we described how to decide whether to borrow or to use savings. If using your own savings appears the wiser alternative, estimating future replacement costs will help eliminate savings illusion.

Replacement cost: The cost of replacing new for old.

To estimate **replacement cost,** you will need three pieces of information: the expected date of replacement, the expected rate of price increase, and the present cost of replacement. Time to replacement may be based on the product's remaining service life, technological change, or simply your desire to replace old with new. You may plan to keep some products, such as refrigerators and water heaters, as long as possible. The dealer or manufacturer may be able to supply you with a realistic estimate of that product's remaining service life. For products that become outmoded by your desire to keep pace with styles or technological change, you will have to provide your own assessment. For example, you can probably depend on there being significant technological changes in electronic equipment, such as computers and camcorders, every three to five years.

The expected future cost of replacement will also depend on the product's present cost and the expected rate of price increase. This latter may be difficult to determine; however, looking at past price increases for similar groups of products may be helpful. The U.S. Bureau of Labor Statistics calculates separate price indexes for selected groups of commodities, some of which are listed in Table 16.1. Before you use these numbers in your calculations, however, you should realize that a price index does not necessarily reflect what is happening to the price of an average product in the marketplace. Price indexes attempt to price products that embody a constant technology. Therefore, price changes resulting from improvements in technology or improvements in quality have no impact on the price index. For example, over the period covered in Table 16.1, appliances and electronic equipment have fallen in price at an annual rate of decline of 1.6 percent. But that doesn't mean that the average price of a camcorder or computer has necessarily fallen. Consumers on average may be spending the same amount on each of these items but in effect be purchasing a highly improved product. For items that embody a more stable technology, such as furniture and bedding, the price index may more accurately reflect what is happening to the price of an average product.

Net replacement cost: Replacement cost less trade-in value.

On products that have a trade-in value, you may want to calculate **net replacement cost.** This is equal to replacement cost less the market value of the trade-in. This is most important when calculating the financial resources needed to purchase a replacement vehicle. Table 16.2 contains estimates of the price of a used car as a percentage of the price of a similar model new car. The percent-

TABLE 16.1 • ANNUAL RATE OF CHANGE IN PRICES OF SELECTED PRODUCTS (1989–1993)

Product	Rate of Change (%)
All items	3.9
Furniture and bedding	2.0
Bedroom furniture	3.0
Sofas	0.7
Living room chairs and tables	2.7
Appliances and electronic equipment	−1.6
Video and audio equipment	−1.6
Televisions	−1.8
Video products other than TV	−5.1
Audio products	0.3
New vehicles	2.7
New cars	2.5
Subcompact	2.5
Compact	2.0
Full size	2.6
Luxury	2.8
New trucks	3.8
Used cars	2.7

SOURCE: Consumer Price Index, Bureau of Labor Statistics.

TABLE 16.2 • THE MARKET PRICE OF A USED CAR AS A PERCENTAGE OF THE MARKET PRICE OF A SIMILAR NEW CAR

Age at End of Year (in years)	Size				
	Large	Intermediate	Compact	Subcompact	Van
0	100%	100%	100%	100%	100%
1	75%	77%	82%	87%	69%
2	60%	63%	69%	75%	55%
3	46%	52%	58%	63%	44%
4	37%	42%	49%	54%	38%
5	29%	34%	41%	45%	32%
6	22%	25%	34%	37%	27%
7	16%	18%	28%	29%	22%
8	10%	13%	22%	21%	17%
9	5%	8%	16%	14%	12%
10	3%	4%	11%	8%	8%
11	1%	2%	5%	3%	4%
12	0%	0%	0%	0%	0%

SOURCE: Adapted from Federal Highway Administration, *Cost of Owning and Operating Automobiles and Vans 1984,* U.S. Department of Transportation, 1986.

ages were calculated by the Federal Highway Administration on the basis of data supplied by the National Automobile Dealers Association (N.A.D.A.) for representative American-made cars. Multiplying the appropriate percentage by the expected value of a similar new car will provide an approximate trade-in value. This is only a very rough estimate. If you would like to find out how your particular make or model is likely to hold its value, you might look at how similar makes and models in previous years have declined in price. You can look that information up in the *N.A.D.A. Official Used Car Guide* or the *Automotive Lease Guide,* available in most libraries.

Suppose you expect that over the next four years the annual rate of price change for a particular good will average 5 percent. If you locate the intersection of the 5 percent column and the row for period 4 in Appendix Table A.1, you will find the number 1.2155. This is the price adjustment factor. At a 5 percent annual rate of change, what costs $10 today will cost about $12.16 four years from now. This can be calculated as follows:

$$\text{Present price} \times \text{price adjustment factor} = \text{future price}$$
$$\$10 \times 1.2155 = \$12.16$$

Auto Replacement Costs for the Steeles

The eventual replacement of the family cars should be analyzed. The Steeles have been paying for their cars through trade-ins and borrowing. In about two years they expect to trade the Honda for a similar new small car. The worksheet in Table 16.3 contains their calculations. They figure it would cost them about $17,000 to purchase a similar compact car now. If inflation is expected to average 5 percent over the next two years, the inflation factor is 1.1025. Thus, the expected price of a similar new car at that time will be $17,000 × 1.1025 = $18,743. Using the deprecia-

TABLE 16.3 • THE STEELES' WORKSHEET FOR AUTOMOBILE REPLACEMENT COST		
CAR: HONDA		
Item	Description	Amount
1	Present cost of replacement car	$17,000
2	Present age of used car	3 years
3	Years to replacement	2 years
4	Age of used car at replacement (item 2 + item 3)	5 years
5	Estimated annual rate of price change	5%
6	Price adjustment factor (see item 3, item 5, and Appendix Table A.1)	1.1025
7	Expected future cost (item 1 × item 6)	$18,742.50
8	Percentage depreciation on used car (item 4 and Table 16.2)	41%
9	Trade-in value of used car (item 7 × item 8)	$7,684.43
10	Net replacement cost (item 7 – item 9)	$11,058.07

tion schedule for compact cars in Table 16.2, the Steeles calculate that a five-year-old compact car should trade in for about 41 percent of $18,743, or $7,684. Thus, the difference of $11,058 is the estimated net replacement cost to be covered by a down payment and an auto loan. If the Steeles had planned to trade up to a more expensive car, they would have separately estimated this price and then subtracted the $7,684 to estimate the potential cash outlay.

You should note that these techniques are used only for estimating future prices. When the time actually comes to trade in and purchase a new car, you should consult the pricing guides mentioned in this chapter.

SELECTING MAJOR HOME APPLIANCES

An efficient selection process must include gathering and evaluating information. Information can be gained from talking to friends, visiting retail outlets, and reading such consumer-oriented magazines as *Consumer Reports* and *Consumer Research* or purchasing one of the numerous buyers' guides. The gathering of this information may require some time, effort, and money.

The results of a Federal Trade Commission study on shopping behavior indicate that the average consumer visits about two stores, and typically compares about three brands, before purchasing a major home appliance. Over half the buyers make a purchase after five days of shopping. Whether this behavior is optimal is difficult to determine. Obviously, shopping should continue as long as additional search costs, including the cost of your time and the cost of transportation, are lower than the additional benefits generated by the search, measured in terms of lower prices or better quality.

The following pieces of information are essential for making an informed decision:

1. Prices of various brands at different stores
2. Available optional features

3. The product service record and service availability
4. The cost of operation and maintenance
5. Warranty coverage

It is unlikely that one purchase will appear superior in all five categories. Therefore, an accurate assessment of the trade-offs will play an important part in the selection process.

Prices and Options

When shopping, be sure to look at the total price. If you are planning to have the appliance delivered and installed, charges for these services as well as any finance charges should all be considered part of the good's total price. In addition, ask the salesperson whether any of the items in which you are interested will be on sale in the near future and whether the store might do better than the listed price. Some large chain stores are known for providing advance information on upcoming sales or for refunding part of the original purchase price if you buy the item immediately preceding the official sale period. Other smaller owner-managed stores are known for providing discounts only when requested.

When making comparisons between brands and within brands, you are likely to confront an array of prices and options. You will have to judge whether the optional feature is worth the added cost. On such items as microwave ovens and videotape recorders, *Consumer Reports* has found that most brands and most models accomplish the basic task for which they were built equally well. Cost differences are centered primarily on optional features, such as electronic memory and pause control. If you plan to use these features often, they may be worth the price. Usually, however, the novelty wears off and they end up as useless but expensive trim on the basic appliance. Those options that really do prove convenient or that provide for added safety are often suggested in the product survey articles in *Consumer Reports* and *Consumer Research*. These articles are also a good source of information on product quality and durability.

The Product Service Record and Service Availability

The results of product surveys conducted by the consumer magazines should help you judge relative performance. Of particular help are frequency-of-repair statistics collected by *Consumer Reports* in an annual survey of its readers. These results can be collected only on goods purchased in previous years, so they are somewhat dated. However, they may still prove useful in judging the problems you are likely to encounter with a general class of goods or the products of a specific manufacturer.

You can generally expect products with complicated mechanical parts, such as washing machines, to require more service than other, largely nonmechanical items, such as ovens. For such service-intensive products, both the service record and the availability of service are worth checking. Does the store that sold you the item provide customer support at a reasonable price? How will problems covered by a warranty be serviced? Are there manufacturer-authorized repair services in the immediate area? The prospect of qualified and convenient service may sometimes be worth a higher purchase price.

Costs of Operation and Maintenance

Your estimate of maintenance costs may be based on suggested service intervals in the owner's manual and independent information on the product's service record. Be very wary of claims on cost savings made by manufacturers: They have often fallen short of the truth. Since 1978 the Federal Trade Commission has been examining products that claim to save energy under the Energy Policy and Conservation Act. Unfortunately, there are many products, and resources for enforcement are limited. The FTC has made significant progress, however, in promulgating energy cost disclosure rules for major home appliances. Since May 1980, the manufacturers of seven appliance categories (refrigerators and refrigerator-freezers, freezers, dishwashers, water heaters, room air conditioners, clothes washers, and furnaces) must affix labels to their products indicating energy consumption under standard Department of Energy tests.

EnergyGuide: A federally mandated sticker indicating an appliance's energy usage.

A sample **EnergyGuide** label is shown in Figure 16.1. In large print is the expected yearly cost based on an average national cost of energy and the needs of a typical household. Also indicated is the range of energy costs for comparable models. If you know the actual cost of energy in your area, you can find a more accurate estimate on the bottom half of the label.

Warranties

Warranty or guarantee: The seller's assumption of responsibility for the quality, character, or suitability of goods sold.

Most consumers do not bother to read warranties. They should, though, because the terms of a warranty can often provide sufficient reasons for selecting one product over another. **Warranty** and **guarantee** have the same meaning. They represent the seller's assumption of responsibility for the quality, character, or suitability of the goods sold. In a world of imperfect information, the buyer cannot know everything about the product being purchased. Therefore, the consumer requires some protection in the event the product does not perform as expected. It is the warranty that provides the needed protection.

"As is": The seller bears absolutely no responsibility for the quality or performance of the good.

Implied warranty: A warranty created by the operation of the law when no express warranty exists.

IMPLIED AND EXPRESS WARRANTIES All products, except those sold **"as is,"** carry implied warranties. An implied warranty is imposed upon the seller by the operation of the law. In other words, the law sets down certain requirements that the seller must live up to. The **implied warranty** will consist of a warranty of merchantability and a warranty of fitness for purpose. *Merchantability* means that the buyer has the right to expect that the good is generally of the same quality as similar goods in its class and that it does what it was built to do. A buyer has the right to expect that a washing machine washes clothes. *Fitness of purpose* means that if the buyer is relying on the seller to select a good for a particular purpose, and the seller has reason to know of that purpose, the good should prove suitable. For example, if the seller knows that the buyer wants a washing machine to wash rugs, then the machine should be able to handle difficult tasks such as cleaning heavy rugs.

Express warranty: An oral or written agreement between buyer and seller concerning the character or performance of the good.

Not all products carry an **express warranty.** An express warranty is contractual in nature; that is, it depends on the written or oral agreement between the buyer and seller. An express warranty need not be in writing, nor is it even necessary for the seller to intend to guarantee the item for an express warranty to exist. Statements of fact and promises expressed by the sales agent or manufacturer either at the time of the sale or in previous advertisements can form the basis for an express

(Name of Corporation)
Model(s) AH503, AH504, AH507
Type of Defrost: Full Automatic

Refrigerator-Freezer
Capacity: 23 Cubic Feet

ENERGYGUIDE

Estimates on the scale are based on a national average electric rate of 4.97¢ per kilowatt hour.

Only models with 22.5 to 24.4 cubic feet are compared in the scale.

Model with lowest energy cost **$68**

$91

THIS MODEL

Model with highest energy cost **$132**

Estimated yearly energy cost

Your cost will vary depending on your local energy rate and how you use the product. This energy cost is based on U.S. Government standard tests.

How much will this model cost you to run yearly?

		Yearly cost **Estimated yearly $ cost shown below**
Cost per kilowatt hour	**2¢**	$36
	4¢	$73
	6¢	$109
	8¢	$146
	10¢	$182
	12¢	$218

Ask your salesperson or local utility for the energy rate (cost per kilowatt hour) in your area.

Important Removal of this label before consumer purchase is a violation of federal law (42 U.S.C. 6302)

(Part No. 371026)

Figure 16.1 Sample EnergyGuide.

Box 16.1 SIMPLIFYING FINANCIAL PLANNING
"Writing" a Wrong with a Complaint Letter

Need the President's Name and the Address of the Firm?
First check to see if the company has a local office. If it does, call and ask for the name and address of its national president. If there is no local listing, *Standard & Poor's Register of Corporations, Directors and Executives* is a good reference source that lists over 37,000 American business firms. The book can be found in most libraries.

Need the Consumer Representative's Name and Address?
See the *Consumer's Resource Handbook* for a listing of many corporate contacts.

Have the Name of Product but Need to Know the Manufacturer?
The *Thomas Registry* lists thousands of products and their manufacturers. This book can also be found in many public libraries.

Your Letter
Include your name, address, and home and work phone numbers.

Type your letter, if possible. If it is handwritten, make sure it is neat and legible.

Make it brief and to the point. Include all pertinent facts (e.g., date of transaction, item involved, store) and what you believe would be a fair and just settlement of the problem. Attach documentation to support your case; be sure to send COPIES, not originals.

Remember, the person reading your letter is not personally responsible for your problem but may be responsible for resolving it. Therefore, avoid writing a sarcastic, threatening, or angry letter; it may lessen your chances of getting the complaint resolved.

Keep a copy of the letter for your records.

SOURCE: U.S. Office of Consumer Affairs, *Consumer's Resource Handbook,* The White House, Washington, D.C., 1986.

Puffery: Persuasive sales talk overly praising the good.

Magnuson-Moss Warranty Act of 1975: Federal law regulating the conditions and limitations contained in express warranties.

warranty. However, you must carefully distinguish statements of fact from what is called **puffery.** This is typical sales talk meant to persuade the customer by overly praising the good. Statements such as, "This is a good buy," are mere puffery and do not carry an express warranty.

The **Magnuson-Moss Warranty Act of 1975,** regulates express written warranties. Before passage of this act, many written warranties contained clauses that relieved the seller of an implied warranty. In many of these situations, consumers would have been better off without an express warranty. One of the purposes of this act was to make such clauses ineffective by prohibiting written warranties from limiting the implied warranty to a shorter period than that covered by the written warranty. However, the seller can still avoid an implied warranty by selling the product "as is."

Full warranty: During a specified time period, purchases are entitled to full protection, including lemon protection and all repair-related costs.

Lemon protection: If the merchandise cannot be repaired after a reasonable number of attempts, the customer can elect to receive either a replacement or a refund.

Limited warranty: Any express warranty that does not meet all of the necessary conditions for a full warranty.

FULL AND LIMITED WARRANTIES Another purpose of the Warranty Act was to set down requirements for full and limited warranties. It is now necessary that all written warranties be labeled either *limited* or *full.*

The **full warranty** label means that consumers are entitled to full remedies for a specified period of time. They may even request a replacement or refund if the warrantor has been given a reasonable number of attempts to fix the product and has been unsuccessful. This provision is termed **lemon protection,** and it is included only in full warranties. The *full* label also means that, during the period specified, consumers will not be charged for parts or labor, or associated transportation and travel. In addition, a full warranty cannot disclaim or limit the duration of implied warranties, be limited to the original owner, require a registration card to provide the date of purchase, or impose an unreasonable requirement as a condition of warranty coverage. Any warranty that does not meet these standards must be labeled a **limited warranty.**

Many products will carry both limited and full warranties. For example, the first year of ownership may be covered by a full warranty, with coverage reduced to a limited warranty in subsequent years. It is also possible that some components of the appliance will be covered by a full warranty, while others will have limited coverage or none. Many consumers mistakenly believe that the term *full* means that all parts are warrantied.

Service contract or extended warranty: For an initial fee, the seller agrees to repair the merchandise, either without charge or at a set charge, for a period beyond the initial warranty.

SHOULD YOU PURCHASE A SERVICE CONTRACT? Whenever you purchase a major home appliance or a car, the salesperson will usually try to sell you a **service contract,** or what is also called an **extended warranty.** This is because service contracts have proved to be highly profitable for sellers and not so profitable for buyers. Unless you are particularly hard on the products you use, the expected cost of repairs is typically much less than the cost of the service contract. For example, an MIT study for the National Science Foundation revealed that the cost of a service contract for a color TV set was almost 10 times the expected cost of repairs, and for a refrigerator it was about 16 times the expected cost of repairs.

A service contract is, in effect, the same as an insurance policy. You are insuring yourself against repairs on your consumer durables. The manufacturer or retailer is betting that the equipment won't break down, and you are betting that it will. In previous chapters we discussed the basic principles of insurance protection. One such principle is that you should concentrate on insuring yourself against major financial calamities and bear any small risks yourself. The breakdown of the washing machine or the need for a valve job may seem major at the time it happens, but it is really minor relative to other financial losses you may suffer.

SELECTING AN AUTOMOBILE

Except for a home, your car is probably the largest single purchase you will make. Therefore, it is appropriate for you to put some time and effort into this decision. To make the correct choice you will have to accurately assess your own needs, evaluate market alternatives, and consider financing options. Having all relevant information written down will prove helpful in making your final decision. Consumers can obtain a useful worksheet, along with background information, in *The Car Book,* available from the U.S. Department of Transportation, National Highway Traffic Safety Administration, Washington, D.C. 20590. Completing the worksheet will force you both to confront your real needs and to identify important points of comparison.

The consumer magazines' coverage of automobiles is similar to that of home appliances. Reading the articles can help you identify those makes and models that are either best buys or especially trouble prone. Particularly helpful are the results of the *Consumer Reports* reader survey, in which consumers are asked to indicate their own experiences.

Pricing Information

The current practices accompanying automobile sales seem to have evolved from the horse trading of the past. A car is one of the few purchases we make that still involves haggling over price. In such market encounters, the person with the best information will usually have the advantage. If you don't do some comparative shopping, you give the seller the advantage.

Monroney sticker price: Legally required price information adhered to the windows of all new cars.
Base price: Price of the car without optional features.
Dealer sticker price: Monroney sticker price plus dealer add-ons.
Invoice price: The price the manufacturer charges the retailer for the car.

NEW CARS Each new car must have the **Monroney sticker price** on a side window. This shows the base price, the manufacturer's installed options with the manufacturer's suggested retail price, the manufacturer's transportation charge, and the fuel economy. The **base price** is the cost of the car without options but includes standard equipment and factory warranty. Some new cars may also have a **dealer sticker price.** This will include such extras as dealer-installed options, additional dealer markup (ADM), dealer preparation, and undercoating. The dealer rarely gets the sticker price for the car.

The most important piece of information you can have when bargaining with the dealer is the **invoice price.** This is the price the manufacturer charges the dealer for the car. However, on some cars the invoice price may be greater than the dealer's final cost. This is because the dealer may receive rebates, allowances, discounts, and incentive awards from the manufacturer.

Many car guides list invoice costs or provide a formula for estimating the invoice cost. Each year the April issue of *Consumer Reports* reviews that year's models. In addition, for a small fee, *Consumer Reports* will send you a computer printout listing the invoice cost for the car and the options you have selected. *Car Facts,* supplied free of charge through many credit unions, also provides information on prices, safety records, and gas mileage. To use estimates of dealer cost provided by consumer groups, it is suggested that you first ask the salesperson for the minimum markup over invoice that is acceptable to the dealership. If this markup is favorable relative to other dealers you have visited, add it to their indicated invoice cost and make a firm offer. Don't waiver from your initial offer. If your money doesn't talk, be ready to walk.

When you purchase a new car, the salesperson is also likely to offer you an extended warranty for an additional charge. For the same reasons stated previously, it is usually not a good buy. Moreover, to a considerable degree the extended warranty may cover repairs already provided for under the regular warranty. A four-year, 48,000-mile extended warranty on a car that has a manufacturer's three-year, 36,000-mile regular warranty extends coverage by only one year and 12,000 miles. The limited additional coverage, however, has not deterred dealers from charging exorbitant prices. The New York attorney general's office found that over half the consumers in that state who purchased extended warranties were charged more than the manufacturer's suggested retail price.

USED CARS If you are considering buying, selling, or trading in a used car, the two most commonly used sources of pricing information are the *National Automobile Dealers Association Official Used Car Guide* and the *Kelley Blue Book Used Car Guide.* These are on hand at most libraries and at banks where car loans are made. They contain the average trade-in or wholesale price and the retail price for many different makes of used cars. Also included are estimated prices for optional equipment.

Your best buy is typically a two- to three-year old used car. This is because the annual percentage depreciation in price is greatest over the first few years. Before selecting a model, you should consult the *Consumer Reports* readers' survey on frequency of repair records also published in the April issue. Obviously, try to avoid makes and models that are not on their recommended list.

A used car at a dealer should have a large sticker called the "Buyers Guide" posted in the window. This will indicate whether the car is covered by a warranty, and if it is, what the warranty includes. About one-half of used cars are sold "as is," meaning there is no warranty. When you purchase a car "as is," you are fully re-

Box 16.2 SAVING MONEY
Use Your Home Equity to Finance Your Car

Home equity loans have become one of the cheapest sources of credit for consumers. Rates on home equity loans are typically about 1.5 to 1.75 percent above the prime rate imposed by major banks. This is slightly below interest rates on new car loans at commercial banks and several points below rates on both new and used cars charged by financing companies.

Besides the attractive interest rate, a home equity loan has another big advantage, the tax advantage. Interest on home equity loans up to $100,000 is tax deductible. If you itemize your deductions (if you have a home you probably do), this can be a substantial savings.

A homeowner can take out a loan by borrowing against the equity in the home, the difference between the market value on the home and the remaining balance on the mortgage. Of course, if you default, you can lose your home. Defaults, however, are low on home equity loans. This is why lenders can offer attractive rates.

One important concern is that you don't trade off long-term home equity debt for short-term enjoyment. With most auto loans the outstanding balance is typically less than the market value of the car. When you use a home equity loan, the repayment schedule is not necessarily tied to the life of the auto. Unless you monitor both your loan balance and the value of the car, you could find yourself in an ever-increasing financial quagmire. You may be burdened with debt on a car you no longer own.

In the past, lenders would not make a home equity loan if your total "loan-to-value" ratio was above 80 to 85 percent. This value provided the lender with a cushion should you not be able to repay your loan. Home prices could fall 15 to 20 percent in a declining market without endangering the loan collateral. Lately, lenders have been making home equity loans that take total outstanding loans up to 100 percent of the appraised value of the home. The catch is that these loans carry a higher interest rate to offset the greater risk of default.

The automakers have noticed the obvious tie-in between equity loans and auto purchases. The financial units of both GM and Ford have home equity loans with credit card–style rebates that count toward your next purchase of a car or light truck. Loans through Ford Consumer Finance earn rebates of 1 percent on the average outstanding balance, up to a maximum annual rebate of $2,500. They can accumulate for up to five years. In addition, home equity loans above $10,000 get an instant $500 rebate.

Borrowers should be wary of the rebate programs for at least two reasons. First, you still have to negotiate for the best possible price with the dealer. The rebates offer no significant benefit if the dealer provides less than the usual discount. Second, the rebate may be no great deal if you are being charged more than a competitive interest rate or higher than usual closing costs on the home equity loan.

REPRESENTATIVE LOAN RATES (MID-YEAR 1996)

Credit card rate	16.53%
New car loan	9.21%
Home equity loan	9.17%
1-year adjustable rate mortgage	5.82%
30-year fixed rate mortgage	8.14%

sponsible for any needed repairs. For those cars that are sold with a warranty, the previous discussion on warranties applies. If the car is still covered by an unexpired manufacturer's warranty, then the manufacturer, not the dealer who sold you the car, is responsible for fulfilling the terms of this warranty. If you have any questions concerning warranty coverage, be sure to ask the dealer to explain the terms of the contract. Also be sure that all the dealer's promises are included in the written warranty.

Rebates and Dealer-Supplied Financing

Manufacturer's rebates and low-interest dealer financing are widely used advertising gimmicks. Once in the showroom, the consumer often finds that these items are being offered in place of the typical dealer discount. The true cost of the car may be unchanged or even greater.

A Federal Trade Commission investigation of promotions for dealer financing turned up numerous examples of unethical and possible illegal activities. In some cases consumers were offered the low rate on only a few cars and only if they made an unusually large down payment. In other cases the typical cash discount was unavailable and the car was loaded with high-cost options. The latest promotional strategy is to apply the low advertised rate only on loans of unusually short duration.

Under some circumstances, however, dealer financing may be a real bargain, particularly if the dealer has arranged a low-cost line of credit through the manufacturer or the local bank. Therefore, it may be worth your time to comparison shop and undertake the illustrated calculations on the worksheet in Table 16.4. For example, suppose you are offered the choice between either below-market financing or a discounted purchase price. Purchase option 1 in Table 16.4 consists of a \$12,000 purchase price with 10 percent down and the remaining balance financed at a below-market annual percentage rate of 5 percent over three years. Under purchase option 2, you receive a \$1,000 discount on the price of the car, but you must supply your own financing. Which is the best deal?

The easiest way to determine the best option is first to search out alternative financing with an identical down payment and identical term. In this example, loans requiring a \$1,200 down payment and 36 months to repay are compared. Given a discount of \$1,000 on option 2, the purchase price would be reduced from \$12,000 to \$11,000. Consequently, as Table 16.4 indicates, if you placed \$1,200 down (slightly over 10 percent) under purchase option 2, you would have to borrow \$9,800.

Suppose that after calling local banks, savings and loan associations, and credit unions, you discover that the best rate on private financing with this down payment and term is at a 10 percent annual percentage rate. Your monthly payments under this alternative would equal \$316.22. (The monthly payment can be calculated using Table 16.5: 9.8 [thousands] × \$32.27 = \$316.25.) This is slightly less than the monthly payment of \$323.68 (10.8 [thousands] × \$29.97 = \$323.68) under purchase option 1.

The total cost of the car will equal the sum of the down payment and the monthly payments. Your monthly payments are less when you borrow \$9,800 at 10 percent than when you borrow \$10,800 at 5 percent. Therefore, given identical down payments, the best buy is the car with the lower purchase price and higher loan rate in this example. Under the preferred option 2, you save \$7.43 per month, a total of \$267.48 over the life of the loan.

TABLE 16.4 • WORKSHEET ON COMPARATIVE AUTO FINANCING

	Purchase Option 1	Purchase Option 2
Price	\$12,000.00	\$ 11,000
Less: Down payment	1,200.00	1,200.00
Equals: Balance due	\$10,800.00	\$ 9,800.00
Interest rate (annual)	5.00%	10.00%
Monthly payment	\$ 323.68	\$ 316.25
Multiplied by: Term (months)	36	36
Total monthly payments	\$11,652.68	\$11,383.86
Plus: Down payment	1,200.00	1,200.00
Equals: Total cost	\$12,852.68	\$12,583.86

TABLE 16.5 • MONTHLY PAYMENTS ON EACH $1,000 BORROWED				
Annual Percentage Rate	Term of Loan (Months)			
	24	36	48	60
3%	$42.98	$29.08	$22.13	$17.97
4%	43.42	29.52	22.58	18.42
5%	43.87	29.97	23.03	18.87
6%	44.32	30.42	23.49	19.33
7%	44.77	30.88	23.95	19.80
8%	45.23	31.34	24.41	20.28
9%	45.68	31.90	24.89	20.76
10%	46.14	32.27	25.36	21.25
11%	46.61	32.74	25.85	21.74
12%	47.07	33.21	26.33	22.24
13%	47.54	33.69	26.83	22.75

A word of caution: Sometimes a lender will offer a loan at an attractive interest rate and then tack on to the monthly payment a charge for credit life insurance. This insurance will pay off the remaining principal on the loan in the event of your death. In many states it is illegal to require that the borrower accept the **credit life insurance.** It is often unnecessary, high-cost insurance, the purpose of which is actually to increase the interest return to the lender. If credit life is being forced upon you, be sure to compare loans according to total monthly payments, including the credit life premium.

Credit life insurance: Pays off the remaining loan balance upon one's death.

THE COSTS OF OWNING AND OPERATING AN AUTOMOBILE

When deciding whether to purchase a car, and when planning your household finances, you will need information on the cost of ownership and operation. Runzheimer International, a management consulting firm, specializes in the collection of data on travel and living costs. Their estimates for the cost of owning and operating a representative compact, standard, and large-size car are given in Figure 16.2. For the owner who purchases a new car and trades it in after four years and 60,000 miles, the cost of owning and operating an automobile is a significant expense. As indicated in Figure 16.2, the owner of a 1995 Ford Taurus would incur over $25,000 in automobile expenses in the four-year period. For budgeting purposes, these expenses may be separated into the fixed cost of ownership and the variable cost of operation.

The Cost of Ownership

Ownership costs are fixed; that is, they do not vary with usage. No matter how much or how little you use the car, these expenses will remain relatively constant. Each of the following is considered a **cost of ownership:** auto insurance; license, registration, taxes; depreciation; and finance charges.

Cost of ownership: Fixed costs that do not vary with usage.

INSURANCE The cost of insurance will depend upon the amount and type of coverage. For a detailed discussion of auto insurance see Chapter 8. Briefly, comprehensive insurance covers you against theft and fire. Collision insurance pays for

YOUR DRIVING COSTS

4-year/60,000-mile cycle	1995 Ford Escort LX 4-cyl. (1.9 liter) 4-door hatchback	1995 Ford Taurus GL 6-cyl. (3 liter) 4-door sedan	1995 Chevrolet Caprice 8-cyl. (4.3 liter) 4-door sedan	Average cost
DETAILS OF CAR COSTS				
Operating Costs	**Cost per Mile**	**Cost per Mile**	**Cost per Mile**	**Cost per Mile**
Gasoline and oil	4.8 cents	6.0 cents	6.6 cents	5.8 cents
Maintenance	2.4 cents	2.6 cents	2.8 cents	2.6 cents
Tires	0.9 cents	1.4 cents	1.4 cents	1.2 cents
	8.1 cents	10.0 cents	10.8 cents	9.6 cents
Ownership Costs	**Cost per Year**	**Cost per Year**	**Cost per Year**	**Cost per Year**
Comprehensive insurance ($250 deductible)	$161	$95	$108	$121
Collision insurance ($500 deductible)	304	211	241	252
Bodily injury and property damage ($100,000, $300,000, $50,000)	410	410	410	410
License, registration, taxes	169	211	228	203
Depreciation	2,636	3,099	3,484	3,073
Finance charge (20% down; loan @ 9.096% /4 yrs.)	545	729	783	686
	$4,225 (or $11.57 per day)	$4,755 (or $13.03 per day)	$5,254 (or $14.40 per day)	$4,745 (or $13.00 per day)
Depreciation for excess mileage per 1,000 miles over 15,000 miles annually	$139	$148	$156	$148
COST PER MILE				
Based on the above figures, the motorist driving 15,000 miles a year would pay:				
15,000 miles	@8.1¢ $1,215	@10.0¢ $1,500	@10.8¢ $1,620	@9.6¢ $1,440
*365 days	@$11.57 4,225	@$13.03 4,755	@$14.40 5,254	@$13.00 4,745
	$5,440	$6,255	$6,874	$6,185
Cost per Mile	**36.3 cents**	**41.7 cents**	**45.8 cents**	**41.2 cents**
The same person driving 20,000 miles a year would pay:				
20,000 miles	@8.1¢ $1,620	@10.0¢ $2,000	@10.8¢ $2,160	@9.6¢ $1,920
*365 days	@$11.57 4,225	@$13.03 4,755	@$14.40 5,254	@$13.00 4,745
Added depreciation per 1,000 over 15,000 miles	@$139 695	@$148 740	@$156 780	@$148 740
	$6,540	$7,495	$8,194	$7,405
Cost per Mile	**32.7 cents**	**37.5 cents**	**41.0 cents**	**37.0 cents**
The same person driving 10,000 miles a year would pay:				
10,000 miles	@8.1¢ $810	@10.0¢ $1,000	@10.8¢ $1,080	@9.6¢ $960
**365 days	@$9.44 3,447	@$10.66 3,891	@$13.61 4,969	@$11.24 4,102
	$4,257	$4,891	$6,049	$5,062
Cost per Mile	**42.6 cents**	**48.9 cents**	**60.5 cents**	**50.6 cents**

*Ownership costs based on a four-year/60,000-mile retention cycle

**Ownership costs based on a six-year/60,000-mile retention cycle

Figure 16.2 Estimating Driving Costs.

SOURCE: Runzheimer International. These data are presented with permission from Runzheimer International, the Rochester, Wisconsin–based management consulting firm.

damage to your car from an accident, regardless of who is at fault. Deductibles on each of these coverages indicate that the insurance company reimburses only losses that exceed this amount.

Property damage and liability insurance protects you from the cost of the harm you may cause to others. The Runzheimer cost estimate of this coverage is based on a policy with limits of $100,000/$300,000/$50,000. The first number sets a limit on the financial responsibility of the insurer for harm to any single individual, the second number limits the insurer's liability for all individuals in a single accident, and the last number sets the liability limit on property damage.

LICENSE, REGISTRATION, TAXES The state in which you live will impose these fees. Each state has its own formula for determining the cost of a license. This can vary depending on the vehicle's weight and type and your intended use of the motor vehicle.

Certificate of title: Legal evidence of your ownership of a motor vehicle.

Certificate of registration: A document indicating that your car is properly registered with the state motor vehicle department.

Depreciation: The reduction in the market value of a motor vehicle due to passage of time, mechanical and physical condition, and number of miles driven.

With the purchase of a car you should receive a **certificate of title.** This authenticates your ownership of the car and should be kept in a safe place. Never leave it in the car, since the car may be stolen. Another important document is the **certificate of registration,** which indicates that the vehicle has been properly registered with your state motor vehicle department. This document should remain in your car.

DEPRECIATION **Depreciation** is the reduction in the market value of the vehicle due to passage of time, mechanical and physical condition, and number of miles driven. While depreciation does vary with usage, it is dependent primarily upon time, and therefore, can be considered a fixed cost for any given year.

Depreciation is the greatest single cost over the four-year holding period. However, as an annual expense it declines steadily throughout the years of ownership. Table 16.2 indicated that a new large-size car will decline to 75 percent of its initial value at the end of the first year and to 60 percent of its initial value by the end of the second year. In the first year, 25 percent of the new-car value is lost, but in the second year, only 15 percent of the new-car value is lost.

Your average annual depreciation will depend on the age of your car and your holding period. If you purchased a new car each year for $20,000 and traded in the old car each year for $15,000, your average annual depreciation would be $5,000. Alternatively, if you purchased a new car every other year for $20,000 and traded in the two-year-old car for $12,000, the depreciation over the two-year period would be $8,000. After the total depreciation is divided by 2, the length of the holding period, the average annual depreciation is $4,000. The difference between average annual depreciation of $5,000 and average annual depreciation of $4,000 represents a yearly savings of $1,000. This is the dollar advantage of having a two-year holding period rather than a one-year holding period. The longer you hold the car, the smaller is your average annual cost of depreciation.

FINANCE CHARGES The finance charges in Figure 16.2 assume that each car is purchased with a 20 percent down payment and financed with a four-year loan at an annual percentage rate (APR) of 9 percent. Over the four-year period, total finance charges will range from $2,180 for the compact car to $3,132 for the large car. If you purchase the car out of savings, you can eliminate these explicit finance charges; however, you give up the interest income you could have earned on those savings. This lost interest would also represent a cost of ownership. Consequently, whether or not you intend to finance the purchase with borrowed funds, you should consider the Runzheimer estimate of finance charges as a real cost of ownership.

OTHER COSTS OF OWNERSHIP Any additional fixed costs that are incurred because of car ownership should also be considered. For example, if you rent a garage to house your car, the rental payments should be included in the cost of ownership. On the other hand, if you would normally live in a home with a garage, whether or not you own a car, then your additional or marginal cost of storage would be zero.

The cost of accessories may also be included. These may consist of such things as extra wheels for snow tires, radios, and trailer hitches. Items that have an effect on mechanical operation can be included under the maintenance component of operating expenses.

Box 16.3

PERSONAL FINANCE NEWS

Late Edition

Auto Shopping at the Cybermall

Surfing the Internet is a poor choice of terms. On the Internet, the main electronic highway, you are more likely to find a deal on an auto than a surfboard. So the next time you are thinking of going car shopping, you might try driving onto the I-way (Information Highway).

Start with the automotive classified page from Yahoo, a directory provider (electronic addresses are listed below). There you will find over 35 listings from AA Discount Auto Brokerage to Wheels On-Line. The sites contain listings for new and used cars and car brokers who claim they can find you the best deal in the land.

The commercial services also have their special areas for auto shoppers. On CompuServe at the AutoNet Showroom, you can discover the dealer's cost on a new car and calculate monthly payments. Through AutoVantage on both CompuServe and America Online you can find the market price for new and used cars and even arrange a purchase.

You may negotiate directly with dealers, or you may engage a car-buying service over the Internet. For a fee, a car-buying service will locate a dealer and prenegotiate an advantageous price. Any purchase, however, should be completed face to face. You still want to kick the tires and make sure you're getting what you were promised.

Even if you don't plan on buying a car from an advertiser on the Internet, it's still a good place to visit. You can easily comparison shop, getting price quotes on several makes and models. This is useful knowledge to have before you hit the real highway and spend several hours driving from one showroom to another.

Automobile-related news groups are another excellent source of information. Current owners discuss both the pros and cons of various makes and models. They point out defects to watch out for and trade information on secret warranties that the dealer won't tell you about.

The home pages for the automakers are a nice place to visit if you want to review the latest makes and models. There's the most recent information on options and specifications. Moreover, with over 60 links to manufacturers listed in Yahoo's directory, it's likely you will find the car of your choice.

Should that dream car turn into a nightmare, the Internet can also provide some help. The Better Business Bureau mediates disputes between manufacturers and disgruntled customers through their Autoline program. Information on the program and the most up-to-date list of participating manufacturers can be found on the BBB Autoline home page.

INTERNET ADDRESSES	
Automotive Classifieds	http://www.yahoo.com/Business_and_ Economy/Classifieds/Automotive/
Buyer's Guides	http://www.yahoo.com/Business_and_ Economy/Products_and_Services/Automotive/ Buyer_s_Guides/
Automotive Manufacturers	http://www.yahoo.com/Business_and_Econ omy/Companies/Automotive/Manufacturers/
BBB Autoline	http://www.bbb.org/council/complaints/BBB autoLine.html
News Groups	rec.autos.marketplace rec.autos.misc

The Cost of Operation

Cost of operation: Variable costs that are directly related to usage.

Costs that are related directly to usage are called *variable costs.* The **cost of operation** includes all variable costs. Figure 16.2 lists the variable cost per mile for each component of operating cost.

GASOLINE AND OIL After the cost of depreciation, this is likely to be your next largest vehicle expense. Your costs should be based on your regional cost of fuel and your car's fuel economy. The data in Figure 16.2 indicate that, at 15,000 miles a year, drivers of compact cars would spend about $270 less on gasoline and oil than drivers of larger cars.

MAINTENANCE AND TIRES The owner's manual or your local mechanic should be able to recommend a maintenance schedule based on the miles you typically drive. Maintenance and tires are not generally covered under an automobile warranty and therefore should be included in the household budget. For older cars on which the warranty has expired, unscheduled repairs and parts replacement should also be given consideration when estimating expenditures.

OTHER OPERATING COSTS Metered curb parking, fees charged for parking lots, and toll charges for highways, tunnels, and bridges may all represent additional operating costs. In an urban environment these costs should not be overlooked; they can represent a significant cost of commuting.

The Total Cost of Ownership and Operation

By adding together the fixed cost of ownership and the variable cost of operation, you can calculate the total cost of the family car. For the mid-size car driven 15,000 miles a year, total annual cost of $6,255 would consist of $4,755 in ownership cost and $1,500 in operating cost. As in this example, the cost of ownership generally represents a larger portion of total auto expenditures than the cost of operation.

On a per mile basis, the total cost per mile of the mid-size car driven 15,000 miles per year is 41.7 cents. This consists of 10 cents per mile in operating costs and 31.7 cents per mile in ownership costs. At this level of usage, ownership cost represents about 76 percent of your auto-related transportation expenses. However, if the car is driven an additional mile, the variable cost of operations will increase by about 10 cents, while the fixed cost of ownership will remain relatively stable. This means that as the car is used more often, the relative importance of ownership cost will decline. It can be seen in Figure 16.2 that, at 20,000 miles per year, the cost of ownership including depreciation declines to about 73 percent.

The Mass Transit Alternative

In highly congested New York City, about 44 percent of the work force uses public transportation to get to work. In less densely populated Indianapolis, only about 3 percent of the work force uses public transportation. This difference can be explained in terms of relative availability, relative cost, and relative convenience of mass transit in each of these cities. If you have a mass transit alternative in your city, you should compare the costs of using a private auto with those of using public transit.

When judging the relative merits of public transit, you should first decide whether its use would permit you to do without owning and operating a motor vehicle. If so, you may weigh the cost of public transit against the total cost of ownership and operation. However, if you find you need the car anyway, then you should weigh the cost of public transit only against the cost of vehicle operation. This is because the cost of ownership is a **sunk cost:** It is something you have to pay whether or not you use the car. Therefore, if you own the car and want to know whether to drive it an additional mile or to use public transit to go the same mile, you should consider only the **marginal,** or additional, **cost** you will incur. In most circumstances the least costly alternative will depend upon the necessity of car ownership.

Sunk cost: A cost that has already been incurred and therefore cannot be changed.

Marginal cost: Additional or incremental cost that will be incurred.

According to Figure 16.2, a mid-size car that has been driven 15,000 miles will cost you 24.8 cents for each additional mile. This will consist of 10 cents for operations and maintenance and 14.8 cents for excess depreciation. In this case, you would contemplate using supplementary mass transit only if the cost per mile fell below 24.8 cents. And even then, the cost savings may not offset any additional inconvenience.

THE LEASING ALTERNATIVE

If you find that you do need a car, but the need exists only for an occasional trip, you might consider an occasional rental as a practical alternative to ownership. By renting you avoid the high fixed cost of ownership, an exorbitant expense for a car that is seldom used.

If you need a car for longer periods of time but wish to hold down the high initial cost of ownership, you might consider leasing. Your current expenses and your periodic payments will be less than if you purchased the same car on credit. When you lease a vehicle, you are only paying rent for the car's long-term use. Your payments are determined primarily by the difference between the initial price of the car and the resale value of the car at the termination of the lease. If you finance a purchase, on the other hand, you are building equity as you pay off the loan principal. When you complete your car loan payments, you own the car. If you sell the car before all the loan payments are completed, you should receive any amount in excess of the loan balance.

There are two types of leasing contracts: closed-end and open-end. Both are covered by regulations specified in the **Consumer Leasing Act of 1977.** This act requires the leasing company (the lessor) to disclose in writing specific information about a consumer lease before you (the lessee) sign the lease agreement.

Consumer Leasing Act of 1977: A federal statute regulating leases on consumer goods.

The Closed-End Lease

The **closed-end lease** is also sometimes called the *net* or *walkaway* lease. You make fixed periodic payments based on your estimated usage. When your lease expires, you simply return the car and pay a surcharge for mileage in excess of your estimate. Unless you have seriously damaged the vehicle, given it more than normal wear, or driven it more miles than the lease permits, you are not responsible for the value of the vehicle at the end of the lease term. Because the lessor is taking the risk as to what the value of the car will be when you return it, your lease payments generally will be higher than they would be under an open-end lease.

Closed-end lease: Your costs are determined at the time you lease the car. Under most circumstances, you are not responsible for the value of the car at the end of the lease.

The Open-End Lease

Open-end lease: The total cost of the lease is unknown until the end of the lease, when the estimated resale value of the car is determined.

The **open-end lease** also has fixed periodic payments; however, the total cost remains unknown until the end of the leasing period. This is because the periodic payments are based on the estimated resale value on the returned car, sometimes called the estimated *residual value*.

When you return the vehicle, the lessor will appraise it and compare the appraised value with the residual value stated in the lease. Under the Consumer Leasing Act, you have the right, at your expense, to obtain an independent appraisal by someone agreed to by both you and the lessor. If you get an independent appraisal, you and the lessor are bound by it.

If the appraised value of the car is the same as, or greater than, the residual value specified in the lease disclosure, you owe nothing. (Your contract will determine whether you get a refund for any excess value. You can ask the lessor to include the right to a refund in your contract.) Alternatively, if the appraisal indicates that the vehicle is worth less than the specified amount, you may have to pay all or a portion of the difference. This cost is often called an *end-of-lease payment*.

You may be able to bargain for lower periodic payments if you agree to have a higher residual value put on the vehicle. Of course, setting a higher residual value increases your risk of having to make a large payment at the end of the lease. To ensure that consumers will not unknowingly enter into agreements with exorbitant end-of-lease payments, the Consumer Leasing Act requires that under most circumstances the end-of-lease payment can be no more than three times the average monthly payment on the lease. However, higher payments can be collected if you agreed to pay a greater amount, there was unreasonable wear or excessive use, or the lessor wins a lawsuit seeking a higher amount.

A Lease/Buy Comparison

Figure 16.3 contains a worksheet for comparing the cost of leasing with that of purchasing a car on credit. The calculations are based on a new car costing $17,000 plus tax. All of the costs associated with owning and operating a car are not shown on the worksheet. It is assumed that the costs of operations, maintenance, repairs, insurance, and registration are the same whether you purchase or lease. Therefore, these costs are irrelevant to the lease/purchase decision. Only costs that affect the decision are relevant costs.

The initial costs associated with leasing a car may include a security deposit, the first and last periodic payments, and a so-called capitalized cost reduction. Only the last item is considered a relevant initial cost. This is because the security deposit will be returned when the lease terminates, and the first and last payments are to be included under continuing relevant costs.

A capitalized cost reduction is, in effect, an advanced payment on the lease. It may or may not be required by the lessor. If you trade in a car you own, the capitalized cost reduction may be set equal to the value of the trade. The more you pay down initially, the lower your periodic payments will be. However, if you make a high initial payment in order to reduce your periodic payments, you lose one important advantage of leasing—the lower initial cost. In the worksheet example, it is assumed that initial decision-relevant costs include a 20 percent down payment and a 6 percent sales tax.

Continuing relevant payments will consist of periodic payments on the lease and auto loan payments on the purchase. In the example, it is assumed that a four-year

Leasing		Purchasing	
Relevant Explicit Initial Costs			
Capitalized cost reduction	$ 0.00	Sales tax	$ 1,020.00
Miscellaneous costs	0.00	Down payment and trade-in	3,400.00
		Miscellaneous costs	0.00
Total explicit initial costs	$ 0.00	Total explicit initial costs	$ 4,420.00
Relevant Explicit Continuing Costs			
Monthly lease payment	$ 290.00	Monthly loan payment	$ 358.14
× Months:	48	× Months	48
Total explicit continuing costs	$13,920.00	Total explicit continuing costs	$17,190.72
Relevant Explicit Final Costs			
Excessive mileage charge	$ 1,200.00	Loan payoff, if applicable	$ 0.00
Excessive wear and tear	0.00	Less estimated residual value	−8,600.00
Adjustment for over-estimated residual value	0.00		
Miscellaneous items	0.00		
Total explicit final costs	$ 1,200.00	Total explicit final costs	$−8,600.00
Relevant Implicit Costs			
Relevant explicit initial costs	$ 0.00	Relevant explicit initial costs	$ 4,420.00
Security deposit	290.00	× After-tax interest rate	.08
Lease prepayments	290.00	Annual implicit costs	$ 353.60
Total initial cash outflow	$ 580.00	× Terms of loan (years)	4
× After-tax interest rate	.08		
Annual implicit costs	$ 46.40		
× Terms of lease (years)	4		
Total implicit costs	$ 185.60	Total implicit costs	$ 1,414.40
Total Relevant Costs			
Explicit initial costs	$ 0.00	Explicit initial costs	$ 4,420.00
Explicit continuing costs	13,920.00	Explicit continuing costs	17,190.72
Explicit final costs	1,200.00	Explicit final costs	−8,600.00
Total explicit costs	$15,120.00	Total explicit costs	$13,010.72
Total implicit costs	185.60	Total implicit costs	1,414.40
Total relevant costs	$15,305.60	Total relevant costs	$14,425.12

Figure 16.3 Worksheet for the lease/buy decision.

lease is being considered, for which periodic payments would total $13,920. The purchase option assumes an initial loan of $13,600 (equal to the difference between the purchase price of $17,000 and the down payment of $3,400). If this were financed over four years at an annual percentage rate of 12 percent, monthly loan payments would total $17,190.72 over the term of the loan.

Final costs at the termination of the lease may include an excess mileage charge and miscellaneous items such as a disposition charge or a fee for excessive wear. Most leases have a mileage cap of 15,000 miles per year. The fee for each additional mile over the mileage cap can vary widely. Closed-end leases may reflect excessive wear on the car in either the excess mileage fee or in an adjustment for an overestimated residual value in the car.

The single final cost on the purchase side of the worksheet consists of the amount needed to pay off any remaining balance on the auto loan. This will be reduced, however, by the estimated resale value on the vehicle at the end of the holding period. At the end of the purchase alternative the consumer has a car worth $8,600, whereas at the end of the lease alternative the consumer owns nothing.

In the last section of the lease/buy worksheet, relevant explicit costs are totaled for each of the options. If you consider just explicit costs, the purchase option looks much more attractive. However, remember that if you decide to purchase the car, your initial costs are far greater. Those funds that were used to make the initial payment on the purchase of the car could have been invested and earned you income. Therefore, you must also take into account the opportunity cost of your initial expenditures in the section of the worksheet entitled "Relevant Implicit costs."

To calculate the implicit cost of each option, you must first total up your initial cash outlay. For the lease alternative this will include your initial relevant expenses plus any lease prepayments or security deposit. Even though the security deposit and lease prepayments are either returned to you in the future or offset future obligations, you have still lost the income these funds could have generated over the term of the lease. If your initial cash outlay for the leasing alternative is $580 and you could have earned an annual after-tax return of 8 percent on these funds, then the total implicit cost is $185.50 ($580 × 0.08 × 4). For the purchase the total implicit cost is $1,414.40. It is larger than under the leasing alternative because it requires a much larger explicit initial cost.

When deciding on an open-end lease, it is suggested that unless you have good reasons for doing otherwise, you should set the estimated resale value on the purchase alternative equal to the estimated residual value in the lease. When figured this way, a downside error in the estimated residual value will wash out and not affect the correct decision. For example, suppose the residual value is $100 less than estimated. The resulting $100 end-of-lease payment will increase the relevant cost of leasing by $100. However, this also means that the trade-in value under the purchase alternative would be $100 less than expected, thus increasing the cost of the purchase alternative by $100. Since the cost of each alternative increases by the same amount, an error in the estimated residual value should not affect your choice.

This worksheet assumes that you will hold the car for the entire term of the contract. However, the Consumers Bankers Association reports that about 30 percent of auto leases are terminated early. In addition to simply desiring a new car, early termination can be triggered by theft or accident. Regardless of the reason for termination, you may be responsible for depreciation in the market value of the car and for additional special charges upon breaking the lease. Be sure you understand just how much you will owe if you decide to return the vehicle before the scheduled expiration of the lease.

Negotiating an Auto Lease

There is a growing concern among consumer advocates that consumers have been duped into paying too much for leases. Consumer groups are urging that lessors provide the consumer standardized information that includes the net (or adjusted) capitalized cost of the lease and the interest rate used to calculate the periodic payments, the "lease factor." The capitalized cost of the lease is supposed to represent the cost of the car. It will depend upon depreciation during the lease and the residual value of the car. This will also include other items related to usage such as taxes, registration, and license fees. The net capitalized cost is the capitalized cost less a capitalized cost reduction that includes your down payment and trade-in. This will be the amount upon which the monthly payments are based.

Unfortunately, in the past there has been no set formula for calculating these costs. Recently, however, there have been two attempts to come up with comparable information on leasing, one by a consumer group and the other by an industry trade association. Ralph Nader's Task Force for Automotive Issues has issued the "Reality Checklist for Vehicle Leasing." The checklist is to be completed by the leasing agency. If each potential lessor completes the form, you will then have comparable data for making an informed comparison. The Reality Checklist, supported by numerous state attorneys general, can be obtained for a small fee by writing to CTF Reality Checklist, P.O. Box 7648, Atlanta, Georgia 30357-0648, or for free on the Internet (see Internet Addresses). The industry trade association, American Financial Services, believes that the Reality Checklist is overly complex. In response, the member credit agencies for the major auto manufacturers have now adopted a simplified common leasing form that is likely to provide compatible information on leasing. Should none of this benefit the consumer, the Federal Reserve Board, a government agency, may soon issue its own disclosure regulations.

Given the nonstandardized information in the marketplace, it is best if you use the worksheet in Figure 16.3 to conduct your own analysis in a five-step process.

1. Don't directly enter into negotiations on a lease. First, identify the lowest price that the dealer will accept for the car. This will represent the capitalized cost.
2. After you have determined the best price you can get, then separately negotiate the value on any trade-in you may have. Given your anticipated down payment and trade-in, you can then estimate net capitalized cost.
3. Check all sources of financing to determine the best interest rate and your needed monthly payments under the purchase option.
4. Check out the resale value from industry publications.
5. Finally, enter into negotiations for the lease, you should then have all the information you need to use the lease/buy comparison worksheet and make an informed decision. Be wary of last-minute changes in the deal that don't leave you time to recheck your calculations. This is when consumers are most susceptible to high-pressure sales techniques that result in wasted dollars.

WHAT IF YOU BOUGHT A LEMON?

Your chance of purchasing a new car with serious problems is about one in 800. Your chance of purchasing a car with at least a few defects is apparently much higher. Most of the complaints in the first year should be covered by the new-car warranty. To ensure that they are corrected, you should be prepared to deal with new-car defects and know how to seek remedial action.

The suggested procedure is to discuss the problem with the dealer first, allowing the firm an adequate opportunity to repair the defect. If the dealer is unwilling to honor the warranty or is taking an unreasonable amount of time to correct the problem, you should then contact the manufacturer. At the auto company, the person you should contact first is often called the *zone representative* or the *area service manager*. If you still do not receive satisfaction, your next step is to contact the consumer representative at the company's headquarters. If neither the dealer nor the manufacturer responds to your request, you may consider going to small claims court, entering arbitration, or hiring an attorney.

Whichever alternative you choose, be prepared to supply adequate records on all your attempts at repair or replacement. Accordingly, be sure you receive a repair slip each time you return the car for service. The receipt should be legible and should contain an accurate statement of your complaint, the date of service, and the attempted repairs. If the dealer suggests you do not need a repair slip because the car is under warranty, insist on your right to receive one. Also, retain copies of all relevant correspondence and a diary recording each related conversation, including the date, the name of the person with whom you discussed your problem, and a summary of what was said.

Secret Warranties

Secret warranty or policy adjustment: An understanding between manufacturers and retailers that certain defects will be repaired at no cost only when confronted with strong consumer complaints.

Warranties were examined previously in the section on major home appliances. Everything stated there holds true for automotive warranties as well. One additional item, however, commonly known as the **secret warranty,** seems to be unique to the automotive industry. It takes effect after the written warranty has expired. Under a secret warranty, the manufacturer repairs certain defects only when customers complain. Other, more docile, customers are not told about this policy and are unfairly charged for repairs.

The industry prefers the term **policy adjustment** to *secret warranty*. Given the way the auto industry treats customers, it is a good idea to complain whenever you think your problem results from faulty workmanship or design. You should ask the zone representative whether policy adjustments have been made on similar problems and whether a policy adjustment would cover your current defect. The Center for Auto Safety collects information on policy adjustments. They may be able to supply you with information on how a manufacturer has previously dealt with similar defects.

Action Plan for the Steeles: The Purchase of a Family Computer

Background The Steeles have been considering the purchase of a family computer. They have been looking for a multipurpose machine that will allow them to bring work home, reduce time spent on personal finances, aid the children in school, and run some really exciting computer games. After reviewing consumer guides, talking with salespeople, and comparison shopping, they have decided on a packaged system that meets their needs. It includes a computer with a relatively fast processor, adequate memory, a color monitor, and a printer. In addition, it comes with a CD-ROM and lots of bundled software. The street price on the entire package is $2,500, and for $300 they can purchase an extended warranty that covers all parts and service for three years.

The Problem The Steeles have given this purchase a high priority. They are willing to cut back on other expenditures in order to purchase a home computer. They know, however, that this is a decision that will have a long-term impact on the family budget. As of now they are not quite sure how this will affect their future finances.

The Plan The Steeles have completed the first step in the purchase of any consumer durable; they have thoroughly researched the product and its market price. Having done their homework, they should realize that the extended warranty is probably not worth the cost. The computer system comes with a one-year full warranty; therefore, the extended warranty really covers only two years. Furthermore, defects are most likely to show up during the first year of operation. Instead of purchasing the extended warranty, they should increase the household maintenance budget by $150 over each of the next two years. By assuming the risk and budgeting for an expected expense, they should come out ahead. The warranty is a high-profit item for the dealer and a low-value item for the consumer.

Before purchasing, they must now decide on whether they can comfortably integrate the expected future cost of operations and maintenance into the family budget. They should consider both required operational expenses and supplemental voluntary expenses that enhance the enjoyment of the product. The printer will require paper and ink cartridges, which can be quite expensive if they are planning to print colorful reports for work and school. They may also want to plan for additional software purchases. The computer came with an impressive list of programs, but over time they may want to update the business software with the latest versions, add programs for specialized tasks, and purchase new computer games as they become bored with the old ones. For these reasons, the Steeles may want to include a line item in their budget for computer-related purchases. Including this expense in the budget will force them to consider how they are going to pay for these future items. Are they going to reduce their contribution to savings, or are they going to give up other consumption-related purchases?

Consumer durables define our lifestyle, and when we bring a new consumer durable into the household we can expect a change in that lifestyle. A computer can whet our appetite for all sorts of accessories such as scanners, faxes, and on-line services. This is fine, as long as we consider the trade-offs we are getting into. We may be willing to take fewer trips to the movies in order to purchase more computer games, trading off one type of entertainment for another.

The Steeles should also consider future replacement cost. This may sound strange, since they haven't even purchased the computer yet. But if this is going to have the impact on family life that they expect, then they are going to have to plan for future upgrading and replacement. The literature the Steeles have reviewed indicates that there seems to be a relatively short life cycle in computers. To run the latest software, they will need to upgrade to a faster computer about every three to five years. The good news is that the price of the basic system incorporating the latest technology seems to have remained reasonably stable. Consequently, they might plan for replacement of the proposed machine in five years. At that time they can either sell the old machine for a few hundred dollars or keep it as a second computer for the kids. If they budget $500 a year for replacement, they should have the needed funds when they upgrade.

In summary, as with all consumer durables, the Steeles should review the household budget before they purchase. They should consider the impact of both ongoing operational expenses and future replacement cost. With adequate consideration, they should avoid any surprise expenses.

Arbitration

In *mediation*, an attempt is made to have the parties to the dispute reach their own agreement. Most consumer protection agencies, such as the Better Business Bureau, will first attempt to resolve the disagreement through mediation. If that doesn't work, arbitration may be entered into.

Arbitration: A process for settling disputes in which an impartial third party mediates and suggests a binding or nonbinding remedy.

Arbitration is a process for settling disputes in which an impartial third party listens to arguments made by both sides and suggests a remedy that may be binding or nonbinding. In consumer-related disputes, the Federal Trade Commission sets down rules to ensure that the arbitration procedure is, in fact, impartial.

If you have a problem with a new car and do not receive satisfaction from the dealer or the manufacturer's representative, or you are dissatisfied with repairs made on a used car, your next step is to consider arbitration. A listing of the major arbitration programs is given in Table 16.6.

Entering arbitration has two significant advantages over using the court system: The process is relatively speedy, and there is no cost to the individual. However, there are also some disadvantages. The arbitrators need not be lawyers or knowledgeable mechanics. Thus, they may not fully understand your problem or your rights as a consumer. Furthermore, they will not award punitive damages or compensatory damages related to such incidentals as lost wages or medical bills resulting from a defective car. Without your own lawyer, you may not know whether you would be entitled to such payments in the regular court system. In addition, by entering arbitration you may be accepting a potential decision that is legally

TABLE 16.6 • ARBITRATION PROGRAMS

BBB Autoline

National participants include: Acura, Alfa Romeo, AM General, Audi, General Motors (Buick, Cadillac, Chevrolet, GMC Truck, Pontiac, Oldsmobile), Honda, Hyundai, Infiniti, Kia, Land Rover, Lexus, Nissan, Porsche, Saturn, Toyota, Volkswagen.

Participants in some states include: BMW, Chrysler, Jaguar, Maserati, Mazda, Mitsubishi, Peugeot, Rolls-Royce, Saab, Sterling, Subaru, Suzuki, Volvo.

Federal guidelines require that Autoline settle disputes within 40 days of when it has the necessary data.

Details available on Autoline from local BBB.

Call 800-955-5100.

Autocap (Automotive Consumer Action Program)

Administered through National Automobile Dealers Association, handles 15 makers of imports.

Call 703-821-7144.

Chrysler and Ford have their own boards for handling complaints:

Chrysler Motors Customer Relations

800-922-1997.

Ford Consumer Appeals Board

313-337-6950 inside Maine.

800-241-8450 outside Maine.

State-run arbitration boards

Many states have arbitration boards that help enforce the lemon laws. State-run boards exist in Connecticut, Florida, Hawaii, Maine, Massachusetts, New York, New Jersey, Texas, Vermont, Washington, and the District of Columbia. Contact your state consumer-protection office for information.

binding. You should realize that your chances of coming out of arbitration with a better offer than that provided by the dealer or manufacturer's representative are only about 50-50.

Lemon Laws

Nearly all states have lemon laws to protect buyers of new cars. A few states even have lemon laws regulating the sale of used cars. In general, lemon laws declare that if a car dealer does not repair substantial defects covered by the new-car warranty within a reasonable period of time, the owner may be entitled to a comparable new car or a refund. A reasonable time is usually defined as four trips to the repair shop for the same problem of a total of 30 days in the repair shop. If the manufacturer or dealer does not supply a new car, the customer may go to court after attempting to arbitrate the matter.

The *Lemon Book,* available through the Center for Auto Safety, explains your rights and remedies and gives a breakdown of lemon laws by state. If your state does not have a lemon law, you can still go to court to enforce performance of express and implied warranties under the Magnuson-Moss Warranty Act, discussed earlier in this chapter.

SUMMARY

Consumer durables provide long-term benefits, while committing us to long-term operational costs and creating the need for long-range planning. Such planning will involve the following questions. What is the future replacement cost likely to be? How much savings in operational costs can various models provide? How much protection do warranties afford? What fixed and variable costs are involved? In this chapter we have examined how each of these questions will affect the purchasing and budgeting of both major home appliances and the family auto.

KEY TERMS

arbitration (p. 464)
"as is" (p. 445)
base price (p. 449)
certificate of title (p. 454)
certificate of registration (p. 454)
closed-end lease (p. 457)
consumer durables (p. 440)
Consumer Leasing Act of 1977 (p. 457)
cost of operation (p. 456)
cost of ownership (p. 452)
credit life insurance (p. 452)
dealer sticker price (p. 449)
depreciation (p. 454)
EnergyGuide (p. 445)
express warranty (p. 445)
extended warranty (p. 448)
full warranty (p. 447)
guarantee (p. 445)
implied warranty (p. 445)
invoice price (p. 449)
lemon protection (p. 447)
limited warranty (p. 447)
Magnuson-Moss Warranty Act of 1975 (p. 447)
marginal cost (p. 457)
Monroney sticker price (p. 449)
net replacement cost (p. 441)
open-end lease (p. 458)
policy adjustment (p. 462)
puffery (p. 447)
replacement cost (p. 440)
savings illusion (p. 440)
secret warranty (p. 462)
service contract (p. 448)
sunk cost (p. 457)
warranty (p. 445)

PROBLEMS AND REVIEW QUESTIONS

1. What special characteristics and budgeting problems do consumer durables present?
2. Suppose it costs you $300 to replace your washing machine at today's prices. If you expect prices to increase by 10 percent over each of the next two years, about how much will it cost you two years from now?
3. Using the depreciation schedule in Table 16.2, and assuming zero inflation, estimate the trade-in value of a $10,000 compact car over each of the next 12 years. Now repeat your calculation, but instead assume a 5 percent yearly inflation rate.
4. Where can you find information on a product's service record and operational costs?
5. Where can you find information on a major appliance's energy usage?
6. What is the difference between an express and an implied warranty?
7. Does an item sold "as is" carry an implied warranty?
8. What requirements must a warranty satisfy before it can be labeled *full?* How do these differ for a limited warranty?
9. You purchase a stereo system from a local department store on the basis of the salesperson's assurance that this system is a "good buy." You later find out that it wasn't such a good buy. The same product is being sold elsewhere at a much lower price. Does the salesperson's statement constitute an express warranty? What action do you now take?
10. Suppose you purchase the stereo system and later find that it plays at only one speed. You also find that nobody manufactures records to be played at that speed. The product was not sold "as is," but you forgot to ask if there was a written warranty. What can you do?
11. What is the greatest cost associated with owning and operating a car?
12. How do you distinguish an ownership cost from an operating cost?
13. You commute 20 miles each day in your own car, and the estimated operational cost per mile is 15 cents. If you used the mass transit system, the same trip would cost you $2. Should you leave your car at home and ride the public transport?
14. Your new station wagon has 14,000 miles on the odometer. The new-car warranty expired at the 12,000-mile mark. Yesterday, while you were driving the car to school, the rear axle broke. The dealer tells you it will cost over $1,000 to have the problem fixed because the warranty has expired. What do you do?
15. Explain secret warranties and lemon protection.

Case 16.1 Ann Barnard Considers Alternative Holding Periods

Ann Barnard typically buys a new car and trades in the old one every five years. Because new cars are so expensive, she has recently been considering a change in her buying habits. She would like to know how much she might save in depreciation costs if instead she purchased a year-old car every four years.

QUESTIONS

1. Using a new-car price of $20,000 and the depreciation schedule for an intermediate-size car in Table 16.2, calculate the annual cost of depreciation given her present buying habits. Now calculate the annual cost of depreciation under the proposed change. What is the annual cost savings? What is the cost savings over the five-year holding period?
2. What other factors should Ann Barnard consider before she changes her buying behavior?

Case 16.2 The Reeds Estimate Replacement Cost

The Reeds just purchased an intermediate-sized new car for $18,000. They plan to trade in this car for a similar new car in five years. The Reeds estimate that inflation should average about 5 percent per year over the next five years.

QUESTIONS

1. Given that inflation averages 5 percent per year over the next five years, what will a similar new car cost five years from now?

2. Under this inflation assumption, what will be the trade-in value on their current car at that time?
3. The Reeds plan to purchase a new car in five years by trading in the then-old car and making up the difference in cash. What is the expected size of the cash payment five years from now?

HELPFUL CONTACTS

American Automobile Association
(See your local directory.)

Better Business Bureau
(See your local directory.)

Center for Auto Safety
2001 S Street, NW, Suite 410, Washington, DC 20009
Clearinghouse for automotive complaints.

National Highway Traffic Safety Administration
Auto Safety Hotline, NEF-11 HL, 400 Seventh St., SW Washington, DC 20590 (telephone 800-424-9393)
Keeps information on manufacturers' recalls and can provide printout of complaints on a particular make and model.

Public Reference, Federal Trade Commission, Washington, DC 20580
Series of pamphlets on consumer issues:

A Consumer Guide to Vehicle Leasing
Facts for Consumers: Auto Service Contracts
Facts for Consumers: New Car Buying Guide
Facts for Consumers: Buying a Used Car
How to Write a Wrong: Complain Effectively and Get Results

INTERNET ADDRESSES

Alamo Rent A Car Rules and Regulations (review the contract before you rent)
http://www.freeways.com/bookit/rules.html

Federal Trade Commission (advice on buying, renting, or leasing an auto)
gopher://gopher.ftc.gov:70/11/ConsumerLine/publications/automobiles

Minnesota's Lemon Law
http://www.ag.state.mn.us/consumer/cars/lemonlaw.html

National Better Business Bureaus (directory of Better Business Bureaus, programs, and services including BBB Autoline)
http://www.bbb.org/council/main/index.html

Reality Checklist for Vehicle Leasing
gopher://gopher.essential.org/00/ftp/pub/csrl/reality_checklist

U.S. Consumer Product Safety Commission (report safety problems and review consumer alerts)
gopher://cpsc.gov/

Yahoo Classified Auto Ads (numerous links to dealers, brokers, and individual owners)
http://www.yahoo.com/Business_and_Economy/Classifieds/Automotive/

Chapter

17

Retirement and Pension Planning: Planning for Your Long-Term Needs

Objectives

1. To evaluate the features of a company pension plan
2. To analyze alternative company retirement plans
3. To list individual tax-deferred methods of saving
4. To estimate your retirement needs
5. To learn how to establish a personal saving plan for retirement

Most financial planners will advise you to begin planning for retirement as soon as you enter the workforce. If you put off retirement planning until your forties and fifties, altering projected retirement benefits during your remaining working years will be much more difficult. In addition, you will have missed most of the tax advantages that come from funding tax-deferred retirement plans.

You probably realize this is good advice, but if you are in your early twenties and retirement is far off into the twenty-first century, you may find it very difficult to follow. Unless you have a crystal ball, forecasting more than five years ahead is usually fruitless. Changes in tax rates, interest rates, inflation rates, and Social Security benefits may all upset well-made retirement plans. For this reason, a retirement plan should not be viewed as something set in concrete. It should change as circumstances change. And the important point to remember is that the sooner you get started, the easier it will be to accommodate that plan to your changing personal and financial environment.

Retirement planning should take into consideration the family's needs and resources over the financial life cycle. Figure 17.1 illustrates a typical family's earnings and expenditures with respect to the age of the primary market worker. During the worker's twenties, thirties, and forties, both income and expenditures will likely increase. Savings accumulated during these early years will have more time to grow and accumulate tax-deferred returns until they are needed in retirement. Unfortunately, this is also the time when the family experiences the significant financial demands of childrearing, culminating with the high cost of a college education. In the fifties, most of the children will have left the household, and there will be a dramatic rise in savings as expenditures drop. Saving will be easier at this time, but the money set aside will have fewer years in which to accumulate returns.

Earnings for the average market worker begin to decline in the early sixties as work time decreases and leisure time increases. Self-employed individuals may experience no clear division between preretirement and postretirement years. Financially, retirement may be said to occur when expenses begin to exceed earnings. Retirement years are ones of dissaving, when the wealth accumulated over the preretirement years is slowly depleted. The standard of living in retirement will depend largely upon the family's accumulated savings, and therefore on plans begun and actions taken many years before.

Figure 17.1
A typical family's earnings and expenditures over the family life cycle.

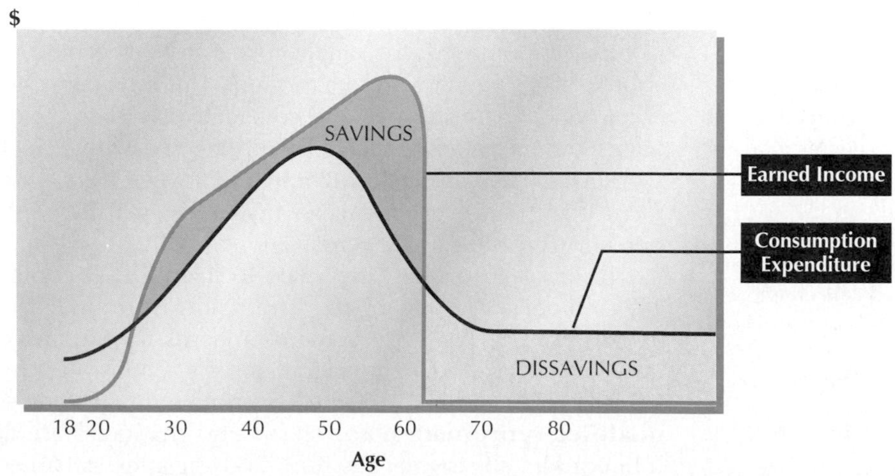

When and how much to save are personal decisions. There is not one "right" retirement plan for everyone. In saving for retirement, you are trading off present consumption for future consumption. How much you plan to save will depend on how much weight you place on each of these needs. Your retirement plan may be to consume everything today and leave nothing for tomorrow. As long as you realize that this decision means you will someday have to survive on minimal benefits provided under an uncertain system of Social Security, we have no quarrel with your choice.

In this chapter, we will first examine the traditional ways of saving for retirement. Once you understand how you can save, we address the question of how much you need to save to achieve your goals.

SAVING AND INVESTING FOR RETIREMENT

Is saving for retirement different from other types of saving? Like most questions in personal finance, this one can be answered with both a yes and a no. It is different because in many cases the government permits it to be treated differently. The nation has an interest in seeing that older Americans are financially independent. To achieve this end, it provides special tax status for funds that it believes are earmarked for this purpose. The tax isn't forgiven; it's just deferred until the funds are needed in your later years.

Retirement saving is also different because the funding need is not immediate. This means the savings can be channeled into less liquid investments that possibly penalize short-term withdrawals but pay a high return on long-term holdings.

Other than these two characteristics, saving and investing for retirement are the same as for any other purpose. Accordingly, investments for retirement should satisfy all of the guidelines for investments discussed in previous chapters. Most important, there should be a proper diversification of holdings, and the acceptable risk-return trade-off should depend on the size of your nest egg. Only after you have provided for a needed safety margin in your later years should you consider speculative deals with potentially more rewarding or more damaging outcomes.

Company Pension Plans

Company-sponsored retirement plans have become an increasingly important source of income for retired workers. Unfortunately, since the mid-1980s there is evidence that private pension coverage may have actually declined. Recent estimates by the Bureau of Labor Statistics reveal that, in firms with more than 100 workers, 78 percent of all full-time employees were covered by at least one retirement plan. However, in smaller businesses with fewer than 100 workers, only 42 percent were similarly covered.

Employee Retirement Income Security Act (ERISA): Federal act regulating funding and coverage guidelines for tax-qualified, employer-sponsored pension plans.

Qualified retirement plan: One that satisfies conditions set down in ERISA and therefore qualifies for special tax advantages.

The passage of the **Employee Retirement Income Security Act (ERISA)** in 1974 eliminated much of the uncertainty surrounding the payment of company benefits. ERISA set down certain standards for funding of company-sponsored retirement plans, including guidelines for employee coverage and contributions. When a plan meets all of the government-mandated requirements, it becomes a **qualified retirement plan.** This means that taxes are deferred on employer contributions to the retirement fund and on interest earned by the retirement fund.

Taxes do not become due until the benefits of the retirement fund are received by the employee.

Because "qualified" plans offer significant tax advantages, almost all company plans satisfy the ERISA requirements. To understand the advantages of tax deferral, look at the example in Table 17.1. The comparison is based upon an assumed flat tax rate of 28 percent. In Case One, the monies placed into the fund and the interest on the fund are taxed; in Case Two the tax is applied when the fund matures at the end of the 20-year period. In the first example, $2,000 in compensation is set aside each year for investment, but only $1,440 can be invested after taxes. Given an assumed pretax interest rate of 10 percent, the effective after-tax interest rate reduces to 7.2 percent. After 20 years this non-tax-deferred investment fund will accumulate to $64,683.27. In Case Two, the full $2,000 of compensation can be invested and return a pretax interest rate of 10 percent. When the fund matures at the end of 20 years, taxes become due. Applying the same 28 percent tax rate to the distributions, we find that you are still over $26,000 ahead on the tax-deferred investment. This is the power of tax deferral.

Notice that the current example assumes your marginal tax rate is the same in both your preretirement years and your postretirement years. If your real income

TABLE 17.1 • THE POWER OF TAX DEFERRAL UNDER A FLAT 28% TAX RATE

Case One: No Deferral of Taxes			
Year	**Contribution after Taxes**	**Interest Income after Taxes (after-tax rate 7.2%)**	**Ending Balance**
1	$1,440	$ 103.68	$ 1,543.68
2	1,440	214.82	3,198.50
3	1,440	333.97	4,972.48
•	•	•	•
•	•	•	•
•	•	•	•
18	1,440	3,593.48	53,502.97
19	1,440	3,955.89	58,898.87
20	1,440	4,344.40	64,683.27
		Taxes due at maturity	(-0-)
		Ending year's balance after taxes	$64,683.27
Case Two: Deferral of Taxes			
Year	**Tax-Deferred Contribution**	**Tax-Deferred Interest Income (tax-deferred rate 10%)**	**Ending Balance**
1	$2,000	$ 100.00	$ 2,200.00
2	2,000	420.00	4,620.00
3	2,000	662.00	7,282.00
•	•	•	•
•	•	•	•
•	•	•	•
18	2,000	9,119.83	100,318.00
19	2,000	10,231.80	112,550.00
20	2,000	11,455.00	126,005.00
		Taxes due at maturity	(–35,281.40)
		Ending year's balance after taxes	$ 90,723.60

declines after retirement, thus placing you in a lower marginal tax bracket, the benefits of tax deferral can be even greater. On the other hand, for the lucky few who might find themselves in a higher marginal tax bracket after retirement, perhaps because of a tax on Social Security earnings, deferral of income taxes may be an unwise choice.

A pension is nothing more than a promissory note. If you have a pension, what you have is a promise that you will receive certain payments at retirement. Before

Box 17.1

PERSONAL FINANCE NEWS

Late Edition

The Pension Annuitants Protection Act of 1994

Some retirees who thought their retirement benefits were protected by the federal government have been unfortunately surprised to find otherwise. When Congress passed the Employee Retirement Income Security Act (ERISA) of 1974 it also created the Pension Benefit Guaranty Corporation (PBGC) to insure pension benefits against loss. PBGC insurance, however, protects tax-qualified defined-benefit plans only up to an annually determined monthly maximum ($2,642 in 1996). Defined-contribution plans, such as 401(k) savings plans, are not covered.

But even those with defined-benefit plans may not always have their benefits guaranteed by the PBGC. Companies can terminate their defined-benefit plans and their responsibility for future defined benefits by purchasing annuities to cover their obligations. Annuities that transfer liability from the employer to the annuity provider are called benefit distribution annuities. They may be purchased when a pension plan is terminated, or they may be purchased for participants who are retiring or leaving employment with vested benefits.

The PBGC sets down regulations that govern plan terminations by requiring employers to adequately fund the promised benefits. But what happens when an employer funds the plan with retirement annuities and then the company issuing the annuities becomes insolvent? It turns out that once an employer receives PBGC approval to terminate a plan, the PBGC no longer insures those benefits.

Jesse and Irma Bell of Sequin, Texas, were receiving a $780.32 monthly pension check because Jesse, 74, had worked 46 years in the oil fields. Those checks ended abruptly in April 1991, when Executive Life, a bankrupt insurer, was taken over by the state of California. Jesse's old employer had converted his pension into an annuity in the now bankrupt company. Fortunately for the Bells and other Executive Life annuitants, the state of California has been able to continue the annuity payments, but only after a 30 percent cut.

In addition to not covering benefit distribution annuities, the PBGC does not guarantee retirement funds in a defined-contribution account. The value of funds invested in defined-contribution plans will depend on the volatility and stability of the underlying investment. This may surprise many employees who have retirement savings invested in guaranteed investment contracts (GICs). A significant percentage, about 60 percent, of 401(k) assets are in GICs. The term *guaranteed* is misleading. These are not guaranteed by the federal government; although, if the issuer is an insurance company, there may be a state guaranty fund providing partial protection.

Even when benefits are uninsured by the PBGC, they still may not be permanently lost. Under regulations made possible by the Pension Annuitants Protection Act of 1994, the PBGC now requires that plan administrators select the safest available annuity provider, unless it is in the interests of participants and beneficiaries to do otherwise. If they act negligently by placing those funds in highly risky investments, they can be held responsible for any subsequent losses. A court may order the employer to pay the promised amounts plus reasonable prejudgement interest.

The Pension Annuitants Protection Act of 1994 also gives the PBGC greater authority to ensure the health of existing pension plans by requiring increased contributions to underfunded plans. In addition, they can require underfunded plans to disclose their financial information to participants, along with information on the limits of Pension Benefit Guaranty coverage.

The Department of Labor is currently suing several employers who may have violated their fiduciary responsibility to safeguard pension assets. So far, the law has withstood court challenges, and it looks as if employees may be compensated for lost benefits due to bankrupt insurers. Jesse Bell, certainly, hopes the Department of Labor will prevail and restore his lost benefits. At 74 years of age, he also probably wishes it doesn't take too long.

the passage of ERISA it was not uncommon to hear of workers nearing retirement losing all of the promised pension benefits they had been depending on. Some firms purposely terminated workers right before retirement so that they would not have to pay pension benefits. Other, better-intentioned firms found they simply could not afford to pay the promised benefits.

ERISA has remedied this situation by requiring that all qualified pension plans be adequately funded and by setting down rules so that workers could not be denied their rights to an expected pension. It has also created the Pension Benefit Guaranty Corporation (PBGC) to insure promised benefits against unexpected loss. However, even after ERISA, it is still possible for an employee to end his or her career without a pension. Furthermore, ERISA does not set standards for minimum benefits. At retirement you may find that your benefits are not as generous as you thought. For these reasons, and because the pension plan is often a valuable component of the salary package, it deserves close examination.

A careful study of the plan documents listed in Figure 17.2 will provide essential information on the operation of your pension plan. If you have trouble reading these documents, the personnel officer or plan administrator may explain the contents.

DEFINED-BENEFIT AND DEFINED-CONTRIBUTION PLANS All pension plans can be classified as defined-benefit plans, defined-contribution plans, or some combination of the two.

Defined-benefit plan: A pension plan that specifies the monthly benefit you will receive at retirement age.

A **defined-benefit plan** specifies the monthly benefit you will receive when you reach retirement age. Each year the employer contributes to a retirement fund an amount necessary to pay for those promised future benefits. The present contribution is actuarially determined; that is, it is based upon assumed investment returns and probabilities of survival.

Figure 17.2 Qualified plan documents.

Participants in qualified plans are entitled to receive certain documents providing important information on the operation of the plan and their particular interest in the plan. In most cases, these documents will be routinely made available. If they are not, you should demand copies of the following:

Summary Plan Description This general overview of how the retirement plan operates should be written in a clear and understandable form. It contains essential information on the structure of the plan, explaining how benefits are calculated, when they may be received, and most important, how you might lose them.

Summary Annual Report It provides updated information on the plan and its financial status. If the pension fund depends upon an underlying portfolio of investments, it should indicate how well those investments performed over the previous year.

Personal Benefits Statement This may be included within the Summary Annual Report. It will indicate the total amount of your pension benefits that are currently accrued and vested. Each participant is entitled to receive an updated statement once a year. If you have not received one in the last 12 months the plan administrator (listed in the Summary Plan Description) must provide it within 30 days upon written request.

Statement of Deferred Vested Benefits for Terminating Employees If you leave your current employer, and you have a vested right to benefits, you should receive a statement describing those rights and benefits. Copies of this statement are kept on file by the Secretary of Health and Human Resources. If you lose your copy, or for some reason the firm will not provide you one, a duplicate is obtainable through the Social Security Administration upon written request.

As illustrated in Figure 17.3, workers can expect a defined-benefit plan to replace about 30 percent of their final salary with a single life annuity. Such plans covered about 56 percent of workers in medium and large firms in 1993. This was considerably down from 87 percent in 1979. This trend is expected to continue as firms attempt to hold down liabilities for future pension payments.

Defined-contribution plan: A pension plan that defines the current pension plan contribution. Future retirement benefits are dependent upon the underlying investments in the retirement fund.

Under a **defined-contribution plan** you are not guaranteed a specific benefit at retirement. Instead, your benefits will depend upon the investment performance of the retirement fund. Employer contributions go into a separate retirement account for each worker, where they accumulate until retirement. The current value of this account should be indicated on the personal benefits statement (see Figure 17.2). About one-half of workers in medium and large firms were participants in 1993.

In most defined-contribution plans, the funds accumulated in the retirement account may be converted at retirement to an annuity that generates lifetime income. The cost of the annuity and the income generated by the annuity will depend on financial factors at the retirement date. Sometimes personal benefits statements for defined-contribution plans will contain an example of the monthly benefits that might be purchased with your retirement account. This example is only an illustration and should not be mistaken for a guaranteed monthly benefit.

Defined-benefit and defined-contribution plans have offsetting advantages and disadvantages. With a defined-benefit plan, you know how much you will receive, but you don't know how much those dollars will be worth. Inflation can severely erode the purchasing power of benefits that currently appear quite respectable. With a defined-contribution plan, you know how much your retirement fund is currently worth, but you don't know how many dollars you will have at retirement. Remember, this will depend upon future contributions and yet-to-be-determined investment returns.

Both defined-benefit and defined-contribution plans can be integrated with the Social Security system. When they are, your company's benefits and contributions

Figure 17.3 Average replacement rates under defined-benefit plans, 1993.
SOURCE: U.S. Dept. of Labor, *Employee Benefits in Medium and Large Private Establishments, 1993,* Bulletin 2456, 1994, Table 147.

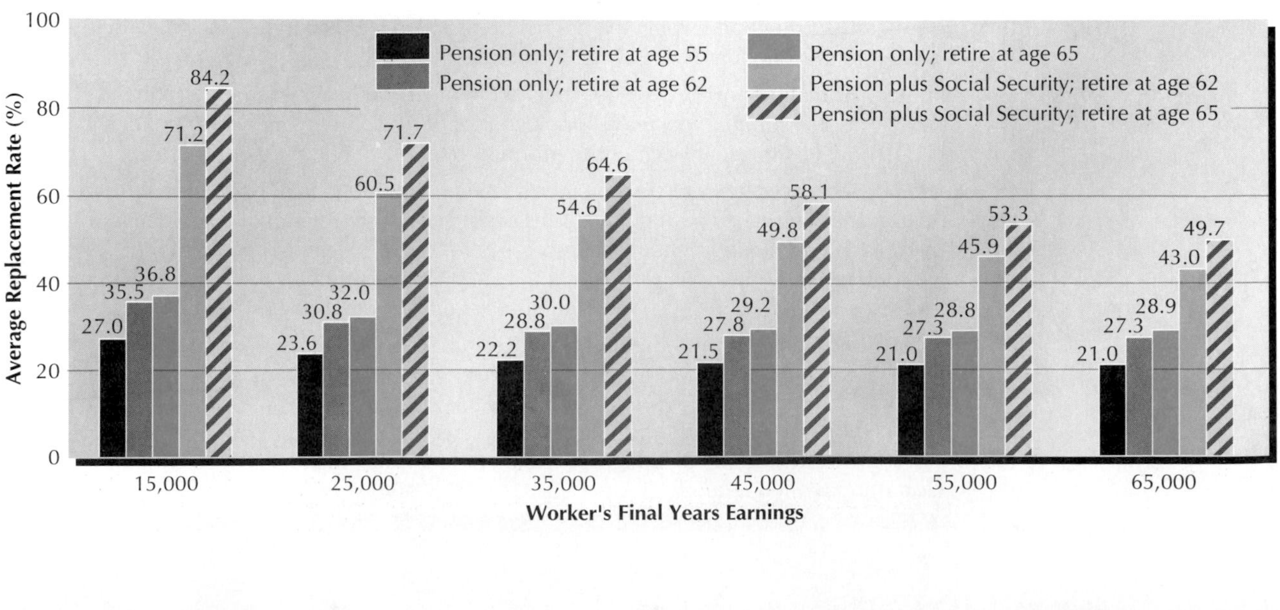

may be less than expected. Defined-benefit plans can be written so that benefit payments from the plan are reduced as Social Security benefits increase. Defined-contribution plans sometimes include part of the Social Security tax in calculating the company's contribution.

CONTRIBUTIONS A few plans require mandatory contributions from employees who wish to participate in the company retirement plan. Those who elect not to participate should find out under what conditions, if any, they may later join. Most do not require employee contributions. However, many defined-contribution plans permit the employee to make a voluntary contribution to the retirement account.

Employee contributions, whether mandatory or voluntary, are not ordinarily deductible against your current income, although the tax on the investment returns while these funds are in the account is deferred. An exception occurs when an employer provides supplementary savings plans such as a 401(k), discussed later.

Accrued benefit: Pension benefits that have been accumulated because of previous credited service.

Vested benefits: Pension benefits that you are entitled to receive regardless of future employment.

VESTING When you participate in a pension plan, you accrue pension benefits. The **accrued benefit** is the benefit that a pension plan participant has accumulated to a particular point in time. Some or all of your accrued benefits may be lost if you leave your present employer. Your rights to your currently promised benefits will depend upon whether they are *vested*. **Vested benefits** are not forfeitable for any reason other than death. You may be fired, or you may quit, but in either case you still retain the right to receive all vested retirement benefits.

ERISA requires that all employee contributions to a retirement plan must be immediately vested. However, there may be a specified waiting period before employer contributions are fully or partially vested. All qualified pension plans must satisfy one of the vesting schedules in Figure 17.4. Under the cliff vesting, no vesting need occur before five years of credited service. After the fifth year, however, all benefits must become fully vested. Graded vesting provides a more gradual approach, with an increasing portion of accrued benefits vested in years three through six. In either case, these represent minimum vesting standards. Many employers allow benefits to vest at a faster pace than is legally required.

Figure 17.4 Minimum vesting requirements.

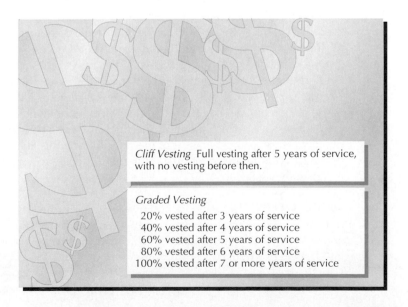

Cliff Vesting Full vesting after 5 years of service, with no vesting before then.

Graded Vesting

20% vested after 3 years of service
40% vested after 4 years of service
60% vested after 5 years of service
80% vested after 6 years of service
100% vested after 7 or more years of service

CREDITED SERVICE It is important that you understand how years of service are defined when determining your rights and future benefits. For several reasons, you may have fewer years of credited service than calendar years of employment. Under all plans, you are credited with a year of service only if you have worked a sufficient number of hours within a 12-month period. The required number of hours, typically 1,000, can be found in the Summary Plan Description.

In the Summary Plan Description you will also find a definition for a break in service. Plans generally require that you work at least 500 hours per 12-month period to avoid a break in service. A break in service may delay the vesting of benefits and cause a forfeiture of nonvested benefits. Under federal law, qualified retirement plans cannot terminate nonvested benefits unless the break in service is greater than five years. Furthermore, firms cannot interrupt vesting for maternity or paternity leaves of one year or less.

Normal retirement age: The age at which you are entitled to full retirement benefits.

Early retirement age: The earliest age at which you can retire with reduced benefits.

RETIREMENT BENEFITS Most plans specify age 65 as **normal retirement age.** At this age, you are eligible to receive the full pension benefits indicated in the plan. Many plans also specify an **early retirement age** at which you can retire with reduced benefits. A common requirement for early retirement benefits is the attainment of age 55 and the completion of 10 years of service. The amount by which your benefits will be reduced will depend upon the time interval between the early retirement age and the normal retirement age. You may be given a schedule of reduced payments or a formula for calculating the reduction factor.

The law forbids an employer from requiring you to retire at any age. If the normal retirement age is 65, you have a right to postpone receiving benefits until age 70. Furthermore, the company plan must provide you with additional retirement benefits for years of service beyond normal retirement age.

Flat benefit method: Pension benefits are equal to a specified percentage of compensation or a specific dollar benefit.

Unit benefit method: Pension benefits depend directly upon units of credited service.

In a defined-benefit plan, retirement benefits at normal retirement age are computed under a flat benefit method, a unit benefit method, or some combination of the two. With the **flat benefit method,** monthly benefits are equal to either a specific percentage of compensation or a specific dollar payment. Most plans use the **unit benefit method,** where length of service is entered directly into the benefit formula. For example, the formula might state that your monthly normal retirement benefit will be $20 times your years of service. Alternatively, it might employ a percentage formula, such as 2 percent of salary times your years of service.

Regardless of whether the flat or unit method is employed, you will receive better inflation protection when benefits are stated not in specific dollars but rather as a percentage of your salary. This is so because your salary at retirement should reflect the higher cost of living at that time. Percentage formulas use either the *career average approach* or the *final average approach*. With the career average approach, percentage benefits are based on your average compensation over all years of service. Most plans use the final average approach. It bases benefits on a percentage of your average compensation over the last three or five years. Since the final average approach responds more rapidly to an inflationary rise in wages, it is usually preferred.

MEDICAL BENEFITS You do not qualify for enrollment in the Medicare program until you are age 65. If you presently have health insurance through your employer and you plan to retire before age 65, be sure you have adequate alternative coverage between when you retire and when you and your spouse turn 65. It helps if your employer provides medical benefits for retired workers. In firms with over 100 employees, about one-half of participants in retirement plans have their med-

Box 17.2 SIMPLIFYING FINANCIAL PLANNING
Checklist of Questions for Your Pension Plan Review

- What type of pension plan do I have (defined-benefit or defined-contribution)? ❑
- Is it a qualified retirement plan covered by ERISA and insured by the PBGC? ❑
- In order to participate, must I contribute to the pension plan? If so, how much? ❑
- Can I make voluntary contributions to my employer's pension plan? What are the tax consequences of these contributions? ❑
- Are my benefits fully vested? If not, how long must I remain employed before they are? ❑
- How many years of credited service have I accumulated? How many hours do I have to work to earn a year of credited service? ❑
- How is a break in service defined? What happens to my benefits if I have a break in service? ❑
- What are my likely benefits at normal retirement age? How much would I receive at normal retirement age if I terminated employment today? ❑
- How are my benefits at normal retirement age calculated? What is the benefit formula? ❑
- Is there an early retirement age? If so, how are my benefits reduced for early retirement? ❑
- If I become disabled before retirement, may I receive disability benefits through the pension plan? ❑
- If I die, will my spouse or dependents receive any payout from my pension plan? ❑
- What are the payout options at retirement? Can I receive a lump-sum distribution at termination or retirement? ❑
- At retirement will I receive a single life annuity or a joint life annuity? If I am to receive a joint life annuity, how will benefits be reduced at the first death? ❑

ical coverage at least partially paid for by their previous employer. Such support, however, may not be unconditional. After experiencing significant increases in the cost of medical insurance, many companies have either trimmed back or eliminated medical coverage provided to retired workers. At the present time it is unclear whether promises made by employers concerning medical benefits for retired workers have the same status as promises regarding pension benefits. This is now being decided in the courts.

Regardless of whether your employer subsidizes medical benefits for retired workers, you still may have the right to continued coverage under a group health plan sponsored by an employer with 20 or more workers. Your rights are set down in the Consolidated Omnibus Reconciliation Act of 1985 (COBRA). For 60 days after retiring, you may elect to continue group health coverage. If you make this election, you can extend the group health coverage for another 18 months, after which the group policy may be converted to an individual policy. Under COBRA, the employer does not have to pay for your insurance after you leave employment. However, by continuing coverage under the employer-sponsored plan, you avoid having to satisfy preexisting conditions clauses that might exclude benefit payments under a new insurance plan.

When you do turn age 65, you most likely will qualify for enrollment in the Medicare program. Moreover, for six months after you turn 65, you cannot be denied private "medigap" insurance because of any preexisting illness. See Chapter 7 for details on both of these programs.

DISABILITY BENEFITS Some company retirement plans also include disability income protection. Contributions by the company to the retirement plan may continue during periods of disability. In other situations, the plan may begin paying out monthly benefits at the onset of the disability, regardless of the employee's age. Furthermore, the monthly benefits may be computed under a more generous disability benefit formula. A review of the sections in Chapter 7 on disability insurance will help you determine the quality of this coverage.

SURVIVORS' BENEFITS ERISA now requires that if you die before your retirement benefits begin, the vested portion of your benefits must be used to provide death benefits for your spouse. It also mandates that married workers automatically be provided a **joint and last survivor annuity** at retirement, unless both spouses elect otherwise. This means that payments will continue as long as either you or your spouse is still alive, although the amount may be reduced after the first death. Federal law requires that monthly payments from the survivor's annuity be more than 50 percent, but less than 100 percent, of the amount paid when both the spouse and the participant were alive. The law also specifies that the benefits cannot be reduced if the surviving spouse remarries. The alternative is a **single life annuity,** for which all payments cease at the pensioner's death. The value of the single life annuity and the joint and last survivor annuity must be actuarially equivalent. That means that the total expected payouts under the two annuity options should be the same. Accordingly, since the potential benefit period under a single life annuity is less than a joint and last survivor annuity, the single life option will provide larger monthly benefits.

Joint and last survivor annuity: Periodic benefits continue as long as you or your spouse is alive.

Single life annuity: All periodic payments cease at the death of the annuitant.

The choice is a difficult one. Do you select larger monthly payments over your life or lower monthly payments over both your life and your spouse's? Before making the decision, you must understand that the expected total payments are actuarially equivalent. Given life expectancies and interest returns, the two annuities are worth the same. Accordingly, if both you and your spouse need the cash flow generated by the joint and survivor annuity and you are both in average health, don't gamble on the single life annuity. You may do better under the single life annuity, but the odds are just as good that you will do worse, in which case the surviving spouse may suffer financial hardships.

DISTRIBUTIONS Distributions from a retirement account may occur for reasons other than just retirement. If you die, become disabled, leave your current employment, or suffer financial hardship, you may be entitled to receive the funds in your retirement plan. The distribution may consist of a single payment, termed a lump-sum distribution, or an annuity, a series of periodic payments. When you receive the distributions, you must pay ordinary income taxes on the proceeds from all tax-deferred accumulations. However, the tax consequences may be postponed further if you roll over the distribution into another tax-deferred retirement account.

If you do take a lump-sum distribution and don't roll it over, all taxes on the benefits will become due at the time of distribution. The lump-sum distribution is eligible, however, for tax-advantageous 5- or 10-year forward income averaging. Under this formula, the tax is based upon the assumption that the distribution would be your only income over a five-year period. For most taxpayers, the use of five-year averaging will reduce the tax on the lump-sum distribution. Of course, choosing an annuity instead of a lump-sum distribution may have even more favorable tax consequences. Those who do take the lump-sum distribution usually have an immediate need for the funds.

An early or late withdrawal of funds from a retirement account may trigger tax penalties in addition to income taxes. In the Tax Reform Act of 1986, Congress imposed a uniform set of penalties on early and late withdrawals from almost all types of group and individual retirement accounts, including those discussed later in this chapter. An early withdrawal is defined as any withdrawal before age $59^1/_2$. With a few exceptions, such as death, disability, excessive medical expenses, or a lifetime annuity, a 10 percent tax penalty is levied on all early withdrawals.

The penalty on late withdrawals is much worse. Payouts from retirement funds must begin by April 1 of the next calendar year after you reach $70^1/_2$. In addition, these payouts must be large enough to distribute the fund over your own or your spouse's life expectancy. If you fail to meet the minimum required distribution, there is an onerous 50 percent tax penalty on the difference between the actual distribution and the minimum required distribution.

Other Company Retirement Plans

Companies may offer savings vehicles that differ from the pension format discussed above in one of two ways: One, they may not provide the same type of scheduled contributions or benefits expected of a long-term pension plan; or, two, they may be used to save for needs other than retirement. Such plans are often offered as a supplement to, rather than an alternative to, a typical pension plan. By not tying the employer or the employee into a scheduled set of contributions, they allow each to supplement the basic benefits afforded by the pension plan whenever possible.

ERISA specifies limits on the total amount contributed to company-sponsored retirement plans by both the employer and employee. The guidelines are complicated but generous. Most middle-income taxpayers are not likely to be affected. For example, the combined limit on defined-contribution plans is currently equal to the lesser of 25 percent of employee compensation or $30,000.

Profit-sharing plan: A defined-contribution plan in which contributions are contingent upon the profitability of the firm.

PROFIT-SHARING PLANS A **profit-sharing plan** is a type of defined-contribution plan whereby the employer makes contributions into an individual employee's account according to a predetermined formula. Qualified profit-sharing plans must satisfy many of the same rules governing qualified pension plans. Unlike a pension plan, however, the employee may not have to wait until retirement to receive distributions. The plan can be set to pay out after a fixed number of years. One disadvantage for planning purposes is that the firm must contribute only when it earns a profit. Thus, the amount the profit-sharing plan will contain at retirement is highly uncertain.

401(k) salary-reduction plan: A savings plan that permits earners to defer the taxability of income until funds are withdrawn.

401(k) SALARY-REDUCTION PLANS In place of, or in addition to, a qualified pension or profit-sharing plan, you may be able to set up a **401(k) salary-reduction plan,** which defers a portion of your compensation for retirement. Although you may currently owe Social Security taxes on the earnings, federal income taxes are deferred until you receive the money.

The maximum tax-deferred employee contribution was limited to $9,240 in 1995. It is adjusted upward each year for increases in the Consumer Price Index. The limit is coordinated with those on SEPs and TSAs discussed below. This means that contributions to other plans may reduce your allowable tax-deferred contribution to a 401(k).

Usually the employer provides a choice of investment vehicles into which the funds may be placed while earning tax-deferred returns. Furthermore, many employers offer matching contributions. These contributions, plus the current reduction in income taxes, typically make salary-reduction plans an excellent long-term investment.

Employee stock ownership plan (ESOP): A savings plan that provides employees benefits in the form of company stock.

EMPLOYEE STOCK OWNERSHIP PLANS (ESOPs) An **employee stock ownership plan (ESOP)** can function in many different ways, but most operate like profit-sharing plans. The difference is that contributions are invested primarily in the employer's stock, and contributions are not necessarily dependent on profits. In addition, all distributions must be made in the form of stock.

An employee stock ownership program is an inappropriate instrument for retirement savings. Because most of the funds are concentrated in the stock of one company, it does not provide any safety through diversification. The value of the fund is likely to swing widely as the company's fortunes change. You could lose both your job and your savings at the same time.

New regulations remedy some of the criticism. Under the Tax Reform Act of 1986, certain employees nearing retirement may elect to place part of their ESOP account in diversified investments.

403(b) tax-sheltered annuity: A tax-advantaged savings plan for employees of nonprofit institutions.

403(B) TAX-SHELTERED ANNUITIES (TSAs) Only employees of nonprofit institutions are eligible for **403(b) tax-sheltered annuities.** Like the 401(k), they require the employee to enter into a salary-reduction agreement with the employer. Taxes on contributions and returns are deferred until the dollars are withdrawn. The limit on employee contributions is currently $9,500. This will increase as the contribution limit on 401(k) plans rises above $9,500.

Simplified employee pension plan (SEP): An employer-sponsored retirement plan utilizing individual retirement accounts.

SIMPLIFIED EMPLOYEE PENSION PLANS (SEPs) A **simplified employee pension plan (SEP)** has advantages for both the employer and employee. For the employer, the paperwork and administrative costs are much less than under a qualified pension plan. For the employee, all amounts deposited in the SEP are immediately vested. As an alternative to a qualified pension plan, the SEP plan permits the employer to set up a tax-deferred individual retirement account for each employee. Into this account the employer can contribute an amount equal to 15 percent of the employee's salary up to a generous annually set maximum. The employee also has the right to make additional tax-deferred contributions. The limit on voluntary contributions is the same as that for 401(k) salary reduction plans.

Individual Retirement Plans

If you do not have a company retirement plan or you would like to supplement a company plan through additional private savings, the benefits of tax deferral can also be achieved through non-corporate-sponsored investments. The rules governing early and late withdrawals from individual retirement plans are generally the same as for company-sponsored plans. Distributions before age $59^1/_2$ incur a 10 percent penalty tax, and insufficient withdrawals after age $70^1/_2$ suffer a 50 percent tax penalty. The four most common are IRAs, Keoghs, retirement annuities, and home ownership.

Individual retirement account (IRA): An individual retirement account that qualifies for special tax treatment under IRS regulations.

INDIVIDUAL RETIREMENT ACCOUNTS (IRAs) The **individual retirement account (IRA)** is a trust or custodial account approved by the Internal Revenue Service. In a trust or custodial relationship, the funds are temporarily held by someone other than the investor. However, you as the investor may still retain control over how the funds are managed. The IRS approval indicates that the form of the IRA satisfies the requirements for special tax treatment. It does not suggest anything about the merits of investing in this particular account. Poorly managed IRAs can offer low returns and high risks while still maintaining IRS approval of their tax status.

Box 17.3 SAVING MONEY
Consolidating Pension Accounts through Rollovers

If you have opened up IRAs over the last several years, or you have pension accounts from previous employers, you probably have trouble keeping track of your retirement savings. Many small accounts can also be costly, since each is likely to charge a management fee. By consolidating these accounts, you can simplify your bookkeeping and achieve some economies of scale in your investments.

With tax-deferred retirement accounts, of course, taxes become due when the funds are withdrawn. Taxes, however, can be deferred further if the funds are redeposited in another tax-deferred retirement account within 60 days. This tax-free transfer of assets from one retirement plan to another is termed a *rollover*. In order to ensure that you don't violate the 60-day limit, it is best to arrange a direct transfer from one account to another, so that you never have receipt of the funds.

A rollover is also useful for deferring taxes on a lump-sum distribution from a qualified retirement plan. A distribution of previously nontaxable contributions to retirement savings might occur upon termination of employment. In most cases, this can have severe tax consequences, if your age is less than 59½ years and you do not roll over these funds into another retirement plan, such as an IRA. You will have to pay both ordinary income taxes and a 10 percent penalty on the funds you receive. Using a tax-free rollover, however, you can avoid the penalty by postponing receipt until after age 59½, and allow your savings to continue earning tax-deferred income.

If you decide to take the distribution and not roll it over, there are still some ways to hold your taxes down. Under certain circumstances, the 10 percent penalty might be avoided. These include disability, receipt of an annuity, exorbitant medical expenses, and payment under a divorce or separation agreement. In addition, the ordinary income tax can be reduced through five-year forward averaging on non-IRA distributions. This allows you to pay the same tax that you would if you received the distribution over five years instead of one. By spreading the income out over five years, you lower the marginal tax rate and the total taxes due. You can use five-year averaging only if you are over 59½ and you have been covered by your employer's retirement plan for at least five years. Furthermore, you can use it only once in your lifetime, so use it wisely.

For the majority of Americans, an IRA is probably the most convenient, and most tax advantageous, means to save individually for retirement. Taxes on income earned by funds in the account are deferred until the earnings are withdrawn. Furthermore, for many workers the annual contributions are either partially or fully deductible against current income. This effectively defers taxes on the contribution until it is withdrawn from the account in later years.

Eligibility. Every individual receiving earned income, or alimony, can contribute to an IRA. The maximum annual contribution is restricted to the lesser of earned income or $2,000. For married couples, each may contribute up to $2,000 of earned income, for a combined total contribution of $4,000. You may even open an IRA for a spouse with no earned income.

Part or all of the IRA may be taken as an adjustment to gross income on your individual tax return. The full amount is deductible for those who are not covered by a retirement plan at work. For those who are, or who are filing a joint return with someone who is, the size of the deduction will depend upon adjusted gross income before the IRA deduction. Singles may deduct the full amount of their contributions when their incomes are less than $25,000. At incomes between $25,000 and $35,000 they are still entitled to a partial deduction. Married couples with combined incomes of less than $40,000 can deduct the full amount. Their IRA deduction is phased out between $40,000 and $50,000. The worksheet for calculating the partial deduction on 1995 federal income taxes is presented in Figure 17.5.

If filing status is:	Enter on line 1:	
Single, or Head of Household	$35,000	
Married-joint return, or Qualifying widow(er)	$50,000	
Married-separate return	$10,000	
1. Amount from above		$ ______
2. Adjusted gross income		______
3. Subtract line 2 from line 1		______
4. Maximum partial deduction. Multiply line 3 by 20% (0.20). If the result is not a multiple of $10, round it to the next highest multiple of $10 (for example, $611.40 rounded to $620). However, if the result is less than $200, but more than zero, enter $200.		$ ______

Figure 17.5 Worksheet for calculating maximum partial deduction. (Use this worksheet only if the adjusted gross income is within phase-out range.)

Taxes on deductible IRA contributions are delayed, not forgiven. When contributions are withdrawn, taxes will become due on the portion of the withdrawal resulting from previously untaxed contributions and investment earnings. A deductible IRA contribution can be an excellent tax-advantageous investment for young adults with moderate incomes. They are able to capture both the immediate benefit of the tax reduction and the long-term benefit of tax deferral over the many years until retirement. As was demonstrated in Table 17.1, the benefits of tax deferral can be substantial.

Investments. You cannot invest your IRA funds in life insurance or in collectibles other than gold or silver U.S. coins. Nor can you borrow from the account, use it as collateral for a loan, or engage in investments that put you at risk for more than the value of the IRA. Other than these few rules, how you invest your IRA is a matter of considerable choice. You can place it in CDs, annuities, mutual funds, or real estate, or you can open a self-directed IRA through a brokerage house and organize your own portfolio of stocks and bonds.

The IRA is only one component of your investment portfolio. Where you should invest your IRA will depend on the risk-return trade-off that is acceptable to you, and the diversity and risk in your non-IRA investments. In general, however, you probably want to consider investments that generate high ordinary income as candidates for inclusion in an IRA. Taxes are deferred on both deductible contributions and investment returns. It makes no sense to use the IRA for investments that generate uncertain tax-postponed capital gains, since taxes are already deferred.

Keogh (HR-10) plan: A tax-deferred pension account for self-employed individuals.

KEOGH (HR-10) PLANS If you derive any of your earnings from self-employment, you can set up a **Keogh (HR-10) plan.** Suppose you work by day for a corporation with a qualified corporate pension plan, but by night you run your own business. Part of the earned income from your self-employment may be tax-sheltered for retirement in a Keogh, even though you are already participating in the corporate retirement plan as an employee.

The limits on contributions to a Keogh are more generous than those governing IRAs. You can contribute 20 percent of your net income from self-employment, up to a maximum nontaxable contribution of $30,000. Rules governing withdrawals and related penalties are about the same as for IRAs.

RETIREMENT ANNUITIES In the early years of the family life cycle, when you have many responsibilities, it is important that you provide an estate for the protection of your survivors. In the later years, when you have fewer family responsibilities, it is more important to protect yourself against the possibility that your estate may run out before your death. Annuities can provide such assurance.

Annuity contract: A contract that provides for some form of periodic payment.

Accumulation period: The term over which the principal in the contract is building.

Annuity contracts sold by life insurance companies are a convenient means of saving for retirement and of providing security in retirement. Coinciding with these two objectives, annuities have two distinct periods: the accumulation period and the liquidation period.

During the **accumulation period** the principal builds through investments and returns on investments, while benefits are deferred. The annuity contract may allow the buyer to make a single investment (a single premium annuity) or a series of investments during the accumulation period.

Fixed annuity: An annuity in which the principal is guaranteed.

You can purchase either fixed or variable annuities. The distinction has to do with the preservation of principal during the accumulation period. The value of a **fixed annuity** can only increase, whereas the value of a variable annuity can move both up and down. Typically, the interest rate on fixed annuities is guaranteed for a short period of time, such as a year. After this initial period, the interest rate can be changed at the discretion of the insurance company, so long as it doesn't fall below some guaranteed minimal interest rate, such as 3 percent.

Variable annuity: The value of the annuity is dependent upon the market performance of a specified investment fund.

The principal in a **variable annuity** is invested in a portfolio of securities. Therefore, the value of a variable annuity will increase or decrease with the changing value of the underlying securities. The future worth of the annuity will depend on the portfolio's financial performance. It if does poorly, you could lose some or all of your principal.

Liquidation period: The term over which the annuity pays out periodic benefits.

Annuity starting date: The date when the annuity begins periodic payments.

When the accumulation period ends, you can typically receive the accumulated cash value in a lump-sum payment or in the form of an annuity. In the **liquidation period** the owner receives the annuity benefit in monthly or annual installments. When you elect the type of payments to be received, you are said to annuitize the contract. The **annuity starting date** is the point in time when the liquidation period begins.

Immediate annuity: Payments begin one period from the current date.

Deferred annuity: Payments are deferred until some later time period.

An **immediate annuity** begins payments one period from the date it is purchased. How much income an annuity might purchase is indicated in Figure 17.6. Annuities that defer benefits until some later period are called **deferred annuities.** During the accumulation period, when benefits are deferred, taxes on the investment buildup of principal are also postponed. This makes deferred annuities a tax-advantageous savings vehicle. As with other retirement accounts, income taxes become due when the tax-deferred accumulations are withdrawn. Likewise, there is a 10 percent tax penalty on early distributions before age $59^1/_2$ The early withdrawal penalty does not apply in cases of death or disability or when payments are received as an annuity over the life of the annuitant or his or her spouse.

In addition to the penalties levied by the government on early withdrawal, the insurance company may impose a surrender charge in the early years. Some policies contain a bailout provision that permits you to surrender the policy without charges if the rate paid on the annuity falls below some initially guaranteed rate. Together, tax penalties and surrender charges restrict the use of annuities to long-term savings objectives, such as retirement.

This doesn't necessarily mean you are stuck with your current annuity. If you have held the annuity for more than five years, the surrender charges should be low or nonexistent. The typical surrender charge is about 7 percent of the investment in the first year and declines by about 1 percent a year until it reaches zero.

Suppose you purchase a single life annuity with a single payment of $100,000. The monthly payments begin immediately and end at your death. How much would you receive each month? The answers below indicate that the older you are and the higher the rate of interest, the better your monthly benefits will be.

Males

	Starting Age		
Interest Rate	60	65	70
9%	$929	$1,026	$1,165
8%	866	964	1,103
7%	803	902	1,041

Females

	Starting Age		
Interest Rate	60	65	70
9%	$847	$910	$1,005
8%	783	847	943
7%	719	784	882

NOTE: Calculations are based on the 1983 Group Annuity Mortality Table published by the Society of Actuaries.

Figure 17.6 How much will $100,000 buy?

In addition, tax penalties can be avoided if you transfer funds from your current annuity into another through what is known as a "1035 exchange." Your new company can help arrange the tax-free transfer. Even with surrender charges, if the previous insurer is paying a low return or is financially unsound, it may be worthwhile to arrange a tax-free reallocation of your funds.

There are many ways you may decide to receive the proceeds from the annuity. You can elect to receive a single life or a joint and last survivor annuity, already discussed in the section on survivors' benefits in qualified retirement plans. Under these options you are assured of receiving benefits no matter how long you (single life annuity) or you and your spouse (joint and last survivor annuity) may live.

Of course, if benefits are based entirely upon survival, the possibility of an early death means you, the annuitant, may never receive the cost of the annuity in expected benefits. For this reason, many annuitants desire a *refund feature*. This guarantees that payments will continue until they have at least refunded the cost of the annuity. Accordingly, should you die during the guaranteed period, payments would continue to your named beneficiary for the remainder of the guaranteed refund period.

The period of guaranteed payments need not coincide with the refund period. Annuities can be written to guarantee any number of payments over 5, 10, 15, or 20 years. Of course, the longer the guarantee period, the smaller will be the annuity payment. A single life annuity with all payments ceasing at death will provide you with the greatest periodic benefit per dollar of cost.

Purchasing an annuity with guaranteed payments does not guarantee that the life insurance company selling the annuity will be around to make those payments. The insurance company is only as secure as its own investments. Given the recent volatility in financial markets, some of those investments may not be as safe as was once thought. This, and the long-term nature of the relationship, make it essential that you check out the financial stability of the company issuing the policy in *Best's*

Insurance Reports. As with life insurance, purchase an annuity only from a company with an A+ rating for financial stability.

Retirement annuities receive the same tax treatment as nondeductible IRA contributions, but there is no limit on the amount you may invest. Taxes on investment earnings are deferred until they are withdrawn during the liquidation period.

HOME OWNERSHIP For many people, home ownership is an integral part of their retirement plan. They look forward to having the mortgage paid off and seeing an end to the monthly mortgage payments. Thus, equity in a home, equal to market value less the mortgage balance, represents an important source of savings for the elderly. The home ownership rate among those in the early retirement ages of 55 to 64 is close to 80 percent.

Obviously, owning a home is considered by many an important means of saving for retirement. Interest payments on the mortgage are tax deductible, and you pay no tax on the appreciation in market value until you sell. Furthermore, taxes on the capital gain arising from the sale may be postponed if you reinvest in another home. The real bonus comes when you sell after age 55, because you are then allowed to exclude from capital gains taxes $125,000 of the gains accumulated over the many years of home ownership. This is a once-in-a-lifetime exclusion, so you should consider your financial situation carefully before taking it. It is fully explained in IRS Publication 523, *Tax Information on Selling Your Home*.

Home ownership can be an important source of savings for the future, but there are some potential disadvantages you should be aware of. Markets may rise and fall, and in efficient financial markets the past may be an inaccurate guide to the future. The housing market did very well in the 1970s as the baby-boom generation entered the age of home ownership. What might happen in the twenty-first century, when these same individuals retire and sell homes that are no longer needed, is highly uncertain. In this potential market, those who rely on the equity in a home for financial support in retirement may be very disappointed.

The main point is that you should always attempt to reduce your risks through diversification. Don't rely on home ownership, or any other single investment, as the only source of retirement income. As one component in a comprehensive and diversified savings plan, it is likely to be a very good, tax-advantageous investment.

Having a good chunk of your retirement savings locked up in your home can also be a problem if you need those savings for maintenance expenditures. A reverse mortgage could let you have your savings and your home at the same time. With a **reverse mortgage,** also called an *equity conversion* loan, the equity in your home serves as collateral for the loan. What makes this loan unique is that repayment of principal and interest is deferred until the house is sold, regardless of when that may be. The loan may provide a line of credit, a lump-sum payment, or, as is the most common option, monthly disbursements. The monthly payout may extend over a fixed number of years or for as long as you remain in the home. When the home is sold, the lender is repaid debt plus interest. The Federal Housing Administration insures reverse mortgages up to about $125,000, thus guaranteeing lenders that the equity will be sufficient to cover the amount owed at sale.

Reverse mortgage: Allows retirees to remain in their home while accessing the home equity for supplemental income.

ESTABLISHING A PERSONAL RETIREMENT PLAN

We have already examined the various forms your retirement savings might take, but we have not yet answered the question of how much to save. The easy response is that you should save enough to meet your goals. All planning involves a statement of goals and a method for achieving those goals. In retirement planning the goal is a specific standard of living in your later years. Your standard is a personal decision. Do you plan to purchase a pleasure yacht and cruise the high seas, or do you plan to live on handouts from charitable organizations?

Obviously, your goals will depend upon more than mere desires. They will be affected by your present income, your ability and willingness to save, and your expected Social Security benefits. To come up with a viable plan, you might begin by setting a goal and then calculating how much you would have to save to achieve it. If the required savings appear out of line with your present abilities, then revise the goal and repeat your calculations. You should eventually arrive at a goal and a level of current savings that balance your immediate and future needs.

Financial planners often state that retirement planning should be thought of as a three-legged stool, with Social Security, company pensions, and private savings providing each of the essential supporting legs.

Social Security Benefits

Part of your retirement planning will be dependent upon our Social Security system. Because of its uncertain operation, some have accused the system of generating social insecurity. The Social Security taxes you pay each year do not go into an investment fund where they accumulate for your retirement years. The Social Security tax is simply a transfer tax. It transfers income from working Americans to those receiving Social Security benefits.

Because there is no investment fund, and because the government retains the power to tax, the system technically cannot go bankrupt. However, the average age of the population is expected to increase into the twenty-first century. There are currently 5 working persons for each elderly person; by the year 2030 there will be only 2.5 working persons for each elderly person. As this trend continues, the government will confront a difficult choice. It must either increase taxes on the working population or reduce benefits. In anticipation of future problems, some changes are already set to go into effect.

RETIREMENT AGE Normal retirement age for full Social Security benefits is currently age 65, but the baby-boom generation will have to wait a little longer. Beginning in 2003, normal retirement age will increase in installments until it reaches age 67 in 2027.

Additional incentives for delayed retirement should also hold down the cost of benefits. For each year you delay receiving benefits beyond age 65 up to age 71, benefits are increased. For those born after 1942, the yearly increase for delayed retirement is 8 percent.

There are no plans to change the early retirement age of 62. However, benefits at early retirement will eventually fall from 80 to 70 percent of monthly benefits at normal retirement age.

RETIREMENT BENEFITS In a complicated manner, Social Security benefits are based on the amount you paid into the system and your age at retirement. The methodology for calculating retirement benefits is contained in Appendix B on the Social Security system. You can save yourself considerable work by having the Social Security Administration estimate your future retirement benefits. How to obtain an estimate of your benefits is also discussed in Appendix B. If you do not yet have a personalized estimate of benefits, you can temporarily use the benchmark estimates in Table 17.2.

Two-earner couples can each qualify separately for a pension, or one may qualify as a dependent on the other's earning record. A dependent spouse at normal retirement age will receive benefits equal to 50 percent of the benefits received by the retired wage earner. Whether you should qualify on your own record or your spouse's will depend on which generates more in retirement benefits.

RETIREMENT TEST The government would like to reserve benefits for those who are truly retired, so it reduces benefit payments as earnings increase. In 1995, those under 65 and receiving retirement benefits could earn up to $8,160 before Social Security checks were reduced by $1 for each $2 earned. Between ages 65 and 69 they could earn $11,280 without reduction. For earnings in excess of this annually determined threshold, Social Security benefits are reduced by $1 for every $3 you earn. Only from age 70 on is there no reduction for earnings.

The retirement test may be necessary to hold down the cost of the Social Security system, but it does have an undesirable side effect. It severely penalizes older Americans who choose to remain in the work force. As a result of the Social Security offset, each dollar earned above the threshold by those aged 65 to 69 is effectively reduced by 33 cents. Furthermore, if the marginal tax rate from combined federal and state taxes is 28 percent, then the government takes 28 additional cents from each incremental dollar of earnings in taxes. The 28 cents in income taxes on earned income and the 33 cents in lost benefits add up to an effective marginal tax on additional earnings of 61 percent. Moreover, this does not take into account a possible increase in taxable Social Security benefits.

TAXATION OF SOCIAL SECURITY BENEFITS Before 1984, Social Security benefits were tax free. Congress then passed a law that subjected up to 50 percent of these benefits to federal income taxes. Beginning in 1994, the maximum amount that could be included in taxable income was raised to 85 percent.

The calculations for determining the taxable portion are complicated. A simplified rule is that if the total of nonbenefit income plus one-half of Social Security benefits exceeds $25,000 to $34,000 for single individuals and $32,000 to $44,000 for married couples, than 50 to 85 percent of the earnings could be taxed.

As stated in the previous section, the combined effect of earned income taxes and the Social Security offset can have a negative impact on work incentives for

TABLE 17.2 • ESTIMATES OF SOCIAL SECURITY RETIREMENT BENEFITS

	Average Annual Social Security–Covered Earnings				
	Less than $10,000	$10,000 –20,000	$20,000 –30,000	$30,000 –50,000	$50,000 and over
Claiming benefits at age 65					
Worker alone	$7,550	$ 9,540	$11,620	$14,620	$16,080
Worker with spouse	9,790	12,390	15,100	18,990	20,900
Claiming benefits at age 62					
Worker alone	6,030	7,630	9,290	11,700	12,860
Worker with spouse	8,860	11,210	13,650	17,170	18,880

high-income retirees. Such workers might end up with only 39 cents of each additional dollar earned. The disincentive is even greater if the earned income results in additional taxation of Social Security benefits. Remember that under the retirement test, an additional dollar of earnings can reduce Social Security benefits by 33 cents. However, the remaining 67 cents, which is not offset by the retirement test, may now be included in taxable income. At a 50 percent inclusion ratio and a 28 percent marginal tax rate this would result in an additional 9 cents (67 × 0.5 × 0.28) in taxes. This could leave working pensioners with as little as 30 cents (39 – 9) out of each marginal dollar of earned income.

Retirees depending on distributions from tax-deferred retirement accounts can mitigate the effects of the tax on Social Security benefits with proper tax planning. First, avoid unnecessarily large distributions in a single year that may put you above the base amount. Second, it may be worthwhile to distribute the account completely before Social Security benefits begin. In this way the principal in the account will not show up as future income, producing taxable Social Security benefits.

COST-OF-LIVING ADJUSTMENTS One particularly attractive characteristic of Social Security retirement pensions is that they are periodically increased to offset the rise in the price level. Most private pensions provide for fixed dollar benefits during retirement. Over time these constant dollar benefits will purchase fewer goods and services. Having Social Security as part of your retirement income ensures you will receive at least partial inflation protection.

Estimating and Saving for Your Retirement Needs

What is needed is a simple process that gets you started planning for retirement in your early years but that can also be refined as you approach retirement, permitting more exact planning as your needs become more apparent. One way of doing this is first to target your retirement needs and then estimate the annual savings necessary to meet that target. Each year, as new information becomes available, it can be incorporated into your retirement planning, and a new savings requirement can be calculated. Although the target may move each year, if you take the indicated steps you should arrive at your retirement goals. In this section we provide two methods for estimating your retirement needs. The first approach simplifies planning by assuming that investment returns and the inflation rate are identical. The second approach involves more-complicated computations but allows you more control over assumed investment returns and assumed rates of inflation.

A SIMPLIFIED APPROACH Younger workers with many years until retirement cannot be certain about economic conditions between now and retirement. They can easily be sidetracked by dwelling on these uncertainties. It is far better to gloss over them with simplifying assumptions, while at the same time building in a safety margin to cover potential misfortunes. This can be accomplished by conservatively assuming that interest rates and inflation rates cancel each other out. Thus, inflation forecasts and complicated financial calculations are eliminated.

Figure 17.7 contains a worksheet that may be used for retirement planning by either a single individual or a household with a single market worker. In households where both spouses have separate retirement plans, and they expect to retire at different ages or dates, separate worksheets may be prepared by each market

		Sample Data		Your Data
1. Current salary		$ 50,000		
2. Percentage of current salary you plan to replace		× 0.60		×
3. Retirement income target		$ 30,000		
4. Minus vested defined benefits		(0)		( )
5. Minus Social Security benefits		($ 17,503)		( )
6. Required supplemental income from investment fund		$ 12,497		
7. Life expectancy (see Table 17.3)		× 26		×
8. Required target investment fund		$324,922		
9. Present target resources				
Keogh	$ 0			
IRA	$20,000			
Defined-contribution plan	$48,320			
General investments	$25,000			
TOTAL		($ 93,320)		( )
10. Required additions to target fund		$231,602		
11. Years to retirement		÷ 20		÷
12. Current annual saving needed to achieve target		$ 11,580		

Figure 17.7
Simplified retirement planning worksheet.

worker. In the current example we are assuming a married couple dependent upon the wages of a single market worker. The market worker plans to retire at age 65, at which time the spouse will be age 63.

Begin your analysis by entering your current salary on line 1. On line 2, estimate the percentage of that salary you would have to replace in order to retain an adequate standard of living during your retirement years. This figure should be based on the assumption that you will not have any work-related expenses or dependent children to support. A good rule of thumb is that you will need about 60 percent of your final salary to retain your current living standard during retirement. If you are planning to have your home fully paid for by then, this percentage may be reduced accordingly.

The retirement income target on line 3 will have to be covered by pension benefits or investment accumulations. To estimate the needed investment fund, first subtract annual pension benefits. Line 4 contains defined-benefit payments from corporate pension plans or independently purchased annuities. Enter only benefits that are vested and accrued—that is, future benefits you would receive at the expected retirement date were you to terminate employment and further contributions today.

An estimate of your Social Security pension benefit can be obtained from the Social Security Administration (see Appendix B). They will prepare estimates of benefits at normal retirement age of 65 and any other retirement age for which you may be planning. The estimates are in today's dollars, unadjusted for future inflation. Consequently, they may be entered directly into Figure 17.7 on line 5. If you do not have a personalized estimate prepared by the Social Security Administration, you can approximate your benefits with one of our estimates listed in Table 17.2.

After subtracting annual payments under government and nongovernment pension programs, you have the annual income you must generate from investments in defined-contribution plans and individual investment accounts.

Table 17.3 contains unisex single and joint life expectancies published by the Internal Revenue Service. The single life expectancy represents the number of years an individual is expected to survive. Of course, 50 percent will live fewer years and 50 percent will live more years. The joint life expectancy is based on two lives; the expected number of years until both are deceased is the joint life expectancy.

Given a married couple age 65 and age 63 at retirement, their joint life expectancy at that date is 26.0 years. Assuming that supplemental income on line 6 is needed over the joint lives, then 26.0 years can be entered on line 7. Multiplying line 6 by line 7 provides the size of the target retirement fund needed to produce the supplemental investment income.

You may wonder what will happen if you live longer than expected. Remember, we are building a safety margin into our estimates by assuming that investment returns just equal the rate of inflation. You should be able to earn a return that exceeds inflation, so the fund should actually last longer than the stated life expectancy. Alternatively, if you choose to purchase a life annuity at this point, the amount in the investment fund should be more than adequate.

The target investment fund on line 8 will change from year to year as your salary and defined-benefit payments change. But as long as you continue to aim for this moving target, you should reach the appropriate amount at retirement. To find out how much you must devote to retirement savings today, you must subtract the amounts you have already accumulated in defined-contribution pension plans, individual retirement accounts, and other savings vehicles that are not reserved to satisfy other purposes. If you then divide the remaining amount on line 10 by the number of years until retirement, you can find the current amount you must devote to additional retirement savings.

If the level of saving indicated on line 12 is greater than you currently wish to undertake, you might instead work backward. Start with your desired level of annual savings and then estimate how much of your present income this would eventually replace in retirement. This reverse procedure will bring your future goals into alignment with your present level of income and expenditure.

The simplified approach outlined in Figure 17.7 is highly conservative. If you consistently earn a return on your savings that exceeds the rise in the cost of living, the simplified approach to retirement planning will cause you to overfund your retirement needs. To take account of such differences, you must be familiar with the concepts of present value and future value discussed in Appendix A. If you are unfamiliar with these terms, you can either skip the next section or review the material in Appendix A before proceeding.

AN ADVANCED APPROACH For those who wish to take the time value of money into consideration—or perhaps observe how sensitive their retirement planning is to the assumed interest rate and inflation rate—the advanced approach outlined in Figure 17.8 is recommended.

TABLE 17.3 • SINGLE AND JOINT LIFE EXPECTANCIES IN YEARS

Single Life Annuity
Life Expectancy
(Earnings Multiple)

Age	50	51	52	53	54	55	56	57	58	59	60	61	62	63	64	65	66	67	68	69	70
	33.1	32.2	31.3	30.4	29.5	28.6	27.7	26.8	25.9	25.0	24.2	23.3	22.5	21.6	20.8	20.0	19.2	18.4	17.6	16.8	16.0

Joint Life Annuity
Joint Life Expectancy
(Earnings Multiple)

Age	50	51	52	53	54	55	56	57	58	59	60	61	62	63	64	65	66	67	68	69	70
50	39.2	38.7	38.3	37.9	37.5	37.1	36.8	36.4	36.1	35.9	35.6	35.4	35.1	34.9	34.8	34.6	34.4	34.3	34.2	34.1	34.0
51		38.2	37.8	37.3	36.9	36.5	36.1	35.8	35.5	35.2	34.9	34.6	34.4	34.2	34.0	33.8	33.6	33.5	33.4	33.2	33.1
52			37.3	36.8	36.4	35.9	35.6	35.2	34.8	34.5	34.2	33.9	33.7	33.5	33.2	33.0	32.9	32.7	32.5	32.4	32.3
53				36.3	35.8	35.4	35.0	34.6	34.2	33.9	33.6	33.3	33.0	32.7	32.5	32.3	32.1	31.9	31.8	31.6	31.5
54					35.3	34.9	34.4	34.0	33.6	33.3	32.9	32.6	32.3	32.0	31.8	31.6	31.4	31.2	31.0	30.8	30.7
55						34.4	33.9	33.5	33.1	32.7	32.3	32.0	31.7	31.4	31.1	30.9	30.6	30.4	30.2	30.1	29.9
56							33.4	33.0	32.5	32.1	31.7	31.4	31.0	30.7	30.4	30.2	29.9	29.7	29.5	29.3	29.1
57								32.5	32.0	31.6	31.2	30.8	30.4	30.1	29.8	29.5	29.2	29.0	28.8	28.6	28.4
58									31.5	31.1	30.6	30.2	29.9	29.5	29.2	28.9	28.6	28.3	28.1	27.8	27.6
59										30.6	30.1	29.7	29.3	28.9	28.6	28.2	27.9	27.6	27.4	27.1	26.9
60											29.7	29.2	28.8	28.4	28.0	27.6	27.3	27.0	26.7	26.5	26.2
61												28.7	28.3	27.8	27.4	27.1	26.7	26.4	26.1	25.8	25.6
62													27.8	27.3	26.9	26.5	26.1	25.8	25.5	25.2	24.9
63														26.9	26.4	26.0	25.6	25.2	24.9	24.6	24.3
64															25.9	25.5	25.1	24.7	24.3	24.0	23.7
65																25.0	24.6	24.2	23.8	23.4	23.1
66																	24.1	23.7	23.3	22.9	22.5
67																		23.2	22.8	22.4	22.0
68																			22.3	21.9	21.5
69																				21.5	21.1
70																					20.6

SOURCE: Internal Revenue Service, Publication 939, Tables V and VI, January 1990.

	Sample Data		Your Data	
6. Required supplemental income from investment fund		$ 12,497		____
7. Income adjustment				
Number of periods until retirement:	20		____	
Inflation rate:	5%		____	
Future value of $1 (see Appendix Table A.1)		× 2.6533		× ____
Future value of supplemental annual income		$ 33,158		____
8. Required funding at retirement				
Number of periods of retirement income:	26		____	
Net discount rate: (after-tax interest rate minus the inflation rate)	3%		____	
Present value at retirement of a $1 inflation adjusted annuity due (see appendix Table A.4)		× 18.4131		× ____
Lump sum needed at retirement to provide annual supplemental income		$610,548		____
9. Future value of retirement resources				
Years to retirement:	20			____
After-tax return on investments:	8%			____
Present retirement resources	$93,320			____
Future value of $1	× 4.6610			× ____
Future value of target resources		434,961		____
10. Additional savings needed at retirement		$175,587		____
Future value of $1 annuity to retirement (see Appendix Table A.2)		÷ 45.762		÷ ____
11. Current annual savings needed to achieve target		$ 3,837		____

Figure 17.8
Advanced retirement planning worksheet.

Advanced retirement planning requires that you first estimate the amount of funding you will need at retirement in tomorrow's dollars. Since the initial calculations under both the simplified and the advanced approaches are the same, Figure 17.8 begins with line 6 from the previous worksheet. The required supplemental income listed on line 6 is in current dollars. To find your income needs in future dollars, future rates of inflation must be taken into account. Appendix Table A.1 provides the future value of $1 compounded over various periods, at several different rates of growth. If there are 20 years to retirement and you assume a 5 percent annual rate of inflation, what cost $1.00 today will cost $2.6533 dollars 20 years from now. When you multiply 2.6533 (the future value of $1) by $12,497 on line 6, you will find that in the year you retire you will actually need supplemental dollar income of $33,158.

Appendix Table A.4 provides the present value of a $1 annuity payable over various periods. If you multiply the present value of a $1 annuity payable over your retirement years by $33,158, you can find how much you would need to fund this annuity at retirement. Of course, if you want your standard of living to remain constant, what you really desire is an annuity that begins at $33,158 and then is adjusted upward each year for any increase in the cost of living. The present value of an inflation-adjusted annuity can be found by using a net discount rate, which is approximately equal to the rate of inflation minus the rate of interest. For example, if you assume an after-tax return on your investments of 8 percent and a rate of inflation of 5 percent, then the net discount rate is 3 percent.

According to Appendix Table A.4, the present value of a $1 annuity payable for 26 years at a net discount rate of 3 percent is $17.8768. However, this is the present value of an annuity that pays out at the end of each year. What you really need in this example is a payment at the beginning of the year in which you retire, and then 25 future payments, each at the beginning of a subsequent year. An annuity that pays out at the beginning of each period is termed an *annuity due*. The present value of an n-period $1 annuity due can be found by taking the present value of an $(n - 1)$-period $1 annuity and adding 1 to it. Accordingly, the present value of a 26-period annuity due at a net discount rate of 3 percent is $18.4131. This is equal to $17.4131 (the present value of a 25-period annuity discounted at 3 percent) plus $1.

Multiplying the present value of a $1 annuity due by the required supplemental income indicates that the lump sum needed at retirement is $610,548. This may be funded by both previously accumulated resources and future savings. Those resources you have already accumulated will continue to earn investment income until they are needed. If you assume that the annual after-tax return on your current resources is 8 percent, then Appendix Table A.1 indicates that $1 of present funding will grow to $4.6610 in 20 years. Therefore, the future value of present resources at retirement will be $434,961 (=$93,320 × 4.6610). Thus, the additional savings needed at retirement will be equal to the difference between future needs and the future value of present resources, or $175,587 (=$610,548 – 434,961).

The future value of a $1 annuity is given in Appendix Table A.2. The value indicates how much you would have in an investment fund after the given number of years, if you deposited $1 in the account each year and the amount deposited earned interest at the indicated rate. For example, the future value of a $1 annual payment made over each of the next 20 years, where these payments earn an annual after-tax return of 8 percent, is $45.762. Dividing $175,587 (the additional savings needed at retirement) by 45.762, you will find that equal annual contributions of $3,837 will cover the shortfall in future funding needs.

You should notice that in this example there is a considerable difference between the required annual savings under the simplified approach and the advanced approach. By assuming resources of $93,320 and then assuming that returns on these resources will beat the rate of inflation by 3 percent over each of the next 20 years, required additional savings are substantially reduced. You are, in effect, assuming that you can provide for much of your retirement needs through real growth in your current portfolio. Of course, should these estimates prove too optimistic, you may have to increase future contributions or else fall short of your target funding.

Action Plan for the Steeles: Reviewing Their Retirement Plans

Background Both Arnold and Sharon should receive Social Security wage earner's pensions when they retire. Furthermore, Arnold has fully vested pension rights at his current job. If he terminated employment today, he could either receive a lump-sum payment of $21,000 or leave the funds in the pension plan for a joint life annuity with survivorship paying $18,000 per year when Arnold reaches age 65, 28 years from now.

The Problem After reviewing their household budget and balance sheet, the Steeles realize that they have not been saving for retirement. They want to know how much they would need to save each year in order to retire at 60 percent of their present income. The benefit statement from the Social Security Administration indicates that they would receive combined benefits of about $19,000. With Arnold's defined-pension benefits of $18,000, their total retirement income in today's dollars would be about $37,000. That is about $10,000 less than what they would like to have in retirement income.

They would want to know how much they would have to save annually in order to provide for the desired supplemental income. Both Arnold and Sharon have 401(k) plans at work that they have not taken advantage of. Neither plan provides any matching contribution by the employer. They expect a future inflation rate of 4 percent and an after-tax return on their savings of 8 percent.

The Plan At retirement 28 years from now, if annual inflation averages 4 percent, the required supplemental income in tomorrow's dollars will be $29,987. Arnold and Sharon's joint life expectancy at retirement is about 26 years. Given a net discount rate of 4 percent (8 percent after-tax return minus 4 percent inflation), the required supplemental fund at retirement is $479,276. Assuming an after-tax return of 8 percent, the future value of a $1 annuity at 28 years from now will be $95.34. Therefore, annual savings of $5,027 (= $479,276/$95.34) will allow the Steeles to satisfy their desired retirement income. Since this is significantly below the contribution ceiling on 401(k) plans, they should be able to use it successfully as a saving vehicle.

SUMMARY

Retirement planning involves an explicit consideration of present versus future needs and an examination of how present resources may be allocated to serve future needs. An important means of saving for retirement is through a company-sponsored pension plan. Other convenient, tax-deferred methods sponsored by employers include profit-sharing plans, salary-reduction agreements, and employee stock ownership plans. Savings may also be channeled through non-company-sponsored plans, such as IRAs and Keoghs. Whatever savings method is used, retirement planning should include a financial goal and a viable savings plan for achieving that goal. The sooner you get started, the easier it will be to alter your plan to meet your changing future needs.

KEY TERMS

accrued benefit (p. 475)
accumulation period (p. 483)
annuity contract (p. 483)
annuity starting date (p. 483)
deferred annuity (p. 483)
defined-benefit plan (p. 473)
defined-contribution plan (p. 474)
early retirement age (p. 476)

Employee Retirement Income Security Act (ERISA) (p. 470)

employee stock ownership plan (ESOP) (p. 480)

fixed annuity (p. 483)

flat benefit method (p. 476)

401(k) salary-reduction plan (p. 479)

403(b) tax-sheltered annuity (p. 480)

immediate annuity (p. 483)

individual retirement account (IRA) (p. 480)

joint and last survivor annuity (p. 478)

Keogh (HR-10) plan (p. 482)

liquidation period (p. 483)

normal retirement age (p. 476)

profit-sharing plan (p. 479)

qualified retirement plan (p. 470)

reverse mortgage (p. 485)

simplified employee pension plan (SEP) (p. 480)

single life annuity (p. 478)

unit benefit method (p. 476)

variable annuity (p. 483)

vested benefits (p. 475)

PROBLEMS AND REVIEW QUESTIONS

1. "Retirement planning should be put off until you can accurately assess your latter-day needs." Do you agree or disagree with this statement? Explain.
2. What does the term *qualified* indicate when describing a pension plan? Why is it important that a pension plan be qualified?
3. What is the difference between a defined-benefit plan and a defined-contribution plan? What are the advantages and disadvantages of each?
4. Why is it important that benefits be vested?
5. What percentage of pension benefits would be vested for an employee with four years of service at age 35 under each of the following vesting standards:
   (*a*) cliff vesting
   (*b*) graded vesting
6. Up to what age must the company provide you with additions to your retirement benefits? You cannot be forced into retirement before what age?
7. Which approach for calculating defined benefits responds more rapidly to the effects of inflation: the career average approach or the final average approach? Why?
8. How does a pension plan differ from a profit-sharing plan?
9. Which tax-deferred retirement plans could a self-employed individual take advantage of?
10. How do fixed annuities differ from variable annuities?
11. Why is it unwise to place the majority of your retirement savings into your home?
12. What is normal retirement age for Social Security benefits? How is this expected to change?
13. A 65-year-old retiree earning $10,000 in part-time employment during 1995 would lose what amount in Social Security benefits, according to the retirement test? Suppose the retiree were 64 years of age; what is the potential loss? Suppose the retiree is 71 years of age; what is the potential loss?
14. Are Social Security benefits tax free? Explain.
15. How much to save today for retirement in the distant future is difficult to determine. How might you simplify the problem?
16. You want to change the mutual fund you have your IRA invested in. How might you change funds without triggering a tax on your withdrawal?
17. When might deferral of taxes on a retirement account be an unwise choice?
18. How does health care planning before age 65 differ from health care planning after age 65?
19. Does the nonemployee spouse have any rights to a pension plan participant's defined benefits?
20. Why do the ages 59½ and 70½ have special significance for qualified retirement plans?

Case 17.1 Steve Deutsch Plans for Retirement

Steve Deutsch's company pension and his expected Social Security benefits are his only sources of retirement income. He would like to retire in 10 years at age 62, but he is worried that these programs will not provide enough in early retirement benefits for him to live in his normal style. He figures he would need to generate an additional income of $10,000 from a supplemental investment fund for him to live comfortably in early retirement. He can use either the simplified or advanced approach to project his retirement needs. He expects that the after-tax returns on his investments will average 9 percent, and future inflation will average 5 percent.

QUESTIONS

1. What is the target amount he would need in this investment fund?
2. What is his current savings target, given the target investment fund?
3. Where might Steve consider placing these additional funds for retirement?

Case 17.2 Janet Myrnic Considers Changing Jobs

Janet Myrnic has been offered an executive position at a competing firm. The salary is substantially above what her present employer is paying. Therefore, it is very likely she will accept the offer.

However, before leaving her old job, she would like to review her participation in that company's pension plan and understand her rights. She has participated in the company's defined-contribution plan for the last five years, during which the employer matched each dollar she contributed to the retirement fund. Combined contributions currently total $11,320.

QUESTIONS

1. Under graded vesting, what percentage of these benefits must be vested?
2. Suppose the entire amount in Janet's retirement account were fully vested; how much is she definitely entitled to receive in a lump-sum payment at termination of employment?
3. Assuming she leaves some funds in the retirement plan, what document should she receive at termination?
4. What are her investment options if she decides to receive a lump-sum payment?

HELPFUL CONTACTS

American Association of Retired Persons
1909 K Street, NW, Washington, DC 20049
A nonprofit organization engaged in lobbying for the interests of retired individuals. For a list of lenders of reverse mortgages, contact the AARP Home Equity Information Center, 601 E Street, NW, Washington, DC 20094.

The National Council for the Aging, Inc.
600 Maryland Avenue, SW, Washington, DC 20024
A nonprofit organization providing programs to improve the economic and social conditions of older people. It monitors local employment agencies for older workers.

INTERNET ADDRESSES

BenefitsLink (information on retirement plans and yellow pages for benefits service providers)
http://www.magicnet.net/benefits/index.html

Gabelli Funds, Inc. (financial calculator for determining needed investment amounts for retirement)
http://www.gabelli.com/Gab_phtml/mfund/saving3.html

Legal Information Institute (links on pension law materials)
http://www.law.cornell.edu/topics/pensions.html

Social Security Online (information on retirement benefits)
http://www.ssa.gov/SSA_Home.html

TIAA-CREF (retirement program for college teachers includes downloadable software for retirement planning)
http://chronicle.merit.edu/.vendors/.tiaa/.home.htm

Chapter 18

Estate Planning: Dividing Up What's Left

Objectives

1. To understand the purpose of a will
2. To appreciate the need for an attorney's help in writing a will
3. To recognize what may happen if you die without a will
4. To be able to plan for transfers outside the will
5. To discuss the different kinds of trusts
6. To explain the relationship between the federal gift tax and the federal estate tax

Death estate: Property and wealth transferred at death.

Upon death, the property you leave is termed your **death estate.** It should be large enough to provide for the care and support of the surviving spouse and children. In Chapter 6, on life insurance, we examined methods for estimating the needed support for survivors and how that support may be funded through accumulated savings and life insurance. However, all your planning and all your saving may accomplish little if your estate is squandered on legal costs or is transferred to the wrong individual. To make sure this does not happen, you will need some expert advice. Estate planning is not a do-it-yourself project. For small estates the help of an attorney may prove sufficient, but for large estates, especially those over $600,000, the aid of either an accountant or a financial planner specializing in estate transfer should also be enlisted.

Estate planning has two basic objectives: one, to transfer your assets at death in a manner consistent with your wishes, and two, to transfer those assets as intact as possible. The first objective can be achieved through a well-thought-out will. Depending on the amount and nature of your wealth, the second objective can be either very simple or very difficult.

TRANSFERRING YOUR ESTATE THROUGH A WILL

Intestate: To die without a valid will.

An overwhelming number of Americans die each year without a valid will. In these situations the deceased is said to have died **intestate.** When this occurs, the state supplies a ready-made will dividing the estate according to that state's laws of intestacy. The division is uniquely determined by each state, but the laws generally follow the format outlined in Figure 18.1.

The chance is very small that the state-mandated distribution of your assets will reflect your own desires. In fact, for many families with minor children, the distribution directed by the state is likely to run counter to the best interest of the family. Typically, under the laws of intestacy a surviving spouse with children receives only one-half to one-third of the estate. The rest is distributed to the children of the deceased. For those who have not yet reached the age of majority, court-appointed trustees will have to manage these funds in the children's interest. The surviving spouse may then be required to gain the agreement of the trustees on how and when these funds may be spent. For most families, this arrangement is undesirable and inconvenient. In addition, the associated administrative and legal costs may use up resources needed to support the surviving spouse and children.

The intentions of the state are good. It ensures that the interest of those least able to defend themselves, minor children, are protected. However, most children don't need protection from their parents. Through the use of a will, we can apportion the estate in a manner that more conveniently and adequately serves the needs of the entire family unit.

The Last Will and Testament

Will: A legal declaration of how you wish your property to be disposed of at your death.

A **will** is a legal declaration of how you wish your property to be disposed of at your death. It should be drawn up only with the supervision of an attorney knowledgeable in estate planning. The presence of an attorney is essential because there are myriad reasons for declaring a will invalid and contesting the distribution of the estate. For example, unless the will is properly witnessed, according to state-mandated guidelines, you may not have a valid will. Should the will be declared

Survivors	Division of Property
Spouse and one child	Spouse and child each receive one-half
Spouse and two or more children	Spouse receives one-third. The other two-thirds is divided equally among the children
Spouse and parents surviving, no children	Spouse receives 50–75% of estate, surviving parents receive the rest
Spouse surviving, no children, and parents deceased	Spouse receives 50–100% of estate, surviving brothers and sisters receive remaining balance
Parents surviving, no spouse or children	Parents receive all
Brother(s) and/or sister(s) surviving, no spouse or children, parents deceased	Brother(s) and/or sister(s) receive equal shares

Figure 18.1 Possible division of estate under intestate provisions.

invalid for any reason, the estate will be distributed under the laws of intestacy. Furthermore, an improperly written will that does not foreclose future court proceedings may be more costly to your intended beneficiaries than dying with no will at all. With the advice and supervision of an attorney, you should be able to avoid this possibility and still accomplish a desirable division of your assets.

Your estate planning objectives will not be achieved if you simply write a will and then forget it. Review the document periodically to ensure that it reflects your current familial status and needs. In addition, be sure to review your will whenever you change your state of residency or your family structure. Don't assume that just because you previously wrote a will with the help of a knowledgeable attorney that it is necessarily still valid. The laws differ among states, and a valid will in one state may be invalid in another.

Testate: To die with a valid will.
Testator: The male author of a valid will.
Testatrix: The female author of a valid will.

A person who leaves a valid will is said to die **testate** and is referred to as either the **testator** or the **testatrix.** The correct suffix depends on whether the person is a male, requiring a *tor* ending, or a female, requiring a *trix* ending. You as the testator or testatrix can accomplish several objectives through the use of a will. You can name the executor for your estate. You can choose the guardian for your children. You can specify how your estate should be divided among beneficiaries. And finally, you can create investment trusts to provide for the future support and welfare of the beneficiaries.

Executor or executrix: The person who manages the distribution of the death estate according to the wishes expressed in the will.

NAMING AN EXECUTOR The person named in the will who manages your estate from the time of death until all the assets are distributed is called the **executor** or **executrix.** Because he or she is given extensive powers to handle your affairs and distribute your property according to your wishes, you must pick someone who is exceedingly trustworthy. Furthermore, discuss your choice with your potential executor, explaining what is required and who might provide additional information on the handling of your estate. This information should also be contained in the "letter of last instructions" discussed later. If you die without a will, or the named executor refuses to serve, the court chooses someone termed the **administrator** or **administratrix** to handle your estate. This choice may not coincide with your own desires.

Administrator or administratrix: The court-appointed manager of the death estate and will.

An executor will normally be paid a fee for services performed, but the person you select may agree to serve free. More important, unless the will specifically states otherwise, the executor will be required to post a bond to cover any poten-

Box 18.1

PERSONAL FINANCE NEWS

Late Edition

Being of Sound Mind and Sound Software

"Create a legal will in under an hour. No stress, no lawyers."

"Create binding legal documents on any PC!"

" . . . the program designed to help you protect your family and your assets."

Do-it-yourself wills can be attractive to personal computer owners. PC users know the power of the PC and the appropriate software to act as an electronic savant doing the owner's bidding. Just think of all the advantages to these programs.

First, there's the privacy of writing a will without having to reveal your wishes to another living soul. Then, there's the peace of mind from knowing you took care of a matter that you have put off for too long. And, finally, there's the satisfaction that for less than $100—and in some cases for much less than that—you can create a legally binding document on a computer and avoid expensive attorney's fees.

But a judge who reviewed the final wills produced by three software packages urges do-it-yourselfers to be careful. Judge George A. Gounaris, a Montgomery County, Ohio, probate judge, said he has seen the heartaches that result when a will maker's intended wishes fail to happen because of a poorly written will.

All three computer-generated wills would hold up in an Ohio probate court, Gounaris said. That wasn't the problem. The judge was concerned about whether each will accurately expressed the wishes of the will maker.

If you do write your own will, then the judge recommends that you have an attorney review it afterward. He recalled the example of a man who decided to write his own will and that of his wife, all in one document. He included all the nice wording found in wills, and then wrote, "In the event I predecease her, all of my estate goes to my wife. In the event my wife predeceases me, all of her estate goes to me."

The will was correct in every way except that paragraph, Gounaris said. The law doesn't provide for the inclusion of one person's will in the middle of another will. In effect, it left his wife with no will. She could die intestate, a legal term for having no will.

The software isn't equipped to explain these fine legal points to the user, who might be unaware of the potential hazard. As another example, the judge cited a case in which the will maker left an estranged son a pittance of money and instructions that it be used to buy a hanging rope. The father wanted to make it clear he thought his son should hang himself.

The son refused to take receipt of the bequest and held up the completion of probate indefinitely, to the dismay of the other relatives—not the deceased's intentions at all.

Had the father retained a lawyer to review his do-it-yourself will, perhaps potential problems with the son and probate could have been avoided. "It's not the computer's will," the judge said. "It's not the lawyer's will. It's your will. And you want it right."

SOURCE: Excerpted from Judith L. Schultz, "Being of Sound Mind and Software," *Dayton Daily News,* February 4, 1991, pp. 10–11.

tial mismanagement of the estate. This is expensive and will eventually be charged to the estate. Assuming you have picked a trustworthy individual, you may waive the need for posting bond in the will.

SPECIFYING GUARDIANSHIP For those who have children, the will is used to name a guardian in the event both parents die before the children reach the age of majority. As in the case of executor, you should make sure the proposed guardian will accept the assigned role. If you leave surviving children without a named guardian, or the named guardian refuses to serve, the court chooses one. In some cases this assignment provides the incentive for a lengthy and emotional custody battle among relatives. A potentially undesirable outcome is that guardianship of the children may be split. Consequently, brothers and sisters may grow up emotionally and physically separated from each other.

DIVIDING THE ESTATE In the will, you also indicate how your property should be disposed of. You may divide your estate up into percentage shares or provide for

Bequest or legacy: Property given by a wish expressed in a will.

Per capita division: One in which the inheritance is divided equally among surviving family members.

Per stirpes division: One in which the inheritance is divided equally among branches of the family.

absolute dollar payments for each beneficiary. You may also make a specific **bequest,** also termed a **legacy,** leaving a specific item of property to a particular individual.

Most property is divided up under either a *per capita* or a *per stirpes* division. Suppose Arnold and Sharon Steele have two grandchildren by their son, John, as illustrated in Figure 18.2. Furthermore, assume John dies before his parents. At Arnold's and Sharon's subsequent death, how will their property be divided among the grandchildren and the surviving daughter, Nancy? The answer will depend upon whether the Steeles specified a per capita or a per stirpes distribution in their will. In a **per capita division,** all of the survivors would share equally. One-third would go to Nancy, and one-third would go to each of the grandchildren. In a **per stirpes division**, each *branch* of the family would share equally. In this example, Nancy would receive one-half of the property, and each of John's children would receive one-quarter.

The way in which the estate is divided may affect estate taxes, inheritance taxes, and the income taxes of beneficiaries. In addition, there are some potential legal problems that should be considered. First, property cannot be left directly to minor children. If you have minor children, you will have to provide for their continued support through some kind of trust arrangement. An attorney can help you formu-

Figure 18.2 Alternative estate distributions.

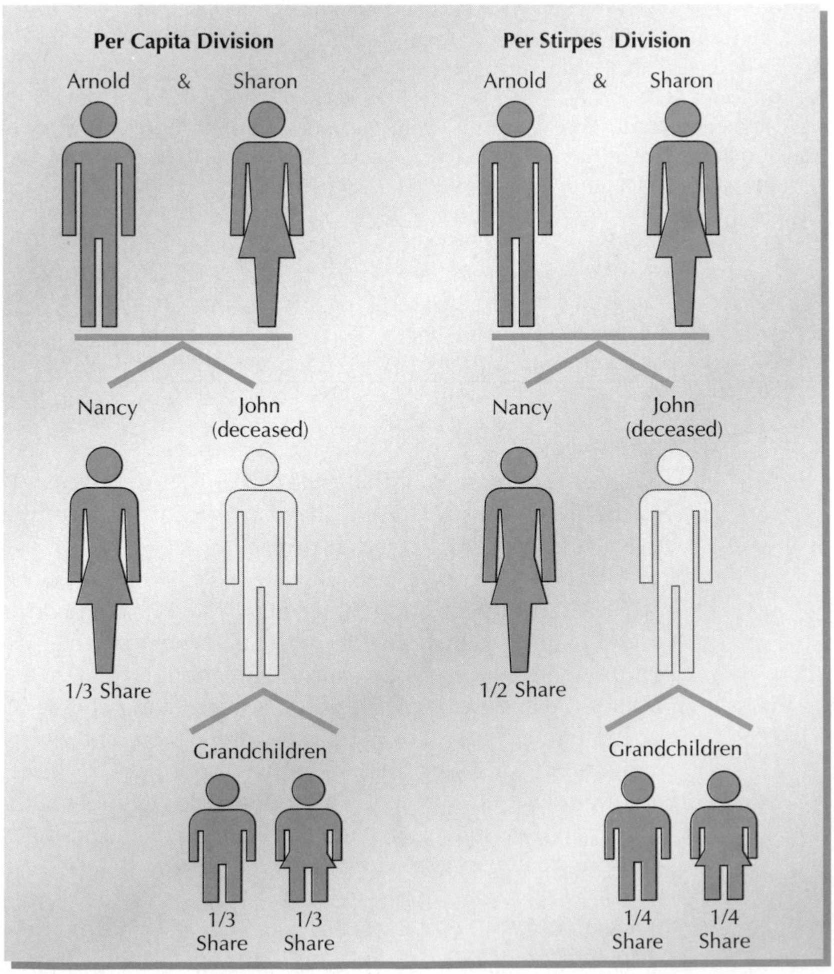

late one that reflects your intentions. Second, who is included and who is not included in your will may determine its validity. Under state law you may have no choice but to leave part of your estate to your spouse. Your failure to do so in your will may later provide the basis for contesting the will's validity. If you wish to leave another close relative, such as a child, out of the will, be sure to state so. Otherwise, this person may successfully argue in court that he or she was inadvertently omitted, meaning the present will is invalid. Obviously, a knowledgeable attorney can provide crucial advice on achieving your estate planning objectives.

Changing or Revoking the Will

Codicil: An amendment to an existing will, modifying or explaining specific items.

If you wish to change only a few specific items in the will, you can do so through a **codicil,** which is usually a one-page document indicating the desired changes in the existing will. Like the initial will, the codicil should also be drawn up and witnessed in a manner satisfying state law. Thus, an attorney should also be used when amending an existing will with a codicil.

For matters that require more than a few simple changes, the old will should be revoked and a new will written. The old will can be revoked by expressly stating so in the new will. What most people do not realize is that a previously valid will may be automatically revoked by a change in family status. Marriage, divorce, or the birth of a child can all automatically revoke an existing will. The exact result of this change will, again, depend upon state law. Naturally, you should consult an attorney whenever family arrangements change.

The Letter of Last Instructions

If you desire, you can leave your relatives with a few well-chosen words, but not in the will, as most TV dramas would have you believe. The will is a tool for attaining certain legal objectives; accordingly, it should not be cluttered up with personal comments. Since the will is a legal document, everything in it is subject to legal interpretation and challenge. Therefore, to minimize the possibility of misinterpretation and conflict, you should not include unnecessary statements. Your last words of wisdom or insult should be contained in the **letter of last instructions.**

Letter of last instructions: A document providing advice on the management of your death estate and the distribution of your assets.

In it you might explain why you structured your bequests as you did, what you hoped to accomplish in the specified distribution of your assets, and what you hope your beneficiaries might accomplish in the future.

The letter of last instructions should also have a more practical objective. It should serve as a road map for your survivors, pointing the way to information on your estate. Since a road map is most useful at the beginning of a trip, inform your beneficiaries where it might be found and keep copies at several locations.

The letter of last instructions should contain an inventory of your assets and the location of important documents, beginning with the location of your will. You may want to keep a copy of the will along with the letter of last instructions. However, the original will should be kept on file at the attorney's office or, where applicable, at the county office with the register of wills and not in your safe deposit box or home. It may take a while before the safe deposit box may be opened after your death, and wills left at home have been known to disappear.

Be sure to provide information on life insurance policies, death and survivor benefits under pension plans, and your financial holdings. Such readily available information can save the executor considerable time and expense when taking inventory of your estate. Also provide the names of individuals who are familiar with the operation of your estate, such as your stockbroker, accountant, lawyer, and financial planner. The executor may have to rely on their help in the management and distribution of your assets.

Probate

Probate: A court process in which assets are transferred according to a will or the laws of intestacy.

Probate is the name for the court process in which assets are transferred subject to the will or the laws of intestacy. A special court, known as the probate court, exists to handle the transferal of death estates. The proceedings in this court may be divided into the seven major steps listed in Figure 18.3.

In the first step the court determines whether a valid will exists. If there is one, the named executor oversees the rest of the process. In the absence of a valid will, the court will appoint an administrator to help manage the probate process.

Lately, many attorneys and financial planners have been strongly critical of the probate process. They have argued that it is too costly and has led to unfortunate delays in the transferal of the death estate, producing a prolonged disruption in the lives of the survivors. Probate costs can average from about 3 to 5 percent of the value of the estate, and it can typically take a year to complete the probate process, with larger estates taking many years. To remedy this situation, two suggestions have been put forth, one for governments and one for individuals. The first proposes a **Uniform Probate Code** for adoption by state legislatures. Some states have already enacted this code, thus reducing some of the cost and delay associated with the probate process. The second suggests that individuals structure their estates so as to avoid probate.

Uniform Probate Code: A code for standardizing the probate process among the states.

Not all property is distributed through the will and the probate process. Property may be passed outside of the will. Since probate costs are usually equal to a percentage of the assets transferred, even a partial transfer of assets outside the will can result in cost savings. However, this need not result in any tax savings. Estate taxes are based on the value of the gross estate, which will include property transferred both within and outside of the will.

TRANSFERRING YOUR ESTATE OUTSIDE THE WILL

One way of transferring property and avoiding probate is to give your assets away while you are still living. Most of us would like to retain control over our property in case of future need, however, so this method isn't always desirable. There are ways in which property may transfer at death, thus leaving us with control while living, and yet still avoiding probate. Joint tenancy, trusts, and contracts are the three most important ways in which this is accomplished. Each has advantages and drawbacks, and none should be entered into just to avoid probate. The indiscrimi-

Figure 18.3
Seven major steps of probate.

1. Validation of will and appointment of executor or administrator
2. Informing heirs and claimants of death
3. Inventory and valuation of property and debts
4. Payments of claims against the estate
5. Determination and payment of taxes due
6. Determination of how the estate is to be divided and who are the legal heirs
7. Division and distribution of estate to heirs

nate use of these estate planning instruments could result in increased tax liabilities, increased estate management costs, and an undesirable distribution of your estate. Accordingly, each should be used with care and forethought, and never as a substitute for a will. Rather, they should be looked upon as individual instruments in your estate planning tool kit.

Joint Tenancy with Right of Survivorship

Joint tenancy: A form of ownership in which each co-owner has an undivided interest in the property and the property passes to the co-owner at death.

When property is held under the form of ownership called *joint tenancy with right of survivorship,* it automatically passes at death to the surviving co-owner. It is not distributed through the will and, therefore, avoids probate. In a **joint tenancy,** each owner has an undivided interest in the property, meaning that each has an equal right to make use of and enjoy the entire property.

Married couples are often joint tenants in the ownership of a home. Having a sizable asset such as the home pass outside of probate can result in a significant cost saving. However, on estates large enough to incur estate taxes, a reduction in probate costs should not be a primary objective, because tax liabilities could be much greater. In these situations, the form of ownership for major assets should be discussed with a knowledgeable attorney or tax analyst.

Most estate planners tend to look upon joint tenancy unfavorably, because too many people use it as a substitute for a will. It is not. Even when most of your assets are held in joint tenancy, you still need a will to specify how the property is to be distributed at the death of the surviving owner. Joint tenants who are husband and wife might die simultaneously in an accident; only a will can specify how the jointly held property would then be disposed of.

Joint tenancy can also present problems in life. In some situations a co-owner can dispose of the property without your knowledge or consent; in others you may need the consent of the co-owner before entering a transaction. This can only make problems worse in troubled marriages or between divorced partners. Furthermore, you should realize that joint tenancy makes your interest in the property liable for claims on the co-owner. When one of the owners is engaged in a business where there are potential liabilities, this tool of estate planning should be avoided.

Married couples with complicated family relationships should also think twice before becoming joint tenants. For example, if both spouses have children from a previous marriage, and all property is held jointly by the couple, the children of the spouse to die first may be left with nothing. The property passes first to the surviving spouse and then probably to the children of the surviving spouse.

Tenancy in common: A form of ownership in which each co-owner has an undivided interest in the property, but the property can be individually transferred.

Joint tenancy should not be confused with other forms of multiple ownership such as *tenancy in common* or *community property*. **Tenancy in common** is similar to joint tenancy in that each owner shares an undivided interest, even when each owns an unequal share. However, an important difference for estate planning is that the property does not necessarily pass to the co-owner(s) at death. Each owner can transfer his or her share in the tenancy in common as desired in both life and death. Thus, ownership will pass through the will the same as individually owned property.

Community property: Recognized in some states, it is property acquired during the marriage by the joint efforts of husband and wife.

Some states employ the concept of **community property.** This is property acquired during the marriage from the joint efforts of husband and wife. Each is assumed to share equally in the ownership of such assets. Upon the death of either spouse, community property is treated much the same as in tenancy in common. The surviving spouse receives one-half of the property. The other half is disposed of through the will of the deceased spouse or through the laws of intestacy.

Trusts

Trust: A legal arrangement in which property is held by one party for the benefit of another.

Trustee: The one who controls the property in a trust.

Beneficiary: The one who is to benefit from the trust.

Fiduciary responsibility: A legal responsibility to manage the trust in the best interests of the beneficiary.

Grantor: The one who establishes and funds the trust.

Testamentary trust: A trust that takes effect at death.

A **trust** is an arrangement whereby the right to property is held by one party, the **trustee,** for the benefit of another, the **beneficiary.** The trustee is said to have a **fiduciary responsibility** to the beneficiary. This means that the trustee has a legal obligation to manage the trust in the best interests of the beneficiary. If the trustee does not honor this obligation, he or she may be held liable for any damages suffered by the beneficiary.

The person who establishes and funds the trust is known as the **grantor.** The grantor may arrange for the trust to become operational either at his or her death or while the grantor is still alive. Each arrangement can play an important role in estate planning.

A trust specified in the will and taking effect at death is called a **testamentary trust.** The most common reason for including a testamentary trust in a will is to provide for the support and care of dependent children. A minor cannot receive the proceeds from an estate directly. When property is left to a minor and the funds are not placed in a testamentary trust, the court will create a trust fund to manage the bequest in the minor's interest. By preempting the court, you can specify who will manage the fund, for what purpose the funds may be used, and when the funds may be paid out.

Inter vivos or living trust: A trust that takes effect during the grantor's lifetime.

Since funding for a testamentary trust must be specified in the will, the trust funds are generally liable for both probate costs and estate taxes. An **inter vivos trust** is one established during the grantor's lifetime and is also termed a **living trust.** Funds in a living trust pass outside the will and the probate process, saving probate costs. This occurs because probate includes only those items held in the name of the deceased. The property in a living trust is held in the name of the trust.

Revocable trust: A trust that can be changed or revoked by the grantor.

Irrevocable trust: A trust that cannot be changed by the grantor once it is established.

Although funds in a living trust escape probate, they still may be taxable as part of the decedent's estate. The deciding factor for estate tax liability is whether the trust fund is *revocable* or *irrevocable.* A **revocable trust** can be changed or revoked by the grantor at any time. In reality the property still remains under the control of the person who established the trust and is therefore part of the deceased's taxable estate. The same is not true for an **irrevocable trust.** The terms of an irrevocable trust cannot be changed after it is established. Thus, the grantor loses all effective future control of the property placed in the trust, which eliminates future estate tax liabilities but creates immediate gift tax liabilities. Naturally, irrevocable trusts should be set up only after considerable forethought.

In a living trust, the grantor, the trustee, and the beneficiary may all be the same person. Setting up a revocable living trust that provides for your own welfare while you are still alive and then for the welfare of your survivors after your death is often suggested in the popular financial literature as an ideal method of avoiding probate. One book on the subject even has tear-out forms for setting up your own living trust.

As discussed previously, estate planning is not a do-it-yourself project. If you are considering setting up a revocable living trust, you would probably be better off if you first discussed the matter with an attorney specializing in estate planning. You might learn that this arrangement has both advantages and disadvantages. Property placed in the trust is not so easily exchanged as property outside the trust. Moreover, if you want an attorney to write the living trust and provide support in funding it, you will find that legal costs exceed those associated with writing a will. Furthermore, even if you have a living trust, you may still need a will. Such things as naming a guardian for your children can be accomplished only through a will.

Box 18.2 SAVING MONEY
Medicaid Planning: Planning to Survive on the Kindness of Others

Medicaid was designed to provide medical assistance to the financial indigent. But with the annual cost of a nursing home stay ranging from a low of about $36,000 to upwards of more than $70,000, persons who need nursing home care can quickly find themselves in that category. Persons with modest estates may have no choice but to qualify for Medicaid eventually.

The goal of Medicaid planning is to avoid having to spend down your assets on nursing home care before you qualify for Medicaid assistance. You may be able to protect your assets by conveying them to a spouse or close relative. Since the assets are no longer in your name, you may then qualify as financial indigent and meet the standards for receiving Medicaid assistance.

The idea of purposely transferring assets to qualify for a program that was meant to help the poor obviously raises some difficult ethical issues. To the extent that the aged are successful in shifting assets and living off the kindness of the government, the effect is to raise the cost of taxes and medical care to the rest of us.

Those who engage in Medicaid planning see it differently. To them it is no different than taking advantage of tax breaks. After all, you are not required to pay more than your fair share, and it's the law that determines your fair share. As long as you don't do anything illegal, it's acceptable. From their point of view, after a lifetime of hard work, the government should do more to help them.

To qualify you must spend down assets to around $2,000. However, your spouse may keep up to about $72,660 in assets, and not all assets are counted. The family home and prepaid funeral expenses may be exempt. The idea is to move funds into noncountable assets and transfer funds that would otherwise be counted.

In an attempt to slow the growing trend in Medicare planning, Congress passed the Omnibus Budget Reconciliation Act of 1993. Its purpose was to make it more difficult for the elderly to transfer assets and still qualify for Medicaid. Under the previous law, assets transferred 30 months before you applied for Medicaid could delay your eligibility. The new law lengthens that "look-back" period to 36 months for most assets, with an even longer period for transfers into certain types of trusts.

Here's how it works. If a transfer takes place within the 36-month look-back period, dated from when you apply for Medicaid, then you are ineligible for Medicaid during some period after the transfer. The number of months you are ineligible will be equal to the amount of the transfer divided by a "cost factor." The cost factor varies from state to state and is supposed to be related to the cost of nursing home care in each state.

For example, if you give away $250,000 during the 36-month period and the cost factor is $3,000, then you are ineligible for Medicaid for 83 ($250,000/$3,000) months from the date of transfer. Alternatively, if you don't apply for Medicaid until 36 months after the transfer, then you are outside the look-back period and you immediately qualify for Medicaid. Assuming that those nursing home expenses are $3,000 a month, waiting 36 months before you apply can enable you to transfer $108,000 ($250,000 − [36 × $3,000]) in funds that might otherwise have gone for nursing home expenses. It's easy to see why even for individuals with modest estates Medicaid planning is expanding.

The trust arrangement in the hands of a knowledgeable estate planner is like a scalpel in the hands of a skilled surgeon. It can accomplish the seemingly impossible in appropriately caring for beneficiaries and in minimizing death taxes. However, in the hands of a layperson it may cause nothing but trouble.

Contractual Transfers

Life insurance policies, retirement plans, and bank accounts are all contractual relationships, the benefits of which can be assigned directly to beneficiaries, thus passing outside the will.

Trustee bank account: A bank account that provides for a contractual transfer of ownership at death.

In states that have adopted the Uniform Probate Code, a bank account with the designation, "Arnold Steele, payable on death to Sharon Steele," would pass directly to Sharon at Arnold's death. In other states the same type of transfer may be accomplished through a **trustee bank account.** The designation for this type of account would be "Arnold Steele, as trustee for Sharon Steele."

Because no trust is actually created, the terminology used in setting up a trustee bank account is confusing. In the present example, Arnold would not owe Sharon any fiduciary responsibility. Moreover, Sharon would have absolutely no right to the bank account while Arnold is alive. However, at his death, the funds in the account would pass directly to Sharon, thus circumventing probate.

DEATH TAXES AND OTHER RELATED TAX ISSUES

Death tax: A tax on property either transferred or received at death.
Estate tax: A tax imposed on the property of the deceased before transfer.
Inheritance tax: A tax paid by the beneficiary on property received as an inheritance.
Gift tax: A tax imposed upon gifts transferred during life.

A tax on the property transferred or received upon the death of the owner is known as a **death tax.** There are two types of death taxes: an estate tax and an inheritance tax. An **estate tax** is imposed on the property of the deceased before it is transferred; an **inheritance tax** is levied on the property when it is received by the beneficiary. At the federal level, only an estate tax exists. However, state governments impose either estate or inheritance taxes, and sometimes both.

Most discussions of death taxes also include an examination of gift taxes. This is because an effective estate or inheritance tax presupposes the existence of a tax on gifts. Without a **gift tax,** any estate taxes can be avoided by simply giving away your belongings before you die.

The Federal Gift Tax

In 1976 Congress passed a unified rate schedule that applies identical tax rates to taxable gifts and taxable estates. The rate structure in Figure 18.4 is progressive, with a maximum rate of 55 percent on taxable estates over $3 million. When you

Figure 18.4
Unified tax rate schedule for estates and gifts.

(A) Taxable Amount Over	(B) Taxable Amount Not Over	(C) Tax on Amount in Column A	(D) Rate of Tax on Excess Over Amount in Column A (%)
0	$ 10,000	0	18
$ 10,000	20,000	$ 1,800	20
20,000	40,000	3,800	22
40,000	60,000	8,200	24
60,000	80,000	13,000	26
80,000	100,000	18,200	28
100,000	150,000	23,800	30
150,000	250,000	38,800	32
250,000	500,000	70,800	34
500,000	750,000	155,800	37
750,000	1,000,000	248,300	39
1,000,000	1,250,000	345,800	41
1,250,000	1,500,000	448,300	43
1,500,000	2,000,000	555,800	45
2,000,000	2,500,000	780,800	49
2,500,000	3,000,000	1,025,800	53
3,000,000	----------	1,290,800	55

consider that the income generating this wealth has already been subject to an income tax, the rates do seem high. However, they apply only after generous exclusions and exemptions and reduction by a unified tax credit on gifts and estates of $192,800. This is enough to completely offset the tax liability on taxable gifts and estates of $600,000 or less.

Taxable gifts: The value of gifts less excludable amounts.

To understand how the federal gift tax and the unified tax credit operate you must first be able to calculate **taxable gifts,** as illustrated in Figure 18.5. Taxable gifts equal the total value of gifts made during the year less the annual exclusion per recipient, gifts to charitable institutions, amounts paid to medical and educational institutions for services provided the recipient, and amounts given to a spouse.

The annual exclusion per recipient is $10,000. Through the yearly application of this exclusion, a good part of many estates can be transferred tax free over the donor's lifetime. For example, suppose you have three children and you transfer $10,000 to each one. Accordingly, $30,000 could be transferred each year without incurring a gift tax. Moreover, if you are married, each spouse is entitled to a $10,000 exclusion per recipient, so that in this situation $60,000 in yearly transfers would escape the gift tax.

Even if you have a taxable gift, you will probably not have to pay a gift tax. For example, if the taxable gifts for this and previous years total less than $600,000, then the unified tax credit could be used to offset the entire amount due.

Box 18.3 SIMPLIFYING FINANCIAL PLANNING
Checklist for Estate Planning Documents

These are the documents that every family should have. They should be current and readily accessible.

- ✔ A Valid Will
  Purpose: To attain a desirable distribution of your estate and establish care for your dependent survivors. Needs to be reviewed whenever there is a change in family status or a significant change in financial resources.
  Location: Your lawyer's safe or in some states with the Registry of Deeds. A copy may be kept at home.
- ✔ Letter of Last Instructions
  Purpose: To provide information on the management and location of your assets. It should contain a financial inventory.
  Location: A copy should be kept with the will or other safe accessible place. Other copies may be distributed to those who must locate and manage your death estate.
- ✔ Durable Power of Attorney
  Purpose: To grant a trusted person, called the agent, the power to handle your financial affairs. A durable power of attorney will remain effective should you become incapacitated. Document older than seven years may need to be updated.
  Location: A copy may be held by the person granted the durable power of attorney. In some states it must be kept on file at the Registry of Deeds. Retain the original in a safe place that your agent will have access to when needed.
- ✔ Living Will
  Purpose: To express your wishes concerning life-sustaining health care if you were terminally ill or permanently unconscious.
  Location: Copies should be held by your physician, your attorney, and close relations.
- ✔ Health Care Durable Power of Attorney
  Purpose: To grant a trusted person the power to make health care decisions for you should you become incapacitated. It allows you to more fully specify your health care wishes than a living will. Document older than seven years may need to be updated.
  Location: A copy held by the person granted the health care power of attorney. Retain the original in a safe place that your agent will have access to.

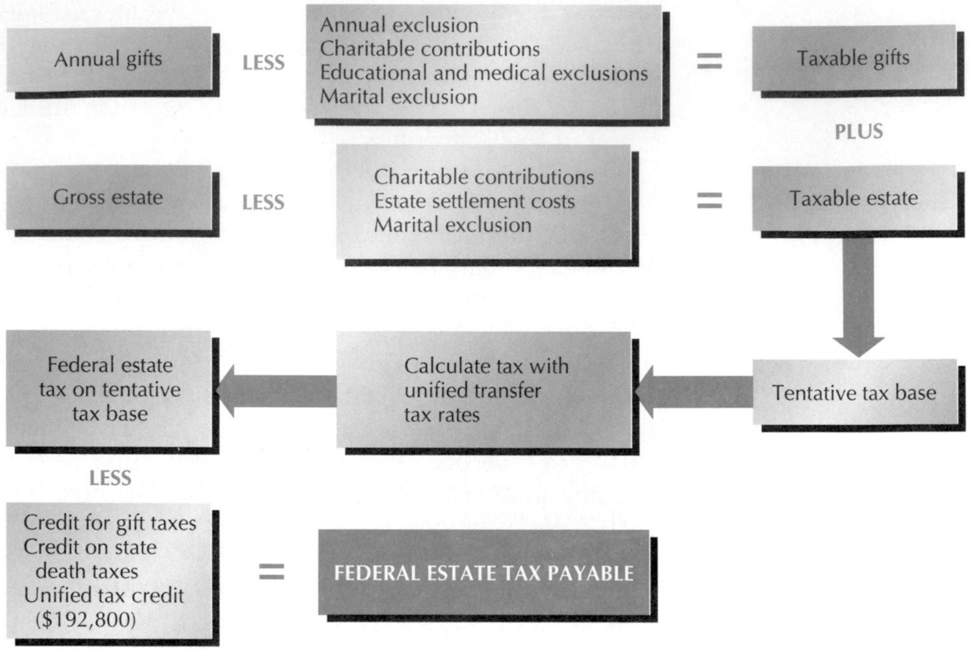

Figure 18.5
Taxable transfers.

The Federal Estate Tax

Taxable estate: The gross estate less excludable amounts.

Gross estate: Everything owned at death less indebtedness.

Marital exclusion: The value of property transferred to the spouse that is excluded from taxable transfers.

That part of the unified tax credit not used to offset gift taxes may be applied to reduce federal estate taxes on the **taxable estate.** To calculate the taxable estate, you must first begin with an estimate of the **gross estate.** This figure equals the value of everything owned at the moment of death, including life insurance proceeds when the policy is owned by the deceased, less indebtedness. The gross estate is then reduced by the marital deduction, estate settlement costs, and charitable contributions to arrive at the taxable estate.

The **marital exclusion** is equal to the value of the property transferred to the spouse. Since 1982 there has been an unlimited deduction for such transfers, whether by gift or at death. Accordingly, regardless of the size of the estate, the property received by one spouse at the death of the other will transfer free of federal estate taxes.

For nonspousal transfers there will be a taxable estate. However, the unused portion of the unified tax credit may eliminate all or most of the tentative estate tax. For example, suppose the last surviving parent is leaving a taxable estate of $500,000, and that this individual made taxable gifts of $200,000. On the combined tentative tax base of $700,000, estate and gift taxes would amount to $229,800. When we subtract from this the unified tax credit of $192,800, federal estate taxes payable are reduced to only $37,000. This is slightly more than 5 percent of the taxable transfers.

However, it is possible that even this minimal tax could have been avoided by transferring part of the estate to the children at the death of the first parent and the remainder of the estate at the death of the second parent. In this manner, $600,000 in transfers could have been excluded at each death, eliminating potential gift and estate taxes on $1,200,000 of taxable transfers.

TRUSTS AND SPOUSAL TRANSFERS Through the use of trusts you can accomplish several important estate planning tasks simultaneously: You can provide for the lifetime support of a surviving spouse, you can determine whether the property used to provide the lifetime support should be included in your own or your spouse's taxable estate, and finally, you can determine who chooses the ultimate beneficiary of the estate at the death of the surviving spouse. The types and characteristics of trusts used for these purposes are summarized in Table 18.1.

Suppose you want to take advantage of the unified tax credit at your death. As explained previously, this would reduce the size of the surviving spouse's taxable estate, possibly eliminating a future estate tax liability. This could be accomplished if you left the property directly to your children. But you hesitate to do this, because you feel the assets might be needed for the support of the surviving spouse. A **bypass trust** (also called a nonmarital trust) could eliminate your dilemma.

Bypass trust: Provides lifetime support for the surviving spouse, but bypasses the death estate of that spouse.

A bypass trust provides for the life support of the surviving spouse. At the death of the surviving spouse, the remainder in the trust passes to beneficiaries named by the initial creator of the trust. Since the surviving spouse has no say in who ultimately receives the trust, the trust would not be included in the death estate of the surviving spouse. The property of the trust therefore bypasses the estate of the surviving spouse. The property in the bypass trust is included in the taxable estate of the creator. However, if the taxable estate of the creator is less than $600,000, the unified tax credit will eliminate all tax liabilities.

Alternatively, suppose you want to take advantage of the marital exclusion and provide for the life support of a surviving spouse. In this case, property used to fund the trust would be excluded from the initial spouse's death estate but included in the estate of the last spouse to die. This could be accomplished through a **marital trust.**

Marital trust: Property qualifies for the marital exclusion but is included in the estate of the last spouse to die.

A marital trust typically provides the surviving spouse with the power to appoint the ultimate beneficiary. Suppose you want to provide for the future support of a surviving spouse. On the other hand, you are worried your spouse might squander your estate or even remarry and leave the remainder to someone other than your children. Therefore, you might want to deny the surviving spouse the right to appoint the ultimate beneficiaries of the trust. A special kind of marital trust called a **Q-TIP** trust (a qualified terminable interest property trust) would satisfy all your objectives. It denies the surviving spouse the right to appoint beneficiaries, while at the same time qualifying for the marital exclusion.

Q-TIP trust: Qualifies for the marital exclusion while also denying the surviving spouse the right to appoint the ultimate beneficiary.

INTERGENERATIONAL TRANSFERS An intergenerational transfer is any transfer of property from one generation to another. A transfer of money from parents to children, or from grandparents to grandchildren, would be an intergenerational transfer.

TABLE 18.1 • TRUSTS AND ESTATE PLANNING

	Qualifies for Marital Deduction	Surviving Spouse Has Right to Appoint Beneficiary	Included in Deceased Spouse's Estate	Included in Surviving Spouse's Estate
Marital trusts				
Power of appointment	Yes	Yes	No	Yes
Q-TIP	Yes	No	No	Yes
Bypass trusts (nonmarital trusts)	No	No	Yes	No

It is possible to make direct transfers and create trusts that skip a generation. For example, a transfer from grandparent to grandchildren while the grandchildren's parents were living would skip a generation. Such transfers would also skip being included in the grandchildren's parents' death estate and thus avoid a whole generation of death/estate taxes. The **Generation Skipping Transfer Tax (GST)** is meant to close this loophole partially by levying a special tax of 50 percent on generation-skipping transfers. The tax is applied, however, only after a liberal $1 million exclusion.

Generation Skipping Transfer Tax (GST): Levies a special tax on estate transfers that attempt to skip a generation.

Federal Income Taxes

Most of us are not wealthy enough to worry about the gift or estate tax. However, the method in which our property is distributed can still be important because it may determine federal income taxes paid by the beneficiaries. In some situations it may be preferable to let the property transfer at death rather than as a gift. For example, suppose Sharon Steele lived in a non-community property state and owned exclusively under her own name some shares of stock with an original cost of $5,000 and a current market value of $15,000. If she sold the shares today, she would have to pay tax on the $10,000 gain in value. However, if she died today, and Arnold received these shares as a death transfer and then subsequently sold the stocks for $15,000, there would be no capital gains tax to pay. This is because the property of the deceased receives a stepped-up cost basis for tax purposes, set by the executor either at the time of death or at an alternative valuation date six months after the death. Thus, if the shares are valued at $15,000 at the time of the death and later sold for the same amount, no capital gains taxes are due.

On the other hand, if Sharon had made Arnold a gift of the stock before her supposed death, there would be a $5,000 cost basis when Arnold sold the stock. The recipient of a gift must assume the donor's cost basis when the property has appreciated in value. The basic rule of thumb is that you let those goods that have appreciated in market value transfer at death rather than as gifts. In this way a new cost basis is established, and potential capital gains taxes are eliminated.

Alternatively, don't bequeath property that has depreciated in value. The beneficiary will not be able to receive the tax benefit from the capital loss. Don't give depreciated property away, either. The best strategy is to take the capital loss yourself. On gifts that have depreciated in value, the cost basis to the recipient is the lower of the cost to the donor or the fair market value at the time the gift was made. Thus, the recipient of a gift that has depreciated in value since it was purchased by the donor would not be able to take the reduction in value before the property was transferred as a loss for tax purposes.

The type of ownership can also influence income tax liabilities for survivors. If the stocks in the previous example were held in joint tenancy by both Arnold and Sharon, instead of being solely owned by Sharon, then only 50 percent of the shares would have received a stepped-up cost basis at the time of Sharon's death. When a husband and wife enter into a joint tenancy, the assumption is that each owns an undivided interest of 50 percent. Therefore, if Arnold subsequently sold the stock for $15,000, he would pay taxes on only half of the $10,000 capital gain.

You would expect taxes to affect community property in the same way as property in joint tenancy, but they don't. If the stocks in the previous example were acquired during the marriage from the joint efforts of Arnold and Sharon, they would be community property, regardless of whose name they were held in. The entire amount of such community property receives a new cost basis at the death of either partner. In this example, the stocks would have a new cost basis of $15,000 even though they were previously held in Sharon's name.

The exception to this rule proves that the tax code, if nothing else, is meant to be consistent. If property is held in joint tenancy by a husband and wife in a community property state, the community interest is negated, and only 50 percent of the property receives a stepped-up basis.

Funds in qualified retirement plans and individual retirement accounts (see Chapter 17) do not receive a stepped-up basis at death. The deceased is said to have had a zero cost basis in these retirement funds. This means that the funds become fully taxable when withdrawn by the beneficiary.

Action Plan for the Steeles: The Need for a Will

Background Most of the Steeles' major assets, including their home, the vehicles, and the bank accounts, are owned by Arnold and Sharon in joint tenancy. The other important assets, such as life insurance policies and retirement accounts, have assigned beneficiaries. Given that the terms of ownership of their assets already provide for their disposition upon the death of either Sharon or Arnold, and that they both would feel comfortable with any of their close relatives assuming the role of guardian, the Steeles have not felt the need to draw up a will.

The Problem Recently, one of Arnold's co-workers, who was not much older than Arnold, suffered a stroke and died. Since he mentioned this news to Sharon, she has been urging Arnold to consult an attorney and have a will drawn up. She now feels they have reached the time in life when they should take a more formal approach to estate planning. However, Arnold still wonders whether the will is worth the cost of the attorney's fee. He has suggested to Sharon they get one of those books with tear-out forms telling you how to write a will without consulting an attorney.

The Plan The Steeles have erred in not having a will drawn up before now. They should contact an attorney specializing in estate planning immediately and have wills drawn up for both of them. If Arnold wants to save money, he should consider changing the oil in the family cars, rather than writing his own will. The attorney's fee is likely to be much less expensive than the financial mess that would ensue were both Arnold and Sharon to die without a valid will. In the absence of a valid will, the courts would have to pick an administrator for the estate, choose a guardian for the children, and set up a trust fund for their future support. Resolving these matters in the will would cut legal expenses and ease the emotional strain on the surviving children.

If Arnold and Sharon both died intestate, the children would divide the estate equally. However, since both Nancy and John are minors, they could not receive the property directly. Rather, it would be placed in a court-appointed trust and utilized according to terms set down by the court. As each reached the age of majority, Nancy and John would receive whatever amount remained in the trust fund.

Instead of having the court determine how these funds will be managed and used for the support of the children, Arnold and Sharon can decide this by creating a testamentary trust through the will. With a little forethought, they can set up a trust fund that would support the children in much the same way as they do now, not the way the court-imposed trust would do it.

The Steeles will not spend equal amounts on the upbringing of Nancy and John. Families usually provide for their children according to each child's needs, aptitudes, and opportunities. For example, if one child requires special medical care or has a special talent for academics or athletics, the parents might decide to allocate a disproportionate share of the family's resources for the improvement of that child. Through a testamentary trust the Steeles could accomplish much the same. The property could be placed in a single fund that provided for the care and support of both children according to need. Only after the younger child reached the age of majority would what was left be divided equally between the children.

Another important item the Steeles could control in a testamentary trust is the time when each child receives the monies held in trust. The fund need not be dissolved when the child reaches the age of majority, but instead could be delayed until some later age. Furthermore, the entire amount does not have to be paid out at one time. One common provision in testamentary trusts is that only one-half of the value of the trust fund is paid out when the child reaches a specific age. Payment of the other half is delayed for about five years. Consequently, if the child squanders the first payment, he or she gets a second chance to manage the second half more carefully.

Another obvious reason the Steeles need a will is so that they can name a potential guardian for the children. They shouldn't assume that surviving relatives, children, and the courts will all come to a mutually agreeable decision. To avoid misunderstandings and costly litigation, they should select a guardian. If both the chosen guardian and the children agree with the decision, this person should be named guardian in the will.

Durable power of attorney: Allows another to act on your behalf, even if you become incapacitated or disabled.

While they are at the lawyer's office having the will drawn up, they should also inquire about a **durable power of attorney.** Most of the Steeles' property is held in joint tenancy. Given the family relationships involved, and tax considerations, this form of ownership may be appropriate for them. However, it could present problems were either Arnold or Sharon to become mentally incapable of making financial decisions. The disposition of jointly held property may require the written consent of both tenants.

A *power of attorney* is a written agreement that allows one individual to act on behalf of another. With a power of attorney, another person could act with the same authority over your financial affairs as you would yourself. Even stronger is a *durable* power of attorney, which does not lapse if you become incapacitated or disabled.

The one major drawback of such an arrangement is that it may delegate to your spouse a little more power than is desirable during ordinary times. Accordingly, a knowledgeable attorney may be able to organize your affairs so that the power of attorney does not become operative unless one spouse becomes mentally incapacitated.

With durable powers of attorney and complete wills, the Steeles should be prepared for some of life's worst setbacks.

Inheritance Taxes

The federal government does not impose an inheritance tax. However, 18 states tax inheritances. In all of them, the rates are structured so that the larger the estate and the more distant the relationship to the deceased, the higher is the tax rate. The exact tax rate and the exemption accorded each beneficiary from the tax differ from state to state.

Inheritance tax statutes generally segregate beneficiaries into classes similar to the following:

- Class 1: Spouse
- Class 2: Parents, children, grandparents, lineal descendants
- Class 3: Brothers and sisters, aunts and uncles
- Class 4: Children of brothers and sisters, children of aunts and uncles
- Class 5: All others

Inheritance taxes should play an important role in estate planning by providing an incentive to leave property to closer relatives. Furthermore, because exemptions are low—in one state $5,000 for a spouse—and because rates can be high on large estates, approaching 30 percent, inheritance taxes also provide an incentive for lifetime gifts.

SUMMARY

Estate planning has two primary objectives: first, to transfer your assets at death in a manner consistent with your wishes; and second, to transfer those assets intact insofar as possible. With the advice of professionals, these goals may be accomplished through the use of a will, joint tenancy, revocable and irrevocable trusts, contractual transfers, and gifts. The benefits and disadvantages of each were examined in this chapter. With proper planning, these methods can be used to minimize the impact on transfers of both death and income taxes.

KEY TERMS

administrator/administratrix (p. 500)
beneficiary (p. 506)
bequest (p. 502)
bypass trust (p. 511)
codicil (p. 503)
community property (p. 505)
death estate (p. 499)
death tax (p. 508)
durable power of attorney (p. 514)
estate tax (p. 508)
executor/executrix (p. 500)
fiduciary responsibility (p. 506)
Generation Skipping Transfer Tax (GST) (p. 512)
gift tax (p. 508)
grantor (p. 506)
gross estate (p. 510)
inheritance tax (p. 508)
inter vivos trust (p. 506)
intestate (p. 499)
irrevocable trust (p. 506)
joint tenancy (p. 505)
legacy (p. 502)
letter of last instructions (p. 503)
living trust (p. 506)
marital exclusion (p. 510)
marital trust (p. 511)
per capita division (p. 502)
per stirpes division (p. 502)
probate (p. 504)
Q-TIP trust (p. 511)
revocable trust (p. 506)
taxable estate (p. 510)
taxable gifts (p. 509)
tenancy in common (p. 505)
testamentary trust (p. 506)
testate (p. 500)
testator/testatrix (p. 500)
trust (p. 506)
trustee (p. 506)
trustee bank account (p. 507)
Uniform Probate Code (p. 504)
will (p. 499)

PROBLEMS AND REVIEW QUESTIONS

1. What are the basic objectives of estate planning?
2. What does it mean to die intestate? How might your estate be divided if you died intestate?
3. What can be accomplished only through the use of a will? How would these matters be handled in the absence of a will?
4. How may a previous will be revoked?
5. When certain changes occur, it is important that you review your will. What are these changes, and why is it important to review your will when they occur?
6. How does the letter of last instructions differ from the last will and testament? What might be included in one but not the other?
7. For estate planning purposes, what is the difference between *joint tenancy* and *tenancy in common*? When might a husband and wife want to avoid joint tenancy?

8. What is a trust? What obligation does the trustee have?
9. What different types of trusts can be created? Explain how each can affect probate costs and estate taxes.
10. There are two common types of death taxes. What are they, and how do they differ?
11. For an estate tax to be effective, what other type of tax must also exist? Why?
12. Suppose a married couple jointly gave $25,000 to a distant relative during the year. How much of this amount would represent a taxable gift? Under what circumstances would the full amount be nontaxable?
13. Discuss the ways in which a married couple might plan to transfer this estate so as to avoid all federal estate and gift taxes.
14. How is the cost basis of a gift determined for income tax purposes?
15. Discuss how previous ownership of assets by the deceased may affect future income taxes paid by the beneficiaries.

Case 18.1 Jim and Nancy Vuduris Purchase a New Home

Jim and Nancy Vuduris recently got married. Each was married before, and each had two children from the previous marriage living with them. Since the new combined family was too large for either of their present homes, they found it necessary to sell the old homes and purchase a single, larger house. They realize that the way in which ownership in the new home is specified will affect their estate planning and future tax liabilities. Accordingly, they plan to consult an attorney before taking title to the new home.

QUESTIONS

1. Why are the sale of the old homes and the purchase of a new home important considerations in their estate plan? What types of problems do such transactions create?
2. What are the several ways in which Jim and Nancy might hold ownership in the new home? How might each of these affect future tax liabilities or the survivor at the death of the first?
3. If Jim were to die intestate, how might his ownership in the home be distributed?

Case 18.2 A Grandchild for the Trebnicks

Last night Linda and Gregg Trebnick received a phone call from their son Matt, telling them their first grandchild had been born, a 10-pound baby girl to be named Marta Trebnick.

The senior Trebnicks have done well over the years. Linda and Gregg invested in some common stocks that have risen enormously in value since they purchased them many years ago. They now have a portfolio of stocks and bonds that is large enough to meet all of their expected retirement needs and then some, but not large enough to make them worry about federal estate taxes. Moreover, they are on a substantial government pension with automatic cost-of-living adjustments.

Given their present financial position, they would like to celebrate the birth by setting up a trust fund to provide for Marta's future college education. They are considering selling some of their stocks that have appreciated in value and placing these funds in the trust.

QUESTIONS

1. Given the types of trust funds discussed in this chapter, which one appears most advantageous for the Trebnicks? Explain why.
2. Setting up the trust will have certain tax implications. What are they?
3. Suppose the Trebnicks had an estate large enough to be potentially liable for estate taxes. Would this affect the choice of the most advantageous trust vehicle? How and why?

INTERNET ADDRESSES

Estate and Gift Tax Law Materials (links prepared by the Legal Information Institute)
http://www.law.cornell.edu/topics/estate_gift_tax.html

Lifenet (calculator for estimating estate taxes)
http://www.lifenet.com/estate.html

Living Wills Infoserve (Canadian registry for living wills)
http://www.sentex.net/~lwr/index.html

Appendix A

Time-Value-of-Money Concepts

In Chapter 1 you were introduced to the basic concepts regarding the time value of money. This appendix provides greater detail about these concepts and it also includes present value and future value of $1 tables.

FUTURE VALUE OF A SINGLE PAYMENT

Finding the future value, *FV*, of a sum of money invested today answers the question: "How much will my money grow if I invest it today and leave it in the investment for a specified number of time periods, assuming it earns a specified rate of return each period?" For example, $100 invested for three years and earning 10 percent each year grows to $133.10, as shown below.

$$FV \text{ end of year } 1 = \$100 + 0.10(\$100) = \$110.00$$
$$FV \text{ end of year } 2 = \$110 + 0.10(\$110) = \$121.00$$
$$FV \text{ end of year } 3 = \$121 + 0.10(\$121) = \$133.10$$

The year-by-year solution is long and unnecessary, because there are two much quicker solutions. If you have a calculator, simply use the *FV* of a single payment formula, which is

$$FV = PV(1.0 + i)^n \qquad \text{(A1)}$$

where

FV = the future value
PV = the present value (the amount invested today)
i = the interest rate per period
n = the number of periods the PV is invested

In the above example, we have

$$FV = \$100(1.0 + 0.10)^3 = \$100(1.10)^3 = \$100(1.331) = \$133.10$$

The other approach for finding an *FV* is to refer to a future value (also called compound value) table. These are widely available, and they show the future value of $1 for various investment periods and rates. Table A.1 illustrates a future value table, and if you go down the left-hand column to period 3 (indicating three holding periods) and across to the 10 percent column, you find the number 1.3310. (Of course, this is the same number we have already calculated.) Since this shows the

TABLE A.1 • FUTURE VALUE (*FV*) OF $1 AT THE END OF *n* PERIODS: $FV = (1.0 + i)^n$

Number of Periods	1%	2%	3%	4%	5%	6%	7%	8%	9%	10%	12%	14%	15%	16%	18%	20%	24%	28%	32%	36%
1	1.0100	1.0200	1.0300	1.0400	1.0500	1.0600	1.0700	1.0800	1.0900	1.1000	1.1200	1.1400	1.1500	1.1600	1.1800	1.2000	1.2400	1.2800	1.3200	1.3600
2	1.0201	1.0404	1.0609	1.0816	1.1025	1.1236	1.1449	1.1664	1.1881	1.2100	1.2544	1.2996	1.3225	1.3456	1.3924	1.4400	1.5376	1.6384	1.7424	1.8496
3	1.0303	1.0612	1.0927	1.1249	1.1576	1.1910	1.2250	1.2597	1.2950	1.3310	1.4049	1.4815	1.5209	1.5609	1.6430	1.7280	1.9066	2.0972	2.3000	2.5155
4	1.0406	1.0824	1.1255	1.1699	1.2155	1.2625	1.3108	1.3605	1.4116	1.4641	1.5735	1.6890	1.7490	1.8106	1.9388	2.0736	2.3642	2.6844	3.0360	3.4210
5	1.0510	1.1041	1.1593	1.2167	1.2763	1.3382	1.4026	1.4693	1.5386	1.6105	1.7623	1.9254	2.0114	2.1003	2.2878	2.4883	2.9316	3.4360	4.0075	4.6526
6	1.0615	1.1262	1.1941	1.2653	1.3401	1.4185	1.5007	1.5869	1.6771	1.7716	1.9738	2.1950	2.3131	2.4364	2.6996	2.9860	3.6352	4.3980	5.2899	6.3275
7	1.0721	1.1487	1.2299	1.3159	1.4071	1.5036	1.6058	1.7138	1.8280	1.9487	2.2107	2.5023	2.6600	2.8262	3.1855	3.5832	4.5077	5.6295	6.9826	8.6054
8	1.0829	1.1717	1.2668	1.3686	1.4775	1.5938	1.7182	1.8509	1.9926	2.1436	2.4760	2.8526	3.0590	3.2784	3.7589	4.2998	5.5895	7.2058	9.2170	11.705
9	1.0937	1.1951	1.3048	1.4233	1.5513	1.6895	1.8385	1.9990	2.1719	2.3579	2.7731	3.2519	3.5179	3.8030	4.4355	5.1598	6.9310	9.2234	12.166	15.916
10	1.1046	1.2190	1.3439	1.4802	1.6289	1.7908	1.9672	2.1589	2.3674	2.5937	3.1058	3.7072	4.0456	4.4114	5.2338	6.1917	8.5944	11.805	16.059	21.646
11	1.1157	1.2434	1.3842	1.5395	1.7103	1.8983	2.1049	2.3316	2.5804	2.8531	3.4785	4.2262	4.6524	5.1173	6.1759	7.4301	10.657	15.111	21.198	29.439
12	1.1268	1.2682	1.4258	1.6010	1.7959	2.0122	2.2522	2.5182	2.8127	3.1384	3.8960	4.8179	5.3502	5.9360	7.2876	8.9161	13.214	19.342	27.982	40.037
13	1.1381	1.2936	1.4685	1.6651	1.8856	2.1329	2.4098	2.7196	3.0658	3.4523	4.3635	5.4924	6.1528	6.8858	8.5994	10.699	16.386	24.758	36.937	54.451
14	1.1495	1.3195	1.5126	1.7317	1.9799	2.2609	2.5785	2.9372	3.3417	3.7975	4.8871	6.2613	7.0757	7.9875	10.147	12.839	20.319	31.691	48.756	74.053
15	1.1610	1.3459	1.5580	1.8009	2.0789	2.3966	2.7590	3.1722	3.6425	4.1772	5.4736	7.1379	8.1371	9.2655	11.973	15.407	25.195	40.564	64.358	100.71
16	1.1726	1.3728	1.6047	1.8730	2.1829	2.5404	2.9522	3.4259	3.9703	4.5950	6.1304	8.1372	9.3576	10.748	14.129	18.488	31.242	51.923	84.953	136.96
17	1.1843	1.4002	1.6528	1.9479	2.2920	2.6928	3.1588	3.7000	4.3276	5.0545	6.8660	9.2765	10.761	12.467	16.672	22.186	38.740	66.461	112.13	186.27
18	1.1961	1.4282	1.7024	2.0258	2.4066	2.8543	3.3799	3.9960	4.7171	5.5599	7.6900	10.575	12.375	14.462	19.673	26.623	48.038	85.070	148.02	253.33
19	1.2081	1.4568	1.7535	2.1068	2.5270	3.0256	3.6165	4.3157	5.1417	6.1159	8.6128	12.055	14.231	16.776	23.214	31.948	59.567	108.89	195.39	344.53
20	1.2202	1.4859	1.8061	2.1911	2.6533	3.2071	3.8697	4.6610	5.6044	6.7275	9.6463	13.743	16.366	19.460	27.393	38.337	73.864	139.37	257.91	468.57
21	1.2324	1.5157	1.8603	2.2788	2.7860	3.3996	4.1406	5.0338	6.1088	7.4002	10.803	15.667	18.821	22.574	32.323	46.005	91.591	178.40	340.44	637.26
22	1.2447	1.5460	1.9161	2.3699	2.9253	3.6035	4.4304	5.4365	6.6586	8.1403	12.100	17.861	21.644	26.186	38.142	55.206	113.57	228.35	449.39	866.67
23	1.2572	1.5769	1.9736	2.4647	3.0715	3.8197	4.7405	5.8715	7.2579	8.9543	13.552	20.361	24.891	30.376	45.007	66.247	140.83	292.30	593.19	1178.6
24	1.2697	1.6084	2.0328	2.5633	3.2251	4.0489	5.0724	6.3412	7.9111	9.8497	15.178	23.212	28.625	35.236	53.108	79.496	174.63	374.14	783.02	1602.9
25	1.2824	1.6406	2.0938	2.6658	3.3864	4.2919	5.4274	6.8485	8.6231	10.834	17.000	26.461	32.918	40.874	62.668	95.396	216.54	478.90	1033.5	2180.0
26	1.2953	1.6734	2.1566	2.7725	3.5557	4.5494	5.8074	7.3964	9.3992	11.918	19.040	30.166	37.856	47.414	73.948	114.47	268.51	612.99	1364.3	2964.9
27	1.3082	1.7069	2.2213	2.8834	3.7335	4.8223	6.2139	7.9881	10.245	13.110	21.324	34.389	43.535	55.000	87.259	137.37	332.95	784.63	1800.9	4032.2
28	1.3213	1.7410	2.2879	2.9987	3.9201	5.1117	6.6488	8.6271	11.167	14.421	23.883	39.204	50.065	63.800	102.96	164.84	412.86	1004.3	2377.2	5483.8
29	1.3345	1.7758	2.3566	3.1187	4.1161	5.4184	7.1143	9.3173	12.172	15.863	26.749	44.693	57.575	74.008	121.50	197.81	511.95	1285.5	3137.9	7458.0
30	1.3478	1.8114	2.4273	3.2434	4.3219	5.7435	7.6123	10.062	13.267	17.449	29.959	50.950	66.211	85.849	143.37	237.37	634.81	1645.5	4142.0	10143.
40	1.4889	2.2080	3.2620	4.8010	7.0400	10.285	14.974	21.724	31.409	45.259	93.050	188.88	267.86	378.72	750.37	1469.7	5455.9	19426.	66520.	*
50	1.6446	2.6916	4.3839	7.1067	11.467	18.420	29.457	46.901	74.357	117.39	289.00	700.23	1083.6	1670.7	3927.3	9100.4	46890.	*	*	*
60	1.8167	3.2810	5.8916	10.519	18.679	32.987	57.946	101.25	176.03	304.48	897.59	2595.9	4383.9	7370.1	20555.	56347.	*	*	*	*

NOTE: n = number of periods; i = interest rate per period.

future value of $1, the final step is to multiply the *FV* of $1 by the amount of dollars invested, as we have already done.

FUTURE VALUE OF A STREAM OF EQUAL PAYMENTS (AN ANNUITY)

Very often an investment program calls for an equal amount invested each period. For example, suppose your budget allows a $100 investment each year. You are curious about how much you will accumulate at the end of three years, assuming you begin making payments at the end of each of the next three years. This total future value is calculated below:

FV of the payment made at the end of year 1 = $\$100(1.10)^2 = \$100(1.21) = \$121.00$
FV of the payment made at the end of year 2 = $\$100(1.10)^1 = \$100(1.10) = \$110.00$
FV of the payment made at the end of year 3 = $100.00
Total future value = $331.00

Just as in the case of the *FV* of a single payment, you can use a formula to find the future value of a stream of equal investments—that is, of an annuity. It is

$$FV = \frac{[(1.0 + i)^n - 1.0] \times A}{i} \tag{A2}$$

where, *FV*, *i*, and *n* have the same meaning as before, and *A* = the amount of the annuity.

Substituting the above values, we have

$$FV = \frac{[(1.0 + 0.10)^3 - 1.0] \times 100}{0.10} = \frac{[(1.10)^3 - 1.0] \times 100}{0.10}$$
$$= \frac{(1.331 - 1.0) \times 100}{0.10} = \frac{0.331 \times 100}{0.10} = \frac{33.10}{0.10} = \$331.10$$

There are also future value of an annuity tables that can be consulted for a quick answer. Table A.2 is an example of such a table. To find the answer to the above example, again simply go down to period 3 and across to the 10 percent column to find the answer for the future value of a $1 annuity invested for three periods at a rate of 10 percent each period. It is 3.31. Multiply the amount of the annuity, $100, by this number to arrive at the correct answer: $331.00.

The above example assumes that the annuity payments begin at the end of the first period. However, you might encounter situations where the payments begin immediately. Let's assume that to be the case using the above example again. This change offers no particular problem: Simply assume four holding periods instead of three and then subtract 1.0 from the *FV* coefficient. In Table A.2, the coefficient for four periods at 10 percent is 4.641. Subtracting 1.0 from this gives 3.641, which is the future value of $1 invested for three periods with payments beginning immediately. So $100 invested in this fashion would grow to $364.10, a somewhat larger amount than in the previous illustration. Of course, this answer makes sense because your money is invested one year longer.

TABLE A.2 • FUTURE VALUE OF $1 ANNUITY: $FV = \left(\frac{(1.0 + i)^n - 1.0}{i}\right)$

Number of Periods	1%	2%	3%	4%	5%	6%	7%	8%	9%	10%	12%	14%	15%	16%	18%	20%	24%	28%	32%	36%
1	1.0000	1.0000	1.0000	1.0000	1.0000	1.0000	1.0000	1.0000	1.0000	1.0000	1.0000	1.0000	1.0000	1.0000	1.0000	1.0000	1.0000	1.0000	1.0000	1.0000
2	2.0100	2.0200	2.0300	2.0400	2.0500	2.0600	2.0700	2.0800	2.0900	2.1000	2.1200	2.1400	2.1500	2.1600	2.1800	2.2000	2.2400	2.2800	2.3200	2.3600
3	3.0301	3.0604	3.0909	3.1216	3.1525	3.1836	3.2149	3.2464	3.2781	3.3100	3.3744	3.4396	3.4725	3.5056	3.5724	3.6400	3.7776	3.9184	4.0624	4.2096
4	4.0604	4.1216	4.1836	4.2465	4.3101	4.3746	4.4399	4.5061	4.5731	4.6410	4.7793	4.9211	4.9934	5.0665	5.2154	5.3680	5.6842	6.0156	6.3624	6.7251
5	5.1010	5.2040	5.3091	5.4163	5.5256	5.6371	5.7507	5.8666	5.9847	6.1051	6.3528	6.6101	6.7424	6.8771	7.1542	7.4416	8.0484	8.6999	9.3983	10.146
6	6.1520	6.3081	6.4684	6.6330	6.8019	6.9753	7.1533	7.3359	7.5233	7.7156	8.1152	8.5355	8.7537	8.9775	9.4420	9.9299	10.980	12.135	13.405	14.798
7	7.2135	7.4343	7.6625	7.8983	8.1420	8.3938	8.6540	8.9228	9.2004	9.4872	10.089	10.730	11.066	11.413	12.141	12.915	14.615	16.533	18.695	21.126
8	8.2857	8.5830	8.8923	9.2142	9.5491	9.8975	10.259	10.636	11.028	11.435	12.299	13.232	13.726	14.240	15.327	16.499	19.122	22.163	25.678	29.731
9	9.3685	9.7546	10.159	10.582	11.026	11.491	11.978	12.487	13.021	13.579	14.775	16.085	16.785	17.518	19.085	20.798	24.712	29.369	34.895	41.435
10	10.462	10.949	11.463	12.006	12.577	13.180	13.816	14.486	15.192	15.937	17.548	19.337	20.303	21.321	23.521	25.958	31.643	38.592	47.061	57.351
11	11.566	12.168	12.807	13.486	14.206	14.971	15.783	16.645	17.560	18.531	20.654	23.044	24.349	25.732	28.755	32.150	40.237	50.398	63.121	78.993
12	12.682	13.412	14.192	15.025	15.917	16.869	17.888	18.977	20.140	21.384	24.133	27.270	29.001	30.850	34.931	39.580	50.894	65.510	84.320	108.43
13	13.809	14.680	15.617	16.626	17.713	18.882	20.140	21.495	22.953	24.522	28.029	32.088	34.351	36.786	42.218	48.496	64.109	84.852	112.30	148.47
14	14.947	15.973	17.086	18.291	19.598	21.015	22.550	24.214	26.019	27.975	32.392	37.581	40.504	43.672	50.818	59.195	80.496	109.61	149.23	202.92
15	16.096	17.293	18.598	20.023	21.578	23.276	25.129	27.152	29.360	31.772	37.279	43.842	47.580	51.659	60.965	72.035	100.81	141.30	197.99	276.97
16	17.257	18.639	20.156	21.824	23.657	25.672	27.888	30.324	33.003	35.949	42.753	50.980	55.717	60.925	72.939	87.442	126.01	181.86	262.35	377.69
17	18.430	20.012	21.761	23.697	25.840	28.212	30.840	33.750	36.973	40.544	48.883	59.117	65.075	71.673	87.068	105.93	157.25	233.79	347.30	514.66
18	19.614	21.412	23.414	25.645	28.132	30.905	33.999	37.450	41.301	45.599	55.749	68.394	75.836	84.140	103.74	128.11	195.99	300.25	459.44	700.93
19	20.810	22.840	25.116	27.671	30.539	33.760	37.379	41.446	46.018	51.159	63.439	78.969	88.211	98.603	123.41	154.74	244.03	385.32	607.47	954.27
20	22.019	24.297	26.870	29.778	33.066	36.785	40.995	45.762	51.160	57.275	72.052	91.024	102.44	115.37	146.62	186.68	303.60	494.21	802.86	1298.8
21	23.239	25.783	28.676	31.969	35.719	39.992	44.865	50.422	56.764	64.002	81.698	104.76	118.81	134.84	174.02	225.02	377.46	633.59	1060.7	1767.3
22	24.471	27.299	30.536	34.248	38.505	43.392	49.005	55.456	62.873	71.402	92.502	120.43	137.63	157.41	206.34	271.03	469.05	811.99	1401.2	2404.6
23	25.716	28.845	32.452	36.617	41.430	46.995	53.436	60.893	69.531	79.543	104.60	138.29	159.27	183.60	244.48	326.23	582.62	1040.3	1850.6	3271.3
24	26.973	30.421	34.426	39.082	44.502	50.815	58.176	66.764	76.789	88.497	118.15	158.65	184.16	213.97	289.49	392.48	723.46	1332.6	2443.8	4449.9
25	28.243	32.030	36.459	41.645	47.727	54.864	63.249	73.105	84.700	98.347	133.33	181.87	212.79	249.21	342.60	471.98	898.09	1706.8	3226.8	6052.9
26	29.525	33.670	38.553	44.311	51.113	59.156	68.676	79.954	93.323	109.18	150.33	208.33	245.71	290.08	405.27	567.37	1114.6	2185.7	4260.4	8233.0
27	30.820	35.344	40.709	47.084	54.669	63.705	74.483	87.350	102.72	121.09	169.37	238.49	283.56	337.50	479.22	681.85	1383.1	2798.7	5624.7	11197.9
28	32.129	37.051	42.930	49.967	58.402	68.528	80.697	95.338	112.96	134.20	190.69	272.88	327.10	392.50	566.48	819.22	1716.0	3583.3	7425.6	15230.2
29	33.450	38.792	45.218	52.966	62.322	73.639	87.346	103.96	124.13	148.63	214.58	312.09	377.16	456.30	669.44	984.06	2128.9	4587.6	9802.9	20714.1
30	34.784	40.568	47.575	56.084	66.438	79.058	94.460	113.28	136.30	164.49	241.33	356.78	434.74	530.31	790.94	1181.8	2640.9	5873.2	12940.	28172.2
40	48.886	60.402	75.401	95.025	120.79	154.76	199.63	259.05	337.88	442.59	767.09	1342.0	1779.0	2360.7	4163.2	7343.8	22728.	69377.	*	*
50	64.463	84.579	112.79	152.66	209.34	290.33	406.52	573.76	815.08	1163.9	2400.0	4994.5	72177.	10435.	21813.	45497.	*	*	*	*
60	81.669	114.05	163.05	237.99	353.58	533.12	813.52	1253.2	1944.7	3034.8	7471.6	18535.	29219.	46057.	*	*	*	*	*	*

NOTE: n = number of periods; i = interest rate per period.

PRESENT VALUE OF A SINGLE PAYMENT

To find the present value, *PV*, of a single payment, you just reverse the process of finding a future value. Referring to Equation (A1), you simply rearrange terms to get

$$PV = \frac{FV}{(1.0 + i)^n} \text{ or } PV = FV \times \frac{1.0}{(1.0 + i)^n} \quad \text{(A3)}$$

Thus, the present value of 133.10 received three years from today is $100.

$$PV = \frac{\$133.10}{(1.0 + 0.10)^3} = \frac{\$133.10}{(1.10)^3} = \frac{\$133.10}{1.331} = \$100$$

Table A.3 shows a present value of $1 table. It is used in exactly the same manner as a future value table. The number in the period 3 row and 10 percent column is 0.7513, which is 1 divided by $(1.10)^3$. Multiplying 0.7513 by $133.10 gives $100.

PRESENT VALUE OF A STREAM OF EQUAL PAYMENTS (AN ANNUITY)

The formula below can be used to calculate the present value of a stream of equal payments to be received beginning at the end of the first period and assuming that each payment is discounted at the discount rate applicable each period.

$$PV = \frac{[1.0 - 1.0/(1.0 + i)^n] \times A}{i} \quad \text{(A4)}$$

If you receive $100 at the end of each of the next three periods, the present value of this stream is

$$\begin{aligned} PV &= \frac{[1.0 - 1.0/(1.0 + 0.10)^3] \times \$100}{0.10} = \frac{[1.0 - 1.0/(1.10)^3] \times \$100}{0.10} \\ &= \frac{[1.0 - (1.0/1.331) \times \$100}{0.10} \\ &= \frac{(1.0 - 0.7513) \times \$100}{0.10} = \frac{0.24869 \times \$100}{0.10} = \frac{\$24.869}{0.10} \\ &= \$248.69 \end{aligned}$$

The same answer can be found by referring to a present value of an annuity table, such as the one in Table A.4, and finding the value for $n = 3$ and $i = 10$ percent. This is 2.4869, and multiplying it by the $100 annuity gives $248.69. Figure A.1 shows some applications of *FV* and *PV* techniques; exercises to test your understanding of the material follow.

TABLE A.3 • PRESENT VALUE OF $1: $PV = \frac{1.0}{(1.0 + i)^n}$

Number of Periods	1%	2%	3%	4%	5%	6%	7%	8%	9%	10%	12%	14%	15%	16%	18%	20%	24%	28%	32%	36%
1	.9901	.9804	.9709	.9615	.9524	.9434	.9346	.9259	.9174	.9091	.8929	.8772	.8696	.8621	.8475	.8333	.8065	.7813	.7576	.7353
2	.9803	.9612	.9426	.9246	.9070	.8900	.8734	.8573	.8417	.8264	.7972	.7695	.7561	.7432	.7182	.6944	.6504	.6104	.5739	.5407
3	.9706	.9423	.9151	.8890	.8638	.8396	.8163	.7938	.7722	.7513	.7118	.6750	.6575	.6407	.6086	.5787	.5245	.4768	.4348	.3975
4	.9610	.9238	.8885	.8548	.8227	.7921	.7629	.7350	.7084	.6830	.6355	.5921	.5718	.5523	.5158	.4823	.4230	.3725	.3294	.2923
5	.9515	.9057	.8626	.8219	.7835	.7473	.7130	.6806	.6499	.6209	.5674	.5194	.4972	.4761	.4371	.4019	.3411	.2910	.2495	.2149
6	.9420	.8880	.8375	.7903	.7462	.7050	.6633	.6302	.5963	.5645	.5066	.4556	.4323	.4104	.3704	.3349	.2751	.2274	.1890	.1580
7	.9327	.8706	.8131	.7599	.7107	.6651	.6227	.5835	.5470	.5132	.4523	.3996	.3759	.3538	.3139	.2791	.2218	.1776	.1432	.1162
8	.9235	.8535	.7894	.7307	.6768	.6274	.5820	.5403	.5019	.4665	.4039	.3506	.3269	.3050	.2660	.2326	.1789	.1388	.1085	.0854
9	.9143	.8368	.7664	.7026	.6446	.5919	.5439	.5002	.4604	.4241	.3606	.3075	.2843	.2630	.2255	.1938	.1443	.1084	.0822	.0628
10	.9053	.8203	.7441	.6756	.6139	.5584	.5083	.4632	.4224	.3855	.3220	.2697	.2472	.2267	.1911	.1615	.1164	.0847	.0623	.0462
11	.8963	.8043	.7224	.6496	.5847	.5268	.4751	.4289	.3875	.3505	.2875	.2366	.2149	.1954	.1619	.1346	.0938	.0662	.0472	.0340
12	.8874	.7885	.7014	.6246	.5568	.4970	.4440	.3971	.3555	.3186	.2567	.2076	.1869	.1685	.1372	.1122	.0757	.0517	.0357	.0250
13	.8787	.7730	.6810	.6006	.5303	.4688	.4150	.3677	.3262	.2897	.2292	.1821	.1625	.1452	.1163	.0935	.0610	.0404	.0271	.0184
14	.8700	.7579	.6611	.5775	.5051	.4423	.3878	.3405	.2992	.2633	.2046	.1597	.1413	.1252	.0985	.0779	.0492	.0316	.0205	.0135
15	.8613	.7430	.6419	.5553	.4810	.4173	.3624	.3152	.2745	.2394	.1827	.1401	.1229	.1079	.0835	.0649	.0397	.0247	.0155	.0099
16	.8528	.7284	.6232	.5339	.4581	.3936	.3387	.2919	.2519	.2176	.1631	.1229	.1069	.0930	.0708	.0541	.0320	.0193	.0118	.0073
17	.8444	.7142	.6050	.5134	.4363	.3714	.3166	.2703	.2311	.1978	.1456	.1078	.0929	.0802	.0600	.0451	.0258	.0150	.0089	.0054
18	.8360	.7002	.5874	.4936	.4155	.3503	.2959	.2502	.2120	.1799	.1300	.0946	.0808	.0691	.0508	.0376	.0208	.0118	.0068	.0039
19	.8277	.6864	.5703	.4746	.3957	.3305	.2765	.2317	.1945	.1635	.1161	.0829	.0703	.0596	.0431	.0313	.0168	.0092	.0051	.0029
20	.8195	.6730	.5537	.4564	.3769	.3118	.2584	.2145	.1784	.1486	.1037	.0728	.0611	.0514	.0365	.0261	.0135	.0072	.0039	.0021
21	.8114	.6598	.5375	.4388	.3589	.2942	.2415	.1987	.1637	.1351	.0926	.0638	.0531	.0443	.0309	.0217	.0109	.0056	.0029	.0016
22	.8034	.6468	.5219	.4220	.3418	.2775	.2257	.1839	.1502	.1228	.0826	.0560	.0462	.0382	.0262	.0181	.0088	.0044	.0022	.0012
23	.7954	.6342	.5067	.4057	.3256	.2618	.2109	.1703	.1378	.1117	.0738	.0491	.0402	.0329	.0222	.0151	.0071	.0034	.0017	.0008
24	.7876	.6217	.4919	.3901	.3101	.2470	.1971	.1577	.1264	.1015	.0659	.0431	.0349	.0284	.0188	.0126	.0057	.0027	.0013	.0006
25	.7798	.6095	.4776	.3751	.2953	.2330	.1842	.1460	.1160	.0923	.0588	.0378	.0304	.0245	.0160	.0105	.0046	.0021	.0010	.0005
26	.7720	.5976	.4637	.3607	.2812	.2198	.1722	.1352	.1064	.0839	.0525	.0331	.0264	.0211	.0135	.0087	.0037	.0016	.0007	.0003
27	.7644	.5859	.4502	.3468	.2678	.2074	.1609	.1252	.0976	.0763	.0469	.0291	.0230	.0182	.0115	.0073	.0030	.0013	.0006	.0002
28	.7568	.5744	.4371	.3335	.2551	.1956	.1504	.1159	.0895	.0693	.0419	.0255	.0200	.0157	.0097	.0061	.0024	.0010	.0004	.0002
29	.7493	.5631	.4243	.3207	.2429	.1846	.1406	.1073	.0822	.0630	.0374	.0224	.0174	.0135	.0082	.0051	.0020	.0008	.0003	.0001
30	.7419	.5521	.4120	.3083	.2314	.1741	.1314	.0994	.0754	.0573	.0334	.0196	.0151	.0116	.0070	.0042	.0016	.0006	.0002	.0001
40	.6717	.4529	.3066	.2083	.1420	.0972	.0668	.0460	.0318	.0221	.0107	.0053	.0037	.0026	.0013	.0007	.0002	.0001	*	*
50	.6080	.3715	.2281	.1407	.0872	.0543	.0339	.0213	.0134	.0085	.0035	.0014	.0009	.0006	.0003	.0001	*	*	*	*
60	.5504	.3048	.1697	.0951	.0535	.0303	.0173	.0099	.0057	.0033	.0011	.0004	.0002	.0001	*	*	*	*	*	*

NOTE: n = number of periods; i = interest rate per period.

TABLE A.4 • PRESENT VALUE OF AN ANNUITY OF $1 PER PERIOD FOR *n* PERIODS; $PV = \dfrac{1.0 - \dfrac{1.0}{(1.0 + i)^n}}{i}$

Number of Periods	1%	2%	3%	4%	5%	6%	7%	8%	9%	10%	12%	14%	15%	16%	18%	20%	24%	28%	32%
1	0.9901	0.9804	0.9709	0.9615	0.9524	0.9434	0.9346	0.9259	0.9174	0.9091	0.8929	0.8772	0.8696	0.8621	0.8475	0.8333	0.8065	0.7813	0.7576
2	1.9704	1.9416	1.9135	1.8861	1.8594	1.8334	1.8080	1.7833	1.7591	1.7355	1.6901	1.6467	1.6257	1.6052	1.5656	1.5278	1.4568	1.3916	1.3315
3	2.9410	2.8839	2.8286	2.7751	2.7232	2.6730	2.6243	2.5771	2.5313	2.4869	2.4018	2.3216	2.2832	2.2459	2.1743	2.1065	1.9813	1.8684	1.7663
4	3.9020	3.8077	3.7171	3.6299	3.5460	3.4651	3.3872	3.3121	3.2397	3.1699	3.0373	2.9137	2.8550	2.7982	2.6901	2.5887	2.4043	2.2410	2.0957
5	4.8534	4.7135	4.5797	4.4518	4.3295	4.2124	4.1002	3.9927	3.8897	3.7908	3.6048	3.4331	3.3522	3.2743	3.1272	2.9906	2.7454	2.5320	2.3452
6	5.7955	5.6014	5.4172	5.2421	5.0757	4.9173	4.7665	4.6229	4.4859	4.3553	4.1114	3.8887	3.7845	3.6847	3.4976	3.3255	3.0205	2.7594	2.5342
7	6.7282	6.4720	6.2303	6.0021	5.7864	5.5824	5.3893	5.2064	5.0330	4.8684	4.5638	4.2883	4.1604	4.0386	3.8115	3.6046	3.2423	3.9370	2.6775
8	7.6517	7.3255	7.0179	6.7327	6.4632	6.2098	5.9713	5.7466	5.5348	5.3349	4.9676	4.6389	4.4873	4.3436	4.0776	3.8372	3.4212	3.0758	2.7860
9	8.5660	8.1622	7.7861	7.4353	7.1078	6.8017	6.5152	6.2469	5.9952	5.7590	5.3282	4.9464	4.7716	4.6065	4.3030	4.0310	3.5655	3.1842	2.8681
10	9.4713	8.9826	8.5302	8.1109	7.7217	7.3601	7.0236	6.7101	6.4177	6.1446	5.6502	5.2161	5.0188	4.8332	4.4941	4.1925	3.6819	3.2689	2.9304
11	10.3676	9.7868	9.2526	8.7605	8.3064	7.8869	7.4987	7.1390	6.8052	6.4951	5.9377	5.4527	5.2337	5.0286	4.6560	4.3721	3.7757	3.3351	2.9776
12	11.2551	10.5753	9.9540	9.3851	8.8633	8.3838	7.9427	7.5361	7.1607	6.8137	6.1944	5.6603	5.4206	5.1971	4.7932	4.4392	3.8514	3.3868	3.0133
13	12.1337	11.3484	10.6350	9.9856	9.3936	8.8527	8.3577	7.9038	7.4869	7.1034	6.4235	5.8424	5.5831	5.3423	4.9095	4.5327	3.9124	2.4272	3.0404
14	13.0037	12.1062	11.2961	10.5631	9.8986	9.2950	8.7455	8.2442	7.7862	7.3667	6.6282	6.0021	5.7245	5.4675	5.0081	4.6106	3.9616	3.4587	3.0609
15	13.8651	12.8493	11.9379	11.1184	10.3797	9.7122	9.1079	8.5595	8.0607	7.6061	6.8109	6.1422	5.8474	5.5755	5.0916	4.6755	4.0013	3.4834	3.0764
16	14.7179	13.5777	12.5611	11.6523	10.8378	10.1059	9.4466	8.8514	8.3126	7.8237	6.9740	6.2651	5.9542	5.6685	5.1624	4.7296	4.0333	3.5026	3.0882
17	15.5623	14.2919	13.1661	12.1657	11.2741	10.4773	9.7632	9.1216	8.5436	8.0216	7.1196	6.3729	6.0472	5.7487	5.2223	4.7746	4.0591	3.5177	3.0971
18	16.3983	14.9920	13.7535	12.6593	11.6896	10.8276	10.0591	9.3719	8.7556	8.2014	7.2497	6.4674	6.1280	5.8178	5.2732	4.8122	4.0799	3.5294	3.1039
19	17.2260	15.6785	14.3238	13,1339	12.0853	11.1581	10.3356	9.6036	8.9501	8.3649	7.3658	6.5504	6.1982	5.8775	5.3162	4.8435	4.0967	3.5386	3.1090
20	18.0456	16.3514	14.8775	13.5903	12.4622	11.4699	10.5940	9.8181	9.1285	8.5136	7.4694	6.6231	6.2593	5.9288	5.3527	4.8696	4.1103	3.5458	3.1129
21	18.8570	17.0112	15.4150	14.0292	12.8212	11.7641	10.8355	10.0168	9.2922	8.6487	7.5620	6.6870	6.3125	5.9731	5.3837	4.8913	4.1212	3.5514	3.1158
22	19.6604	17.6580	15.9369	14.4511	13.1630	12.0416	11.0612	10.2007	9.4424	8.7715	7.6446	6.7429	6.3587	6.0113	5.4099	4.9094	4.1300	3.5558	3.1180
23	20.4558	18.2922	16.4436	14.8568	13.4886	12.3034	11.2722	10.3711	9.5802	8.8832	7.7184	6.7921	6.3988	6.0442	5.4321	4.9245	4.1371	3.5592	3.1197
24	21.2434	18.9139	16.9355	15.2470	13.7986	12.5504	11.4693	10.5288	9.7066	8.9847	7.7843	6.8351	6.4338	6.0726	5.4509	4.9371	4.1428	3.5619	3.1210
25	22.0232	19.5325	17.4131	15.6221	14.0939	12.7834	11.6536	10.6748	9.8226	9.0770	7.8431	6.8729	6.4641	6.0971	5.4669	4.9476	4.1474	3.5640	3.1220
26	22.7952	20.1210	17.8768	15.9828	14.3752	13.0032	11.8258	10.8100	9.9290	9.1609	7.8957	6.9061	6.4906	6.1182	5.4804	4.9563	4.1511	3.5656	3.1227
27	23.5596	20.7069	18.3270	16.3296	14.6430	13.2105	11.9867	10.9352	10.0266	9.2372	7.9426	6.9352	6.5135	6.1364	5.4919	4.9636	4.1542	3.5669	3.1233
28	24.3164	21.2813	18.7641	16.6631	14.8981	13.4062	12.1371	11.0511	10.1161	9.3066	7.9844	6.9607	6.5335	6.1520	5.5016	4.9697	4.1566	3.5679	3.1237
29	25.0658	21.8444	19.1885	16.9837	15.1411	13.5907	12.2777	11.1584	10.1983	9.3696	8.0218	6.9830	6.5509	6.1656	5.5098	4.9747	4.1585	3.5687	3.1240
30	25.8077	22.3965	19.6004	17.2920	15.3725	13.7648	12.4090	11.2578	10.2737	9.4268	8.0552	7.0027	6.5660	6.1772	5.5168	4.9789	4.1601	3.5693	3.1242
40	32.8347	27.3555	23.1148	19.7928	17.1591	15.0463	13.3317	11.9246	10.7574	9.7791	8.2438	7.1050	6.6418	6.2335	5.5482	4.9966	4.1659	3.5712	3.1250
50	39.1961	31.4236	25.7298	21.4822	18.2559	15.7619	13.8007	12.2335	10.9617	9.9148	8.3045	7.1327	6.6605	6.2463	5.5541	4.9995	4.1666	3.5714	3.1250
60	44.9550	34.7609	27.6756	22.6235	18.9293	16.1614	14.0392	12.3766	11.0480	9.9672	8.3240	7.1401	6.6651	6.2492	5.5553	4.9999	4.1667	3.5714	3.1250

NOTE: n = number of periods; i = interest rate per period.

Problem	Solution
1. Alicia invests $350 today and expects to earn 20% on the investment each year for the next 20 years. How much will she have?	Find the future value, *FV*, of $1 for 20% and 20 years; 38.337. Multiply 38.337 times $350 to get the answer; it is $13,417.95.
2. Manuel's uncle plans to give him a graduation present of $500 at graduation or $700 three years later if Manuel agrees to complete a graduate program. Considering the value of the gift only, and assuming Manuel could invest at 8% in each of the three years, which is the better alternative?	You can use either future or present value of $1 tables. Using the former, find the *FV* for 8% and three years; it is 1.2597. The future value of $500 is $629.85 ($500 × 1.2597). Since this is less than $700, Manuel is better off waiting three years for his uncle's gift. If you use the present value of $1, you find the present value coefficient for 8% and three years; it is 0.7938. You then find the present value, *PV*, of $700, which is $555.66 (0.7938 × $700). Since the present value is greater than the immediate $500, Manuel should accept the future $700.
3. Gunther's stockbroker is trying to convince Gunther to purchase a security that will be worth $10,000 in 30 years. The cost of the security today is $1,500. Gunther isn't sure whether this is a good or bad investment, but believes he could make a better decision if he knew the approximate rate of return on the investment. What is it?	You can find a rate of return by dividing the future value of an investment by its cost to arrive at a future value of $1 coefficient. Relate this coefficient then to the number of periods and the approximate value of *i*. You have a coefficient of 6.667 ($10,000/$1,500). Since the number of periods is 30, go across the 30 row until you come as close as possible to 6.667. As you see, the corresponds to an *i* value of 6%, which is 5.7435. Since 6.667 is somewhat larger than 5.7435, you conclude the rate of return is greater than 6% but far less than 8% (in which case the coefficient would be 10.0620). As a rough approximation, you conclude it is about 6.5%. (You could use more accurate interpolation techniques, but such accuracy is not necessary in many cases. Moreover, for greater accuracy you should use expanded tables or an appropriate calculating device.)

Figure A.1
Some applications of *FV* and *PV* techniques.

EXERCISES

1. You receive $500 in graduation presents and plan to invest it for your retirement in 40 years. Assuming you can earn 8 percent interest each year, how much will you have at retirement? (Answer: $10,862.) How much will you have if you could earn 12 percent each year? (Answer: $46,526.)
2. Suppose you cannot make an immediate investment for retirement but can afford $100 each year for the next 30 years, with the first payment starting in one year. Assuming a 14 percent investment rate each year, how much will you accumulate at the end of 30 years? (Answer: $35,678.) Suppose your target was to accumulate $50,000; how much

must you invest each year? (Answer: $140.14.) Suppose your target was $50,000 but you had only 20 years and could earn only 10 percent each year. What would be your yearly contribution? (Answer: $872.98.)

3. You are thinking of buying a zero coupon bond. It matures in 10 years for $1,000, pays no yearly interest, and currently costs $200. You look at other similar bonds and see that they are yielding 16 percent. Since you feel the zero coupon bond should also yield 16 percent, the most you are willing to pay for it is ________________. (Answer: $226.70.) Should you or should you not buy the bond? (Answer: Should.) Suppose you bought the bond and interest rates fell immediately afterward, such that your bond yielded only 10 percent based on its current market price. How much would its current market price be? (Answer: $385.50.)
4. You are thinking of buying an annuity to provide future income to your spouse in the event of your death. The insurance company selling the annuity offers two alternatives: The first calls for an immediate payment of $10,000, and the other requires annual payments of $1,500 for the next 10 years with payments beginning in one year. You are pretty sure you can invest your money at 6 percent interest each year for the next 10 years. If this is true, which alternative should you prefer? (Answer: The first, since the present value of the second is $11,040, which is greater than $10,000.) Suppose you could earn 10 percent; now which would be better? (Answer: The second; its present value is $9,217.)

Appendix B

The Social Security System

Social Security was never meant to replace your private pension plan or eliminate the need for retirement planning. However, the amount you receive from private disability insurance or a private pension plan may depend on your Social Security benefits. Even when payments under these plans are not contingent on Social Security benefits, the need for private protection will be dependent upon the size of the governmentally supplied safety net. Your private disability insurance, life insurance, and retirement planning may all depend upon how much you can expect to receive from Social Security.

The Social Security Administration supplies estimates of benefits to all upon request. To receive an estimate of your future Social Security benefits, you need only contact the nearest Social Security office listed in your telephone directory. Ask them to send you Form SSA-7004, known as a "Request for Earnings and Benefit Estimate Statement." A few weeks after returning this form, you should receive a "Personal Earnings and Benefit Estimate Statement." This statement will contain the following information:

- Your total covered earnings from 1937 to 1950
- A year-by-year statement of your covered earnings from 1951 to the present
- Estimates of your retirement benefits at different ages
- Estimates of your survivor and disability benefits
- The number of credits you need to be insured for each type of Social Security, and the total credits you have earned to date

The estimates provided by the Social Security Administration are in today's dollars of purchasing power. This makes it possible for you to judge what standard of living these benefits might support. The actual amount you receive in future dollars will depend upon future inflation, your future labor force experience and, of course, the generosity of some future U.S. Congress.

You should check the earnings statement. It's estimated that one person in 13 has not had covered earnings credited correctly. Old W-2 forms and tax returns can provide proof of historical earnings. A certified copy of any tax return you filed within the last six years can be obtained by sending IRS Form 4506.

The purpose of this appendix is to explain how your Social Security benefits are determined. Because the best we can do here is summarize the calculations and rules for estimating benefits, and because the benefits will change as a result of inflation and changes in the laws, this is only an estimate. The actual benefits you are to receive can be calculated only at the time you are to receive them with the aid of an informed employee of the Social Security system.

The rules governing eligibility and benefits are very complicated. For this reason, you should contact the nearest office of the Social Security Administration when there is the slightest possibility that you may receive benefits. Accordingly, you should check on potential benefits if:

1. You are unable to work because of an illness or injury that is expected to last a year or longer
2. You are 62 or older or plan to retire
3. You are within three months of age 65 even if you don't plan to retire
4. You experience a death in the family
5. Your spouse or your dependent children suffer permanent kidney failure
6. You are a dependent of someone who is eligible for benefits

Not all individuals in these categories will qualify for benefits. Furthermore, those who do qualify may find benefits reduced or eliminated because of other income received. However, given the likelihood of benefits, it is best to check.

WHO IS COVERED BY SOCIAL SECURITY?

The objective of the Social Security system is to provide universal coverage for all workers. If you have held a nongovernment job, you have most likely paid some funds into the system, entitling you and your family to potential benefits. Previously, federal workers were not covered, and nonprofit private and public institutions were permitted to opt out of the system. Since 1984, however, all new federal employees are required to become members, and no additional nonprofit institutions are allowed to leave the system.

For one of several reasons, covered workers, their dependents, and their survivors may all be entitled to benefits from the Social Security system. To be eligible for the entire range of potential benefits, a worker must be "fully insured." This requirement is satisfied when the worker has sufficient *quarters of coverage*. Before 1978, a quarter of coverage was awarded for each calendar quarter in which the worker received \$50 or more of covered earnings. After 1978, quarters of coverage were based on annual earnings. In 1995, a worker was credited with one quarter of coverage for each \$630 earned during the year up to a maximum of four quarters in one year. The amounts needed for a quarter of coverage are adjusted each year for the change in the wage level. Values for the intervening years are given in Table B.1.

Fully Insured at Retirement

To receive benefits that are contingent on the covered worker's reaching retirement age, the worker must be fully insured at retirement. For workers currently reaching age 62, *fully insured* is achieved with 40 quarters of coverage (10 years of covered wages).

TABLE B.1 • EARNINGS NEEDED FOR ONE QUARTER OF COVERAGE	
Year	Dollar Amount
1977	50
1978	250
1979	260
1980	290
1981	310
1982	340
1983	370
1984	390
1985	410
1986	440
1987	460
1988	470
1989	500
1990	520
1991	540
1992	570
1993	590
1994	620
1995	630
1996	640

Fully Insured at the Onset of Disability

Only those who satisfy the Social Security Administration's stringent requirements may receive disability benefits. To qualify for Social Security disability, you must have a physical or mental impairment that prevents you from doing any substantial gainful activity and that is expected to last at least 12 months or is expected to result in death. In 1995, substantial gainful activity was defined as any work that resulted in a monthly income above $500. For disabled workers or families of disabled workers who meet this strict definition, the insured worker must also be both fully insured and disability insured before being eligible for benefits. Monthly disability benefits begin at the sixth month of disability.

The test to determine whether the worker is fully insured at the onset of the disability is the same as that for retirement, except that the age at the onset of the disability is used instead of age 62 and a minimum of six quarters of coverage must exist. For example, if a worker became disabled at age 30, there would be eight complete years between age 21 and age 30. Therefore, this person would need eight complete quarters of coverage to be fully insured.

To be "disability insured," this person must have been recently employed. Those within three years of their twenty-first birthday must have six quarters of coverage within the immediate 12 quarters to be disability insured. Those under 31 must have earned coverage in at least half of the quarters, beginning with the quarter after that in which they turned age 21 and ending with the quarter in which they became disabled. All others must meet what is called the 20/40 test. They must have 20 quarters of coverage in the immediately preceding 40 quarters.

To receive benefits, the worker must be both fully insured and disability insured. As you can see, it is possible to be fully insured, which would entitle you to retirement benefits, without being disability insured. With 10 years of covered work you would be fully insured. However, unless five of those years were within the last 10 years before the onset of the disability, you would not be disability insured and, consequently, you would be ineligible for disability benefits.

One last point: Those who do not qualify for benefits based on their own earnings history may still qualify based on a parent's earnings record. This is possible if the disability occurred before age 22.

Fully Insured at Death

In order for survivors of a covered worker to be entitled to the full range of Social Security survivors' benefits, the covered worker must be fully insured at death. The fully insured test at death is the same as for fully insured at disability except that age at death is substituted for age at onset of disability. There must be a quarter of coverage for each year between age 21 and age at death, with a maximum of 40 quarters of coverage and a minimum of six quarters of coverage.

Currently Insured

When determining whether a worker is fully insured, only those quarters of coverage accumulated after age 21 are counted. Accordingly, many young workers who have already spent considerable time in covered employment may not be fully insured. In order to ensure that families of young workers would not be unfairly denied benefits, Congress created another category of insureds called *currently insured*. This status applies only at death. Its purpose is to provide benefits to survivors of young workers even though the covered workers may not be fully insured. For widow(er)s with dependent children and dependent children to be entitled to survivors' benefits, the deceased worker need only be currently insured. Persons are currently insured if they have at least six quarters of coverage during the last 13 quarters before they died, became disabled, or retired.

CALCULATION OF BENEFITS

Benefit payments are generally related to past earnings of the covered worker. The actual computation of the benefits is an involved, four-phase process that includes the following:

1. Indexing past earnings
2. Calculating average indexed monthly earnings (AIME)
3. Calculating the primary insurance amount (PIA)
4. Calculating the basic monthly benefit

The following discussion will explain how the Social Security Administration calculates your benefit. If you would like to calculate your own, you can get out a pencil and paper or you can obtain a DOS program called ANYPIA by contacting the nearest Social Security office. The program may also be downloaded for free from Social Security Online (http://www.ssa.gov).

Indexing Past Earnings

A sample worksheet for estimating average indexed monthly earnings is given in Table B.2. The data on the worksheet are for a worker who became disabled and became eligible for benefits in 1995 at age 28. Column 1 includes each year since 1950, or each year between when the covered worker turned 21 and the one before the covered worker became disabled, reached age 62, or died. These years are called the "base computation years." In column 2, earnings in each of these years are listed. If you are making the calculation for yourself and you don't know your previous earnings, you can receive a record of your past covered wages by contacting the Social Security Administration.

The maximum amount of wages covered by Social Security taxes for each of the base computation years is entered in column 3. The needed values can be found in Table B.3. Only wages up to these amounts will count toward the calculation of your Social Security benefits. Therefore, the lesser of the wages in column 2 and column 3 is entered in column 4. These are called *covered wages*.

The next step is to multiply the wages in column 4 by the wage index in column 5 (see Table B.3 for wage index values). The Social Security Administration revises this index each year for changes in the national wage level. The purpose of this adjustment is to increase the value of wages earned in the early years so that recent wages, which are more heavily dominated by inflation, do not overly influence the calculation of benefits. The correct index will depend upon the last year of covered earnings. The index-adjusted wage is entered in column 6.

Calculating Average Indexed Monthly Earnings

Before you calculate average earnings, you are allowed to exclude several years in which earnings were low. This prevents a few bad years of earnings from significantly reducing your benefits payments. You may drop one-fifth of the base computation years (disregard any fraction) up to a maximum of five, but no less than

TABLE B.2 • WORKSHEET FOR CALCULATING AVERAGE INDEXED MONTHLY EARNINGS

(1) Base Computation Year	(2) Gross Wages	(3) Maximum Taxable Wages	(4) Covered Wages	(5) Wage Index	(6) Indexed Wages	(7) Indexed Wages in Benefit Computation Year
1989	$46,438	$48,000	$46,438	1.1509049	$53,445.72	—
1990	49,689	51,300	49,689	1.1000900	54,662.00	—
1991	53,167	53,400	53,167	1.0605673	56,387.04	56,387.04
1992	56,889	55,500	55,500	1.0086002	55,977.31	55,977.31
1993	60,871	57,600	57,600	1.0000000	57,600.00	57,600.00
1994	65,132	60,600	60,600	1.0000000	60,600.00	60,600.00
					Total wages in benefit computation years =	$230,564.35
					Months in benefit computation years =	48
						$4,803.42
					AIME =	$4,803.00

TABLE B.3 • DATA FOR CALCULATING AIME

Year	Annual Maximum Taxable Earnings	Average Annual National Wage	Wage Index*
1996	$62,700	—	
1995	61,200	—	
1994	60,600	23,753.53	1.0000000
1993	57,600	23,132.67	1.0000000
1992	55,500	22,935.42	1.0086002
1991	53,400	21,811.60	1.0605673
1990	51,300	21,027.98	1.1000900
1989	48,000	20,099.55	1.1509049
1988	45,000	19,334.04	1.1964737
1987	43,800	18,426.51	1.2554016
1986	42,000	17,321.82	1.3354642
1985	39,600	16,822.51	1.3751022
1984	37,800	16,135.07	1.4336889
1983	35,700	15,239.24	1.5179674
1982	32,400	14,531.34	1.5919158
1981	29,700	13.773.10	1.6795543
1980	25,900	12,513.46	1.8486230
1979	22,900	11,479.46	2.0151357
1978	17,700	10,556.03	2.1914176
1977	16,500	9,779.44	2.3654391
1976	15,300	9,226.48	2.5072043
1975	14,100	8,630.92	2.6802091
1974	13,200	8,030.76	2.8805082
1973	10,800	7,580.16	3.0517390
1972	9,000	7,133.80	3.2426855
1971	7,800	6,497.08	3.5604718
1970	7,800	6,186.24	3.7393748
1969	7,800	5,893.76	3.9249427
1968	7,800	5,571.76	4.1517707
1967	6,600	5,213.44	4.4371221
1966	6,600	4,938.36	4.6842818
1965	4,800	4,658.72	4.9654562
1964	4,800	4,576.32	5.0548629
1963	4,800	4,396.64	5.2614428
1962	4,800	4,291.40	5.3904716
1961	4,800	4,086.76	5.6603936
1960	4,800	4,007.12	5.7728918

*Factors for workers who were first eligible (attained age 62, became disabled, or died) in 1995.

two. The years that are left, those with the highest indexed earnings, are called the *benefit computation years*.

The final step in calculating average indexed monthly earnings is to sum wages over the benefit computation years in column 7, and divide this value by the number of months in the benefit computation years. The resulting figure rounded to the next lower dollar is averaged indexed monthly earnings (AIME).

Calculating the Primary Insurance Amount

Once you have calculated AIME, you may next compute the primary insurance amount (PIA). To compute the PIA you need the AIME and a percentage formula published by the Social Security Administration. For example, in 1995 the PIA was equal to 90 percent of the first $426 of AIME, plus 32 percent of the $2,141 of AIME, plus 15 percent of everything over $2,567 of AIME. Given an AIME of $4,803, the PIA rounded to the next lower dime would be $1,403.90, computed as follows:

90% of $426	=	$ 383.40
32% of 2,141	=	685.12
15% of 2,236	=	335.40
		$1,403.92
PIA	=	$1,403.90

The level of monthly wages at which the percentage applied changes is called the *bend point*. Each year the bend points are revised to reflect changes in the national wage level.

Some workers who receive a pension for noncovered employment and who are also eligible for Social Security retirement benefits must apply a different formula for calculating the PIA. The alternative benefit formula reduces the percentage factor on the first bracket from 90 percent to 40 percent.

Calculating the Basic Monthly Benefit

The primary insurance amount is a very important figure, because all monthly benefit payments will be based on a percentage of the PIA. For example, a fully insured worker retiring at age 65 would receive an initial benefit payment equal to 100 percent of the PIA. Furthermore, the spouse of this pensioner could receive a spousal benefit beginning at age 65 equal to 50 percent of the PIA. Some other basic monthly benefits expressed as a percentage of the PIA are listed in Table B.4. Unless the sum of the individual benefits due family members exceeds the family

TABLE B.4 • BASIC MONTHLY BENEFITS AS A PERCENTAGE OF THE PRIMARY INSURANCE AMOUNT OF FULLY INSURED WORKER

Status	Percentage
Retired worker at 65	100
Disabled worker	100
Spouse or divorced spouse of retired worker at 65	50
Spouse of disabled worker with dependent children	50
Child of retired or disabled worker	50
Surviving spouse or surviving divorced spouse of retired worker at 65	100
Sole parent of deceased worker	82.5
Each of two dependent parents of a deceased worker	75
Child of a deceased worker	75
Surviving spouse with dependent children	75

maximum (see Table B.6), monthly benefits payable to each member of the family would generally be based on the indicated percentage of the PIA.

ADJUSTMENTS TO MONTHLY BENEFITS

For numerous reasons, the monthly benefits payable may not be equal to the percentage of the PIA indicated in Table B.4. Several adjustments can either increase or decrease the actual monthly benefit. Below we discuss some of the more common ones.

Cost-of-Living Adjustments

In January of each year, Social Security benefits are adjusted for increases in the cost of living. If the Social Security trust fund is above a stated level, the adjustments are calculated according to changes in the Consumer Price Index; otherwise, the increase is based on the lesser of the rise in the CPI or in the national wage level.

Retirement Age and Reduction for Early Retirement

The retirement age at which unreduced retirement benefits are first available is currently age 65. This is when a monthly pension equal to 100 percent of the primary insurance amount would begin.

Congress has scheduled a change in normal retirement age. It is set to increase two months a year for workers reaching age 62 between 2000 and 2005, remain fixed at age 66 for those reaching age 62 between 2006 and 2016, and then again increase two months a year for those reaching age 62 between 2017 and 2022. For all those reaching age 62 after 2022, normal retirement age will be 67. The effect of the age requirements is illustrated in Table B.5.

Insured workers may elect to retire before reaching normal retirement age. However, monthly benefit payments will be adjusted downward from the PIA for each month early retirement precedes normal retirement age. An eligible worker can now retire at age 62 with 80 percent of the benefits received at the normal retirement age of 65. As shown in Table B.5, this is also scheduled to change over the next few decades, with age 62 benefits for a retired worker eventually falling to only 70 percent of the primary insurance amount.

Increase for Delayed Retirement

Delaying retirement past normal retirement age can result in an increase in monthly benefits for each month retirement is delayed between normal retirement age and age 70. For those who reached 62 between December 1978 and January 1987, the delayed retirement credit is equal to 3 percent for each year, or 1/4 percent for each month retirement is delayed. For those reaching 62 after 1986, the delayed retirement credit is 3 1/2 percent per year or 2/3 percent per month up to age 70. From then on, the delayed retirement credit is set to increase steadily until 2008, when it reaches 8 percent for each year of delayed retirement.

TABLE B.5 • NORMAL RETIREMENT AGE AND AGE 62 BENEFITS

	Retirement Age (Years/Months)		Age 62 Benefits as Percent of PIA*	
Year of Birth	Worker/ Spouse	Widow(er)	Worker	Spouse
1937 (same as prior law)	65/0	65/0	80.0	37.5
1938	65/2	65/0	79.2	37.1
1939	65/4	65/0	78.3	36.7
1940	65/6	65/2	77.5	36.2
1941	65/8	65/4	76.7	35.8
1942	65/10	65/6	75.8	35.4
1943	66/0	65/8	75.0	35.0
1944	66/0	65/10	75.0	35.0
1945–1954	66/0	66/0	75.0	35.0
1955	66/2	66/0	74.2	34.6
1956	66/4	66/0	73.3	34.2
1957	66/6	66/2	72.5	33.8
1958	66/8	66/4	71.7	33.3
1959	66/10	66/6	70.8	32.9
1960	67/0	66/8	70.0	32.5
1961	67/0	66/10	70.0	32.5
1962 and after	67/0	67/0	70.0	32.5

*Reduced retirement benefits will continue to be available to workers (and spouses) beginning at age 62 but at a greater reduction. For workers and spouses, the prior-law reduction factors (5/9ths of 1 percent per month for workers and 25/36ths of 1 percent per month for spouses) are retained for the first 36 months of benefits before age 65 and a new factor (5/12ths of 1 percent) is applied for each additional month. For older survivors, reduced benefits continue to be available at age 60 with the monthly reduction adjusted for each age cohort so as to maintain a 28.5 percent reduction at age 60—the same maximum reduction as occurred under prior law.

SOURCE: *Social Security Bulletin,* July 1983, p. 30.

Adjustment for the Family Maximum

The *family maximum* is the maximum amount that can be paid one family—excluding payments to divorced spouses—in monthly benefits based on one worker's earnings record. There is one family maximum for survivors' and retirement benefits and another one for disability benefits.

The family maximum for survivors' and retirement benefits is calculated in a manner similar to that for figuring the PIA. However, the bend points and the percentages are unique.

In 1995 the family maximum was equal to 150 percent of the first $544 of the PIA, plus 272 percent of the PIA in excess of $544 but not in excess of $785, plus 134 percent of the PIA in excess of $785 but not in excess of $1,024, plus 175 percent of the PIA in excess of $1,024. For example, given a primary insurance amount of $1,403.90 in 1995, the maximum that could be paid out in family survivors' benefits was $2,461.40 after rounding to the next lower dime.

150% of $544 =	$ 816.00
274% of ($785 – $544) =	660.34
134% of ($1,024 – $785) =	320.26
175% of ($1,403.90 – $1,024) =	664.83
	$2,461.43
Family maximum =	$2,461.40

TABLE B.6 • EXAMPLE OF ADJUSTMENT FOR FAMILY MAXIMUM			
	Original Benefit	Adjusted Benefit (Four Child Family)	Adjusted Benefit (Three Child Family)
Insured	$1,403.90	$1,403.90	$1,403.90
Spouse	701.95	140.38	175.48
1st child	701.95	140.38	175.48
2nd child	701.95	140.38	175.48
3rd child	701.95	140.38	175.48
4th child	701.95	140.38	—
Total	$4,913.65	$2,105.80	$2,105.80

The family maximum for a family with an insured disabled worker is calculated in a different manner. It is equal to the lesser of 150 percent of the PIA, or 85 percent of the AIME, but never less than the PIA. Using the sample calculations for a disabled worker, the maximum family benefit would be equal to 150 percent of $1,403.90 (PIA), or $2,105.80.

When the total basic benefits due to a single family exceed the relevant maximum, then benefits paid all family members except the insured worker are reduced proportionately to bring total benefits in line with the family maximum. Total benefits due a disabled worker with a dependent spouse and four children, and a primary insurance amount of $1,403.90, would seemingly total $4,913.65. Table B.6 demonstrates how these benefits would be adjusted for a family maximum of $2,105.80, and how they subsequently would be adjusted after one child left the household.

Earnings Test

Social Security retirement benefits are for those who have truly retired from the work force. Likewise, benefits for survivors or dependents are for those truly in need. Accordingly, for recipients under age 65, benefits are reduced by $1 for each $2 of earnings above an annually determined amount ($8,160 in 1995). Retirees between age 65 to 69 have benefits reduced by $1 for each $3 of earnings above a higher exemption ($11,280 in 1995). There is no earnings test for those age 70 and above. They may earn any amount without fear of benefit reduction.

Index